Interference in Sovereign Affairs and the Discursive Economy of International Law

Developments in International Law

VOLUME 81

The titles published in this series are listed at *brill.com/diil*

Interference in Sovereign Affairs and the Discursive Economy of International Law

By

Frédéric Mégret

BRILL | NIJHOFF

LEIDEN | BOSTON

Library of Congress Cataloging-in-Publication Data

Names: Mégret, Frédéric, author.
Title: Interference in sovereign affairs and the discursive economy of international law / by Frédéric Mégret, full professor, Hans & Tamar Oppenheimer Chair in public international law, Center for Human Rights and Legal Pluralism, Faculty of Law, McGill University.
Description: Boston : Brill, 2025. | Series: Developments in international law; 81 | Includes bibliographical references and index. | Summary: Interference in sovereign affairs is everywhere but nowhere at the same time. Whether it is pressure on public officials, conditionality in development assistance, criticism of states' human rights record, psychological or propaganda operations, instrumentalization of diasporas, international organization supervision, unilateral sanctions, election interference or meddling diplomats, the phenomenon is as amorphous as it is diffuse. But what if it was the lens that we use to capture interference that was the problem? How do the tools of international law blind us to the reality of certain phenomena? The urgency of understanding interference on its own terms has never been greater, and it requires nothing less than a reimagining of the sort of discursive investments on which international law relies.
Identifiers: LCCN 2024061839 | ISBN 9789004532724 (hardback) | ISBN 9789004532731 (ebook)
Subjects: LCSH: International law–Economic aspects. | International law–Political aspects. | Globalization–Economic aspects. | Sovereignty–Economic aspects. | International economic relations. | Investments, Foreign–Legal aspects.
Classification: LCC KZ1252 .M44 2025 | DDC 341.3–dc23/eng/20241230
LC record available at https://lccn.loc.gov/2024061839

Typeface for the Latin, Greek, and Cyrillic scripts: "Brill". See and download: brill.com/brill-typeface.

ISSN 0924-5332
ISBN 978-90-04-53272-4 (hardback)
ISBN 978-90-04-53273-1 (e-book)
DOI 10.1163/9789004532731

This book is printed on acid-free paper and produced in a sustainable manner.

Printed by Printforce, the Netherlands

Contents

Acknowledgement

This book was originally developed as an article in the wake of interference in the 2016 U.S. elections, but already with a view to expanding its scope beyond that single incident. Before I knew it, the article had spun out of control and become too long to be publishable in a journal. In many ways, the topic is the gift that kept giving, such is the extent to which it has forcefully returned to the forefront of international legal concerns, but also to which it is a prism to revisit many of the central tenets of the international legal order. The more I pulled threads, the more the entire fabric of international law seemed to unravel. I credit Pia Husch, who visited McGill as a graduate trainee, for rekindling my interest in my own project and encouraging me to push through, as well as enlightening conversations. A shout out to my colleague and friend Evan Fox-Decent for encouraging me to pursue this monograph.

An early version of this project benefited from the feedback of Evan Criddle, Paul Stephan, Alexander Greenawalt, Nancy Combs, Jay Butler, Kish Vinayagamoorthy, and Odette Lienau at William & Mary's International Law Workshop in 2018. Later, the broad ideas that had begun to inform the book were exposed in 2023 at the University of Hong Kong at the invitation of Kuzi Charamba ('The Return of Interference in Sovereign Affairs and International Law'). At the invitation of Päl Wrange, I then had the opportunity to push some of these arguments further at the Stockholm Centre for International Law and Justice ('The New Interference in Sovereign Affairs and International Law'). I also gave an opening lecture for the Master 'Droit, gouvernance et digital' at the Issy-les-Moulineaux campus of the Université Catholique de Lille on 'Interference 2.0' for which I thank Delphine Dogot. Finally, Sundhya Pahuja gave me the opportunity to present my thinking on the notion of 'Corporate interference' at the Beehive seminar of the Laureate Program on Global Corporations and International Law of the Law School, University of Melbourne, in May 2024.

Funding for this research was provided by the SSHRC and the Hans & Tamar Oppenheimer Chair in Public International Law. I am thankful to both for the help provided. The book was completed whilst holding the Samuel Rubin Visiting Professorship at the Columbia Law School, and I am grateful for the welcome I received there.

I am indebted to Wanshu Cong for invaluable help and, in particular, translations from the Chinese. Isabella Spano, my trusted research assistant, did an incredible job of complementing research and editing of the final product.

Nicolas Kamran did me the huge favor of reading a full early draft of the manuscript, and his keen and critical eye was key to the final product.

I am forever indebted to Jean-Daniel and Sabine for their trust. A special thought for Mina and Darius who sometimes complain that 'daddy works too much'. To both, when you read this one day, I hope you will see my labor for what it was. Finally, much gratitude to Niloufar, eshgham, for her loving support.

The book is dedicated to the memory of Xavier Ricard Lanata.

Bolton Est, May 2024.

INTRODUCTION

The World-Making Character of Interference and Non-interference

> The subject of intervention is one of the vaguest branches of international law. We are told that intervention is a right; that it is a crime; that is the rule; that it is the exception; that it is never permissible at all.[1]

From accusations of Russian meddling in the U.S. 2016 election to complaints about the recognition by Western states of Juan Guaidó as the head of the Venezuelan state; from the outlawing of foreign funding of NGOs in such diverse countries as Russia, Egypt, Hungary, Georgia or Israel to European development aid conditionality; from African complaints that an LGBTQ+ agenda is being thrust upon them, to allegations of Chinese students reporting to Beijing on sensitive comments made by lecturers in Australia: the venerable question of interference in sovereign affairs, once vaguely redolent of intractable but antiquated Cold War controversies, has made a remarkable and explosive comeback on the international stage. It has done so in a context of renewed anxiety about sovereignty, democratic institutions, and the international legal order itself. Indeed, such incidents may well only be the emerging part of an iceberg whose dimensions international lawyers are barely beginning to assess, even as they are called upon to articulate, navigate and negotiate claims about interference and non-interference anew. Where does interference stand in international law? And, more importantly, where does international law stand, in the midst of conspicuous and pervasive interference?

It has become common to deplore the fact that the norm of non-intervention is more honored in the breach than anything else[2] (as the International Court

1 PH Winfield, 'The History of Intervention in International Law' (1922) 3 British Year Book of International Law 130, 130.

2 Chen Yifeng, 'The Customary Nature of the Principle of Non-Intervention: A Methodological Note' (2014) 2 Renmin Chinese Law Review 319.

 | DOI:10.1163/9789004532731_002

of Justice (ICJ) put it in a quaint euphemism, 'examples of trespass against this principle are not infrequent').[3] This is as it may, and certainly the blatantness of some forms of interference and the contrast between stated principles and practice can be galling.[4] But the denunciation of violations can also be trite. Even breaches can be productive moments for international law, which loves nothing more, famously, than a good crisis.[5] Do breaches betray a project in decay, perhaps a comical disconnect of legal scholarship from reality, or the continued relevance of norms precisely because they bear the full onslaught of international politics? A norm can be frequently breached yet nonetheless solid in other ways, if nothing else as a reference point for international legal action and arguments—although, evidently, that may not be granting much. A norm may also evidently be ambiguous, but in ways that are productive and dynamic. The most contested and ambiguous norms of international law may also be the most interesting, and so the worthiest of scholarly consideration.

1 What It Means to 'Constitute'

What will matter in this book is what both compliance with and violation of the norm reveal about how it constructs international legal reality, a reality constantly articulated through international legal argumentation.[6] In that respect, it is posited that the rule of non-intervention matters less because it is demonstrably respected than because it is a constitutive legal rule, one which tells us how the 'game' of international law is supposed to be played.[7] The norm, if nothing else, shapes the world we live in and, in that respect at least, international law is a self-fulfilling prophecy whose constructive incidence largely precedes and even relativizes its violations. One does not begin to understand the reality of international law until one takes the full measure of its 'world-making' character, namely the power of its inter-subjective

3 *Military and Paramilitary Activities in and against Nicaragua* (*Nicaragua v United States*) (*Merits*) [1986] ICJ Rep 14 [202].

4 On the importance of what states do when it comes to interference rather than merely what they say, see Thomas M Franck and Edward Weisband, 'The Johnson and Brezhnev Doctrines: The Law You Make May Be Your Own' (1969) 22 Stanford Law Review 979.

5 Hilary Charlesworth, 'International Law: A Discipline of Crisis' (2002) 65 The Modern Law Review 377.

6 Anthony Clark Arend, 'Do Legal Rules Matter--International Law and International Politics' (1997) 38 Virginia Journal of International Law 107.

7 Stephen A Kocs, 'Explaining the Strategic Behavior of States: International Law as System Structure' (1994) 38 International Studies Quarterly 535.

understandings about the very conditions under which breaches might occur (rather than just the existence of such breaches or what to do about them).[8]

Specifically, interference is a 'constitutive' claim because it builds a world in which something known as interference can matter and exist. To put it differently, the idea of interference would not exist but for international law and the way it already posits that there is such a thing as sovereignty. Interference provides a label to structure unrelated factoids into a plausible legal claim. We would not know interference as 'interference'—at least the interference we know, as we know it—were it not for international law. This means, crucially, that there is no 'interference' as an international relations phenomenon in the abstract (any more than there is statehood, war, international organizations, or a High Seas outside of legal regimes that constructs all of these things as existing), merely a pure legal claim that something understood as interference is problematic. That sovereignty is then understood as a broad claim against a certain form of interference is less revealing of an intractable chicken-and-egg problem than a reflection of the reality that concepts only exist to the extent that they are propped up by others. To deal with interference, then, is not to deploy international law to rein in an international politics imagined as 'out there', but to create the conditions for an international politics of interference and non-interference by furnishing the conceptual apparatus wherein such a politics can even make sense.

What will be crucial, then, is the existence of an already shared 'culture' of both interference and non-interference, part positive norms but also part aesthetics, posture, and calculation. This is connected to the recent interest in 'frames of reference':[9] what matters is the conditions of possibility of interference as a norm that makes it possible to even think of non-interference as a category and even a project. The norm is already woven into the world it then seeks to capture.[10] Moreover, someone, somewhere had to think of 'interference' as an idea worth investing in for some end.[11] This is also what makes

---

8 Guy Fiti Sinclair, 'A Better Way of World Making? International Law and Development at the United Nations' in Ruth Buchanan, Luis Eslava and Sundhya Pahuja (eds), *Oxford Handbook of International Law and Development* (Oxford University Press 2023); Negar Mansouri, 'International Organizations and World Making Practices: Some Notes on Method' (2022) 19 International Organizations Law Review 528.

9 Andrea Bianchi and Moshe Hirsch (eds), *International Law's Invisible Frames: Social Cognition and Knowledge Production in International Legal Processes* (Oxford University Press 2021).

10 Jean d'Aspremont, 'A Wordly Law in a Legal World' in Andrea Bianchi and Moshe Hirsch (eds), *International Law's Invisible Frames: Social Cognition and Knowledge Production in International Legal Processes* (Oxford University Press 2021).

11 Ruth Buchanan and others, 'Making and Remaking the World Anew: International Law and the Development Project' in Ruth Buchanan, Luis Eslava and Sundhya Pahuja

it possible to think of interference and non-interference as always embedded in a certain conception of *relations* between states and projects therein: non-interference would not mean anything if there was a single state. And it is also, powerfully, what makes it possible to *not* see certain forms of behavior as interference, thus lending a cloak of invisibility to certain phenomena that can then except themselves from the critique they otherwise so generously dole out. In other words, what constitutes interference is not a once-and-for-all stable framework to be applied to various 'real world' instances (as in the standard positivist mindset), but itself the product of a competition—all the more intense that it is often hidden—over its definition.

The norm of non-intervention, then, matters, if at all, not particularly because it is respected but because of the intensity of political, symbolic and legal investments it is the object of. Notably, this book will be premised on the need to avoid at least three related temptations. A first temptation is the notion that the norm of non-intervention is not itself the problem and that what is are its violation by egotistic and misguided sovereigns. This is a classic move by international lawyers: the fault lies entirely in an international politics deemed external to the law itself. If only sovereigns treated rules with more deference (even reverence!), then the problem would simply go away. That diagnosis is of course not entirely wrong, which is why it can also be subtly misleading if taken at face value: states do indeed, perhaps often, violate the law, renege on their commitments and, of course, try to get away with it, in the process further muddling the distinction between norm-compliance and norm-violation. Any minimally realistic account of international law must surely take this as a given and attend to the difficult work of parsing different forms of interaction with norms. The book will not discount the value that lies in the posture of invoking the norm of non-intervention to critique what it designates.

But the problem is that this vision takes for granted that international law is not already saturated with international politics and not guilty of the sins it denounces. As such it ignores the extent to which international law is deeply compromised in the production of its conditions of existence and even of its own violation. As will appear in the book, the norm of non-intervention is in a sense exactly where states want it to be—or at least where certain constellations of powerful states manage it to be at various junctions. A vision of 'politics' as the party-spoiler thus provides at best an unhelpful blueprint to navigate the complexities of living with and through international law, one

(eds), *The Oxford Handbook of International Law and Development* (Oxford University Press 2023).

not only prone to wishful thinking ('if only states.') and *faux* indignation, but dispensing with the hard work of muddling through the complexities of the real. As Chen Yifeng reminds us, '[t]he conflict between the rule and practice of non-intervention cannot simply be regarded as a problem for international politics, which as such per se lies outside of the concern of international lawyers'.[12] The norm of non-intervention, is what it is—warts and all—not by accident but by design. International law cannot, in other words, claim innocence from the worlds it produces. International lawyers interested in the work that interference does must be ready to get their 'hands dirty' by seeing it as a product of the strategies and rhetorical investments that international law makes possible.

A second temptation is, at the opposite extreme, the 'technicist' or dogmatic urge to reduce problems with the nom of non-intervention to some glitches in the international legal software that will be remedied if only the conceptual 'bug' can be removed. There is of course always a need for more clarity and the many efforts at dissecting the meaning of intervention bring a worthwhile contribution to our understanding of the law. Distinctions such as that between *lex ferenda* and *lex lata* are worth keeping in mind as broad indicators of the sort of work that international lawyers are routinely expected to do.[13] Again, it will not be claimed here that the classical doctrinal pursuits of international law are mindless and fruitless; they are in fact very much the medium through which claims of intervention and interference can be made sense of. The problem is that focusing on them over-emphasizes the merely formal dimensions of the norm of non-intervention. The 'elusive essence' of intervention[14] cannot be captured through pure interpretation, deductive reasoning from first principles, or observation of state practice. It must be reconstructed as first and foremost a praxis, a way of arguing about sovereignty when the circumstances require and the values at stake justify it that comes into focus in the encounter between rules and real-world events.

As one invariably finds, moreover, the challenge is not just with non-intervention's lack of juridical clarity. The confused state in which the norm of non-intervention/non-interference finds itself as a result of legal controversy is a factor, real and galling as it is, but it is also a result of the ultimately

12 Yifeng (n 2) 322.

13 Richard B Lillich, 'The Status of Economic Coercion under International Law: United Nations Norms' (1977) 12 Texas International Law Journal 17, 17.

14 Martina Buscemi and Elena Carpanelli, 'The "Elusive Essence" of the Principle of Non-Intervention in Light of Recent Practice: The Cases of Venezuela and Hong Kong' (2021) 79 Questions of International Law 1.

irreconcilable values and interests that the norm purports to reconcile. The ability of a rule such as non-intervention to paper over these differences is limited; it provides, at best, a precariously stitched veil to hide some of the contradictions involved in ascertaining, for example, whether intervention is really intervention or the implementation of a human rights international obligation; whether it is still intervention when carried out by corporate actors; or what measures are authorized and desirable to offset it. Interpreting the norm 'better' or coming up with a 'better' understanding of its sources are important pursuits, but not for the simplicist positivist reasons that are sometimes presume. It cannot ultimately defer the moment of reckoning wherein the circular logic of the law faces its limit. 'Clarity' or 'determinacy' are overrated dimensions of law if they are obtained only at the cost of folding reality into a one-dimensional mould that ultimately says more about observer biases than the object at stake.

A third temptation is that the problem is one of policy or normative thinking that can simply be addressed by coming up with a better, more insightful moral or political theory of what the norm of non-intervention *really* seeks to protect. There is some merit, evidently, to the idea that international law, perhaps precisely when it comes to hard-to-define notions such as interference, is, in the inimitable jargon of the New Haven school, a 'dynamic process of authoritative decision-making'.[15] As will be seen, there is no dearth of sophisticated theorizing that envisages the problem of interference as one of conflict between human rights and sovereignty,[16] or that calls for a reassessment of the value of self-determination[17] or that proposes to reaffirm conditions of coexistence between states,[18] each with their assorted prescriptions.

Again, the problem is not that normative theorizing is not useful or productive, and indeed there is much need for actualizing the normative categories with which we analyze the incidence of the norm. Having said that, much normative theorizing in this vein, whether extolling the inherent value of sovereignty, democracy, self-determination or human rights, ultimately cannot hide its provenance and, often, the provincialism of its assumptions. It only makes

15 Rosalyn Higgins, 'Intervention and International Law' in Hedley Bull (ed), *Intervention in world politics* (Clarendon Press 1984).

16 Lori Fisler Damrosch, 'Politics Across Borders: Nonintervention and Nonforcible Influence over Domestic Affairs' (1989) 83 American Journal of International Law 1.

17 Jens David Ohlin, *Election Interference: International Law and the Future of Democracy* (Cambridge University Press 2020).

18 Cecilia Yue Wu, 'Challenging Paternalistic Interference: The Case for Non-Intervention in a Globalized World' (2024) 65 Harvard International Law Journal 253.

sense against the background of typically unstated preferences for a particular version of international legal liberalism (or any other of a range of non-liberal view of international law) that themselves invoke ever more abstract and arbitrary preferences. It neglects the problem of incommensurability of international values in a world of states. And of course, it occasionally does not even pretend that it offers a specifically legal, at least *de lege* lata, understanding of international law.[19]

In short, jurisprudence alone cannot 'theorize away' these conflicts from some neutral Archimedean standpoint in a thoroughly pluralist world where interference and intervention are bound to mean very different things for different constituencies. Such is the paradox, namely that any comprehensive moral theory of non-intervention relies on a comprehensive theory of international society that is simply never fully available and, perhaps, even dangerous. If we knew what the ultimate end of international society was, then we would not need an international society and the international law that comes with it. We could safely abandon a world of sovereign states to embrace a cosmopolitan global *polis* where, in turn, non-intervention would be relatively meaningless since it would have dissolved the notion that there is anything significant to interfere with (as opposed to something to be governed). The norm of non-intervention exists precisely because the international system is a pluralist one; and precisely because it is a pluralist one, in turn, non-intervention will mean different things to different states, and therefore never the same thing for all. This is the tragedy of anarchy understood as pluralism: that it creates a world that would require the very principles that its existence cannot ultimately ground,[20] and is thus constantly at risk of degenerating into anomia and aporia.

In that respect, the endless quest to 'further define' an international rule such as non-intervention may seem somewhat fruitless, or at least Sisyphean. As Wolfgang Friedmann deplored already in the 1960s, '[b]ecause the traditional rules of international law provide no rules for these new types of intervention [author's note: the non-forcible kind], and because it is extremely difficult to assess the legality or illegality of various forms of interference with national sovereignty, the net result of the many debates of this question has

19 For a criticism of the New Haven school in that vein, see Adam Roberts, 'Intervention: Beyond "Dictatorial Interference"', *The Empire of Security and the Safety of the People* (Routledge 2006) 166.

20 Martti Koskenniemi, *From Apology to Utopia: The Structure of International Legal Argument* (Cambridge University Press 2006).

understandably been very meagre'.[21] Indeed, it has more recently been noted that a 'combination of such legal uncertainty, insuperable political dissent, a turbulent historical background and divergent geostrategic ambitions has proved and still proves to be a toxic mixture' for the international legal conversation around intervention in civil wars.[22]

At the same time, international law should also never let a good crisis go to waste. Engaging the toxicity as itself a symptom of international law's hangovers seems a worthy project in this moment of reinvention. What may be understood as the current 'crisis' of interference, revealed most starkly with electoral interference in the U.S. 2016 election campaign and the Brexit referendum but not reducible to either of these events, can help sharpen our understanding of why a certain kind of interference mattered then and for what reasons. 'Exceptional interference' of this kind and the sort of panic it elicited can then be usefully contrasted with 'everyday interference': the interference that appears so banal it almost goes undetected. There are energies to reclaim even and perhaps even more in the moment of radical doubt about the rule of non-intervention, such as it is, and the light it can shed on the broader practice of interference.

2 The Rule of Non-intervention, the Practice of Interference

This book's premise is that the destabilization of the norm of non-intervention—a destabilization that has been long in the making and is, in fact, endemic to the norm itself—is an opportunity to rethink its meaning in international relations and law. There is much more to non-intervention than the norm of non-intervention. In the process, one will be called upon to reexamine how everything that makes the norm of non-intervention both intelligible and central is constantly being negotiated as a result of the changing nature of actual interference. Non-intervention is not a fixed norm in a mobile world; it is, very much, a moving part amongst many moving parts. Although this can be dizzying, artificial fixity, notably the fixity of certain well-trodden discursive moves (for example, seeking to infer non-interference from the

21 Wolfgang Friedmann, *The Changing Structure of International Law* (New York, Columbia University Press 1964) 270.

22 Christina Nowak, 'The Changing Law of Non-Intervention in Civil Wars—Assessing the Production of Legality in State Practice after 2011' (2018) 5 Journal on the Use of Force and International Law 40, 41.

meaning of sovereignty, or focusing obsessively on a 1980s ICJ case,[23] etc.), can also provide a very misleading sense of certainty. International legal scholarship must stare down the abyss of international politics and, if not relish, at least accept the ensuing vertigo to produce a jurisprudence that hews closely to both sociological and normative developments.

The book's central move, in an effort to disrupt facile and repetitive conversations, will be to deliberately emphasize the idea of *interference* rather than specifically the rule of non-intervention. 'Interference' and 'intervention' are often used interchangeably[24] and the idea that their distinction could be crucial in international law is of uncertain vintage and, in fact, rarely spelt explicitly as such. 'Interference' will be used here in tension with 'intervention' even though the two sometimes operate on a continuum. The contention is that the focus of international law on intervention's *violation* of sovereignty, despite being doctrinally the most significant, does not do justice to what have become much more ambiguous concerns about the *displacement* of sovereignty and its many ramifications. As the book will emphasize, there is also an evident politics to defining the problem as one of merely intervention, one that seems almost destined to pre-empt claims about the demands of friendly relations between states and to keep the genie of intervention firmly into the box if not of the use of force, at least of coercion. To focus on interference, by contrast, is to be less fixated on the crises of intervention and more open to the manifold ways in which interference already structures international relations, in ways that are legally productive even as they are not always reducible to a legal/illegal framing.

This shift, it is hoped, will allow the book to depart inductively from the socio-legal reality of a phenomenon in international relations rather than deductively from a purportedly canonical rule of international law. It will do so as part of a commitment to understanding international phenomena on their own terms as it were, and to ask questions about how said phenomena challenge international law, rather than trying to fit, as has often been the case, irreducible phenomena into the rigid categories of international law. As such, it will also seek to do justice to the fact that interference is at least as much a

23 ibid 43. ('As a matter of principle, the ongoing resort to the ICJ's Nicaragua ruling, which has to be regarded as a product of the Cold War era, seems paradoxical and unreflective, given that the world has dramatically changed since 1986').

24 John Linarelli, 'An Examination of the Proposed Crime of Intervention in the Draft Code of Crimes against the Peace and Security of Mankind Lead Articles' (1995) 18 Suffolk Transnational Law Review 1; Antonios Tzanakopoulos, 'The Right to Be Free from Economic Coercion' (2015) 4 Cambridge International Law Journal 616, 622–623.

category of international legal understanding as it is an actual phenomenon. To frame something as interference is already to problematize it as such, the phenomenon does not exist independently of our attempts to grapple with it. Interference is further reframing some crucial categories of international law because of the way it retroacts on prevailing understandings of sovereignty that were supposed to be at its basis all along. As a complex international, transnational and global phenomenon, it needs to be understood not merely through international law but as a result of the interaction of domestic, human rights and constitutional legal orders and therefore the ongoing transformation of global law.

At its simplest, interference can be understood as a process of meddling with matters that are plausibly argued as belonging to another state to the point of displacing the decisional power of the normal sovereign. It includes a series of acts and processes that are imagined as encroaching on states' sovereignty as a result of other states' actions that fall short of coercive force or even the most blatant forms of coercive intervention. The litmus test for interference, then, is not coercion (although coercive intervention is, a fortiori, also a form of interference) but a more subtle displacement, which Lori Damrosch once described as 'non-forcible influence over domestic affairs'.[25] In its classic vein, it included, for example, financing of foreign political parties and corruption of foreign public officials, unilateral economic pressure, or propaganda operations which by themselves already created a host of unresolved questions. In its new form, as will be seen, it includes disinformation campaigns, cyber destabilization, or manipulation of diasporas that further contribute to destructuring the norm of non-intervention. Each new way of interfering brings unexpected attention to a facet of sovereignty that had been neglected before, which was never already entirely contained in the concept of sovereignty and which precipitates a rearticulation of its fundamentals (fundamentals which turn out to be as contingent as the debates they trigger).

The new interference adds the complexity that it operates in a grey zone between the state and the non-state, the domestic and the foreign, or the municipal and the international. But the new interference, as will be seen, is itself a product of the international legal mind—no less real for being so, but also remarkably elusive because the categories of understanding one uses to apprehend it are precisely what is constantly evaporating. This is, to be clear, a phenomenon whose contours have often proved to be difficult to pin down, yet only because international law has only ever provided a problematic set

25 Damrosch (n 16).

of keys to understand what intervention is or is not. One way of doing so will be to see interference as the principal source of a range of anxieties about the disruption of the imagined operation of sovereignty and, notably, the public sphere—in other words, seeing the phenomenon through the reaction to it, as a sort of Rorschach test of prevailing international legal attitudes. Indeed, the new interference is to some extent a phantasmagorical creation of the international legal mind. It not only creates concerns about sovereignty; it *is* a concern about sovereignty.

The book therefore makes the choice to focus on this relatively less visible, more ordinary form of intervention—run of the mill interference, if one can call it like that—that operates very much in the shadow of more notorious debates about intervention. This errs more closely to the French *ingérence*, a term ironically once resurrected to justify the possibility of interfering in the affairs of states that endangered their populations[26] but which today might as well describe an endemic if pathological condition of international relations. It is in that penumbral domain that behavior arises which proves to be the most testing, but perhaps also the most interesting, for international law. The relevant rule of international law is routinely still referred to as the rule of non-intervention even as, as the book will argue, there is much ambiguity between claims about a rule of non-intervention and the existence of a rule of non-interference. The point will not be to further police that distinction by denying or reifying it, but to understand what it says about sovereignty that we struggle to distinguish between the two.

The book's starting point, at any rate, is the real and growing gap between the rule of non-intervention such as it has arguably become historically entrenched in international law and the phenomenon it is supposed to regulate: the mismatch, that is, between the prohibition against intervention and the reality of interference. The question is what this mismatch speaks to intellectually. It could be a symptom of the intellectual decadence of international law, just as it could manifest the law's ability to renew its categories. In that respect, although the book may provide some answers to readers interested in how to *deal* with interference, it is clearly less interested in being a 'how to' guide than it is in teasing out the depths of complexity that result from such a mismatch. More than anything else, it will be dedicated to the intuition that international law is never only about regulating intervention or interference but always, in the process, of arbitrating what counts as such. Although the debate has been marked in the last three decades by a dominant international

26 Mario Bettati, *Le droit d'ingérence: Mutation de l'ordre international* (Odile Jacob 1996).

legal script that has constructed the conversation as one about the extent to which states should bypass other's sovereignty to safeguard human rights, it has in other times and other places been about the proper role of corporations, the demands of decolonization, the defense of democracy, the continuity of trade relations, the dangers of resort to force, or the regulation of cyberspace.

Deciding on the terms of that debate and what it is mostly *about*, then, is a privilege embedded in international law and the discursive practices it enables. Scholarship can provide a much-needed critical distance from the *discourses* of intervention and interference, if it is not to fall prey to the breathless search for policy relevance. As will become apparent, interference provides an opportunity to revisit old debates that have never left the international scene, and that will not simply go away as a result of being ignored or dismissed. Curiously for a notion as seemingly central to international law, it has been the object of relatively few systematic scholarly developments. There is, for example, considerable writing specifically on the use of force as a form of unlawful intervention[27] and, notably, on the quite specific but always prolific matter of intervention in civil wars.[28] And whilst there are certainly a number of worthy general attempts to frame the principle of non-intervention,[29]

27 Anne Orford, *Reading Humanitarian Intervention: Human Rights and the Use of Force in International Law* (Cambridge University Press 2003); Christine Gray, *International Law and the Use of Force* (3rd edn, Oxford University Press 2018); Cornelius Friesendorf, *International Intervention and the Use of Force* (Ubiquity Press 2012); Martha Finnemore, *The Purpose of Intervention: Changing Beliefs about the Use of Force* (Cornell University Press 2003); Barry M Benjamin, 'Unilateral Humanitarian Intervention: Legalizing the Use of Force to Prevent Human Rights Atrocities Note' (1992) 16 Fordham International Law Journal 120; Philip Alston and Euan Macdonald (eds), *Human Rights, Intervention, and the Use of Force* (Oxford University Press 2008).

28 Chiara Redaelli, *Intervention in Civil Wars: Effectiveness, Legitimacy, and Human Rights* (Hart Publishing 2020); Gregory H Fox, 'Intervention by Invitation' in Marc Weller (ed), *The Oxford Handbook of the Use of Force in International Law* (Oxford University Press 2015); Théodore Christakis and Karine Bannelier, 'Volenti non fit injuria? Les effets du consentement à l'intervention militaire' (2004) 50 Annuaire Français de Droit International 102; Mohamed Bennouna, *Le consentement à l'ingérence militaire dans les conflits internes* (Librairie Générale de Droit et de Jurisprudence 1974); Christopher J Le Mon, 'Unilateral Intervention by Invitation in Civil Wars: The Effective Control Test Tested Papers from the Center for International Studies at New York University School of Law: Junior Fellows' Notes' (2002) 35 New York University Journal of International Law and Politics 741; Erika de Wet, 'The Modern Practice of Intervention by Invitation in Africa and Its Implications for the Prohibition of the Use of Force' (2015) 26 European Journal of International Law 979.

29 The general literature, compared to a range of international law issues that might seem relatively less important, is rather limited. Momir B Milojević, 'The Principle of Non-Interference in the Internal Affairs of States' (2000) 1 Facta Universitatis, Series: Law and

there has been far less writing on practices less intrusive than the use of force let alone non-coercive intervention,[30] aside from a quite specific literature on the recognition of break-out states[31] and governments[32] that is itself of course not unrelated to questions of state and inter-state violence. This may be as a result of the overarching emphasis on force in international law and on coercion in debates about intervention. The point is that the dominance of non-intervention as the framing norm in international law has become an increasingly uneasy fit for non-forcible, subterranean and diffuse 'mere' interference. It may be that pinning down the definition of interference is simply 'too close for comfort' for international law, demanding that one home in on concepts that many international lawyers had rather keep fuzzy for epistemological and strategic reasons. Whatever the cause, there is a surfeit of literature on forceful intervention and a clear deficit on its non-forceful variant, as well as a tendency to see the latter only in the shadow of the former.

Politics 427; Marcelo Kohen, 'The Principle of Non-Intervention 25 Years after the Nicaragua Judgment' (2012) 25 Leiden Journal of International Law 157; Maziar Jamnejad and Michael Wood, 'The Principle of Non-Intervention' (2009) 22 Leiden Journal of International Law 345; Karl Josef Partsch, 'Das Völkerrechtliche Nichteinmischungsprinzip: Zur Praxis Der Organisation Der Afrikanischen Einheit (OAU) Und Des Afrikanischen Staatenverkehrs. By Philip Kunig. Baden-Baden: Nomos-Verlagsgesellschaft, 1981. Pp. 449. DM 77' (1984) 78 American Journal of International Law 972; Damrosch (n 16); Ellery C Stowell, *Intervention in International Law* (J Bryne 1921); Oran Young, 'Systemic Bases of Intervention' in John Norton Moore and Wolfgang Friedmann (eds), *Law and Civil War in the Modern World* (Johns Hopkins Press 1974); Nicolai A Ouchakov, *La Compétence Interne Des Etats et La Non-Intervention Dans Le Droit International Contemporain*, vol 141 (Brill Nijhoff 1974); Tom J Farer, 'Problems of an International Law of Intervention' (1968) 3 Stanford Journal of International Studies 20; Ann Van Wynen Thomas and Aaron Joshua Thomas, *Non-Intervention: The Law and Its Import in the Americas* (Southern Methodist University Press 1956); Higgins, 'Intervention and International Law' (n 15).

30 One notable early exception is Damrosch (n 16).

31 Stefan Oeter, 'The Role of Recognition and Non-Recognition with Regard to Secession' in Chirstian Walter, Antje von Ungern-Sternberg and Kavus Abushov (eds), *Self-Determination and Secession in International Law* (Oxford University Press 2014); David Turns, 'The Stimson Doctrine of Non-Recognition: Its Historical Genesis and Influence on Contemporary International Law' (2003) 2 Chinese Journal of International Law 105; John Dugard, *Recognition and the United Nations* (Grotius Publications 1987).

32 Stefan Talmon, *Recognition of Governments in International Law: With Particular Reference to Governments in Exile* (Clarendon Press 2001); Jose Serralvo, 'Government Recognition and International Humanitarian Law Applicability in Post-Gaddafi Libya' in Terry D Gill (ed), *Yearbook of International Humanitarian Law*, vol 18 (Asser Press 2015); MJ Peterson, 'Recognition of Governments Should Not Be Abolished' (1983) 77 American Journal of International Law 31.

It may also be that this gap in the literature is not entirely coincidental and reflects a global political economy of scholarship: some states, notably Western, have historically placed such a heavy focus on regulating uses of force that they have tended to correspondingly neglect and even minimize forms of intervention, let alone interference, short of force.[33] By contrast, it is states of the Global South that have been on the receiving end not only of forceful intervention but also of all manner of interference who have been most adamant that the latter phenomenon should be taken with the seriousness it deserves. The proposed extension of the rules of non-intervention beyond the use of force was, in turn, long discredited by Western states as 'unnecessary and impractical in the light of modern realities'.[34] To envisage non-intervention critically in this day and age, then, is also, in the words of Patrick Quinton-Brown, to 'decoloniz[e] intervention' including by 'decoloniz[ing] the intervention concept itself' beyond tired tropes about 'saving strangers'.[35] This entails understanding how both discourses of intervention and non-intervention have historically served to orient thinking in particular, pre-determined, and oft problematic directions.

At the same time, even the agenda of re-discovery of genealogies of intervention and non-intervention is being overtaken by the changing nature of the phenomenon, one that has increasingly blurred its contours and reawakened dormant conversations. Decolonization cannot be merely a rediscovery of a mythical past (perhaps one in which polities did not interfere with each other because they did not interact with each other) and must itself come clean about its preferred theory of international interaction. Simultaneously and as a result of the considerable change in the nature of interference that this book will seek to explore, the issue of interference has, in a sort of delicious irony, for the first time come back to haunt the West itself. The intuition is increasingly that the more interesting and problematic forms of interference may arise in a grey zone between war and peace, somewhat short of military intervention but above ordinary violations of sovereignty.[36] It is not clear, however, that

33 In fact, some Western states have long considered that the 'classic conception of non-intervention had already been absorbed by the prohibition of the threat or use of force', essentially rendering the question redundant. Edward McWhinney, 'The "New" Countries and the "New" International Law: The United Nations' Special Conference on Friendly Relations and Co-Operation among States' (1966) 60 American Journal of International Law 1, 23.

34 ibid 10.

35 Patrick Quinton-Brown, *Intervention before Interventionism: A Global Genealogy* (Oxford University Press 2024) 6.

36 Myres S McDougal and Florentino P Feliciano, 'International Coercion and World Public Order: The General Principles of the Law of War' (1957) 67 The Yale Law Journal 771.

international law is ready for a further dilution of what constitutes intervention or that it has the tools to capture what is new and problematic about the 'new' interference. Interference, such as it is, may ultimately prove resistant to consistent regulation, hamstrung by a commitment to a legality/illegality model that does not always do justice to an understanding of behavior as being 'more or less' legal.

If nothing else, then, there is an evident temporality and geopolitics to the invocation of interference in a context where 'the principle of non-interference has always been a protection for the smaller countries against the major ones'.[37] The question is not merely what interference is, but who magnifies or minimizes it, when, how and why. Despite the ensuing unequal scholarly interest, the notion is constantly invoked and has long played quite a central part in international affairs, if only—although as this book will argue, this is hardly inconsequential—as a rhetorical device. The only certainty is that states agree on the troublesome existence of interference and the corresponding non-intervention rule, even as they significantly disagree on the former's gravity and the latter's scope.[38] This is problematic in a context where accusations of interference are often banded out loosely, and where the stakes of interference being proven are considerable. Yet it is not entirely unexpected either: in international law, universal consensus about a concept's existence and importance is often directly correlated to fundamental disagreement about its foundation, scope and nature (to wit, international law itself, sovereignty, *jus cogens*, etc.).[39] In fact, there is a degree to which the debate about intervention and interference is not so much about those notions in and of themselves than it is, more or less obliquely, a constantly rehearsed debate about sovereignty in international law itself.[40] The shadowy nature of interference makes it harder

37 Georges-Henri Soutou, 'Was There a European Order in the Twentieth Century? From the Concert of Europe to the End of the Cold War' (2000) 9 Contemporary European History 329, 352.

38 Disagreement as to the scope of the rule of non-intervention is to the point that some international law scholars have long disputed its very existence, see e.g., Anthony D'Amato, 'There Is No Norm of Intervention or Non-Intervention in International Law' (2001) 7 International Legal Theory 33.

39 Frédéric Mégret, 'L'articulation Entre Tribunaux Pénaux Internationaux et Juridictions Nationales: Centralité et Ambiguïté Dans l'ordre Juridique International' (PhD Thesis, Graduate Institute of International Studies (University of Geneva) and Université Panthéon-Sorbonne (Paris I) 2006).

40 W Michael Reisman, 'Coercion and Self-Determination: Construing Charter Article 2(4)' (1984) 78 American Journal of International Law 642.

to apprehend as a phenomenon, but also sheds light in striking ways on dominant conceptions of law and their limitations.

It is against this already uncertain background that the debate has of late morphed into something even more complicated as a result of the diversification of actors involved in interference, their sometimes-nebulous character, and the always amorphous nature of the very sovereignty they target. The resulting brew—at once toxic and deeply dependent on the structures of globalization—raises questions about what clarity international law might bring to the matter and, in turn, about the role of international law itself in maintaining a sense that interference is indeed a meaningful category of analysis. In short, what will be described in more detail in Chapter 1 as the 'new interference' and that lends its title to the book is characterized by its complexity and its ubiquity; a sense of the great harms it may bring compounded by doubts about how to deal with it—the daunting realization that 'it has become increasingly difficult to deal with nuanced activities that may cause unprecedented harms'.[41] The new interference has not so much replaced the old intervention as it has added a layer of novelty and complexity to an already ill-understood phenomenon. This further complication of the question has not only done little to clarify its international legal meaning; it has, as this book will contend, tended to *radicalize* the contradictions that lie at the heart of the concept.

3 The 'New Interference' and International Law

The elusiveness of the phenomenon may be compounded by the sort of intellectual work that has (not) gone into trying to capture it. One of the great afflictions of international legal thinking, as once famously decried by Hilary Charlesworth, is its 'crisis mentality'.[42] International lawyers run from one crisis to another, breathlessly offering prescriptions that often turn out to be little more than patches. The 'crisis' can quickly and more problematically become the default mode of international legal scholarship.[43] And in the 'solution' to

41 Ido Kilovaty, 'Doxfare: Politically Motivated Leaks and the Future of the Norm on Non-Intervention in the Era of Weaponized Information' (2018) 9 Harvard National Security Journal 146, 147.

42 Charlesworth (n 5).

43 See e.g., Frédéric Mégret, 'COVID and the Crisis Mode in International Legal Scholarship' in Makane Moïse Mbengue and Jean d'Aspremont (eds), *Crisis Narratives in International Law* (Brill Nijhoff 2021).

every crisis lie, arguably, the seeds of the next crisis. The debate on interference has certainly not always escaped that curse: pursued with a renewed vigor in the West in the wake of Russian and Chinese meddling with elections in the U.S. and Europe from the mid-2010s, it has sometimes been reduced to a conversation about interference in democratic processes, often understood as Western. This has been revealing of the international legal profession's short memory span and unwillingness to confront its past in a context where the least that can be said is that interference is nothing new.

Moreover, the debate has seemed to run behind its shadow, shoring up support for vigorous new policies in a climate of moral panic about the imagined considerable risks that such interference portends for, notably, democracy, the rule of law and human rights. This will not have assuaged concerns that the discourse on interference has a dynamic of its own that is not reducible to the phenomenon itself (whatever that is), and can be seen as having its roots in long term concerns about sovereign control. It is part of a dynamic fed by and that feeds into anxieties that say as much about the state of target societies (notably in terms of strident inequality, weakened democracy, immigration crisis, etc.)[44] as it is based on an entirely sober assessment of the scale of the problem. Not all the direst predictions, in particular, have turned out to be true. For example, although the U.S. intelligence community does believe that Russia and Iran have carried out influence operations during elections, it found 'no indications that any foreign actor attempted to alter any technical aspect of the voting process in the 2020 U.S. elections, including voter registration, casting ballots, vote tabulation, or reporting results'.[45] When it comes to interference, the worst is not always the most probable, even as the 'worst' has its uses as a rhetorical device to agitate for action and reaction.

In that light, international law is often presented as one solution among others to the problem of interference. This may minimize the extent to which interference only exists, on a basic analytical level, as a function of a system that already has committed to the notion that there is such a thing as 'domestic affairs' with which other states can meaningfully interfere from without. It also neglects the extent to which that system has tended to deeply and fundamentally normalize intervention, long before it concerned itself with its

44 Igor Istomin, 'Why Do We Talk So Much about Foreign Interference?' (*Davis Center for Russian and European Studies*, 17 April 2021) <https://daviscenter.fas.harvard.edu/insights/why-do-we-talk-so-much-about-foreign-interference> accessed 15 June 2024.

45 National Intelligence Council, 'Foreign Threats to the 2020 U.S. Federal Elections (Declassified)' <https://www.dni.gov/files/ODNI/documents/assessments/ICA-declass-16MAR21.pdf> accessed 11 January 2024.

problematic character. Often missing, moreover, has been a critical distance from the phenomenon, a sense of the West's own looming presence in moves to previously generalize interference in the affairs of other states, or any sense of the complex negative feedback loops that combating interference might create for the very things one seeks to protect.[46] There is more than a fleeting sense, moreover, of international law pursuing its own shadow in the strenuous effort to define interference. Indeed, to the extent that:

> any violation of the rules of international law represents in some way an interference in matters within the jurisdiction of other States, one might well subsume virtually the whole of international law into the principle of non-intervention. [...] It is quite clear that [...] the principle of non-intervention is, at one and the same time, all or nothing.[47]

The time seems opportune, at any rate, to take a step back from the particulars of this or that controversy implicating interference, in order to adopt a more panoramic and critical view on the evolution of the phenomenon, one that connects the dots between its various manifestations into a more compelling narrative. The question of what constitutes interference in the affairs of sovereign states is both a historical, political, even philosophical one, even as it is also, ultimately, a legal question; it raises issues of jurisprudence, politics and ethics but also of domestic, transnational and international law in their own right. The question is not how one can disentangle international law from international politics, but how one can better understand the former as a function of the latter.[48] Indeed, the debate is interwoven with North-South and at least formerly East-West rivalries; it involves calculations, deceit and trickery; and it is, crucially, a *strategic* debate involving questions about how far each actor in the international system is willing to complain about others' interference or, relatedly, to justify its own interference. That the debate is ideologically highly complex and contrived is perhaps best shown by the fact that in recent history it was U.S. President Donald Trump—a populist, and one arguably systematically committed to reasserting sovereignty against the

---

46 Evelyn Douek, 'The Free Speech Blind Spot: Foreign Election Interference on Social Media' in Jens David Ohlin and Duncan B Hollis (eds), *Defending Democracies: Combating Foreign Election Interference in a Digital Age* (Oxford University Press 2021).

47 Benedetto Conforti, 'The Principle of Non-Intervention' in Mohammed Bedjaoui (ed), *International Law: Achievements and Prospects* (UNESCO 1991) 467.

48 Martti Koskenniemi, 'The Politics of International Law–20 Years Later' (2009) 20 European Journal of International Law 7.

liberal international legal order—who has been simultaneously accused of having benefited most from, and even invited, systematic incursions into that very sovereignty.[49]

In the midst of that maelstrom, international lawyers are often asked for clear answers that they may feel ill-suited to provide, at the risk of being overrun by other fields of expertise. One enduring assumption throughout seems to nonetheless have been that international law must perforce have *something* useful to say about interference. As this book will ultimately suggest, it is not, in fact, absolutely evident that international law—as opposed to a mixture of domestic law or various national security measures mixed in with elements of transnational law—should necessarily have pride of place in ascertaining the contours of interference and proposing a response to it. The international law debate on non-intervention brings its own biases (cooperation, rivalry, etc.) that focus on a few select dynamics. To tackle interference on its own terms is also to let the object 'speak back' to the paradigm and to make way for the devising of different tools of inquiry. If the norm of non-intervention, for example, spoke to an imagined system of hard sovereignties strenuously impeding intervention in each others' affairs, then a hypothetical norm of non-interference speaks to an imagined reality of diffuse, porous and inter-connected entities that are involved in a much more complex endeavor to distinguish themselves from each other. In that respect, interference is less interesting in itself than for what it says about the dynamics of unification and fragmentation and the multi-secular effort of polities to differentiate themselves ('my sovereignty is not yours') even as they absorb themselves in common schemes and only exist, in a sense, as a result of each other.

But one should not too readily assume that, because international law can lay claim to the concept of non-intervention as its own, it does not, in turn, defer to neighboring branches of law and other disciplines to fully ascertain its meaning. What is needed is an unprecedented integration of international law, human rights law and constitutional law that combines both the horizontal dimensions of non-intervention and its vertical components. For instance, what counts as interference may as well be recast as a constitutional law matter, one involving each state in the definition of what *it* considers to be interference. No more may be needed for states to domestically channel resources to resisting foreign attempts to influence their elections than such a unilateral domestic law determination. International law offers at best a framework

49 Uri Friedman, 'The Call Was Coming From Inside the White House' [2019] *The Atlantic* <https://www.theatlantic.com/politics/archive/2019/09/how-trumps-ukraine-call-invited-election-interference/598963/> accessed 26 December 2023.

and states can, for their own reasons, go above and beyond it. In the end, the impasses of the debate on interference may lead to nothing more than a reassertion of the fundamental rights of states and the basic prerogatives of sovereignty,[50] a more or less calculated flight from international law just as international law seems more necessary than ever. In doing so, however, states may well saw the branch on which they are sitting, only indulging in their own symbolic aggrandizement at the cost of undermining what makes them states within a community of states in the first place. This book will accordingly navigate international law, human rights and constitutional law somewhat freely because of a conviction that interference is at its most interesting when it does not merely provide an opportunity to prove the credentials of any particular discipline but, in a sense, shapes a discipline of its own.

At the same time, to the extent that states want to complain about interference in their domestic affairs (and as we will see, they often do), it is true that they must per necessity invoke the usages of international law for the purposes of communicating their complaint effectively to other states. To make a claim about interference to another state at least, then, is to complain about something that is *illegal under international law* or at least against its spirit, that requires minimum objectivization, if that claim is not simply to be dismissed as an instance of parochial interest-maximization. But note here that nor is it clear that classical international law—the standard prescriptions to deal with state-to-state relations—is still the most compelling response to the ills of interference and the puzzles of non-interference, notably because of the way it sometimes unhelpfully posits that there is such a thing as stable state-to-state relations that provide a kind of undisputed yardstick to measure the worrisome character of interference. Because interference is just as likely to be inter-societal, because it may turn out to affect populations or individuals more than states, and because it is often more trans-national than international, one may need to adjust one's lens accordingly. International law can quickly turn out to be part of the problem.

As the book will show, interference has become one of the most intriguing prisms to observe the tensions between that traditional international law and models of international law emphasizing the primacy of cosmopolitan human rights on the one hand, and the rise of private and transnational regulation on the other. These contending paradigms, however, do not themselves provide clear and uncontested answers to the riddle of interference. As will appear, for example, and contra a traditional view of human rights as relatively justifying

50 Yue Wu (n 18).

interference by third states, human rights can be and are invoked in defense of an agenda of resisting interference.[51] As to transnational regulation, whilst it may add a layer of control of private actors, it is not at all clear it is in any way dedicated to the traditional defense of a sovereign preserve that was a hallmark of the norm of non-intervention. Quite the contrary may be true, and the new interference, beyond the immediate regulation of its object, may also be based on an implicit claim that international law is unsuited to the task, almost designed to trigger a regulatory response that is as much beyond as it is against international law as a mode of ordering.

As has been noted by many commentators, even on its own international legal terms the rhetoric of interference often exhibits a strange mix of solemn grandstanding and haphazard and fragmented practice.[52] Some debates at the U.N. sound as if they are merely going through the motions when it comes to the issue: resolutions are adopted year after year that seem to have little bearing on what states do or even complain about, as if the proclamation of non-interference operated on a symbolic level of its own, disconnected from the day-to-day of international life; yesterday's forms of intervention are still an abiding concern for many states even as today's interference is an emerging one for others; champions of non-interference one day are enthusiastic practitioners of it the next (and vice versa). Is 'interference', perhaps by its very relational nature, a notion too elusive for serious international legal argumentation? Could the concept be so vague as to be unhelpful and even dangerous? Are states even talking about the same thing when they invoke interference? What of 'popular' understandings of interference that are not aligned with expert international legal definitions?

Faced with these questions, international lawyers have sought to transcend the relatively anemic status of the academic conversation on the topic. They have tackled the notion's content, deploying some of the familiar tools of international legal argumentations. A first wave of post-Cold War scholarship sought to address the issue at a time when claims about interference were only beginning to be heard in the West and the brunt of the complaint about interference was still carried by post-colonial states. For example, Lori Damrosch wrote one of the seminal and still most interesting articles on the question in the American Journal of International Law, outlining the complex relations between non-interference and non-forcible influence.[53] More recently, Maziar Jamnejad and Michael Wood contributed a significant article in the

51 Damrosch (n 16) 35.
52 Damrosch (n 16); Jamnejad and Wood (n 29).
53 Damrosch (n 16).

Leiden Journal of International Law on the content of the principle, emphasizing both treaty and non-treaty practice as well as circumstances that may preclude the wrongfulness of intervention.[54] Useful and worthy as these early efforts may have been, they were nonetheless undertaken before the current storm in which the new interference arose. They also provide a classical treatment of the question under public international law that does not always fully acknowledge international law's own mutations into something quite different from what it was once understood as meaning.

It is not clear, however, that the new wave of scholarship devoted to interference has always made decisive headway either. In that respect, whilst there has now been a raft of international legal discussions of, for example, Russian meddling in the U.S. 2016 election[55] and the question of election interference more generally,[56] these accounts typically discuss this sort of interference in isolation from the broader historical debate on intervention. The relentless focus on interference in Western elections is, in fact, often strikingly a-historical, as if the post-2016 debate could be addressed largely on its own late-modern terms. That a-historicism is blatant and sometimes crass: reading discussions of recent episodes of interference in the U.S., one would never get a sense that the rule of non-intervention was anything but a bland rule of international law that simply flows from sovereignty. One would not get a sense, in particular, that debates about intervention and non-intervention have long structured the very meaning of what it meant to be a member of the international community, what one might expect from 'sovereignty' and a series of major tussles—between North and South, East and West—over, essentially, who would get interfered with and who would not. Specifically, one lacks any sense of the connection of interference to the history of imperialism, the lasting traumas it has left in its wake, and the rather rich irony that states have long been on the producing end of interference now bitterly complain that they are on its receiving end.

54 Jamnejad and Wood (n 29).

55 Michael N Schmitt, 'Grey Zones in the International Law of Cyberspace' (2017) 42 Yale Journal of International Law Online 1; Steven J Barela, 'Zero Shades of Grey: Russian-Ops Violate International Law' (*Just Security*, 29 March 2018) <https://www.justsecurity.org/54340/shades-grey-russian-ops-violate-international-law/> accessed 20 September 2018; David P Fidler, 'The U.S. Election Hacks, Cybersecurity, and International Law' (2016) 110 AJIL Unbound 337.

56 Jens David Ohlin and Duncan B Hollis (eds), *Defending democracies: combating foreign election interference in a digital age* (Oxford University Press 2021).

A significant and related track of scholarship has for several years now discussed questions of sovereign cybersecurity,[57] most notoriously in the framework of the first Tallinn Manual[58] and in connection to armed conflict.[59] Cyberspace is certainly a complicating factor in the interference equation, both the *means* and a *medium* whose very nature may change the meaning of interference. Some of these debates should loom reasonably large in any current assessment of the magnitude of the problem of interference and will inform the present discussion and will be covered in some depth in this book. There ought to be real questioning, however, as to whether this specific technological lens is fundamentally a game changer when it comes to interference or merely raises anew, and in slightly different form, questions that have long haunted international law. As to the focus on armed conflict via cyberattack it represents in some ways the most dramatic form of interference in cyberspace, but the international law on the use of force is a paradigm that comes with its own distortions and leaves out forms of interference that are no less worrying merely because they do not reach the level of an armed conflict.[60]

A certain tendency to focus breathlessly on the latest technological development can, at any rate, end up neglecting the extent to which technology is not so much the driver of change as one of its manifestations, not to mention the extent to which earlier technologies of interference were just as intrusive.[61] It can also reinforce the discipline's fixation on 'novelty' as the driver of intellectual investments, a novelty whose erasures and political provenance are only too clear. This book will thus seek to locate the question of cyber-meddling within larger developments about interference, and will resist focusing *only* on what is in the end merely the latest chapter in a much longer history. In resisting this tendency, the book hopes to move the debate away from the recent rediscovery of interference to reclaim a *temps long* of interference's practices

57 MA Xinmin, 'What Kind of Internet Order Do We Need?' (2015) 14 Chinese Journal of International Law 399; Murdoch Watney, 'Challenges Pertaining to Cyber War under International Law', *2014 Third International Conference on Cyber Security, Cyber Warfare and Digital Forensic* (*CyberSec*) (2014); Jozef Valuch and Ondrej Hamulak, 'Cyber Operations During the Conflict in Ukraine and the Role of International' in Sergey Sayapin and Evhen Tsybulenko (eds), *The Use of Force against Ukraine and International Law: Jus Ad Bellum, Jus In Bello, Jus Post Bellum* (Asser Press 2018).

58 *Tallinn Manual on the International Law Applicable to Cyber Warfare* (Cambridge University Press 2013).

59 Valuch and Hamulak (n 57).

60 Jean d'Aspremont, 'Cyber Operations and International Law: An Interventionist Legal Thought' (2016) 21 Journal of Conflict & Security Law 575.

61 Patrick CR Terry, 'Voting by Proxy—Meddling in Foreign Elections and Public International Law' (2022) 29 Indiana Journal of Global Legal Studies 69, 70.

that does justice to its historical normality and geographic ubiquity. This will in some ways weigh down the exercise with a heavier historical and theoretical apparatus, but will also hopefully avoid the sort of fetishization of novelty which has of late become a hallmark of the study of interference.

One impression that emerges from this incipient scholarship on interference, moreover, is an unmistakable sense of national and cultural parochialism. The emphasis on the Anglo-American or European responses to interference, in particular, fails to engage, at least on an equal footing, with claims about interference that have been made by a variety of countries and constituencies over at least the last 70 years. As such, it ironically sometimes fails to contextualize what is new and specific about its object and ends up being provincial and tone-deaf about the urgency with which other arguments about interference have been made for decades by less well represented constituencies.[62] This also leads to an artificial dialogue in which one side's claims about interference are taken seriously and the others' are seen as mere political posturing, a conversation that fundamentally neglects their common provenance and, indeed, dialectical relationship. It is often dependent on a very linear and simplistic narrative of intervention (used to be allowed, became prohibited, now contested, etc.) that does not do justice to the various oscillations between interference and non-interference and the permutations of positions that occur across time.[63]

Contextualizing the current debates as merely the latest round in decades long conversations can, on the contrary, help highlight both the specificities and continuities of the 'new interference'. This will involve, in particular, taking seriously and genealogically a long tradition of hostility to interference rooted in Third World, Non-Aligned and Latin America and Afro-Asian struggles,[64] but also paying attention to the ambivalence of that tradition and the late reneging on some of its principles for a not altogether discernible outcome. The book will argue, in fact, that historical and geographic myopia about the issue of interference explains in part why a seemingly simple question (what is interference and what might be unlawful about it?) turns out to be more intractable than it ought to be. It also suggests why responses that are politically given to those questions are difficult to generalize and lead to dead ends.

62 For a helpful recent attempt to go back in time and revisit today's interference debate in light of the past decades of exchanges, see Stephen Townley, 'Intervention's Idiosyncrasies: The Need for a New Approach to Understanding Sub-Forcible Intervention' (2018) 42 Fordham International Law Journal 1167.

63 Quinton-Brown (n 35).

64 ibid.

Engaging the history of interference and non-interference, both intellectual and diplomatic, entails a commitment to context and timing. It means taking seriously the huge distortions in the scholarly production on the issue, and their reflection of material, racial, cultural prejudices manifest in universities, think tanks and journals. One must specifically and constantly attend to these distortions by mentally compensating for absences and gaps in the literature that result from the habitus of the international legal profession.

Most of the literature on non-interference, furthermore, has drawn on a conventional legal positivist methodology that seems increasingly under threat as a result of the very ubiquitous and contradictory character of interference claims and the diversification of actors involved in it. It has tended to remain mired in international lawyers' linguistic obsession with text or the spoken word at the expense of context and acts; and by its very nature it has tended to constantly focus attention on the state, as if the question raised by interference were not precisely whether the state ought to be the appropriate unity of analysis. To be clear, ascertaining the content of the rule on non-interference in this conventional way remains a topical and useful task in and of itself, at least as part of a more complex enquiry. It requires one to abide by the disciplining effects of international law, including its injunction to understand the law as grounded in the reality of international relations whilst clinging to some normative claim and putting one's mind to the exercise in good faith. Notwithstanding the well-known and amply debated limitations of that methodological framework,[65] it no doubt produces effects, perhaps even salutary effects, in one's locutor. This book will thus not shun from engaging some of the linguistic games that are the inevitable lot of any practitioner trying to make sense of what interference means here and there.

At the same time, that methodology is heavily reliant on discourses of sovereignty that are, both ontologically and epistemologically, the very thing that interference not only undermines but, arguably, transcends. It is an exercise, moreover, which in its desire to posit a strong distinction between what is legal and what is illegal runs into some familiar limitations. Often the resonance that is sought by branding something as 'illegal' rings hollow because that dramatic *effet d'annonce* is followed by more of a whimper than a bang. Often also, the emphasis on compliance eludes the many shades of grey between compliance and violation: over-compliance, grudging compliance, *faux* compliance, accidental compliance, violation as challenge to the norm, violation for valid reasons, etc. In addition, focusing on a simplistic concept of compliance

65 Koskenniemi, *From Apology to Utopia* (n 20).

has several drawbacks: self-righteousness, non-irony, crisis mentality, one-upmanship and, above all, a failure to acknowledge and even deception about one's own motivations and agenda. As the debate over interference often reminds us, much scholarship in international law is oblivious to its ideological blind spots and thus constantly at risk of being instrumentalized by the powers-that-be.

The illusion of international legal clarity, then, tends to be too often the project on which international legal scholarship embarks, with dubious results and even legitimacy. Leaving aside notorious doubts about the intellectual sustainability of such moves,[66] this will not do away with underlying and often unresolved normative issues: how does one distinguish between good faith or bad faith protests against interference? States simply grandstanding and genuine identification of a norm? What is the rule supposed to prohibit in the first place and what is its finality? How does it relate to that most contested of concepts, sovereignty? What are the politics of international law associated with making or countering claims of interference? Maybe no state denies that the norm of non-intervention exists, but what good does this do if states are fundamentally at odds over what interference is? A purely customary elucidation of the norm, conclusive as it may be in theory on international law's own doctrinal terms, still leaves much to be desired. What is gained in terms of certainty about the norm's existence, is immediately lost in terms of precision about its content. In trying to discern the contours of interference, international law sees only itself in the mirror.

To echo the earlier point of the dangers of looking for resolution outside of international law, however, others have sought to frame the issue entirely as a series of policy dilemmas.[67] The question is how one would want to define interference and on the basis of what objectives. This has the merit of bringing to the fore the extent to which any definition of interference is in itself a high-stake endeavor: to define is itself a political act that stands to ultimately have real implications in the world by, henceforth, counting some behavior as interference and other not. This policy-oriented approach does get U.S. closer

66 Martti Koskenniemi, 'The Pull of the Mainstream' (1990) 88 Michigan Law Review 1946.

67 For an analysis almost wholly in the terms of policy dilemmas, in the manner of the New Haven school, see Farer, 'Problems of an International Law of Intervention' (n 29). Also Louis Henkin and others, 'Force, Intervention, and Neutrality in Contemporary International Law' (1963) 57 Proceedings of the American Society of International Law at Its Annual Meeting (1921–1969) 147; Florentino P Feliciano, 'Conflicting Orders and the Appraisal of Resort to Coercion' (1959) 53 Proceedings of the American Society of International Law at Its Annual Meeting (1921–1969) 153.

to the notion that the definition of interference is agentic, circumstantial and relational. But it also neglects the extent to which international lawyers are not merely at liberty to define what constitutes interference as what makes most sense from a policy perspective, irrespective of the existing normative pre-commitments of the discipline. The blatant instrumentalism involved often barely hides its political provenance, in a context where states do need to objectivize what counts as interference if their arguments are to carry at all with other states.

At the other end of the spectrum, significant work has begun to emerge at the intersection of international law and normative theory in a more jurisprudential vein. The writings of Jens Ohlin come to mind as having sought to think deeply about what interference means but also ought to mean.[68] Earlier work in the English School of international relations, notably RJ Vincent's magnus opus on intervention, also forged a trailblazing path in terms of the larger normative resonance of the theme in an international society of states.[69] That work and its broader inspiration will inform this book. It has the merit of moving U.S. beyond the naive instrumentalism of policy approaches that feign to believe that an uncomplex and unproblematic theory of why interference is banned is widely available, and of course of narrow positivist approaches. But as will appear, the particular conclusions that some of these authors reach are still in need of further critical attention, particularly in light of the rapidly evolving nature of the debate and the unintended consequences that may derive from, in particular, too a-historical and uncritical a liberal focus.

Rather than a strictly doctrinal, policy-oriented or jurisprudential approach, then, this book will stake its ambition on a more critical vision of the dilemmas of interference. In this, it hopes to make the most of what other scholars might treat as merely the frustrating 'crooked timber' of international relations, which it will chose instead to see as the very substance of such relations' dynamism. Instead of simply deploring the debate's contradictions—'but [a] natural consequence of the darkness which besets a subject, at no time clear and even now in a fluid condition'—[70] as a pure manifestation of the supremacy of unprincipled politics, it will treat it as a starting point and symptom of the complex antinomies that the commitment to non-interference leads anyone trying to make sense of the notion into. The non-conclusive character of many of these debates, at any rate, should be familiar from the major rupture-lines of international co-existence in the crucible of competing sovereignties: one

68 Ohlin, *Election Interference: International Law and the Future of Democracy* (n 17).
69 RJ Vincent, *Nonintervention and International Order* (Princeton University Press 1974).
70 Winfield (n 1) 130.

state's terrorism is another's freedom fighter; one state's aggression is another's self-defence; and one state's interference, then, is another's benign influence.[71] Contra the suggestion that 'we' at least 'know intervention/interference when we see it', it will suggest that a hard look at the ambiguities of that debate provides an opportunity to reexamine the nature of that 'we' and to challenge the intuition that different constituencies have the same thing in mind when they speak of either.

The *structuring* rather than strictly determinative nature of such antinomies, then, is what is clear; although what is being structured and how exactly is precisely the task at hand. Most claims of interference and non-interference, for example, are often just that: claims that are made by one state to another, although with little prospect of conventional resolution, and where resolution may not even be the stake of the dispute. Posing, virtue-signalling, grandstanding, evading, distracting, dividing, deflecting, are all part of conversations that states have and by which they manage both their appetite for interference in maximization of their national interest and their horror at being interfered with at the expense of their sovereignty. States disagree about whether interference has indeed occurred and often seem happy to leave it at that, giving the whole debate a sort of permanently unresolved quality: ships crossing each other in the dark, then, as the dominant metaphor of debates about interference. One would have to assume, still, that there is something to making these claims *qua* legal claims; otherwise, why would states bother making them, often with an evident sense of urgency and entitlement?

Claims about interference and non-interference, in this context, are made in earnest and not just as political window-dressing, all the more so that there is real uncertainty about the right position because either side might, in fact, be right. A claim about interference can, in a sense, be its own end: merely saying something to the effect of: 'I am sovereign, respect me!' Moreover, the indeterminacy of the debate means that rhetorically swaying one's audience (whichever it be imagined to be) is the true stake, and one worth devoting energy to, one that may even allow for simultaneous winners. One may simply be playing to a different audience, international or even domestic. In some ways, the claim about interference is the very fundamental, constitutional claim of international law: that by which the sovereign comes into being, not as a self-contained or internally instituted entity but as one claiming recognition as such from others. States, in a sense, are only ever complaining about

71 Charles G Fenwick, 'Intervention: Individual and Collective' (1945) 39 American Journal of International Law 645.

interference; it is their *raison d'être*. And in claiming, like the monarchs of yesteryear, que 'l'Etat, c'est moi' they are invariably required to concede that 'l'Etat, c'est toi *aussi*'.

Drawing on a tradition that emphasizes the discursive, communicative and relational nature of international legal argumentation,[72] this book proposes to treat the non-interference norm as a rich rhetorical terrain that constitutes the international legal field, rather than the other way round.[73] Rhetorical performances about interference represent a highly ritualized exercise of symbolic border delimitation through which the ongoing meaning of sovereignty is constantly being renegotiated. Rather than merely protecting sovereignty, they tell U.S. something about what sovereignty is considered to *be* at any point in time ('I *am* a sovereign because I call out your interference on this or that ground'). Sovereigns that decline to protest interference, by contrast, consign themselves not only to political irrelevance but risk undermining the very foundations of their (precarious) statehood. A robust practice of non-interference (complaining about it, not engaging in it) is the tapestry that must logically sustain the claim that sovereignty exists in a meaningful way.

Claims about interference, therefore, have a role in structuring international law, at least as much as they are structured by international law. A debate about *relations* between subjects imagined as givens (what is interference between states?) turns out to be a debate about the *identit(ies)* of those subjects (what is sovereignty as refracted by interference?). As a result, the book aims less at providing the precise contours of the notion than to highlight non-interference's ongoing constitutive role in international law and affairs and, in particular, the co-constitutive role it has for other concepts (most notably, sovereignty). Rather than asking the conventional positivist question of 'what is interference?', it will ask the typically constructivist question of 'what does the claim of (non)interference *do*?'[74] Or, put slightly differently, it will speculate about

---

72 For a recent overview of how the contribution of Chaim Perelman to the study of the rhetoric of law could be adapted to international legal argument, see Ian Scobbie, 'Rhetoric, Persuasion, and Interpretation in International Law' in Andrea Bianchi, Daniel Peat and Matthew Windsor (eds), *Interpretation in International Law* (Oxford University Press 2015).

73 Martti Koskenniemi, 'International Law and Hegemony: A Reconfiguration' (2004) 17 Cambridge Review of International Affairs 197.

74 For an application of constructivist method in relation to the norm of non-interference, see Nikolas Busse, 'Constructivism and Southeast Asian Security' (1999) 12 The Pacific Review 39; Paul D Williams, 'From Non-Intervention to Non-Indifference: The Origins and Development of the African Union's Security Culture' (2007) 106 African Affairs 253.

what it *means* to invoke non-interference against the background of a dense tapestry of semantic performances: to be sovereign is to act like one.

As per this book's title, I propose, based on various strands of my previous work,[75] the notion of a *discursive economy* as a conceit for what I believe is going on in the background. The idea of a discursive economy is of a system, typically characteristic of languages, the main function of which is to produce meaning. Production of meaning is the central stake of much social activity. Meaning mediates the world of things and the world of ideas through interconnected symbols. Understanding law as a discursive economy—as opposed to a system of rules or a particular type of morality—makes it possible to fully engage its meaning-producing function. Meaning feeds off consistency but also rupture, analogy but also contrast. It is patterned rather than systematically organized. The contention is that the law, as a system of signs, is on some level *only* a system of meaning. The production of meaning is extremely fluid but also imposes its constraints. One cannot say *anything*, or at least one says anything at the risk of undermining one's status as locutor, and perhaps the status of the language itself. But one can constantly rearrange the chairs on the deck in an effort to orient the overall meaning of the system.

To speak of international law as discursive economy rather than simply a language has two effects. First, it focuses on *discourse*, the *act* of invoking, channelling and projecting language rather than just language itself. As such, it brings attention to how language is used in creative and productive ways that are not reducible to linguistic laws. It highlights, in particular, that there are two forms of intervention in and through language: as a locutor interested in obtaining particular effects (e.g., in our case, condemning interference, protesting one's non-interference) and as a sort of decentralized trustee for that language, mindful of the ramifications of language use and diffusely aware of one's long term impact on it. In the latter role, every locutor is responsible for the ways in which the pursuit of interest (by others but particularly one's own) through language may ultimately undermine the ability of that language to convey anything. For example, one ultimately cannot have the full

75 See, in particular, Frédéric Mégret, 'Thinking About What International Humanitarian Lawyers "Do": An Examination of the Laws of War as a Field of Professional Practice' in Wouter Werner, Marieke de Hoon and Alexis Galan (eds), *The Law of International Lawyers; Reflections on the Work of Martti Koskenniemi* (2017); Frédéric Mégret, 'Alston in Alabama: Towards a Theory of International Human Rights Law Praxis' in Nehal Bhuta and others (eds), *The Struggle for Human Rights—Law, Politics, Practice. Essays in Honor of Philip Alston* (2021); Frédéric Mégret, 'International Criminal Law and the Symbolic Economy of Stigma' (International Nuremberg Principles Academy, 5 August 2023).

benefit of denouncing intervention in one's own affairs if one has otherwise consistently eviscerated the notion of intervention through overuse or use at counter-purpose.

As such, the focus on discourse emphasizes its repetitive and iterative dimension. One does not only use discourse once but many times over time, in ways that constantly affect one's prospective ability to use language in the future even as it shines back on one's past uses of language. Stylistically, the greatest dangers that trustees for a language must guard against is the dilution of words through overuse or the collapse of the semantic categories that constitute it. For example, if everything becomes intervention, then nothing is intervention. The word loses any trenchancy. Moreover, if the distinctions between interaction, influence, interference, intervention, coercion and use of force are blurred, then none of these words can fulfill their ideal analytical function. This is despite the considerable temptation for slippage through either hyperbole or euphemism and, for example, recharacterizing what might at first brush seem the less worrying phenomenon in the terms of the more worrying one. At the same time, an ultra sparing and restrictive use of language (using intervention only to describe the most grotesquely coercive forms of intervention) can deprive language of its function in another way, by preventing it from having any effect in the world. It involves a form of denying the word to the world that not only risks consigning it to irrelevance, but prompts the unchained reemergence of language elsewhere and weakens one's ability to continue to invest productively in language. This also underscores the extent to which discourse is the site of competition between actors over who has the last word on language, who speaks its most genuine version, and who gets to deploy it against whom.

Second, the notion of a discursive *economy* makes the most of the idea that international law discourse is the management of a form of symbolic scarcity. Locutors seek to prevent the devaluation of language through excess or insufficient use. Language is accordingly the object of a range of symbolic investments over time. These investments can be affective (the 'passion' for non-interference, the *noblesse oblige* of intervention, etc.), interested (how does having a given position on interference maximize my national interest), strategic (how will my position on intervention in this realm affect my standing on interference in this other) or aesthetic. Investments can be constant or evolutive. They are always based on certain expectations for returns, that may or may not materialize. They are relatively path driven and come with their own inertias: investing in a certain usage of international law does not bind one to such usages forever but makes it harder to suddenly change course because it will expose contradiction as well as inherently weaken language (one cannot say one thing and its contrary). Contradiction, ambivalence and ambiguity are all postures that can be occupied within the discursive field to maximize one's ability to redeploy investments.

Investing in meaning is an inherently speculative activity in that one cannot actually know in advance what the yield of a particular discourse is (will it turn out, retrospectively, to have been a good investment to emphasize the distinctiveness of intervention from the use of force on the one side and mere interference on the other?). Social actors sometimes come out on top, and sometimes stand to lose much, including credibility, reputation and dignity. But language does sustain a form of constant exchange between parties in which "words" are produced, given, and received. In this process, the value of words can be enhanced through their rarity or cheapened through their over-use. Actors are aware at any given time of what they are trying to say through international law and also, more diffusely, of the costs of saying anything through international law, including in terms of forsaken opportunities to make other arguments in other circumstances or to invoke vernaculars entirely other than international law (international morality and international politics).

Language can be the object of speculative bubbles and crashes but is also remarkably enduring over time as a basic currency of international relations. Language structures rather than it determines outcomes. Language belongs to its locutors but has a life of its own. Language, in short, produces autonomous and sui generis effects that are not reducible to actors' strategy or the structure of the world, whatever either of those may be. How international actors engage with, manipulate but also entrust their destinies to discursive outcomes, then, is both the great mystery of international law. It makes it possible to prod the depths of contradiction that beset international law discourse, its infuriating circularity, whilst living with and even rejoicing in the antinomies it produces.[76]

Instead of seeing a trade-off between the consistency of the concept, its optimality, and its social relevance, for example, the book will argue, perhaps provocatively, that the norm of non-interference *is socially relevant precisely despite and sometimes even because of its inconsistency.* Inconsistency allows the norm to, over time, justify both non-interference (as its name would seem to suggest) but also interference, against a background where international law remains fundamentally indecisive about whether either is always problematic and why. Inconsistency is precisely the dynamic tool that states require to organize their relations through law.[77] That inconsistency produces significant

76 Koskenniemi, *From Apology to Utopia* (n 20).

77 ibid.

social effects should be of the highest interest to international lawyers, perhaps all the more so that they despair of the possibility of coming up with a single comprehensive theory of what constitutes unlawful interference. It also brings a retort of sorts to those skeptical of international law, albeit not necessarily the kind typically favored by international lawyers: the inconsistency of interference and non-interference claims is constitutive of the reality of sovereignty, even in its most confusing, inconclusive form.

This is, to be sure, not the same as haphazardness: there is a real method to (non) interference's folly (as one would expect from a patterned discourse), that which emerges over time from repeated points of agreement as well as persistent areas of opposition. Taking inconsistency seriously, then, involves paying attention to the discursive and argumentative strategies in and of themselves rather than their imagined foundation in an external reality or epistemological discipline. Indeed, even as states disagree about its scope, states—and quite possibly a range of other actors—constantly make claims and counterclaims about whether interference has occurred, which at least reveal the sort of reasoning that they believe they need to craft in order to make such claims stick. It is these debates—rich, constantly renewed, and contradictory—that constitute the norm of non-interference, rather than any particular answer to the question they seem to presuppose, especially one focused on over-interpreting a few disparate positive law sources. The norm of non-interference, in other words, is not the answer to a question that precedes it (e.g., this is how far a state may meddle in the affairs of another state), but the question that follows the question-begging answer (i.e., what does claiming that a state is meddling in one's affairs reveal?)

In short, therefore, the book aims to remedy three fundamental flaws in the ongoing debate about interference. First, its presentism and a-historicism, which leads to a situation in which one is constantly at risk of being delusional about the debate's novelty and reinventing the wheel. More worryingly, a lack of awareness of the past of interference (including one's own past) risks neglecting the extent to which one cannot simply adopt the position that the exigencies of the moment seem to require without bringing to the fore unresolved historical questions, as well as one's deep compromissions in already making interference and non-interference what they are. Second, a failure to pay attention to the constitutive dimensions of non-intervention, by focusing on the merely regulatory dimension of the norm, constantly and infuriatingly shifts the goal post on what it simultaneously constitutes (defines, delineates, describes, etc.). In taking for granted a sense of an already existing and immutable sovereignty to (not) be interfered with, it fails to apprehend the extent to which sovereignty is as much shaped by interference (and pushbacks against it) as it is simplistically violated by it. Third, the lack of attention to the strategic and not merely norm-complying dimensions of defining interference gives much more importance to the voice of scholarly international lawyers than it deserves. It neglects the extent to which all definition of interference is an expression of foreign legal policy[78] that is much more about calculating angles than implementing international law in any straightforward way, let alone out of fidelity to it. The norm of non-interference is 'what states make of it' and, as we shall see, they have decided to make strikingly different things of it in different circumstances.

In the process, the book will make three recurring and interrelated claims. First, that the debate has and arguably should continue to shift from non-intervention to a broader conversation about non-interference. This is an ambitious but also slightly disconcerting and potentially problematic move that may give the impression that one is chasing shadows. Second the claim will be that, even as the discourse about interference has been rekindled, it has seemed to constantly and perversely deprive itself of an object, as what constitutes both inherently domestic affairs and interference therewith has never seemed more elusive. This raises crucial questions about whether there is anything worth defending about the notion of domestic affairs and whether that claim has not been chronically overrun by a voluntary submission to the international gaze. Third, the argument will be that the discourse of human rights, fundamentally problematizing the horizontal emphasis of international law, provides U.S. with a way of renewing our understanding of what is specifically problematic about interference and how we might go about identifying it. The book falls far short of providing a fully-fledged human rights theory of non-interference, but it does hope to be a step in the direction of understanding interference beyond the, increasingly problematic, public international law canon.

Each of the book's parts seeks to remedy some theoretical and methodological shortcoming of the debate to this point. The first part provides a synthetic and dialectic overview of the history of claims about non-interference in sovereign affairs in order to contextualize the concept's evolution, suggesting that claims about interference have often changed camp and ideological flavor. This means that, over time, states have been called upon to argue against their own earlier case, at no point more so than in the last decade characterized by

78 Frédéric Mégret, 'Foreign Legal Policy as the Background to Foreign Relations Law? Revisiting Guy de Lacharrière's La Politique Juridique Extérieure' in Helmut Philipp Aust and Thomas Kleinlein (eds), *Encounters between Foreign Relations Law and International Law: Bridges and Boundaries* (Cambridge University Press 2021).

the 'new interference'. In exposing this process, the book sheds light on the fundamentally unstable and politically ambiguous character of the notion of interference as well as the particular nature of the shamelessness that characterizes the *répartie* on interference (Part 1). The book then analyzes how the new interference radicalizes old questions of international law, leading to a flurry of renewed claims about both the nature of the *domaine réservé* and what it takes to interfere with it. The most significant conclusion here is that the 'game' of interference in conditions of both globalization and great power rivalry, changing geopolitical balance, mutual dependency on a common informational infrastructure, and imbrication of public spheres, has fundamentally changed. This has created renewed illegibility and significant dangers for both those who seek to wield and limit interference, in a context where interference constantly invokes a host of correlated concepts that themselves know of no stable meaning outside discursive claims made, precisely, through claims of 'interference' (Part 2). Finally, the last part highlights a number of strategic dilemmas that the renewed threat of interference raises, including the risk that one's incoherence in arguing against interference even as one continues to interfere will be exposed, or the possibility that states will over-react and harm significant domestic and international legal interests in the process. It is thus a contribution to how the process of dealing with the problem of perceived interference also contributes to constructing and even amplifying it. Interference, ultimately, has no meaning separate from the strategies that actors deploy to make sense of it (Part 3).

The conclusion will hint at the difficulty of taking interference as such seriously as a category of international law, but also the difficulty of not taking it seriously. There is a fundamental tension between the logic of independence and inter-dependence that has long been at the core of international law and that is exposed with renewed and in some ways unprecedented virulence by the new interference debate. Integrating the traditional international law on intervention with a broader focus on interference is one step towards rekindling a broader interest in how the sovereignty of all states is being interfered with almost all the time by all states. To really make headway, moreover, one must expand the analysis of interference towards both constitutional and international human rights law to understand how thinking about interference also requires U.S. to assess the frameworks that we typically deploy to understand it. Interference unfolds not just horizontally between states but also vertically between state and society and, as it were, 'diagonally' through transnational flows that are not reducible to international law's traditional public law-heavy framing. These developments mean that international lawyers constantly run the risk of missing the mark, of addressing yesterday's problem rather than today's or a future rather than current problem. The book will thus weigh on the possibility of, henceforth, living with the reality of interference in ways that are normatively sustainable and productive, even in a world where the polysemy of interference proves impossible to transcend.

A final preliminary note is in order. The book will leave aside several areas connected to the principle of non-interference. The first is the use of force, which is of course strictly prohibited and regulated as such and constitutes a particularly manifest case of interference. It also belongs, however, to a domain too ample, too distinctive, and too well broached already to be dealt with in any useful way here. Whilst not discounting the danger of the 'lesser' forms of interference to serve as a laboratory for and morph into violent intervention—indeed the tendency of the 'new interference' to occasionally collapse (as in cyberspace) the distinction between violent and non-violent interference—[79] there is reason to think that the relative importance of the norm against forcible intervention may have to be discounted in an age where hacking into political parties' headquarters and releasing emails or recognizing an opposition leader as the presumptive head of state may simply be a more effective and far less costly way of imposing one's will on another sovereign. The book will also for the most part leave aside any systematic discussion of state jurisdiction, whether civil or criminal, prescriptive, adjudicative or enforcement. These issues will be mentioned in passing as providing pointers for what constitutes the legitimate domain of the sovereign but this is an area that would be worthy of entirely separate developments and is, at any rate, extensively covered by the literature.

The point of interference is that it is less than a use of force and more than a mere a violation of sovereignty, something more in the nature, as we will see, of a substitution to and perversion of the sovereign. It is in this ever-sensitive grey area that constitutes neither evidently armed intervention nor obvious jurisdictional encroachment that the most testing challenges for the international legal order arguably arise.

---

79 See e.g., Christian Henderson, 'The Arab Spring and the Notion of External State Sovereignty in International Law' (2014) 35 Liverpool Law Review 175.

PART 1

Interference and Non-interference: A Short History

This first part aims to give the bare outline of one possible way of recounting the role that claims of interference and non-interference have played in the history of international law. It does so to provide a broad framing narrative on which the book's legal analysis can subsequently be grafted. Its basic goal is to emphasize the specific historicity of the debate on interference, as involving both elements of continuity and rupture in the discursive economy of international law.[80] On the one hand, there is a risk of making today's interference more like the old than it really is, relying on a sort of venerable and eternal legal conception of intervention that does not do justice to its fragmented historical unfolding; on the other hand, there is a 'presentist' risk of making the 'new interference' appear as irreducible and unique when, to some extent, it merely refracts older conversations. This part will foreground the agency of various actors in precipitating particular influential accounts of what interference is, as well as some of the structural factors that have made the problem more or less urgent. Finally, it will show how real-world developments have been mediated by a series of stylized conversations on the proper perimeter of non-intervention. History, it turns out, is a particularly opportune space to observe long term investments in certain discourses of non-intervention, their subversion, and their renewal.

1 Non-interference's Conditions of Possibility

The default position in a pre- or a-Westphalian, typically imperial, world was widely understood to have been one of relatively wanton interference across jurisdiction, notably on a vertical basis, specifically by the Papacy and the Holy Roman Emperor (although this constant meddling of all in the affairs of all is only anachronistically and retrospectively understood as interference). As Nicolai Alexandrovitch Ouchakov put it, '[d]ans les conditions de la hiérarchie féodale, ce qui était indiscutable c'était le droit du suzerain d'intervenir dans les affaires de son vassal. Les guerres intestines féodales s'opposaient à l'établissement du principe de non-intervention'.[81] In other words, there could not be a strong concept of interference in a system that did not simultaneously know of a strong concept of sovereignty. Interference was also a widespread 'horizontal' phenomenon as various potentates intruded with various degrees

80 Jyoti Rattan, 'Changing Dimensions of Intervention Under International Law: A Critical Analysis' (2019) 9 Sage Open 1.

81 Ouchakov (n 29) 5. ['Under the conditions of the feudal hierarchy, what was indisputable was the right of the suzerain to intervene in the affairs of his vassal. Feudal internecine wars opposed the establishment of the principle of non-intervention'].

 | DOI:10.1163/9789004532731_003

of authority on the affairs of others, the point being that this interference was not specifically or legally as problematic in a system where jurisdiction was fundamentally overlapping and ill-differentiated. In particular, the systematic overlap of territorial and personal jurisdiction ensured conditions in which the very bases for a reserved sphere of competency were often lacking.

By contrast, the Treaty of Westphalia is widely understood as having internationally consecrated sovereignty and, more specifically, a principle of non-interference at least from Papal jurisdiction: *rex est imperator in regno suo*. Simultaneously, the principle of *ejus regio cujos religio* solidified an understanding of then emerging sovereigns as realms of competency onto themselves. Non-interference was gradually buttressed through appeals to the freedom of nations who should not tread on the affairs of other nations. As Christian Wolff put it, 'to interfere in the government of another [...] is opposed to the natural liberty of nations'.[82] Emerich de Vattel is typically associated with more profoundly marking the turn to a conception of non-interference and non-intervention in sovereign affairs,[83] arguing that:

> It is an evident consequence of the liberty and independence of nations, that all have a right to be governed as they think proper, and that no state has the smallest right to interfere in the government of another. Of all the rights that can belong to a nation, sovereignty is, doubtless, the most precious, and that which other nations ought the most scrupulously to respect, if they would not do her an injury. [...] It does not then belong to any foreign power to take cognisance of the administration of that sovereign, to set himself up for a judge of his conduct, and to oblige him to alter it. If he loads his subjects with taxes, and if he treats them with severity, the nation alone is concerned in the business; and no other is called upon to oblige him to amend his conduct, and follow more wise and equitable maxims.[84]

82 Cited in Thomas and Thomas (n 29) 5.

83 Simone Zurbuchen, 'Vattel's "Law of Nations" and the Principle of Non-Intervention' (2010) 31 Grotiana 69.

84 Emer de Vattel, *The Law of Nations, or, Principles of the Law of Nature, Applied to the Conduct and Affairs of Nations and Sovereigns, with Three Early Essays on the Origin and Nature of Natural Law and on Luxury* (Béla Kapossy and Richard Whatmore eds, Liberty Fund, Incorporated 2008) 289–290.

Non-interference, then, involved both a duty to restrain oneself from interference and a right to complain of any such interference. Taking that reasoning to its logical consequence, Vattel went as far as to argue that:

> The Spaniards violated all rules when they set themselves up as judges of the Inca Athualpa. If that prince had violated the law of nations with respect to them, they would have had a right to punish him. But they accused him of having put some of his subjects to death, of having had several wives, etc.—things, for which he was not at all accountable to them.[85]

That broad assessment of early modernity as having foreshadowed notions of non-interference must nonetheless be nuanced in at least three ways, each relevant to our understanding of non-interference as a series of interrelated practices and normative arrangements for the international legal order. First, the image was obviously, even in the European hinterland, a considerable historical simplification.[86] The Holy Roman Empire and its complex relations of meddling with its constituent entities would continue to exist for another 150 years after Westphalia. The constitution of nation-states had barely begun for most of Europe even as non-interference began to emerge as a kind of ideational map to what might characterize the emerging political reality.[87] Foreign meddling remained rife as late as the 19th Century, whether by French revolutionaries or conservative monarchies bent on restoring or protecting the *Ancien Régime*. Even as Vattel fortified notions of non-intervention conceptually, he was also one of the principal artisans of a conception of 'just war' that allowed foreign powers to come to the rescue of national revolts against tyranny.[88] In short, claims to non-interference were to an extent messy, ambiguous and *ad hoc*.

Second, non-interference was also embedded in a series of guarantees, in particular of the rights of minorities, that paradoxically safeguarded the

---

85 ibid 290.

86 Derek Croxton, 'The Peace of Westphalia of 1648 and the Origins of Sovereignty' (1999) 21 The International History Review 569.

87 Jennifer Pitts, 'Intervention and Sovereign Equality: Legacies of Vattel' in Jennifer M Welsh and Stefano Recchia (eds), *Just and Unjust Military Intervention: European Thinkers from Vitoria to Mill* (Cambridge University Press 2013).

88 de Vattel (n 84) 290. ('But if the prince, by violating the fundamental laws, gives his subjects a legal right to resist him,—if tyranny becoming insupportable obliges the nation to rise in their own defence,—every foreign power has a right to succour an oppressed people who implore their assistance').

possibility of collective interference.[89] Debates about humanitarian intervention, often presented as a hallmark of the late 20th Century, were fundamental as early as the 17th and up to the 19th Century, in the writings of Grotius, Wheaton, Bluntschli, Phillimore, Bonfils, Fauchille, Rolin-Jaequemyns, and others.[90] They often revolved around the idea of a 'right of' vested in an emerging 'international community', as illustrated notably by Western efforts to preserve Greek independence against Ottoman attempts to suppress it.[91] They continued to largely structure the international legal conversation, even as the principle of non-intervention was increasingly proclaimed, underlining the fundamental contradiction between a system of equals (sovereigns) and one structured by common values (the international community).[92] Hence, overall, non-interference was, perhaps unsurprisingly, always implicated not only in patterns of continuing interference but in claims about its legitimacy in the name of protecting sovereignty itself.[93] These belie any facile and linear evolution of the international system from one default position to another and stress the continuity between some of today's most vigorous debates and those of earlier times. Instead, this part hopes to shed light on the reality that nothing of the claim about non-interference's constitutive character for the international legal order is lost by paying close attention to the attendant quasi-universality of legitimized interference.

Third, the realm of sovereign statehood was fundamentally and not only contingently limited to parts of the Western world, and thus so was the scope of intervention. The conquest of the Americas, in particular, although it had led to some soul searching about whether 'Indians' had a soul and were worthy

89 Brendan Simms, '"A False Principle in the Law of Nations": State Sovereignty, [German] Liberty and Intervention in the Age of Westphalia and Burke' in Brendan Simms and DJB Trim (eds), *Humanitarian Intervention: A History* (Cambridge University Press 2011).

90 Richard Tuck, 'Grotius, Hobbes, and Pufendorf on Humanitarian Intervention' in Jennifer M Welsh and Stefano Recchia (eds), *Just and Unjust Military Intervention: European Thinkers from Vitoria to Mill* (Cambridge University Press 2013).

91 Gustave Rolin-Jaequemyns, 'Note Sur La Théorie Du Droit D'Intervention, à Propos d'une Lettre de M. Le Professeur Arntz' (1876) 8 Revue de Droit International et de Législation Comparée 673.

92 Daniel Marc Segesser, 'Humanitarian Intervention and the Issue of State Sovereignty in the Discourse of Legal Experts between the 1830s and the First World War' in Fabian Klose (ed), *The Emergence of Humanitarian Intervention: Ideas and Practice from the Nineteenth Century to the Present* (Cambridge University Press 2015).

93 Stefan Kroll, 'The Legal Justification of International Intervention: Theories of Community and Admissibility' in Fabian Klose (ed), *The Emergence of Humanitarian Intervention: Ideas and Practice from the Nineteenth Century to the Present* (Cambridge University Press 2015).

of sovereignty, ultimately arose entirely outside the discourses of intervention, such as they were. There could not, to put it simply, be intervention or interference in the affairs of a people that were not sovereign in the first place. In other words, whatever norm of non-interference gradually began to crystalize around Westphalia was thoroughly compatible with the systematic denial of even a path to sovereignty for non-European peoples.[94] Europe would continue to engage in wanton processes of interference with its semi-periphery, as illustrated for example in the capitulation regimes and the ability it heralded for European powers to protection their compatriots and coreligionists extra-territorially as part of the 'Eastern question' but also recurring 'humanitarian interventions'.[95] This is no mean caveat to a theory of non-intervention that otherwise claims quite a hegemonic hold on the international legal psyche. And of course, colonialism, ironically itself justified as an intervention to combat slavery,[96] erased the very possibility of intervention by denying the sovereignty of most the peoples of Asia and Africa. It was thus only in peculiar, intermediary cases, notably that of the young republics of the Americas, that non-interference was to be claimed in the very process of independence struggles.

2 Non-interference and State Building

In due course, ideas about non-intervention in international law would be given renewed vigor as a result of state building projects, independence struggles and a republican ethos that has foregrounded the self-sufficient, self-referential, and exclusive nature of sovereignty.[97] Non-interference is not alien to a certain spirit of prickly nationalism but also fully subsumable, to its credit, within a core aspiration to democracy. The spirit of non-interference shone most brightly, arguably, in newly independent states, notably the nascent U.S.

---

94 Antony Anghie, *Imperialism, Sovereignty and the Making of International Law* (Cambridge University Press 2007); Edward Keene, *Beyond the Anarchical Society: Grotius, Colonialism and Order in World Politics* (Cambridge University Press 2002).

95 Davide Rodogno, *Against Massacre: Humanitarian Interventions in the Ottoman Empire, 1815–1914* (Princeton University Press 2012).

96 Fabian Klose, *In the Cause of Humanity: A History of Humanitarian Intervention in the Long Nineteenth Century* (Cambridge University Press 2022).

97 In that sense, many of the developments that made the international system 'Westphalian' occurred long after the actual Peace of Westphalia, notably in the 19th Century. See Andreas Osiander, 'Sovereignty, International Relations, and the Westphalian Myth' (2001) 55 International Organization 251.

Republic, keen on cutting off ties to former imperial or colonial powers. Early on, Thomas Jefferson had been warned by John Adams of 'foreign Interference, Intrigue [and] Influence' as common ills.[98] Alexander Hamilton intimated the danger of 'cabal, intrigue and corruption' that might be 'expected to make their approaches from more than one quarter, but chiefly from the desire in foreign powers to gain an improper ascendant in our councils'.[99] It was famously President George Washington, in his farewell address, who warned against 'the insidious wiles of foreign influence' and insisted that 'the jealousy of a free people ought to be *constantly* awake, since history and experience prove [...] one of the most baneful foes of Republican Government'.[100]

If nothing else, these early concerns shaped the U.S.'s constitutional destiny, an insistence on non-interference springing from the realm of sovereignty rather than the 'dictates' of international law. Nonetheless, it also manifested an emerging 'externalisation of sovereignty' whereby that internal claim to self-determination increasingly needed to be recognized internationally and could, in fact, not fail to be so recognized as, specifically, a form of independence from other states.[101] One cannot long constitute non-interference—at least under international law—merely as a claim from within, or a claim that oneself (and oneself only) not be interfered with. The one noticeable incidence of international law in that respect is its ability to gradually demand generalization of claims made by merely some states to all states. But this move was never a foregone conclusion and was always less accomplished, not only in practice but normatively, than the positivist and retrospective international legal rendering of it suggests. More often than not, it seemed that the very possibility of non-interference required the occasional massive interference, if only to uphold the system on which the former was premised.

A nascent international law was nonetheless invoked and called upon to delineate, police and arbitrate competing claims to intervention and non-intervention (to use the favored term of that era), at no time more clearly than

98 Mary A Giunta, J Dane Hartgrove and Mary-Jane M Dowd, *The Emerging Nation: A Documentary History of the Foreign Relations of the United States Under the Articles of Confederation, 1780–1789* (National Historical Publications and Records Commission 1996) 667.

99 Alexander Hamilton, 'No. 68: The Mode of Electing the President', *The Federalist Papers* (Open Road Integrated Media 2020).

100 Matthew Spalding and Patrick J Garrity, *A Sacred Union of Citizens: George Washington's Farewell Address and the American Character* (Rowman & Littlefield 1996) 53.

101 Stephane Beaulac, *The Power of Language in the Making of International Law: The Word Sovereignty in Bodin and Vattel and the Myth of Westphalia* (Brill Nijhoff 2004).

in the 19th Century.[102] One of the great debates that structured 19th Century Europe was the degree to which revolutionary regimes should be allowed to promote, spread and protect their views in other states. The French revolution had proclaimed its profound hostility to foreign-driven *restauration*, but itself did not shy away from promoting its model given that '[l]e peuple français est l'ami et l'allié naturel des peuples libres',[103] illustrating a typical ambiguity around notions of intervention. Napoleon Bonaparte's imperial adventure and his attempt to propagate some version of the French revolutionary fervour was faced with a united resistance from dynastic regimes banding together to make sure that he would be defeated and that never again would they be threatened by such noxious exports—a form of non-intervention *avant la lettre*. Nonetheless, the Holy Alliance's efforts to put a lid to liberal change, through conservative interference if need be, gradually gave way to the Concert of Europe's more collectivized and accommodating tolerance of some change (and therefore reticence to *restaurative* interference), notably under the influence of the United Kingdom.[104] Ideas about non-intervention could not wholly be contained, and they indeed tended to spread.

That is, unless that change came from Haiti and involved a slave revolt, in which case considerable efforts were deployed so that that particular example would not propagate to other slave-owning colonies. This would, in turn, justify continuous interference in the affairs of Haiti, including the exacting by France, the former colonial power, of an extortionate indemnity. Ironically, where precocious recognition of governments would become the classic problem of the international law, the issue in the case of Haiti was that it was denied recognition altogether long after it had acquired de facto and de jure independence, notably by the U.S. until 1862. This meant that it could in a sense never fully accede to the dignity of being able to even claim not to be interfered with (one cannot interfere with, in a sense, what one does not even recognize to be a state and one cannot not be interfered with if one is not considered a sovereign).[105]

---

102 Stephen D Krasner, *Sovereignty: Organized Hypocrisy* (Princeton University Press 1999).

103 Acte constitutionnel du 24 juin 1793, art 118 (France).

104 Matthias Schulz, 'Cultures of Peace and Security from the Vienna Congress to the Twenty-First Century: Characteristics and Dilemmas' in Beatrice de Graaf, Brian Vick and Ido de Haan (eds), *Securing Europe after Napoleon: 1815 and the New European Security Culture* (Cambridge University Press 2019).

105 Frédéric Mégret, '"Racial Panics" and the Constitution of (White) International Law' in Devon Carbado and others (eds), *Race, Racism, and International Law: Critical Race Theory in Global Context* (forthcoming).

A similar fate would await future colonies in the second half of the 19th Century, engendered through a series of technologies of encroachment on what had often been sustained polities with their own claim to sovereignty. Finally, in the semi-periphery, durable patterns of intervention and interference were sustained by unequal treaties with the Ottoman Empire, China, Persia or Japan. Their autonomy thus remained somewhat illusory since they had not shown themselves 'worthy' of non-interference. In short, international law would deploy a series of interventionist moves dedicated to making sure that, even as the 'international' conception became hegemonic in the West, systematic efforts were devoted to making sure that entire regions would simultaneously 'become less of the world'[106] and thus relatively less entitled to non-intervention. To deny the benefit of the principle of non-intervention in this context amounted to nothing less than denying statehood.

3 Historicizing Interference and Non-interference

This part will focus on relatively late developments, notably from the late 19th to early 21st Century, for it is during this period that latent debates on to the notion of non-interference gained significant traction and were increasingly formulated in terms of international law. One can distinguish an early phase of debates about interference spearheaded by Latin American creole concerns with sovereignty; a second wave emerging as a result of the Cold War and decolonization; and a third wave emerging since the end of the Cold War. The increased salience of interference has reflected a variety of phenomena: the fact that there was, plainly put, much of it or at least that it developed a more pernicious character in a context of significant interdependence; the fact that sovereignty's contours were increasingly reshaped by new states with strong independence agendas; and the fact that, although the debate had until then been overshadowed by the one about the use of force, a number of developments made less flagrant forms of interference not just possible, but also more likely. Finally, as we will see, the 'new interference' of the last decade, an interference that has increasingly targeted the democratic and liberal systems of Western states, has considerably renewed interest in the notion by changing its nature and provenance.

Contra a feigned 'discovery' of the dangers of interference by some Western commentators, this first part is grounded in an understanding that interference

106 Samera Esmeir, 'On Becoming Less of the World' (2018) 8 History of the Present 88.

has been the lot of most states most of the time and, in a sense, their default condition.[107] In that respect, the hidden stake of debates about interference in not what the term means in the absolute but, at any one time, who gets to interfere and who gets to be interfered with. Conversations around interference constitute some states' sovereignty as 'interferable' and others' as 'non-interferable'. By the same token, the insistence on the norm of non-intervention has often entailed, beyond day-to-day praxis, a *performance* of independence, one that is all the more likely to be activated that it rests against not-so-distant memories of imperial domination, gunboat diplomacy and subservience that are prompt to be rekindled at the slightest whiff of *déjà vu*.[108]

As will be seen, the story is partly one of the broad interference compact that structured the international legal order for a long time being challenged and even in some respects reversed and collapsing. But this should not blind U.S. to the extent to which the norm has always been challenged and contested, more valid for some than for others, and displayed chronically uncertain contours. As interference becomes more ubiquitous, it is prompting a late reappraisal of the value of non-intervention, even as, ironically, that moment may already have passed. The question, at any rate, often appears to be whether some states can live with conditions of interference that they have historically imposed on others. The normalization of interference, in turn, begs the question of what is so wrong with interference; or at least why the problem is more prevalent than previously acknowledged and why it was previously not treated with the seriousness it deserved. The discursive economy of international law that is triggered as result involves revisiting the past, producing origin stories and exalting foundational myths in the crucible of the present.

The story recounted here will be conceptual and dialectical rather than strictly chronological. It seeks to reconstruct the debate on interference as a series of situated and temporal rhetorical 'moves' by various actors in the international system involved and often profoundly invested in its discursive economy. This is done with a view to emphasizing the importance of context—actors, time, stage, audience—wherein claims about interference or non-interference are made, as well as their fundamentally relational character. Every claim to non-interference is typically a response to a claim of interference, both legally and politically. What this short history highlights, then, is a basic theme of this book, namely that over time actors adopt both pro

107 Lori A Ringhand, 'Foreign Election Interference: Comparative Approaches to a Global Challenge' (2021) 20 Election Law Journal: Rules, Politics, and Policy 1.

108 Stefano Saluzzo, 'The Principle of Non-Intervention and the Battle over Hong Kong' (2021) 79 Questions of International Law 27.

and anti-interference arguments and typically try to have it both ways discursively: to interfere in the affairs of other states whilst seeking to minimize influence in theirs. This then creates systemic indeterminacy but also an intriguing rough stability of the norm over time, as well as possibilities for its challenge and unsettling. Highlighting the early development of the concept of non-interference (Chapter 1) will therefore set the stage for an understanding of the changes in the conceptual and rhetorical terrain that the 'new interference' arguably brings into sharper focus (Chapter 2).

CHAPTER 1

The Emergence of Non-interference as a Norm in International Law

1 Introduction

1.1 *The Relative Early Irrelevance of Non-intervention*

The notion of non-interference was not unheard of up to the early 20th Century, but it was framed quite differently. There existed in the 19th Century such a thing as an international law *of* intervention, the principle of which was often explicitly anticipated in bilateral treaties, such as the U.S. treaty with Panama which allowed the U.S. to intervene to protect 'treaty rights, national interests and safety and the interests of collective civilization'.[109] Intervention was thus woven into a broad political economy of imperial relations. In 1878, the Balkan states had agreed in the Berlin treaty to establish civil and political rights for all of their people, notably Jews and Muslims, in exchange for the recognition of their independence,[110] in ways that powerfully normalized Western intervention rooted in a perception of the 'semi-civilized' nature of those nations.[111] This normalization and even extolling of the virtues of intervention provided a very uncertain foundation for its flourishing.

If anything, as Paul Behrens has shown, the origins of the norm of non-interference are to be sought in an earlier age in exquisite diplomatic usages and, notably, the burgeoning practice of ambassadors and diplomats of 'minding their own (sovereign's) business' by not intruding on that of their hosts, even as one understands that it may very much have been their motivation to do so.[112] For ambassadors to not interfere in the affairs of the host states and for host states to not interfere in the affairs of sending states by imprisoning or executing their emissaries spoke to an early, highly institutionalized and

109 Theodore Roosevelt, 'Document 310 in "Papers Relating to the Foreign Relations of the United States, With the Annual Message of the President Transmitted to Congress December 7, 1903"' <https://history.state.gov/historicaldocuments/frus1903/d310> accessed 12 January 2024.

110 Eric D Weitz, *A World Divided: The Global Struggle for Human Rights in the Age of Nation-States* (Princeton University Press 2019) 168–169.

111 Ntina Tzouvala, '"These Ancient Arenas of Racial Struggles": International Law and the Balkans, 1878–1949' (2018) 29 European Journal of International Law 1149.

112 Paul Behrens, *Diplomatic Interference and the Law* (Bloomsbury Publishing 2016).

 | DOI:10.1163/9789004532731_004

prototypical mutual agreement to not interfere. The incidence of such precedents, however, remained limited to the particular circumstances of foreign officials being allowed to operate on the territory of other states. They did not amount to a full-fledged rule of non-interference which remained, in conditions of significant power asymmetry, an elusive aspiration for most.

Even in the 19th Century, however, there emerged early concerns with the excesses of interference. Contra continental powers' appetite for intervention in the affairs of other states to crush emerging revolutionary favor, a constant of British diplomacy was support for the notion that states should not interfere in the affairs of other states. Although that concern was specifically expressed about the fate of Christian subjects of the Ottoman Empire, there was some more general reservation about licencing in advance forms of strong interference. Furthermore, the debate on intervention witnessed an evident shift as it migrated across the Atlantic from Europe to the Americas, where newfound sensitivities, both of the young U.S. republic[113] but also increasingly of the Latin American republics, strongly contributed to reshaping the tonality of the international legal conversation. Who the participants were to these various conversations and how they came to them had a significant impact on the renewal of discursive economies.

After the First World War, Eastern European states 'responded loudly with criticism over [the treaties'] meddling in international affairs'.[114] But these early protests tended to emanate from the semi-periphery and as such did not make much of a dent into the edifice of international law and the consensus view about the legality, in most cases, of intervention. The states that emerged eventually had to accept the regimes of scrutiny that were foisted on them as a condition of their being treated as sovereigns, an opportunity they could not afford to let pass and that made them legitimate targets of intervention as the price for being taken seriously as states. At least the resulting regimes of minority protection were internationalized under the League rather than continuing age-old patterns of state-to-state interference, but the difference was in practice subtle. At any rate, Eastern European states' protests could be countered by the international community's insistence that a failure to take minority matters seriously in an earlier era had led to serious political dislocation and war. Their vulnerability to interference had not only been agreed to: it was in the interests of peace and even statehood.

113 Thomas and Thomas (n 29).

114 Carole Fink, 'The League of Nations and the Minorities Question' (1995) 157 World Affairs 197, 199.

1.2 *The Rise of Non-intervention as a Concern*

Several factors have historically contributed to the relative prominence of 'interference' in 20th Century discourse. First, as long as interference was rife and defining it was paradoxically unidentifiable as such. It could not have been considered to run against international law because many of its targets were not, in fact, sovereign. In a world of Empires and colonization, the prohibition of interference must surely count as nonsensical since independence is not the organizing principle in the first place. This left of course the possibility of interference within and amongst parts of the Western heartland or, as already mentioned, in its near periphery, but that interference at least occurred within a certain civilizational proximity. Interference only makes sense fully as a concept of international law in a world in which the promise of sovereignty has been significantly actualized. The rise of the Latin American republics, Japan, Turkey, and by the mid-20th Century of a variety of previously colonized African and Asian nations, has thus unleashed powerful anti-interventionist forces that have busied themselves with shaping the international legal agenda around the issue. Anti-imperial and decolonization struggles, in particular, became a central site of the reevaluation and upgrading of the norm of non-intervention to something resembling its default status today as a central point of reference of international law.

Second, the issue was for a long time overshadowed by the question of the prohibition on the use of force and armed intervention. By contrast, the prohibition of the use of force in international relations by the U.N. Charter has ushered in an era where that form of intervention is proscribed on its own ground (not exclusive of the possibility that it could also be treated as interference). This has created a renewed interest in what actions below the use of force are susceptible to nonetheless still constitute intervention or interference, a category that is otherwise 'difficult to individuate'.[115] One possibility is that the relative success of the norm against the use of armed force in international law pushed interference 'underground' as it were, multiplying and, in fact, encouraging forms of interference that no longer had a blatantly armed character. As is a common observation in criminology, transgressors adapt to and internalize evolving prohibitions, finding new ways to achieve their aims whilst minimizing the costs of being found on the wrong side of the law.[116] In

115 Natalino Ronzitti, 'Sanctions as Instruments of Coercive Diplomacy: An International Law Perspective' in Natalino Ronzitti (ed), *Coercive Diplomacy, Sanctions and International Law* (Brill Nijhoff 2016) 4.

116 Oona A Hathaway and Scott J Shapiro, *The Internationalists: How a Radical Plan to Outlaw War Remade the World* (Simon & Schuster 2017).

that light, technological developments (e.g., the radio, the internet) have made it increasingly possible to obtain some of the political effects that might traditionally have been obtained through war through lesser means and at lesser risk. This underscores a sense that international law is often chasing developments and sometimes focused on prohibiting behavior that is no longer the essence of a transgression.

Third, ideological polarization and fragmentation has certainly been a potent factor in making interference felt for what it is. The more polarized the international system, the more jealous states are likely to be of their sovereign prerogatives and the more sensitive to the fact that others are interfering with them, thus raising the rhetorical temperature in debates about interference. Whatever its status, interference is less likely to be felt in an environment in which states partake of a broad common ideological agenda, whichever it may be. In a cosmopolitan world order, for example, interference could be conceptualized as merely the actualization of a common aspiration to which various parties agree to hold each other accountable (for example, human rights); in short, it is hardly likely to be felt like interference. In a highly Westphalian world, by contrast, interference is the weapon by which states, particularly powerful states, actively meddle in the sovereign fate of others even as others have more grounding to complain about it. Somewhere in between, a highly plural world both maximizes the odds that a number of agents will lay claim to sovereign status and yet feel deeply constrained in that aspiration by the interference of others. Non-intervention, in this context, can be understood as 'the way in which strong states fulfill the obligation to accept the equality of weak states'[117]—deeply aspirational no doubt, but increasingly established as the operative ideal towards which an 'international society' of equals should strive.

1.3 *Recognitions of Insurgency, Belligerency, Governments and New States*

The case for the norm of non-intervention has always been built against particularly blatant forms of interference that have characterized certain eras of the international system. One (somewhat neglected) early barometer of the temperature of international law on such matters, at least in Europe, was the emerging international law of extradition. Liberal powers, notably Great Britain, refused to extradite for 'political offences', especially of a revolutionary kind. This was supposedly out of their natural sympathies for those seeking

117 Richard A Falk, *Legal Order in a Violent World* (Princeton University Press 2019) 204.

to overthrow tyrannical regimes but was also justified by virtue of not wishing to be seen as concurring to the realization of other states' sovereignty, i.e., a form of non-interference. Different regimes thought of political criminality very differently so that no state should be forced, as a result of extradition commitments, to concur to the realization of another state's sovereignty by, as it were, consenting to the extra-territorial application of repugnant foreign criminal laws to persons within its jurisdiction. At the same time, and somewhat paradoxically, the refusal to extradite was understood as a refusal to be drawn into the affairs of the requesting state (paradoxical, because that state was in a sense inviting that interference by itself requesting extradition). Hence it has been argued that the 'soundest basis' for refusing to extradite political offenders 'is furnished by the fundamental idea of neutrality and non-interference in the internal affairs' since it is 'the indisputable right of every State to keep out, not only of wars between foreign States, but also of internal political troubles across the frontiers and to avoid any action which may endanger its good relations with a foreign State for the present time or for the future'.[118]

Having said that, one of the primary ways in which debates about interference manifested themselves early was through the question of the recognition of situations of belligerency in civil wars, or even of insurgents or new states. These are issues that are different but nonetheless raise broadly similar questions from the angle of interference and non-interference. Although the question has become less conspicuous over time, there is a sense in which this kind of recognition raised the paradigmatic question of interference early on through a narrow and practical prism, since it involved nothing less than pronouncement regarding the very sovereignty of another state and its legitimate government. In failing to recognize a situation of belligerency, one might be faulted for failing to recognize an actual armed conflict and the fundamental uncertainty it created about power in a territory; in precociously recognizing a belligerency or even new authorities, however, one might easily be faulted for having interfered in the affairs of another state in the most fundamental way. This raised questions for the state wherein the fighting occurred, but also questions of legal foreign policy for third states who often only got one chance at calibrating their response properly.

This begged for identifiable criteria by which one might separate wrongful and rightful recognition not susceptible to the accusation of interference. In theory, the bar was set quite high. As Hersch Lauterpacht put it, 'it

118 Hermann Mannheim, 'Some Recent Problems in the Law of Extradition' (1935) 21 Transactions of the Grotius Society 109, 121–122.

is universally admitted that in the case of a civil war or a war of secession it is contrary to international law to grant to the insurgent community full recognition as a government or a State. So long as the issue has not been definitely decided in favour of the rebellious party, recognition is premature and unlawful'.[119] Recognition of a situation of belligerency (which amounts to a recognition that there is indeed a war and that the rebels are not to be treated as mere criminals) was not necessarily a form of interference, if its motivation was grounded in a defensible interest of an intervening state. The question was whether the recognizing state had justifiable reasons of its own for such recognition, for example, the need to safeguard the security of its nationals by dealing with the groups that effectively controlled part of a territory. Moreover, the trend was towards establishing objective criteria to ground a recognition of belligerency (control of territory, responsible authority, etc.).[120] If such a recognition proceeded—typically, because of a degree of de facto governmental control—rather than a merely political preference for the rebels, then what might otherwise have been treated as interference could be recast as the normal and even necessary operation of international law.

But when and how international law allows states to recognize a situation of belligerency, withdraw their recognition of a foreign government, or come to the conclusion that a new state has been created on the territory of a previously existing one, remain vexed questions. Perhaps one of the best-known early cases of this sort of dilemma was in relation to Latin American states seeking to overthrow their European colonizers. Dilemmas involving the recognition of belligerents, governments, and states proved to activate a very delicate diplomatic calculus. The Monroe doctrine was characteristically cautious and insisted that revolting colonies should not be recognized until the 'movement assumed such a steady and consistent form as to make the success of the provinces probable'.[121] Too late a recognition would defeat the purpose of international law as mandating that one deal with actually sovereign entities; too early a recognition, however, could amount to an enormous *faux pas*

119 Hersch Lauterpacht, 'Recognition of Insurgents as a De Facto Government' (1939) 3 The Modern Law Review 1, 6.

120 Hersch Lauterpacht, *Recognition in International Law* (Cambridge University Press 1947) 176.

121 Cited in Vernon A O'Rourke, 'Recognition of Belligerency and the Spanish War' (1937) 31 The American Journal of International Law 398, 405.

against the existing colonial power or government. The delicacy of the matter was, precisely, that it involved 'a question of the state of affairs in another nation'.[122]

It was notably persistent efforts in Cuba to overthrow the Spanish colonial government that helped sharpen the issue. The Cuban situation, characterized by intermittent and uncertain uprisings, confronted the U.S. presidency with a recurring challenge. On the one hand, the U.S. government's sympathies clearly lay with the people of Cuba—or, at least, the absence of a European colonial power in the U.S.'s vicinity. At the same time, the U.S. was wary that by recognizing an insurgent group too soon—indeed, one that might well not prevail—it would expose itself to the reproach from Spain that it was interfering in its affairs (that it could be accused, in other words, of 'a gratuitous demonstration of moral support to the rebellion' not justified by the circumstances). As one commentator put it, recognizing the Cuban rebels as belligerents 'is a serious step, involving grave international consequences; such a step must not be taken as a mere holiday pastime, in gayety of heart at the appearance of a new popular uprising; if it is to be taken, it must be with the utmost care, and with a knowledge of its legal bearings and of its consequences'.[123]

This raised 'the great international question, at what time and under what circumstances to recognize a new power as entitled to a place among the family of nations'.[124] For President Grant, the hidden purpose of Cuban *émigrés* in the U.S. was 'to embroil this Government in complications and possible hostilities with Spain [...] under the deceptive and apparently plausible demand for a mere recognition of belligerency'.[125] Highlighting the importance of neutrality going back to Jefferson, as well as the U.S.'s governments efforts against filibustering and the consequences that could flow for U.S. interests, he emphasized that 'the question of belligerency is one of fact not to be decided by sympathies for or prejudices against either party'.[126] As Lawrence put it, 'the one thing other states have to consider is whether the new government created by the revolution commands the obedience of the people of the state'—not to be

122 Joseph H Beale, Jr, 'Recognition of Cuban Belligerency' (1895) 9 Harvard Law Review 406, 407.

123 ibid 406.

124 Francis Wharton, *A Digest of the International Law of the United States: Taken from Documents Issued by Presidents and Secretaries of State, and from Decisions of Federal Courts and Opinions of Attorneys-General* (Government Printing Office 1886) 386.

125 ibid 385.

126 Wharton (n 124) 387.

mistaken with any bias in favor of one government over the other—but 'in no case have they a right to interfere with it'.[127]

Notably, this required that an identifiable situation of 'war' be found to have emerged, which itself required:

> above all, a de facto political organization of the insurgents sufficient in character and resources to constitute it, if left to itself, a state among nations capable of discharging the duties of a state, and of meeting the just responsibilities it may incur as such toward other powers in the discharge of its national duties.[128]

Recognition of belligerency when there was not, in fact, a such groups let alone a war would make the U.S. 'guilty of an unfriendly, almost a hostile act toward Spain'.[129] Unsatisfied in 1870 that the Cuban insurgents had reached that level of control, Grant was ultimately happy to consider this as essentially still a Spanish imperial matter. By 1898, however, and confronted with a somewhat changing situation, Congress felt that the chronic inability of Spain to enforce its jurisdiction as well as the right of the people of Cuba to something resembling independence meant that U.S. force could in fact be used to oust Spain altogether. This shows the extent to which recognition can be a self-fulfilling prophecy and engender its own dynamics.

Similar issues have continued to occasionally agitate international practice, notably around the recognition of governments. For example, many European governments had to decide during the Spanish civil war whether to recognize the nationalist insurgency of General Franco or the legitimate Republican government. They were careful to at best recognize the nationalist faction as insurgent and in control of parts of Spain for limited purposes, lest they violate 'the prohibition of premature recognition [as a] rule of international law'.[130] Only in the final days of the Civil war could they conclusively throw their weight behind the nationalists. The general tendency has clearly been towards a strong condemnation of supporting any side (and particularly the rebel side) in civil wars, and especially to do 'prematurely' so as long as the

---

127 Thomas Joseph Lawrence, *The Principles of International Law* (2nd edn, Macmillan 1895) 130.

128 Wharton (n 124) 387.

129 Amos S Hershey, 'The Recognition of Cuban Belligerency' (1896) 7 The ANNALS of the American Academy of Political and Social Science 74, 81.

130 Lauterpacht, 'Recognition of Insurgents as a De Facto Government' (n 119) 8.

facts on the ground do not justify it.[131] This was especially the case of course when a state goes from recognizing to supporting a party to a conflict, as the U.S. did in Vietnam, albeit of what seemed for a while at least to be the legitimate government.[132]

The incidence of such rules is equally relevant outside any armed conflict when it comes to the recognition of foreign governments following coups or disputed elections. Particularly problematic from the point of view of interference are situations where foreign states recognize another head of state than the one that holds de facto power. This happened more recently when a raft of Western and Latin American states recognized Juan Guaidó as President of Venezuela despite Nicolás Maduro having been already sworn in, much to the chagrin of a number of other states invoking the lack of effectivity of his control.[133] Not only did this lead to cascading problems across a variety of institutions and jurisdictions[134] but, in being based seemingly on little else than the political preference of recognizing states for a particular head of state and their criticism of elections, it seemed to push the envelope of the international law of recognition. It is true that there is a trend in recognition towards favoring elements of the legitimacy of regimes over and above the evaluation of actual control,[135] which has long been suspected of bringing in a more qualitative—and thus problematic—evaluation of the adequacy of such regimes.[136] Nonetheless, the long-competing U.S. Tobar (non-recognition of rebel coups) and Estrada (change of government is entirely an internal matter)

131 Institut de Droit International, 'The Principle of Non-Intervention in Civil Wars', *Session of Wiesbaden* (1975).

132 Tom J Farer, 'Harnessing Rogue Elephants: A Short Discourse on Foreign Intervention in Civil Strife' (1969) 82 Harvard Law Review 511.

133 Jack McNally, 'Representation, Recognition, Resistance: Rival Governments Before the International Court of Justice' (2023) 61 Columbia Journal of Transnational Law 267.

134 Félix A Quintero Vollmer, 'International Law or International Politics? The Guaidó v. Maduro Conundrum at the Inter-American Development Bank' (2020) 51 The University of Miami Inter-American Law Review 117; Laura Rees-Evans and Rhys Carvosso, 'Legal Consequences of and Approaches to the Question of Recognition of a Government of a State: Disputes Involving Venezuela' (2021) 36 ICSID Review-Foreign Investment Law Journal 563; Réka A Papp, 'Representation of States in Investment Arbitrations Involving Governments Competing for International Recognition' in Tobias Ackermann and Sebastian Wuschka (eds), *Investments in Conflict Zones* (Brill Nijhoff 2020).

135 Rizwanul Islam, 'The Murky State Practice on Recognition of Governments and the National Unity Government in Myanmar' (2022) 44 Houston Journal of International Law 447.

136 Charles G Fenwick, 'The Recognition of New Governments Instituted by Force' (1944) 38 American Journal of International Law 448.

doctrines[137] which can be seen as more generally structuring international law has gradually given way to a certain ascendency of the latter over the former.[138]

Finally, some of the same dynamics apply to the recognition of states as such. Schematically, failure to recognize a state that has objectively emerged may be deemed to be interference with it, even though by hypothesis its sovereignty may not have been subjectively recognized; or a separate state may be recognized too early, at the risk of the larger sovereign from which it emerges protesting that its affairs are being grossly interfered with (for example, the U.K.'s arguably early recognition of Italy as the government of Ethiopia in 1938 and, *a contrario*, the U.S.'s refusal to recognize Manchukuo).[139] Again, the details of such interference or non-interference matter less than the fact that both recognition and lack of it can be analyzed as, in ultimate analysis, raising quintessential questions of intervention that go to the heart of the rule and what it means to be a sovereign. In that respect, both the law of recognition and interference are shaped by the overall discursive economy of international law and, notably, the prohibition of annexation, the deference to the *uti possidetis* principle and the recognition of the intangibility of borders.[140] Recognition in violation of these principles is all the more likely to be qualified as interference and worse if force was involved, but one cannot help notice how claims about intervention or lack of it are rooted in elemental considerations about whether there is sovereignty at all.

2 Interference within Non-interference and the Paradoxical Logic of Spheres

The specifics of diverse modalities of recognition aside, the relative caution in recognizing insurgents, belligerents, governments and states, is a special case of the broader problem of interference, one that reaches for the very essence of what it means to be sovereign. It involves weighing effectivity against legitimacy in ways that can each potentially be described as manifesting undue

137 Donald Marquand Dozer, 'Recognition in Contemporary Inter-American Relations' (1966) 8 Journal of Inter-American Studies 318.

138 Federico Jarast, 'Is Democracy in Peril in the Americas?: The Demise of Tobar and the Resurrection of Estrada' (2021) 45 Fletcher Forum of World Affairs 17; Charles L Cochran, 'The Estrada Doctrine and United States Policy' (1973) 5 Lawyer of the Americas 27.

139 Arnold D McNair, 'Stimson Doctrine of Non-Recognition' (1933) 14 British Year Book of International Law 65.

140 James Wilford Garner, 'Non-Recognition of Illegal Territorial Annexations and Claims to Sovereignty' (1936) 30 American Journal of International Law 679.

interference and thus brings attention to the constant risk of getting one's linguistic investments in international law wrong. As it happens and to make matters more complicated, it must be read in conjunction with the broader economy of imperial relations and the emergence of at least spaces within which all foreign interference is viewed with deep suspicion.

Intriguingly, many claims to non-interference have been simultaneously hegemonic in nature, arguing, essentially, for a limited right to not being interfered with whilst interfering with others. The history of both U.S. and Soviet imperialisms in the 20th Century provides evidence of this complex, nested character of the emergence of the norm of non-interference within broader imperial constellations, as a paradoxical double claim to exercise regional dominance in the process of keeping other powers at bay from that dominance. This brings attention to how early claims in favor of non-interference involved a simultaneous claim to rightful interference, as well as invoking the language of spheres, regionalism, stability and even ideological alignment. It shows the inherently precarious, contradictory and deeply problematic nature of these early investments in the language of non-interference.

2.1 *From the Monroe Doctrine to the Roosevelt Corollary*

Early investments in the discursive economy of non-intervention served to delimit the border between legitimate foreign policy and illicit intervention, but in ways that have had an ambivalent relationship to the powerfully assertive hegemonic practices of regional powers. The Monroe doctrine, and an attendant concern that the Old World should not interfere in the affairs of the New World (just as the New would not interfere in the affairs of the Old), is a classic illustration of this phenomenon, including as it relates to recognition. In that respect, the relative scruple in not interfering in the affairs of foreign powers—in not anticipating, at least, on the contest of arms—was typically combined with strong assertions about the need for other states to respect the U.S. sphere of competence, and a clear sense that European powers were destined to eventually desist from exerting influence on the region (nowhere more so, arguably, than in relation to Cuba), especially if their failures of control objectively created dangers for foreign nationals. The de facto control of governments was thus in practice often superseded by a sense of the illegitimacy of remaining European control which militated, all other things being equal, for recognition of independence governments—but paradoxically, on account of their imagined subservience to U.S. regional hegemony. Latin American republics could be forgiven for thinking that they merely traded one form of interference with another, albeit under the auspices of a newfound regional umbrella against interference.

The Monroe doctrine did ensure that Latin American states could push back against some of the more blatant forms of 'extra-continental' interference, as President Benito Juarez did against the Emperor Maximilian and French support in 1865. Theodore Roosevelt was clear that 'any country whose people conduct themselves well can count upon our hearty friendship' and that 'if a nation shows that it knows how to act with reasonable efficiency and decency in social relations and political matters, if it keeps order and pays it obligations, it need fear no interference from the United States'.[141] There was much denial that, in proclaiming the Monroe doctrine the U.S., had intended to arrogate for itself any kind of control over the hemisphere. Elihu Root went as far as to claim that any resulting limitations to the sovereignty of Latin American republics was merely a condition of their independence and added nothing to that which already existed under international law.[142] The disinterestedness of the U.S. in maintaining the *pax americana* was insistently proclaimed[143] as was the lack of connection between the doctrine stricto sensu and the occasional imperialist lapse of the U.S.[144] Moreover, any suggestion that the doctrine had engendered imperial copycats (notably in the case of Japan) was vigorously denied.[145]

At the same time, though the Monroe doctrine may have nominally focused on non-interference, it also often translated into a renewed claim by the U.S. to, fundamentally, exercise a kind of *droit de regard* in the sphere of the Latin American republics (as it did in 1904 in Santo Domingo, in 1911 in Nicaragua and in Haiti several times, all in the name, ironically, of preventing 'interference'). This was made spectacularly clear in the so-called 'Roosevelt Corollary' to the Monroe doctrine (1904), which anticipated and justified unilateral intervention in cases of 'chronic wrong-doing or an impotence which results in the general loosening of the ties of civilized society'. This would 'ultimately require intervention by some civilized nation, and in the Western Hemisphere the adherence of the United States to the Monroe Doctrine may force the United States, however reluctantly [...] to the exercise of an international police

141 Theodore Roosevelt, 'Theodore Roosevelt's Corollary to the Monroe Doctrine (1905)' <https://www.archives.gov/milestone-documents/roosevelt-corollary> accessed 14 June 2023.

142 Elihu Root, 'The Real Monroe Doctrine' (1914) 8 Proceedings of the American Society of International Law at Its Annual Meeting (1907–1917) 6, 15.

143 JM Callahan, 'The Modern Meaning of the Monroe Doctrine' (1914) 4 The Journal of Race Development 359.

144 A Pearce Higgins, 'The Monroe Doctrine' (1924) 5 British Year Book of International Law 103, 116–117.

145 Gilbert Reid, 'An Imitation Monroe Doctrine' (1915) 6 The Journal of Race Development 12.

power'.[146] Even in relation to Europe, the doctrine was eventually defended as not having condoned complete isolationism and as justifying U.S. intervention were the need to defend American rights to arise.[147]

The apparently paradoxical reference to the Monroe doctrine in relation to non-interference can be understood in light of the perception that failure by the U.S. to intervene would sooner or later encourage extra-hemispheric powers to do so. 'Interfere or risk being interfered with', then, seems to have been the implicit logic. The 'Roosevelt Corollary' emerged, for example, against the background of European states seeking to obtain reimbursement of debts from Central and South American states (notably Venezuela, Colombia, and Santo Domingo), and U.S. efforts to avert such an outcome. This was arguably less out of respect for Latin American sovereignty than out of a concern that European creditors would be pushed towards intervention if the U.S. did not strongly signal its displeasure in advance, thus endangering peace. Indeed, the underlying claims of the doctrine were spelled out by Elihu Root somewhat implausibly under international law as based on the idea that 'the exercise of the right of self-protection may and frequently does extend in its effect beyond the limits of the territorial jurisdiction of the state exercising it'.[148]

In effect, this justified a form of 'interference within non-interference' in the Americas, exercised as a broad international police power by the U.S. For Roosevelt, this was based an obligation to 'accept certain responsibilities along with the rights which [the Monroe Doctrine] confers'. Even though 'it cannot be too often and too emphatically asserted that the United States has not the slightest desire for territorial aggrandizement at the expense of any of its southern neighbors' and that it would not 'treat the Monroe doctrine as an excuse for such aggrandizement on its part', Roosevelt argued, it would be 'incompatible with international equity for the United States to refuse to allow other powers to take the only means at their disposal of satisfying the claims of their creditors and yet to refuse, itself, to take any such steps'. For the U.S. to intervene in the affairs of American States to recover debts, 'provided that action does not take the shape of interference with their form of government', was merely a recognition of the fact that in relation to money claims the U.S. had become 'a party in interest'.[149] As if, in final analysis, the claim of

146 Roosevelt, 'Theodore Roosevelt's Corollary to the Monroe Doctrine (1905)' (n 141).

147 John B Whitton, 'Isolation: An Obsolete Principle of the Monroe Doctrine' (1932) 15 International Conciliation 211.

148 Root (n 142) 11.

149 Theodore Roosevelt, 'Message from the President of the United States, Transmitting a Protocol of an Agreement between the United States and the Dominican Republic, Providing for the Collection and Disbursement by the United States of the Customs

non-interference could not be separated from the claim of a right to interfere and vice versa.

2.2 *The Brezhnev Doctrine and Socialist Internationalism*

Whilst the Monroe doctrine gradually declined in the inter-war, similarly complex claims to interference/non-interference on a regional or ideological basis have since been entertained, albeit by different global powers. A structurally congenial series of claims coincided with the emergence of the Soviet Empire and its eventual decline. The USSR was behind some of the early efforts to define what might not count as interference, in pursuit of a communist vision of international law. On the one hand, the Soviets were at the forefront of developing ideas about their right to interfere in their near-abroad, particularly after the Second World War. On the other hand, they, insisted on the importance of sovereignty and 'peaceful coexistence' with reactionary states. For Brezhnev, for example, 'the socialist states stand for strict respect for the sovereignty of all countries' and 'emphatically oppose interference in the affairs of any states'.

Yet the Soviet Union also sought, characteristically, to transcend notions of non-interference altogether when it came to fellow communist states. This they did by anchoring sovereignty in a higher communal bond, that of 'socialist internationalism', and a corresponding downgrading of formal sovereignty. This was because 'the establishment and defense of the sovereignty of states that have embarked upon the road of building socialism is of particular importance for U.S. communists'. When such states were threatened by the 'forces of imperialism and reaction', it was in fact 'the maintenance of socialist sovereignty' that was at stake and, whatever the bourgeois 'clamor over "defense of sovereignty"', the Soviet Union had to defend the 'common law governing socialist construction'.[150]

This is how, for example, one famous article in Pravda understood the then emerging 'Brezhnev doctrine' in 1968, scolding those who endorsed 'an abstract, non-class approach to the question of sovereignty and the rights of nations to self-determination':

> none of their decisions should do harm either to socialism in their own county or to the fundamental interests of other socialist countries and

Revenues of the Dominican Republic, Signed on February 7, 1905' 334–335 <https://history.state.gov/historicaldocuments/frus1905/d325> accessed 12 January 2024.

150 Speech of Leonid Brezhnev on 12 November 1968 at the Fifth Polish Communist Party Congress. Cited in Stephen M Schwebel, 'The Brezhnev Doctrine Repealed and Peaceful Co-Existence Enacted' (1972) 66 American Journal of International Law 816, 816–817.

> of the entire working-class movement which [is] striving for socialism. This means that each Communist Party is responsible not only to its own people but also to all the socialist countries and to the entire communist movement. [...] Just as, in Lenin's words, a man, living in a society, cannot be free from that society, so this or that socialist state, existing in the system of other states making up the socialist community, cannot be free from the common interests of that community. The sovereignty of each socialist country cannot be set up in opposition to the interests of the socialist world and the interests of the world revolutionary movement. [...] The weakening of any links in the world socialist system directly affects all the socialist countries, which cannot look on indifferently when this happens.[151]

In essence, it was the Czechoslovak reformists who had undermined Czechoslovak sovereignty from within, leading the Soviet Union to intervene in an act of friendship to protect the will of the working class ... The Brezhnev doctrine was of course about forceful intervention, but it *a fortiori* licensed lesser forms of interference. What is worth noting in passing is the striking structural similarity of such formulations[152] with what would become, as we will see later, the rhetoric of human rights-infused international law (with one difference of course, namely its relative socialist parochialism and lack of explicitly universal ambition). As Brezhnev himself put it after the Soviet repressions in Hungary and later Czechoslovakia:

> when internal and external forces, hostile to socialism, seek to reverse the development of any socialist country whatsoever in the direction of the restoration of the capitalist order, when a threat to the cause of socialism arises in that country, a threat to the security of the socialist commonwealth as a whole—this already becomes not only a problem of the people of the country concerned, but also a common problem and the concern of all socialist countries.[153]

---

151 Sergei Kovalov, 'Sovereignty and the International Duties of Socialist Countries' (1970) 23 Chronique de politique étrangère 247, 247–248. (English translation of the original Russian article published in Pravda on September 26, 1968).

152 Jean-Pierre Massias, 'La doctrine Brejnev et le droit d'ingérence' (2013) 57 Droits 75.

153 Schwebel, 'The Brezhnev Doctrine Repealed and Peaceful Co-Existence Enacted' (n 150) 816–817.

The Brezhnev doctrine was received by international lawyers outside the Soviet camp as a blatant violation of the U.N. Charter, and in contradiction with what had until then been the pro-sovereignty tenets of Soviet foreign policy.[154] The Soviet Union did try to reconcile its commitment to sovereignty with its new-found defense of intervention, insisting in its draft definition of aggression which was debated at the U.N. soon after the invasion of Czechoslovakia that 'encroachment by one state on another's social and political achievements is aggression only when it involves states with different social systems'.[155] The suggestion was that peaceful coexistence and hence non-interference applied to relations with bourgeois states (despite early intimations that this would be impossible), whilst the socialist group was governed by 'socialist internationalism'.

Although on one level anathema to Charter principles of international law, this was of course consonant with a broader tradition of imperial conceptions of interference and could thus build on the simmering discursive legacies of previous rhetorical investments. To make matters worse and in parallel, the U.S. during the Cold War had hardly discontinued its own old patterns of interference, merely renovating them under the banner of anti-Communism. For example, Kennedy made it clear that:

> Should it ever appear that the Inter-American doctrine of non-interference merely conceals or excuses the policy of non-action, that the nations of this hemisphere should fail to meet their commitment against outside Communist penetration, then I want it clearly understood that this Government will not hesitate in meeting its primary obligations which are the security of our nation.[156]

In this quite startling statement, Kennedy made it clear that non-interference in the affairs of Latin American states was conditional on they themselves effectively standing up for non-interference by the Soviet bloc in their affairs. The Reagan Doctrine, as formulated by the then President in his State of the Union of Address of 6 February 1985, proclaimed that:

---

154 Stephen G Glazer, 'The Brezhnev Doctrine' (1971) 5 International Lawyer (ABA) 169.

155 Cited in ibid 173.

156 John F Kennedy, 'Address before the American Society of Newspaper Editors' (Washington, DC, 20 April 1961) <https://www.jfklibrary.org/archives/other-resources/john-f-kennedy-speeches/american-society-of-newspaper-editors-19610420> accessed 21 April 2024.

> We must stand by all our democratic allies. And we must not break faith with those who are risking their lives—in every continent, from Afghanistan to Nicaragua—to defy Soviet-supported aggression and secure rights which have been ours from birth. The Sandinista dictatorship of Nicaragua, with full Cuban-Soviet bloc support, not only persecutes its people, the church, and denies a free press, but arms and provides bases for Communist terrorists attacking neighboring states. Support for freedom fighters is self-defense and totally consistent with the OAS and U.N. Charters.[157]

This was a stark reminder that the Monroe Doctrine had never fully gone and that non-interference would be sustained, if at all, at the price of interference.[158] At the time, it led to a spirited debate on whether the Brezhnev and Reagan doctrines were indeed that different. Michael Reisman, for example, found neither doctrine to be fully inconsistent with international law, and both to rely, not entirely *contra legem* in his view, on notions of defensive zones. As he put it in the characteristically apologetic jargon of the New Haven school:

> Insofar as any of these doctrines reserve for one state the right to limit or attenuate the political independence of another state, they are inconsistent with the U.N. Charter. If your conception of international law stops with the textual examination of the Charter, you need not go any further. But if your conception of international law is one that relates the aggregate concerns of the entire system for the maintenance of minimum order and the options available to achieve this, then your inquiry about the lawfulness of these two doctrines has only begun.[159]

Reisman then went on to explain how the threat of nuclear annihilation meant that the two superpowers had to make 'certain arrangements between themselves and that these arrangements are the conditions sine qua non of all the rest of international law'. Although they could not quite dictate to third

157 Ronald Reagan, 'Address Before a Joint Session of the Congress on the State of the Union' (Washington, DC, 6 February 1985) <https://www.reaganlibrary.gov/archives/speech/address-joint-session-congress-state-union-february-1985> accessed 21 April 2024.

158 W Michael Reisman, 'Old Wine in New Bottles: The Reagan and Brezhnev Doctrines in Contemporary International Law and Practice' (1988) 13 Yale Journal of International Law 171.

159 William D Rogers and others, 'The Brezhnev Doctrine and the Reagan Doctrine: Apples and Oranges?' (1987) 81 Proceedings of the Annual Meeting (American Society of International Law) 561, 565.

countries what their exact policies could be, nor could these countries align themselves with ideologies incompatible with their political and geographic destiny.

This claim of special rights in world affairs nonetheless sat oddly with core tenets of the international legal system as illustrated in the U.N. Charter, notably the sovereignty and equality of states. It amounted to little more than a denial of the full sovereignty of other countries, all be it purportedly to rescue them from socialist overthrow.[160] Both the continued echoes of the Monroe Doctrine and the emerging claims of the Brezhnev doctrine, then, made for an awkward coexistence with international law, betraying a form of mimetism that was also a form of race to the bottom.[161] Indeed, contra Reisman, Thomas Franck was wary of the sort of contagion that the Monroe doctrine had unleashed historically, and the risk that the U.S. was finally receiving a taste of its own medicine ('our policymakers at the time of the Guatemalan, Cuban, and Dominican crises gave a conceptual definition to our actions which, without distortion or embroidery, was turned back on U.S. as the Brezhnev Doctrine').[162] The U.S. could invoke the U.N. Charter against the claims of the 'socialist community' as much as it wanted, but this process was ultimately the inevitable result of a logic of spheres which had long been set in motion by the U.S. and of which international law had conserved the memory.

2.3 *An International Normalization?*

Towards the end of the Cold War, the Soviet Union gradually realigned itself with a more egalitarian understanding of non-interference, namely that it applied to all states, including those in the Eastern bloc, notably Poland which was then in the throes of the Solidarity movement.[163] In 1989, in a speech to the Council of Europe, Mikhail Gorbachev insisted that:

> Social and political orders in one country or another changed in the past and may change in the future. But this change is the exclusive affair of the people of that country and is their choice. Any interference in domestic

160 Nicholas Rostow, 'Law and the Use of Force by States: The Brezhnev Doctrine' (1980) 7 Yale Journal of World Public Order 209.

161 Schwebel, 'The Brezhnev Doctrine Repealed and Peaceful Co-Existence Enacted' (n 150).

162 Franck and Weisband (n 4) 982.

163 Jan Skórzyński, 'The Doctrine of Non-Interference: The Self-Limiting Revolution of Solidarity and the Gorbachev's Policy of "New Thinking"' [2017] Divinatio 103.

> affairs and any attempts to restrict the sovereignty of states, both friend and allies or any others, are inadmissible.[164]

In other words, both the Monroe and Brezhnev doctrine eventually eroded and even crumbled in a context of reassertion of sovereignty of those countries that had been their targets. This led to a gradual normalization of the principle of non-intervention internally to both spheres and acceptance of the notion that it applied at the level of every state, in line with the promise of the Charter. The case against intervention made by vassal states can be seen as having exploited particularly blatant contradictions in both doctrines, as so many claims to interfere whilst not being interfered with that eventually betrayed their logical inconsistency and discursive one-sidedness.

At the same time, however, and beyond superpower interferences with their immediate spheres of competence, the Cold War had also been the site of some of the most blatant and toxic forms of interference in the Third World, including support for coups deposing leaders and support for friendly dictators.[165] By contrast, this normalized intervention in ways that could make it difficult for the international legal observer to discern the continuing contours of a norm of non-intervention, if it actually continued to exist in the crucible of superpower rivalry. Not only struggles for independence, but their intermingling with ideologically motivated revolutions and their deliberate transnational propagation seemed to fundamentally rewrite the rules of the international 'game'. As Lou Henkin deplored, somewhat despondently:

> One may ask whether even peaceful competition between East and West for the allegiance or support of other nations is consistent with the principle that they are or should be independent, equal, sovereign nations. What becomes of rules against intervention when Communist expansion takes the form of subversion, development and backing of local Communist parties, or military support for rebellion in which local Communist parties play a substantial [role]; or when the United States in turn intervenes to support non-Communist regimes?[166]

164 Cited in Bennett Kovrig, *Of Walls and Bridges: The United States and Eastern Europe* (New York University Press 1991) 153.

165 William Blum, *Killing Hope: U.S. Military and CIA Interventions Since World War II* (Zed Books 2003).

166 Henkin and others (n 67) 155.

In effect, the U.S. and the Soviet Union were frequently associated with dramatic such instances of intervention in the domestic affairs of states, including Iran, Chile, Indonesia, Guatemala, the Democratic Republic of Congo, the Dominican Republic, Cuba, Nicaragua, Brazil, Argentina, Chile and others. This often followed intense efforts by these states to reclaim their full independence, notably through policies of nationalization and attempts to steer a separate geopolitical course.[167] Some of the coups that resulted had the aim of removing icons of non-interference, often then swiftly replaced by sycophants and a reversal of all their previous non-interference policies through the reassertion of relations of *clientele*. In that respect, interference might not immediately appear as such to the extent it was consented to formally by pliant local relays. Yet in effect, for example, U.S. support of the Republic of Vietnam to offset Soviet and Chinese support of the Viet Minh entrenched a situation of superpower dependency based on ongoing patterns of interference.

Finally, claims of imperial non-interference must be seen in light of the twilight of European extra-maritime empires. Ironically, given the larger-than-life role that the norm of non-interference would in due course achieve in the political trajectories of decolonized states, non-interference long served the purpose for France, the U.K., the Netherlands and Portugal of keeping international onlookers at a distance from their colonial possessions. For France in particular, the Algerian war did not even fall within the remit of the United Nations, let alone of other states who would clearly have interfered with its *domaine réservé* in taking a stance on the 'internal' conflict that opposed it to the Front de Libération Nationale.[168] Even the treatment by South Africa of black South Africans was considered a fundamental internal matter by that country's government.[169] It was, by contrast, national liberation movements and their allies who argued vigorously for a politics of *intervention* in the name of colonized peoples' solidarity, albeit on the basis that colonial situations were not properly qualified as internal in the first place and that it was colonial

167 Sundhya Pahuja and Cait Storr, 'Rethinking Iran and International Law: The Anglo-Iranian Oil Company Case Revisited', *The International Legal Order: Current Needs and Possible Responses* (Brill Nijhoff 2017).

168 Maurice Flory, 'Algérie et Droit international' (1959) 5 Annuaire Français de Droit International 817, 820.

169 Bonny Ibhawoh, 'Seeking the Political Kingdom: Universal Human Rights and the Anti-Colonial Movement in Africa' in A Dirk Moses, Marco Duranti and Roland Burke (eds), *Decolonization, Self-Determination, and the Rise of Global Human Rights Politics* (Cambridge University Press 2020) 43–44.

powers who had engaged in old patterns of interference.[170] It will bear remembering that investment in the logic of intervention by the South itself, given its later almost complete identification with non-intervention. Simultaneously, the irony for European colonial powers is that their stance against interference in their colonial possessions coincided with an increasing openness to the significance of supranational human rights protections within the European environment and its potential extra-territorial reach.[171] So much so, in fact, that one of the hidden stakes of forging a European human rights system has been described as ensuring that it did not extend to the colonies.[172]

3 Deprovincializing Non-interference? Cosmopolitanization and the Role of Human Rights

Even as the norm of non-interference witnessed a gradual if ambiguous consolidation, it was simultaneously being contested in the crucible of East-West rivalry, from one very specific and distinct angle. This was evident in Western efforts to normatively redefine the outer limits of sovereignty and interference in the dynamic context of the Cold War, particularly in Europe, as part of efforts at *détente* that had long emphasized the potential of minding human rights to deflate situations threatening international peace and security. It is notably through the medium of human rights discourse, a discourse that was largely conceptualized in an international and universalist mode, that new tools were developed to pry open the sovereignty of certain states.[173] Part good faith projection of a particular liberal culture, part Trojan horse for Western designs, human rights emerged as possibly the single most important factor in redefining the parameters of intervention and non-intervention. Their intrusion brings attention to how semantic fields interact through discourse to produce new variants of existing norms and to further complexify an already fraught field.

170 Fabian Klose, *Human Rights in the Shadow of Colonial Violence: The Wars of Independence in Kenya and Algeria* (University of Pennsylvania Press 2013) 6.

171 See e.g., ibid 34.

172 ibid 5.

173 Rasmus Mariager, Karl Molin and Kjersti Brathagen (eds), *Human Rights in Europe during the Cold War* (Routledge 2014).

3.1 *The Helsinki Conference as Formative Episode*

The Final Act of the Helsinki Conference on Security and Cooperation in Europe of 1975 is often presented as a watershed moment for the evolving construction of the norm of non-interference. Indeed, it is perhaps in connection to that one, now largely neglected treaty, that most early international legal writing has been produced discussing the question of interference[174] and that the sources of much contemporary thinking—and equivocation—about the issue can be traced. Its adoption and subsequent practice shed light on the *quid pro quos* of how interference can be recharacterized through human rights and the importance of misunderstandings in the discursive economy. Although the Act proclaimed the principle of non-intervention, as was duly noted by the ICJ in the Nicaragua case, principle 7 also immediately went on to affirm certain fundamental rights of humans.[175] States committed to respect freedom of thought, conscience, religion, and belief, as well as minority rights. The ambiguity of this formulation in a context of intense polarization soon produced radically diverging interpretations, as the meaning of intervention was parsed to distinguish it from mere legal influence.

For the West, the list of protected rights trumped the prohibition on non-interference, making the USSR's domestic political record fair game for discussion. That reading was based on the notion that the Final Act prohibited only 'intervention', which was to be understood as involving coercion, unlike the broader term 'interference' which would have implied that states could not concern themselves with something that was not their business more generally. The Soviets, or so the story goes, having only one word in Russian to describe the two, failed to press hard enough for a prohibition of non-interference and in the process only got the much narrower prohibition of non-intervention. Nonetheless, they subsequently sought to draw a line between states committing to respect rights and legalizing interference from other states.[176] At the

174 Lauri Hannikainen, 'Human Rights and Non-Intervention in the Final Act of the CSCE' (1979) 48 Nordic Journal of International Law 27. See also Marc J Bossuyt, 'Human Rights and Non-Intervention in Domestic Matters' (1985) 35 Review—International Commission of Jurists 45; Arie Bloed and Pieter van Dijk (eds), *Essays on Human Rights in the Helsinki Process*, vol 5 (Brill Nijhoff 1985); Conforti (n 47).

175 Organization for Security and Co-operation in Europe (OSCE) 'Conference on Security and Co-operation in Europe Final Act—Declaration on Principles Guiding Relations between Participating States' (Helsinki 1 August 1975) 14 ILM 1292 (Helsinki Final Act) principles 6 and 7.

176 Arie Bloed and Pieter van Dijk, 'Human Rights and Non-Intervention' in Arie Bloed and Pieter van Dijk (eds), *Essays on Human Rights in the Helsinki Process* (Brill Nijhoff 1985). Some legal scholars supported this interpretation, noting that there was little in the document that specifically supported interference. See Hannikainen (n 174) 29.

Belgrade follow-up meeting, these various positions were tested as the debate continued about whether human rights criticism or lack of it would be more conducive to *détente*. The U.S. accused Eastern bloc states of significant rights violations, naming and describing them in detail. By contrast, the Europeans described human rights violations in general terms, not specifying who they considered at fault.[177]

In either case, the opening up of state sovereignty to human rights scrutiny could be seen as creating what constructivist international relations theorists have identified as 'rhetorical entrapment'[178] for states wary of being scrutinized by others, but whose instinct was to also respond, however indignantly, to such scrutiny. If they responded to the substance of the accusations, they could be considered to have acquiesced to at least the legality of criticizing them; if they responded in kind by counter-critiquing their critiques' own human rights record (as, no doubt, they had long been tempted to), they could be considered to have proceeded on the very assumptions that they purported to criticize others for making. The Eastern bloc was wary of falling into this trap, but eventually the temptation to give Western states a taste of their own medicine was too strong and Socialist states simply joined the fray, thereby implying that they had mollified their position on the issue in principle and, quite possibly if implicitly, that criticism of their own human rights record was no longer fundamentally beyond bounds.

Soon enough, international lawyers extrapolated far more dramatic consequences from these ad hoc developments, insisting that the seeds of human rights not being part of the *domaine réservé* had been sowed as early as the proclamation of the Universal Declaration and had even slowly gained customary status.[179] The Final Act assumed a sort of emblematic function, whilst the idea of human rights as 'fair game' has since become very central to claims about what constitutes (or rather, does not constitute) interference. This initial move was in due course buttressed by a vast conceptual and doctrinal edifice

177 'The Belgrade Follow-Up Meeting of the Conference on Security and Co-Operation in Europe: 4 October 1977—8 March 1978' (1978) 9 Bulletin of Peace Proposals 183.

178 Thomas Risse-Kappen and Kathryn Sikkink, 'The Socialization of International Human Rights Norms into Domestic Practices: Introduction' in Thomas Risse-Kappen, Stephen C Ropp and Kathryn Sikkink (eds), *The Power of Human Rights: International Norms and Domestic Change* (Cambridge University Press 1999) 28.

179 Dominic McGoldrick, 'The Principle of Non-Intervention: Human Rights' in Vaughan Lowe and Colin Warbrick (eds), *The United Nations and the Principles of International Law* (Routledge 1994).

that has consistently portrayed human rights obligations as *erga omnes*[180] or, at least in specific regional arrangements, as a 'collective guarantee'.[181] Clearly a state violating human rights is not ground for armed intervention, as the ICJ noted in the Nicaragua case,[182] but this at least allows for other states to express concern about such violations. Even if the invocation of human rights had initially been purely strategic and even if there had been misunderstandings about what it meant for interference, the Helsinki episode opened a breach in the wall of non-intervention that was not about to be filled.

3.2 *Between Humanitarianism and droits-de-l'hommisme*

At any rate, the idea that involvement in what would otherwise be considered the sovereign affairs of another state does not qualify as interference if it is inspired by human rights has achieved considerable currency since. Even in the heyday of the Third World driven debate on non-interference (expounded later in this book), states from that group recognized that the norm 'could not be construed to mean that a country could violate the fundamental human rights of its citizens without that violation becoming the concern of the entire world community'.[183] That evolution is reflected, notably, in the *Institut de Droit International's* 1989 resolution on 'The Protection of Human Rights and the Principle of Non-Intervention in Internal Affairs of States'.[184] The resolution notes that the obligation to observe human rights, particularly as contained in the Universal Declaration 'is incumbent upon every State in relation to the international community as a whole, and every State has a legal interest in the protection of human rights. The obligation further implies a duty of solidarity among all States to ensure as rapidly as possible the effective protection of human rights throughout the world'.[185] This was understood as meaning specifically that '[a] State acting in breach of its obligations in the sphere of human rights cannot evade its international responsibility by claiming that such matters are essentially within its domestic jurisdiction'.[186]

---

180 Yoram Dinstein, 'The Erga Omnes Applicability of Human Rights' (1992) 30 Archiv des Völkerrechts 16.

181 Antônio Augusto Cançado Trindade, *International Law for Humankind: Towards a New Jus Gentium* (2nd edn, Brill Nijhoff 2010) 315.

182 *Nicaragua v United States* (n 3) [268].

183 UNGA Sixth Committee (22nd Session) 'Summary record of the 1001st meeting' (17 November 1967) U.N. Doc A/C.6/SR.1001, para 2.

184 Institut de Droit International, 'The Protection of Human Rights and the Principle of Non-Intervention in Internal Affairs of States', *Session of Santiago de Compostela* (1989).

185 ibid 1.

186 ibid 2.

As a result, the broad arc of human rights promotion in international law has consisted in arguing that human rights are fundamentally a matter of international concern, and therefore never beyond international scrutiny. This was already evident in an older humanitarian tradition that denied that offers of humanitarian assistance could be seen as interference. For example, parties to the 1949 Geneva conventions must 'allow the free passage of shipments of medicine and material, as well as objects necessary for religious worship, intended only for the civilian population of another party, even if the latter is its adversary'.[187] So long as such assistance is impartial, it 'shall not be regarded as interference in the armed conflict or as unfriendly acts'.[188] It is true that the situation is more sensitive in the case of non-international armed conflict, as has been already mentioned in relation to recognitions of belligerency and the like, but even there offers of assistance should not be considered to constitute interference.[189] Preempting claims of interference in the name of widely shared international values, thus, was one of the early ways in which the norm of non-intervention was partly hollowed out and humanitarian concerns provide as good a basis as any to make that point.

This older humanitarian tradition, however, has increasingly been taken over by a more modern human rights sensitivity that has uncoupled the debate on interference from the ultimately quite specific concern with armed conflict. A clear line was long drawn between a broad notional commitment to human rights as a matter of substantive concern of all states, but not leading to any method of enforcement that might interfere with sovereign affairs. Early efforts to secure international rights of individual petition—let alone judicial standing by victims of human rights violations—were sidelined. At best, in the U.N., the initial focus was on massive or systematic violations, and those that specifically endangered international peace and security. Between states,

---

187 Geneva Convention Relative to the Protection of Civilian Persons in Time of War (adopted 12 August 1949, entered into force 21 October 1950) 75 UNTS 287 (Fourth Geneva Convention) art 23.

188 Protocol Additional to the Geneva Conventions of 12 August 1949, and relating to the Protection of Victims of International Armed Conflicts (adopted 8 June 1977, entered into force 7 December 1978) 1125 UNTS 3 (AP I) art 70.

189 Protocol Additional to the Geneva Conventions of 12 August 1949, and relating to the Protection of Victims of Non-International Armed Conflicts (adopted 8 June 1977, entered into force 7 December 1978) 1125 UNTS 609 (AP II) art 3(2). See also *Nicaragua v United States* (n 3) [242]; Declaration on Principles of International Law concerning Friendly Relations and Co-operation among States in accordance with the Charter of the United Nations, UNGA Res 2625 (XXV) (24 October 1970) U.N. Doc A/RES/2625 (1970 Declaration on Friendly Relations).

the matter was even trickier and every concession was negotiated inch by inch. The position of Socialist states for example was extremely cautious, and although they agreed that an 'opinion' by a State about another State's human rights performance 'should not be considered to constitute intervention but to be part of the normal communication between States', they also emphasized that 'it should be clear that such communication should not include demands, pressure or campaigns'.[190]

By and large, however, that prudence has increasingly been displaced, not least because of the fall of the Soviet Union, by a much more sustained attempt to exceptionalize human rights from the suspicion of interference. A typical if rather abstract statement of what is understood by many to be the end result, perhaps all the more interesting that it is made by a Russian author, is provided by Vladimir Kartashin:

> The principles of sovereignty and non-interference with domestic affairs are limited in modern international law by human rights, peoples' rights, and individual rights. In this context, efforts put forth by both the international community and particular States to ensure fundamental rights and freedoms all over the world cannot be viewed as interference with domestic affair [...] No State has the right to violate fundamental human rights and freedoms, while invoking State sovereignty. When the said rights are violated, the principles of sovereignty and non-interference can be restricted to such an extent as necessary for putting an end to these violations.[191]

Numerous sweeping statements to the same effect can be found in the international legal literature that not only purport to subtract all matters of human rights from the *domaine réservé* (portraying it increasingly as almost an empty shell) but make sovereignty itself conditional upon respect for rights.[192] The notion that human rights are a common concern and that therefore external action in their favor is relatively less likely to be understood as a form of interference is almost routinely invoked internationally.

---

190 Hannikainen (n 174) 34.

191 Vladimir A Kartashkin, 'Humanitarian Intervention in the Globalizing World' (2005) 5 Baltic Yearbook of International Law 27, 33.

192 Hallie Ludsin, 'Returning Sovereignty to the People' (2013) 46 Vanderbilt Journal of Transnational Law 97.

3.3 *A Droit d'Ingérence?*

One particularly strong offshoot of that early 1990s line of thought, somewhere on the fault line of humanitarianism and human rights, was a notably francophone agitation around a right of interference (*droit d'ingérence*) or even a duty of interference (*devoir d'ingérence*) when particular humanitarian catastrophes threatened.[193] That limited foray was constantly at risk of being abusively generalized in ways that would have reduced the prohibition on intervention to very little. Going against the grain of a generation of Third World leaders who had emphasized the importance and even the normative primacy of sovereignty as a site of self-determination, the 'French doctors' insisted, notably following the Biafra episode, that post-colonial sovereignty had too often been allowed to become the problem, at the expense of a culture of rights.[194]

By the 1990s, this fed into increasingly muscular discourses of interventionism that resurrected earlier imperial visions of a 'right of intervention' sustained by the 'civilizing mission' in a context of emphasis on the gravity of international crimes. In the words of Tony Blair:

> The most pressing foreign policy problem we face is to identify the circumstances in which we should get actively involved in other people's conflicts. Non-interference has long been considered an important principle of international order. And it is not one we would want to jettison too readily. One state should not feel it has the right to change the political system of another or foment subversion or seize pieces of territory to which it feels it should have some claim. But the principle of non-interference must be qualified in important respects. Acts of genocide can never be a purely internal matter.[195]

In rhetorical terms at least, and taking into account only such statements, the domain of what might be considered interference had been considerably reduced.[196] Human rights, their broad scope and vagueness, have thus lent themselves well to significant patterns of intrusion or at least of redefining

193 Bettati (n 26).

194 Jessica Whyte, 'Liberté sans Frontières, French Humanitarianism, and the Neoliberal Critique of Third Worldism' in A Dirk Moses, Marco Duranti and Roland Burke (eds), *Decolonization, Self-Determination, and the Rise of Global Human Rights Politics* (Cambridge University Press 2020).

195 Tony Blair, 'The Blair Doctrine' (1999) <https://archive.globalpolicy.org/empire/humanint/1999/0422blair.htm> accessed 8 January 2024.

196 Fernando R Tesón, *Humanitarian Intervention: An Inquiry into Law and Morality* (Transnational Publishers 1997).

what potentially constitutes interference.[197] States have for example been emboldened to more systematically and forcefully raise human rights concerns in bilateral relations,[198] even as the governance of human rights has no doubt been multilateralized, on both a regional and universal basis. Moreover, the prototypical form of reasoning on interference associated with human rights has been extended significantly. For instance, it has since the 90s been reinforced (dubiously as it happens, but the discursive investment is nonetheless real) by the argument that there is a 'right to democracy',[199] leading specifically to a multiplication of programs of democratic assistance but also the occasional 'pro-democracy' intervention.[200] Sovereignty itself has been redefined as a form of 'responsibility' that ought not to be rigidly opposed to necessary humanitarian interventions,[201] opening yet more avenues for potential incursions within it.[202]

Indeed, the investment in the relative weakening of the rule of non-interference and the reduction of the scope of the *domaine réservé* evident in this trend have been powerfully framed in the background, often problematically, by the strongly connected debate on the use of force[203] and the renewed interest in humanitarian intervention and the legitimation of an international role in correcting and remedying atrocities.[204] As then Secretary General of the United Nations Javier Perez de Cuellar put it in 1991:

> [T]he principle of non-interference with the essential domestic jurisdiction of states cannot be regarded as a protective barrier behind which human rights could be massively or systematically violated with impunity

197 RJ Vincent and Peter Wilson, 'Beyond Non-Intervention' in Ian Forbes and Mark Hoffman (eds), *Political Theory, International Relations, and the Ethics of Intervention* (Palgrave Macmillan U.K. 1993).

198 Jerome J Shestack and Roberta Cohen, 'International Human Rights: A Role for the United States Symposium: Human Rights and United States Foreign Policy' (1973) 14 Virginia Journal of International Law 673, 685.

199 Thomas M Franck, 'The Emerging Right to Democratic Governance' (1992) 86 American Journal of International Law 46.

200 Michael McFaul, 'Democracy Promotion as a World Value' (2004) 28 The Washington Quarterly 147.

201 Francis M Deng and others, *Sovereignty as Responsibility: Conflict Management in Africa* (Brookings Institution 2010).

202 Amy E Eckert, 'The Non-Intervention Principle and International Humanitarian Interventions' (2001) 7 International Legal Theory 49.

203 Dino Kritsiotis, 'Close Encounters of a Sovereign Kind' (2009) 20 European Journal of International Law 299.

204 Orford (n 27).

> [...] The case for not impinging on the sovereignty, territorial integrity and political independence of States is by itself indubitably strong. But it would only be weakened if it were to carry the implication that sovereignty, even in this day and age, includes the right of mass slaughter or of launching systematic campaigns of decimation or forced exodus of civilian populations.[205]

If states can bomb to save a population from its imminent demise or even to bring about democracy or combat 'illegitimate regimes',[206] then a fortiori one would think they can also intervene preventively through means not entailing the use of force in order to avert such a disaster. In fact, the R2P concept's strong preference for non-forceful means suggests that, at least when major atrocities are involved, interference is not only legal, but welcome.[207]

In conclusion, human rights have proved, rhetorically at least, an important vehicle to shift the form of what is considered acceptable intervention and interference towards the end of the Cold War and as part of a relatively brief post-Cold War interlude. They did so as part of a unipolar moment that sheds doubt on the shift's longevity and sustainability as an inflexion of international law, but they did substantially contribute to blur the normative terrain, with Kosovo as an absolute high point of confusion around the competing claims of intervention and human rights, especially in the West.[208] By purporting to make human rights the litmus test of international law, they shifted the conversation away from intervention-nonintervention to a conversation about

---

205 UNGA, Report of the Secretary-General on the Work of the Organization (13 September 1991) U.N. Doc A/46/1, 5.

206 Lori Fisler Damrosch and David J Scheffer, *Law and Force in The New International Order* (Avalon Publishing 1991).

207 The idea that humanitarian intervention more narrowly involves a clear relativization of the principle of non-interference is evident in much political discourse. See for example Blair (n 195).

208 Richard A Falk, 'Kosovo, World Order, and the Future of International Law' (1999) 93 American Journal of International Law 847; Louis Henkin, 'Kosovo and the Law of "Humanitarian Intervention"' (1999) 93 American Journal of International Law 824; Abraham D Sofaer, 'International Law and Kosovo' (2000) 36 Stanford Journal of International Law 1; Ian Brownlie and Christine J Apperley, 'Kosovo Crisis Inquiry: Memorandum on the International Law Aspects' (2000) 49 International & Comparative Law Quarterly 878; Thomas M Franck, 'Lessons of Kosovo' (1999) 93 American Journal of International Law 857; Patrick Thornberry, '"Come, Friendly Bombs ...": International Law in Kosovo' in Kyril Drezov, Bulent Gokay and Michael Waller (eds), *Kosovo: The Politics of Delusion* (Routledge 2001); Christine M Chinkin, 'Kosovo: A "Good" or "Bad" War?' (1999) 93 American Journal of International Law 841.

the proper scope of human rights. Nonetheless, these developments towards shrinking the domain of interference through vigorous assertions of the scope of human rights must be read in light of earlier and simultaneous efforts to reassert the value of non-interference for the times that suggest that every move to push definitions in one direction is met by an opposite push in the other direction.

4 Push-Back: The Third-World Attempt at Sanctification of Non-interference

Although on one level 'deprovincializing' intervention by connecting it to global values such as human rights, it is worth noting that the investment in an expanded terrain of intervention was not without several ambiguities. First, the cosmopolitanism of human rights was also, in many ways, the provincialism of the liberal West, projected onto the world and imagining itself as endowed with a messianic mission to reform international law. Second and as such, this projection was much less a novelty than it is presented as being since the 1990s, and in fact reconnects with the long arc of international law, all the way from its early genesis in Spanish scholastics to 19th Century *interventions d'humanité*. In other words, international law has always and not just recently been about promoting higher values that transcend states and occasionally justify incursions in the affairs of particular members of the international community. Third, in claiming the mantel of international human rights law relatively late in the day to better justify intervention, the West was in fact only one-upping the Third World which had itself long sought to cast the right to self-determination and the struggle against colonization and racist regimes as themselves fully human rights pursuits that could justify both intervention and non-intervention. In short, the West does not have a monopoly of human rights-infused understandings of international law, only a certain commanding authority over a particular liberal narrative of human rights in the international sphere. Its promotion of a particular vision of intervention after the Cold War was also a 'reappropriation' of a theme that had dangerously slipped from its control as the Third World intermittently took the normative lead in defining intervention and non-intervention.[209]

209 Quinton-Brown (n 35) 11–12.

4.1 *From the Americas to the United Nations*

The effort to reframe interference as legitimate intervention, in particular via human rights, has long coexisted and had to contend with a considerable rhetorical effort in the *opposite* direction. Starting in the early twentieth Century, Latin American Republics had strongly pushed back against the notion that states could use compulsory measures to collect public debts (for their own reasons, evidently, and not as part of subservience to the Monroe Doctrine). The Drago and Calvo Doctrines, in particular, condemned not only armed intervention but, in the case of the latter, even diplomatic manoeuvres that could be conceived as inimical to sovereignty.[210] Calvo, the Argentine foreign minister, condemned European powers for following a different set of rules outside Europe than they had within it and, essentially, minimizing the territorial sovereignty of South American states for the benefit, of all things, of private interests.[211] Although about more than just interference, this precedent set the stage for a tradition of claims for the full benefits of sovereignty from states in the semi-periphery that would eventually be taken up by others and considerably change the economy of non-intervention.

In the inter-war, faced with ever more hegemonic claims asserted under the Monroe doctrine, Latin American states had attempted to formalise the prohibition of non-interference as part of an effort at resistance against U.S. hegemony through a form of regional international law. Article 8 of the Montevideo Convention of 1933, better known for its stipulation of the basic requirements of statehood, stipulated that '[n]o State has the right to intervene in the internal or external affairs of another'.[212] This was the 'great achievement' of the Montevideo Convention by Latin American international lawyers for whom it had been 'a central goal [...] of the classical period'.[213] The achievement was notable because it 'did not lay down existing law, but created new law'[214] or at least translated into positive international law what had until then been mostly the ruminations of international legal scholars. The Convention was at the time a major success in obtaining grudging U.S. renouncement, as part

---

210 Amos S Hershey, 'The Calvo and Drago Doctrines' (1907) 1 American Journal of International Law 26.

211 Carlos Calvo, *Le Droit International Théorique et Pratique*, vol 5 (4th edn, Rousseau 1887) 350–351.

212 Montevideo Convention on Rights and Duties of States adopted by the Seventh International Conference of American States (adopted 26 December 1933, entered into force 26 December 1934) 165 LNTS 19 (Montevideo Convention) art 8.

213 ibid.

214 Arnulf Becker Lorca, *Mestizo International Law: A Global Intellectual History 1842–1933* (Cambridge University Press 2014) 309.

of Roosevelt's 'good neighbor' policy, to the Monroe doctrine, even though it was hardly the last chapter in a long litany of U.S. interventions.[215] Perhaps even more dramatically, the Charter of the Organization of American States solemnly proclaimed in 1951 that:

> No State or group of States has the right to intervene, directly or indirectly, for any reason whatever, in the internal or external affairs of any other State. The foregoing principle prohibits not only armed force but also any other form of interference or attempted threat against the personality of the State or against its political, economic, and cultural elements.[216]

In other words, the contribution of Latin America to nascent ideas of non-intervention as a universal ideal and not merely the privilege of Western European nations or the U.S. was decisive.

This would in due course influence efforts undertaken at the nascent United Nations to shape a doctrine of prohibited intervention: 'Could not what had been done in America on the continental scale be repeated on a world scale?'[217] asked Jesús Yepes of Colombia before the International Law Commission (ILC). The U.N. Charter set the tone for the international law of non-interference in the second half of the twentieth Century. It did not contain any specific provision to that effect, but the condemnation of the 'threat or use of force' in Article 2(4)[218] and the notion that, at least as regards the U.N. itself, '[n]othing contained in the present Charter shall authorize [it] to intervene in matters which are essentially within the domestic jurisdiction of any state'[219] set a certain baseline, to which this book will return. The prohibition on the use of force arguably 'absorbed much of the classic conception of intervention' thus endowing it with renewed strength,[220] although this would also paradoxically for a long time be the bane of efforts to define intervention as a sui generis phenomenon. It also led to somewhat quixotic and ultimately largely unsuccessful efforts by the Third World to include economic coercion as a use of force prohibited by Article 2(4) of the U.N. Charter, that may in fact

215 Sumner Welles, 'Intervention and Interventions' (1947) 26 Foreign Affairs 116.

216 Charter of the Organization of American States (as amended) (adopted 20 April 1948, entered into force 13 December 1951) 119 UNTS 3 (OAS Charter) art 19.

217 Yearbook of the International Law Commission (ILC) (1950) vol I, 160, para 50c.

218 U.N. Charter, art 2(4).

219 U.N. Charter, art 2(7).

220 UNGA Special Committee on Principles of International Law Concerning Friendly Relations and Co-Operation Among States (23 October 1964) U.N. Doc A/AC.119/SR.26 (Mr Sinclair, United Kingdom), 5.

have delayed a reckoning with forms of intervention that were neither purely violent nor purely economic.

At any rate, the evolving definition of intervention was also a function of norm-entrepreneurship and various ideological projects at orienting international law's discursive development. Throughout the second half of the 20th Century in particular, states or groups of states traded arguments, and sometimes switched roles, often in response to particular crises (decolonization, the OPEP embargo, sanctions against South Africa or Nicaragua, etc.). These served to temporarily focus ideas but also often had the effect of overdetermining particular states' strategies in the moment, at the risk of later cornering them into more dramatic positions than they found served their long-term national interest. Some measure of backtracking has therefore always attended the development of international law on such issues, an early measure perhaps of the difficulty of maintaining a consistent stance on non-intervention especially, as is the case of many states, when one is potentially both on the giving and receiving end of intervention. Ironically, although the non-intervention gospel was partly descended from European ideas about self-determination and sovereignty, it was 'Third World jurists [who] soon realised that traditional ideas about statehood, self-determination and non-interference could be employed in their interest as they had once been employed in the interests of their colonial masters'[221] (in truth, of course, they could also lay claim to their own normative traditions of self-determination).

Claims about non-interference would thus become intertwined and sometimes mired in the decolonial agenda of the 60s and 70s. The formidable achievement of the Third World was to have bundled together a commitment to self-determination, human rights and sovereignty and made them the basis for an agenda of non-intervention. This gave a particular tenor to Cold War anti-interference projects that sought to keep foreign powers at bay to effect colonial emancipation, albeit not always avoiding the trap of enlisting the support of other foreign powers to intervene in the process. In essence, that discourse was flexible and could be turned against itself or create a degree of systemic inconsistency: the sovereignty of newly decolonized states was sacrosanct to be sure, but Apartheid South Africa's or colonial France's were not. Yet this could be reconstructed as not, in fact, a contradiction: the point was that non-intervention was meaningless in international law without a sense of what values non-intervention was supposed to promote and, on that score,

221 Martti Koskenniemi, 'International Law in the World of Ideas' in James Crawford and Martti Koskenniemi (eds), *The Cambridge Companion to International Law* (Cambridge University Press 2012) 55–56.

there was little doubt for the Third World about what those values were (just as it had been clear to Western states that one could intervene in the sovereign affairs of the Soviet Union on account of human rights, but not in their own). Against the fetishism of form, the Third World proposed a broad solidaristic agenda of non-intervention *and* intervention in the service of its particular designs.[222]

At the same time, one should not underestimate the extent to which non-interference had already been presaged and tested, as has already been hinted, by claims of imperial and hegemonic powers to themselves guarantee spaces within which interference was anathema. During the Cold War, both superpowers made it clear they would strongly resent interference in their sovereign affairs, as well as those of their *protégés*. Beyond the Brezhnev doctrine within the Eastern bloc, the organizing principle in the Soviet Union's relationship to the West was meant to be that of 'peaceful coexistence', i.e., one where the default international principle of non-interference applied. According to the terms of the 1972 Moscow declaration, for example, '[d]ifferences in ideology and in the social systems of the USA and the USSR are not obstacles to the bilateral development of normal relations based on the principles of sovereignty, equality, non-interference in internal affairs and mutual advantage'.[223] The normalization of relations between the two blocs and the era of East-West *détente* certainly gave an air of plausibility to renewed claims about non-interference, even if of course these claims had an air of pure rhetoric about them.

But despite the at least nominal and, occasionally, strategic and, of course, somewhat dubious support of the superpowers for the idea of non-interference at least as it applied to them, the brunt of the effort to uphold the principle was largely shouldered by newly decolonized states, many of which operated as part of the non-aligned group. Claims about non-interference, for example were central to the political tonality of the Bandung conference.[224] In 1957, the U.N. General Assembly (UNGA) adopted the resolution on 'Peaceful and Neighbourly Relations among States',[225] the first of many such landmark documents to foreground non-interference. The famous 1960 'Declaration on the Granting of Independence to Colonial Countries and Peoples',[226] although it

222 Quinton-Brown (n 35) 11.

223 Cited in Schwebel, 'The Brezhnev Doctrine Repealed and Peaceful Co-Existence Enacted' (n 150) 818.

224 Final Communiqué of the Asian-African Conference of Bandung (24 April 1955) s G, principle 4; Roland Burke, *Decolonization and the Evolution of International Human Rights* (University of Pennsylvania Press 2010) 25.

225 UNGA Res 1236 (XII) (14 December 1957) U.N. Doc A/RES/1236.

226 UNGA Res 1514 (XV) (14 December 1960) U.N. Doc A/RES/1514.

only addressed interference in passing given its basic goal of securing sovereignty for newly independent states, also set the tone. These instruments will be dissected in more detail later in the book, but suffice it to note here that, although they can never be entirely dissociated from the conditions of their emergence, they set a particular tone in international law and would become very difficult to contradict explicitly in the ensuing decades.

Newly independent states were particularly concerned about continued military intervention, but also outside support for secessionist groups and the issue of economic and financial coercion. They pursued a complex strategy that involved investments first in the definition of aggression and, when that failed, in intervention/interference as such. Throughout that era, debates about whether the prohibition of the use of force included coercive economic measures or whether the latter were only capable of violating the norm of non-intervention (or perhaps not even that) were connected: once the Third World failed to achieve consensus about aggression including economic coercion, it shifted to ensuring that the latter would at least be included as a violation of the prohibition of intervention. The proximity between ongoing debates on the use of force and interference may have had the effect of tainting the latter in more categorical claims than warranted. As argued by Stephen Townley, it inclined the Third World to think of intervention as very much a black-and-white rule, possibly at the cost of illusory claims to clarity.[227] In many ways, however, the debate on the use of force was of a different nature; although it incorporated an underlying claim about intervention, it was and remains quite distinct. Still, these overlapping debates tended to reinforce rather than detract from each other on the long term.

4.2 *The Emerging International Legal Formalization of Non-interference*

The question of intervention was litigated again and again whether on its own terms or indirectly via a wide range of issues including the draft Code of Offences against the Peace and Security of Mankind, the validity of treaties, sovereignty over natural resources, self-determination, aggression, unilateral sanctions, or propaganda activities. As such, it remains one of the guiding threads to understand the last decades of debates in international law and their tendency to almost obsessively entertain the same issues, at times with very little attention to how the conversation constantly reinvents the wheel. Intervention and interference have truly served as mirrors within which sovereignty contemplates itself, elusively seeking to capture the essence of a

227 Townley (n 62).

phenomenon that in the end often tends to merely refract the anxieties of the observer. But they have also captured the intensity of divisions that preside over international law's destiny, in a context of Third World insurgency, gross meddling and North-South as well as East-West divides.[228] In particular, the debate has radicalized interrogations at the heart of sovereignty that see it as either exclusive or interdependent, a power or a responsibility, a freedom or an obligation.

These interrogations have no doubt sustained the division of the world into stereotypical blocs but, beyond diplomatic theatrics, have also proved prone to cut across groups and even reverse over time—a particular refrain of this book. An early high point of the non-intervention agenda was the 1954 Draft Code of Offences against the Peace and Security of Mankind. Seen from the perspective of today's sensitivity, it is striking to see a range of behavior characteristic of intervention being held up as among the most central international offences and, even though one should not make too much of such formal details, preceding the enumeration of crimes against humanity and war crimes. In addition to the 'usual suspects' of fomenting strife or terrorist activity in another state's territory, the Draft Code included '[t]he intervention by the authorities of a State in the internal or external affairs of another State, by means of coercive measures of an economic or political character in order to force its will and thereby obtain advantages of any kind'.[229]

But it is General Assembly resolution 2131 (XX) of the 21 December 1965 titled 'Declaration on the Inadmissibility of Intervention in the Domestic Affairs of States and the Protection of their Independence and Sovereignty' (hereafter, 1965 Declaration on the Inadmissibility of Intervention) that truly set the tone.[230] The resolution, which was promoted by states such as Egypt, Colombia and India, was adopted by 109 votes to none. It deplored not only 'armed intervention' but also 'direct or indirect forms of interference threatening the sovereign personality and the political independence of States'.[231] It has been described as 'the adumbration of highly abstract primary principles

228 Samuel Moyn and Umut Özsu, 'The Historical Origins and Setting of the Friendly Relations Declaration' in Jorge E Viñuales (ed), *The U.N. Friendly Relations Declaration at 50: An Assessment of the Fundamental Principles of International Law* (Cambridge University Press 2020).

229 Draft Code of Offences against the Peace and Security of Mankind, 1954, Article 9.

230 UNGA Res 2131 (XX) (21 December 1965) U.N. Doc A/RES/20/2131 (1965 Declaration on the Inadmissibility of Intervention).

231 ibid.

at the expense of detailed secondary principles and rules',[232] but was at least that. It emphasized that '[n]o State has the right to intervene, directly or indirectly, for any reason whatever, in the internal or external affairs of any State'.[233] Notably, the resolution proclaimed very broadly that:

> No State may use or encourage the use of economic, political or any other type of measures to coerce another State in order to obtain from it the subordination of the exercise of its sovereign rights or to secure from it advantages of any kind. Also, no State shall organize, assist, foment, finance, incite or tolerate subversive, terrorist, or armed activities directed towards the violent overthrow of the regime of another State, or interfere in civil strife in another State.[234]

In 1970, the General Assembly confirmed and amplified that stance through the adoption of the landmark 'Declaration on Principles of International Law concerning Friendly Relations and Cooperation among States' (hereafter, 1970 Declaration on Friendly Relations).[235] The resolution was adopted without a vote and is generally seen as authoritative. Although quite focused on the principle of prohibition of armed intervention, it also insisted in no uncertain terms that: 'No State or group of States has the right to intervene, directly or indirectly, for any reason whatever, in the internal or external affairs of any other State'. This included 'all other forms of interference or attempted threats against the personality of the State or against its political, economic and cultural elements, are in violation of international law'.[236]

Finally, in 1981, the General Assembly adopted the 'Declaration on the Inadmissibility of Intervention and Interference in the Internal Affairs of States' (hereafter, 1981 Declaration on the Inadmissibility of Intervention and Interference), a resolution of more uncertain status under international law.[237] In retrospect, this may have been the high point of a certain strident view against interference, one deeply wedded to Third World politics. Numerous less

---

232 Edward McWhinney, 'Declaration on the Inadmissibility of Intervention in the Domestic Affairs of States and the Protection of Their Independence and Sovereignty General Assembly Resolution 2131 (XX)', s 2 <https://legal.un.org/avl/ha/ga_2131-xx/ga_2131-xx.html> accessed 8 January 2024.

233 1965 Declaration on the Inadmissibility of Intervention, para 1.

234 ibid, art 2.

235 1970 Declaration on Friendly Relations.

236 ibid.

237 UNGA Res 36/103 (9 December 1981) A/RES/36/103 (1981 Declaration on the Inadmissibility of Intervention and Interference).

significant but similar sounding resolutions were adopted during that era.[238] Also of note is that, from the 1950s to the early 1990s, the ILC debated repeatedly, as part of its effort on a Code of Crimes against the Peace and Security of Mankind, the possibility of including a crime of intervention. That effort almost came to pass, but it eventually failed alongside the broader project of the Code, nonetheless leaving a trace of its particular investment in the discursive economy of international law. In short, it would not be an exaggeration to say that throughout much of the decolonization era and the Cold War, the definition of intervention and interference was the explicit or implicit stake of many symbolic exchanges wherein some states sought to negotiate their newfound independence and others sought to temper their enthusiasm.

Although mostly supported by the Soviet bloc and the non-aligned, the strong stance against interference also had its supporters in the West. These included realists who thought that mixing human rights concerns with international diplomacy would be problematic. For example, the Nixon administration opposed the Jackson Amendment which would have denied most-favored nation treatment to the USSR on human rights grounds, precisely on the basis that it would constitute inappropriate interference.[239] Even the Helsinki Final Act of the Conference on Security and Co-operation in Europe, which as we have seen is often understood as having heralded a much more central role for human rights, stipulated that '[t]he participating States will refrain from any intervention, direct or indirect, individual or collective, in the internal or external affairs falling within the domestic jurisdiction of another participating State'.[240] In other words, both sides were prone to at least pay lip service to the notion of non-interference, and every move to interfere also included a countervailing move to appear to be restraining interference.

---

238 UNGA Res 31/91 (14 December 1976) U.N. Doc A/RES/31/91; UNGA Res 32/152 (19 December 1977) U.N. Doc A/RES/32/153; UNGA Res 33/74 (15 December 1978) U.N. Doc A/RES/33/74; UNGA Res 34/101 (14 December 1979) U.N. Doc A/RES/34/101; UNGA Res 35/159 (12 December 1980) U.N. Doc A/RES/35/159; Report of the Secretary-General, 'Non-Interference in the Internal Affairs of States' (4 October 1979) U.N. Doc A/34/192; UNGA Res 44/147 (15 December 1989) U.N. Doc A/RES/44/147; UNGA Res 45/151 (18 December 1990) U.N. Doc A/RES/45/151; UNGA Res 46/130 (17 December 1991) U.N. Doc A/RES/46/130; UNGA Res 47/130 (18 December 1992) U.N. Doc A/RES/47/130; UNGA Res 48/124 (20 December 1993) U.N. Doc A/RES/48/124; UNGA Res 50/172 (22 December 1995) U.N. Doc A/RES/50/172; UNGA Res 52/119 (12 December 1997) U.N. Doc A/RES/52/119; UNGA Res 54/168 (17 December 1999) U.N. Doc A/RES/54/168; UNGA Res 56/154 (19 December 2001) U.N. Doc A/RES/56/154; UNGA Res 66/186 (22 December 2011) U.N. Doc A/RES/66/186.

239 Shestack and Cohen (n 198) 684.

240 Helsinki Final Act, principle 6.

Many of the relevant resolutions were adopted as a result of the considerable weight of the non-aligned and Socialist worlds in the General Assembly and thus bore all the hallmarks of that vast and historical norm-entrepreneurship. As such, they certainly contributed to the ongoing and dynamic shaping of the norm of non-interference in expansive directions, even as the extent to which they instantly crystallized international law remained open to doubt. They adroitly framed their claim within the canon of international law to be able to invoke its legacy and to appear to be merely articulating the obvious, or at least to be prolonging and generalizing trends that had long been latent. They were often deliberately anchored in and justified in terms of some of the broad goals of the U.N. Charter, notably international peace and security. The first preambular paragraph of the Friendly Relations resolution, for example, emphasized the 'conviction':

> that the strict observance by States of the obligation not to intervene in the affairs of any other State is an essential condition to ensure that nations live in peace with one another, since the practice of any form of intervention not only violates the spirit and the letter of the Charter, but also leads to the creation of situations which threaten international peace and security.[241]

In particular, the attempt to make a compelling case for non-interference was linked to the general argument against creating exceptions to the strict prohibition on the use of force. Where humanitarian intervention has often been based on the notion that states' human rights records are of international concern, the reassertion of both a strict prohibition on the use of force and a strict prohibition on interference have often gone hand in hand. Third world states, in essence, insisted that the burden to prove that an exception to the strict rule against non-intervention existed should be shifted to states trying to make that case, who then would have to contend with an increasingly solidified custom in the opposite direction.

The case against interference gained strong support unexpectedly as Nicaragua sued the U.S. for its support for the contras. Coming towards the end of that Cold War era, the case provided a unique and much contested opportunity to tease out the differences between use of force, intervention and interference. In its *Nicaragua v United States* ruling, where the Court prefaced its

241 1970 Declaration on Friendly Relations, 122.

reasoning, in relation at least to the case of support by the U.S. for opposition forces in Nicaragua, that:

> It ha[d] to consider whether there might be indications of a practice illustrative of belief in a kind of general right for States to intervene, directly or indirectly, with or without armed force, in support of an internal opposition in another State, whose cause appeared particularly worthy by reason of the political and moral values with which it was identified. For such a general right to come into existence would involve a fundamental modification of the customary law principle of non-intervention.[242]

Although sometimes primarily remembered for holding that the U.S. was not responsible for using force against Nicaragua given its lack of 'effective control' over the Contras, the case is perhaps just as notable for its corollary finding: namely, that the U.S. had undoubtedly intervened unlawfully in the affairs of Nicaragua. We will return to some of the details of these findings, many of which remain as instructive today as they were then, in due course. The case has been interpreted and is remembered as 'a major decision against hegemonic subordination of small, regional, "other" states and peoples'.[243] Its conclusion that intervention had occurred would thus resonate throughout the decades and provide a unique judicial confirmation of the solidity of the norm even as, perhaps predictably, it would fail to silence persistent debates about the nature and scope of non-intervention.

4.3 *The Continuing Fate of Non-interference*

Finally, it is worth noting the central role that the norm of interference has assumed in structuring South-South cooperation and integration. Whilst this can be easily forgotten in often Western-centric sources that are much more focused on the incidence of human rights, the reality is that the Global South has often been remarkably consistent in following through on big proclamations of non-interference, notably *inter se*. Outside the already mentioned inter-American origin of the principle, one early manifestation had been the Five Principles of Peaceful Coexistence (Panchsheel) which formed the basis of the Sino-Indian treaty of 1955 and whose third principle emphasized

242 *Nicaragua v United States* (n 3) [206].

243 Henry J III Richardson, 'Critical Perspectives on Intervention Symposium: The International Law and Politics of External Intervention in Internal Conflict: Keynote Address' (2014) 29 Maryland Journal of International Law 12, 23.

'mutual non-interference in each other's internal affairs'.[244] More recently, the Shanghai Cooperation Organization,[245] ASEAN,[246] the Forum on China-Africa Cooperation,[247] the Boao Forum for Asia,[248] the China-Arab States Cooperation Forum (CACF)[249] and even China's Belt and Road Initiative[250] all invoke non-interference almost religiously. Indeed, it is sometimes claimed that China is the true guardian of the principle of non-interference when the West has largely given up on it,[251] even though that claim needs to be taken with a grain of salt. At the very least, then, non-interference also has a very strong regional and inter-regional flavor that suggests pertinent sub-universal levels of discourse and practice. At the same time and ironically non-interference is sometimes paired with what may appear to be regionally imperial ventures.

In short, in taking advantage of their automatic majority at the General Assembly, states in an earlier era of decolonization did propose a radically alternative vision to a world where interference had almost been the default rule. In doing so they managed to shore up support for an at least rhetorical affirmation of a strong norm of non-intervention and, as we will see, non-interference, even as the influence of human rights was starting to be felt. At the same time, they may have overshot and been pushing their luck somewhat with broad definitions of interference that they could little claim had an obvious basis in customary international law. Predictably, the more intense the affirmation of the sanctity of principles, the more evasive General Assembly resolutions were

244 Chandrasekhar Dasgupta, 'A Brief History of Panchsheel' (2016) 51 Economic and Political Weekly 26.

245 Shanghai Cooperation Organisation [SCO], 'Qingdao Declaration of the Council of Heads of State of Shanghai Cooperation Organisation' <http://www.china.org.cn/chinese/2018-07/05/content_53968548.htm> accessed 14 February 2019.

246 Lee Jones, 'ASEAN's Unchanged Melody? The Theory and Practice of 'Non-Interference'in Southeast Asia' (2010) 23 The Pacific Review 479; Robin Ramcharan, 'ASEAN and Non-Interference: A Principle Maintained' (2000) 22 Contemporary Southeast Asia 60.

247 Forum on China-Africa Cooperation [FOCAC], 'Beijing Declaration: Toward an Even Stronger China-Africa Community with a Shared Future' <http://www.focac.org/eng/zywx_1/zywj/201809/t20180912_8079765.htm> accessed 14 February 2019.

248 Jinping Xi, 'Towards a Community of Common Destiny and A New Future of Asia' (Boao Forum for Asia Annual Conference, Boao, 28 March 2015) <http://www.xinhuanet.com//english/2015-03/29/c_134106145.htm> accessed 14 February 2019.

249 Jinping Xi, 'Carrying Forward the Spirit of China-Arab Friendship and Jointly Building a China-Arab Community with a Shared Future in the New Era' (China-Arab States Summit, Riyadh, 9 December 2022) <https://english.news.cn/20221210/9c4e2500c7da4a6b84f11b57bfb64ef9/c.html> accessed 8 January 2024.

250 Xi (n 248).

251 Yang Zewei, 'Role of Panchsheel in Building International Order' (2004) 8 World Affairs: The Journal of International Issues 35.

about their precise content. More fundamentally, the risk was of imagining a world in which coercion of any kind does not and should not exist and then constantly taking umbrage to any change in the existing pattern of bilateral or multilateral relations, even as the international system has in a sense always been structurally coercive. Certainly, the effort to enshrine a renewed commitment to non-interference in international law through the sheer force of majority vote and repetition or within the confines of regional efforts has hardly been an unqualified universal success—no more, however, than the effort to entirely exclude human rights scrutiny from the suspicion of interference.

Although all states were rhetorically committed to non-interference in that momentous high point of General Assembly life, they were also quick to disagree on the scope of what it included, especially in the most sensitive zone that goes to the heart of this book: interference that does not involve the use of force or support for rebels; can credibly portray itself as speaking the language of human rights; and is sufficiently discreet and indirect to avoid easy detection. Moreover, the progress of the anti-interference agenda was in retrospect hardly cast in stone. By and large, Western states historically opposed strong assertions of the norm and often voted against or abstained from the landmark resolutions that emerged in the 1970s and 1980s. By the 1990s, the non-interference wave had begun to recede under strong opposition. This was particularly evident in the debates on a Draft Code of Offences Against the Peace and Security of Mankind which had been resurrected at the ILC after a long dormancy since the 1950s. By the Commission's forty-seventh session, no less than six of the previously 12 crimes of the report had been omitted, 5 of which were very characteristic of the earlier anti-interference agenda (the threat of aggression; intervention; colonial domination and other forms of alien domination; apartheid; the recruitment, use, financing and training of mercenaries; and wilful and severe damage to the environment). The face of international criminal law had thus begun to be normalized along much more conventional liberal cosmopolitan lines that would in due course emphasize only 'atrocity crimes'. Ironically, the latter have since even further corroded the prohibition of intervention by rekindling the register of humanitarian intervention and interference.[252]

Nonetheless, the status of non-interference as a norm of international law has remained relatively well-ingrained and, despite differences, the broad parameters of the conversation have come to be largely agreed upon. In a sense, although it temporarily went out of fashion during the hubristic days of the

252 Sarah Riley Case and Frédéric Mégret, 'The Colour of Jus Cogens' in Mohsen al Attar, Claire Smith and Ata Hindi (eds), *Emancipating International Law: Confronting the Violence of Racialised Boundaries* (Oxford University Press Forthcoming).

'New International Order' of the 1990s, the non-aligned world has remained remarkably and consistently attached to the notion of non-interference, laying the ground for it to make a comeback of sorts.[253] One area where this has manifested itself, revealing a clear fault line between the Global South and the Western world in the process, is around the debate on 'unilateral coercive measures'. For the former, unilateral sanctions are clearly an 'imposition by some States of their will on other States'[254] and 'tools for economic pressure'.[255] The General Assembly's Third Committee has a long practice, at the instigation of the Non-Aligned Movement, of adopting resolutions on 'Human rights and unilateral coercive measures' that lambast such measures for their negative impact on international relations but also specifically for being in violation of international law; simultaneously, the Second Committee, on the initiative of the Group of 77 and China, adopts annual resolutions on 'Unilateral economic measures as a means of political and economic coercion against developing countries' as a violation of the principle of non-intervention.

The West systematically voted against the above-mentioned resolutions in ways that may have created an uneasy stalemate. States may have 'agreed to disagree' rather than arrived at anything like a shared position. But there is more. As we will see, the irony is that Third World states, which long complained of the nefarious character of interference even if it did not make it to the level of intervention (to the scepticism of the West), may have been strangely prescient. Their intuition that intervention was (or ought to be understood as) a much broader issue than the sole emphasis on armed coercion or even just coercion suggests they may have been right all along. As will be seen, many Western states themselves have increasingly and routinely described interference in critical terms. They have done so for their own reasons but in ways that have illustrated the fundamental reversibility of positions. In the process, they have potentially added to the register of condemned intervention an entire panoply of new modalities.

---

253 Sholto Byrnes, 'Non-Interference or the Responsibility to Protect?' [2016] The National <https://www.thenationalnews.com/opinion/non-interference-or-the-responsibility-to-protect-1.144234> accessed 27 December 2023.

254 'Declaration of the Russian Federation and the People's Republic of China on the Promotion of International Law' (25 June 2016), para 6. For the full English text see Kenneth Anderson, 'Text of Russia-China Joint Declaration on Promotion and Principles of International Law' (*Lawfare*, 7 July 2016) <https://www.lawfaremedia.org/article/text-russia-china-joint-declaration-promotion-and-principles-international-law> accessed 28 June 2024.

255 UNGA Res 51/103 (3 March 1997) U.N. Doc A/RES/51/103.

CHAPTER 2

The Rise of the 'New' Interference

1 Introduction

The story of non-interference in international law could have been left there—and indeed it briefly seemed to stabilize towards the end of the Cold War in an uneasy *entre-deux* between camps. The norm of non-interference continued to be proclaimed ritually albeit without the gusto with which it had previously been invested. The U.S.'s intervention in Nicaraguan affairs—essentially funding and supporting a rebel group—had nothing subtle about it and still had the air of a use of force, albeit a covert one. Occurring as it did towards the end of the Cold War, it thus did not necessarily fully presage what was to come, as part of a much more complex geopolitical, technological, and ideational metamorphosis of interference.

Yet a new set of dynamics soon emerged, which has significantly contributed to both reenergize and complicate the issue. The current state of interference can be conceptualized as the product of a series of moves unfolding since the 2000s, which have seen the subjects, targets and nature of interference change dramatically but also, as a result, some of the normative dilemmas it raises. These developments suggest that the debate does not keep repeating itself across time in exactly the same terms, not only as a result of the evolving conditions and underlying politics of the international system, but also of the constantly shifting discursive dynamics of the debate itself. That debate is shaped by both material and ideational elements and has certainly witnessed an intensification. At the same time, the 'operating system' of international law appears somewhat dated, most clearly sanctioning behavior—forceful intervention, support for rebels or terrorist groups, etc.—that continues to exist, of course, but no longer defines the most challenging questions of the times. Its concepts have changed little, even as the origin, nature, and modalities of interference have been profoundly reinvented, notably in a non-coercive or non-clearly-coercive direction.

This chapter will seek to highlight the contours of the debate on interference as it has developed since the end of the Cold War. Although borrowing from the old, the 'new' interference is characterized by an acceleration of interference flows, the multiplication of its places of origin, and the diversification of the normative registers that are drawn upon to both oppose it and justify it. In particular, the problem has mushroomed from a fairly blatant form

 | DOI:10.1163/9789004532731_005

of state-to-state coercion to a form of ubiquitous interference by a variety of actors with all in a context of global interdependence where '[s]ome act of every nation may send its reverberations everywhere',[256] making it difficult to understand what is being interfered with, let alone who is doing the interfering. This has also arguably given the phenomenon a much more central and preoccupying role in global affairs, eve as it has unleashed dynamics that make it problematic to pin down and combat. At the same time, the chapter will underscore the extent to which the new interference is also an *effet de discours*, the result of discursive investments that make it what it is and that need to be understood in their own terms.

2 The End of the Cold War and the Uncertain Fate of Interference

The controversy over interference had gone briefly dormant in the early 1990s at the end of the Cold War, in a context where democracy and human rights promotion no longer seemed controversial—where they no longer seemed, in short, to constitute interference. With the sovereignty of former Eastern bloc states significantly weakened, few were able or even willing to seriously push back.[257] The clout of the Third World also seemed to wane as a result of the disinvestment of the Soviet Union and the acceptance of liberal reforms by some leaders in the non-interference camp. Considerable energy was invested in 'liberalization' and its emphasis on multi-facetted domestic reform. Intervention was, for a while, barely mentioned. Influence was at any rate increasingly channelled through civil society and NGOs, making it harder to detect and identify. Emboldened by its Cold War successes, the West also stood more steadfastly in favor of a number of foreign opposition groups with relatively little pushback. In this overture for what in other times might have been described as an agenda of interference, the debate abated temporarily for lack of parties to it.

2.1 *Renewed Interference?*

Interference has been increasingly mediated through complex international and institutional arrangements that made it less conspicuous. The Final Act of the CSCE had opened a treaty breach which was gradually expanded after the Cold War to encompass North-South relations, notably through

256 Henkin and others (n 67) 156.
257 Bill Bowring, 'Human Rights and Eastern Europe' in Angela Hegarty and Siobhan Leonard (eds), *A Human Rights Agenda for the 21st Century* (Cavendish 1999) 339.

'conditionality'.[258] For example, when the E.U. and a number of African, Caribbean and Pacific (ACP) states signed the first Lomé agreement in 1975, it had emphasized non-interference in the sovereign affairs of ACP states and 'mutual respect' between partners; development was thus treated as an issue separate from democracy and human rights. This soon created disquiet within the European Communities in the face of what were perceived as significant rights violations by some beneficiary regimes. An attempt to include conditionality in Lomé II was rejected by ACP states as a form of interference, but by 1984 when Lomé III was signed, a human rights clause was first included in the Preamble, and by Lomé IV, human rights were included in Article 5 of the treaty—no doubt as a result of the changing power dynamics and the deep economic crisis that affected African states. Emphasizing non-interference, the former 'reflex of countries in order to halt human rights criticisms during the Cold War' now seemed like 'somewhat of an old-fashioned plea'.[259]

The net result was that the 'E.U.'s denunciation of human rights violations in any ACP state became legal within the ambit of the Convention and was no longer, ipso facto, regarded as interference in the internal affairs of such country'.[260] This underlined the grudging abdication of one side to the argument and the extent to which, in the right geopolitical circumstances, what at any given time constituted interference could be readjusted by political consensus. After 1989, the scope of interference was extended to democracy, the rule of law, and 'good governance',[261] to much continued misgivings from ACP states.[262] The replacement of the Lomé framework by the Cotonou agreement of 23 June 2000 further expanded the scope of conditionality to include conformity with a range of market reform demands.[263] Although they reluctantly accepted the principle that human rights were relevant to development cooperation, a

258 Dieter Sepp, 'Promoting Human Rights and Democratic Transition in Africa' (2000) 7 Javnost—The Public 81.

259 Elena Fierro, *European Union's Approach to Human Rights Conditionality in Practice* (Brill Nijhoff 2003) 304.

260 Bolade M Eyinla, 'The European Union and the Application of Political Conditionality in Sub-Sahara Africa' (1999) 54 Africa: Rivista Trimestrale di Studi e Documentazione dell'Istituto Italiano per l'Africa e l'Oriente 581, 587.

261 Gordon Crawford, 'Human Rights and Democracy in E.U. Development Co-Operation: Towards Fair and Equal Treatment' in Marjorie Lister (ed), *European Union Development Policy* (St Martin's Press 1998).

262 Eyinla (n 260).

263 Stephen R Hurt, 'Co-Operation and Coercion? The Cotonou Agreement between the European Union and ACP States and the End of the Lomé Convention' (2003) 24 Third World Quarterly 161.

number of states challenged the possibility for the then European communities to adopt sanctioning measures unilaterally, with limited success.

It should be said that, although interference often came from the West, the debate has had broader regional dimensions. Organizations such as ASEAN, which have centrally committed to non-interference, have found themselves feeling the limits of that approach in instances such as Myanmar, and heeding calls to move in at least a slightly more interventionist direction[264]—at the risk of being called out for violating their own 'ASEAN way'.[265] The African Union has itself evolved from a traditional stance emphasizing non-intervention to one increasingly emphasizing non-indifference, with the possibility of intervention explicitly recognized by the Malabo Protocol.[266] The earlier strictly non-interventionist stance of the Organization of African Unity had hampered its ability to have a positive bearing on the Biafra and Rwandan crises for example, not to mention the human toll in Uganda, Eritrea, the Democratic Republic of Congo or Darfur. In Burundi, Sudan, Somalia, the Comoros, or Gambia, African states under the African Union have shown an increasing willingness to enforce peacekeeping mandates,[267] all the way to a sort of 'right of intervention' in cases of atrocity crimes.[268]

2.2 *Renewed Pushback?*

At any rate, there is little doubt that interference did remain a live issue in the background, sometimes neglected only as a result of excessive focus on Western sources. A liberal interventionist agenda, the 'Washington consensus', Western NGOs proselytizing, or NATO expansion have all produced a sentiment of renewed meddling in domestic affairs and corresponding erosion of sovereignty leading to a renewed pushback against 'interference' which began to manifest itself in the late 1990s as Western solicitousness was increasingly

264 Jeannie Henderson, *Reassessing ASEAN* (Oxford University Press 1999); John Arendshorst, 'The Dilemma of Non-Interference: Myanmar, Human Rights, and the ASEAN Charter' (2009) 8 Northwestern Journal of International Human Rights 102; Hiro Katsumata, 'Why Is ASEAN Diplomacy Changing? From "Non-Interference" to "Open and Frank Discussions"' (2004) 44 Asian Survey 237.

265 Gillian Goh, 'The "ASEAN Way"' (2000) 13 Pacific Review 439.

266 Marina Sharpe, 'From Non-Interference to Non-Indifference: The African Union and the Responsibility to Protect' (International Refugee Rights Initiative 2017).

267 Williams (n 74); Migai Akech, 'Regional Mechanisms and Intra-State Conflicts: Implementing the African Union's Principle of Non-Indifference?' (2020) 4 Strathmore Law Journal 141; Ben Kioko, 'The Right of Intervention under the African Union's Constitutive Act: From Non-Interference to Non-Intervention' (2003) 85 International Review of the Red Cross 807.

268 Williams (n 74).

reframed as obnoxious. Interference was sometimes normalized through extra-territorial legislative measures purporting to promote democracy or human rights.[269] It also occasionally borrowed more discreet and subterranean pathways. The so-called 'color revolutions' (Yugoslavia in 2000, Georgia in 2003, Ukraine in 2004, and Kirgizstan in 2005) which successfully toppled authoritarian regimes through protests, for example, were seen as part of a new, supple form of Western interference that did not always say its name. Although local protest movements in those contexts had domestic roots and legitimacy, their toolkit of nonviolent resistance was often understood to result from outside advice and to constitute a particularly devious form of interference,[270] all the way to the 'destruction of statehood'.[271] Similarly, a foreign hand was often suspected in relation to the 'Arab Spring' events of 2011.[272] The fight against 'unilateral sanctions' also emerged as a rallying cry for many states in the Global South (and, particularly, Russia) furious at what they saw as a wholly unjustified and illegal practice.[273]

After a period in which it seemed to go in abeyance, the agenda of non-interference has thus been resurrected with a vengeance in a context where the 'the dominant discourse once again is about defending state borders and putting up walls'.[274] This is part based on the rekindling of a Global South sensitivity about non-interference and a perception that international law continues to effectively arbitrate the line between interference and non-interference, in ways that prolong imperial, colonial and racial legacies.[275] But in part it is also because agendas of non-interference have taken root in less expected political spaces. They have sought to ground themselves in popular opinion

---

269 Claire M Diallo, 'The U.S. Empire: Is Any Sovereign Nation Safe after the Russian and Belarus Democracy Acts Notes' (2006) 91 Iowa Law Review 673.

270 AG Lisitsyn-Svetlanov, 'Legal immunities of "color revolutions"' (2016) 3 Russian Journal of Legal Studies 32.

271 Tero Lundstedt, 'The Destruction of Statehood and the Color Revolutions under Russian International Law Doctrine' (2021) 8 Groningen Journal of International Law 228.

272 Gamal M Selim, 'The United States and the Arab Spring: The Dynamics of Political Engineering' (2013) 35 Arab Studies Quarterly 255.

273 Idriss Jazairy, 'Unilateral Economic Sanctions, International Law, and Human Rights' (2019) 33 Ethics & International Affairs 291; Michael Mastanduno, 'Extraterritorial Sanctions: Managing "Hyper-Unilateralism" in U.S. Foreign Policy' in Stewart Patrick and Shepard Forman (eds), *Multilateralism and U.S. Foreign Policy: Ambivalent Engagement* (Lynne Rienner Publishers 2002); Ivan N Timofeev, 'Unilateral and Extraterritorial Sanctions Policy: The Russian Dimension', *Research Handbook on Unilateral and Extraterritorial Sanctions* (Edward Elgar Publishing 2021).

274 Quinton-Brown (n 35) 1.

275 Richardson (n 243).

and even populist politics in a variety of countries. Although the Kosovo crisis focused much attention on foreign armed intervention and certainly acted as a lightning rod for broader concerns about interference, for example, it is worth noting that immediately before it, Serbia had organized a referendum on 'foreign mediation in Kosovo', which asked voters to answer the question 'Do you approve the participation of foreign representatives in solving the problems in Kosovo and Metohija?':[276] 96,5% voted in the negative.[277] One area where popular sentiment has been invoked to whip up passions against interference is LBGTQ+ rights which have been portrayed as manifesting a 'corrupting' agenda by the West seeking to impose its mores to a recalcitrant former Soviet bloc or Africa.[278]

In some sectors, the opposition to interference has gradually reached fever pitch, in ways that have often been ill-appreciated in the West. It has taken a more instantaneous, public, and knee-jerk form accentuated by the globalization of communications. One anecdotally revealing novelty has been the tendency for the pushback by governmental actors to express itself in real time on Twitter. Following French President Macron's criticism of the elections in Venezuela, for example, that country's foreign minister immediately fired a fairly typical series of tweets including:

> (1/3) President @EmmanuelMacron, on May 20th, millions of Venezuelans are going to democratically elect the President of our Republic through the most transparent and secure electoral system in the world. We demand respect for the internal affairs of Venezuela.[279]

Although tweeting about such issues seems to reduce complaints about interference to ultra-public sound bites, it also functions as an instant window into

276 Teuta Vodo and Eleni Stathopoulou, 'A Comparative Perspective on the Balkan Constitutions and the Space Provided for the Citizens' (2015) 8 Journal of Comparative Politics 20, 28.

277 'Serb "no" to Foreign Mediation in Kosovo' *BBC News* (23 April 1998) <http://news.bbc.co.uk/2/hi/special_report/1998/kosovo/82713.stm> accessed 16 June 2023.

278 Emil Edenborg, 'Anti-Gender Politics as Discourse Coalitions: Russia's Domestic and International Promotion of "Traditional Values"' (2023) 70 Problems of Post-Communism 175; Sarah K Dreier, 'Resisting Rights to Renounce Imperialism: East African Churches' Strategic Symbolic Resistance to LGBTQ Inclusion' (2018) 62 International Studies Quarterly 423.

279 'Macron Riles Venezuela with Presidential Election Criticism' [2018] RFI <http://en.rfi.fr/20180404-macron-criticises-venezuela-presidential-election-arreaza-maduro> accessed 14 February 2019.

the apparent thinking of political leaders and diplomats on these issues. In the process, it suggests that claims of interference can still translate into real popular appeal, even as they simultaneously speak a diplomatic language steeped into the usages of international society.

Moreover, although the complaint about interference has typically come from governments, it has often been echoed or found relays in local civil society actors, notably conservative groups. For example, in Georgia, a meeting of the plenary session of the World Congress of Families in 2016 pleaded loudly against interference by the West's 'fanatical liberal ideology', to argue for abortion and against LGBTQ+ rights.[280] One of the characteristics of the new pushback against interference is indeed its tendency to draw on 'GONGOs' that relay the governmental message whilst further undermining the status of independent NGOs. That pushback has often espoused lines of 'civilizational' confrontation that oppose agendas imagined as 'foreign' or 'colonial' to agendas portrayed as 'national' or 'indigenous', often with a strong emphasis on gender issues.[281]

The controversy about the potential harms of interference, then, may only have been briefly dormant. This has created the conditions to periodically reactivate a reflex of defiance against foreign interference that has translated in a range of legal initiatives. Formally, complaints about interference have regularly featured in ICJ pleadings. For example, in the proceedings instituted by Ecuador against Mexico on 29 April 2024, Ecuador argued that through Mexico's 'Head of State making false and injurious statements calling into question the legitimacy of the elections in Ecuador, Mexico has breached the principle of non-interference in the internal affairs of other States. This is an affront against the democratic institutions of Ecuador and Ecuador's inalienable right to choose its political system'.[282] Uganda was previously found by the ICJ to not only have violated the prohibition on the use of force against the Democratic Republic of Congo, but also to have engaged in unlawful interference in its internal affairs.[283]

280 Robert Coalson, '"Family Values" Congress Brings Pro-Moscow Message to Georgia' *Radio Free Europe/Radio Liberty* (17 May 2016) <https://www.rferl.org/a/georgia-confress-families-antigay-moscow-oligarchs-bush/27741199.html> accessed 2 September 2018.

281 Yolaine Frossard de Saugy, '"We Are Not Gays": Regime Preservation and the Politicization of Identity in Mugabe's Zimbabwe' (2022) 65 African Studies Review 591; Jeremy Youde, 'Patriotic History and Anti-LGBT Rhetoric in Zimbabwean Politics' (2017) 51 Canadian Journal of African Studies / Revue canadienne des études africaines 61.

282 *Proceedings instituted by Ecuador against Mexico on 29 April 2024* (*Republic of Ecuador v United Mexican States*) (*Application instituting proceedings*) ICJ 195-20240429-APP-01-00-EN [48].

283 *Armed Activities on the Territory of the Congo* (*Democratic Republic of the Congo v Uganda*) (*Judgment*) [2005] ICJ Rep 168.

Furthermore, the pushback has adopted renovated, international forms, giving the theme a continued resonance. From the 1990s onwards, many states in the Global South mobilized first against the *droit/devoir d'ingérence* and then against increasingly claims about the breath of humanitarian interventions.[284] The Third World was very active when notions such as humanitarian intervention were being discussed with renewed intensity in the West. The Foreign Ministers of the Group of 77 produced a Ministerial Declaration in 1999 which 'rejected the so-called right of humanitarian intervention, which has no basis in the U.N. Charter or in international law'.[285] Of course, such a statement is specifically about a particular form of use of force but there is no doubt that, indirectly, it is also about condemning interference in the affairs of states. Of particular note is the fact that, long before concerns about Russian meddling with U.S. elections emerged (and typically ignored in the context of that debate), a number of states expressed strong concern in the General Assembly, manifested in several resolutions,[286] about interference with elections.

More recently, the Group of Friends in Defense of the Charter of the United Nations (which includes Algeria, Angola, Belarus, Bolivia, Burundi, Cambodia, China, Cuba, Equatorial Guinea, Ethiopia, North Korea, Eritrea, Iran, Laos, Mali, Namibia, Nicaragua, Russia, Saint Vincent and the Grenadines, South Africa, Palestine, Syria, Venezuela, Vietnam and Zimbabwe) was established in July 2021 in New York. Although broadly set up to support the U.N. Charter and multilateralism over the use of force, it also emphasizes 'timeless principles; such as self-determination, sovereign equality, [and] non-intervention in the internal affairs of States'.[287] This sort of agenda was well in evidence,

284 Bernhard Graefrath, 'Ingérence et droit international' in Marie-Dominique Perrot (ed), *Dérives humanitaires : États d'urgence et droit d'ingérence* (Graduate Institute Publications 1994).

285 'Declaration on the Occasion of the Twenty-Third Annual Ministerial Meeting of the Group of 77' (1999) para 69 <http://www.g77.org/doc/Decl1999.html> accessed 14 February 2019.

286 UNGA Res 44/147 (1989); UNGA Res 45/151 (1990); UNGA Res 46/130 (1991); UNGA Res 47/130 (1992); UNGA Res 48/124 (1993); UNGA Res 50/172 (1995); UNGA Res 52/119 (1997); UNGA Res 54/168 (1999); UNGA Res 56/154 (2001).

287 Group of Friends in Defense of the Charter of the United Nations, 'Statement Delivered by the Delegation of the Bolivarian Republic of Venezuela during the Debate on Agenda Item 83, Entitled "Report of the Special Committee on the Charter of the United Nations and on the Strengthening of the Role of the Organization" within the Framework of the Sixth Committee of the General Assembly of the United Nations' (New York, 3 November 2022) para 3 <https://www.gof-uncharter.org/_files/ugd/6140e8_6761e1152de648b592a3b9580815be0e.pdf> accessed 12 January 2024.

for example, in the debate over what the Security Council should do about Venezuela, where a number of states accused the U.S. of seeking to reinstate the 'racist' Monroe Doctrine. Another manifestation of this trend is the effort by Russia and others, as early as 1999, to put the question of 'Developments in the field of information and telecommunications in the context of international security' on the U.N.'s agenda.[288] Six Groups of Governmental Experts (GGEs) have since been created which have focused specifically on threats from cyberspace and the sort of measures that states could adopt to resist them. Although initially that effort seemed mostly focused on the danger of the 'the misuse or exploitation of information resources or technologies for criminal or terrorist purposes',[289] it has gradually morphed into a broader concern with interference by other states,[290] even as it has struggled to capture that interference.[291] In short, although not as dominant as it once was the anti-intervention agenda still manages to mount sustained campaigns to shore up support for the norm.

2.3 *The Rise of the Anti-interference State*

Concerns about interference are, moreover, evident in domestic state initiatives as well, in a context where internal deeds may often speak louder than international words. The Russian Senate's 'Provisional Commission on Protecting State Sovereignty and Preventing Foreign Interference' is an example.[292] Civil society has particularly been a target of the ensuing fallout. The Declaration on Friendly Relations had already highlighted that 'no State shall [...] interfere in civil life in another State'.[293] Some states have seized on this in an effort to hamper or significantly dampen NGO activity by increasing registration obligations or loosely limiting how foreign civil society organizations can operate,[294]

288 UNGA Res 53/70 (4 January 1999) U.N. Doc A/RES/53/70.

289 ibid.

290 This is particularly clear in UNGA, 'Report of the Group of Governmental Experts on Developments in the Field of Information and Telecommunications in the Context of International Security' (22 July 2015) U.N. Doc A/70/174 (Report on International Security Developments in IT).

291 Vera Rusinova, 'Qualification of the Harmful Use of Information and Communications Technologies Under International Law: In Search of a Consensus' (2022) 1 Russian Journal of World Politics and Law of Nations 32.

292 Alexander Borzenko, 'A Russian Senate Commission Has Recommended a Whole Series of Government Responses to "Western Meddling"' *Meduza* (4 June 2018) <https://meduza.io/en/feature/2018/06/04/a-russian-senate-commission-has-recommended-a-whole-series-of-government-responses-to-western-meddling> accessed 14 March 2019.

293 1970 Declaration on Friendly Relations, 123.

294 Carl Gershman and Michael Allen, 'New Threats to Freedom: The Assault on Democracy Assistance' (2006) 17 Journal of Democracy 36.

often specifically targeting either Western NGOs or Western funding. The most visible countries in this drive include, Russia, China, Egypt, Venezuela, Belarus, Zimbabwe, Tunisia (pre-revolution), Hungary, and Israel. In China, for example, although foreign NGOs are in principle permitted to work in a variety of fields, they 'must not endanger China's national unity, security, or ethnic unity; and must not harm China's national interests, societal public interest', and 'must not engage in or fund for-profit, political, or religious activities'.[295]

The main manifestations of this trend have been onerous registration and reporting obligations, funding or activity restrictions, and generally increased government oversight.[296] Often, foreign and international NGOs have seen their regime aligned with the less favorable one of local NGOs, who are subject to significant scrutiny. Foreign funded NGOs have been raided and in some cases their personnel detained. They have been branded as foreign agents representing outside interests. For example, the Russian Foreign Agents Law, adopted in 2012 at the beginning of President Putin's third term, created a federal register of civil society groups deemed 'foreign agents'. Foreign agents are defined as those receiving material support from sources outside Russia or as suspected of so doing and engaging in 'political activity'. They must label their publications as such and are subjected to onerous reporting, auditing and accounting obligations, under threat of criminal sanctions, including a prison term of up to two years.

All of these efforts to restrain interference, no doubt, coincide with a sharpening of the discourse of interference on the grounds of human rights. The latter is understood as a discourse of openness that strongly challenges the notion that states have any legitimacy in denying support to human rights groups, almost suggesting that they have an obligation to welcome human rights influence on their territory. For example, one Human Rights Watch report in the context of the Russian NGO law excoriates 'interference' but understood as the interference of Russia with its own NGOs rather than any sense that Russia might have misgivings about funding of civil society on its territory (specifically describing the principle of non-interference as the principle that 'Government officials should not interfere in the activity of NGOs').[297] Faced

295 Law of the People's Republic of China on the Administration of Activities of Overseas Nongovernmental Organizations in the Mainland of China adopted 28 April 2016, <https://www.registrationchina.com/articles/law/administration-of-activities-of-overseas-ngo-in-china/> accessed 20 January 2024.

296 Gershman and Allen (n 294).

297 Human Rights Watch, 'An Uncivil Approach to Civil Society' (2009) 65 <https://www.hrw.org/sites/default/files/reports/russia0609webwcover.pdf> accessed 19 June 2023.

with such a discourse, states have been tempted to reaffirm and even 'perform' their sovereignty strongly, reinstating a nostalgic sense of the state as defined by its ability to exclude external influences, often portrayed as corrupting of local mores.

The push back against interference has, in turn, led to a 'pushback against the pushback' as Western states increasingly, for example, express misgivings about the authoritarian leaning tendencies of the cyber-agenda promoted by Russia and China,[298] deny that unilateral sanctions are a form of interference, or stand by R2P as evidence of a certain latitude to intervene. There is little doubt, then, that these forays and the reaction to them are intimately linked and feed into each other prompting a recurring cycle of interference and counter-interference, as well as reactive and coordinated attempts to influence the regulatory framework within which they arise. The tit-for-tat dynamic of that conversation tends to radicalize positions in ways that cause considerable strain to international law.

3 Blowback: Revenge of the South?

The banality of both these claims to interference and the push back against them suggests a certain continuity with the Cold War, despite a short interlude. They also suggest that despite the effort to fundamentally reshape the notion of interference in light of human rights concerns, less has changed than may appear on the surface. In short, states remain keenly attached to the norm of non-interference when they stand to be affected by interference, even as they are evidently less so when they are purveyors of interference. Claims that human rights justify considerable interference are very unequally accepted and their uncritical repetition by international lawyers does not do justice to the depth of anti-interference sentiment. This is even as interference has mutated perhaps precisely to elude detection, creating new debates about what is or is not properly considered interference. It is in this moment that claims about interference and non-interference have also been caught up in the profound geopolitical realignment of the world away from the unipolar moment. Most spectacularly, a number of Global South states have begun engaging in their

298 Alex Grigsby, 'Unpacking the Competing Russian and U.S. Cyberspace Resolutions at the United Nations' (*Council on Foreign Relations*, 29 October 2018) <https://www.cfr.org/blog/unpacking-competing-russian-and-us-cyberspace-resolutions-united-nations> accessed 11 March 2019.

own kind of interference, at the risk of upsetting ideological fault lines that had arguably structured the debate for decades.

3.1 *'Off Script' Interference*

Traditionally, interference was very much conceived as a manifestation of the powerful, understood mostly as Western states, and their hegemonic politics. Writing in the early 1920s but in what might as well have been a description of today's Venezuelan crisis, P.H. Winfield noted that '[t]he most frequent infractions of the rule [of non-interference] have occurred […] because the weakness produced by internal dissensions renders a state an easy prey to the designs of an unscrupulous neighbour'.[299] Indeed, Richard Falk once argued, somewhat bizarrely, that interference implied 'that the allegedly intervening state possessed superior strength'. In other words, one could interfere 'down' from a position of domination but not up from a position of subordination ('it would not be intelligible to talk of Cuba intervening in the internal affairs of the United States').[300] At the same time, the Global South is not without its own long tradition of quasi-interventionism in favor of anti-imperial, anti-colonial and anti-racist struggles. As has been rediscovered, for example, the Indian National Congress of Nehru was strongly supportive of intervention in the Spanish Civil War which it rightly understood as prefiguring a global struggle against fascism.[301] Some of the oft-quoted instances of supposed 'humanitarian intervention' (Tanzania's invasion of Uganda and Vietnam's invasion of Kampuchea) arose in the Global South.[302]

One also witnesses, over time, a softening of the Latin American stance against non-interference over time, at least inter se, as part of a commitment to regional solidarity and the collective responsibility to prevent backsliding of democracy, mediated through regional integration. This was, to begin with at least, mostly crystallized by the OAS's anti-communist stance and its resolve that the interventionism of the Soviet bloc should be met by a counter-push.

---

299 Winfield (n 1) 136–137.

300 Falk, *Legal Order in a Violent World* (n 117) 204.

301 Michael P Ortiz, 'Spain! Why? Jawaharlal Nehru, Non-Intervention, and the Spanish Civil War' (2019) 49 European History Quarterly 445.

302 Michael Leifer, 'Vietnam's Intervention in Kampuchea: The Rights of State v. the Rights of People' in Ian Forbes and Mark Hoffman (eds), *Political Theory, International Relations, and the Ethics of Intervention* (Palgrave Macmillan U.K. 1993); Oliver Furley and Roy May, 'Tanzania's Military Intervention in Uganda' in Oliver Furley and Roy May (eds), *African Interventionist States* (Routledge 2017).

The exclusion of Cuba from the OAS manifested this sensitivity[303] which one might have traditionally associated more with U.S. influence. It led to a variety of initiatives to protect OAS states from 'subversive intervention' based on the notion that if subversion of governments was involved then the OAS could intervene.[304] Although 'American states recognized that non-intervention was excellent in theory' they also found that it 'could be as dangerous to the sovereignty and political independence of an American state as was the doctrine of intervention'. Therefore, 'an alternative to individual intervention was found in the doctrine of collective intervention, bringing with it a continentalization of the Monroe Doctrine'.[305] Throughout, decisions by the OAS to legitimize intervention had, ambiguously, anti-interference or anti-subversion as their goal. The earlier anti-Communist focus of the OAS has since gradually shifted towards a commitment to preserving democracy against rigid claims of non-interference.[306]

This tentative interventionism would more broadly receive a boost in the decolonization era, as part of an effort to affirm the Third World's sovereignty and independence. Already in the 1970s, the OPEP oil shock had given Western states an inkling of their vulnerabilities as a result of their dependency on Gulf petroleum. In effect, the Third World was only too willing to engage in what it might in other times and circumstances have described as interference, for the purpose of enforcing its particular vision of a just international legal order. To wit also, support for other decolonial struggles on what colonizing powers at least then saw as being their territory. This manifested a 'direct repudiation of the duty to refrain from evaluating the contending claims of the factions in an internal war' that international law had traditionally sought to impose, replacing its evaluation of the 'factual character of the conflict' by one of the 'justice of certain insurgent causes'.[307] Intervention to promote self-determination suddenly seemed like it could emancipate itself from the criticism that the

303 Quincy Wright, 'Intervention and Cuba in 1961' (1961) 55 Proceedings of the American Society of International Law at Its Annual Meeting (1921–1969) 2.

304 AJ Thomas, 'The Organization of American States and Subversive Intervention' (1961) 55 Proceedings of the American Society of International Law at Its Annual Meeting (1921–1969) 19.

305 ibid 22–23.

306 M Margaret Ball, 'Issue for the Americas: Non-Intervention v. Human Rights and the Preservation of Democratic Institutions' (1961) 15 International Organization 21.

307 Falk, *Legal Order in a Violent World* (n 117) 125.

Third World had previously lavished on any intervention. To request intervention was, in fact, a right of peoples unjustly denied their freedom.[308]

Throughout the Cold War, Cuba for example did not hesitate to engage in foreign interventions in favor of rebel groups to spread revolution whether in Nicaragua, Bolivia, Panama, Grenada, the Dominican Republic, Angola, Guinea-Bissau, Mozambique, the Democratic Republic of the Congo, Ethiopia, Algeria, Yemen, Iraq and Syria. To be clear, this interventionism was simultaneously based on a clearly articulated anti-interventionism when it came to its own affairs and proclamations of fraternity when it came to the affairs of others it sought to help. In the shadow of these South-South interventions, African leaders did also call on Western powers to not support Portugal's retrograde policies or uphold the power of white Rhodesians against the black majority or defend South-Africa's continued occupation of Namibia. Moreover, they were adamant that political insurgencies outside the narrow framework of decolonization should not receive any outside support. It remains that a program of intervention was very much inscribed at the heart of the revolutionary decolonial project, on the basis of solidarity between colonized peoples. Such interventions are ripe for scholarly reappraisal as laying waste to the idea that internationalist interventionism is some sort of Western monopoly, when communism, anti-racism and anti-imperialism have just as well furnished arguments for their own interventionism.[309]

It is instructive in that respect to see how some Third World scholars went out of their way at the time to emphasize that the Friendly Declaration had never intended to exclude coercive economic measures. In particular, it could not possibly compromise sovereignty of their natural resources which they could dispose of them as they wished (including, as the case may be, by refusing to sell them to their enemies).[310] The 1973–1974 OPEP oil embargo episode is often neglected in the context of recent discussions of interference but was an early sign that the Third World might flex whatever interfering muscle it had on account of its own overwhelming priorities and those of the international legal order it imagined. It led to the 'uncomfortable', 'shocking' and 'disturbing'

308 Malcolm Shaw, 'International Law and Intervention in Africa' (1985) 8 International Relations 341.

309 Patrick Quinton-Brown, 'Interventionist or Internationalist? Coercion, Self-Determination, and Humanitarianism in Third World Practice' (2023) 37 International Relations 251.

310 Ibrahim FI Shihata, 'Destination Embargo of Arab Oil: Its Legality Under International Law' (1974) 68 American Journal of International Law 591, 617–618.

discovery in the West that it too could be 'vulnerable to such pressures'.[311] In other words, the study of the history of intervention in international law was always ill-served by simplistic and often self-serving narratives that pit a naturally interventionist 'North' v an inherently anti-interventionist 'South', even as such a vision captures something of imperialist asymmetries. If anything, moreover, that opposition has become even less pertinent to understand the dynamics of interference.

In fact, it is worth noting that the West, which has generally been more associated, via the politics of imperialism, with a stance gladly diminishing the *domaine réservé* of states it sought to influence, was in the first decades after the Second World War one of the main protagonists of the 'domestic jurisdiction' exception to the competency of the United Nations. It was Britain, France, the Netherlands and South Africa, for example, which sought to cloak their late colonial enterprises under the mantel of domestic jurisdiction, *against* Third World claims that questions of self-determination, anti-racism and human rights, had once and for all been internationalized. One of the central symbolic stakes of decolonization, in a sense, was whether self-determination and the violence it sometimes engendered ought to be treated as a domestic or international issue. The West's rearguard battle in that respect manifested itself in protests and even walkouts and a somewhat desperate conservative defense of the status quo (Article 2(7) as the 'documentary shield of the custodians of the colonial system').[312] Ultimately, it could not fend off the Asio-African and Latin American groups' clout and their success in at least nominally internationalizing situations which they felt encroached on their emerging sovereignty.[313] Much role-play and even role reversal therefore seems possible between different groups on the international political exchequer in these crucial decades.

3.2 *The Reversal of Interference Fluxes*

What remained largely inconceivable, even in this Cold War setting, was the possibility that states in the Global South—outside, perhaps, the specific issue of Soviet propaganda—could themselves turn into purveyors of interference. Yet the truly novel element is that, even as the Global South remains adamant

311 Richard B Bilder, 'Comments on the Legality of the Arab Oil Boycott' (1977) 12 Texas International Law Journal 41, 45.

312 Inis L Claude, Jr, 'Domestic Jurisdiction and Colonialism' in Martin Kilson (ed), *New States in the Modern World* (Harvard University Press 1975) 123.

313 Georges Abi-Saab, 'The Newly Independent States and the Scope of Domestic Jurisdiction' (1960) 54 Proceedings of the American Society of International Law at Its Annual Meeting (1921–1969) 84, 88.

about the sanctity of the norm, it has, as it were, moved on the offensive. What has thus made the debate about interference so lively today is arguably a dramatic reversal in the flows of interference. Already in 1989, Lori Fisler Damrosch presciently noted that '[s]ome of the very states that have been objects of superpower attention are themselves trying to influence political developments beyond their borders'[314]—a phenomenon that has, if anything, only intensified exponentially since and which may be one of the single most dramatic contribution to the renewal of the intervention genre. The reality is that global patterns of interference today are much more complicated than a neo-imperial or neo-colonial model would suggest. In addition to the powerful no doubt continuing to prey upon the weak, the 'new interference' has also become one of the preferred weapons of the weak against the powerful, offering potentially high return at relatively low costs.[315]

Whereas interference had for many decades (if not centuries) seemed to flow principally from the Global North/West to the East/South, those flows have been significantly reversed, revealing traditional targets of interference to themselves be engaging in their own powerful form of meddling and, in the process, turning the table on the traditional 'interferers'. This was evident as early as the 1980s when for the first time foreign direct investment in the West, notably by Japan, created conditions in which countries such as the U.S. stood to be vulnerable to at least certain forms of corporate interference by actors seeking to safeguard their investments there.[316] In addition, continuing forms of South-South interference have increasingly manifested themselves, as states like China or Russia reprise and reinvent interference tactics to subjugate states within their sphere of influence. Even Latin American states, themselves historically at the cutting edge of promoting a norm of non-intervention in their relations to the U.S., have of late invested in their own register of interference, through such contraptions as the 'Lima group' in relation to Venezuela.[317] Unilateral sanctions by Bahrain, Egypt, the United Arab Emirates and Saudi Arabia against Qatar also show that the geography of what can be plausibly

314 Damrosch (n 16) 2.

315 Igor Istomin, 'How Not to Interfere in Another Country's Domestic Politics' (2022) 98 International Affairs 1677.

316 Celeste M Murphy, 'Searching for a Coherent National Policy: The Problem of Foreign Money in United States Politics Notes' (1996) 3 Buffalo Journal of International Law 541.

317 Andrea Valentina Dias Bolivar, 'The U.S. Unilateral Coercive Measures Imposed in Latin America: A Study Based on the Experience of Cuba, Nicaragua, and Venezuela' (2022) 5 Sorbonne Student Law Review—Revue juridique des étudiants de la Sorbonne 26.

described as interference[318] has broadened significantly in scope. In short, a consistent stance against interference is not, in fact, a reliable predictor of whether one will engage in interference or not.

In an age, furthermore, when the technological, economic, and political barriers to interference have been significantly lowered—an age, in fact, where interference might as well, although a bit improbably, be the doing of 'somebody sitting on their bed that weighs 400 pounds'[319]— interference has had an uncanny tendency to flow back from the periphery to the core. Aided by the lowering of the cost of interference, many states, notably Russia[320] and China,[321] have developed their own sophisticated interference agendas, especially targeting electoral processes. Perhaps the most vivid proof of this phenomenon is that interference now affects the heart of the hegemonic power, prompting, in turn, a renewed but this time largely defensive effort by the U.S. to (re)assert a norm of non-interference. In addition, the new interference has tended to prey on a distinct type of vulnerability: not so much that of small states, as that of relatively 'open' states and the possibilities that they afford to those agents from outside who would seek to alter their path. As Henning Lahmann put it:

> What makes the situation entirely different from the Cold War era is that, because of their intrinsic openness, liberal democracies are inherently more vulnerable than authoritarian or totalitarian systems with tight public structures that can more easily control the streams of information. In this sense, the old asymmetry has been reversed.[322]

The motivation for this renewed interest in interfering with Western, particularly, domestic politics, is multifaceted.[323] In some cases, the aim is merely to

---

318 Alexandra Hofer and Luca Ferro, 'Sanctioning Qatar: Coercive Interference in the State's Domaine Réservé?' (*EJIL: Talk!*, 30 June 2017) <https://www.ejiltalk.org/sanctioning-qatar-coercive-interference-in-the-states-domaine-reserve/> accessed 21 June 2024.

319 Krishnadev Calamur, 'Some of the People Trump Has Blamed for Russia's 2016 Election Hack' [2018] *The Atlantic* <https://www.theatlantic.com/international/archive/2018/07/trump-russia-hack/565445/> accessed 26 September 2018.

320 Select Committee on Intelligence of the United States Senate, 'Russian Active Measures Campaigns and Interference in the 2016 U.S. Elections' (2018) Senate Report 116–290 <https://www.intelligence.senate.gov/publications/report-select-committee-intelligence-united-states-senate-russian-active-measures> accessed 12 January 2024.

321 Edward J Barss, *Chinese Election Interference in Taiwan* (Routledge 2022).

322 Henning Lahmann, 'Information Operations and the Question of Illegitimate Interference under International Law' (2020) 53 Israel Law Review 189, 199–200.

323 Zephyr Teachout, 'Extraterritorial Electioneering and the Globalization of American Elections' (2009) 27 Berkeley Journal of International Law 162, 182 ff.

have specific foreign laws changed; in other cases, it may be to more broadly have a government that is friendly and supportive of one's goals; and in yet other cases it may be to lastingly cause harm to and weaken an adversary. Some interfering states have certainly had more ominous aims than merely propping up any particular law or candidate, including sowing doubt and confusion about the target's governance processes, autonomy, and democracy. Interference is partly desirable simply because it is available, especially in asymmetric contexts. It is a relatively facile way to impact the trajectory of foreign states, render their foreign policy less hostile or more subservient, as well as weaken them more fundamentally. Interference can certainly have a disruptive or even debilitative effect.

This at least partial reversal of the ways of the world is a phenomenon that is visible elsewhere and that is part of a broader realignment. For example, it has been argued that the reversal of migration patterns globally in the last 80 years is the single most decisive factor to explain the metamorphosis of international mobility law from one that presumed a broad right of entry into all lands to one that has been reinvented as securing borders at all costs.[324] Similarly, French philosopher and anthropologist Xavier Ricard argues in 'La tropicalisation du monde' that the West's ways are finally coming home to roost, as technologies once developed in the crucible of Western imperialism are now redirected at it with a vengeance.[325] This major shift is deprovincializing intervention, showing it to be less a specifically Western modality of international relations than a big or mid-power technology.

This fundamental realignment is precipitating at least two, symmetric changes. On the one hand, rising powers such as China with extensive dealings on the African continent and significant geopolitical and geoeconomic interests in the stability, openness or friendliness of major partners and rivals have found themselves starting to subtly renegotiate their own historical commitment to non-interference.[326] On the other hand, powers traditionally associated with relatively wanton interference in the affairs of others have had to develop their own mechanisms for coping with interference, including a much

324 Frédéric Mégret, 'The Contingency of International Migration Law: "Freedom of Movement", Race, and Imperial Legacies' in Ingo Venzke and Kevin Jon Heller (eds), *Contingency in International Law: On the Possibility of Different Legal Histories* (Oxford University Press 2021).

325 Xavier Ricard Lanata, *La tropicalisation du monde* (Presses Universitaires de France 2019).

326 Chen Zheng, 'China Debates the Non-Interference Principle' (2016) 9 The Chinese Journal of International Politics 349; Zhongying Pang, 'China's Non-Intervention Question' (2009) 1 Global Responsibility to Protect 237.

more nuanced, if not contrite, discourse on intervention, even as they have periodically been tempted by their own forms of isolationism.

3.3 *Benign or Malign?*

Some of the manifestations of this trend towards reversing interference flows have been benign and, from an international law and human rights point of view, probably even welcome. To seek to influence the affairs of other states in in a sense the banal lot of all international relations. It has been practiced for centuries and is in many ways ratified by international law, especially those segments that emphasize not just bare coexistence but the finality of the international legal project as being enhanced cooperation, community and even integration. And it will appear to many observers somewhat deserved, for example, that the West should occasionally get a taste of its own medicine, particularly when it comes to human rights criticism. The very resemblance of interference to what are in other respects perfectly legitimate patterns of mutual influencing are, as will see, one of the secrets of why the question remains so intractable in a context where it may be difficult to have one without the other.

An intriguing illustration of the kind of brusque reversal involved is the Chinese effort at producing an annual report on the U.S. human rights record[327] as a sort of *répartie* to the State Department's own practice of compiling country human rights reports. This sort of retort is unobjectionable in principle given the West's track record in criticizing China for its own performance, although the fact that only a U.S. report is produced suggests some narrow political finality. In that respect, human rights-based 'meddling' can be seen as having at least created various opportunities for the reciprocal discussion of issues of common concern, especially in such multilateral contexts as the Human Rights Council. It is difficult for the West to impugn this newfound interest in criticizing its own record given its own historical insistence that human rights issues are not off limits.[328] This reflects a salutary if nascent decentralization of the monitoring and implementation of human rights. It is further confirmation that if some states' human rights record can be criticized,

---

327 'Human Rights Record of the United States in 2017' (The State Council Information Office of the People's Republic of China 2018) <http://english.scio.gov.cn/scionews/2018-04/25/content_50960455.htm> accessed 12 January 2024.

328 Li Yunlong, Chang Jian, and Liu Huawen, 'West Not the Guardian of Human Rights' *China Daily* (15 March 2016) <http://www.chinadaily.com.cn/opinion/2016-03/15/content_23866802.htm> accessed 2 September 2018.

then all states' record can be criticized without being suspected pro tanto of interference.

Some interference operations, however, equalizing of the opportunities for intervention as they may be, appear far more problematic. The most emblematic development has been meddling in elections, a worrying phenomenon whose full contours have yet to be wholly ascertained.[329] This is distinct from foreign support to elections (although quite how distinct will be discussed later) in that it does not seek, ideal-typically, to merely help uphold the fairness of voting. It includes both partisan interventions favoring the election of one candidate and more general attempts to destabilize a foreign democratic system. The 2016 U.S. election is perhaps best-known case of this phenomenon.[330] The hacking and then release of DNC e-mails was meant to favor a particular candidate in the election. Russia is typically the state that has been most accused of engaging in such practices but, by some accounts, China is even more active[331] and Iran[332] and others are active players. Other elections that have arguably been targeted include Canada's,[333] Taiwan's,[334] France's,[335] Australia's,[336] and several in Africa

329 Kristina Lyn Heitkamp, *Interference in Elections* (Greenhaven Publishing LLC 2018).

330 Robert S Mueller, 'Report on the Investigation into Russian Interference in the 2016 Presidential Election' (U.S. Department of Justice 2019) <https://www.justice.gov/archives/sco/file/1373816/dl> accessed 4 January 2014.

331 Jonas Parello-Plesner, 'The Chinese Communist Party's Foreign Interference Operations: How the U.S. and Other Democracies Should Respond' (Hudson Institute 2018) 3 <https://s3.amazonaws.com/media.hudson.org/files/publications/JonasFINAL.pdf> accessed 2 September 2018.

332 Sam Sabin, 'Iran Has Surprisingly Become the Dominating Threat of the 2024 U.S. Election Cycle' (*Axios*, 16 August 2024) <https://www.axios.com/2024/08/16/iran-foreign-interference-2024-presidential-election> accessed 15 September 2024.

333 'Foreign Interference' *The Globe and Mail* (22 December 2023) <https://www.theglobeandmail.com/topics/foreign-interference/> accessed 28 December 2023.

334 Lily Kuo, 'Taiwan's Citizens Battle pro-China Fake News Campaigns as Election Nears' *The Guardian* (30 December 2019) <https://www.theguardian.com/world/2019/dec/30/taiwan-presidential-election-referendum-on-ties-with-china> accessed 28 December 2023.

335 Sacha Houlié, 'Rapport Public Fait Au Nom de La Délégation Parlementaire Au Renseignement Relatif à l'activité de La Délégation Parlementaire Au Renseignement Pour l'année 2022–2023' (Délégation parlementaire au renseignement 2023) 1454/810 <https://www.assemblee-nationale.fr/dyn/16/rapports/dpr/l16b1454_rapport-information> accessed 4 January 2024.

336 Joint Standing Committee on Electoral Matters, 'Report on the Conduct of the 2019 Federal Election and Matters Related Thereto' (Parliament of the Commonwealth of Australia 2020) <https://www.aph.gov.au/Parliamentary_Business/Committees/Joint/Electoral_Matters/2019Federalelection/Report> accessed 28 December 2023.

notably,[337] to the point that election interference has been described as a 'global challenge'.[338] It is not of course as if previous instances of Western interference in elections had themselves always been benign, as will be discussed later. But the phenomenon is pervasive, sufficiently under-the-radar to activate ramping anxiety and, at any rate, worrying regardless of whether foreign interference operations have, in fact, swayed elections, a question that is still disputed.

There is a sense, moreover, that this is only the most recent and spectacular manifestation of a broader phenomenon. Beyond specific elections, interference can be characterized as a broad attempt to shape the democratic and political life of other countries through manipulations of the public sphere or even the information space. In some cases, concerns about interference have fed into a kind of generalized defiance of foreign actors, as European actors in particular call for the erection of new borders to guard against the corrosive influence of ill-intentioned meddlers, in ways that often seem to emulate the 'fortress Europe' mentality so visible in the immigration sphere. As will be seen, the discourse of non-interference is not without its own sinister and, in some cases, frankly xenophobic, racist, or antisemitic undertones. In fact, the 'militarized discourse' about foreign interference 'is also marked by an "invasion" framing that vilifies and denigrates the value of "foreign" speech'.[339] In that, reactions to interference in both the West and the Global South tend to borrow from the same playbook, with interference both a reality and a scarecrow susceptible to shape domestic dynamics, sometimes on the basis of perception alone.

To be clear from the outset, then, there may be a certain duplicity in excessively denouncing a state of affairs that one has, in effect, willingly brought about. In an ironic twist, much of what passes for interference is not that easy to distinguish from much of what has gone on under the banner of liberal reform for the last few decades in the East and in the South. The very possibility of the new interference exists largely as a function of decades of globalization that have rendered societies—very deliberately, one would think—vulnerable to it. Societies, under that view, have brought interference upon themselves after bringing it onto others. Specifically, interference often borrows heavily from an earlier Cold War playbook that has been recycled for the times. It is also worth noting that excessive accusations of interference may themselves

337 Africa Center for Strategic Studies, 'Tracking Russian Interference to Derail Democracy in Africa' (Africa Center for Strategic Studies 2023) <https://africacenter.org/spotlight/russia-interference-undermine-democracy-africa/> accessed 28 December 2023.

338 Ringhand (n 107).

339 Douek (n 46) 266.

have their political uses. Politicians may be keen on whipping up a frenzy of denunciation against particular international adversaries; or they may be only too intent on suggesting that their domestic rivals have in fact benefited from foreign interference operations to more readily discredit them; finally, they may be interested in undermining the results of elections by invoking vague and unprovable suspicions of meddling with election infrastructure, thus sabotaging the credibility of their own democratic institutions.[340]

In other words, the very scope of unwanted interference is still a matter of debate and in some ways not knowing how far it extends is part of what makes it so daunting and may trigger states to overreact. The central stake of the interference debate is, in fact, its proper scope. There is at times an element of moral panic involved as the reaction to interference is magnified beyond reason, becoming its own political force in the process. In the midst of this frenzy, claims of broad interference at least reinforce the notion that there is such a thing as a broad norm against it, perhaps even beyond mere intervention and extending to a newfound concern with interference more broadly understood. But the magnification of interference, the tendency to see it everywhere, also ensure that the charge of intervention will lose some of its potency—a classic case of self-defeatingly undermining one's own case. And it remains that Western states and, perhaps more damningly, scholars have shown a remarkable obliviousness to the irony that an agenda of non-interference once embraced by the Third World is now being reclaimed forcefully by states that have historically been most associated with interfering.[341] There is of course something a bit rich here: states that have spent the best of the last 200 years interfering in the affairs of other states now find that being on the receiving end of such interference is unconscionable.

The bottom line, though, is that concerns that had long been a battle cry of the Third World now appear to be increasingly shared in the West as well. This

---

340 On the lack of finding of interference with election infrastructure during the 2020 U.S. election, see U.S. Department of Justice and U.S. Department of Homeland Security, 'Key Findings and Recommendations from the Joint Report of the Department of Justice and the Department of Homeland Security on Foreign Interference Targeting Election Infrastructure or Political Organization, Campaign, or Candidate Infrastructure Related to the 2020 U.S. Federal Election' (2021) <https://www.dhs.gov/publication/key-findings-and-recommendations-foreign-interference-related-2020-us-federal-elections> accessed 12 January 2024.

341 To be exact, that irony is frequently remarked upon but in passing and in ways that do not seem particularly politically sophisticated or productive. William Ossoff, 'Hacking the Domaine Réservé: The Rule of Non-Intervention and Political Interference in Cyberspace' (2021) 62 Harvard International Law Journal 295, 296.

abrupt reversal of dynamics has not entirely changed the terms of the debate, but it has forced each side, belatedly, to reassess how its own traditional stance might complicate the sort of position it feels it needs to adopt in the moment. One can speculate that, all other things being equal, states that had previously minimized the worrisome character of interference may be inclined to upgrade their alarm whilst states that insisted on the need to combat all forms of interference may moderate their zeal to that effect. This has also changed some of the ways in which concern about interference is manifested. For example, the West seems to have been careful to distinguish its own current worries from the old decolonial tradition of concern with interference in sovereign affairs as a more subtle and complex concern with disruption to democratic life. If that seems like excessive finessing, it does not detract from the fact that the concern is real, including in how it reshapes the West's attitude to the rest of the world.

Nonetheless, both the late Western and earlier and ongoing Third World concerns are genuine and, rather than simply denouncing their contradictions and hypocrisy, one may welcome the opportunity for a sober reassessment of what non-interference might mean in this day and age. There is a strong emerging feeling that one is indeed dealing with a new phenomenon, one whose dimensions remain ill-understood, and which creates considerable potential for overreaction. This is partly because the 'usual suspects' of interference have changed sides—although in itself that is a mere political development which should not have much of an impact on international law; but it is also because, in reactivating dramatically opposed world views, the 'new interference' has laid to waste (*again*, arguably) any notion that the norm against intervention operated against unproblematic assumptions about what interference really is. As such, the new interference activates anxieties with particular intensity and, more generally, acts as a crucial test of the regulatory ambitions of international law as mediated by its discursive economy.

4 Late International Legal Anxieties

The shift in the pattern and orientation of interference has coincided with an arguably deeper mutation of its nature as well as the ways it can be apprehended legally. In that respect, interference is an evolving construct, one shaped by the encounter between, presumably, some real-world practices and the particular cognitive frames that go into describing it as such. Interference is also a concern because it consistently produces knowledge claims about its existence and its gravity that belie a range of assumptions about international law. For example, the very notion of interference presumes that there is something to interfere with—that is, that there is a somewhat neatly delineated and irreducible domestic sphere of political, social, or economic activity that can ultimately be usefully distinguished from the 'international'. In a sense, sovereignty itself is, as will be explored in more detail in the next chapter, constituted by what it imagines itself to be protecting against. It is that very premise, however, that has increasingly come into question during the period of intense globalization that arose during the 1990s. If all political, social, and economic processes are being globalized, if there is nothing left to states than an enmeshed confusion of functions, then how could one possibly speak of interference?

In this context, it is important, even as one acknowledges the elements of rupture in the new interference, to resist a diagnosis that would see today's version of it as entirely unprecedented. Interference has in a sense always been complex, diffuse, and omnipresent. Interference did not await Russian electoral manipulation or Chinese pressures on the diaspora to be a challenge for international law. For example, as early as 1976, the General Assembly condemned 'all forms of overt, subtle and highly sophisticated techniques of coercion, subversion and defamation aimed at disrupting the political, social or economic order of other States'[342] in ways that could be transposed verbatim to the current situation. The discourse of 'newness' can, in fact, be a way of promoting a short-sighted view of the history of interference, one that lets the West too easily off the hook of the practices it now purports to condemn so resolutely. Nonetheless, it will serve the intellectual purpose of this book well to at least reflect candidly on the current character of the 'new interference', as it has manifested itself in the last decade. As will become clear, the omnipresence of that interference and its often entangled and mimetic character belie any facile political narrative about its significance and therefore the kind of challenge it portends for international law.

One central intuition is that claims about interference now operate against the background of an international society that has mutated considerably: since the end of the Cold War through an unprecedented wave of globalization; since 9/11 through the global deployment of a repressive anti-terrorism agenda; and since the COVID pandemic through a profound reorganization of supply chains. All the while, the international system has been facing increasingly dire threats as a result of climate change and the tragedy of the commons. The key, then, is that it is not so much (or just) interference that is new

342 UNGA Res 31/91 (14 December 1976) para 4.

than its perception, against the background of fundamental ideational and geopolitical realignments about what is imagined to be the default position of the international legal system. Interference profoundly prods and tests the degree to which states are willing to accept a certain degree of openness to the world as a fundamental condition of international interaction. It is mediated by discourses that emphasize the merits or shortfalls of more or less 'open' societies.[343] And as such, it breeds a degree of conceptual disorientation for sovereign actors in particular, who often seem at a loss as to how to respond to new and unforeseen challenges that constantly push what might be considered to fall under that heading.[344]

Paradigmatically, the 'open society' is one that cannot truly know of interference because it objectively welcomes it, or is at least incapable or unwilling to distinguish what comes from 'outside' from what comes from 'inside', and even what is welcome from what is not. The open society is naturally dedicated to its constitutive openness, to contradiction even, as a form of emancipation from tribalism.[345] That there are evident advantages to openness in terms of trade, culture or even politics is evident. In the process, at the same time, society's outside contours blend with those of its environment. For example, the ubiquity of foreign direct investment makes it hard to know what in the economy is domestic and what is foreign; the imbrication of populations as a result of migrations relativizes distinctions such as that between citizens and foreigners; the emergence of global issues makes it challenging to know where the frontier lies between national and international stakes. There thus emerges a fundamental contradiction between the logic of entanglements implicit in globalization and of political autarchy implicit in sovereignty, and a need to mediate between both. Obviously that tension has been playing out for quite a while—for as long, arguably, as international law itself. But historical phases of relatively more intense bouts of globalization have brough it to the fore, as has certainly been the case during the latest iteration. Analytically, this can help highlight what might be some of the key defining features of the new interference.

---

343 See e.g., Willmoore Kendall, 'The "Open Society" and Its Fallacies' (1960) 54 The American Political Science Review 972; Michael Ignatieff and Stefan Roch (eds), *Rethinking Open Society* (Central European University Press 2018); Christof Royer and Liviu Matei (eds), *Open Society Unresolved: The Contemporary Relevance of a Contested Idea* (Central European University Press 2023).

344 Sean J Wright, 'Reexamining Criminal Prosecutions under the Foreign Nationals Ban' (2018) 32 Notre Dame Journal of Law, Ethics & Public Policy 563.

345 Karl R Popper, *The Open Society and Its Enemies* (Princeton University Press 2020).

4.1 *New Provenance*

First, *the origin of interference is increasingly hard to trace*. Interference might traditionally have been thought of as arising first and foremost in the crucible of state-to-state relations or, quite possibly, as a result of diplomatic work carried out by embassies and consulates.[346] It is, however, increasingly engaged in by shadowy agencies whose connection to governments is deliberately made unclear. Sometimes, this leads to 'false front engagement' where actors pose as other than who they are. In a sense, some will argue that this is merely turning the West's own recipes against it (think of the role of Radio Free Europe and its connections to the CIA during the Cold War, for example),[347] but the degree of outsourcing certainly makes it difficult to know who is behind some recent campaigns. Interference sometimes proceeds from largely private actors[348] that do not fit well within the traditional inter-state paradigm, and that thoroughly confuse/conflate the registers of public and private agency.[349] To not know where interference comes from is not only to run into a technical problem of attribution; it is, on a deeper level, to not (quite) know whether what is happening is even properly defined and understood as interference.

Often, the existence of intermediaries between the state accused of interfering and the state that claims to be interfered with will create an extra layer of plausible deniability. In a context where soft power had long been extolled in the West as both harmless and efficient, it can unleash a peculiar form of dark soft power.[350] One intelligence report, for example, described 'Moscow's

---

346 Behrens, *Diplomatic Interference and the Law* (n 112).

347 Anne-Chantal Lepeuple, '"Radio Free Europe" et "Radio Liberty" (1950–1994)' [1995] Vingtième Siècle. Revue d'histoire 31.

348 For example, the Russian 'Internet Research Agency'. See indictment at *United States of America v Internet Research Agency LLC and others*, No 1:18-cr-00032 (DDC 2018) <https://www.justice.gov/d9/fieldable-panel-panes/basic-panes/attachments/2018/02/16/internet_research_agency_indictment.pdf> accessed 14 February 2019.

349 For example, the claimed collaboration between former elements of the Russian GRU and Wikileaks in the 2016 Russian electoral campaign. See Natasha Bertrand, 'The Shadowy Operative at the Center of the Russia Scandal' [2008] *The Atlantic* <https://www.theatlantic.com/politics/archive/2018/03/the-shadowy-operative-at-the-center-of-the-russia-scandal/556823/> accessed 11 February 2019. See also, on the potential links between a Russian oligarch close to Vladimir Putin and an internet 'troll farm' that was active in the campaign to interfere with the Russian election, ibid.

350 Elaine Kamarck, 'Malevolent Soft Power, AI, and the Threat to Democracy' *Brookings* (29 November 2018) <https://www.brookings.edu/research/malevolent-soft-power-ai-and-the-threat-to-democracy/> accessed 14 February 2019; Joseph Nye, 'For Russia, Some Hard Lessons in the Use of Soft Power' *The Globe and Mail* (12 May 2017) <https://www.theglobeandmail.com/opinion/soft-power-hard-lessons/article34958109/> accessed 14 February 2019.

influence campaign', as following a 'messaging strategy that blends covert intelligence operations—such as cyber activity—with overt efforts by the Russian Government agencies, state owned media, third party intermediaries, and paid social media users or "trolls"'.[351] If nothing else, the feeling of vulnerability of democracies has been intensified by use of 'social media and other mass communication technologies that cannot be traced to particular foreign states at a level that is actionable'.[352] By the same token, the extolling of 'soft power' as surely preferable to violence and as ultimately merely a sophisticated mode of diffusing outcomes surely has prepared the ground for confusion about what exactly is wrong about which soft power. Clearly the fact that it emanates from one's enemies is not sufficient to disqualify something which has long been a motif of pride in U.S. foreign relations for example.

Even outside the conventional range of soft power, there are a range of both old fashioned and rejuvenated ways in which sophisticated actors can make the most of the pressure points of democracies. For example, support for local candidates through anonymized and straw financial donors and consultants could result in outcomes that have a tipping role at the level of national politics.[353] Foreign lobbying of legislatures will often resort to local consultants who provide a front of respectability and obscure the sources of their mandates. Paradoxically, seemingly 'above board' practices thriving on the openness of international relations and democratic governance may be even harder to detect. Patterns of sustained efforts at swaying allies' political course provide a particularly difficult test case for the new interference since they seem to operate within the bonds of amity and even the normal functioning of democracy. Hence the role of AIPAC in the U.S. has turned out to be particularly contentious given its acting in support of and in close connection with (although arguably not on behalf of) a foreign ally, to the point of trying to unseat certain members of Congress, albeit on the basis of domestic donations.[354]

351 Intelligence Community Assessment, 'Assessing Russian Activities and Intentions in Recent U.S. Elections' (2017) ICA 2017-01D II.

352 David Johnston, 'First Report—The Right Honourable David Johnston, Independent Special Rapporteur on Foreign Interference' (2023) 13 <https://www.canada.ca/content/dam/di-id/documents/rpt/rapporteur/Independent-Special-Rapporteur%20-Report-eng.pdf> accessed 21 November 2023.

353 Wright, 'Reexamining Criminal Prosecutions under the Foreign Nationals Ban' (n 344).

354 Kate Kelly and Kenneth P Vogel, 'Pro-Israel Lobby Faces Challenges Amid Gaza War and Shifting Politics' *The New York Times* (13 March 2024) <https://www.nytimes.com/2024/03/13/us/politics/aipac-israel-gaza-democrats-republicans.html> accessed 6 September 2024.

At the same time, the West's own role in very diffuse processes of regime change has brought attention on the difficulty of pinning down blame on particular operations that are perceived by some as blatantly inimical.[355] Whilst the U.S., for example, has funded a range of foundations and media in countries where it had geopolitical interests, it is also true that '[i]n the case of the color revolutions, significantly, revolutionary activity was largely a by-product of Western influence, without necessarily [being] orchestrated by the West':[356] clearly interference by civilizational osmosis is far beyond what should count as intervention under international law, even if it raises questions about who has the power to effect such change and how. Moreover, not every outcome that can be seen as inimical to one's foreign policy can be easily chalked up to foreign interference: in that respect, the tendency to see the 'hand of Moscow' or the 'hand of Washington' behind every political transition can grossly underestimate the significance of local dynamics and agency. This is especially so given that there is an evident politics to loudly denouncing something as interference in order to solidify one's own power.[357] In short, even where a significant inter-state rivalry subtext exists, it will not always be clear that there has even been an interference, let alone who it can be attributed to, especially when political change is brought about through massive local mobilization.

It is also worth noting that whilst international law is traditionally quite focused on a public, state-to-state form of interference, major corporations, not just domestic but international, have also deployed considerable means of their own to influence political outcomes. Interference in the affairs of states by corporations is nothing new and was once even caricatural in its intensity and brazenness, notably in the waning years of colonialism and during the Cold War. For example, International Telephone and Telegraph (ITT) was accused of attempting to impede the election of Salvador Allende to the presidency of Chile to prevent nationalization of foreign investments, going as far as to offer 1 million $ to the CIA to fund the candidate of the opposition. Allende had on that occasion denounced before UNCTAD III the 'powerful corruptive influence on the public institutions in rich and poor countries alike' and the 'flagrant intervention' by ITT in Chile's internal affairs.[358] The Union des Mines

355 Andrei Manoilo and Oleg Karpovich, *Color Revolutions: Techniques in Breaking Down Modern Political Regimes* (AuthorHouse 2015); Lisitsyn-Svetlanov (n 270).

356 Valery Solovei, 'Color Revolutions and Russia' in Adam Przeworski (ed), *Democracy in a Russian Mirror* (Cambridge University Press 2015) 80.

357 Kirill Petrov, 'Elites and Color Revolutions: The Logic of Russia's Response' (2020) 5 Russian Politics 426.

358 United Nations Conference on Trade and Development (UNCTAD) 'Address Delivered by Mr Salvador Allende Gossens, President of Chile at the Inaugural Ceremony on 13 April

du Katanga in the Congo and United Fruit in Central America had previously served a similarly toxic role as 'states within the state'. Gulf Oil also paid $ 3 million to a South Korean Presidential candidate to buy votes.[359] More recently, it has emerged that Chinese businesses are by far the largest foreign-linked donors to both major Australian political parties.[360]

International law is still very much lagging behind such developments. Efforts to adopt a U.N. Code of Conduct on Transnational Corporations largely stumbled with the end of the Cold War[361] and the initiative fell into oblivion. Ironically, the more recent trend to endow corporations with human rights responsibilities may objectively encourage them to interfere in the domestic affairs of host states as a function of complying with their growing international law obligations and their resulting quasi-public clout.[362] This leaves unanswered questions about the agency of corporations, the materiality of their continued interference, and the degree of its illegitimacy, in a context where it is only to be expected that private actors would have an interest in influencing the regulatory framework in host states.

Finally, a significant and relatively new development is the use of diasporas as vectors, willing or unwilling, of interference, sometimes in close connection to states. This is particularly evident in Australia and Canada, two countries with large expatriate or foreign-origin populations, segments of which have sometimes been instrumentalized by their state of origin to weigh on local political outcomes. The Chinese Communist Party (CCP), for example, has long been active, through its United Front Work Department which is part of the Ministry of Overseas Chinese Affairs, as well as its consulates in exercising control over Chinese community organizations abroad. By courting those organizations and supporting them, they can exact subtle forms of allegiance from some diaspora members. These will then participate in local political affairs qua Chinese community organizations and, sometimes, push elements

---

1972' in *Proceedings of the United Nations Conference on Trade and Development* (United Nations 1973) 353, para 58.

359 Richard D Lyons, 'Gulf Oil Admits It Illegaly Gave 5 Million Abroad' *New York Times* (17 May 1975) <https://www.nytimes.com/1975/05/17/archives/gulf-oil-admits-it-illegally-gave-5million-abroad-top-executive.html> accessed 28 December 2023.

360 Chris Uhlmann, 'Groups with Strong Ties to China Are Major Political Donors' *ABC News* (21 August 2016) <https://www.abc.net.au/news/2016-08-21/australian-groups-strong-ties-china-political-donations/7768012> accessed 8 September 2023.

361 United Nations Centre on Transnational Corporations, *The United Nations Code of Conduct on Transnational Corporations* (United Nations 1986) art 15.

362 John M Kline, 'Political Activities by Transnational Corporations: Bright Lines versus Grey Boundaries' (2003) 12 Transnational Corporations 1.

of the Chinese foreign policy agenda such as moderating accusations concerning Xinjiang, Tibet, or Hong Kong, supporting CCP claims to sovereignty over the South China Seas, or opposing Taiwan. There have also been scandals in Canada concerning cash-for-access events involving members of the Chinese diaspora with CCP connections.[363] For example, it has been alleged that China has actively promoted 'incubators' for Chinese Canadian political candidates under the guise of 'educat[ing] newcomers about Canadian democracy'.[364]

Repressive action sometimes ensues for members of the diaspora who do not toe the party line.[365] Local politicians of Chinese origin who have an oppositional stance towards Beijing have been known to be ostracized and threatened under pressure from local consulates or through WeChat campaigns, a medium controlled and heavily monitored by Beijing. For example, ominously, Canadian Conservative MP Michael Chong was allegedly harassed by the Chinese government after he voted in favor of a motion in the House of Commons condemning China's treatment of its Uyghur minority as a genocide. Information about his relatives in China was collected for the purpose of intimidating him.[366] China has also been accused of orienting local Chinese-language media that have considerable influence with the Chinese community to steer voting patterns in local and national elections. The point here is not to assess the veracity of all of such allegations but to note that, even if only partially true, these suggest a genuine qualitative shift in some of the patterns and channels of interference, one far removed from ideas that interference would necessarily be the exclusive doing of government agents.

363 Andrew Greene, Henry Belot and Ursula Malone, 'Chinese Billionaire Paid $55,000 for Lunch with Shorten' *ABC News* (11 December 2017) <https://www.abc.net.au/news/2017-12-12/chinese-billionaire-paid-$55,000-for-lunch-with-shorten/9248342> accessed 8 September 2023; Robert Fife and Steven Chase, 'Trudeau Attended Cash-for-Access Fundraiser with Chinese Billionaires' *The Globe and Mail* (22 November 2016) <https://www.theglobeandmail.com/news/politics/trudeau-attended-cash-for-access-fundraiser-with-chinese-billionaires/article32971362/> accessed 8 September 2023.

364 Tom Blackwell, 'New Group with Beijing Links to Promote Friendly Candidates in Canadian Elections' *National Post* (26 November 2022) <https://nationalpost.com/news/china-friendly-candidates-canadian-elections> accessed 21 November 2023.

365 Robert Fife and Steven Chase, 'CSIS Warns China's Operation Fox Hunt Is Targeting Canada's Chinese Community' *The Globe and Mail* (10 November 2020) <https://www.theglobeandmail.com/politics/article-csis-warns-chinas-operation-fox-hunt-is-targeting-canadas-chinese/> accessed 8 September 2023.

366 Leyland Cecco, 'Canadian Lawmaker Says China Targeted His Family for Harassment' *The Guardian* (3 May 2023) <https://www.theguardian.com/world/2023/may/03/michael-chong-justin-trudeau-harassment-canada-china> accessed 28 December 2023.

4.2 *New Targets*

Second, *interference is increasingly diffuse in terms of its targets*. Interference had traditionally targeted foreign governments and possibly, via propaganda, public opinions; it had often sought to exact a particular outcome, but it had not particularly targeted the *systems and infrastructure* that form the bedrock of states' political, economic, and social life. The switch from targeting the state to targeting society, and from targeting the government to targeting democracy, operates a fundamental renewal of the interference genre (e.g.: 'hacking democracy').[367] This includes harming electoral systems per se, for example by interfering with vote counting machines but also simply funding from outside corrupt election management bodies that one knows will renew existing governments; turning political parties and candidates into proxies and vectors of foreign influence; or confusing or infiltrating the media in order to sway the political process. Acting more generally on the 'informational environment' of target societies stretches the definition of interference to breaking point in a context where a wide range of actors are arguably constantly and legitimately in the process of doing just that. This creates the conditions for a fundamental disorientation of the norm of intervention.

It should be noted that this trend of bypassing the host state to exert influence directly on society is certainly not anodyne, but nor is it, in its generality, particularly novel. It meshes well, in a neoliberal era, with a trend towards the diminution of the role of the state. For example, much global governance since the 1990s is part of a movement towards disintermediation and of reaching out directly to local partners, in ways that bypass central governments. This has long been evident in the development sector where donors sometimes deliberately try to avoid said governments, often on account of a perception of their corruptness and inefficiency.[368] It is also apparent, tellingly, in the security sector itself where particular agencies, notably those deemed less corruptible, are supported from abroad, in ways that blur the separation between intervener and intervened. The Mérida initiative, which provides direct U.S. funding to Mexican law-enforcement agencies for the purposes of border policing, for example, has been analyzed by Peter Finkenbusch as:

> a powerful critique of Mexican sovereignty as the right to self-government and non-intervention. It articulates a profound scepticism towards

---

367 Thomas Rid and Ben Buchanan, 'Hacking Democracy Voting: Uses & Abuses' (2018) 38 SAIS Review of International Affairs 3.

368 Michael Riegner, 'Development Cooperation and the City' in Helmut Philipp Aust and Janne E Nijman (eds), *Research Handbook on International Law and Cities* (2021).

> classic liberal notions of political autonomy and national interest, presenting them as cumbersome administrative obstacles. Thus, while traditional notions of sovereignty have not disappeared entirely and might regain strength in the future, the Merida Initiative shifted the discourse of Mexican sovereignty from rights to capacity. Importantly, sovereignty-as-capacity silenced the critique of international involvement as illegal trespassing and restricted the policy debate to technical issues.[369]

The systematic bypassing of quasi-governmental authorities is also evident in the delivery of humanitarian aid, to Gaza for example.[370] Albeit a special case, this underscores the reality of post-interventionist practices of interference wherein local authorities struggle to even establish an initial claim to sovereignty as a result of their systematic circumvention. Seen against the background of this normalized bypassing of the state, then, 'intervention' may not elicit the same reaction of shock that it once did or at least need to be understood less as the exceptional contravention of a clear rule than as the default modus operandi for most states, most of the time.

Separately, interference has reactivated never settled but momentous anxieties about the mismatch between state, territory and society. In the traditional model, the state is imagined as a unitary actor whose sovereignty acts as a sort of shield as far as the rest of the world is concerned, and whose integrity is violated each time it is pierced. This vision owes much to a legal-formalistic take on the state as a bundle of public prerogatives exercised by a central administration, as well as nationalist assumptions about the unitary character of peoples and a neat delineation between the domestic and the international spheres. But this assumes too readily a sort of alignment between the state and society, sovereignty and population, etc. It also assumes that local populations and actors, for example, will be at one with their state when it comes to resisting interference. The better view is that the state is already constantly undergoing dynamics of fragmentation and contestation, and that just because the government is opposed to outside interference does not mean that local civilian forces are also. This problematizes the question of who one is imagined to be interfering with, and raises the possibility that even as the government resents a particular form of interference, a part of the population may welcome it.

---

369 Peter Finkenbusch, 'The Demise of the Intervention Paradigm—Resilience Thinking in the Merida Initiative' [2017] Conflict, Security & Development 313, 314.

370 Tamer Qarmout, *Delivering Aid Without Government: International Aid and Civil Society Engagement in the Recovery and Reconstruction of the Gaza Strip* (Springer 2017) 8–10.

The overall impression is, at any rate, one in which direct government to government relations are being bypassed by a mix of state-to-society and society-to-society modes of transnational influence/interference, evading the safeguards habitually deployed to protect the integrity of, notably, the executive branch. Donations to political parties by foreigners, paid junkets for parliamentarians,[371] or nominations of former senior politicians to boards of major foreign public companies[372] (once described as the 'capture of elites by foreign interests, facilitated by the non-restriction of "revolving doors" between the E.U. institutions and autocratic countries')[373] all belong to this emerging intermediary echelon of interference that does not fall evidently under espionage, bribery or even intimidation.[374] The foreign funding of political parties, in particular, especially when it is covert and aimed at disrupting political stability is widely perceived to inflict grave—but elusive—distortions on the operation of democracy.[375] This is all occurring, note, in allegedly 'free' societies that have long glorified the liberty of individual agents to engage in a range of self-interested economic activities without having their intentions second-guessed and that are normally hesitant about policing the operation of democracy for fear that this could quickly become tyrannical.

These developments have occurred, moreover, in ways that have fundamentally renewed the register of interference and the sense of what it is targeting. For example, whereas the (now quite ubiquitous) financing from abroad of political parties and candidates was once seen as the key problem,[376] that concern has been eclipsed by the sophistication of information manipulation

371 'Globe Editorial: When Politicians Accept "Free" Trips, Democracy Pays' *The Globe and Mail* (2 December 2017) <https://www.theglobeandmail.com/opinion/editorials/globe-editorial-when-politicians-accept-free-trips-democracy-pays/article37169152/> accessed 8 September 2023.

372 Laurenz Gehrke, 'Former German Chancellor Schröder Nominated for Gazprom Board' *POLITICO* (4 February 2022) <https://www.politico.eu/article/outrage-germany-ex-chancellor-schroder-gazprom-board-nomination/> accessed 8 September 2023.

373 European Parliament resolution of 1 June 2023 on foreign interference in all democratic processes in the European Union, including disinformation (2022/2075(INI)) [2023] OJ C/2023/1226 ('2023 Resolution on Foreign Interference in the EU'), para BT.

374 Chris Uhlmann and Caitlyn Gribbin, 'PM Orders Inquiry amid Revelations ASIO Warned Parties about Chinese Donations' *ABC News* (5 June 2017) <https://www.abc.net.au/news/2017-06-06/turnbull-orders-inquiry-following-revelation-asio-warned-parties/8592308> accessed 8 September 2023.

375 European Parliament resolution of 9 March 2022 on foreign interference in all democratic processes in the European Union, including disinformation (2020/2268(INI)) [2022] OJ C347/9 ('2022 Resolution on Foreign Interference in the EU'), para BE.

376 Fritz Plasser and Gunda Plasser, *Global Political Campaigning: A Worldwide Analysis of Campaign Professionals and Their Practices* (Praeger 2002).

operations, in ways that make the former appear almost quaint. Interference with academic milieus as a sort of soft underbelly of sovereignty (whether via Beijing aligned Confucius Institutes or Dehli aligned Bharatiya Janata Party-affiliated Akhil Bharatiya Vidyarthi Parishad) is a significant example of a form of interference that bypasses more obvious political targets by seeking to orient the production of expertise and research but that does not fit easily in the international legal vernacular. This creates new challenges for understanding what is problematic about interference, in a context where pressures on students and academics, however problematic they may be in principle, may seem of quite a different nature than interference in *sovereign* affairs. This not to mention the way in which an agenda of resistance to academic interference may run against academic freedom.

Targeting social networks, producing fake news, accrediting rumors, or infrastructure exploitation is an enterprise that is both broader in its breadth, potentially far more corrosive, and yet harder to detect. This 'infrastructural interference' may seek particular outcomes, but it may also be a goal in itself, that of simply weakening the legibility of local politics and their democratic apparatus. In some cases, the medium used to interfere is itself the infrastructure, so ubiquitous and central to modern life have social networks become for example, so that inevitably questions of substitution will arise (who would replace TikTok if it were banned in the U.S.?). As has been noted in the Canadian context, '[r]ecent history suggests that interference may be designed with the intent to sow distrust and confusion, potentially undermining voters' confidence in the process or willingness to vote, not necessarily to affect *the result* of the election'.[377] The European Parliament put it even more starkly, claiming that interference will:

> mislead and deceive citizens and affect their voting behaviour, amplify divisive debates, divide, polarise and exploit the vulnerabilities of societies, promote hate speech, worsen the situation of vulnerable groups which are more likely to become victims of disinformation, distort the integrity of democratic elections and referendums, sow distrust in national governments, public authorities and the liberal democratic order.[378]

---

377 *Debates of the Senate*, 42–1, Vol 150 (6 November 2018) 6742 (Stéphane Perrault) [Canada]. My emphasis.

378 2022 Resolution on Foreign Interference in the E.U. (n 357), para E.

In short, interference's targets and even demands are increasingly unclear, augmenting the risk of overreaction or of responding to the wrong threat or of treating all threats as belonging to some broad generic category when each must be assessed on its own terms.

4.3 *New Means*

Third, interference has tended to occur through a variety of new means that have accentuated its intrusive potential even as they have become harder to detect. Where previously:

> the administrative agencies of one country [could not] reach inside another country in an effort to bring about desired change. The techniques of informal access [...] are distinguished by precisely this capacity and that explains the increase in their number and importance. These techniques include information programs, cultural exchange programs, many kinds of economic aid, technical assistance in many forms, military training missions, military civic action programs, political warfare, economic warfare, psychological warfare, and the organization of insurgency and internal warfare.[379]

Compared to relatively 'crude' early forms of interference (such as the provision of bags of money to local political operatives),[380] then, the new interference seems more sophisticated if less evidently deliberate. This includes so-called 'hybrid' operations that combine different actors, conventional and unconventional means, and real-world disturbances and disinformation, all whilst seeking to remain below the threshold of detection.[381] At the same time, influence has taken increasingly soft and diffuse forms, notably as part of 'cultural diplomacy' such as Chinese state-run Confucius Institutes.[382] It often includes a highly covert character and sometimes draws on astroturfing techniques that make it appear as emanating from other sources. For example, it was revealed

---

379 Andrew M Scott, 'Nonintervention and Conditional Intervention' (1968) 22 Journal of International Affairs 208, 209.

380 Dov H Levin, 'Partisan Electoral Interventions by the Great Powers: Introducing the PEIG Dataset' (2016) 36 Conflict Management and Peace Science 88.

381 Ondřej Filipec, 'Multilevel Analysis of the 2021 Poland–Belarus Border Crisis in the Context of Hybrid Threats' (2022) 8 Central European Journal of Politics 1.

382 Naima Green-Riley, 'The State Department Labeled China's Confucius Programs a Bad Influence on U.S. Students. What's the Story?' *Washington Post* (25 August 2020) <https://www.washingtonpost.com/politics/2020/08/24/state-department-labeled-chinas-confucius-programs-bad-influence-us-students-whats-story/> accessed 10 January 2024.

that, as part of a strategy to shore up support for its war in Gaza, Israel, via its Ministry for Diasporas, had engineered a sophisticated operation on the basis of fake social network accounts to sway Democratic lawmakers in the U.S.[383] The hybrid character of certain operations is even more explicitly conveyed by their drawing on both real and cyber components. One such example of a hybrid threat is the transportation of migrants to European borders (from Belarus to Poland, Lithuania and Latvia) with a view to polarizing and weakening European societies[384] or efforts to steer polarization through 'anti-gender' disinformation targeting the LGBTQ+ community in an attempt to make it a wedge issue. 'Clandestine diplomacy', 'geoeconomics' and 'disinformation' are combined to divide target countries and thus weaken their resilience and the integrity of their political debates.[385] Doxing,[386] 'weaponized skepticism',[387] impersonation,[388] coexist as part of a toxic cocktail of destabilization that sometimes barely needs to hide its manipulative character (for public opinions to suspect they are being manipulated may be enough to sow democratic doubt). Even hostage diplomacy, consisting in the more or less arbitrary capture of foreign nationals in order to pressure their country, can be seen as a modality of the broader register of interference.[389]

New technologies have also featured prominently in the arsenal of the new interference, at times coming close to defining it because of the way the medium itself seems to fundamentally change its modalities. The internet has had an outsize role, and its impact has been to thoroughly redefine notions of territoriality central to the traditional prohibition on interference. As Barrie Sander

383 Sheera Frenkel, 'Israel Secretly Targets U.S. Lawmakers with Influence Campaign on Gaza War' *The New York Times* (5 June 2024) <https://www.nytimes.com/2024/06/05/technology/israel-campaign-gaza-social-media.html> accessed 5 June 2024.

384 Reis Thebault, 'Belarus's Weaponization of Migration Is a Desperate "Attack on the Democratic World," Lithuanian President Says' *Washington Post* (12 August 2021) <https://www.washingtonpost.com/world/europe/belarus-migrants-lithuania-fence/2021/08/12/bd39dd60-faab-11eb-911c-524bc8b68f17_story.html> accessed 10 January 2024.

385 Mikael Wigell, 'Hybrid Interference as a Wedge Strategy: A Theory of External Interference in Liberal Democracy' (2019) 95 International affairs 255.

386 Kilovaty, 'Doxfare: Politically Motivated Leaks and the Future of the Norm on Non-Intervention in the Era of Weaponized Information' (n 41).

387 Regina Rini, 'Weaponized Skepticism: An Analysis of Social Media Deception as Applied Political Epistemology' in Elizabeth Edenberg and Michael Hannon (eds), *Political Epistemology* (Oxford University Press 2021).

388 Brian Friedberg and Joan Donovan, 'On the Internet, Nobody Knows You're a Bot: Pseudoanonymous Influence Operations and Networked Social Movements' (2019) 6 Journal of Design and Science.

389 2022 Resolution on Foreign Interference in the E.U. (n 337), para BZ.

notes, cyberspace 'is an enabling environment that allows actors to transmit information to large audiences at low cost, near instantaneously, through multiple distribution points, across borders and with heightened opportunities for anonymity'.[390] Although the impact of such technologies can be overstated, compared to quaint Cold War mass mailing or radio programs, the operation of thousands of servers, the possibility of concealing one's identity, the utter decentralization of cyberspace, and the wide receptivity of users mean that subversion efforts have a much easier time bypassing state filters and directly connecting with ordinary citizens. Rather than massive cyber-attacks amounting to a use of force, as has often been feared, it is the ubiquity of 'low-intensity cyber operations' that has, in its ambiguity and stealth, intensified concerns and raised growing questions for international lawyers.[391]

As the European Parliament put it, in a powerful statement linking the diverging genres of old and new modes of intervention, acts of interference can take:

> many forms, including disinformation, the suppression of information, the manipulation of social media platforms and their algorithms, terms and conditions, and advertising systems, cyberattacks, hack-and-leak operations to gain access to voter information and interfere with the legitimacy of the electoral process, threats against and the harassment of journalists, researchers, politicians and members of civil society organisations, covert donations and loans to political parties, campaigns favouring specific candidates, organisations and media outlets, fake or proxy media outlets and organisations, elite capture and co-optation, 'dirty' money, fake personas and identities, pressure to self-censor, the abusive exploitation of historical, religious and cultural narratives, pressure on educational and cultural institutions, taking control of critical infrastructure, pressuring foreign nationals living in the E.U., the instrumentalisation of migrants and espionage; whereas these tactics are often combined for greater effect.[392]

390 Barrie Sander, 'Democracy Under the Influence: Paradigms of State Responsibility for Cyber Influence Operations on Elections' (2019) 18 Chinese Journal of International Law 1, 3–4.

391 Sean Watts, 'Low-Intensity Cyber Operations and the Principle of Non-Intervention' in Jens David Ohlin, Kevin Govern and Claire Finkelstein (eds), *Cyber War: Law and Ethics for Virtual Conflicts* (Oxford University Press 2015).

392 2022 Resolution on Foreign Interference in the E.U. (n 337), para G.

Interference has thus tended to reveal the intense vulnerability of domestic political spaces to foreign manipulation and to lead some to frame the issue increasingly as one of security. It has gone so far as to blur the distinction between interference/intervention and the use of force, in contexts where the former can be as destructive and threatening as conventional military attacks. This has led to spirited debates, for example, on whether election interference is an act of war, a form of prohibited coercive intervention, a violation of sovereignty, a mere attempt at legally influencing or should fall within its own category.[393] The insidious character of this interference may also be that it uses apparently innocuous means, but in a way and with finalities that make them problematic. 'Information', for example, is on one level either a value or a commodity freely circulating; but it is also a tool that can be 'weaponized' as part of 'information operations' and 'information wars'. It is at times as if the new interference were deliberately trying to skirt the limitations of the prohibition on intervention by confusing its regulatory sensors.

All in all, interference in cyberspace has certainly tended to relativize the distinction between peace time and war time, the use of force and initiatives that are merely hostile, or the criminal and the illegal, with potentially destabilizing consequences. Of course, interference is not alone in confusing those registers and arguably only succeeds because they have already been destabilized in globalized post-modernity. The new interference does not replace as much as it prolongs and multiplies the old, creating a sort of 'perfect storm' of interference: even as ever-more sophisticated efforts at cyber-hacking emerge, for example, one still needs to contend with old-fashioned and even comparatively venerable questions such as when to recognize an opposition leader as the head of state (as in the case of Venezuela), or whether political parties should accept foreign funding or whether unilateral sanctions are illegal. This reactivates with a vengeance old and never resolved problems even as it poses new ones whose terms are hard to reconcile with the traditional discourse of interference. It can lead actors to tie themselves into knots as they try to synthesize the old and the new, their attempts at influence and their resistance to interference, and the public and private dimensions of their domestic spheres. Interference, in short, is not simply a new challenge *for* international law; it is, in more ways than one, a challenge *to* international law because it problematizes international law's categories of understanding: sovereignty, community interest, human rights, etc. Indeed, what is or is not interference is increasingly

---

393 Julia Brooks, 'Election Interference Under International Law' (2020) 52 Journal of International Law and Politics Online Forum 1.

calling into question not only some central assumptions of international law but the very usefulness of the fragmenting state as a socio-legal fiction.

The emphasis on technologies, however, can be unduly narrow and neglect the extent to which it is also as a result of new and specific *normative* technologies within which interference is embedded that make it seem so elusive. For example, concerns with interference coincide with the rise of discourses on 'sovereignty as responsibility'[394] that themselves make sovereignty (and therefore non-interference) heavily dependent on the ability to abide by the *cahier des charges* of a 'good sovereign' and render any claim to non-interference precarious and even conditional. Although an earlier 1990s discourse tended to pit 'human security' and 'intervention' against each other in somewhat caricatural terms, moreover, emerging discourses of *resilience* 'operate conceptually by reinterpreting external intervention as productive of capable and securing subjects' so that 'human security does away with the liberal binary of intervention/non-intervention'.[395] In short, even as interference is being normalized it is also being invisibilized, in a normative environment that, henceforth, struggles to detect it for what it is and even to name it.

The challenge, therefore, is not just a policy or positive law one, but one that is more deeply normative in that the parameters of what counts as interference are constantly rearticulated to shed light on why one should care. At the same time, we do not have, it seems, a compelling and widely accepted theory of why interference, beyond being presumptively illegal, might be problematic in principle. Consider, to begin with, that whilst interference is typically seen as an unmitigated harm, its actual incidence in any given case will vary: interference could, for example, occasionally produce 'good' effects but still be problematic; or interference could certainly be well-intentioned yet toxic. The critique of bad intentions (the 'pretext problem') which seemed so relevant in the case of blatant interventions,[396] only goes so far. It is true that there may be something particularly galling about claiming to interfere on certain grounds when one is in fact pursuing other ends. But not only are the intentions of states when interfering complex and multi-facetted, it is also not evident that they should be conclusive of the harmful character of interference as a matter of international legal theory.

---

394 Philip Cunliffe, 'Sovereignty and the Politics of Responsibility' in Christopher Bickerton, Philip Cunliffe and Alexander Gourevitch (eds), *Politics Without Sovereignty: A Critique of Contemporary International Relations* (Routledge 2006).

395 David Chandler, 'Resilience and Human Security: The Post-Interventionist Paradigm' (2012) 43 Security Dialogue 213, 221.

396 Yue Wu (n 18) s II. A.

Or consider that what might otherwise be described as interference may have been requested by the state itself. Evidently, assistance cannot be *that* problematic in that last scenario: one cannot complain of the very thing one has welcomed.[397] Aside from canonical cases of 'intervention by invitation', much interference of even the new kind occurs, in fact, at the behest or with the complicity of local constituencies, including governmental elites, for largely self-serving reasons. For example, political parties in the U.K. have supported foreign donations or made it harder to ban them,[398] even as they increasingly rely on thinktanks that are obscurely foreign funded.[399] In India, the two leading political parties successfully lobbied to exempt themselves with retrospective effect from a law prohibiting foreign funding, even though the same law continues to apply to NGOs.[400] In Israel, the Likud has opposed a bill extending the existing election propaganda law to online content that would have required the identification of ads and donations.[401] Much of the furore in Canada about electoral interference was not only that possibility in itself, but the fact that one party (the Liberals) objectively stood to benefit from it and, arguably, turned a blind eye to it.[402]

Obviously, 'interference by invitation' from a particular political constituency does not necessarily make interference generally welcome or legal, as we will see in greater detail in the next part. There is never it seems a shortage of shadowy forces willing to hand over the keys of sovereignty to external actors for their short-term gain.[403] Not even interference or intervention at the

397 Robert Y Jennings and Arthur Watts (eds), *Oppenheim's International Law*, vol 1 (9th edn, Oxford University Press 2008) 435.

398 Ben Quinn, 'Government Defeats Move to Tighten U.K. Foreign Donations Law' *The Guardian* (3 May 2023) <https://www.theguardian.com/politics/2023/may/03/government-defeats-move-to-tighten-uk-foreign-donations-law> accessed 28 August 2023.

399 Rob Evans and others, 'Wealthy U.S. Donors Gave Millions to Rightwing U.K. Groups' *The Guardian* (29 November 2019) <https://www.theguardian.com/politics/2019/nov/29/wealthy-us-donors-gave-millions-to-rightwing-uk-groups> accessed 26 April 2024.

400 Zeenat Saberin, 'India Parties Now Can Get Foreign Funding, Activists Say Not OK' *Aljazeera* (11 April 2018) <https://www.aljazeera.com/features/2018/4/11/india-parties-now-can-get-foreign-funding-activists-say-not-ok> accessed 28 August 2023.

401 Toi Staff, 'Election Judge Bars Anonymous Internet Ads despite Likud Objection' *The Times of Israel* (28 February 2019) <https://www.timesofisrael.com/election-judge-bars-anonymous-internet-adds-despite-likud-objection/> accessed 19 December 2023.

402 John Ivison, 'Did Liberals Conspire with China's Election Interference?' *National Post* (1 March 2023) <https://nationalpost.com/opinion/trudeau-liberals-conspire-china-election-interference> accessed 21 November 2023.

403 Greta Bedekovics, 'The Far Right's Invitation for Foreign Interference in U.S. Elections' (*Center for American Progress*, 6 June 2024) <https://www.americanprogress.org/article/the-far-rights-invitation-for-foreign-interference-in-u-s-elections/> accessed 15 June 2024.

invitation of the state concerned necessarily even redeemed such an invitation, especially given legacies of states being 'made to invite' such meddling (e.g., Afghanistan dubiously soliciting Soviet intervention). The invitation could be nothing more than the doing of a puppet government inviting interference in a sovereignty which it had no business alienating. Or, more radically, it could reflect the reality that a state is not, in fact, a state, at least not one worthy of recognition under international law.[404] At the same time, the existence of such invitations, highlighting some possible domestic source of legitimacy for what might otherwise be meddling, objectively muddles the waters of why intervention or interference are specifically condemnable given the evidence that some groups at least seek to channel it internally. This is particularly the case, as we will see, to the extent that the invitation has significant popular backing.

One classic international legal argument in this context might be that at least no state seems to be challenging the norm of non-intervention as such. Indeed, it has even been argued that, for one thing, most CIA fomented coups were covert, which suggested rising 'credibility and hypocrisy costs associated with brazen violations of the nonintervention principle' and its international law status.[405] This may not be much a defense of the rule, though, the sort of lip service to virtue that passes for social recognition. At the end of the day, it was not exactly a progress that coups were covert, and this could even count as a perverse effect of international law. It may suggest, nonetheless, that the norm continues to have a structuring role and its status to be nominally well-entrenched even in conditions where its meaning is perpetually under contestation. Non-interference continues to act as a prism for international relations and is understood as a legitimate frame of reference despite persistent doubts about its content. States engage in legal controversies about its meaning if nothing else so they can win the argument that what they are doing in other states is not interference but that what other states are attempting to do on their territory is.

What remains interesting, for the purposes of the rest of this book, is why states do nonetheless formulate at least some of their opposition to interference and some of their support for non-interference through international law. The temptation to frame (if not settle) questions of interference or non-interference in international legal terms is a strong and, it turns out, extremely tempting one. States seemingly cannot avoid anchoring their arguments about

404 Suk-Jung Han, 'The Problem of Sovereignty: Manchukuo, 1932–1937' (2004) 12 Positions: East Asia Cultures Critique 457.

405 Michael Poznansky, *In the Shadow of International Law: Secrecy and Regime Change in the Postwar World* (Oxford University Press 2020) 5.

interference in a horizon of common international legal references because this is typically the only one available when dealing with other states. To do so helps generalize their preferences but also, more positively, hints at the need for rules that can withstand the test of time and structure international relations. Some discursive investments, in particular, may achieve short term gains but at the risk of impairing the ability of international law to act as a sustainable discourse. And even though the international law of non-interference may be muddled and confused, it still captures a fundamental intuition about how the system ought to operate. Over time, the norm—if not agreement about its exact content and application—is reinforced by its systematic invocation not as decisional but as framing. States may even gravitate towards a sort of rough middle ground, even as they constantly try to push the envelope of how it ought to be interpreted in particular cases.

Having said that, because what constitutes interference in the first place is a fundamentally contested concept, the question is never as simple as merely 'applying' an unproblematic norm of non-interference to particular facts but, almost always, to argue for a certain vision of non-interference: one is always, simultaneously, a norm 'applier' and a norm 'promoter'. In doing so, one is forced to come clean as it were about one's implicit assumptions for and in international law. During the relatively stylized struggles of the Cold War, particularly in traditional interstate conditions with a limited number of players, a reasonably clear sense of what constituted internal affairs, and quite evident technical limitations to the degree of interference that states could orchestrate, the norm of non-intervention was at least consistently held up as an international legal ideal. Most importantly, the terms of its contestation and the kind of linguistic games it permitted were fairly accepted, lending an air of stability to the debate. That stability, however, relatively superficial as it may have been, has been further destabilized by the conditions in which the 'new interference' operates, conditions that create considerable doubt about non-intervention's continued relevance in international law. Does non-intervention promise too much as a norm? Is it being supplanted, perhaps, by a broader norm of non-interference?

PART 2

The Age of Interference: Questions for International Law

The new interference has not entirely superseded the old intervention and in fact sometimes merely recycles part of it. Even as international law is increasingly dealing with complex questions arising from, for example, cyber hacking of information systems, the question of the illegality of supporting rebels in a foreign country or of the opportune character of recognizing a rebel group as the legitimate government of a state, or the degree to which human rights shatter the bounds of what constitutes interference, or the possibility that politicians will straightforwardly be corrupted by foreign powers all certainly remain topical. More often than not, it is the imbrication of these issues, their very hybrid character, that makes them particularly intractable. What is clear at least is that the traditional focus on use of force has long given way to an 'infinite variety of forms of intervention that violate daily the theoretical principles of non-interference', particularly of an economic kind.[406] Regrouping behind a dogmatic defense of non-intervention may not be the most fruitful strategy.

Interference, at any rate, is creating considerable systemic instability within international law as a result of its propensity to corrode categories. As international law seeks to paper over the deep divisions that have given rise to the notion of non-intervention, it inevitably compromises itself into a series of classic tautological postures that merely define intervention as intervention.[407] Although claims that the definition of interference/intervention is fundamentally vague are rife (the definition of intervention is 'riddled with definitional ambiguity and conceptual uncertainty', points one author),[408] it should also be noted that claims of vagueness can on occasion be greatly exaggerated and are not without their own political uses. The politics of what counts as vague and what counts as precise are themselves instrumentalized. There is no reason to think, in particular, that intervention or interference are any vaguer than a range of concepts on which international law routinely relies, first and foremost among which sovereignty: no more but no less either and in ways that reactivate latent tensions barely suppressed by attention to form.

406 Wolfgang Friedmann, 'Intervention and the Developing Countries' (1969) 10 Virginia Journal of International Law 205, 209.

407 Karl Zemanek, 'Human Rights Protection vs. Non-Intervention: A Perennial Conflict?' in Lal Chad Vohrah and others (eds), *Man's Inhumanity to Man. Essays on International Law in Honour of Antonio Cassese* (Brill 2003) 961.

408 Mohamed S Helal, 'On Coercion in International Law' (2019) 52 NYU Journal of International Law and Politics 1, 47.

 | DOI 10.1163/9789004532731_006

Still, one can at least agree that the latest round of developments on the issue of interference cannot be said to arise against the background of an already once and for all stabilized debate. As Part 1 has shown, the very scope of intervention has been hotly contested historically, and efforts at definition have arisen if anything on the edge of major geopolitical fault lines. Recent debates about interference writ large tend to reactivate, sometimes at cross purpose, earlier debates rather than simply drawing on their uncontested legacies. Much international legal argumentation also evokes more or less painful memories and is constantly at risk of being overtaken by them. Investments in the discursive economy of international law always occur in an echo chamber of past investments against which they stand to be evaluated, making it hard to distinguish signal from noise and constantly creating distortions in messaging. Whilst the previous part has highlighted the importance of the historical genesis of debates about non-intervention and cautioned against the temptation of a *tabula rasa* or at least of reinventing the wheel, the past is both hugely informative even as it is, ultimately, a poor guide to the present.

For example, early international legal scholars were obsessed with very broad questions about humanitarian intervention, foregrounding the issue of the use of force and visions of dire life-and-death struggles between a tyrant and its population. They could not be said to have had an eye for the sort of low-intensity, ubiquitous and under-the-radar everyday interference that has arguably become a hallmark of interference's cyber variant. One will need to proceed carefully, hence, when moving back and forth between the past and the present, as if Grotius or Vattel could be understood to speak directly to our modern conditions. Recognizing the influence of earlier debates on intervention should not entail surrendering uncritically to those debates as if they could be extracted from their historicity. At the same time, there is clearly a structural dimension to those conversations as they have occurred over the centuries, one that pits a variety of stylized figures of speech and reference points (sovereignty, the international interest, etc.). Understanding not just the tenor but the particular rhythm and cyclical structure of these debates is key to understanding them qua debates that often have a life of their own beyond actual world events.

For all the appearance of consensus around at least a broad, structuring norm of non-intervention, moreover, states have at best agreed to disagree about its actual scope, through processes of recurrent deferral, constructive ambiguity, and creative interpretation. One should be alive to the possibility, always real in international law, that the definition of what constitutes interference, like the notion of sovereignty to which it so evidently relates, is itself beyond international law altogether, standing to be expressed rather than defined, and by pure acts of sovereign will rather than cut-and-dry rules of international law.[409] RJ Vincent, himself not an international lawyer, cautioned:

> If the principle of nonintervention retains a place in contemporary international law, it is not, if it ever has been, as a clear injunction against a particular act. The values it draws attention to and protects are those included under the rubric of the principle of state sovereignty, such as the rights of a state to territorial integrity and political independence. Standing guard over such imprecisely defined rights and requiring respect for them in a sort of legal shorthand, the principle appeals more perhaps to governments than it does to jurists.[410]

Be that as it may, the notion that intervention is legal, essentially, if states say it is or simply get away with whatever interpretation they favor, is distinctly unappealing to the legal mind. It seems to rely on some strong assertion of the doctrine of fundamental rights of states, notably on grounds of self-preservation or even interest maximization, that international law has long aspired to move away from.[411] It may be true that the norm of non-intervention 'however true at a sufficiently general level of abstraction, is perhaps too general to be helpful',[412] but it is still international lawyers' task to make sense of it. Of course, the question is worth asking whether international law can ever effectuate a critical return on the substratum of sovereignty to which it gives expression and, as it were, regulate its own constitutive concepts. Does international law rule sovereignty or does it merely derive from it? And if sovereignty does exist only on the basis of international legal regulation, then is there any inherent bar to interference that is not entirely dependent on the operation of international law?

409 Vincent (n 69) ch 8.

410 ibid 310.

411 Tzanakopoulos (n 24); Niki Aloupi, 'The Right to Non-Intervention and Non-Interference' (2015) 4 Cambridge International Law Journal 566.

412 Vincent (n 69) 311.

1 Non-interference as Argumentative Claim

Rather than addressing those questions from an entirely theoretical perspective, intellectual inquiry into the matter may be better served by the sort of approach that the actors of the international system have themselves brought to it: asserting occasionally, no doubt, a sort of prerogative to interfere writlarge (or at least to decide for themselves what constitutes interference) but also, more often than not, finessing each others' arguments about what constitutes interference, claiming that they are not violating international law even as others are, or reimagining a concept of interference for the times, etc. The norm of non-intervention does act as 'a slogan of protest and legitimation' and it is as such that 'it recommends itself to governments as a serviceable tool of international politics'.[413] Where international relations theorists may see only window-dressing, international lawyers are prone to see window dressing *and* something else (or perhaps what one might understand as normatively productive window dressing). That elusive *je ne sais quoi* involves validity claims, rhetorical in the strong meaning of the word, which engage their locutors and tie them into justificatory exercises that are never entirely reducible to whatever politics gave rise to them.[414]

In short, legal talk may be cheap, but it is not gratuitous either, to the extent that it constructs interest and even identity. Inevitably, states will have encountered some of the standard limitations and force of international legal argument in the process of protesting intervention or non-intervention: on the one hand, the temptation of a rigid and imperative rule which, almost invariably, ends up being too strict for its own good and leads to its own gradual destructuring through the introduction of ever more exceptions; on the other hand, the temptation of casuistry, wherein any sense of the overall direction of international law is lost but that body of rules at least cannot be faulted for its lack of flexibility. Over time, one can see a range of approaches to the metaproblem of how to define intervention. A conventional one is obviously positivist and tends to emphasize non-intervention as a rule with a clear core despite its hazy penumbra. This can be traced to a dynamic early Latin-American tradition and its uptake by the General Assembly, for example, which has long sought to draw red lines when it comes to intervention.[415] Another approach is

413 ibid 310.

414 Thomas M Franck and Edward Weisband, *Word Politics: Verbal Strategy Among the Superpowers* (Oxford University Press 1971).

415 On the influence of that Latin-American connection to the bias in favor of a rules-oriented conception of non-intervention, see Townley (n 62).

more interested in the 'world order' finalities of proscribing intervention and leans towards a multi-factor analysis that often ends up being associated with the exercise of U.S. power.[416]

Inevitably, the former is accused of being too rigid for the 'complex' circumstances of the world, whilst the latter is constantly suspected of leaving too much discretion to the decision-maker, especially the powerful. Inevitably also, different conceptions of interference proceed from characteristically unstated assumptions about the default state of international relations: to those who see only an ongoing competition between prickly sovereigns, the bar of what constitutes intervention may well be set very low; to those who see interdependence as the natural equilibrium state of international relations, interference will often seem a benign sin. How, then, might international law help U.S. understand the 'new interference' and how does it stand to be affected by it? How can one do justice to the intuition that international law not only regulates but constitutes the new interference by providing states and international lawyers with the vocabulary that allows them to understand (and misunderstand) it as such in the first place?

If nothing else, international law affirms the undisputed existence of *some* norm of non-intervention and perhaps of non-interference as well. Whatever doubts one may have about its contents, those typically do not extend to its existence, which is repeatedly emphasized as well established under customary international law. At the same time, establishing the norm's very legality invariably involves some contortions given the norms' apparently constant violations. This is at times reminiscent of how other, purportedly central norms of the international legal order such as the prohibition of torture are often proved (or not). The central puzzle is how to establish the existence of a norm in the face of consistent evidence that it is honored in the breach. Faced with much contrary practice that seems to undermine the norm's existence, international lawyers engage in a series of related moves.

First, they recast the record in terms of a glass half-full: it is easier to detect violations of the norm of interference, than the ordinary, banal and invisible compliance with it. In practice, needless to say, most states, to paraphrase Henkin, are not intervening with the affairs of most states most of the time (although that does not make the instances when they do so less problematic).[417] States may not get much credit for this given the range of actual reasons beyond deferral to the law why they are interfering, but it should still

416 Farer, 'Harnessing Rogue Elephants' (n 132).

417 Louis Henkin, *How Nations Behave: Law and Foreign Policy* (2nd edn, Columbia University Press 1979) 47.

count as practice.[418] Moreover, lawyers tend to discount the significance of violations, so long as states are not brazen about such violations and, in fact, '[defend their] conduct by appealing to exceptions or justifications contained within the rule itself'.[419]

Second and subsidiarily, international lawyers relatively diminish the value of practice. This was the path elected by the ICJ for example in the Nicaragua case, which notoriously led it to lower the threshold of concurrent practice precisely in relation to intervention by highlighting that 'it is not to be expected that [...] the application of the rules in question should have been perfect, in the sense that States should have refrained, with complete consistency, from [...] intervention in each other's internal affairs'. Indeed, 'for a rule to be established as customary' practice need not be 'in absolutely rigorous conformity with the rule' and it is 'sufficient that the conduct of States should, in general, be consistent with such rules'.[420] It is striking, then, that this locus classicus of international law emerged as part an attempt to pin down the status of non-intervention, testifying in a sense to the esteem in which the norm is held even as strict compliance with it is a constant motif of doubt. General compliance is of course as difficult to prove as it is to disprove, and quickly points back less to actual practice than a sense of the norm's immanent value or societal importance.

Third, international lawyers invoke—against the scarcity, unreliability and contradictory character of practice—the countervailing weight of *opinio juris*.[421] Again, the ICJ indicated that 'instances of State conduct inconsistent with a given rule should generally have been treated as breaches of that rule, not as indications of the recognition of a new rule'.[422] For example, the methodological focus has often been on the relevance of 'protests' against interference in ascertaining the contours of the norm.[423] 'We may not know what interference is exactly, but states at least seem to recognize it when they see it', goes the intuition. Converging statements in international fora then provide the added veneer of multilateral *opinio juris* needed to dispel any doubt that the norm is indeed dear to a great many states. On that score of course, states have been very active in condemning intervention and interference in general

418 Yifeng (n 2) 337.
419 *Nicaragua v United States* (n 3) [186].
420 ibid.
421 Bruno Simma and Philip Alston, 'The Sources of Human Rights Law: Custom, Jus Cogens, and General Principles' (1988) 12 Australian Yearbook of International Law 82.
422 *Nicaragua v United States* (n 3) [186].
423 Yifeng (n 2) 324.

terms. State practice and recognition of its salience are merely presented as a form of confirmation of what is already obvious in the U.N. Charter, for example. General Assembly resolutions, whatever one may think of the motives for their adoption, may not make international law but provide ample evidence of what states are willing to recognize as such: even if their deeds do not provide a normatively ambitious yardstick, they can at least be held to their words.[424]

From grounded first and foremost in practice, then, the foundation of the rule in customary international law is eventually said to 'translate [...] the ideal and expectation of international society into a normative requirement of positive law': in short, if non-intervention did not exist, it should be invented as a necessary feature of 'the general legal conscience'.[425] This classic deductive move potentially elevates non-intervention to the level of an axiomatic constitutional principle of the international legal order ('a structural principle of international law derived from the basic structure of international society'),[426] essentially freeing it up from the constraints and pitfalls of classical custom. It meshes well with the temptation of seeing the principle of non-intervention as one of *jus cogens* and therefore as not even amenable to the vagaries of contrary practice or, for that matter, *opinio juris*.[427] The natural law inspiration of such a move are evident, although that can be finessed by merely insisting that the principle of non-intervention is a necessary analytical 'corollary', as the ICJ put it, 'of the principle of the sovereign equality of States'.[428] It remains difficult to understand what it would mean for the principle of non-interference to really have *jus cogens* nature, given that sovereignty surely involves the ability to modulate and even surrender said sovereignty but the reference is often really only meant to authenticate the entrenchment of non-intervention.

Much of the doctrinal and real-world action, however, lies elsewhere, in the act of filling 'intervention' and 'interference' as empty vessels with meaning and then specifying that meaning in particular circumstances. International law also provides a bare definition of what is prohibited under the banner of non-intervention specifically, which this second part will broadly entertain, even as it seeks to push the definition of intervention to incorporate a more generic understanding of interference. That definitional exercise is of course crucial

---

424 Xuan W Tay, 'Reconstructing the Principle of Non-Intervention and Non-Interference—Electoral Disinformation, Nicaragua, and the Quilt-Work Approach' (2022) 40 Berkeley Journal of International Law 39, 54–60.

425 Yifeng (n 2) 326.

426 ibid 330.

427 See, in that respect, *Nicaragua v United States*, Separate Opinion by José Sette-Camara, 199.

428 *Nicaragua v United States* (n 3) [202].

in itself. It points to the importance of holding on to an intermediary category that is not equated with use of force (with potentially dire consequences) yet not reducible to ordinary violations of sovereignty either (which fail to convey the particular gravity of what is involved in interfering as a form of substitution to the sovereign). An ill-defined norm of non-intervention will be 'either weak or so amorphous as to not be subject to rational or general delimitation'.[429] But the definitional exercise is also crucial because of everything that describing something as unlawful interference/intervention potentially unleashes. For example, countermeasures will only be justifiable under international law if another state has violated its obligations in the first place, so that lowering the threshold of illegality too much may also generate undesirable or at least disproportionate reactions.[430] Note also that to the extent that it was once considered that intervention might count as one of the crimes in a Code of Crimes against the Peace and Security of Mankind, concerns of *nullum crimen sine lege* may also arise.[431]

This exercise in elucidating the meaning of intervention and interference is never purely definitional in the intellectual sense of the term, but one that stands to have actual effects in and on the world, including in terms of engaging responsibility, apportioning blame for harms, and shaping responses. Moreover, the question is not only what intervention *is*, but what the discourse of intervention *permits* (in other words, what is *not* intervention). States are constantly called upon to police the outer-perimeter of intervention (particularly as it morphs into mere interference) and interference, in ways that implicitly licence what does not fall within their range. This was, for example, the thinking that presumably presided over Western efforts during the negotiation of the 1970 Declaration on Friendly Relations, namely that economic coercion was better left, at best, to the realm of non-intervention rather than the use of force, lest dangerous escalations be encouraged (i.e., armed reprisals).[432] The assimilation of even blatantly coercive economic interference to uses of force was seen as potentially explosive for the international legal order, and presented as dubiously grounded in the law.[433] Ironically, it was Western

429 Linarelli (n 24) 2.

430 The question arises, notably, in relation to low level cyber interference. Watts (n 391).

431 Yearbook of the ILC (1950) vol I, 160, para 51; Linarelli (n 24) 40.

432 Hartmut Brosche, 'The Arab Oil Embargo and United States Pressure against Chile: Economic and Political Coercion and the Charter of the United Nations' (1974) 7 Case Western Reserve Journal of International Law 3; Helal (n 408).

433 Tom J Farer, 'Political and Economic Coercion in Contemporary International Law' (1985) 79 American Journal of International Law 405.

international lawyers who, in turn, pivoted completely during the 1973 OPEP oil embargo. Many were then willing to contemplate that economic coercion in the form of subtraction of a key commodity was indeed tantamount to a use of force.[434] Julius Stone even implied that the 1973 oil boycott might have allowed the U.S. to exercise self-defence.[435]

In that respect, there is no gainsaying that:

> each state tends to expound a doctrine of nonintervention which is framed with reference to those particular forces in world politics which seem to present an actual or potential challenge to its own sovereignty or, more broadly, to the maintenance or propagation of its conception of international order.[436]

But to point this out without more is trite. The definitional exercise is not only a policy-oriented strategic one in which states merely seek to maximize their interests. Simply because a particular understanding of intervention or interference is conducive to one's national interest does not mean that one can abstract oneself from the work of making the argument under international law. This involves, as it should, erudite conversations about the sources of international law and their hierarchy.[437] The norm of non-intervention is included in treaties, both bilateral[438] and, increasingly, multilateral; it is certainly susceptible to a lively conversation about its status under customary international law; and Courts, notably in the European context, have begun to wade in on its scope and permissible responses to it, against the ever looming background of the ICJ's crucial ruling in *Nicaragua v United States*.[439]

At the same time as these sources are deployed to ascertain the meaning of intervention and interference, these notions further problematize classic

434 Paul Stephen Dempsey, 'Economic Aggression & Self-Defense in International Law: The Arab Oil Weapon and Alternative American Responses Thereto' (1977) 9 Case Western Reserve Journal of International Law 253, 263–267.

435 Julius Stone, *Conflict Through Consensus: United Nations Approaches to Aggression* (Johns Hopkins University Press 1977).

436 Vincent (n 69) 314.

437 Yifeng (n 2).

438 For example, as early as 1921, a bilateral treaty between the Soviet Union and Persia anticipated that 'in consideration of the fact that each nation has the right to determine freely its political destiny, each of the two Contracting Parties formally expresses its desire to abstain from any intervention in the internal affairs of the Other'. Treaty of Friendship (Russian Soviet Federal Socialist Republic–Persia) (26 February 1921) 9 LNTS 383 art 4.

439 *Nicaragua v United States* (n 3).

problems in the doctrine of sources such as the distinction between *opinio juris* and motives,[440] resort to extra-legal considerations in justifying adherence to norms,[441] or the role of silence.[442] A more general concern relates to the evolving understanding of customary or conventional norms of non-intervention, one's implicit theory of change in international law, and the severability of particular formalistic understandings of interference from the historical intellectual context that gave rise to them. In that respect, invoking the Friendly Declaration liberally today, for example, as if it spoke to the reality of the moment, involves a hefty dose of anachronism and, perhaps, bad faith. For some the Declaration needs to be expurgated of 'dated cliches, much favoured by non-aligned countries at the time, like anti-colonialism, anti-imperialism, anti-apartheid, et cetera'.[443] For others, the Declaration may be precisely a conduit to reactivate such ideas, a testimony to a bygone era that nonetheless speaks across time to the sort of world one might yet reinvent. Although the debate on intervention and interference is not unique in raising acute challenges to the elucidation of norms, there is also reason to think that the closer one gets to the very core of what sovereignty means, the more elusive the tools of international law seem to be to the task.[444]

Nonetheless, at least three fundamental ambiguities have presided over the emergence of the norm of non-intervention and non-interference in international law and continue to permeate its operation. The first is that for a long time, it was clear that there was a 'right' of intervention. This means that international lawyers have had to, over the course of the 20th Century, simultaneously dismantle that claim even as they sought prop up the alternative case for non-intervention. Of course, a so-called right of intervention may now seem like it is a very dated concept but, in fact, discourses around humanitarian intervention or R2P tend to resurrect a sense that it is actually a necessity and an obligation in some cases. There is no shortage of supplementary reasons why states imagine that, notwithstanding the demise of a right of intervention,

---

440 Dapo Akande and Zachary Vermeer, 'The Airstrikes against Islamic State in Iraq and the Alleged Prohibition on Military Assistance to Governments in Civil Wars' (*EJIL: Talk!*, 2 February 2015) <https://www.ejiltalk.org/the-airstrikes-against-islamic-state-in-iraq-and-the-alleged-prohibition-on-military-assistance-to-governments-in-civil-wars/> accessed 10 July 2024.

441 Nowak (n 22).

442 Luca Ferro, 'The Doctrine of "Negative Equality" and the Silent Majority of States' (2021) 8 Journal on the Use of Force and International Law 4.

443 Zemanek (n 407) 960.

444 Mégret, 'L'articulation Entre Tribunaux Pénaux Internationaux et Juridictions Nationales: Centralité et Ambiguïté Dans l'ordre Juridique International' (n 39).

that right nonetheless persists in some form whether as a result of failures of sovereignty,[445] the need to protect one's nationals[446] or, indeed, systematic human rights violations.[447] In other words, the 'right of intervention' has never entirely disappeared from conversations even as those have shifted to outlining a prohibition of intervention. This means that international law tends to be haunted by very contrasting images of what non-intervention requires and that these debates, to a surprising degree, are still being litigated today in very much the same way they were decades ago, if not longer.

Second, non-intervention, perhaps surprisingly, has a rather ambiguous footing in the U.N. Charter itself. The Charter specifies in no uncertain terms that states should refrain from the use of force (Article 2(4)) and that the U.N. itself should not interfere in domestic affairs (Article 2(7)), but the principle of non-interference by states into the affairs of other states is not explicitly mentioned and evidently falls within neither. If anything, the foundation of non-intervention lies in fundamental principles of international law, and notably its necessary correlation with sovereignty and the equality of states, although on a level of generality that is unlikely to help elucidate its content. That content can also be reconstructed deductively, at least in part, on the basis of the customary prohibition of the use of force, the right of self-determination or the requirement of settling disputes peacefully.[448] Still, for a principle as central as non-intervention is often presented as being, it is somewhat unsettling that it has not secured a more incontrovertible place under the Charter. This may of course always have been an indication of its contentious character.

Third, conversations about the norm's status inevitably include discussions of the customary value of various General Assembly resolutions that most notoriously proclaimed it. Resolutions are clearly an important indicator of *opinio juris* (especially when, as the Friendly Relations Declaration, they are adopted by consensus and claim to be merely interpreting the U.N. Charter) and perhaps even a manifestation of international practice, but it bears underlining that they do not in and of themselves make law. In addition to resolutions being adopted, then, it is worth bearing in mind who voted for them and

445 Steven E Goldman, 'A Right of Intervention Based upon Impaired Sovereignty' (1994) 156 World Affairs 124.

446 Jean Raby, 'The Right of Intervention for the Protection of Nationals: Reassessing the Doctrinal Debate' (1989) 30 Les Cahiers de droit 441.

447 Richard B Lillich, 'Intervention to Protect Human Rights' (1969) 15 McGill Law Journal 205.

448 Dire Tladi, 'The Duty Not to Intervene in Matters within Domestic Jurisdiction' in Jorge E Viñuales (ed), *The U.N. Friendly Relations Declaration at 50: An Assessment of the Fundamental Principles of International Law* (Cambridge University Press 2020) 90.

for what reason. For example, states' support of a variety of anti-intervention resolutions, notably the later 1976 Declaration on Non-Interference and the 1981 Declaration on the Inadmissibility of Intervention and Interference, was often ambiguous and did not necessarily involve a recognition that the resulting principles were part of international law. Lawmaking by General Assembly resolutions has long raised fraught epistemic issues[449] that caution against assuming that repetitiousness necessarily international law makes. To this day, the attempt to 'legislate' international law through the sheer weight of Assembly majorities or joint statements, for example in relation to unilateral economic sanctions,[450] remains a very ambiguous exercise that may say more about international politics than international law making. Indeed, the largely hortatory character of such instruments as the Friendly Declaration suggest that it was never designed, perhaps quite wisely, to resolve the issues that its implementation would raise, let alone to provide a precise road map for the multifarious problems that would arise decades later around the proper scope of interference.[451]

Behind the doctrinal debate on sources, the debate on intervention and interference has always involved an implicit meta-debate about authorship and what might be described as the 'engineering' of norms of international law. The question is, also, *who* decides on its content, when and why—in other words, who gets to be the locutor of international norms. For example, after the Declaration on Intervention (Resolution 2131) was adopted by the General Assembly, six Western states insisted that they did not consider it to be a full statement of international law and that the drafting Committee of the Friendly Declaration should seek to define it more precisely. By contrast, Chile and the UAR sponsored a resolution enjoining the Committee to 'abide by' the

449 Gregory J Kerwin, 'The Role of United Nations General Assembly Resolutions in Determining Principles of International Law in United States Courts' (1983) 1983 Duke Law Journal 876; Christopher C Joyner, 'UN General Assembly Resolutions and International Law: Rethinking the Contemporary Dynamics of Norm-Creation' (1981) 11 California Western International Law Journal 445; Rossana Deplano, 'The Riddle of Custom: General Assembly Resolutions' in Sufyan Droubi and Jean d'Aspremont (eds), *International organisations, non-State actors, and the formation of customary international law* (Manchester University Press 2020); Stephen M Schwebel, 'The Effect of Resolutions of the U.N. General Assembly on Customary International Law' (1979) 73 Proceedings of the ASIL Annual Meeting 301.

450 'Joint Communiqué of the 14th Meeting of the Foreign Ministers of the Russian Federation, the Republic of India and the People's Republic of China' (*Ministry of Foreign Affairs of the People's Republic of China*, 19 April 2016) <https://www.mfa.gov.cn/eng/wjdt_665385/2649_665393/201604/t20160419_679455.html> accessed 13 July 2024.

451 Zemanek (n 407) 955.

terms of Resolution 2131.[452] During the negotiation of the Friendly Relations Declaration, states were also divided between those who wanted a more precise definition of both the *domaine réservé* and intervention and those who argued that it would be 'unwise and unprofitable' to go into specifics.[453] In more recent times, with the appetite for the General Assembly for such grand proclamations waning and in a context of fragmentation of international law, the adoption of norms on non-interference has taken an increasingly sectorial approach (elections, cyberspace, human rights, etc.) driven by loose ad hoc coalitions. These contestations reveal the extent to which the formulation of a norm of non-interference is also, quite simply, an ongoing project of certain states and certain international lawyers, at any given time, one that involves a degree of platform building.

Given the tentative status of the new interference and the extent to which the international community has struggled to keep up with developments surrounding it, it will come as no surprise that the normative production around the norm also includes rather large swathes of soft-law, whether as part of the broader Talinn exercise on the international law applicable to cyberspace,[454] the 'Oxford Process' and its adoption of a 'Statement on International Law Protections Against Foreign Electoral Interference Through Digital Means',[455] the E.U. High Level Expert Group on Fake News and Online Disinformation,[456] or a joint declaration by various special rapporteurs on freedom of expression.[457] Also of note are the voluntary and non-binding—but of course

452 Piet-Hein Houben, 'Principles of International Law Concerning Friendly Relations and Co-Operation Among States' (1967) 61 American Journal of International Law 703, 717–718.

453 UNGA, 'Report of the Special Committee on Principles of International Law concerning Friendly Relations and Cooperation among States' (16 November 1964) U.N. Doc A/5746 (Report on Friendly Relations and Cooperation among States) paras 230–240.

454 *Tallinn Manual 2.0 on the International Law Applicable to Cyber Operations* (2nd edn, Cambridge University Press 2017).

455 'The Oxford Statement on International Law Protections Against Foreign Electoral Interference' (*Oxford Institute for Ethics, Law and Armed Conflict*) <https://www.elac.ox.ac.uk/the-oxford-process/the-statements-overview/the-oxford-statement-on-international-law-protections-against-foreign-electoral-interference/> accessed 18 December 2023.

456 'A Multi-Dimensional Approach to Disinformation: Report of the Independent High Level Group on Fake News and Online Disinformation' (European Commission 2018) <https://digital-strategy.ec.europa.eu/en/library/final-report-high-level-expert-group-fake-news-and-online-disinformation> accessed 26 January 2024.

457 U.N. Special Rapporteur on Freedom of Opinion and Expression, OSCE Representative on Freedom of the Media, OAS Special Rapporteur on Freedom of Expression and ACHPR Special Rapporteur on Freedom of Expression and Access to Information, 'Joint Declaration on Freedom of Expression and Elections in the Digital Age' (2020).

potentially at some point adding to more—United Nations Groups of Governmental Experts' effort to develop the U.N. norms of responsible state behaviour in cyberspace in the context of international security[458] or the U.N. Open-ended working group (U.N. OEWG) on developments in the field of information and telecommunications in the context of international security. The actual status of that soft law is an object of perennial discussion.[459] Such initiatives seek to capture norms as they evolve, possibly in response to the haphazard and indecisive nature of the emergence of custom, even as they evidently cannot pre-empt the full development of customary international norms by states themselves.

2 The Framing Role of International Law

Beyond attention to strict sources doctrine lie a number of deeper methodological issues about how international law should deal with change at all. This involves both a reaffirmation of the validity of the status quo and a recurring, if guarded, emphasis on the need for the law's adaptation to exogenous shocks. As will be seen, an oft-repeated argument in relation to the new interference is that it requires adaptation to changing circumstances. The starting point is generally the most established international law, sometimes relying on little more than a few sentences of an international judgment rendered in very different times (e.g., the ICJ's judgment in *Nicaragua v United States*). Invariably, though, that judgment is deemed to fall short in some respect and to not have anticipated radical new scenarios, such as interference in cyberspace.[460] The *domaine réservé* or the requirement of coercion are, for example, presented as unduly narrow, prompting calls for adaptation. The law's development is caught between fidelity to an illustrious past and adaptation to a dangerous present.

This then creates a degree of methodological strain. One cannot, obviously, simply change the law because such a change commends itself intellectually. Hence a number of strategies to adapt emerge whilst clinging to the law as it is imagined to have been to this point, sometimes at the cost of significant

458 UNGA Report on International Security Developments in IT (2015) A/70/174.

459 Sejal Parmar, 'The Significance of the Joint Declarations on Freedom of Expression' (2019) 37 Netherlands Quarterly of Human Rights 178.

460 In fact, the ICJ itself made it clear that it was only dealing with the case at hand and could of course not conceivably have been trying to address all possible issues of intervention outside the ultimately quite specific circumstances of *Nicaragua v United States* (n 3).

complications. As we will seen in more detail in this part, the 'domaine réservé' is reinvented as the 'domaine privilégié', for example;[461] the target of interference is reinterpreted as being self-determination rather than sovereignty;[462] coercion is reimagined as something else than quite coercion.[463] Sometimes this is justified on hermeneutic grounds, reinterpreting the corpus of international law based on evolving circumstances—there are few concepts of international law that cannot periodically be rejigged for the needs of the moment; sometimes it is based on policy argument and a distinct if obscure sense by international lawyers of the 'necessities of international life' (e.g., international law must allow for interaction whilst not allowing domination); and, more often than not, it is elaborated on the basis of incipient state practice and statements if not quite forming customary international law, at least helping guess where it might crystalize in the future. This rearrangement of the decks is what the creative practice of international law is made of; but it is also, no doubt, a precarious exercise.[464]

Perhaps just as importantly, international law gives the norm a certain status within the international legal order as a placeholder for certain aspirational values, notably the idea that sovereignty stands for a form of independence from others, even if that independence then needs to be sustained by a degree of rule-complying and even cooperative behavior. As such, it might even be said that (a degree of) non-intervention is not only a rule of international law but a pre-condition to sovereignty and therefore of international law's very existence. For instance, the existence of interference may have a role *ab initio* in establishing whether an entity is a state at all for the purposes of international law, notably in establishing the Montevideo requirement of *government* of a population over a territory. Although a state might suffer interference to the point of being a 'client' state but still a state,[465] the existence of systemic interference would belie the notion that an entity was effectively independently governing, and therefore qualified as a state at all. By the same

461 Thibault Moulin, 'Reviving the Principle of Non-Intervention in Cyberspace: The Path Forward' (2020) 25 Journal of Conflict & Security Law 423.

462 Ohlin, *Election Interference: International Law and the Future of Democracy* (n 17).

463 Marko Milanovic, 'Revisiting Coercion as an Element of Prohibited Intervention in International Law' (2023) 117 American Journal of International Law 601.

464 Frédéric Mégret, 'Thinking About What International Humanitarian Lawyers "Do": An Examination of the Laws of War as a Field of Professional Practice' in Wouter Werner, Marieke de Hoon and Alexis Galan (eds), *The Law of International Lawyers; Reflections on the Work of Martti Koskenniemi* (Cambridge University Press 2017).

465 James Crawford and Ian Brownlie, *Brownlie's Principles of Public International Law* (9th edn, Oxford University Press 2019) 120.

token, to claim that a state that allows itself to be a victim of interference 'is not much of a state' and can therefore be discounted for the purposes of international law's protection from interference, is manifestly wrong on account of the ambitions of international law in propping up the sovereignty of all.[466]

At the same time, any affirmation of non-interference must contend with the reality that no state—not even North Korea—is, as it were, an island-onto-itself. This is what has long cautioned prudence in the face of quixotic proclamations by states of their 'right to be left alone'. As Lou Henkin put it:

> In the system of states, perfect autonomy for any state is an impossible ideal. Big Powers, and even some smaller ones, impinge on other states by the fact of their existence. In modem times in particular, though the independence of states remains an ideal, the system is characterized by a tangle of interdependence. For almost any state, being let alone conflicts with its other values; to realize its own vision of The Good a state requires communication, trade and other relations with other states.[467]

Squaring the circle of how to be autonomous in a world of non-autonomy, then, is arguably the 'primary purpose of international law'.[468] This makes for a realistic and ambitious normative project, but one that is likely to be beset by ambivalence from the outset. The debate about interference and the norm itself arise precisely on the fault line of these tectonics.

International law also paves the way to a somewhat dogmatic debate on the status of the norm of non-intervention or non-interference and whether the concept has an autonomous nature as a fundamental right of states independently of sovereignty itself.[469] That conversation has at least the merit of stressing that the debate over non-interference is nothing but a version of the general debate on the exact nature of sovereignty.[470] It has been argued,

---

466 See Quincy Wright, 'Subversive Intervention' (1960) 54 American Journal of International Law 521, 530. ('It may, indeed, be said that if a state is so inefficient, corrupt or naive in its administration that outside influences of this kind, unsupported by military threats or invasions, can destroy its independence, it ought not to claim the prerogatives of a sovereign state. However, there are many inexperienced states in existence, and if they are to enjoy peaceful co-existence they must be protected by international law against subversive intervention').

467 Louis Henkin, *International Law: Politics and Values* (Brill Nijhoff 1995) 109.

468 ibid.

469 Stephen C Neff, 'The Dormancy, Rise and Decline of Fundamental Liberties of States' (2015) 4 Cambridge International Law Journal 482, 496–497.

470 Aloupi (n 411).

drawing on the Friendly Relations Declaration's mention of an 'inalienable right' that the *domaine réservé* should be treated as a fundamental right of states rather than merely a residual notion describing what states have not committed to international law.[471] The suggestion is that there are 'decisions so fundamental to a state's character that a state cannot relinquish them under international law'.[472] This can be seen as part of a late (anachronistic?) rekindling of interest in the idea of fundamental rights of states and its notion of an antecedent, irreducible domain ascertainable at will.[473] It would protect states' sovereignty against themselves as it were that is, even if they had compromised some of it through international commitments.

This process of sanctification of sovereignty has been a recurring move, from Latin American states in the first half of the 20th Century[474] to the decolonizing world in the second, all the way to being, unsuccessfully, on the agenda of the United Nations.[475] But the notion, which was already contested at the time as a bit of a misnomer and as underestimating the indebtedness of sovereignty to international law,[476] is hard to square with both the voluntarism and the aspiration to social life of international law. As to the former, the fact that states may *want* to relinquish part of their sovereignty and that the ability to do so is presumably entailed in sovereignty itself suggests that it would be difficult to oppose the 'fundamental rights of states' against the manifest willingness of states in another direction. As to the latter, the assertion of an imperious *domaine réservé* simply sits oddly with the reality that '[o]nce States have recognized each other's existence; have adjusted themselves to the necessity of intercourse; and have acknowledged mutual rights and obligations, they have ceased to be truly independent'.[477] Insisting on some residual and actionable uber-*domaine réservé*, for all the notion's rhetorical appeal as a 'textual package of protest or resistance', does not herald the promise of any significant theoretical innovation,[478] could hold international law hostage to wholly capricious

471 Yue Wu (n 18) s III. A.
472 ibid 274.
473 Daniel H Joyner and Marco Roscini, 'Is There Any Room for the Doctrine of Fundamental Rights of States in Today's International Law?' (2015) 4 Cambridge International Law Journal 467.
474 Alejandro Alvarez, 'The State's Right of Self-Preservation' (1919) 3 St Louis Law Review 113.
475 U.N. Secretary-General, 'Preparatory Study Concerning a Draft Declaration on the Rights and Duties of States' (15 December 1948) U.N. Doc A/CN.4/2, 1948.
476 Philip Marshall Brown, 'The Rights of States under International Law' (1916) 26 The Yale Law Journal 85.
477 ibid 88.
478 Jean d'Aspremont, 'The Doctrine of Fundamental Rights of States and Anthropomorphic Thinking in International Law' (2015) 4 Cambridge International Law Journal 501.

reassertions of sovereignty, and does not add anything to the primary rule of non-intervention.

Although the rule of non-intervention is certainly a cardinal and constitutive one, and although some neighboring concepts such as self-determination have been found to have *jus cogens* and *opinio juris* status, it is also doubtful that this is the case of non-intervention. Two states could, however improbably, clearly decide to 'lower the guard' between themselves and facilitate interference in each other's affairs to a greater degree than otherwise contemplated if they wanted to (arguably, this is in fact the basis of much regional organization); and third states are unlikely to be justified in intervening to complain of the interference suffered by another state on account of the notion that non-interference is owed to all (this could appear to be in itself a form of interference; after all, surely it is the prerogative of the state primarily concerned to *not* complain of interference). This decisively sets up the status of the non-interference as occupying a somewhat intermediary status: central, important, and constitutive but also non-imperative, negotiable, and open ended.

This is reflected in the relatively contrived and long-running parallel debate about whether to include intervention in a Code of Crimes against the Peace and Security of Mankind, one which highlighted the profoundly political character of that debate. Intervention featured in Special Rapporteur Doudou Thiam's annual reports to the ILC for a decade, and was supported by various Third World and non-aligned international lawyers who:

> expressed the view that blatant acts of intervention were still a contemporary fact of life, often with the express or thinly disguised aim of destabilizing States in complete disregard of the massive suffering of the populations of the targeted States, and that concerns regarding the lack of precision required by criminal law missed the point that there had been hardly any other acts in the history of mankind which had caused so much misery to millions of underprivileged people and which were almost universally acknowledged to be crimes.[479]

By the mid-1990s, however, the winds had changed and Western international lawyers had begun to significantly push back against its inclusion specifically as a crime, notwithstanding its undoubted status as a norm of international law. As the ILC noted:

---

479 Report of the International Law Commission on the work of its forty-seventh session, 2 May–21 July 1995, Official Records of the General Assembly, Fiftieth session, Supplement No.10, para. 76.

> There was general agreement as to the importance of non-intervention as a fundamental principle of contemporary international law recognized in various international instruments [...] However, the view was also expressed that the principle was of limited scope, owing in particular to the decline in the number of situations qualifying as internal affairs and to the emergence of situations, affecting human rights in particular, in which the internal jurisdiction exception was unwarranted. Some members favoured the Special Rapporteur's proposed deletion of article 17 because of the nebulous character of the underlying concept and lack of rigour required by criminal law.[480]

More usefully, international law might help understand whether every interference or only some instances are illegal, for example outlining cases where a state does not engage its responsibility because acts that might otherwise constitute unlawful intervention or interference are in fact precluded from being illegal by the invocation of self-defence or as lawful countermeasures in response to an international wrongful act, or as the implementation of international sanctions decided by the United Nations. In such circumstances, the strong association between the otherwise interfering act and the invocation of international law trumps any potential finding of illegality. That is, so long as measures to implement sanctions do not exceed their mandate, or countermeasures do not end up violating human rights, for example. Evidently, the use of force in self-help is broadly prohibited, but the use of non-forcible coercion may be permissible in response to unlawful behavior by other states. But the situation of unilateral sanctions that are not directly implementing a Security Council resolution,[481] let alone some recognized international normative objective, is also dubious.

International law may also assist in helping outline a regime applicable to violations of the rule of non-intervention. That regime is by and large shaped by the secondary rules of state responsibility, which occasionally gesture if not at intervention per se, at least at coercion. For example, the ILC Articles on Responsibility of States for Internationally Wrongful Acts exclude responsibility where a State has consented to a wrongful act, except where consent was not 'freely given' or is 'vitiated by [...] coercion'.[482] Moreover, a number of

480 Ibid, para. 75.

481 Alexandra Hofer, 'The "Curiouser and Curiouser" Legal Nature of Non-UN Sanctions: The Case of the U.S. Sanctions against Russia' (2018) 23 Journal of Conflict & Security Law 75.

482 ILC 'Draft Articles on Responsibility of States for Internationally Wrongful Acts—With Commentaries' (2001) Yearbook of the ILC, vol 2, Part 2, 73.

specific consequences of intervention can be detected. This is notably the case in relation to treaty law and the negotiation process of the Vienna Convention. There, Article 52's prohibition of coercion of state representatives through acts or threats leads to the conclusion that 'a consent so obtained must be treated as absolutely void in order to ensure that the victim of the coercion should afterwards be in a position freely to determine its future relations with the State which coerced it'.[483] In other words, intervention sometimes appears indirectly as a function of other discursive investments rather than the central object of attention.

At the same time, Article 52 was felt by many non-aligned states to not go far enough and, in the face of deadlock at the Vienna conference, a 'Declaration on the Prohibition of Military, Political or Economic Coercion' was adopted and appended to the Convention.[484] That Declaration catered to long-held Third World misgivings about unequal treaties and gunboat diplomacy,[485] in the face of much Western opposition based on the importance of the stability of treaties. The former insisted that various forms of economic pressure might well invalidate treaties, whereas the latter considered that only a use of force in violation of the U.N. Charter would. Notwithstanding that dichotomy, the invalidity of agreements on the basis of the use of force or coercion has been invoked by Western commentators, for example in relation to the U.S.-Iran Hostage Settlement Agreement.[486] Moreover, article 52 has sometimes been criticized for defining coercion too narrowly, in a context where economic and political pressures, when reaching a certain threshold, ought to be taken seriously as causes of nullity of treaties.[487]

International law, more subtly, helps crystallize understandings of what is potentially *wrong* about interference, evolving as that sentiment may be. Interference was reviled in the era of decolonization because it suggested the continuity of age-old patterns of meddling in the affairs of the Third World, denial of its newfound sovereignty, and racism. Indeed, as already mentioned,

483 ILC 'Draft Articles on the Law of Treaties with Commentaries' (1966) *Yearbook of the ILC*, vol 2, 239, para 5.

484 Frédéric Mégret, 'Declaration on the Prohibition of Military, Political or Economic Coercion in the Conclusion of Treaties' in Olivier Corten and Pierre Klein (eds), *The Vienna Conventions on the Law of Treaties: A Commentary*, vol 2 (Oxford University Press 2011).

485 Stuart S Malawer, *Imposed Treaties and International Law* (William S Hein & Co 1977).

486 James Redwine, 'The Effect of Duress on the Iranian Hostage Settlement Agreement' (1981) 14 Vanderbilt Journal of Transnational Law 847.

487 Guilherme Del Negro, 'The Validity of Treaties Concluded under Coercion of the State: Sketching a TWAIL Critique' (2017) 10 European Journal of Legal Studies 39.

Western states not only claimed that intervention, including by force, was legal but that it was a *right*. In condemning the U.K.'s sweep for mines in Albanian territorial waters in the Corfu Channel case, the ICJ found, by contrast, that 'the alleged right of intervention as the manifestation of a policy of force, such as has, in the past, given rise to most serious abuses and such as cannot, whatever be the present defects in international organization, find a place in international law'. Specifically, it would in many cases, 'from the nature of things, [...] be reserved for the most powerful States', a non-starter for an international law based on equality.[488] Intervention, then, was associated with the strong-arming tactics of the powerful, where non-intervention sought to protect a vision of sovereigns as equals. Even as the use of force has been condemned on its own grounds, the fact that every use of force continues to be, in addition, an unwanted intervention in domestic affairs, provides an extra layer of understanding of what is wrong with such instances.[489] To this day, moreover, intervention and interference are frowned upon on their own terms even if they do not entail a use of force. In their simplest form, they manifest a type of arrogance that inflicts an indignity on the receiver, regardless of its intent or manifestations.[490]

The footing for condemning interference, particularly of the new kind, is less clear, perhaps because the nature of that interference is itself less clear. Note that the new interference is almost by definition less steeped in arrogance: it at least does not claim to some higher wisdom and its largely covert character seems incompatible with civilizational posturing. What is striking is nonetheless the abundance of rhetorical moves that point to the new interference's toxic character. An explicit link is sometimes drawn between interference and insecurity, with interference frequently described as a form of 'hybrid warfare'. Russia for example has been taken to task for its 'disinformation of an unparalleled malice and magnitude across both traditional media outlets and social media platforms, in order to deceive its citizens at home and the international community on the eve of and during its war of aggression against Ukraine [...] proving that even information can be weaponised'.[491] There is a growing tendency to frame interference as potentially a threat to international

488 *Corfu Channel Case (United Kingdom of Great Britain and Northern Ireland v Albania) (Merits)* [1949] ICJ Rep 4 [35].

489 On the negative incidence of aggression for sovereignty and self-determination, see Frédéric Mégret, 'What Is the Specific Evil of Aggression?' in Claus Kress and Stefan Barriga (eds), *The Crime of Aggression: A Commentary* (Cambridge University Press 2016).

490 Yue Wu (n 18) s II. B.

491 2022 Resolution on Foreign Interference in the E.U. (n 337), para C.

peace and security[492] or to the 'rules-based international order'.[493] As an extension of that language of threats, the European Parliament speaks of 'information manipulation and the spread of disinformation' as 'creat[ing] economic dependencies that can be exploited for political aims' and as 'a prime tool for destabilising and weakening targeted counterparts, or boosting one's own competitive advantage through the establishment of channels of influence, supply chain dependencies, blackmail or coercion', thus 'causing direct and indirect economic damage that has not been systematically assessed'.[494]

It is worth nothing how vague and scattered some of these assertions are, even as they point to strongly felt sentiments. In many ways, their formulation replicates, unwittingly or at least not self-reflexively, the language that Global South states have long used to complain about interference in their own affairs. One constant may be a shift away from a concern with interference as affecting external political independence to one with interference as affecting the very operation of the state, notably the democratic state, and in very intimate ways. The gravity of interference has been presented by the European Union for example as the fact that it is 'threatening the political stability and integrity of the E.U. and its Member States' in ways that warrant creating specific European sanctions.[495] Transparency International has argued that the line between interference in domestic affairs and straightforward corruption is a thin one.[496] The G7 has framed 'malign behavior and hostile

492 Samuel Jarvis, 'The R2P and Atrocity Prevention: Contesting Human Rights as a Threat to International Peace and Security' (2023) 8 European Journal of International Security 243, 246–247 and Supplementary Materials; Camino Kavanagh, 'The United Nations, Cyberspace and International Peace and Security: Responding to Complexity in the 21st Century' (UNIDIR 2017) 25 <https://unidir.org/files/publication/pdfs/the-united-nations-cyberspace-and-international-peace-and-security-en-691.pdf> accessed 27 January 2024. See also, 2021 National Security Strategy (Russia) ('the use of information-communication technologies for interference in the internal affairs of states […] poses a threat to international peace and security') cited in Samuel Charap and Reinhard Krumm (eds), *Proposals to Address Political Interference: Outcomes of a Trilateral Dialogue* (RAND 2023) 16.

493 'Foreign Ministers Communiqué' (G7 Foreign Ministers Meetings, Saint Malo, France, 6 April 2019).

494 2022 Resolution on Foreign Interference in the E.U. (n 337), para H.

495 Kate Jones, 'Legal Loopholes and the Risk of Foreign Interference' (European Union 2023) PE 702.575, 14.

496 Lucas Amin and José María Marín, 'Recommendation on Political Financing for OGP Action Plans' (Transparency International 2020) <https://www.transparency.org/files/content/activity/Rec_on_Political_Integrity_for_OGP_action_plans_-_FINAL.pdf> accessed 1 March 2024.

interference by state and non-state actors' that seek to create "chaos" as a threat to democracy'.[497]

Most remarkably, the new interference has also tended to be reframed on the basis of its negative impact on human rights. The European Parliament largely eschews the traditional vernacular of interference in sovereign affairs as a violation of sovereignty when it claims that 'foreign interference constitutes a serious violation of the universal values and principles on which the Union is founded, such as human dignity, freedom, equality, solidarity, respect for human rights and fundamental freedoms, democracy and the rule of law'.[498] There has also been a discrete awakening of interest in how interference may constitute a violation of the human rights of a population by the state interfering:[499] aside from the question of the extra-territorial application of human rights, the question is which rights exactly are violated as a result of interference.

It stands to reason that the inter-state vernacular of interference can be translated into that of human rights by emphasizing, for example, self-determination but also privacy, freedom of thought, freedom of access to information, political rights including the right to genuine elections, etc.[500] This reframing is notable for how it solicits the language of rights very much against the grain of its more traditional use to justify forms of interference. But it has echoes of a certain tradition, typically championed by the Third World, that draws a strong connection between self-determination, possibly popular democracy, and a rights culture. In other words, the shift from a mere concern with sovereignty to a concern with how interference affects human rights is part and parcel of a more general attempt to reframe international law in the service of the rights project,[501] even as it is of course not free from the ambiguities of such a project.

At any rate, as we will see, these rationalizations of what is wrong about interference are not always compatible, even though they can be deployed

497 'Foreign Ministers Communiqué' (n 493).

498 2022 Resolution on Foreign Interference in the E.U. (n 337), para A.

499 Ido Kilovaty, 'Cybersecurity Abroad: Election Interference and the Extraterritoriality of Human Rights Treaty ObligationsIdo Kilovaty' in Jens David Ohlin and Duncan B Hollis (eds), *Defending Democracies: Combating Foreign Election Interference in a Digital Age* (Oxford University Press 2021).

500 For an analysis of the rights violated, in particular, by election interference, see Jacqueline Van De Velde, 'The Dangers of Forceful Countermeasures as a Response to Cyber Election Interference: Jacqueline Van De Velde' in Jens David Ohlin and Duncan B Hollis (eds), *Defending Democracies: Combating Foreign Election Interference in a Digital Age* (Oxford University Press 2021) 223–224.

501 Trindade (n 181).

by the same actors in different circumstances. What these framings of interference do is act as a sort of 'call to arms' to states (or regional organisations speaking in their name like the E.U.) that seek to protect themselves, outlining a specific role for international cooperation in guarding against interference. For example, the European Parliament has insisted that 'it is the duty of the E.U. and its Member States to defend all citizens and infrastructure, as well as their democratic systems' to develop a better ability to 'prevent, detect, attribute, counter and sanction' interference.[502] In that respect, if nothing else, interference provides powerful opportunities for states to (re)*perform* their sovereignty against external threats, even outside any actual situation of war, in line for example with increasingly dramatic policing of physical borders against migrants. Against that background, the question of definition is the site of a sort of perpetual return, which alternates between grand but abstract principles (sovereignty, self-determination, equality, independence, and non-intervention) and more fractured efforts to pin down the notion in particular contexts.

It remains that the continued production of meaning around the norm of non-interference can be seen as powerfully shaped by at least three dynamics. First, the dynamics of asymmetry. It is not only that some states interfere in the affairs of others more than others and that 'the principle of non-intervention had a special importance for the smaller countries and particularly those which had emerged from colonial domination';[503] it is also that the very ability to define what constitutes interference in the first place is heavily guarded, and that some states have, over time, had the upper-hand over its formulation. The Third and non-aligned worlds have exerted a considerable influence on the definition of what constitutes interference, in large part due to sheer numerical superiority. In that respect, it is certainly true that the norm is 'the favourite norm of the weak and the small' given both their vested interest in its development and their ability to muster majorities in, inter alia, the General Assembly.[504] But the West's role, either historically as normalizing interference in the affairs of others, or resisting calls to define it further, or more recently attempting to exceptionalize interference in its own affairs, has also been considerable. And what it has not contributed in terms of normative entrepreneurialism it has sometimes more than compensated for through sheer inertia.

Second, the dynamics of contestation. One should be alert to how asymmetries structure the ability of some states to contest the interference of which

502 2022 Resolution on Foreign Interference in the E.U. (n 337), para L.

503 McWhinney (n 33) 23.

504 Henkin, *International Law* (n 467) 110.

they are targets, an exercise that remains more fraught than may appear at first. States that are in a situation of dependency vis-à-vis others are relatively less likely to want to 'stir the pot' and endanger whatever ongoing and valuable relationship they may have with the interfering state. This is why the debate between African and Caribbean states and the European Union about human rights conditionality has been so fraught. Moreover, even as non-interference is seen as a precondition of friendly relations between states, making claims that another state is interfering in one's affairs may appear hostile. Some states, therefore, have opted to be quite diplomatic about how they assess interference, at the expense of some consistency in their position and therefore of clarity for international law. At any rate, the 'state' is a fiction—and while it is fair to assume that states may, all other things being equal, be intent on promoting strong non-interference norms towards themselves, they may be internally divided as to how problematic interference really is, and the extent to which it is worth a diplomatic crisis in any given circumstance.

Third, the dynamics of reciprocity. To the extent that a norm of non-interference develops over time, this process remains uniquely dependent on and reactive to the reciprocal demands of international relations and how they shape the making of international law. In principle, there is no more compelling notion than the idea that one should not interfere any more than one is willing to be interfered with. As Quincy Wright once put it, '[i]nternational law cannot protect the new states of Asia and Africa from subversive intervention by Communist states without protecting the Communist states of Eastern Europe from subversive intervention by democratic states of the West'.[505] Certainly, states that are blatant about their interference in the affairs of other states will be in a weak position to protest interference in theirs. Note that this is not a point about the ethics of international law or a condemnation of hypocrisy per se (although hypocrisy there is, and it is condemnable separately). Rather, it points to the underlying normative basis of complying with any norm of international law understood as a form of stylized cooperation and how reciprocity structures the very legal character of norms.

Reciprocity when it comes to non-interference, is not the clearly outlined 'specific reciprocity' of states exchanging, as it were, a similar degree of 'non-interference' or 'interference', an idea that would be clearly nonsensical; rather it is, at best, the 'diffuse reciprocity' characteristic of 'generally accepted standards of behavior' for which Robert Keohane has argued 'the definition of equivalence is less precise, one's partners may be viewed as a group rather than as

505 Wright, 'Subversive Intervention' (n 466) 531.

particular actors, and the sequence of events is less narrowly bounded'.[506] Such diffuse reciprocity is highly vulnerable to misunderstandings in a context where, if nothing else, reciprocity requires a certain visibility about what one is being reciprocal about. Non-reciprocity can be carefully nurtured over time, albeit in inherently unstable ways. The potential and limits of defining interference as part of these dynamics also points to some classic limitations of cooperation as a basis for international law: rules about non-interference should exist regardless of whether each side 'keeps its side of the bargain'. One cannot exclude that over time some states have much more to lose than others from the indecisive state in which the law of non-interference is left in.

Yet ultimately, even though some states stand to gain more in the 'game' of interference (typically because their ability to interfere usefully with others is greater than other state's ability to interfere with them), all states simultaneously have a presumptive shared interest in an effective norm of non-interference that solidifies their authority and existence. Indeed, in the kind of iterative conditions that characterize contemporary international relations, a 'one-time opportunistic gain' obtained by interfering in the affairs of another state may not be worth a future of non-cooperation multiplying the structural risks of interference.[507] Conditions where most states can interfere with other states most of the time (and not only big powers) may bring to the fore both more fraught and, paradoxically, productive conditions. The fact that interference has increasingly been brought to the heart of the hegemon, that its influence is felt where it was not typically felt before, might ultimately herald a reinforcement of the norm. The asymmetry of actual interference always led to an asymmetry of normative efforts at defining it, whereas an interference that is felt everywhere might precipitate a more unanimous and equanimous response.[508]

Ultimately, the *social* rather than merely reciprocal character of such obligations (to the extent that one does not interfere, it is not for anyone's *particular* benefit, but on account of collective values) casts them as involving something more than a rough haggling ('I will not interfere with you, if you do not interfere with me'). Circumscribing non-interference requires that one take seriously its principled justification as well as its positive law validity and not simply its nature as a transactional good. In that respect, the constraint of

506 Robert O Keohane, 'Reciprocity in International Relations' (1986) 40 International Organization 1, 5.

507 Andrew T Guzman, *How International Law Works: A Rational Choice Theory* (Oxford University Press 2008) 42.

508 Such is, at least, the guarded optimism of some authors. See Ossoff (n 341) 296.

the discourse of legal justification is that one cannot simply invoke an interpretation 'because it maximises one's interest', even if that is the reason why one actually invokes it. Nor is invoking reciprocity the way game theorists do is a substitute for engaging the interpretative riddles that are the bane of international lawyers, and that refocus the debate on *normative* rather than merely rational interest considerations—thus resisting the conflation of the two. The claim about non-interference (or valid interference) is ultimately at heart a normative claim that must be taken seriously as such.

This then suggests a vision of international law that does not rely on sovereigns simply 'seeing' their own deep interest through the thicket of artificial semantic controversies that they have themselves generated, but that takes those controversies seriously as entailing discursive commitments to norms. The content of the non-interference norm stands to be specified over time through its repeated exposure to real world circumstances that require legal agents to articulate claims and counterclaims. This means that, to begin with, states must actually bother to make a normative case (as opposed to expecting the case to 'make itself' through the automatic operation of interest coordination or interpretative reasoning); second, they must do so from a standpoint that is systemic rather than merely agent-based, stylistically at least taking into account the interests of the system of international law; third, they must produce rules not merely for the contingent circumstances of the present, but that they are willing to live with over time, in the sure knowledge that their words may well come back to haunt them.

It is worth stressing here that one of the major underlying debates about interference concerns the label under which it fits. The traditional understanding sees the rule of non-intervention as quite a capacious 'cluster of normative regulations, including both the general principle and a set of sub-principles, rules and institutions, which prohibit intervention of different kinds in various concrete circumstances'.[509] In that perspective, non-intervention is the master-concept, and a range of factual practices can eventually be subsumed under it. The clearest normative commitment certainly concerns the prohibition of non-intervention as such, where interference is often merely seen as the factual predicate to violate that norm. In this view, interference and intervention overlap only partly: all intervention involves de facto some kind of interference, but not all interference strictly violates the rule of non-intervention. Interference exists in a grey zone, somewhat below actual prohibited intervention: neither

509 Yifeng (n 2) 319.

particularly encouraged, nor particularly stigmatized, but not unmistakably illegal.

But from a socio-legal perspective at least, starting from intervention to try and analyze interference may be a case of trying to fit a square peg in a round hole. Intervention has a deliberate and intentional connotation that points to an era of direct meddling on the territory of foreign states by big powers. This is evident in use of the term 'armed intervention', albeit presumably only one particularly troublesome modality thereof, which describes various types of military attack launched against states' territory. Intervention, as we will see, also crucially foregrounds the notion of 'coercion' which may turn out to be a particularly awkward fit for the 'new interference', given that in that last case the target state is not most meaningfully described as being coerced. Interference refers to the encroachment on a state's 'affairs' and its 'independence' in ways that are not necessarily territorial and not necessarily or usefully understood as coercive. To speak of interference as if it were merely an instance of intervention, then, can create confusion and promote an excessively narrow approach to the problem at hand. In many ways, the debate is not just to define intervention and interference separately but to define them jointly and in relation to each other.

3 The Distinctiveness of Interference

One of the contributions of this chapter, in line with the broader objectives of the book, will be that interference is arguably not simply a way of committing intervention but has long, if ambiguously, been prohibited or at least legally frowned upon in its own right alongside intervention. Thus, although part of the literature understandably continues to take the prohibition of non-intervention and its emphasis on coercion as its systematic reference point, non-interference has long discretely coexisted as a distinct norm of international law of somewhat uncertain status. It may be, in fact, that thinking productively about interference offers an opportunity to enrich our register beyond dichotomous appeals to legality or illegality, perhaps along the lines of certain behavior being more or less legal. The point of such an approach is not to only identify violations stricto sensu but to delineate areas that are troubling for international law, that warrant a response of some sort, and that suggest ways in which states may legally respond. This sort of modified Lotus approach implies that just because something is not always or unambiguously prohibited in international law, does not necessarily mean that it is never problematic and that anything goes in terms of the exercise of sovereign powers.

There is much anecdotal evidence of the seriousness with which interference has long been taken as a feature of international relations that ought to be a concern for international law. The tipping point seems to have been when intervention, with all its explicit and brute force, ceased to be the only and dominant concern among international lawyers. Paradoxically, this opened new vistas for taking seriously something that was not quite intervention but still more than an ordinary violation of sovereignty. Particularly in the post-colonial moment, blatant repression of the sovereignty of newly independent states sometimes gave way to much more subtle forms of corrupting intrusion that required new vocabularies. The Third World was certainly not blind to this new dimension and did much to put it at the forefront of the international legal agenda, much to the chagrin of the West which typically argued that it unduly expanded the category of intervention to issues that had little relation to its core. In due course, the West, which had long militated for a watertight distinction between 'prohibited intervention' and 'mere interference' has sought to in turn water down that distinction in an effort to appraise the 'new interference' in the moment it was most affected by it.

To wit: whilst the 1965 Declaration on the Inadmissibility of Intervention condemned the use of force, intervention, and coercion in no uncertain terms, it also underlined the right of all states to exercise their right of self-determination 'without any foreign pressure';[510] the 1970 Declaration on Friendly Relations finds that not only 'armed intervention' but 'all other forms of interference [...] are in violation of international law';[511] the 1981 Declaration on the Inadmissibility of Intervention *and* Interference,[512] albeit not the most consensual international instrument on the issue (22 Western states opposed it), makes it very clear that the two are considered to be distinct notions, or at least distinct facets of the same overarching principle. Aside from intervention, the latter specifically targets 'direct or indirect forms of interference threatening the sovereign personality and the independence of states' and underscores '[t]he duty of a State to refrain from any action or attempt in whatever form or under whatever pretext to destabilize or to undermine the stability of another State or of any of its institutions'.[513] It is also worth noting that in the African Union[514] or

510 1965 Declaration on the Inadmissibility of Intervention, para 6.

511 1970 Declaration on Friendly Relations, 123.

512 1981 Declaration on the Inadmissibility of Intervention and Interference.

513 ibid, s 2 (e).

514 Organization of African Unity, Constitutive Act of the African Union (adopted 1 July 2000, entered into force 26 May 2001) 2158 UNTS 3 (AU Constitutive Act), art 4 (g).

ASEAN[515] contexts, it is specifically and routinely interference as much if not more than intervention that is condemned.

Scholarly treatment of the question also suggests that, for some jurisconsults, at least there is both a norm of non-intervention and a norm of non-interference.[516] Oppenheim, himself a defender of the notion that '[i]nterference pure and simple is not intervention', nonetheless recognized that the 1970 Declaration on Friendly Relations 'appears to prescribe a less rigorous standard' by prohibiting interference as such.[517] Quincy Wright once detailed the existence of a rule prohibiting 'subversive intervention', describing it in terms that suggested he had something strikingly different in mind than intervention resembling interference.[518] Moreover, states do complain more generally about interference as well as intervention in ways that suggest that they find the former legally problematic, even if for separate reasons. In fact, the focus on intervention reflects a historical bias that has tended to either take coercion as the be-all and end-all of interference, in ways that have dubiously erased much more complex international legacies of interference. As David Gerber put it:

> Because the course of international relations during the past century and a half has focused attention on the use of the non-interference principle almost exclusively in the context of coercion, many have assumed this is the only context in which it is properly applied. In fact, the concept has been used primarily to distinguish between legitimate exercises of

515 Charter of the Association of Southeast Asian Nations (adopted 20 November 2007, entered into force 15 December 2008) 2624 UNTS 223 (ASEAN Charter), art 2.

516 Indeed, much of the secondary literature, routinely talks of both the principles of non-intervention *and* non-interference. Xuan W Tay, 'Reconstructing the Principle of Non-Intervention and Non-Interference-Electoral Disinformation, Nicaragua, and the Quilt-Work Approach' (2022) 40 Berkeley Journal of International Law 39; Kioko (n 267); Miwa Hirono, Yang Jiang and Marc Lanteigne, 'China's New Roles and Behaviour in Conflict-Affected Regions: Reconsidering Non-Interference and Non-Intervention' (2019) 239 The China Quarterly 573; Eric Corthay, 'The ASEAN Doctrine of Non-Interference in Light of the Fundamental Principle of Non-Intervention' (2015) 17 Asian-Pacific Law & Policy Journal 1; Aloupi (n 411). Occasionally, the literature *only* refers to the principle of non-interference. Momir Milojevic, 'The Principle of Non-Interference in the Internal Affairs of States' (1997) 1 Facta Universitatis, Series: Law and Politics 427.

517 Jennings and Watts (n 397) 432.

518 Wright, 'Subversive Intervention' (n 466) 530. ('[U]tilizing radio waves and other forms of communication, infiltrating into the government and political organizations, and directing minority parties committed to their doctrines, to influence the domestic politics of a state in such a way that a small minority can gain control of the government contrary to the wishes of most of the population').

> influence by one state over another state and unlawful coercion of one state by another.[519]

But the relative hyper-visibility of coercion has obscured concerns that have emerged with a vengeance in the last decades, from expansive assertions of jurisdiction to infrastructural domination or hybrid information operations, i.e. precisely those concerns associated with the 'new interference'.

In short, there is at least some uncertainty as to whether there is a single rule of non-intervention—possibly quite capacious and erring towards the inclusion of practices of interference—or whether that rule has not, perhaps for a long time, been complemented by a distinct rule of non-interference, minimized only as a result of the persistent biases of Western infused international legal scholarship. The possible existence of such a parallel rule of non-interference might be decried, a little gratuitously, as a manifestation of the 'tendency to dilute the principle of non-intervention by Latin American and Afro-Asian States [...] aimed at rendering illegal conduct and actions which fall within the normal activity of foreign relations'.[520] It is true that, a recurring refrain in the literature is to the effect that the broader a norm of interference, the more likely it is to be violated all the time, raising questions about both its pedigree, character and relevance. Maybe non-interference is better consigned to the realm of political or ethical principles that structure international relations over time—a social norm, no doubt, but one lacking the compelling legal character of the rule of non-intervention. Much of the resistance to taking interference seriously under international law is framed in this way, as based on the need to keep registers apart and thus not collapse the discursive economy of international law.

However, one would have to recognize that such structured iteration, including disagreement but gradual honing in on proscribed behavior, is precisely the stuff that, over time, customary norms are made of. The reality is that states in the Global South have long felt that the non-intervention rule, in its classical formulation, was too narrow and that they have expressed this sensitivity in unmistakably legal terms. The dilution concern when it comes to intervention can, in fact, be minimized if one sees the prohibition of interference as a distinct (albeit closely related) norm under international law. Rather than watering down intervention, highlighting a distinct rule of non-interference has the opposite effect: it creates space for two, distinct yet complementary norms,

---

519 David J Gerber, 'Beyond Balancing: International Law Restraints on the Reach of National Laws' (1984) 10 Yale Journal of International Law 185, 211.

520 Ronzitti (n 115) 4.

with separate rationales and scope. At any rate, resistance to the emergence of a distinct norm of interference cannot be entirely dependent on concerns with watering down the norm, if such be the concerted intention of a significant number of states.

Interference short of intervention may not be as grave but it is undoubtedly a motif of storied and distinct concern that should be taken for what it is, not least in the context of renewed anxieties associated with the new interference. It points if nothing else to the fact that interference violates the *sovereignty* of the state that is being interfered with even if not quite in 'intervening' ways. Indeed, the prohibition of interference may not require a specific rule: one may be able to chalk it up to the principle of sovereignty and the way it has long been understood to operate as a primary rule in itself. Despite some occasional misgivings in that respect, the notion that cyber-interference for example, if nothing else violates the target state's sovereignty[521] should be assessed as part of a much more expansive register of interference (through campaign funding, diaspora mediation, economic coercion, etc.).

Of course, that a rule of non-interference exists side by side with the rule of non-intervention makes it no less difficult to pin down, but difficulty in ascertaining a definition is not per se an argument that a rule does not exist. What the agitation around interference does point to is the existence of a range of concerns that are not captured by either a minimalist emphasis on violations of sovereignty or a maximalist emphasis on coercion (let alone of a use of force). The proper scope of these concerns is hard to ascertain in the abstract, but they have long included, for example, more symbolic forms of interference in a state's sovereign affairs that give a good intuitive idea of what is involved. These give a taste of the sort of fundamental sleight that is involved, and the degree to which it implicates nothing less than the very definition of sovereignty. Interference has less to do with coercion than it has to do with displacement, usurpation and a sense of not minding one's business.

For example, when Général de Gaulle famously told a crowd of Québecers 'vive le Québec libre!' upon his first visit to Canada, Ottawa correctly assessed that this was more than an offence to protocol—a genuine affront to Canada's sovereignty and interference therein.[522] There has rightly been 'diplomatic

521 Michael N Schmitt and Liis Vihul, 'Sovereignty in Cyberspace: Lex Lata Vel Non?' (2017) 111 AJIL Unbound 213; Michael Schmitt, 'In Defense of Sovereignty in Cyberspace' (*Just Security*, 8 May 2018) <https://www.justsecurity.org/55876/defense-sovereignty-cyberspace/> accessed 10 September 2023.

522 Jérémie Cornut, 'Les relations diplomatiques France-Canada-Québec 50 ans après "Vive le Québec Libre !"' (2017) 9 IdeAs.

protest when governments or high officers indulge in libelous or propagandistic utterances which would weaken or disrupt the internal order of a friendly state'.[523] Recently, an entire book by Paul Behrens was devoted to theorizing the delicate matter of 'diplomatic interference' as entailing such legally loaded *faux pas*.[524] And of course, the broad arc of concerns associated with the 'new interference' fall squarely within that *entre deux* of problematic if elusive international conduct that clearly implicates international legal principles even if not always clearly identified rules. Thus, as David Gerber puts it, '[t]he confusion relating to terminology and usage [...] should not be allowed to obscure the fundamental point that the legal principles relating to intervention, or coercive interference, are merely specific applications of the general principle of non-interference'.[525]

Perhaps tellingly, these debates highlight that definitions of interference are reliant on implicit assumptions about what is imagined to be the default state of the international system. These suggest that all concepts of intervention or non-intervention are indebted to broad political conceptions of the world,[526] even as those can be invoked at cross-purpose.[527] Under what one might describe as the particularly influential 'cosmopolitan' model of international law, the key descriptors of international relations are interdependence and integration, giving rise to a situation in which most states' affairs are imagined to already be other states' affairs, if only because most issues have become global. Under that view, the element of interference tends to be minimized, based on strong assumptions that it is going to be complicated and not particularly desirable to seek to highlight the odd interference that tips into illegality. For another, more communitarian or 'nationalist' model, by contrast, the key words are independence, self-determination, and pluralism. In that model, the default state of the international system is still very much imagined to be one of self-contained sovereigns keen on protecting their domestic sphere from outside incursions. On that view, otherwise anodyne forms of influence and meddling are relatively more likely to be seen as illicit forms of interference.

The point here is not that one can ascertain with any finality which model most corresponds to the reality of international affairs; merely that such

523 Wright, 'Subversive Intervention' (n 466) 532.

524 Behrens, *Diplomatic Interference and the Law* (n 112).

525 Gerber (n 519) 212.

526 Catherine Lu, 'Cosmopolitanism, Liberalism and Intervention' in Catherine Lu, *Just and Unjust Interventions in World Politics* (Palgrave Macmillan U.K. 2006).

527 Alexis Heraclides and Ada Dialla, *Humanitarian Intervention in the Long Nineteenth Century: Setting the Precedent* (Manchester University Press 2017).

models underscore the sort of mental work that goes into describing certain conduct as interference or not. Both models, moreover, comport a risk of 'leakage' in the categories of the other. For example, whilst 'cosmopolitan' and 'nationalist' models may be neat ideal-typical paradigms, the world is neither descriptively entirely cosmopolitan nor nationalist. For example, most 'strictly' domestic violence is, in fact, not strictly domestic, whether it has been largely determined by outside factors, or whether it stands to impact other states. The idea that crises in Myanmar, Sudan, Gaza or Ukraine are purely domestic matters is almost nonsensical as soon as other states are called upon to shoulder some of the burden—not even through any particular intrusiveness on their part—of other countries' woes, such as refugee flows, environmental harm or regional destabilization. In practice, then, the conversation about interference is a sort of echo chamber for underlying claims about the reality and ends of international society that often remain unacknowledged in international legal conversations.

On a more policy-oriented level, the struggle over the definition of interference/intervention involves a stylized push and shove between two competing temptations. On the one hand, to define interference too narrowly will risk depriving states of protections that their sovereignty arguably deserves; it will also expose the definitional exercise to the reproach that it is, for example, unduly Western-centric, highlighting only the most grotesque forms of intervention at the expense of its day-to-day reality as experienced by weaker nations. This formed the basis of long-standing efforts by the Third World to include all forms of coercion and indeed of interference in the definition of non-intervention beyond, notably, the exclusive focus on the use of force (or by encompassing intervention within the use of force). It points to an evident politics of the rarefication of the definition of intervention, one whose suspicious timing and sometimes blatant opportunism served a design of continued domination. Although the rarefication of intervention serves a clear structural purpose in terms of maintaining the integrity of an international norm, it also clear has its ideological provenance and uses.

On the other hand, to define intervention too broadly will the risk dilution and meaninglessness. As Roberto Cordova of Mexico cautioned during the ILC debates on a Draft Code of Crimes against the Peace and Security of Mankind: 'Any attempt to define such intervention [note: beyond the use of force] would be faced with such a host of state activities that the whole of international relations would be involved'.[528] For Hersch Lauterpacht, the risk

528 Yearbook of the ILC (1950) vol I, 160, para 54.

was also that 'perfectly legitimate and normal manifestations of international life [would] be regarded as offenses' in a context where such activity 'consisted to a large extent of economic and political measures taken by one State to exert pressure on another so as to influence its will'.[529] Such a danger is also visible, for example, in the recent move by the French defense ministry to define prohibited intervention in cyberspace by reference to the fact that it merely produces 'harm'[530] or China's view that what is problematic about interference is that it 'undermin[es] [its] political, economic and social stability'.[531] Similarly, it has been argued that outlawing any surveillance of host states by diplomats by drawing on the 'lawful means' caveat to their power under the Vienna Convention on Diplomatic and Consular Relations would 'negate the very function anticipated by the treaty'.[532] Only a narrow definition of non-intervention, in this view, preserves the unique stigma that surrounds it, avoids having a chilling effect on legitimate activity, and ensures that whatever extension of its meaning it captures are the object of strong condemnation.

Note also that definitions, from a policy perspective, are not merely taken at face value, but with an attention to their structural and symbolic ramifications. The move to a mere 'harm' model of intervention, for example, threatens to dilute the notion beyond repair in an international system where all too often the advantages of some at secured at the cost of disadvantages to others. An excessive focus on harm might then well produce a chilling effect on otherwise desirable and innocent interactions between states and, increasingly, societies. This was, at any rate, the consistent position of Western states during the negotiations of the Friendly Relations Declaration, raising as it did, in their view, the specter of deterring normal relations between states.[533] Note that the

529 Yearbook of the ILC (1954) vol I, 151, para 20.

530 'International Law Applied to Operations in Cyberspace' (French Ministry of Defense 2019) 7.

531 People's Republic of China, 'China's Submissions to the Open-Ended Working Group on Developments in the Field of Information and Telecommunications in the Context of International Security' (Open-Ended Working Group on Developments in the Field of Information and Telecommunications in the Context of International Security 2019) <https://front.un-arm.org/wp-content/uploads/2019/09/china-submissions-oewg-en.pdf> accessed 17 May 2024.

532 Craig Forcese, 'Spies without Borders: International Law and Intelligence Collection' (2011) 5 Journal of National Security Law & Policy 179, 200.

533 Report on Friendly Relations and Cooperation among States (1964) A/5746, para 205 (UK) ('in an interdependent world, it is inevitable and desirable that States will be concerned with and will seek to influence the actions and policies of other States, and that the objective of international law is not to prevent such activity but rather to ensure that it is compatible with the sovereign equality of States and self-determination of their peoples').

argument goes both ways. Diluting intervention might also, conceivably, not serve the agenda of weaker states well by undermining the unique status of the prohibition on the use of force and coercive intervention and creating further confusion among categories. 'Policy', even as harnessed to international law, hardly points to unequivocal means, let alone ends, that would guide the development of the definition of interference and its highlighting as a unique category in uncontentious directions separate from politics.

More doctrinally, then, the prohibition of non-interference/non-intervention in domestic affairs has long involved a sort of double-helix debate: first, what are *domestic affairs*? Second, what is *prohibited intervention*? This characterization is so massively accepted as to be unavoidable, although this part will argue that it is far from unproblematic. The issues are distinct but closely connected and at times the same result can be achieved through both routes (for example, human rights norms might be understood to entail that something is not within the *domaine* or that it is not prohibited). As Mohammed Helal has compellingly argued, the definition of intervention fundamentally anticipates, to begin with, the 'pursuit of unlawful ends through unlawful means'.[534] In some ways, resort to unlawful means is the most decisive because it refers to the 'doing' part of intervention (one cannot intervene unlawfully without doing *something*), but on its own it cannot constitute intervention. At the same time, if it is unlawful then it is presumably already illegal on its own *lex specialis* grounds so that characterizing it as intervention does not add much, except by specifying the status of that illegality. It is a priori only the pairing of unlawful means with the encroachment on protected domestic affairs that tips this illegal (but banal) behavior into the terrain of intervention/interference.

Still, as Helal warns, one should keep an open mind to the possibility that actions targeting the domestic affair of states but that are not separately illegal might nonetheless constitute a form of interference.[535] This argument had been anticipated by Eric David who argued that there was a compelling case that discretionary measures that were licit per se (for example, mere retorsion or diplomatic sanctions), could become illicit if not adopted in good faith or as an abuse of right.[536] In fact, this may be precisely the challenge of the new interference, namely that it involves behavior that is not evidently per se illegal but which, seen in its totality and with an attention both to its purpose and effects, has the consequence of displacing, destabilizing or usurping a target

534 Helal (n 408) 47.

535 Helal's work is full of references to such dilemmas. Helal (n 408).

536 Eric David, 'Portée et Limite Du Principe de Non-Intervention' (1990) 23 Revue Belge de Droit International / Belgian Review of International Law 350, 359–360.

state's sovereignty. One way to think of this is as operating on a sliding scale. Some behavior is already illegal on its face and therefore the threshold it needs to cross to be considered a form of intervention is relatively low. This is the case, evidently, of uses of force but also, in most cases, of forceful assistance to rebel groups which almost by nature already encroaches on the sovereign's monopoly of jurisdiction. At the other end of the spectrum, some behavior is so manifestly *not* illegal that notwithstanding the fact it intersects with the *domaine réservé* it cannot be constitutive of even a low-level form of interference and is better characterized as innocuous influence. This includes much diplomatic activity even if perceived as hostile or unhelpful, broad support for independent and impartial NGOs, etc.

In the rather spacious in-between, however, one finds modalities of action that are neither blatantly legal nor illegal but which may raise red flags as 'more or less legal' depending on their goal, characteristics and context. These include the full range of the old and new interference from financing of political parties and propaganda operations, to sophisticated cybercampaigns or pressures on the diaspora. What matters when evaluating the legality of such measures is not so much the measures themselves as their inscription in broader designs and combination with a range of measures. Such a more casuistic approach to intervention was arguably pioneered by Erid David who emphasized that, particularly in the harder cases of non-coercive interference, what is needed is a very fine-tuned attention to how certain policies may or may not cross the threshold into inference. For example, welcoming exiled dissidents on one's territory is not interference even as arming them is, but the *entre deux* (allowing them to engage in hostile propaganda towards their state of origin) is a more undecided question.[537] Moreover, that analysis must per necessity depend on the *lex specialis* involved (use of force, economic sanctions, diplomatic relations, etc.) and a careful pondering of how it is being specifically disrupted by particular measures.

This is also the approach recommended by Giuseppe Puma in relation to Venezuela, for example. According to that author's very sound methodology, the problem is not merely Western sanctions as such which, under one reading at least, can be seen as broadly discretionary. The issue is that these sanctions come to amplify an already unlawful and misplaced recognition of a politician who does not effectively govern Venezuela. Hence what is needed is to assess 'the unlawfulness of the context as a whole' and even to treat that sequence as a wrongful act 'of a composite nature' in the sense of Article 15 of the ILC

537 ibid 356.

Draft on State Responsibility.[538] A mechanistic emphasis on the traditional elements of coercion, dutifully but automatically weighing said elements separately, cannot replace a more holistic attention to what is effectively happening to the sovereignty of a target state in any given case. It risks being tone deaf to the political undertones of both protestations of innocence that there has been interference and the ruffled feathers of a sovereignty denied. The stakes of the new interference demand that international lawyers elevate their game in terms of a multi-pronged analysis of concurrent factors of disruption, even if this sort of analysis by *faisceau d'indices* does not always come to them naturally.

Still, for what it is worth, it will serve international lawyers' purpose well to analyze both whether something falls within in the *domaine* and whether measure complained of encroaches upon it separately. The emphasis on defining domestic affairs seeks to delimit the frontiers of what are internal matters properly so-called, and what matters belong to the international realm. This then requires an assessment of what it actually takes to encroach on that, already separately defined, *domaine réservé*. Despite this theoretical distinction, the notions tend to constantly be interpreted in relation to each other[539] so that the debate often adopts a slightly circuitous quality: an interference is illegal if it interferes with something with which it should not interfere. Moreover, the definition of what it takes to encroach on the *domaine réservé* (coercion, manipulation, substitution, etc.) retro-acts on what intervention is imagined to intervene with, highlighting some prior-conception of the sort of hold that states are expected to have on their *domaine réservé* (control, authority, stability, etc.). This part of the book will have to contend as much as possible with this typical feature of international definitional exercises, and it will do so by somewhat artificially treating each category apart on its own analytical terms.

The intrinsically unstable nature of the definition of intervention/interference and the fact that it is spread across both the understanding of inherent domestic jurisdiction and the nature of behavior intruding with it does suggest that claims that are likely to garner most traction are those that powerfully combine arguments on both levels. For example, a claim that behavior was both related to a fundamentally domestic matter (e.g., national security) and was coercive (e.g., involving threats) would be particularly strong; by contrast, a claim that behavior was merely ill-intentioned and concerned something

538 Giuseppe Puma, 'The Principle of Non-Intervention in the Face of the Venezuelan Crisis' (2021) 79 Questions of International Law 5, 24–25.

539 Behrens, *Diplomatic Interference and the Law* (n 112).

that was on the outer reaches of domestic jurisdiction would be less likely to get traction. In between, all kinds of scenarios arise that suggest a not atypical but certainly difficult balancing act, especially if one is willing to contemplate how interference arises on a spectrum of gravity. What this underscores, however, is the reality long ago stressed by Rosalind Higgins that intervention arises, if anything, along a spectrum wherein 'not every maximalist intervention is unlawful and not every minimalist intrusion is lawful'.[540]

As was hinted in the introduction, the *a priori* inconclusive character of the legal debate as traditionally understood should not excessively concern us. The point from a constructivist lens is that norms continue to have effects even when they are far from conclusive because of the investments they are the object of. There is no concept of non-interference in the absolute that international lawyers can determine by 'observing' the relevant rules. Treaty sources on interference generally go little beyond condemning it. There is a relatively rich customary basis to non-interference, but it is scattered and diffuse compared to state practice in relation to armed intervention (although even the latter is riddled with contradiction as a result). States may not always indicate that they are protesting another state's behavior *as* interference and may sometimes decide that they had rather not be too specific about the normative basis of their opposition, for example because they engage in similar behavior. In that respect, interference works a bit like espionage: states routinely engage in it, may condemn it in others when they catch them, but are wary of stigmatizing it in broad strokes given their own involvement in the practice.[541]

This part will seek to identify the constitutive effects of the norm of non-interference as the result of various social practices of defending the principle and opposing it which, over time, delineate a role for the concept. It is not merely that there is a 'debate about the rule' but that 'the rule is the debate', albeit one structured by the rule that it purports to have as its object. Therein lies the broad social utility and relevance of debates such as the one about interference, namely that they shed light on themselves. In the process, the debate contributes to specify, indirectly, the neighboring principles it invariably relies on. Debates about interference do not proceed from an unproblematic understanding of, say, sovereignty; rather they constitute that sovereignty. Put differently, debates about sovereignty are nothing but debates about who can and who cannot be interfered with, when and how; in turn, of course, that

540 Rosalyn Higgins, *Themes and Theories: Selected Essays, Speeches, and Writings in International Law* (Oxford University Press 2009) 273.

541 A John Radsan, 'The Unresolved Equation of Espionage and International Law' (2007) 28 Michigan Journal of International Law 595, 606.

also means that debates about interference are themselves nothing more than debates about the proper justification, status and scope of sovereignty. This does not minimize the purely formal and doctrinal components of that conversation; but it does locate them in a broader thicket of controversies and may even urge international lawyers to have fewer mediated and mediating conversations.

In the international arena, moreover, claims about interference or the absence of it live or die based on the willingness of actors to make them, and the degree to which others are, in turn, impressed by them. Rather than hard and fast rules, exchanges reveal a series of pressure and inflexion points, moments where lawfulness is more or less assured but, more importantly, where both parties are dialogically involved in the construction of a common legal world. For example, there will be types of interference that states will at least not have the audacity to condone, denying that they were involved in them on the facts: this will provide a certain normative succour by establishing, in the negative, that such behavior is generally not deemed to be legal. By contrast, there will be accusations that some states will be happy to contest on a normative level, denying that there is anything untoward about something which they have no problem acknowledging that they do. There will also be debates that will be abandoned because they are not deemed worth having, claims that some states will not let go because they feel strongly that they go to the heart of some international value, and issues which parties are happy to sit down at a table to discuss. Both what states say and do not say, actions and omissions, matter in structuring the norm. Indeed, as Barrie Sander has noted in the context of sovereign anxieties about cyber-interference, we also need to pay attention to the weight of silences in circumscribing the contours of customary law.[542]

Note that in a context where it is sometimes unclear how to ascertain the content of the rule, it may be even less clear how it is to be complied with or enforced, making the whole exercise appear potentially superfluous. But this perhaps reverses the order of things: it is often when international law is complied with or enforced that we obtain a sense of where its material definitions stand in the first place. In other words, it is those situations where states, as it were, are willing to 'put their money where their mouth is' that may give U.S. a rough indication of when they are really willing to stand for the rule and believe they have a good cause to do so, and where by contrast invocation of

542 Barrie Sander, 'The Sound of Silence: International Law and the Governance of Peacetime Cyber Operations' in Tomáš Minárik and others (eds), *11th International Conference on Cyber Conflict: Silent Battle, CyCon 2019*, vol 900 (NATO CCD COE Publications 2019).

the rule is mere posturing because states are not ultimately willing to follow through with consequences. Even with neither compliance nor enforcement, moreover, we remain with the basic rhetorical claims made by various parties and the reactions of their various audiences as a highly significant source of documentation of the norm.

Increasingly, one must contend with the fact that who these audiences are is one of the defining stakes of international law. Here, on must also entertain the startling claim that one can no longer pretend that states have a monopoly even of what constitutes interference in their affairs. This part will therefore show how the debate about interference produces dichotomies whose effects persist over time and seem immune to dialectical resolution even as they are productive for international relations. It envisages the extent to which arguments about both the notion of the *domaine réservé* (Chapter 3) and what constitutes unlawful interference (Chapter 4) need to be reassessed in view of the fundamental characteristics of the 'new interference'. The central question is whether the new interference constitutes a 'paradigm shift'[543] in a context of diminished enthusiasm or at least sober reassessment of globalization, open societies, and communication technologies, in the process significantly pushing the frontiers of the non-intervention principle; or whether it will merely serve to reconduct a status quo about international law, by rekindling concerns that have long, in fact, structured it.

543 Lahmann (n 322) 198.

CHAPTER 3

Prodding the Breadth and Depth of the Evolving *Domaine Réservé*: What Is Left?

1 Introduction: Ceci N'est Pas un Domaine Réservé …

The idea that there is such a thing as the *domaine réservé* is central to the history and the operation of international law. For all the regular announcements about its demise, it has endured with remarkable constancy as an idea[544] and is at least implicit in many of the claims that are made against intervention and interference. It appeared as early as Article 15(8) of the Covenant of the League of Nations, and is evident in Article 2(7) of the U.N. Charter, which will be examined later as specific instances of the somewhat distinct legal register limiting the intervention of international organizations. Article 36(2) of the Statute of the International Court of Justice makes it possible for states, in what is more specifically a form of protection against interference by other states (albeit mediated by international adjudication), to impose conditions to their recognition of its jurisdiction. A number of states have done so based on a standard reservation to the effect that their recognition excludes 'disputes with regard to questions which by international law fall exclusively within their jurisdiction'.[545]

At the same time, the quintessentially elusive nature of the *domaine* is frequently remarked upon, once leading d'Amato to note that 'the claim of domestic jurisdiction has an impact that is more psychological than legal'.[546] Like the famous 'ceci n'est pas une pipe' by Magritte, the concept seems to escape capture just as it is presented most matter-of-factly. The basic relativity of the idea was famously underlined by the Permanent Court of International

544 Baptiste Jouzier, 'Déclin et persistance de la théorie du domaine réservé: le constat d'un rôle de "transition" du domaine réservé' (2020) 33 Revue québécoise de droit international / Quebec Journal of International Law / Revista quebequense de derecho internacional 53.

545 JHW Verzijl, 'The Competence of the International Court of Justice' (1957) 1 David Davies Memorial Institute of International Studies. Annual memorial lecture 39; Hersch Lauterpacht, 'The Doctrine of Non-Justiciable Disputes in International Law' [1928] Economica 277.

546 Anthony D'Amato, 'Domestic Jurisdiction' in Rudolf Dolzer and others (eds), *Encyclopedia of Public International Law* (1987) 136.

 | DOI:10.1163/9789004532731_007

Justice (PCIJ) itself in the Nationality Decrees case: 'the question whether a certain matter is or is not solely within the jurisdiction of a State is an essentially relative question'.[547] For the ICJ, '[a] prohibited intervention must [...] be one bearing on matters in which each State is permitted, by the principle of State sovereignty, to decide freely' which at least points to some prior, exclusive notion of sovereignty, but in ways that are somewhat circular.[548] What does it actually mean for a state to act freely on certain matters, to what extent can it constrain its own freedom, and what does international law have to say on the matter as distinct from each state? Indeed, the added notion that '[a] State's domestic policy falls within its exclusive jurisdiction, provided of course that it does not violate any obligation of international law'[549] seems to bring the question full circle.

What is clear is that the very notion of interference supposes that there is something distinctive to be interfered with. In that respect, the discursive investment in interference is as much about claiming such a *domaine*, than encroachment on the *domaine* is a precondition to establishing interference. One classic example already discussed as part of the historical genealogy of interference is the very recognition of governments and a fortiori states: both to deny it when it is due or to grant it too early to the wrong entity are not abusively described as forms of intervention:[550] they interfere with the very identity of the state as a Montevideo-style, self-governing entity. Beyond that, the domestic domain is imagined as a self-contained, self-referential and self-propelled sphere of exclusive authority. Whether it is the state, the people or the demos, international law is nominally committed to ensuring a core of sovereigns' 'political independence'. That notion, indefatigably propped up by international law more than it is a readily observable political fact, has to simultaneously contend with the reality of an interdependent world that constantly belies the exclusiveness of the domestic sphere. Not only is the border between the domestic and the foreign a porous one, but domestic processes constantly invite, mix with and interact with international, transnational and global ones. And this is to say nothing of the fact that the borders in question are not mostly territorial, but metaphorical borders, borders of the mind that uneasily seek to characterize certain matters as domestic by opposition to those understood as international. Still, the claim to a *domaine*, whether it is

547 *Nationality Decrees Issued in Tunis and Morocco* (*Great Britain v France*) (*Nationality Decrees case*) (1923) 4 PCIJ Series B 24.

548 *Nicaragua v United States* (n 3) [205].

549 ibid [133].

550 David (n 536) 357.

aggrandizing one's own or diminishing that of others, is in itself a constant of international legal performance.

1.1 *Essence, Residue or Practice?*

On one sociological-leaning account, the definition of what is interference in international law is closely tied to the very definition and evolution of sovereignty via the *domaine réservé*. It is, arguably, a prism to observe how that concept is constituted over time. For the PCIJ, the question of whether a matter was within a state's sole jurisdiction or not 'depends upon the development of international relations',[551] perhaps the most question-begging obiter in the history of international adjudication. The fact that the rule is so closely tied to the very definition of what it seeks to protect, however, makes it an intrinsically difficult notion to pin down. Moreover, although it is one thing to argue 'externally' that the definition of the *domaine réservé* is dependent on the evolution of international relations, this surely cannot count as much of a legal argument from an 'internal' perspective. There is a certain inherently implausibility to the notion that states engage in a sort of guess work writ-large to ascertain the evolving conditions of their sovereignty based on the nature of international relations. The 'evolution of international relations' cannot exist independently of certain rules of legal recognition (typically, of treaty and customary international law) that would allow the powers that be to arbitrate between different conceptions thereof, of which there are no doubt many.

Thus, in some ways the definition adopted by the *Institut de droit international* (IDI) in 1954 at least has the merit of refocusing on international law:

> The 'reserved domain' is the domain of state activities where the jurisdiction of the state is not bound by international law. The extent of this domain depends on international law and varies according to its development.[552]

Note, however, how that definition in turn seems to revert to circularity: the *domaine* is what international law says it is. Tautology abounds. One senses that the vagueness surrounding the definition of the *domaine* is not entirely accidental, of course, maintaining as it does a certain flexibility around its future interpretation, even as it maximizes the odds of misunderstandings.

551 *Nationality Decrees case* (n 547) 24.

552 Institut de Droit International, *Annuaire de L'Institut de Droit International*, vol 45 (II) (BALE Editions juridiques et sociologiques SA 1954) 199 <https://www.idi-iil.org/app/uploads/2017/05/4025-45B-OCR-min.pdf> accessed 3 July 2024.

Not much has changed, it seems, since Vattel's early treatment of the question, rich with caveats and exceptions, to the effect that:

> Enfin, toutes ces choses n'intéressant que la nation, aucune puissance étrangère n'est en droit de s'en mêler, ni ne doit y intervenir, autrement que par ses bons offices, à moins qu'elle n'en soit requise, ou que des raisons particulières ne l'y appellent.[553]

It sometimes seems as if such obtuse formulations, essentially designating as protected the issues that are only the interest of one nation, are in fact deliberate. As has been pointed out, the 1970 Declaration on Friendly Relations' provisions on the issue were 'drafted in extremely vague terms' and the 'wording was so general that it was impossible to establish what matters fell within the reserved domain'.[554] Even the comparatively easy exercise of defining what might constitute interference by diplomats *qua* agents does not fare much better, beset as it is by ambiguities.[555] As to the notion that matters fall within the domain of a state 'because international law allows it to',[556] it is again largely question begging. The idea that certain domains are 'in principle regulated by international law' or 'inherently domestic' or 'flow from sovereignty' has not aged well either, as will see, beholden as it seems to be to either simplistic sociology or question-begging normativism. It is not only that any range of questions are susceptible to the requirements of international life but that there is nothing intrinsic to any question (not even private law, not even nationality, not even national security) that earmarks it fundamentally as part of a domestic preserve.[557] Even the fundamental organization of the state is not an area of complete freedom since every state must, in fine, both continue to qualify as a state and abide by its international legal obligations to others, under customary international law if nothing else.

---

553 Emer de Vattel, *Le droit des gens ou principes de la naturelle appliqués a la conduite et aux affaires des nations et des souverains*, vol I (Carnegie Institute of Washington 1916) bk II ch IV, s 54.

554 T King, 'Human Rights in the Development Policy of the European Community: Towards a European World Order?', *Netherlands Yearbook of International Law*, vol 28 (TMC Asser Press 1997) 62.

555 Paul Behrens, 'The Duty of Non-Interference' in Paul Behrens (ed), *Diplomatic Law in a New Millennium* (Oxford University Press 2017).

556 Satvinder S Juss, 'Nationality Law, Sovereignty, and the Doctrine of Exclusive Domestic Jurisdiction' (1994) 9 Florida Journal of International Law 219, 229.

557 Georges Abi-Saab, 'Some Thoughts on the Principle of Non-Intervention' in Karel Wellens (ed), *International Law: Theory and Practice: Essays in Honour of Eric Suy* (Brill 1998) 230.

For these reasons, the question of what is the *domaine réservé* and how it evolves is a theoretically and practically daunting one. The notion has sometimes seemed to acquire an almost mythical normative status (enhanced, perhaps, by 'the patina of precision in its French rendering')[558] that is simply not matched by the reality of international practice. The latter, one suspects, is deeply mired in transactional processes and a tendency to simultaneously idealize and sacrifice the *domaine*. Even the intuitive appeal of the idea of the *domaine* as a largely *residual* prerogative hardly does justice to the fact that the domestic sphere cannot be merely defined by the negative as that-which-is-not-regulated-internationally: just quite what that sphere is must go beyond the happenstance of what has, at any given time, been 'surrendered' to international law. At any rate, the residual approach to the *domaine* leaves aside questions about what parts of their *domaine* states can and actually have internationalized and, symmetrically, what areas they can reclaim as their own and which have, arguably, become part of an internationalize domain.

Brad Roth's notion of sovereignty as being 'best understood as a retention of ultimate authority: a presumptive monopoly of the last word on what counts as public order within the state's territory' gets U.S. closer to the mark, including in its insistence that, despite voluntary commitments to international law, 'renunciations are exceptions; they do not swallow the rule'.[559] This sort of reading is sustained by anterior normative assumptions about the voluntary and reversible character of certain types of internationalization. Contra a vision of international law commitment as entailing a sort of ratchet effect towards ever greater ties, it emphasizes the fact that 'renouncing a practice does not, [...] imply renouncing the domestic legal authority to resume the practice, notwithstanding the consequent cost to national honor or to national interests'.[560]

This leaves out the possibility, however, that the *domaine*, like the sovereignty it claims to capture, only ever exists already as a delegation from and at the mercy of international law, so that even its basic existence is already internationalized. There are few matters, moreover, that do not appear to be simultaneously domestic and international in equal measure, and figuring which came first is a debate that will inevitably have a chicken-and-egg quality. That is, unless, like Henri Rollin, one anticipates the existence of a vague *domaine intermédiaire*, somewhere between the *domaine réservé* and the *domaine*

558 Ossoff (n 341) 307.

559 Brad R Roth, 'Democratization's Discontents: Rediscovering the Virtues of the Non-Intervention Norm' (2022) 23 Chicago Journal of International Law 161, 166.

560 ibid 166–167.

réglementé,[561] but in ways that get U.S. no closer to addressing the perplexities of the *domaine*. In short, the painful hesitation about what exactly is part of the *domaine* is a byproduct not only in changes in the function of the state, but of the obtuseness of the prior debate about what these functions should be as a function of statehood under international law.

One way of thinking about the broad dynamics of the *domaine réservé*, then, is as part of an area that is susceptible to both enabling and limiting international norms and that can thus more or less be clung to or reclaimed. A common intuition is that the *domaine réservé* is only so big as the scope of international law is small or vice versa. The idea that the *domaine réservé* has historically shrunk as a result of the 'internationalization of domestic law'[562] is a banal cliché of the discipline. Over time, questions that were once treated routinely as part of domestic affairs (non-international armed conflicts, human rights, immigration, and nationality for example), so the story goes, have been increasingly understood as also in significant part international ones. It is true that there are fewer types of issues that have not at some point in time been the object of international law's prescriptions.[563] Some branches of international law, notably international human rights law, seem susceptible to very broad understandings that overlap with much of domestic law (constitutional, criminal, family, etc.).

However, this speaks to the *idea* of the *domaine* rather than its actual content in the particular circumstances of given states, who may or may not have shrunk their *domaine* in the broad ways that it is understood to have shrunk tendentially and on a macro level. Bemoaning or praising this phenomenon often involves trading in sociolegal generalities even as the *domaine réservé* does not mean much in abstract or universal terms. The litmus test for whether something is in the *domaine réservé*, cannot be that at one time or other 'states' (by which must necessarily be understood 'some' states) have seen fit to regulate a broad area under international law. By that count, there would barely be any *domaine* left. Even when it comes to human rights, there is nothing inherent to the idea that these are beyond the *domaine réservé* and, indeed, most of their history was marked by striking assertions to the contrary, mollified if

561 Henri Rolin, *Les Principes de Droit International Public*, vol 77 (Brill Nijhoff 1950) 384.

562 Diane P Wood and others, 'The Internationalization of Domestic Law: The Shrinking Domaine Réservé' (1993) 87 Proceedings of the Annual Meeting (American Society of International Law) 553.

563 Philip Kunig, 'Intervention, Prohibition Of', *Max Planck Encyclopedia of Public International Law* (Oxford University Press 2008) para 4.

at all in very gradual and ambiguous ways.[564] There is nothing in theory or practice that cannot fall under international law but nor is there anything that must fall under it. One also needs to account for the fact that even when an area has been subjected to international regulation, the latter may itself defer back to sovereignty through various mechanisms (e.g., the margin of appreciation, subsidiarity).

Rather, it is suggested that the *domaine réservé* of any state at any moment can be understood as whatever such state has decided to cling to as a decidedly sovereign matter, in ways that are not in violation of general international law, its specific international law commitments, or that it is not prevented from doing by peremptory norms of international law. This is something which the ICJ stressed in the Nicaragua case when it emphasized that '[a] State's domestic policy falls within its exclusive jurisdiction, *provided of course that it does not violate any obligation of international law*'.[565] There is no matter that is inherently within the *domaine réservé* for the purposes of understanding interference, then, only a series of issues that may or may not happen to have been subjected to international law, largely as a result of state voluntarism,[566] as well as a small core of issues (e.g., whether to commit genocide or not) that can never be defined as national through sovereign fiat. Mixed issues that are jointly regulated by domestic and international law are better understood as having been internationalized for the purposes of assessing interference.

This does mean, conversely, that a state cannot claim as part of the *domaine* something which it has previously subjected to international law without violating its obligations (which, if nothing else, indicate that a matter is properly international), not to mention contradicting itself. In other words, one cannot have it both ways: for example, ratifying expansive human rights treaties whilst claiming that human rights are strictly part of the *domaine* (leaving aside, for the time being, issues of the detail of implementation and margin of appreciation). In that respect, states clearly undertake international commitments at their peril, furnishing the international community the whip with which to browbeat them into submission, as it were. A state that complains that another is not honoring its international commitments towards itself or in general

564 See e.g., Elisabeth T Geibel, 'International Protection of Individual Human Rights: Implications of Individual Status' (1978) 1 Houston Journal of International Law 55.

565 *Nicaragua v United States* (n 3) [258]. My emphasis.

566 Jerzy Kranz, 'Réflexions Sur La Souveraineté' in Jerzy Makarczyk (ed), *Theory of International Law at the Threshold of the 21st Century: Essays in honour of Krzysztof Skubiszewski* (Kluwer Law International 1996).

when it comes to *opinio juris* obligations is never, within those bounds, interfering with its sovereign affairs.

By the same token, the canard that 'nothing is sovereign, everything is international' needs to be relativized and scrutinized closely from a legal perspective. It is one thing to say that some norms of international human rights law have customary and even *jus cogens* status; it is another to claim that every human rights issue is henceforth susceptible to justify outside interference in the same way and to the same extent. There is a distance between the 'stratospheric' vision of international human rights as a cosmopolitan project in the making and attention to the manifold ways in which human rights, in theory and practice, involve multiple levels of deferring to lower local authority and jurisdiction. Attention to how any given state has chosen to 'internationalize' certain domestic matters and keep others sovereign—an attention that involves a close reading of state practices and assorted expectations—should thus be *de rigueur*.

Moreover, it is worth noting that the criterion of 'international commitment' is a crude one: a state's commitment to its international obligations does not give other states an unlimited latitude to interfere all the way with how that state honors those international obligations. Simply because violating international law is not part of the *domaine* and third states are in principle on solid ground that they are not necessarily interfering when they complain of such violations does not mean that they can engage in meddling wantonly. Evidently, if a state violates some human rights of its population, for example, this does not allow outside interveners to substitute their powers to its own—even if it does mean, for example, that third states can, without being accused of interfering, at least invoke international law, diplomatically protest such violations, and in some cases adopt counter measures.

In the end, not even the legal internationalization of certain matters, real and significant though it may be, is a blank cheque to truly meddle. What will often be crucial in evaluating the existence of interference is the degree to which it is not only certain broad issue areas that have been made the object of international commitments, but also their monitoring, implementation, and enforcement, and to what degree. In that respect, states that have deliberately 'invited' international attention cannot unproblematically, when push comes to shove, disentangle themselves from such earlier invitation. Still, one must contend with the fact that committing to international obligations means merely that, and that any internationalization of the *domaine* will often be understood by states as susceptible to strict voluntarist construction. In particular, substantive internationalization of certain matters cannot be automatically equated with any degree of third-party enforcement.

One temptation is that defining the *domaine* will require some kind of painstaking exercise in inventory. It may be true that, as Ziegler put it, '[a]n exhaustive delimitation of the scope of *domaine réservé* would [...] require a complete survey of international law in order to define what is outside its ambit, and would amount to writing a history on State sovereignty and international law itself, including that of all treaties concluded'.[567] Yet this could also be an exaggeration in that one can probably distinguish between issues that states have on occasion freely decided to regulate through international law (but which they could presumably decide to reassert total sovereignty over), and dimensions of statehood that by their very nature fall under customary or even peremptory international law and cannot but be regulated internationally. Still, such an exercise of careful scrutiny of the areas that have actually remained domestic and those that, as a result of states at any given time binding themselves or the exigencies of international life, have become internationalized is, in fact, regularly engaged in as suggesting the plausible character of certain matters being domestic to begin with. One author writing in the 1950s listed 'the security of a state, internal and external; the form of a state government and its internal administration; the size and nature of its armed forces; matters concerning its citizenship, naturalization and immigration; tariff policies; treatment of minorities within a state; the economic and social policies of a state'.[568]

Resort to an inventory, almost bound to be over or under-inclusive, does capture the extreme capaciousness of the notion of domestic *domaine* in a context where there are few areas that could not, or indeed have not at some point or place, been largely domestic or largely international. Yet even there one must contend with the capricious and fundamentally reversible nature of any international delegation, not to mention the poorly understood normative incidence of such developments. Simply because states subject certain functions to international regulation or scrutiny does not mean much as such, and certainly is not evidence of *opinio juris* that they should. Many areas, moreover, might be substantively internationalized yet exclusively domestically implemented, in ways that make determining their international or domestic character a difficult task. Indeed, that reality belies any notion that simply because human rights, for example, have been proclaimed internationally then they are 'ex hypothesi no longer in the reserved domain of jurisdiction' where 'States do

567 Katja S Ziegler, 'Domaine Réservé', *Max Planck Encyclopedia of Public International Law* (2013).

568 MS Rajan, 'The Question of Defining "Domestic Jurisdiction"' (1959) 1 International Studies 248, 262.

in fact recognize that even though a "matter" may be governed by an international obligation, it may under some circumstances be regarded as appropriate for domestic action alone'.[569] The 'relativity' of human rights, then, is occasionally underscored as not trumping the 'national sovereign rights'.[570]

One way of thinking about the *domaine réservé*, then, is more principled, focused on assessing whether certain matters can be described as *inherently* domestic. This is, in nature, a more theoretical and almost philosophical exercise. It borrows from the notion of 'inherently sovereign' functions. Elsewhere, I have argued for the potential and the limits of such a notion,[571] one nonetheless distinct from the claim that some matters are specifically domestic as opposed to sovereign or governmental. To be sure, there are a range of matters that are, in line with the enumerative approach above, routinely thought to be largely domestic. States have interior ministries whose focus in very much on domestic affairs. Entire parts of the law seem like they exist largely on their own domestic terms. Even as these areas stand to be influenced by their international environment and international law, it might be argued that they remain principally (rather than exclusively) domestic matters.

It is also sometimes argued that Article 2(7)'s description of 'matters which are *essentially* within the domestic jurisdiction of a State' suggests that there is some minimal consensus of states on such matters, at least in the peculiar multilateral context of the U.N. The ICJ also spoke of matters 'not, in principle, regulated by international law' as if there were issues that could be described as inherently domestic.[572] The *domaine* is described as the 'essential and irreducible sphere which is somehow related to sovereignty and thus may be positively defined',[573] one perhaps even entailing that 'states possess a certain bundle of inherent rights which they are not entitled to dispose of freely in the exercise of their sovereignty'.[574] The idea of the inalienability of certain rights is certainly a germane one in this context, and it may refer to those functions without whose exercise a state would cease to be a state and that it cannot, therefore, decline to exercise. Alf Verdross, whilst taking note of the skepticism towards the idea of an inherent *domaine*, claimed that there are 'some matters

569 Oscar Schachter, *International Law in Theory and Practice*, vol 178 (Brill Nijhoff 1982) 330.

570 Jianming Shen, 'National Sovereignty and Human Rights in a Positive Law Context' (2000) 26 Brooklyn Journal of International Law 417, 431–432.

571 Frédéric Mégret, 'Are There "Inherently Sovereign Functions" in International Law?' (2021) 115 American Journal of International Law 452.

572 ibid.

573 Tzanakopoulos (n 24) 630.

574 ibid 632.

which must be governed in principle by domestic law because self-governing states need a sphere of autonomy' and that '[i]t is impossible to suppress the whole autonomy of states without changing the character of international law itself'.[575] Even the PCIJ in the Decrees in Tunis and Morocco case, which is better known for highlighting the utter contingency of all determinations as to the *domaine*, granted that nationality fell 'in principle' under domestic law. State practice[576] in relation to interference and the Tallinn Manual 2.0[577] suggest the occasional more recent rekindling of thinking in terms of 'matters of an inherently sovereign nature' for the purposes of pinning down interference.

This does set the bar quite high, given the evident willingness of many states to outsource functions that one might otherwise think were very much (once) central to sovereignty. Although it gestures to a sort of habitual understanding of certain matters as being domestic, a theory of inherently domestic matters is nonetheless a difficult one to defend consistently. Such a theory needs to be able to draw a hard line to argue that, as a matter of international law, certain matters are always rightly treated as first, foremost, and perhaps even irreversibly domestic. The obvious stumbling block is definitional and goes to the root difficulty of defining even the most a priori sovereign matters as decisively so in a context where domestic law has never come as much under the influence of international law. Essentialist theories of the *domaine* thus fare quite badly,[578] even when it comes to ordinary areas of domestic law that one might have thought would be immune from internationalization.

For example, criminal or family law may seem like they are entirely about matters occurring on the territory and more often than not among nationals of the state concerned, and yet they are saturated by framing international obligations, whether of extradition or human rights. Consider drug offences: on the one hand, seemingly very national; on the other hand, deeply structured for decades by the U.N. narcotics conventions. A contrario, it may well be, for example, that an interference with the 'external action' of a state is less evidently of an 'infringemen[t] of [its] independence' since it only implicates its

575 Alfred Verdross, 'The Plea of Domestic Jurisdiction before an International Tribunal and a Political Organ of the United Nations' (1968) 28 Heidelberg Journal of International Law 33, 36.

576 'Australia's International Cyber and Critical Tech Engagement Strategy' (Australian Department of Foreign Affairs and Trade 2021) 98 <https://www.dfat.gov.au/sites/default/files/international-cyber-critical-technology-engagement-strategy-2021.pdf> accessed 3 July 2024.

577 *Tallinn Manual 2.0 on the International Law Applicable to Cyber Operations* (n 454) 20.

578 D'Amato (n 546).

international relations;[579] the ICJ, for example, found in the Interpretation of Peace Treaties Advisory Opinion that '[t]he interpretation of the terms of a treaty for this purpose could not be considered as a question essentially within the domestic jurisdiction of a State. It is a question of international law which, by its very nature, lies within the competence of the Court'.[580] Yet clearly and paradoxically foreign policy is simultaneously a good contender for an inherently national matter protected from outside interference given its centrality to statecraft and high politics.

In reality, a critical and historical reading of the history of international law, and of the state within it, suggests that states (and non-state actors) have over time assumed a large number of functions, none of which can lay claim to being fundamentally and necessarily domestic (most notably, states have outsourced even their use of force to mercenaries and the like). Moreover, they have done so precisely on the basis of their sovereignty to do so as part of what might be understood as the 'sovereignty paradox', namely the idea that sovereignty entails the right to be 'less' as well as 'more' sovereign.[581] The malleability of what counts as a sovereign function and what does not thus cautions against investing too much in an ontological conception of the *domaine réservé* which the practice of international law cannot really sustain except as a rough rule of thumb.

As Stephen C McCaffrey, the U.S. member of the ILC in the 1980s, put it, 'the distinction between the internal and external affairs of a State [is] now antiquated'.[582] There is an inherent fluidity to notions like the 'domestic' and the 'foreign' that bodes ill of the ability to draw red lines between the two. For every power to do something domestically, it seems, there is a corresponding international obligation to do it in a certain way. Most state governance is a thorough hybrid of the domestic and the international, even leaving aside canonical questions about whether sovereignty itself only exists as a by-product of international law or as a necessary precedent to it. In reality, just as there are few areas of government that have not been privatized at some point, there are few areas that could not or have not been at some point internationalized—sovereign will notwithstanding.

This is true 'vertically' (in relation to the international community), and 'horizontally' (in relation to other states). As the PCIJ put it in the Nationality

579 Lawrence (n 127) 134.

580 *Interpretation of Peace Treaties with Bulgaria, Hungary and Romania (Advisory Opinion)* (1950) [1950] ICJ Rep 65, 70–71.

581 Mégret, 'Are There "Inherently Sovereign Functions" in International Law?' (n 571).

582 Yearbook of the ILC (1985) vol I, 55, para 51.

Decrees case, not even the conferral of nationality is incapable of being subjected to international rules,[583] and indeed there has been much talk since of the internationalization of citizenship laws.[584] For the Court, it was already axiomatic at the time that 'it may well happen that, in a matter which, like that of nationality, is not, in principle, regulated by international law, the right of a State to use its discretion is nevertheless restricted by obligations which it may have undertaken towards other States'.[585] It is even conceivable that matters of high politics would be outsourced to an international organization (as in the UN's international administration of Kosovo) or, for that matter, to another state. Consider, for example, that Andorra or the Vatican's defense—surely, by most accounts, an inherently domestic matter—has long been delegated to France and Spain and Italy respectively. But this in turn suggests that '[i]n essence, the distinction between domestic and international concern is a function of diplomatic history rather than principle'.[586]

Not even the use of a state's own territory is purely a matter of domestic jurisdiction since states have riparian obligations towards other states sharing the same river, jus ad bellum obligations to not allow armed groups to attack other states from their territory, and environmental obligations to not cause cross-border harm to other states. It might be argued that there is still, whatever the extent of internationalization, an irreducible area of at least discretionary power of implementation manifested by theories of subsidiarity and the margin of appreciation that point a contrario to what is 'inherently domestic'.[587] Yet in hindsight this may well be a relatively marginal power, where the bigger, framing development is that international human rights law now arguably not only constrains every facet of domestic regulatory power but does so largely on the basis of customary international law. As Thomas Buergenthal put it, the view that human rights 'are by their very nature domestic issues [...] and consequently non "internationalizable"' certainly finds 'no support in contemporary international law' so that '[i]t is clear today that under international

583 *Nationality Decrees case* (n 547).

584 Linda Bosniak, 'Citizenship Denationalized' (2000) 7 Indiana Journal of Global Legal Studies 447; Peter J Spiro, 'A New International Law of Citizenship' (2011) 105 American Journal of International Law 694.

585 *Nationality Decrees case* (n 547) 24.

586 Ralph G Steinhardt, 'The Role of International Law as a Canon of Domestic Statutory Construction' (1990) 43 Vanderbilt Law Review 1103, 1177.

587 Courtney Hillebrecht, 'Implementing International Human Rights Law at Home: Domestic Politics and the European Court of Human Rights' (2012) 13 Human Rights Review 279.

law neither "human rights" nor any other subject matter is deemed to be inherently domestic in nature'.[588]

Although it is tempting to take 'solely' or 'essentially' in the definition of domestic jurisdiction as pointing to some inherent and almost philosophically tangible dimension, then, most authors tend to agree with Kelsen's common sensical intuition that:

> Just as there are no matters which, by their very nature, are 'solely' within the domestic jurisdiction of the states, there are no matters which by their very nature are 'in principle' not regulated by international law. There is no 'principle' according to which certain matters cannot or must not regulated by international law. [...] There are [...] even no matters which are actually not 'regulated' by international law, if the term is taken not only in its positive but also in its negative sense. There are only matters in respect to which there is no norm of customary or conventional international law by which an obligation is imposed upon a state to behave in a certain way in respect to a certain matter. Then, and only then, the matter is solely or exclusively—but not 'essentially'—within the domestic jurisdiction of the state.[589]

At best, then, the idea that certain areas fall in principle under domestic law, is merely an—easily—reversible presumption (put differently, 'domestic jurisdiction means little more than a general community concession of primary, but not exclusive, competence over matters arising and intimately concerned with aspects of the internal public order of states').[590] The problem is that if no matter is ever inherently domestic, then no matter is inherently international either, and a theory of the difference between the *domaine réservé* and matters of 'international concern' will forever be suspended on the fault line between the two, including as it is policed by voluntarism on the one hand, and the exigencies of international life on the other.

Contra definition of an essence of the *domaine*, international law has thus seemingly long evolved towards a more modest 'residual' and 'interactional' understanding: what is domestic is domestic not because it is inherently so

588 Thomas Buergenthal, 'Domestic Jurisdiction, Intervention, and Human Rights: The International Law Perspective' in Peter Brown and Douglas MacLean (eds), *Human Rights and U.S. Foreign Policy: Principles and Applications* (Lexington Books 1979) 113–114.

589 Hans Kelsen, *Principles of International Law* (2nd edn, Rinehart & Co 1966) 197–198.

590 Myres S McDougal and W Michael Reisman, 'Rhodesia and the United Nations: The Lawfulness of International Concern' (1968) 62 American Journal of International Law 1, 15.

but only because the state has not subjected it to international obligations. This 'communicating vessels' vision of the *domaine* is illustrated by Fenwick's quasi-geometric formulation of it: the *domaine* is the 'sum total of national interests minus the interests governed by international law. In one sense, therefore, the scope of domestic questions is in inverse ratio to the scope of international law; the wider the latter the narrower the former, and vice versa'.[591] Although the formulation is elegant and hints at some constitutional notion of 'reserved powers', it does seem to envisage matters being either domestic or international in ways that sit oddly with a sensitivity that emphasizes the mixed character, certainly in late modernity, of much governance. As such, it does not shed light on a wide register of activity that states might conceivably and defensibly consider to be broadly within their sovereignty but that are the object of increased penetration by international law.

Terms such as 'principally' have historically done the difficult work of mediating characterizations about just how domestic any exercise of power is, perhaps pointing that certain matters' 'center of gravity' falls more on one side or the other. As Fenwick observed, there are few areas where 'a question primarily domestic [cannot] shad[e] off into an international question' if only because one state's domestic affairs inevitably intrude into another's. But his observation that Cuba's mismanagement by Spain before 1898 'constituted a standing nuisance to the United States, and it was clear that Spain could not be allowed to waive aside the complaint of the United States by raising the point of "domestic jurisdiction"'[592] is a reminder that a range of domestic matters can quickly be rebranded as foreign intrusions for self-serving imperial ends. The distinction between an exercise and an abuse of domestic jurisdiction, in particular, inevitably raises anew fundamental questions about sovereignty and international law, and the limits of a system based on the freedom of its constituents that must nonetheless attend to insistent demands for order between them. The slippery slope towards positing a range of prior duties of sovereignty, all the way to the 'unwilling or unable' standard is a reminder that the sovereignty of some can quickly lapse into something that is 'at the discretion' of others.[593]

591 Charles G Fenwick, 'The Scope of Domestic Questions in International Law' (1925) 19 American Journal of International Law 143, 144.

592 ibid 145.

593 Ntina Tzouvala, 'The "Unwilling or Unable" Doctrine and the Political Economy of the War on Terror' (2023) 14 Humanity: An International Journal of Human Rights, Humanitarianism, and Development 19.

In fact, international legal scholars gladly—and not altogether helpfully—acknowledge that the notion of the *domaine* is, if not an empty vessel, at least a placeholder for evolving expectations about statehood, although that inherent vagueness is supposed to do nothing, quite the contrary, to undermine its resilience.[594] What counts as domestic is susceptible to the accident of ongoing determinations by states and international organizations. The exact content of the *domaine réservé* is constantly being negotiated by states, precisely through claims about interference and non-interference. It emerges as one of these ideas that international law relies on even as it can never—and perhaps should not—entirely define it. It is a *category notion* that has an inherently relative character. The PCIJ has specifically indicated that its 'relativity' relates to 'the development of international relations',[595] a rare but unavoidable recognition of the determinative role of international social conditions on the actual content of the law. At the very least, then, the *domaine réservé* is less a pure concept that one can define in the abstract than a sort of relational quality that emerges in the course of international interaction: paradoxically, the sovereign heart of hearts only really comes into being, if at all, through shared social expectations. This then speaks to its unmistakable reality, but also its evanescent character.

1.2 *The Many Facets of the Domaine Réservé*

At any rate, the question remains how international law might assist in delineating the evolving contours of the notion, given the reality that claims and counterclaims are constantly being made about certain matters falling fundamentally within or outside of sovereignty. These claims, crucially, are not merely claims about what the notion entails in the abstract, but special claims about what it entails concretely in actual circumstances. Note that, analytically, the idea of the *domaine réservé* implies at minimum a normative commitment to the notion that there is such a thing, so that one cannot simply 'define it away'. by contrast for example the 'end product' of cosmopolitan theories may well be 'a situation in which the principle of nonintervention has nothing left to protect'.[596] Even as one cannot 'define away' the *domaine réservé*, one cannot, by contrast, define it into existence by a sheer act of will. Although it is sometimes said that states have considerable latitude about what they consider as belonging to the *domaine* and therefore as beyond outside scrutiny,[597]

594 Jouzier (n 544).

595 *Nationality Decrees case* (n 547) 24.

596 Vincent (n 69) 296.

597 Lyman M Tondel Jr, 'The Connally Reservation Should Be Repealed' (1960) 46 American Bar Association Journal 726.

in reality there are limitations to how much states can redefine certain matters as fundamentally domestic when faced with the demands of international law and, perhaps more crucially, of other states. Paradoxically, the definition of the *domaine* is not part of the *domaine* since it must involve objectifiable elements of international law.

The *domaine réservé* might first be seen as referring to matters that are essentially *domestic*. Much of domestic organization, governance, and law is at first glance largely internal in that sense. But what is domestic is increasingly elusive. It may be that purely private law is the natural realm of domesticity but even such an assumption has long been proved to be misleading. If nothing else, transnational situations involving individuals across borders have long created problems of conflict of law and jurisdiction which suggest that no state may claim a monopoly over their regulation. Moreover, such issues, far from merely involving problems of coordination between sovereigns, are immersed in the regulation of public international law.[598] This is explored further in the next subsection as an outgrowth of the international law of jurisdiction. Even the criminal law, the traditional realm of the state's public ordering through the monopoly of legitimate violence, is increasingly globalized both in relation to international and transnational crimes. This is not to mention deep normative misgivings by feminists in particular about the extent to which certain matters have historically been defined as domestic or international.[599] Rather than defined by where or in relation to what matters it occurs, then, the *domaine réservé* is better understood as referring to a *modality* of exercising power. It is not a territorial, geographic or even functional notion as much as one that refers to a particular legal claim that certain matters are still for a state to decide at the expense of any other.

One of the most evident manifestations of this is that, paradoxically given the otherwise inter-national nature of the matter, the domaine includes a state's international relations and its very ability to conduct an independent foreign policy. For example, the European Community identified as early as 1982 that the Soviet pipeline embargo was an 'unacceptable interference' in its foreign affairs.[600] Subsequently, the E.U. provided an amicus curiae in a case challenging the Massachusetts Burma Law of 1996 (imposing sanctions on

598 Karen Knop, 'Lorimer's Private Citizens of the World' (2016) 27 European Journal of International Law 447.

599 Hilary Charlesworth, 'Feminist Methods in International Law' (1999) 93 American Journal of International Law 379.

600 'European Communities: Comments on the U.S. Regulations Concerning Trade with the USSR' (1982) 21 International Legal Materials 891, para 10.

Burma) arguing that the law 'constitutes a direct interference with the ability of the E.U. to cooperate and carry out foreign trade with the United States [...]. The Massachusetts Burma Law is thus aimed at influencing the foreign policy choices of the Union and its Member States'.[601] In that case, the interference was particularly pronounced since it emanated from a sub-state entity that had no authority engaging in foreign affairs in the first place (not even, arguably, under U.S. constitutional law), but one can imagine situations where a third state meddles unduly in the bilateral relations of two others, prying on *their* joint affairs. The ability to conduct foreign relations on one's own terms typically involves, by extension, an ability to do so confidentially and whilst retaining control over sensitive information, in ways that suggest that spying is naturally prone to and analyzable as a form of interference ('A sovereign government has the right to develop its domestic and foreign affairs policies *unobserved* by a foreign power').[602]

An interesting quirk in that respect that one should probably not make too much of is the fact that diplomats are only, under the Vienna Convention on Diplomatic Relations, required to not interfere with the 'internal affairs' of host states because it was understood by British delegate Fitzmaurice during debates before the ILC that it is the duty of diplomats 'precisely, if not to interfere, at least to concern themselves with its foreign policy'.[603] This would still presumably prevent diplomats from usurping the foreign policy of a host state—its very decisional power as opposed to this or that policy commitment—through reprehensible means. What the Vienna Convention hints at is merely the truism that robust engagement with another state's foreign policy as a result of one's own foreign policy can under no conceivable theory be understood as a form of intervention or even interference. Two states negotiating their relations cannot claim that the other is hereby interfering in its affairs. The suspicion of interference would *a fortiori* not apply to *bona fide* offers already anticipated by international law (*bons offices*, mediation, etc.) as part of the ordinary resolution of disputes, but could apply to various types of political arm-bending by either state.

---

601 Cited in MCW Pinto, 'Asian-African Legal Consultative Committee Bi-Annual Survey of Activities 1997–1999' in BS Chimni and others (eds), *Asian Yearbook of International Law*, vol 8 (Brill Nijhoff 1998) 240.

602 Patrick Terry, '"Absolute Friends": United States Espionage Against Germany and Public International Law' (2015) 28 Revue québécoise de droit international / Quebec Journal of International Law / Revista quebequense de derecho internacional 173, 197. Author's emphasis.

603 Yearbook of the ILC (1957) vol I, 145, para 76.

Note in addition that, in the pursuit of foreign policy, to complain that another state violates international law, especially towards oneself but also towards the international community as a whole, can never be a form of interference. This is so particularly in the context of expanded notions of international standing to complain as a result of the recognition of *erga omnes* obligations. On the whole, then, the fact that foreign relations are thoroughly international in nature is not exclusive of the fact that their determination is still the separate province of every state and that they can, as a result, be an object of interference. In short, there is interference to the extent that one encroaches not so much on a particular quality of issues *ratione materiae* or *ratione loci*, but on a certain field of decisional power that belongs to another sovereign. It is that power to decide—claimed, nurtured and protected rather than inherent—that is really what the prohibition of intervention seeks to protect.

This still leaves considerable ambiguity about how far such power extends, especially when it relates to overlapping competencies. There are essentially two ways to think about the *domaine réservé* which need to be borne in mind going forward. One is by 'horizontal' reference to one's own domestic affairs as being distinct from those of *other states*; the other is by 'vertical' reference to one's domestic affairs being distinct from the international legal realm and the obligations it imposes.[604] The definition of the *domaine*, at any moment, arises as a function of tensions between these two axes: a matter that would otherwise be domestic vis-à-vis another state may no longer be so if it has been internationalized through law; but a matter that has been internationalized as one of compliance with general international law might still insulate a state vis-à-vis the claims of third states that have no recognizable interest in upholding the norm and could thus be seen as interfering in doing so. Rather than merely grandstanding about what constitutes interference in the absolute, states can thus be seen as constantly mediating between these two dimensions of interference as part of a sophisticated praxis of defending, promoting and affirming the(ir) *domaine* in the process of protesting intervention/interference.

In the classical tradition, the horizontal dimension of non-interference stands to be influenced by but ultimately trumps vertical considerations in a spirit of healthy pluralism. Disagreement—even strong disagreement based on the interpretation of international standards—with a state's domestic regime does not normally allow interference. As the ICJ recognized in the 1986 *Nicaragua v United States* case, '[t]he Court cannot contemplate the creation

604 Milojevic (n 516) 428.

of a new rule opening up a right of intervention by one State against another on the ground that the latter has opted for some particular ideology or political system'.[605] This was despite the U.S. Congress's characterization of the Nicaragua regime as a 'totalitarian Communist dictatorship'. As the Court put it, by contrast, '[h]owever the regime in Nicaragua be defined, adherence by a State to any particular doctrine does not constitute a violation of customary international law; to hold otherwise would make nonsense of the fundamental principle of State sovereignty, on which the whole of international law rests, and the freedom of choice of the political, social, economic and cultural system of a State'.[606] There was to be, therefore, no principle of legitimate 'ideological intervention' and states were fundamentally bound to respect other states' choice of regime.

On that horizontal and most historically prototypical axis, the basic intuition is that, in state-to-state relations, domestic affairs are typically the domain of one state and therefore, almost by definition, cannot be of another's. For example, matters unfolding on the territory of one state do not typically unfold on the territory of another sovereign. They are at least *that* state's domestic affairs in that they are not (and cannot be) simultaneously another state's domestic affairs. This dimension of domesticity is important because claims about interference, and certainly the ones about which this book is most concerned, arise mostly as a result of state-to-state relations rather than in relation to broad international obligations. At the same time, the claim that matters are fundamentally domestic must be taken with a pinch of salt: in practice there are many and arguably more and more situations that straddle territories, not to mention that territory itself has become a more complex and bifurcated concept. International criminal law, for example, provides many examples of situations where many states have jurisdiction (and therefore, a fortiori, interest) in a particular case: because the crime was committed on their territory, by or against one of their nationals, not to mention in ways that offend the conscience of humankind. Anti-trust law, anti-bribery efforts, and sanctions are other interesting examples of global regulatory reach.

As appears from the above, one of the paradoxes of sovereignty, as it is mediated by international criminal law, is that it has long demanded some degree of cooperation. States enforce their sovereignty, in part, through agreements with other sovereigns, for example when it comes to judicial cooperation and extradition. They can thus never fully claim these domains as their own, at least if

605 *Nicaragua v United States* (n 3) [263].
606 ibid.

they remain committed (as, for the most part, they must) to extending their jurisdictional reach to situations in which they have a sovereign interest. And they can certainly not claim that they are being interfered with when cooperation is being pursued through instruments that they themselves have ratified. Moreover, these common areas are themselves quite susceptible to capture by supranational regulation, and not merely conventional horizontal coordination between sovereigns. Nonetheless, even areas of joint concern outline *a contrario* some objects that must, hypothetically, be the sole concern of a given sovereign, to the exclusion of any other, if we take a world of states as our point of departure (for example a domestic crime committed by a national against a fellow national on the territory of the state, or questions of sentencing).

One way of thinking of interference in the *domaine réservé* beyond esoteric invocations of its essence is by equating it with interference with certain *organs* of the state. So, for example, interference in the decisions of the executive, the deliberations of the legislature, or the independence of the judiciary might all constitute a form of prohibited interference or even intervention. None of these examples are implausible. As to legislatures, there have been concerns in Italy for example that the Holy See, as a result of its 'perennial temptation [...] to bend state legal systems to its own world view, without admitting the democratic pluralism that [...] characterizes a principle of contemporary legal civilization', sent a secret *note verbale* to the Italian government to try and weigh against a law to combat sex, gender and sexual orientation discrimination.[607] In Australia and in Canada, concerns have been expressed about possible Chinese interference with either the election of members of Parliament or the excessive closeness between elected officials and the Chinese embassy.[608] This has culminated in explosive allegations of treason against unnamed 'semi-witting or witting' Canadian lawmakers in June of 2024.[609] Whatever one makes of the particulars of such accusations, they are certainly on very solid ground when flagging parliamentary processes as part of an inner sanctum of sovereignty that is not to be meddled with.

---

607 Pierluigi Consorti, 'Holy See vs Italy and Gender Discrimination: An Example of Diplomatic Meddling' (2021) 8 Soft Power: Revista Euro-Americana de Theoria e Historia de la Politica 287.

608 Chloe Yeung and Vina Nadjibulla, 'Briefing Note: Canada's Public Inquiry into Foreign Interference—Phase One Hearings' (*Asia Pacific Foundation of Canada*, 18 April 2024) <https://www.asiapacific.ca/publication/briefing-note-canadas-public-inquiry-foreign-interference> accessed 18 April 2024.

609 Zi-Ann Lum, 'Canada's Parliament Rocked by Allegations of Treason' *Politico* (10 June 2024) <https://www.politico.com/news/2024/06/10/canada-parliament-treason-allegations-00162163> accessed 11 June 2024.

The executive is also evidently highly sensitive, especially when collusion is aided from within. A head of state or member of government could be suspected of doing the bidding of another state. Famously, Viktor Yanukovych, the President of Ukraine, was seen as beholden to the Kremlin, to the point of being convicted for treason as a result of having invited Russian troops to invade his country.[610] One of the lingering accusations against Donald Trump first as candidate then as President of the U.S. was of collusion with Russia.[611] There have been concerns in Canada that party membership could be interfered with from abroad to cast ballots in the choice of prime minister.[612] Indeed, laws prohibiting senior office holder from having dual nationality (problematically, as will be seen) have had such a risk in mind. Former Georgian President Mikheil Saakshvili first abandoned his Georgian citizenship to take up an anti-corruption assignment in Ukraine and then had his Ukrainian citizenship canceled.[613] One source of the political crisis in the Ivory Coast revolved around the 'ivoirité' of candidate to the Presidency Ouattara.[614] Finally, note that the judiciary is also increasingly a target of direct and indirect forms of transnational interference that cast its independence in an entirely new light.[615]

Furthermore, the diplomatic service itself could in some cases turn out to be a relatively soft target for interference, operating at counter-purpose by being used to represent the interests of the host state in the sending state. For example, the dismissal of a French ambassador in Hungary on the basis of his excessively pro-Hungarian stance,[616] or the firm rebuttal by the U.S. embassy

---

610 Andrew Roth, 'Ukraine's Ex-President Viktor Yanukovych Found Guilty of Treason' *The Guardian* (25 January 2019) <https://www.theguardian.com/world/2019/jan/25/ukraine-ex-president-viktor-yanukovych-found-guilty-of-treason> accessed 17 April 2024.

611 Julian Borger and others, 'Trump Denies Collusion with Russia but Says He "Speaks for Himself"' *The Guardian* (19 May 2017) <https://www.theguardian.com/us-news/2017/may/18/trump-strays-white-house-message-mueller-witch-hunt> accessed 17 April 2024.

612 Ronaldo Au-Yeung and Alsu Tagirova, 'Beyond General Elections: How Could Foreign Actors Influence the Prime Ministership?' (2024) 79 International Journal 149.

613 Andy J Semotiuk, 'Can A Political Leader Hold Dual Citizenship and Avoid Conflicting Loyalties?' [2017] *Forbes* <https://www.forbes.com/sites/andyjsemotiuk/2017/07/31/mikheil-saakashvili-and-the-problem-of-dual-citizenship/> accessed 20 February 2024.

614 Alfred Babo, 'Ivoirité and Citizenship in Ivory Coast: The Controversial Policy of Authenticity' in Benjamin N Lawrance and Jacqueline Stevens (eds), *Citizenship in Question: Evidentiary Birthright and Statelessness* (Duke University Press 2017).

615 Frédéric Mégret, 'The Independence of Justice in the Cauldron of International Relations' (2022) 85 The Modern Law Review 368.

616 Marc Semo and Blaise Gauquelin, 'Eric Fournier, l'ambassadeur de France qui admirait trop Orban' *Le Monde* (4 July 2018) <https://www.lemonde.fr/europe/article/2018/07/04/eric-fournier-l-ambassadeur-de-france-qui-admirait-trop-orban_5325654_3214.html> accessed 20 February 2024.

in London that it was somehow available as a channel to act on behalf of local donors back in DC,[617] both point to this potential danger. Beyond strictly organs of the state, various intermediary bodies tasked with crucial national functions such as political parties, industry, or universities, could also, in turn, be susceptible to their own forms of capture. These can be targeted as such and directly or as an indirect way to disrupt the state. As we will see, this raises difficult boundary-delimiting questions about whether various *corps intermédiaires*, civil society or even public opinion at large can be understood as encompassed within the *domaine*, even as one may have qualms about equating them with the state. But there is little doubt that the new interference has adapted and is not simply concerned with the most caricatural form of intervention in the workings of public bodies.

One interesting thought here is that interference could be with particular organs or, more troublingly, with the separation of power between such organs itself. Attempts to reach out to particular bodies at cross-purpose or in defiance of their assigned role, for example, can feed on constitutional rivalries and create a degree of impropriety. For example, successive speeches given by Israeli Prime Minister Netanyahu to the U.S. Congress have acted as flashpoints between the latter and the U.S. Presidency. Although Congress is within its right to invite foreign heads of states (albeit normally in consultation with the White House), the timing and nature of the speeches was suspected of being designed to undermine U.S. presidential authority over foreign policy.[618] In a related genre, the great offence of de Gaulle's visit in Canada was not to have expressed support for Québec's independence but to have sailed rather than flown and through the St Laurent to Québec city rather than Ottawa, seemingly addressing himself first and foremost to the Québec population rather than to the Canadian Prime Minister. Such examples show that interference of this kind is more complex than targeting one organ of government and can involve something more in the nature of finding pressure points at the intersection of different organs.

Along similar lines, initiatives that bypass part of the responsible organs in order to foster a direct cooperation with them can, even when well-intended and partly welcome in the host country, create constitutional dissonance there and manifest a form of interference. An interesting example is provided by the

617 Ernest Mason Satow, *Satow's Diplomatic Practice* (Ivor Roberts ed, 6th edn, Oxford University Press 2009) 152.

618 Zack Beauchamp, 'The Netanyahu Speech Controversy, Explained' *Vox* (2 March 2015) <https://www.vox.com/2015/3/2/8130977/netanyahu-speech-explained> accessed 23 June 2024.

Mérida initiative, essentially a set of U.S. Congressional acts allocating funds directly to Mexican law enforcement agencies in order to combat drug cartels. Although welcomed and facilitated by a Mexican executive order, the initiative essentially bypasses the Mexican Senate's power to approve treaties. In such a case, it is almost as if host state authorities circumvent some of their own constitutional limitations in order to effect international cooperation that can nonetheless be seen, under one reading, as invasive and qualifying as a form of intervention.[619] Whether the U.S. should allow itself to be drawn into the domestic affairs of another state—even, as it seems, at its invitation—is an open and delicate question. It remains that the U.S. is directly funding Mexican agencies, on the basis of sovereign priorities that may be partly shared by Mexico but that are ultimately those of the U.S. Congress, to whose deliberations Mexican authorities are evidently not privy.

On a vertical axis, the scope of international regulation and the fact that few issues are not at least partly regulated by it risk, by the same token, consigning the notion of *domaine réservé* to a vanishing horizon. As mentioned, it can never be a form of intervention or interference for a state to invoke a violation of international law by another and nor can a state invoke matters otherwise being within its domain as a justification of a violation of international law. In the former case, a matter is no longer exclusively part of its *domaine* given that it also affects the sovereignty of another in ways now mediated by international law; in all cases, a matter cannot be part of the *domaine* by definition if it stands to be regulated under international law (admittedly, that may be precisely the issue in dispute but that is a different question). This is reinforced by a sense that certain obligations are imperative (*jus cogens*) and of interest to the entire international community (*erga omnes*), laying waste to any notion that states can meaningfully cling to certain issues as inherently domestic and sovereign even if they wanted to.

This trend has been accelerated by a perception that, at least in the U.N. context, a number of developments that might be understood as domestic affect international peace and security in ways that make claims as to their essentially domestic character even more doubtful. To make matters more complicated, 'international concern' has at times shifted away from identifying 'international obligations' or 'international situations', to highlighting 'international values': genocide would be of 'international concern' even if the state where it was alleged to have been committed was not a party to the Genocide

619 Alba Izadó León Hernández, 'When Cooperation and Intervention Meet: Sovereignty in the Mexico-United States Relationship' (2011) 3 Amsterdam Law Forum 54.

Convention and even if it occurred entirely on its territory. The decoupling of a strict juridical understanding of what counts as fundamentally domestic and a more political understanding of what issues are of 'international concern' to the U.N.—a phenomenon amply encouraged, as we will see later, by the practice of international organizations themselves—has the potential to fundamentally expand the realm of defensible intervention, providing overtures even on the state-to-state horizonal axis.

These substantive framings have repercussions jurisdictionally. A state suing another before the ICJ for breaches of international law is not interfering with the affairs of the state sued (even though the matter may be one that involves otherwise very intimate sovereign decisions) on two counts: first because the violation of an obligation owed to it means that the affected state's own sovereignty is affected; second because it can never be a defense to an international law violation that it concerns a matter that a state deems to fall entirely within its domestic affairs. Per hypothesis, the organization of a state's *domaine réservé*, whatever it be deemed to be, can never be a justification for violating international law. One also senses that, when it comes to advisory opinions that stand to impact what are in effect also intensely disputed bilateral disputes, sensitivities of at least one party about interference in their sovereign affairs will be relatively heightened. For example, Israel and a number of other states argued before the ICJ that its issuance of an advisory opinion on the occupied Palestinian territory would '*interfere* with the Israeli-Palestinian negotiation process'.[620] The ICJ, however, has stuck to its long-standing relatively formalist position that it is not interfering in sovereign affairs in such cases since it is not, in fact, dealing with a contentious question.[621] The *erga omnes* nature of the obligations at stake and the fact that Palestine denied that interference arose (that there, were, in fact, any negotiations to interfere with) reinforced a sense that whatever encroachment arose was justified.

It is true that under normal conditions, the bilateral relationship of one state to another may open each to litigation from the other but it is at least within *both* their sovereign affairs to the exclusion of those of third states. This suggests, analytically, a certain 'privatization' of bilateral relations between the relevant states. As Doudou Thiam once noted, '[i]t was difficult to exclude from international relations the influence which certain States had on other States and which was sometimes mutual. That influence created a kind of privileged relationship between them that authorized certain forms of intervention

620 para. 38. Author's emphasis.

621 Advisory Opinion on the Interpretation of Peace Treaties with Bulgaria, Hungary and Romania (Peace Treaties).

which were acceptable to the States concerned'.[622] In other words, interference can be by agreement and reciprocal, opening-up spaces of mutual influence that delineate special regimes of interaction. Even as non-intervention is a customary rule of international law, states can adjust their expectations between themselves; but, simultaneously, the fact that they do is not an invitation for third states who are not privy to that arrangement to do the same.

This is manifested and amplified in stylized fashion in the ICJ's jurisdictional rules and their effort to protect state consent to its jurisdiction. Based on the Monetary Gold principle, third states cannot be drawn into a dispute that they are not a party to, as to do so would interfere with their refusal, as the case may be, to submit a dispute to the Court. Moreover, based on Article 59, the Court's judgments bind only the parties in a dispute. By the same token, however, third states can intervene if they have an 'interest of a legal nature' that could be affected by a dispute (Article 62 of the Court's Statute) or when the construction of a Convention to which they are party is at stake (Article 63). Although not typically analyzed from a non-interference perspective and on one level merely the teasing out of the implications of sovereignty in a jurisdictional context,[623] this delicate bundle of rules can be seen as dedicated to preventing unwarranted interference by third states in the disputes of others, whilst acknowledging that an actual 'intervention' is legal and desirable where such disputes would interfere with the affairs or interests of third states.

This underscores, specifically when it comes to the interpretation of international law, the strong elements of communal interest in its interpretation and the difficulty of states claiming certain disputes as entirely their own both when the actual rights of other states are implicated but also when the broader *inter partes* interests in the relevant treaty are at stake.[624] At the same time, a notable extension of this still quite bilateral or at least multi-lateral framing of jurisdictional disputes before the Court rule is the existence of obligations *erga omnes*, particularly but perhaps not only *inter partes*, and the possibility that third states have an interest, including jurisdictional, in the enforcement of obligations owed to the international community as a whole. This is evident in the cases brought by Gambia against Myanmar and South Africa against Israel

622 Report of the International Law Commission on the work of its fortieth session, 9 May–29 July 1988, Official Records of the General Assembly, Forty-third session, Supplement No. 10, para. 232.

623 CM Chinkin, 'Third-Party Intervention Before the International Court of Justice' (1986) 80 American Journal of International Law 495.

624 Paolo Palchetti, 'Opening the International Court of Justice to Third States: Intervention and Beyond' (2002) 6 Max Planck Yearbook of United Nations Law 139.

on the basis of the Genocide Convention. It has also justified an increasingly significant practice of mass intervention by third states, notably when it comes to alleged breaches of the Genocide Convention. Although such a practice is not without its critics,[625] it does make it increasingly hard to claim that certain violations of peremptory norms affect only the parties directly impacted by them. This increased internationalization of matters that might otherwise have been shielded jurisdictionally by the *inter partes* character of disputes further testifies to the difficulty of drawing neat lines between an imagined *domaine* and matters falling under international law.

1.3 *The International Law of Jurisdiction as Approximation of the Domaine*

Another way of thinking about the *domaine réservé* is more functional and rooted in the operation of international law and the day-to-day guarding of the ideational contours of sovereignty. One rough and remarkably apposite matrix in that respect is provided by the venerable international law of jurisdiction,[626] a branch of international law closely tied to the exercise of sovereignty yet not often thought of in terms of interference. Notwithstanding, claims as to jurisdiction do operate ideal-typically much like non-interference, namely by delineating a sphere of exclusivity and requiring that a state desist, as the PCIJ put it, from 'exercis[ing] its power in any form in the territory of another State'.[627] It is, as it were, 'joined at the hip' with intervention via their common connection to the principle of sovereignty and the idea of a domestic sphere. In effect, intervention has been described as 'really being a problem of jurisdiction'.[628]

To exercise jurisdiction excessively broadly over matters that more naturally pertain to another state's sphere of competence, then, is to risk a particularly obnoxious form of interference. As David Gerber pointed out:

> When a state attaches legal consequences to conduct in another state, it exercises control over that conduct, and when such control affects essential interests in the foreign state, it may constitute an interference with

---

625 'Article 63 Intervention Before the International Court of Justice: New Developments and the Way Forward' (*Opinio Juris*, 26 July 2024) <https://opiniojuris.org/2024/07/26/article-63-intervention-before-the-international-court-of-justice-new-developments-and-the-way-forward/> accessed 29 July 2024.

626 Gerber (n 519).

627 *The Case of the SS 'Lotus' (France v Turkey)* (1927) 10 PCIJ Series A, 18.

628 Higgins, *Themes and Theories* (n 540) 274.

> the sovereign rights of that foreign state. Consequently, the principle of non-interference is properly applicable to the exercise of jurisdiction.[629]

Highlighting a state's a priori jurisdiction is thus a necessary first step to protecting from non-interference in that it helps circumscribe the *domaine. A contrario*, making the point that a matter is not within a foreign state's jurisdiction is key to justifying one's interference. The substantive dimensions of what constitutes jurisdiction are then prolonged and amplified by procedural rules such as the exhaustion of local remedies that protect against unwanted and illegal encroachment.[630] The international law of jurisdiction has, in fact, long proved a sophisticated testing ground for competing claims about competency that have turned out to be eye-opening when it comes to issues—of which there is no shortage, in an interdependent world—that have a transnational impact and thus conceivably implicate more than one sovereign. Both the movement of persons and the operation of the global economy are such instances, and if nothing else their mediation through private international law has long hinted at the artificiality of rigidly separated *domaines* and the inevitability of conciliation of the assertion of different sovereignties at least at the margins. At the same time, capitulations regimes, imperial proclamations concerning the 'protection of nationals', or gunboat diplomacy have long created festering concerns about specifically jurisdictional forms of interference in the semi-periphery that have provided some of the very impetus for the emergence of strong expectations about non-intervention.[631]

Famously, jurisdiction entails prescriptive, adjudicative, and enforcement dimensions. Enforcement jurisdiction is less evidently analyzed under an interference prism since it is, plainly and simply, a violation of sovereignty, and better understood as such. To the extent that enforcement jurisdiction is attached to the other two, however, it will also show itself to be highly dependent on prior claims to material jurisdiction. When it comes to the prescriptive and adjudicative bases, the condition that international law imposes on a state being able to assert jurisdiction is that the exercise of its sovereignty have a nexus with a given issue or, put differently, that the issue have a nexus to its sovereignty.[632] Although typically justified under the international law of

629 Gerber (n 519) 212.

630 D'Amato (n 546).

631 Pär Kristoffer Cassel, *Grounds of Judgment: Extraterritoriality and Imperial Power in Nineteenth-Century China and Japan* (Oxford University Press 2011).

632 Cedric Ryngaert, 'The Concept of Jurisdiction in International Law' in Alexander Orakhelashvili (ed), *Research Handbook on Jurisdiction and Immunities in International Law* (Edward Elgar Publishing 2015).

jurisdiction, it is clear that the requirement of such a nexus is intimately tied to the need to avoid interference and that 'the principles of jurisdiction already constitute a specific manifestation of the principle of nonintervention'.[633]

As Jennings put it, to allow 'the extraterritorial exercise of jurisdiction [...] to extend to the point where the local law is supplanted' is effectively to allow 'interference by one State in the affairs of another'.[634] In such circumstances, exercise of jurisdiction can constitute an 'abuse of rights if the State claiming jurisdiction had no legitimate interest in enforcing its own law and if the enforcement of its law would cause serious mischief in another State'.[635] Indeed, for a state to treat an offender whose wrongful behavior occurred abroad 'according to its own notions, rather than those of the place where he did the acts, not only would be unjust, but would be an interference with the authority of another sovereign, contrary to the comity of nations, which the other state concerned justly might resent'.[636] By contrast, states which can assert a connection to the subject matter they claim to exercise jurisdiction over have at least a *prima facie* claim to rightfully exercise jurisdiction. This may count as a useful approximation, then, of some of the circumstances wherein interference, jurisdictional or not, might be deemed problematic.

Jurisdiction can sometimes be justified, moreover, to the extent that certain areas of overlap do exist, evidently, in an interdependent world, such that states have an interest of their own in situations that, in part at least, unfold simultaneously on the territory of other states. Consider exercises of extra-territorial jurisdiction over one's nationals abroad or as a result of the actions of one's agents or because of an expansive conception of protecting the states' interests abroad (e.g., 'effects' jurisdiction). Nationality underscores broad claims of prescriptive, adjudicative and enforcement jurisdiction that clearly evidence a strong prima facie nexus. The principle of nationality has long played a key role in legitimately expanding the realm of states' extra-territorial jurisdiction, whether legislatively (domestic laws apply to nationals abroad), judicially or a result of executive diplomatic protection. It is largely accepted, for example, that states have jurisdiction not only over crimes committed on their territory

633 Tom Ruys and Cedric Ryngaert, 'Secondary Sanctions: A Weapon out of Control? The International Legality of, and European Responses to, U.S. Secondary Sanctions' [2020] British Yearbook of International Law 1, 10.

634 Robert Y Jennings, 'Extraterritorial Jurisdiction and the United States Antitrust Laws' (1957) 33 British Year Book of International Law 146, 153.

635 Michael Akehurst, 'Jurisdiction in International Law' (1972) 46 British Year Book of International Law 145, 208.

636 *American Banana Co v United Fruit Co*, 213 U.S. 347, 356 (1909).

(other states have no cause for complaining that their nationals are prosecuted for the like) but over crimes committed *by* their nationals or even *against* their nationals. Evidently, states have a strong interest in how their nationals are treated and even how they behave themselves abroad,[637] that leads to a very strong case for their jurisdiction. This includes for example expansive understandings of passive personality jurisdiction as a form of protection of one's nationals.[638]

It is notable that even the international law of nationality long evolved towards requiring a 'genuine connection' upstream precisely out of wariness that nationality would be manipulated by states to arrogate further jurisdiction for themselves and therefore engage in abusive interference. Such an inspiration was manifest for example the Nottebohm case and the Court's reluctance to allow diplomatic protection to proceed on the basis of what it deemed to be a tenuous link of nationality between Nottebohm and Liechtenstein. Although that case is often cited as an illustration of the tendency to consider the law of nationality as not exclusively a domestic matter (and thus an instance of international shrinking of the *domaine réservé*), it is also noteworthy for its willingness to rein in what might otherwise have been an unsubstantiated quasi-interference with the sovereign affairs of Guatemala, with Nottebohm bringing in Liechtenstein into a dispute that it could ill claim jurisdiction over.[639] Similarly, even in the Barcelona Traction case, which is otherwise heralded as the first explicit formalization of the notion of *erga omnes* obligations, the Court denied Belgium the ability to invoke diplomatic protection on behalf of shareholders, against the background of persistent fears about unwanted interference.[640]

The international law of nationality, therefore, both provides opportunities for assertions of extra-territorial jurisdiction and limitations thereto based on implicit ideas about interference. States can definitely exercise jurisdiction over their nationals and who qualifies as such, but should not be allowed to too liberally grant their nationality as a prelude to interfering in the affairs of other states. One problematic recent example is the trend known as 'passportization'

637 Frédéric Mégret, '"Do Not Do Abroad What You Would Not Do at Home?": An Exploration of the Rationales for Extraterritorial Criminal Jurisdiction over a State's Nationals' (2020) 57 Canadian Yearbook of International Law/Annuaire canadien de droit international 1.

638 Adeno Addis, 'Community and Jurisdictional Authority', *Beyond Territoriality* (Brill Nijhoff 2012).

639 *Nottebohm* (*Liechtenstein v Guatemala*) [1955] ICJ Rep 4.

640 Nigel S Rodley, 'Corporate Nationality and the Diplomatic Protection of Multinational Enterprises: The Barcelona Traction Case Comment' (1971) 47 Indiana Law Journal 70.

by which states, notably Hungary and Russia, have granted their citizenship or equivalent rights to foreign nationals, often ethnic-kin that are seen as part of their broader diaspora and in ways that may stoke irredentist passions. Although it has been argued that even the law of nationality has become increasingly internationalized,[641] there is little doubt that in principle there are few issues that come as close to the heart of sovereignty on one's territory as the monopoly of who gets to become a national. Granting one's nationality liberally may not be illegal and indeed dual nationality has been increasingly recognized; but to do so in ways that disrupt the ability of another state to govern its nationals as part of a 'weaponization of citizenship'[642] and even agendas of territorial aggrandizement is an 'abuse of right'[643] that can clearly constitute intervention/interference. The international law of jurisdiction, then, is constrained by the international law on non-intervention, and vice-versa.

In the case of Russia, the granting of passports has, in fact, been a step immediately prior to the deployment of troops, de facto invasion, and illegal annexation. In such scenarios, the assertion of jurisdiction that granting of citizenship then permits (organizing elections and referenda, granting social benefits, etc.) entrenches the usurpation of the sovereignty of the target state even deeper. Asked about the legality of Hungary's Status law and more generally the 'preferential treatment of kin-minorities', the Venice Commission found that, although 'the mere fact that the addressees of a piece of legislation are foreign citizens does not [...] constitute an infringement of the principle of territorial sovereignty', the extra-territorial application of this particular law made its legitimacy 'not so straightforward'.[644] This included the Commission voicing doubt about the power of Hungary to empower non-governmental organisations with ties to the Hungarian state to establish Magyar origin, at least without the consent of host states. Even though there might well exist a nexus between a state and its ethnic kin, unilateral granting of citizenship can amount to a 'personal' rather than 'territorial' annexation.[645] It can

641 Spiro (n 584).

642 Neha Jain, 'Weaponised Citizenship: Should International Law Restrict Oppressive Nationality Attribution?' (2023) Robert Schuman Centre for Advanced Studies Research Paper 2023/54 <https://ssrn.com/abstract=4584093> accessed 2 February 2024.

643 Anne Peters, 'Passportisation: Risks for International Law and Stability—Part I' (*EJIL: Talk!*, 9 May 2019) <https://www.ejiltalk.org/passportisation-risks-for-internatio nal-law-and-stability-part-one/> accessed 20 February 2022.

644 Venice Commission, 48th Plenary Session, Venice, 19–20 October 2001, Report on the Preferential Treatment of National Minorities by Their Kin-State, 22 October 2001. CDL-INF (2001) 19, 16–17.

645 Peters (n 643).

subsequently and problematically legitimize extensive claims based on the 'protection' of nationals abroad.[646]

Extra-territorial jurisdiction can also notoriously and more contentiously be based on the basis of its 'effects' on a state. Anti-trust regulation, long a thorn in the relations of the U.S. with some of its main commercial partners, provides a classic example thereof. For anti-trust purposes, the U.S. considers the global activities of multinational companies registered in the U.S. This may then have an impact on foreign jurisdiction and has at times been described as a form of interference in the affairs of other states, especially the more tenuous link to the state's territory. This is even more so when sanctions interdict behavior by foreign corporations or individuals in their own country that may even have been required of them under domestic law or undertaken at the state's initiative (the thorny problem known as 'secondary sanctions').[647] Pushed to their extreme, the 'effects' doctrines of jurisdiction can have the consequence of installing parallel foreign legislation to that of the territorial state.[648] They manifest a subtle displacement of the ability of that state's expectations of a quasi-monopoly of regulation on its territory. By framing the whole world as the appropriate scale to compute impact on one's jurisdiction, they are a slippery slope towards at least symbolic encroachment on the sovereignty of other states.

From a regulatory perspective, at the same time, it is true that stopping regulation 'at the water's edge' would defeat the purpose of, for example, effective anti-trust efforts, blinding the regulatory state to the extra-territorial ramifications of the actions of foreign actors operating on its territory. More importantly, from an international law perspective, so long as a state can invoke that behavior elsewhere has a direct and substantial impact on it, it will be on relatively strong grounds to assert jurisdiction. Failure to 'intervene' through appropriate jurisdictional assertion could in essence force a state to allow itself to be 'intervened with'. Often, it is unmistakably the 'nationality principle' that has done the work here, allowing states to extend jurisdiction extra-territorially to the acts of their nationals or nationally incorporated companies abroad. This

646 Patricio Barbirotto, 'The Russian Citizenship Law in Ukraine and International Law' (*Opinio Juris*, 6 October 2022) <https://opiniojuris.org/2022/10/06/the-russian-citizenship-law-in-ukraine-and-international-law/> accessed 20 February 2024.

647 James Wilson Perkins, 'In Re Japanese Electronic Products Antitrust Litigation: Sovereign Compulsion, Act of State, and the Extraterritorial Reach of the United States Antitrust Laws Comment' (1986) 36 American University Law Review 721.

648 GW Haight, 'Antitrust Laws and the Territorial Principle' (1957) 11 Vanderbilt Law Review 27.

is not particularly contentious to the extent that states may elect that they do have a continuing interest in how their nationals operate abroad,[649] which does not raise non-intervention red flags.[650] Clearly, by contrast, to regulate the doings of aliens in their own country of nationality is likely to be seen as an unwarranted form of interference, unless justifiable under some conception of 'objective territory' focusing on where certain behavior takes effect.[651]

In addition to the fact that the matter is one of key concern to the allegedly interfering state's sovereignty, note also that the paucity of effects of a claimed 'interference' on another state could be relevant as part of a subtle weighing exercise. For example, France successfully caused an evolution of Canadian foreign policy which at one point considered the holding of elections for the French, Italian and Tunisian abroad on its territory to be an inimical form of interference. As was argued in response, France's assertion of sovereignty over Canadian territory was extremely nominal, whereas organizing elections for its expatriate population effected a significant democratic entitlement. The holding of French elections did not interfere with the holding of Canadian elections and the fact there existed a 'North American constituency' for French electoral purposes that included Canada hardly affected Canadian jurisdiction.[652] Clearly an interdependent world must make way for some degree of conciliation between parallel and overlapping rather than necessarily clashing sovereign interests, a case reinforced by the parallel and overlapping operation of various democracies.

The problem is when extra-territorial reach of a state starts subjecting notably foreign nationals to the competing pull of various, possibly contradictory legal injunctions. This is why secondary sanctions that stand to punish foreign subjects for violations of laws of another state, for example, are particularly problematic.[653] Even when they, more or less dubiously, invoke the authority of general international law, it is not the sanctioning state's role to castigate

649 Mégret, '"Do Not Do Abroad What You Would Not Do at Home?"' (n 637).

650 Martin Ratcovich, 'Extraterritorial Criminalisation and Non-Intervention: Sweden's Criminal Measures against the Purchase of Sex Abroad' (2019) 88 Nordic Journal of International Law 398.

651 Jennings (n 634) 50–51.

652 Frédéric Mégret and Raphaël Girard, 'Diasporas, Extraterritorial Representation, and the Right to Vote' (2015) 52 Canadian Yearbook of international Law/Annuaire canadien de droit international 185.

653 Patrick CR Terry, 'Enforcing U.S. Foreign Policy by Imposing Unilateral Secondary Sanctions: Is Might Right in Public International Law?' (2020) 30 Washington International Law Journal 1; Ruys and Ryngaert (n 633); Cécile Fabre, 'Secondary Economic Sanctions' (2016) 69 Current Legal Problems 259.

other third states for not doing more and certainly to punish private parties that have little a priori connection to its jurisdiction. To the extent that compliance with such sanctions is considered inimical to the policies of the host state, then it is no wonder that it sees them as in violation of the rule of non-intervention.[654] Consider, for example, the U.S.'s application of criminal law to entities doing business with Iran or Cuba even though such entities are based outside the U.S. As Julia Schmidt points out:

> The U.S. extra-territorial sanctions not only limit economic opportunities for European businesses, who are essentially asked by the U.S. measures to choose between trade with the USA and trade with Iran, but they also interfere with the foreign policy choices of the European Union (E.U.) and of its Member States who support the JCPOA and legitimate trade with Iran.[655]

Europe, in other terms, is impeded from continuing to abide by the 2015 JCPOA framework and trading with Iran by the U.S.'s change of mind about that agreement, and willingness to reimpose sanctions on Iran. Similarly, the Helms-Burton Act and its sanction of non-U.S. companies that do business in Cuba 'is viewed by the E.U. to impede its ongoing dialogue with Cuba' and thus to interfere with its foreign policy.[656] More fundamentally, U.S. extra-territorial sanctions can be considered as targeted sanctions against actors in other states because they:

> not only disregard the foreign policy choices of sovereign actors worldwide that do not want to limit trade with Iran and Cuba, but they aim to replace those foreign policy choices with U.S. foreign policy preferences, and they put pressure on foreign actors to change their foreign policies towards both Iran and Cuba in line with U.S. foreign policy goals through the medium of natural and legal persons that are constrained by the extra-territorial legislation.[657]

The sense that the international law of jurisdiction delineates a sphere close to that of the *domaine* goes a long way back. For example, one early Asian African

---

654 Ruys and Ryngaert (n 633) 9.

655 Julia Schmidt, 'The Legality of Unilateral Extra-Territorial Sanctions under International Law' (2022) 27 Journal of Conflict & Security Law 53, 55.

656 ibid.

657 ibid 70.

Legal Consultative Committee's meeting stressed the importance, for the purposes of not interfering, of establishing a 'genuine or substantial link between the State and the activity regulated'.[658] Respecting the limits of one's jurisdiction provides a rough guide as to how not to interfere. To recapitulate, although assertions of judicial competence outside the recognized bases of jurisdiction are typically treated as merely that—abuses of jurisdiction—there is simultaneously a clear sense that what is at stake is *also* more broadly forms of interference with the affairs of other states: particularly extravagant forms of interference, in fact, given that, far from occurring under the radar, they purport to exercise power fully in line with international law.

So ingrained is the need *not* to interfere with other state's jurisdiction, that states or their organs have sometimes manifested significant scruple in making sure that they do not tread on other states' affairs. This is evident in the internalization of 'comity' as a catch word for an injunction of good international citizenship in deferring to the sovereignty of others.[659] It is especially manifest with courts as sometimes guardians of the sovereignty of others (occasionally against the wishes of their own executives or legislatures) that have both resisted the application of their law to foreign situations and welcomed the application of foreign law to domestic situations. As an example of the latter, the whole of private international law can be seen as, inter alia, a form of deference to the claims of other sovereigns to situations having taken root or maintaining significant connection to their authority.[660] As an example of the former, one can point out to a long practice of refusing to weigh on matters that implicate the sovereignty of other states (immunities, non-justiciability, foreign affairs exception, political question doctrine, act of state, *forum non conveniens*)[661] even in cases with a purportedly transnational or universal component.[662]

This is at least partly and implicitly on account that such cases are better addressed either by foreign courts or through the unique medium of foreign

658 Pinto (n 601) 234.

659 FA Mann, 'Comity' in FA Mann, *Foreign Affairs in English Courts* (Oxford University Press 1986). Also, *Buck v Attorney General* [1965] EWCA Civ J0212-3, [1965] Ch 745.

660 James Edelman and Madeleine Salinger, 'Comity in Private International Law and Fundamental Principles of Justice' in Andrew Dickinson and Edwin Peel (eds), *A Conflict Of Laws Companion* (Oxford University Press 2021).

661 David Epstein and Charles S Baldwin, 'Selected Limitations on the Jurisdiction of U.S. Courts' in David Epstein and Charles S Baldwin, *International Litigation: A Guide to Jurisdiction, Practice, and Strategy* (4th edn, Brill Nijhoff 2010).

662 Chris Thomale, 'The Forgotten Discipline of Private International Law: Lessons from Kiobel v Royal Dutch Petroleum—Part 1' (2016) 7 Transnational Legal Theory 155.

policy, but the basic goal is still to avoid violating the rule of non-intervention. Although deference to one's own executive rather than to a foreign sovereign is typically involved—making non-interference at best an indirect byproduct of a constitutional scruple—one should also acknowledge a long tradition to the effect that courts should not 'sit in judgment [as] custos morum of the whole world' as the foundation for this restraint.[663] As the U.S. Supreme Court put it in the Empagran case, courts should avoid applying U.S. law extra-territorially when to do so would cause a 'serious risk of interference with a foreign nation's ability independently to regulate its own commercial affairs'.[664] In that respect, doctrines of avoidance admittedly first and foremost seek to navigate the separation of power and the risk of an 'interference' with the executive, but the incidence on foreign states' sovereignty remains pertinent indirectly for all intents and purposes.[665] Courts have also occasionally been reluctant to construe their state's laws as having extra-territorial effect,[666] especially when the jurisdictional connection is weak,[667] and even been reluctant to grant the executive the authority to exercise power in ways that might predictably intrude on the sovereignty of others.[668]

One area of adjudicative jurisdiction that is premised on a strong international mandate and has long created genuine, if sometimes exaggerated, concerns with interference, is universal jurisdiction. The question is closely tied to the conditions under which universal jurisdiction may be exercised at all under international law. Many claims that universal jurisdiction is, in fact and in law, interfering with the affairs of states have been loosely made. States

663 *United States v La Jeune Eugenie*, 26 F Cas 832, 847 (CCD Mass 1822).

664 *F Hoffmann-La Roche Ltd v Empagran SA*, 542 U.S. 155, 162 (2004).

665 Sharon Weill, 'The Avoiding Role of National Courts: Law as a Political Doctrine' in Sharon Weill, *The Role of National Courts in Applying International Humanitarian Law* (Oxford University Press 2014) 114; pointing out that a court can refrain from exercising jurisdiction 'in order not to interfere in its own government's international policies or in matters pertaining to the sovereignty of third states'.

666 Jonathan Turley, 'When in Rome: Multinational Misconduct and the Presumption against Extraterritoriality' (1989) 84 Northwestern University Law Review 598. Extraterritorial jurisdiction has specifically been rejected as an 'interference with the authority of another sovereign, contrary to the comity of nations', *American Banana v United Fruits* (n 604) 356.

667 Linda S Mullenix, 'Personal Jurisdiction Stops Here: Cabining the Extraterritorial Reach of American Courts William Richman Dedication Issue' (2013) 45 University of Toledo Law Review 705.

668 Forcese (n 532) 180. (Citing the Canadian Supreme Court declining to grant the Canadian secret services a warrant to search foreign premises because it would amount to 'authorizing activities that are inconsistent with and likely to breach the binding customary principles of territorial sovereign equality and non-intervention', rules that have 'evolved to protect the sovereignty of nation states against interference from other states').

routinely insist that the principles of 'sovereign equality and non-interference in internal affairs [should] be strictly observed during any judicial proceedings, including the exercise of universal jurisdiction'.[669] The African Union has complained of at least certain uses of universal jurisdiction, most notably those targeting incumbent heads of state or those that might disrupt peace efforts. Immunities are sometimes specifically understood as a way of guarding against interference.[670]

In the *Congo v Belgium* case, for example, Congo clearly posed the question of the arrest warrant against foreign Minister Yerodia as one of interference, notably by heavily underlining that the very purpose of immunities was to prevent an 'ingérence étrangère'[671] (Belgium responded orally and a bit flippantly that the DRC could simply change foreign minister). Beyond the technical question of incumbent ministers' immunity, this was the real subtext of that entire controversy. The Congolese ad hoc judge, Judge Bula-Bula, himself revealingly a scholar of the question of interference,[672] flagged the evident 'ingérence judiciaire' and emphasized Belgium's continuing history of interference in the affairs of the DRC since independence and what he described as a 'political judicial intervention' by Belgium that fit into this pattern.[673] Judges Higgins, Kooijmans, and Buergenthal in their joint separate opinion also noted that the need to punish those guilty of the gravest crimes had to be weighed against 'the interest of the community of States to [...] act freely on the inter-State level without unwarranted interference'.[674]

There is no doubt, then, that on some level principles of universal jurisdiction disrupt the 'business as usual' dimension of the exercise of jurisdiction whose *raison d'être* is 'the typical resul[t] [...] of a balancing of sovereignty

---

669 'Debate Reveals Rift in Speakers' Understanding of Universal Jurisdiction Scope, Application, as Sixth Committee Takes Up Report on Principle' (*UN Meetings Coverage and Press Releases*, 13 October 2023) <https://press.un.org/en/2023/gal3692.doc.htm> accessed 16 December 2023. See also the interventions of the representatives of Egypt and Cuba, ibid.

670 Avneesh Kumar, 'Scope of Sovereign Immunity in International Law' (2012) 14–15 Romanian Journal of International Law 106, 107–108.

671 *Arrest Warrant of 11 April 2000* (*Republic of the Congo v Belgium*) (*Memorial of the Democratic Republic of the Congo*) (15 May 2001) [47, 73].

672 Sayeman Bula-Bula, 'L'idée d'ingérence à La Lumière Du Nouvel Ordre Mondial' (1994) 6 African Journal of International and Comparative Law 14.

673 *Arrest Warrant of 11 April 2000* (*Republic of the Congo v Belgium*) (*Separate opinion of Judge ad hoc Bula-Bula*) (2001) [2002] ICJ Rep 3 [23–25, 89].

674 *Arrest Warrant of 11 April 2000* (*Republic of the Congo v Belgium*) (*Joint separate opinion of Judges Higgins, Kooijmans and Buergenthal*) (2001) [2002] ICJ Rep 3 [75].

between States and prohibited interference with internal affairs'.[675] It is one thing to find that individuals can be materially liable under international law directly, but it is another to infer from that premise that all domestic courts in the world have jurisdiction over them and that they can override immunities in doing so. Similar arguments are made in relation to so-called universal 'civil' jurisdiction and the danger that laws such as the U.S. Alien Tort Statute will lead to the displacement of foreign law and attendant interference in other sovereigns' affairs.[676] Contra a traditional model of private international law focused on the careful apportioning of competencies, the distribution of laws transnationally and the deference of comity, claims made on behalf of universal jurisdiction have a profoundly corrosive effect on the idea of the *domaine*.

The quite influential cosmopolitan argument is that universal jurisdiction cannot by definition be construed as a form of interference. That is, the very point of universal jurisdiction is that it can be exercised absent any of the normal bases for jurisdiction (territorial, personal or even protective) merely on the basis of some fundamental community interest in the repression of certain international crimes. For Antonio Cassese, the insistence on non-interference when it comes to universal jurisdiction corresponds to an 'archaic conception', in light of the 'modern view, based on the need to further universal values'.[677] It has even been argued that there is no conflict of jurisdiction at all since 'the State exercising universal jurisdiction merely enforces shared normative and legal commitments of all', such that the state with national jurisdiction 'can claim no sovereign interference'.[678] The temptation, then, is to largely wish away the concern about interference on the basis of universal jurisdiction's incontrovertible status in international law.

By the same token, there will remain a number of questions on the margins of universal jurisdiction, including the many areas where its precise scope is disputed, where claims of interference are bound to resurface. These include first the list of crimes that are actually susceptible to universal jurisdiction; second, the existence of a requirement that even if a crime was not committed on the territory, by a national or against a national of the state purporting to

675 Luc Reydams, *Universal Jurisdiction: International and Municipal Legal Perspectives* (Oxford University Press 2003) 23.

676 Paul Barker, 'Universal Civil Jurisdiction and the Extraterritorial Reach of the Alien Tort Statute: The Case of Kiobel before the United States Supreme Court' (2012) 20 University of Miami International and Comparative Law Review 1.

677 Antonio Cassese, *International Criminal Law* (Oxford University Press 2003) 292.

678 Anthony J Colangelo, 'Universal Jurisdiction as an International False Conflict of Laws' (2008) 30 Michigan Journal of International Law 881, 883.

exercise it, the person prosecuted will have at least have some connection to that state's territory; and third, the question of sovereign immunities as they apply to heads of states and members of governments, even to some degree after they have left office.[679] In the civil realm, doubt remains about the very possibility of asserting universal jurisdiction[680] that are specifically framed as entailing questions of interference,[681] despite the cognizance of possible national interests in ensuring respect for international law.[682]

All of these persistent questions, which are as such beyond the reach of this book, raise issues about whether universal jurisdiction is validly exercised in any given circumstance and, if not, whether that can be usefully understood as a form of prohibited intervention. Even forum courts have occasionally been sensitive to the possibility that universal jurisdiction might constitute such an intervention in the affairs of other states, and have sought to limit its reach to cases where a clear connexity exists with their sovereignty (passive personality jurisdiction),[683] or where the courts of the state where the crimes

679 Naomi Roht-Arriaza, 'Universal Jurisdiction: Steps Forward, Steps Back' (2004) 17 Leiden Journal of International Law 375; Bernard Ntahiraja, 'The Legality and Scope of Universal Jurisdiction in Criminal Matters: Is There Any Question to Answer?' (2022) 91 Nordic Journal of International Law 390; AP Van der Mei, 'Punish the Wicked, Constrain the Righteous: Some Comments on the Future of Universal Jurisdiction' (2002) 22 University of Ghana Law Journal 78; David A Tallman, 'Universal Jurisdiction: Lessons from Belgium's Experience' in Jane E Stromseth (ed), *Accountability for Atrocities: National and International Responses* (Brill Nijhoff 2003).

680 Paul David Mora, 'The Alien Tort Statute after Kiobel: The Possibility for Unlawful Assertions of Universal Civil Jurisdiction Still Remains' (2014) 63 International and Comparative Law Quarterly 699.

681 Brief of the Governments of the Kingdom of the Netherlands and the United Kingdom of Great Britain and Northern Ireland as Amici Curiae Supporting Neither Party, *Kiobel v Royal Dutch Petroleum*, 569 U.S. 108 (2013) (No 10-1491); Brief of the Federal Republic of Germany as Amicus Curiae Supporting Respondents, *Kiobel v Royal Dutch Petroleum*, 569 U.S. 108 (2013) (No 10–1491). See also Jochen von Bernstorff, Marc Jacob and John Dingfelder Stone, 'The Alien Tort Statute before the U.S. Supreme Court in the Kiobel Case: Does International Law Prohibit U.S. Courts to Exercise Extraterritorial Civil Jurisdiction over Human Rights Abuses Committed Outside of the US?' (2012) 72 Heidelberg Journal of International Law 579, 584. ('This does not imply that the exercise of adjudicative jurisdiction beyond these bases is necessarily unlawful; it is, however, more likely to intervene unduly in the internal affairs of another state. Jurisdictional competence under international law thus is a relational concept, which in a community of sovereign nation states has to be applied in line with the principle of nonintervention as its ultimate legal limitation').

682 Robert Cryer, 'Come Together? Civil and Criminal Jurisdiction in Kiobel from an International Law Perspective' (2014) 12 Journal of International Criminal Justice 579.

683 Supreme Court of Spain (Penal Chamber) Judgment No 327/2003 (25 February 2003) [Guatemala Genocide case].

were committed were unwilling or unable to exercise their jurisdiction.[684] The Belgium parliament also rolled back its war crimes law, partly out of concerns about interference in the affairs of other states (and, it should be said, the concern that foreign states would in turn interfere with its affairs).[685] That these questions about the proper scope of universal jurisdiction cannot be put to rest once and for all is a reminder that they delineate an area of regular contention over the proper meaning and scope of interference. Characteristically, the debate has since tended to migrate towards a discussion in terms of 'abuse of universal jurisdiction' rather than universal jurisdiction itself being a form of interference.[686] It remains that 'the State claiming an exorbitant universal jurisdiction may well interfere with the sovereignty of other jurisdictionally involved States—most notably, territorial and national States—through the unauthorized projection of domestic law into their territories or over their nationals'.[687]

The reach of the debate extends more generally to the question of sovereign immunity, and the risk that suing states, including for their responsibility in committing or condoning international crimes, will also specifically constitute interference (or, as one U.S. Court put it, 'the rationale for sovereign immunity essentially boils down to substantial bothersome interference with the operation of government').[688] There is little doubt that the long arc of human rights and humanitarianism bends towards a relative minimization of the traditional non-interference interest incarnated in sovereign immunity rules and towards the legitimization of incursions in what in other times would have unmistakably been considered domestic affairs.[689] Again, the point is not to explore those questions in detail here but to bring attention to the fact that getting the policy and law prescription right is widely understood to involve fundamental questions of non-intervention: were it not for the exceptional cover

---

684 Supreme Court of Spain (Penal Chamber) Judgment No 712/2003 (20 May 2003) [Peruvian Genocide case].

685 Annemie Schaus and Pascale Vielle, 'La Belgique, Justicier Du Monde' (2002) 2002 Politique, Revue de débats 8.

686 'Debate Reveals Rift in Speakers' Understanding of Universal Jurisdiction Scope, Application, as Sixth Committee Takes Up Report on Principle' (n 669).

687 Colangelo (n 678) 884.

688 *Littell v Morton*, 445 F2d 1207, 1214 (4th Cir 1971). Also, James Samuel Sable, 'Sovereign Immunity: A Battleground of Competing Considerations' (1980) 12 Southwestern University Law Review 457.

689 Anne L Clunan, 'Redefining Sovereignty: Humanitarianism's Challenge to Sovereign Immunity' in Noha Shawki and Michaelene Cox (eds), *Negotiating Sovereignty and Human Rights: Actors and Issues in Contemporary Human Rights Policy* (Routledge 2009).

of international law in the case of international crimes, intervention would be involved. In short, the trajectory of universal jurisdiction in international law is emblematic of the sort of underlying debates on interference it mediates: walking a tight line between universally mandated exercises of jurisdiction and the ever real risk of overstepping the delicate boundaries of other states' jurisdiction.

Finally, it is worth noting that aside from their strict construction, few international commitments are cast in stone, and most are reversible, allowing states to periodically reinvest what they understand as the *domaine* with gusto. Functions may be re-domesticated, and there is little sense of the fundamental irreversibility of many international commitments, on the basis of voluntaristic premises. The phenomenon sometimes described as the 'backlash' against international norms can be analyzed, in that respect, as a sort of brusque requalification of certain matters as, in fact, belonging to a rekindled *domaine réservé* and as guarding against perceived interference.[690] Certain areas of domestic law and practice can certainly be re-nationalized at relatively short notice, although the travails of Brexit show how much work of disentangling this can lead to. The only exception is that one cannot ever claim that something is part of (what would otherwise be) the *domaine réservé* that touches on *jus cogens* norms: committing genocide, for example, can never revert to states' domestic discretion, if it ever belonged there. Moreover, just as generalities such as 'nothing is sovereign, everything is international' should raise eyebrows, so should the converse 'nothing is international, everything is sovereign'. States only successfully define what is sovereign for international law purposes as a result of a making successful international arguments to that effect.

The *domaine réservé* is still significantly defined by acts of voluntarism as much as the treaties and custom that purport to draw limit it. Moreover, it is not so much that claims about interference are made against unproblematic assumptions about what the *domaine réservé* is, but that such claims constantly and implicitly constitute the *domaine réservé* whose protection they invoke. To methodologically reconstruct the *domaine*, then, involves paying attention

690 On the observable trend of *domaine réservé* expansion, opposite to the expansion of international law, Wood and others (n 562) 554. ('I think, both with regard to the shift in terms of state practice and with regard to the adoption of international conventions, that there is also contrary evidence I find more overwhelming; that the *domaine réservé* is in fact expanding, and that there is a shift toward differentiation'). See also ibid 563. ('[N]ational laws may be shaping the content of international regulation, perhaps even expanding areas of primacy for national law ').

to when, why and how claims about non-interference are made, but also to scrutinize occasions where such claims are made at least implicitly even when the term is not used. It also involves moving beyond repetitious and circuitous claims about interference to ground its study in a more textured exploration of its day-to-day socio-legal performance, contextualizing the *domaine* in the evolution of conceptions about the state and its competencies. If anything, as we will see, the 'new interference' has further compromised the notion that we can give a fixed meaning to inherently domestic jurisdiction in conditions of interdependence, as illustrated in the following efforts to define it by reference to a certain conception of statehood (2), of human rights (3) and of national self-determination (4).

2 Minimal State/Total State

The *domaine reservé* is traditionally understood to refer to matters falling within a state's jurisdiction and to thus be, theoretically and a priori, beyond international law. The way in which this division of labor is understood is that matters not regulated by international law are *ipso facto* considered to have remained part of the state's domain. That assessment is thus in nature dynamic, albeit perhaps a little crudely dichotomous. According to the ICJ, among 'such choices, which must remain free ones' features 'the choice of a political, economic, social and cultural system, and the formulation of foreign policy'.[691] Areas traditionally considered to fall within domestic jurisdiction include matters that closely follow the fundamental organization of statehood: territorial and border control; the relationship to one's population and, in particular, conferral or withdrawal of nationality; the general organization of government; foreign relations; the use of force; core economic policy, etc. This emphasis on both the basic building block of statehood and a more qualitative approach to its organization is visible in the Charter of the Organization of American States (hereafter, OAS Charter) which prohibits 'any other form of interference or attempted threat against the personality of the State or against its political, economic and cultural elements'.[692] It thus includes both the organization of certain sectors of national life and a more ponderous interest in 'self-government'.[693]

---

691 *Nicaragua v United States* (n 3) [205].
692 OAS Charter, art 15.
693 Teachout (n 323) s IV. A.

2.1 *Mutations of Sovereignty*

Certainly, the fundamental features of a state's organization still seem largely within its prerogative. Nonetheless, the development of the state in the last couple of centuries is marked by contradictory trends towards both the inflation and the minimization of its role. This has led to state to oscillate between internationalization and renationalization of the *domaine réservé*. The state, in a pluralistic international system, exists on a spectrum: on the one hand, the 'minimal' state is one that seems to have conceded that there is very little that is inherent to statehood and that is therefore content with a decidedly shrunk *domaine*; on the other hand, the 'total state' considers that everything implicates the core of its sovereignty and that therefore even the slightest intrusion encroaches on its *domaine*. Each of these approaches translates into a different attitude to interference, somewhere between paranoia about the slightest meddling and a more lackadaisical attitude to what makes the state the state. International law unhelpfully speaks of interference as if it applied or was perceived similarly in all states, where clearly its incidence is shaped by a tremendous variety of models of statehood.

The question of the *domaine réservé* must be understood in relation to the long-term evolution of the state, notably in the 20th and 21st Century. That evolution is marked, notably, by a paradoxical growth and retreat of the state's intervention in the economy. As is well known, the state has increasingly become a leading economic actor, borrowing on international financial markets, engaging in development policies, and purchasing and selling goods and services. It has also engaged in policies of welfare and development that formalize its fiduciary role as a provider for populations. But at the same time as it has does so, the state has also been thoroughly 'normalized', divesting itself of its aura as a sovereign persona in order to better engage in business. This has led to a notable *dédoublement* between the state's traditional functions *de jure imperii* (where immunities typically apply) and its new functions *de jure gestionis* (where immunities typically do not apply). Such a functional division of the state is typically considered to be a condition prior to its engagements with international markets, which would be unlikely to do business with it if they had no guarantee of remedy. Immunities typically continue to hold, but only if and when adjudication by domestic courts would be 'wholly inconsistent with the dignity of the foreign state and an interference with its sovereign functions'.[694] Moreover the state has gladly disaggregated itself through

694 *Sengupta v Republic of India* (1983) 64 ILR 352, 361. See also, *British Consulate-General in Naples v Toglia* (1989) 101 ILR 379, 383.

outsourcing and privatization, leading to an ongoing lack of clarity about whether it is still in charge, and whether the relevant matters are still part of the *domaine*.[695]

Although these notions have come up particularly in the relatively narrow context of immunities, they certainly also outline a more deliberately reduced *domaine* substantively. The shrinking public stature of the state in matters economic coexists with ongoing concerns, conversely, that the economy itself is susceptible to interference and must be protected as such. This echoes long-standing notions, going as far back as the East India Company,[696] about whether it might be *corporations* themselves that should be free from interference. This quite startling inversion of non-interference proceeds from neo-liberal premises that have consecrated the idea that states should adopt a *laissez faire* approach to the economy's operation and have elevated free markets to an almost metaphysical level of independence. But it may also be a reflection of the extent to which state sovereignty and 'corporate sovereignty' have long been intertwined so that the latter is naturally driven to claim the immunities that have been associated with the former.[697] At any rate, the generalization of claims of non-interference beyond the state paradoxically fragilizes the state's own.

Another area of complexification of statehood relates to the tendency of the state to fragment itself 'upwards' by delegating a broad range of functions to international organizations. Although the net costs of this move in terms of sovereignty can be exaggerated,[698] it does at least further relativize any strong notion that such functions are inherently or even contingently domestic. States will find it hard, in particular, to brusquely reclaim as domestic matters that have long been the object of joint governance with various regional or international organizations, even if such matters were 'originally' or at some point domestic. The fact that international organizations functions remain, under most readings, powers of attribution subject to the exigencies of voluntarism, should not obscure the fact that in reality such competencies are quite

695 Kuzi Charamba and Frédéric Mégret, 'Wagner, PMSCs, and the Limits of Transnational Governance' (*Lawfare*, 13 April 2023) <https://www.lawfaremedia.org/article/wagner-pmscs-and-limits-transnational-governance> accessed 11 June 2024.

696 John Dalrymple, *The Proper Limits of the Government's Interference with the Affairs of the East-India Company, Attempted to Be Assigned: With Some Few Reflections Extorted by, and on, the Distracted State of the Times* (Leopold Classic Library 2017).

697 Joshua Barkan, *Corporate Sovereignty: Law and Government under Capitalism* (U of Minnesota Press 2013).

698 Oona A Hathaway, 'International Delegation and State Sovereignty' (2008) 71 Law and Contemporary Problems 115.

dynamic and have had a strong tendency to more or less stealthily expand beyond their original conception. This book will return later to what it might mean to think of interference as 'vertical' rather than 'horizontal'. Suffice it to note here that the drawn-out, painful process of Brexit shows just how hard it is to disentangle one's *domaine* from such supranational commitments even as such a pull-out is unmistakably, in part, framed through the vernacular of resisting interference by reclaiming one's sovereignty.[699]

Perhaps more importantly, international law has guaranteed the conditions for an increasing overlap between the *ratione materiae* scope of international and domestic law, weakening the idea that domestic law has anything like an inherent domain. The next section will explore specifically the normative function of international human rights law in objectively shrinking the *domaine réservé*, but in practice the socio-legal effects of that move are there for all to see, making it difficult to protest a range of interventionist practices that invoke human rights. Or consider migration. Although it is seemingly largely accepted that states have the utmost control over migration policy, this was certainly not always the case, and an argument can increasingly be made that even that prerogative is not exclusive.[700] The same is true of something as seemingly intimately tied to sovereignty as the law of nationality,[701] whose associations with the *domaine réservé* have been challenged by assertions of a human right to citizenship.[702] Indeed, even the fundamental modalities of states' organizations are increasingly subjected, directly or indirectly, to international law in the context of international administration, structural adjustment, or democratic exigencies.

On the other hand, and contrary to the conventional but dated and simplistic globalization narrative of the ever-shrinking-*domaine-réservé*, the process goes both ways and can certainly include brusque reassertions of sovereign prerogatives over certain sectors, as well as the continuous maintenance of

---

699 Jed Odermatt, 'Brexit and International Legal Sovereignty' in Juan Santos Vara and Ramses A Wessel (eds), *The Routledge Handbook on the International Dimension of Brexit* (Routledge 2020); Ardi Kolah, 'What Is Meant by 'Sovereignty'and How Important Was It in Influencing the Outcome of the Brexit Trade Negotiations?' <https://pureadmin.qub.ac.uk/ws/files/234180935/Kolah_WP_Proposal_FINAL_1.2.21.pdf> accessed 31 May 2024; John Agnew, 'Taking Back Control? The Myth of Territorial Sovereignty and the Brexit Fiasco' (2020) 8 Territory, Politics, Governance 259.

700 Mégret, 'The Contingency of International Migration Law: "Freedom of Movement", Race, and Imperial Legacies' (n 324).

701 Barbara von Rütte, *The Human Right to Citizenship: Situating the Right to Citizenship within International and Regional Human Rights Law* (Brill Nijhoff 2022) 3; Spiro (n 584).

702 von Rütte (n 701) ch 3.

authority by some states over matters they have clearly signaled as, as far as they are concerned, fundamentally domestic. States have recurrently been tempted to redefine certain areas as part of their inherent domain, all the more so that they have felt certain prerogatives to be threatened, and in the process have sought to draw red lines against interference. Even if they have done so with mixed results (as in the case of Brexit), this attests to an ever-present countervailing trend to re-nationalize in the face of the constant demands of internationalization. That such re-nationalization is even conceivable suggests that the *domaine* never went away and that the incursions of international law were always, to some degree, more contingent than is suggested by more cosmopolitan narratives.

That process of re-nationalization also, it should be said, has deep roots in anti-colonial and anti-imperial resistance. For example, newly decolonized states often insisted that nationalization of natural resources was fundamentally their prerogative and not one regulated by international law. The exercise of that right, moreover, was closely tied to the right of self-determination of peoples[703] and any resistance to it framed as a form of interference. Certainly, the claim that states asserting sovereignty over their natural resources were interfering with the continued proprietary interests, via corporate proxies, of receding colonial powers was treated with contempt. At the same time, the right to exercise such sovereignty has long been constrained, first by obligations of compensation in the case of nationalization (although contested at the time precisely as a form of interference),[704] second by international environmental obligations, and third by ongoing processes of privatization that have blurred the extent to which sovereignty over natural resources conserves a definite public quality. So much so, arguably, that the initial emancipatory impetus has now been strongly mitigated by onerous obligations that relativize

703 Nico Schrijver, 'Self-Determination of Peoples and Sovereignty over Natural Wealth and Resources' in United Nations Human Rights Office of the High Commissioner, *Realizing the Right to Development: Essays in Commemoration of 25 Years of the United Nations Declaration on the Right to Development* (United Nations Publications 2013).

704 In response to U.S. insistence that expropriation should lead to 'appropriate compensation', the Hungarian delegate at the General Assembly emphasized that 'Any decision relating to whether and how much compensation should be paid was essentially an internal affair of the state concerned, which therefore was the sole judge in the matter and could brook no outside interference whatsoever in the exercise of its sovereignty'. See UNGA Second Committee (17th Session) 'Consideration of the Draft Resolution of the Commission on Permanent Sovereignty over Natural Resources' (20 November 1962) U.N. Doc A/C.2/SR.846, para 2.

any rigid notion that control over resources is essentially a domestic issue.[705] Still, a claim to an at least residual sovereignty over functions or resources points to a potential core of non-interference, maybe a sort of presumptive *domaine réservé* or of an original claim to determining certain issues even if that claim can be ceded or relativized.

2.2 *The Attempted Sanctuarization of the Domestic Domain*

More recently, it is particularly in the security and defense sector that a certain process of sanctuarization of the *domaine réservé* has occurred. This involves attempts to deliberately signal to other states what areas one will consider off limits, something which may not always go without saying. It includes an insistence notably in the context of cyber operations that interference with 'critical infrastructure' will be treated as a red line. This follows repeated attacks, for example against the Australian federal government, the Ukraine power grid, U.S. elections, or Iranian uranium enrichment efforts. Although a separate debate is whether some of these attacks are susceptible of constituting armed attacks, the question here is whether in their 'low level' version they can also constitute mere interference. The concern is that cyber-attacks may weaken the systems of particular states but also the general infrastructure of large swathes of both the national and the global economy. The use of the term 'critical infrastructure' by Western states and organizations has spread rapidly in the last few years. It sometimes appears as a sort of *domaine réservé* within the *domaine réservé*, with strong overtones of national security. The European Union, for one, defines critical infrastructure quite broadly as:

> an asset, system or part thereof located in Member States which is essential for the maintenance of vital societal functions, health, safety, security, economic or social well-being of people, and the disruption or destruction of which would have a significant impact in a Member State as a result of the failure to maintain those functions.[706]

For the U.N., this includes domains as diverse as 'the generation, transmission and distribution of energy, air and maritime transport, banking and financial services, e-commerce, water supply, food distribution and public health'.[707] As

705 Nico Schrijver, *Sovereignty Over Natural Resources: Balancing Rights and Duties* (Cambridge University Press 1997).

706 Council Directive 2008/114/EC of 8 December 2008 on the identification and designation of European critical infrastructures and the assessment of the need to improve their protection [2008] OJ L345/75 art 2.

707 UNGA Res 58/199 (23 December 2003) U.N. Doc A/RES/58/199, 1.

can be seen, few areas of a state's economy might not be understood as related to or even dependent on some sort of critical infrastructure. This is even as the building and the upkeep of that infrastructure still routinely relies on international trade, supply chain and tenders that shed doubt on the extent to which it can be neatly nationalized by mere virtue of being described as 'critical'.

An interesting case in point is cyberspace, which has increasingly been described in terms of being a critical infrastructure,[708] most notably by the Department of Homeland Security in the U.S.[709] There has been a rampant tendency to claim sovereignty over certain areas of cyber-space ('cyber-sovereignty'), in ways that seek to bring the language of *domaine réservé* to an area that seems a priori deeply unsuited to it. This has led to efforts to reclaim what is understood to be 'domestic' about information and communication technologies. This is not so much physical infrastructure let alone a space, as a series of sovereign functions, wherever they be exercised.[710] One of the remarkably intractable issues of the moment, however, is the elusiveness of cyberspace and the fact that it clearly exists in ways that transcend any given state. In fact, much of that infrastructure may not have been developed by or the benefit of, nor belong to any particular sovereign. National pretense of jurisdiction over cyberspace, therefore, may lay claim to something that is not (or no longer) for states to claim sovereignty over. Moreover, much cyber infrastructure is of dual use in a context where the state relies on very much the same networks and facilities as private actors.

Whether such virtual Maginot lines will ever provide anything more than an illusory security is therefore open to question, in a context where cyber-sovereignty as a concept remains as catchy as it is elusive. The potential is nonetheless for a considerable, at least symbolic, renationalization of entire spheres of social and economic activity as a result of the effort to guard against interference, notably under the banner of 'securitization'—welding together

708 Moritz Weiss and Felix Biermann, 'Cyberspace and the Protection of Critical National Infrastructure' (2023) 26 Journal of Economic Policy Reform 250; William D O'Neil, 'Cyberspace and Infrastructure' in Franklin D Kramer, Stuart H Starr and Larry K Wentz (eds), *Cyberpower and National Security* (Potomac Books 2009); Sean M Condron, 'Getting It Right: Protecting American Critical Infrastructure in Cyberspace' (2007) 20 Harvard Journal of Law & Technology 403.

709 U.S. Department of Homeland Security, 'Secure Cyberspace and Critical Infrastructure' <https://www.dhs.gov/secure-cyberspace-and-critical-infrastructure> accessed 7 November 2023.

710 Vera Rusinova, 'Principle of the Sovereign Equality of States in the Digital Realm' in Andrey Baykov and Elena Zinovieva (eds), *Digital International Relations* (Palgrave Macmillan 2023).

elements of national security, economic protectionism, nationalism, and the reinvention of the state as a shield protecting against outside interference. Such renationalization processes have effects even if they are not normatively consistent or conceptually coherent: to a significant extent, they construct their reality. To be clear, moreover, the contention is that the boundaries of the *domaine réservé* are being shifted strategically to preempt interference, rather than interference simply 'happening' because something is naturally within the *domaine*. It is the shifting boundaries of the *domaine*, artificial and constructed as they are, that contribute, over time, to shape what is understood as interference and what is not. The posture precedes the definition.

Indeed, the fortunes of the idea of *domaine réservé* are tied to the expansion of the role of the state in other, even more remarkable ways. Even as one of the major developments of globalization had been a neo-liberal prying of the economy away from any sense of sovereign monopoly (and sometimes of any meaningful sovereign participation), concerns about interference are invoked to reinvent a neo-patrimonial state devoted to the absorption of entire swaths of the national economy under its protective umbrella. The operation of the economy as such more generally has thus increasingly been the object of attempts at protection from interference as part of the *domaine réservé*, in ways that are not mandated but arguably do not offend any particular international rule head on. Such a re-appropriation stands to considerably expand the scope of what can be presented, potentially and if need be at least, as domestic affairs, as the state extends its neo-mercantilist tentacles through a mixture of national security and trade-restrictive measures.

On some level, the general operation of the economy would seem to be the sector lending itself least, especially in conditions of globalization, to claims of exclusivity, an evaluation reinforced by the broad evolution of states themselves towards their *de jure gestionis* roles. Yet states have increasingly been tempted, beyond even their own occasional forays qua commercial actors, to designate entire sectors of their economy as scheduled for special protection from interference on account of their strategic character. For example, the Australian Government Department of Home Affairs insists that '[t]he strength of Australian industry—its economic, commercial and technological innovation and success—also makes it a target for foreign interference' and that it is 'committed to supporting industry to make informed and measured decisions on its international engagements and business endeavors, and to understand their exposure to foreign interference risks'. The sectors in question include 'biomedical, education, advanced research and manufacturing, oil, gas and energy, mining equipment, technologies and services, and food and agribusiness'.[711] Similarly, Canada has highlighted as under threat of 'foreign interference and espionage [...] the biopharmaceutical industry, healthcare, supply chains, and research and development'.[712] The European Parliament has expressed concern about 'risk of economic dependence, but also espionage and sabotage, with foreign companies acquiring influence over E.U. critical infrastructure' pointing out notably the fact that 'Chinese shipping companies have acquired majority or sizeable interests in over 20 European ports'.[713] Energy dependency also features prominently among weaknesses that may eventually lead to interference.

This sort of broad securitization has led to wariness in the West of such companies as Huawei and its dominance of 'critical' 5G technology,[714] perhaps one of the most striking test cases of the 'new interference' and what that framing portends. The wariness is also evident in relation to artificial intelligence, quantum computing or even social networks (TikTok, Wechat).[715] It can extend liberally to the entire media industry as when the European Parliament bemoans the fact that 'China has invested almost EUR 3 billion in European media firms over the last 10 years, without an adequate response from the E.U. and its Member States', a move that entails 'considerable risks for the integrity of European democracies and interference by other countries in the EU's domestic affairs'.[716] Beyond suspicions of trade protectionism, the notion that certain technologies have become so crucial to states' sovereign operation that they need to be incubated, nurtured, and protected domestically as if they were coterminous with the performance of sovereignty is a startling development in what potentially counts as part of the *domaine*. And no doubt also, these performative assertions of what belongs to the *domaine* set the stage for ever-growing claims of interference: what is considered fundamentally domestic over time participates in the ongoing construction of what counts as interference.

711 Australian Government, 'Department of Home Affairs' (*Department of Home Affairs Website*) <https://www.homeaffairs.gov.au> accessed 18 June 2023.

712 Public Safety Canada, 'Foreign Interference' (Government of Canada 2021) <https://www.publicsafety.gc.ca/cnt/trnsprnc/brfng-mtrls/prlmntry-bndrs/20210722/015/index-en.aspx> accessed 18 June 2023.

713 2023 Resolution on Foreign Interference in the E.U. (n 335), para AR.

714 Gregory J Moore, 'Huawei, Cyber-Sovereignty and Liberal Norms: China's Challenge to the West/Democracies' (2023) 28 Journal of Chinese Political Science 151.

715 'Annual Threat Assessment of the U.S. Intelligence Community' (Office of the Director of National Intelligence 2024) 12.

716 2023 Resolution on Foreign Interference in the E.U. (n 335), para W.

It is hard to see what sectors are not covered, then, by concerns about interference, with something akin to the cloak of *domaine réservé* loosely invoked to deploy wide ranging defensive measures against perceived foreign threats. This translates into heightened scrutiny of foreign direct investment, including screening for malignant or otherwise problematic takeovers. For example, India restricts Bangladeshi or Pakistani investors from purchasing Indian companies without prior government approval, entirely excluding certain sectors such as defense, space, or atomic energy.[717] The U.S. Federal Government has an interagency committee tasked with reviewing transactions involving foreign investment in the U.S., including real estate transactions, to determine whether they might have an impact on national security notably because they might be connected to military or port installations.[718] Canada has proposed to 'subject all foreign investments by state owned enterprises, or private investors assessed as being closely tied to or subject to direction from foreign governments, to enhanced scrutiny' from a national security perspective.[719] Internationally, the quite permissive 'national security' exception to international trade law allows states parties to not 'furnish any information the disclosure of which it considers contrary to its essential security interests', notably in relation to 'fissionable materials or the materials from which they are derived' or 'traffics in arms, ammunition and implements of war'.[720] In other words, interference may increasingly be presented as constituted through strategic economic initiatives by hostile powers that seek (or are portrayed as seeking) to increase dependency and vulnerability to outside inputs.

Contra this trend, then are, efforts to systematically rebrand the economy as part of some irreducible national *domaine*. Ultimately, efforts at sanctuarizing the economy underline the difficulty of designating certain sectors as part of an industrial inner sanctum under conditions of neo-liberalism that

---

717 Reserve Bank of India, Foreign Exchange Management (Transfer or Issue of Security by a Person Resident Outside India) Regulations, Notification No FEMA 20(R)/2017-RB, 2017.

718 Brandt JC Pasco, 'United States National Security Reviews of Foreign Direct Investment: From Classified Programmes to Critical Infrastructure, This Is What the Committee on Foreign Investment in the United States Cares About' (2014) 29 ICSID Review—Foreign Investment Law Journal 350. To be clear, the framing concern here is national security rather than interference or intervention stricto sensu but the performance of protecting sovereign from foreign encroachments is essentially the same and it is frequently related to concerns with foreign powers rather than merely economic advantage.

719 Public Safety Canada (n 712).

720 The General Agreement on Tariffs and Trade (30 October 1947) 55 UNTS 187 (GATT 1947) art XXI.

have long otherwise emphasized the importance of free competition across borders. The deeply integrated nature of supply chains, even when it comes to strategic sectors, means that drawing lines between the national and the foreign, the critical and the non-critical remains challenging, especially in a context where there is always reason to fear manipulation of national security agendas for protectionist motives. Dependency on global supply chains may certainly create vulnerabilities—if nothing else to boycotts or sanctions—that may affect national independence, but it is at least an open question whether these vulnerabilities create questions of interference specifically as opposed to merely competition. What 'economic sovereignty' means is thus highly debatable, given that vulnerabilities as a result of the international division of labor will have long been freely consented to by states as part of the purported benefits of international trade.[721] Hence although dependency may be understood as a constraint, it was invariably at some point a choice and it will be difficult to fault other states for taking advantage of it, especially when one does the same.

There are, moreover, questions about whether that renationalization can work on its own terms and, more importantly, about the kind of domestic outlook that an all-of-society response to interference can produce. This is particularly the case for institutions that operate at some distance from the state and that can get swept up in an anti-interference drive even as they are highly dependent on continued exchange with the exterior. Consider the example of universities, arguably among the institutions that have most, historically, turned towards the outside on the basis of autonomously driven research agendas and an ethos of open exchange. Many academic institutions in the West have of late become aware of attempts to interfere with their research from abroad (although interference is sometimes confused with industrial or security espionage,[722] which are not the same thing), notably by foreign universities that are, for their part, tightly state-controlled. Whereas threats to academic independence were traditionally seen as coming from within, they have increasingly been identified as emanating from transnational sources.

721 Paul Hérault, 'Strengthening Sovereignty in the Era of Global Value Chains' (IFRI 2021) <https://www.ifri.org/sites/default/files/atoms/files/herault_global_value_chains_2021.pdf> accessed 24 January 2024.

722 Although the issue is different, it arguably stems from the same source, namely that some states exercise particularly tight control over their universities for foreign policy purposes. See e.g., Kasra Aarabi, 'Iran Is Exploiting Our Universities More than Whitehall Imagines' *The Jewish Chronicle* (13 July 2023) <https://www.thejc.com/lets-talk/iran-is-exploiting-our-universities-more-than-whitehall-imagines-okg32c03> accessed 18 February 2024.

Particular incidents, such as the temporary disinvitation of the Dalai Lama by the University of Sydney apparently following pressures from the local Chinese consulate, suggest a real potential for transnational intrusion, at least when it comes to the choice of certain high-profile speakers.[723] The transnational impact of interference on students, notably those who have sought an escape from oppressive conditions but who continue to be at the mercy of the long-arm of their government on foreign campuses, is not negligible either.[724] Although not the same thing as interference, scientific and industrial espionage in laboratories has also been a recurrent fear that evokes ways in which a country's scientific investments and priorities can be disrupted by ill-meaning foreign powers.[725] The fear is that universities, especially given their dependence on outside sources of funding, will prove to be a soft underbelly for the purposes of a certain form of foreign intellectual hijacking. This is evidently a difficult form of interference to respond to and not simply on account of university's own preference for openness, given its diffuseness and easy-mistakability for exactly the sort of free and open exchange that the academic world presupposes.

Although such scenarios are alarming, they have also often been captured by host states keen on claiming the academic sector as a kind of extension of themselves through the jargon of 'critical infrastructure'. This has given rise to initiatives aimed if nothing else at affirming universities' commitment to certain values, to protect them from such interference.[726] The Canadian National Security Guidelines for Research Partnerships (2021) is a good example of how governments can and do work with the university sector to mitigate potential threats, for example by screening some applications for grants that are deemed problematic, identifying foreign labs that pose a

723 Adam Harvey, 'Uni under Fire for Pulling Pin on Dalai Lama Event' *ABC News* (17 April 2013) <https://www.abc.net.au/news/2013-04-17/uni-under-fire-for-pulling-pin-on-dalai-lama-event/4635720> accessed 17 February 2024.

724 Sophie McNeill, '"They Don't Understand the Fear We Have": How China's Long Reach of Repression Undermines Academic Freedom at Australia's Universities' (Human Rights Watch 2021) <https://www.hrw.org/sites/default/files/media_2021/07/australia0621_web.pdf> accessed 18 February 2024.

725 Jorge Marinho and Júlio Ventura, 'Foreign Influence and Academic Espionage: Portugal's University of Lisbon Perspective' (*Diplomat magazine*, 1 October 2023) <https://diplomatmagazine.eu/2023/10/01/foreign-influence-and-academic-espionage/> accessed 16 June 2024.

726 Association of American Universities (AAU), 'America's Leading Research Universities Committed to Protecting Nation's Values and Prosperity' <https://www.aau.edu/newsroom/press-releases/americas-leading-research-universities-committed-protecting-nations-values> accessed 6 March 2024.

threat,[727] and enhancing data security. Australia has set up a 'University Foreign Interference Taskforce' that monitors security risks for the academic sector, notably on-campus intimidation, harassment, censorship or intimidation. Efforts have been undertaken to enhance the national security literacy of universities and to encourage reporting of suspicious activity.[728]

Such initiatives, whilst welcome on some level, also potentially put university agendas on a collision course with their own ambition to act as places of open access to knowledge and debate and the state's willingness to see them as pawns in a broader integrated strategy of non-interference. Although these moves may not be as dramatic as the 'Red Scare' of the 1950s in the U.S., they are somewhat reminiscent of it. Then, the National Council for American Education had sought to 'eradicate Socialism, Communism and all forms of Marxism from the schools and colleges of America, and to stimulate sound American education'.[729] Subversive professors were identified and harassed by Congress. Harvard was denounced as 'Kremlin on the Charles'.[730] The Educational Policies Commission found that Communists should not be employed in academia because they had surrendered their integrity. The effects on academic freedom were considerable. The American Civil Liberties Union, despite being emphatic that it harbored no sympathy for communists, deplored the blanket ban from teaching as 'ill-conceived, unrealistic and dangerous'. The fear was that '[s]tudents would be enlisted in the search for heresy, as they have been. Classrooms would no longer be free; teachers would be driven to a cautious conformity to avoid suspicion of "dangerous thoughts"'.[731]

---

727 Joanna Chiu, 'Canada Set to Name Foreign Labs, Universities That Pose Risk to National Security' *Toronto Star* (8 May 2023) <https://www.thestar.com/news/canada/canada-set-to-name-foreign-labs-universities-that-pose-risk-to-national-security/article_4344a58d-f9f0-5e93-8604-82529aaff253.html> accessed 5 July 2024.

728 'Protect Your Research: Collaborate with Care' (Australian Security Intelligence Organisation (ASIO) 2023) <https://www.asio.gov.au/system/files/2023-05/Protect%20Your%20Research%2C%20Collaborate%20with%20Care%20-%20Booklet.pdf> accessed 18 February 2024.

729 National Council for American Education, *Must American Youth Be Taught That Communism and Socialism Are Superior to Americanism? The Answer of the National Council for American Education Is No!* (National Council for American Education 1952) 2 <http://archive.org/details/1952MustAmericanYouth> accessed 5 July 2024.

730 Ben W Heineman, Jr, 'The University in the McCarthy Era' *The Harvard Crimson* (17 June 1965) <https://www.thecrimson.com/article/1965/6/17/the-university-in-the-mccarthy-era/> accessed 6 March 2024.

731 Committee on Academic Freedom of the American Civil Liberties Union, 'Statement from the Committee on Academic Freedom of the American Civil Liberties Union' (12 July 1949) <https://oac.cdlib.org/ark:/13030/hb4d5nb612/?brand=oac4> accessed 6 March 2024.

'Re-nationalizing' scholarly research, especially in an age where it has otherwise become so global and devoted to the creed of openness, is potentially a highly problematic proposal. It can, by reaction, over-commit universities to a certain alignment with the national security agenda of their own state. It can lead to a chronic suspicion of foreign students and academics and specifically of certain nationalities or even ethnicities. In Australia, for example, Human Rights Watch has deplored that the portrayal of Chinese students as 'unthinking, untrustworthy, manipulable defenders of the Chinese Communist Party' combined with the failure of host institutions to protect their academic freedom has led to a steep rise in racism.[732] Re-nationalization depends on the definition of threats that are constantly evolving and that could be exaggerated in ways that have a stifling impact on research.[733] If nothing else, it can result in very significant loss of funding. Most importantly, it is in tension with a logic of engagement, mutuality and curiosity that requires a willingness to be innovative with international partnerships.[734] Already, some research projects have had to be abandoned, such as the University of Waterloo's partnership with Huawei in Canada.[735] And it is not clear that, for all these measures, the threat of interference has actually receded.[736] This will require careful navigation by relevant actors both within and beyond universities to make sure that a heavy-handed response does not end up making the remedy worse than the ill.[737]

---

732 McNeill (n 723) 5.

733 Brian Owens, 'Researchers Decry a Lack of Clarity under National Security Risk Assessments' *University Affairs* (21 March 2023) <https://universityaffairs.ca/news/news-article/researchers-decry-a-lack-of-clarity-under-national-security-risk-assessments/> accessed 6 March 2024.

734 ibid.

735 Joanna Chiu, 'University of Waterloo Ends Research Partnerships with Huawei, amid Security Concerns over China' *Toronto Star* (19 July 2023) <https://www.thestar.com/news/canada/university-of-waterloo-to-end-research-partnership-with-chinese-tech-giant-huawei/article_d7e7f352-a6d5-5353-bee6-8429df4b2be7.html> accessed 17 February 2024.

736 Brendan Walker-Munro, 'Why Universities Are Still at Risk for Foreign Interference' (*The Interpreter*, 7 August 2023) <https://www.lowyinstitute.org/the-interpreter/why-universities-are-still-risk-foreign-interference> accessed 6 March 2024.

737 See Parliamentary Joint Committee on Intelligence and Security, 'Inquiry into National Security Risks Affecting the Australian Higher Education and Research Sector' (Commonwealth of Australia 2022) 117 <https://parlinfo.aph.gov.au/parlInfo/download/committees/reportjnt/024611/toc_pdf/InquiryintonationalsecurityrisksaffectingtheAustralianhighereducationandresearchsector.pdf;fileType=application%2Fpdf> accessed 2 February 2024. ('[N]ational security and academic freedoms/international engagement are not zero-sum concepts but complementary').

2.3 *(Re)nationalizing Politics?*

Academic freedom and exchange, in fact, can be seen as a laboratory—a sort of canary in the mine—for broader debates about societies' openness in times of interference when it comes to the notion of national politics, especially the democratic kind. This has led to significant soul searching as the feasibility of such a project comes into focus. Partly the argument is that it is simply too late already, that there is too much leakage between the domestic and the foreign to, for example, make relocating democracy forcefully in the *civis* feasible (or even reasserting the sovereignty of 'sovereignty'), let alone appealing. Partly the argument is that it will be hard to have it both ways and to condemn what one has oneself invited. For example, it is often domestic political parties, the very parties tasked with adopting laws to limit interference, who have most directly benefited from foreign funding and who seek to maintain their ability to access it.[738] Another argument is that nationalization of something such as cyberspace is inherently problematic and defeats the prized openness of the digital revolution as part of a commitment to open societies. Finally, another argument is that openness and closure, in addition to being susceptible to deep inertias, are difficult to effect on a sectoral basis as if, for example, the openness of economic, security, and democratic spheres were not already deeply interconnected.

Indeed, as part of the move to guard against the dangers of interference, one witnesses a strong retreat to (and imagining of) what might be described as a sort of core decisional power, and its irreducible delineation of a domain of 'freedom of choice of the political, social, economic and cultural system of a State'.[739] This what Georges Abi-Saab described as the 'hardcore' of sovereignty, understood as the 'sovereign right of "self-organization"'.[740] This rediscovery and even sacralization of sovereignty can feed into a sort of nostalgia for and fantasy of the 'pure' sovereign state, one uncorrupted by 'toxic' foreign interferences and whose fate is entirely in its own hands. This is evident, for example, in the Russian foreign agent registration law, which focuses almost obsessively on organizations that 'participate in political activity in Russia'. This then leads to a temptation to expand the *domaine* to encompass any NGO whose 'goals and tasks [...] create threats to the sovereignty, political independency, territorial integrity, national unity, cultural heritage, and national interests of the

738 Quinn (n 398).
739 *Nicaragua v United States* (n 3) [263].
740 Abi-Saab (n 557) 229.

Russian Federation'.[741] The focus on decision-making is strategically understandable and does point to an intrinsic dimension of what statehood, historically, was supposed to be about; but it can lead to a hyper valorization of the state's monopoly over its own affairs, as well as breed a culture of suspicion that instrumentalizes wariness with the outside to better repress the inside.

Nor is this move, worryingly, restricted to autocratic states; the liberal response has also been to sanctuarize certain irreducible dimensions of the exercise of political power, even if in more narrow and less totalizing ways. It is democracy itself, in particular, that has been strongly reclaimed as *national* (the normative case for seeing democracy as a foundation for non-interference claims will be examined in the next section; I am only interested here in the ways claims about democracy serve to effectively make arguments about the scope of the state's *domaine*).[742] A priori, democracy is a natural candidate for the *domaine réservé* given its central connection to self-determination and governance. Interference has been described as 'vitiat[ing] the public debate around elections and other democratic processes and [...] prevent[ing] citizens from making informed choices or discourage[ing] them from political participation altogether' as well as being 'a direct threat to fair democratic political competition'.[743] Somewhat distinct from democracy lato sensu, a quite compelling case has certainly been made that elections specifically and their organization, as 'the highest and most significant moment of expression of domestic jurisdiction',[744] belong to a certain inner sanctum.

The idea of a 'self-enclosed and autochthonous territory over which the *demos* governs',[745] however, has itself long been put into question. Normatively, as will be discussed further, there may be a certain wariness with conceiving of democracy in purely national terms or self-determination as a fully self-referential process. This may still leave the sovereign ultimately in charge, if nothing else in that it organizes elections and political life. But note some important tensions. Democracy relies in large part on the state *desisting* from

---

741 Federal Law of n 121-FZ of 23 July 2012 on Amendments to Certain Legislative Acts of the Russian Federation in the Regulation of Nonprofit Organizations Acting as a Foreign Agent, para 2 i-d.

742 Jamie Fly, Laura Rosenberger and David Salvo, 'Policy Blueprint for Countering Authoritarian Interference in Democracies' (Alliance for Securing Democracy 2018).

743 2023 Resolution on Foreign Interference in the E.U. (n 335), para AW.

744 Annachiara Rotondo and Pierluigi Salvati, 'Fake News, (Dis)Information, and the Principle of Nonintervention: Scope, Limits, and Possible Responses to Cyber Election Interference in Times of Competition' [2019] The Cyber Defense Review 209, 210.

745 Seyla Benhabib, *The Rights of Others: Aliens, Residents, and Citizens* (Cambridge University Press 2004) 216.

encroaching on the pluralism of political life by imposing its preferences. Part of the vulnerability and even collapse of democratic institutions in the West and beyond has arisen precisely when the state has used its leverage to influence democratic outcomes (from gerrymandering to improperly using public office or budget to campaign or attempts to interfere with the judicial process, for example). An overbearingly protective state is one that can quickly kill the golden goose. The threat of interference, moreover, can be invoked to justify a degree of 'democratic paternalism', one in which the state acts, both potentially positively and ominously, as a sort of 'guardian' of democracy, for example by deciding which foreign information or influence is accessible to the citizenry. And of course, the forceful movement of the state into all walks of life is associated historically with the rise of totalitarianism.

Simultaneously, the need for democracy and its protection have increasingly been internationalized so that democracy may well be inherently domestic but also paradoxically fundamentally enchased in international norms. International election monitoring, whether by international organizations or third states, attests to an ongoing global and transnational interest in the proper conduct of elections. Some states have also bound themselves internationally to achieve democratic standards and to protect themselves from democratic backsliding, in a context where such backsliding is an increasingly global risk.[746] This is, of course, entirely distinct from the eminently contested debate on whether states can intervene to restore democracy in others. Indeed, pro-democratic interference can still be very much problematic interference. Nonetheless, the willingness to internationalize a fundamental concern for democracy at least relativizes the idea that what is problematic about such scrutiny is that it is foreign, when in fact international monitoring is sometimes the only protection against elections being stolen.[747] It belies the notion that the state is alone in maintaining democracy's integrity or that the best way to do so is to block out outside influences.

Moving beyond the protection of both merely sovereignty or only democracy, is a genre of arguments that extends the *domaine* to the public sphere more generally. One idea in this context is that the *domaine réservé* should be

746 Robert Mickey, Steven Levitisky and Lucan Ahmad Way, 'Is America Still Safe for Democracy? Why the United States Is in Danger of Backsliding' (2017) 96 Foreign Affairs 20.

747 Although it is worth noting that the line between monitoring and meddling can sometimes be a subtle one, at least in that monitoring always has an effect on local electors. Sarah Sunn Bush and Lauren Prather, *Monitors and Meddlers: How Foreign Actors Influence Local Trust in Elections* (Cambridge University Press 2022).

redescribed as the '*domaine privilégié*' and include, as part of a revamped inner sanctum that triggers claims of interference, protection of 'the free choice and the stability of a political, economic, social or cultural system from foreign attacks'.[748] This includes a basic sense of sovereignty but also a sort of capacious and even proprietary embrace of dimensions extending beyond the traditional public sphere. As argued quite strikingly by Thibault Moulin, drawing on both a new spin on the 'fundamental rights of states' as well as the notion of necessity, there has long been a tolerance in international law for states protecting certain fundamental interests which extend beyond the mere operation of the government.[749] This arguably militates for a broad understanding of the *domaine* since the rule of non-intervention, as it were, cannot go *less* far than international law otherwise already does in its general defense of sovereignty. This could extend, for example, to more proprietary claims from the sovereign about the public sphere and the need to isolate the debates that occur within it from their exterior, and it could lead to the state assuming a more protective function of private actors that are seen as coextensive to its sphere of competence.

Doctrinally, it is not clear that such a construct is very wise: non-intervention is a rule of international law, necessity is a regime precluding illegality, and the 'rights of state' is an antiquated notion that, pushed to its extreme, can spell the end of international law. Amalgamating the three is not without its dangers. Normatively, it is also problematic in that, as will be discussed in more detail later, it can have the effect of making the public sphere and civil society subservient to the needs of the sovereign to protect its *domaine* réservé, potentially frustrating democracy and peoples' demands for openness. But at least the notion of the '*domaine privilégié*' testifies to the sheer plasticity of what is at any given time considered part of the *domaine*. It shows how, in particular, grave and dire circumstances can lead to swift recharacterization of what was previously international as domestic. The appeal of the theory is also that states are not compelled to watch passively as some of the underlying bases of their self-determining selves are undermined: in effect, the very definition of non-interference and sovereignty are being shaped by the response to the new-interference, and an appeal to voluntarism remains the crux of any attempt at delineating the notion.

If followed, this is nonetheless a remarkable extension of what constitutes the *domaine*. On one reading, it is an extension that may be rendered inevitable

748 Moulin (n 461) 433.

749 ibid.

precisely by the heavy reliance of the post-modern state on an array of privately managed externalities. It is a reminder that although international law's conception of the state is rather thin (a government ruling a population on a territory), domestic conceptions of the state as a site of collective life anchored by a number of political, economic, social, and cultural referents are much richer. They include underlying ideas about self-determination and the extent to which sovereignty is supposed to serve it. Rather than the mere protection of sovereignty, the theory points to a certain *irreducibility* of national life that may be worth protecting in and of itself. Pursued to its logical consequence, however, the idea that many areas of domestic life are part of the *domaine réservé* can lead to an unsustainable encroachment of the public upon the private and goes against a decades if not centuries long effort at treating sovereignty as not merely a private sphere immune from outside scrutiny. And concretely, although interference is typically conceived as occurring against the sovereign or a people's self-determination, the question has increasingly arisen as to whether interference can also target purely private interests in the host state.

Clearly, if we take seriously the idea that the state is composed not only of its government but of its *forces vives*, then there is no limit to the ways in which a foreign state can interfere with the latter. And, indeed, Moulin argues that his conception of *domaine privilégié* means that there can be interference against the 'political organisation of the state', 'internal and external security', 'major economic interests', 'public services' and even 'the environment'. In purporting to create a considerable protective bubble for entire sectors of domestic social life, the notion of the *domaine privilégié* could be just the theory that the norm of non-interference needs. Yet it also carries the risk of its more expansive iterations becoming a recipe for a capacious nationalism that contains the seeds of a new protectionist totalitarianism. What if dictators, oligarchs or plutocrats, having captured the state, then use the claim of non-interference to solidify their essentially privatized vision of sovereignty? Such is, at any rate, the paradigmatic risk of 'total states' propped up by a discourse of non-intervention that seeks to ratify internationally the *fait accompli* of their stranglehold on power: it may either justify a neo-corporatist embrace of the private sphere, or it may unduly sanctify private power as public.

It is true that there may be cases where the imbrication between certain private actors and a sense of the self-directed character of a polity is so intimate that interfering with said private actors is co-extensive with interfering with sovereignty. In other words, interfering directly with private actors within a state could be a way of interfering indirectly with the polity and, by extension, the state. Consider for example the notorious case of the hacking of U.S. company Sony Pictures Entertainment in 2014 by North Korean agents, apparently to deter the company from releasing a movie that was deemed insulting to that state's leader. After Sony cancelled the launch, then President Obama did not hesitate, as head of state, to invoke the broader language of interference. He insisted that '[w]e cannot have a society where some dictator someplace can start imposing censorship here in the United States' and saying he regretted that Sony had not consulted with the government first,[750] whilst John Kerry described it as a violation of 'international norms'.[751] In doing so, the U.S. government seemed to requalify what might have been seen as merely a violation of U.S. domestic law into a matter of constitutional integrity and, possibly, of international law. At least one author has described the hack as unmistakably a violation of sovereignty, although not necessarily a violation of the rule of non-intervention.[752]

At the same time, the matter was not pursued publicly with North Korea as a question of interference let alone intervention under international law per se. No countermeasures are known to have been adopted, Obama clarified that he did not consider it to be an 'act of war', and international lawyers would have had a hard time describing it as a form of intervention *de lege lata*. The situation may be different where the company has a more strategic role or raises key questions of national security (e.g., Boeing) or where what is targeted is not a single company but an entire sector of the economy.[753] This suggests that there is at least a lack of clarity about whether the rule of non-interference is violated when only private interests are targeted (irrespective of the fact that other rules may be violated), and some trepidation about invoking the mantle of the *domaine réservé* to push back against this more *sui generis* state-to-private actor form of interference. It is also a reminder that there is a risk in elevating such matters to the level of public international law when they may just as well be treated under domestic criminal law, for example. In short, just

750 Zeke J Miller, 'Obama Says Sony "Made a Mistake" Pulling "The Interview"' [2014] *TIME* <https://time.com/3642459/sony-hack-the-interview-barack-obama/> accessed 3 January 2024.

751 John Kerry, 'Condemning Cyber-Attack by North Korea' (*US Department of State*, 19 December 2014) <2009-2017.state.gov/secretary/remarks/2014/12/235444.htm> accessed 1 February 2024.

752 Clare Sullivan, 'The 2014 Sony Hack and the Role of International Law' (2016) 8 Journal of National Security Law and Policy 437.

753 Harriet Moynihan, 'The Application of International Law to State Cyberattacks: Sovereignty and Non-Intervention' [2019] Research Paper, International Law Programme, Chatham House para 118 <https://www.chathamhouse.org/sites/default/files/publications/research/2019-11-29-Intl-Law-Cyberattacks.pdf> accessed 3 January 2024.

because the reach of the modern state has tended to be extensive does not mean that every move to broaden the scope of the *domaine réservé* should be accepted uncritically.

3 Human Rights/Democracy

Beyond the ambition to apportion primarily domestic and international domains based on some functional criteria linked to the nature of the state itself, efforts have long gone into putting the distinction on firmer principled footing, notably by making it hinge on some deeper human rights rationale. As we will see, however, human rights do not provide, despite or perhaps because of the high demands they impose on states, a consistent signpost for delimiting the *domaine réservé*. This is on account of the varying degrees to which different states are committed to human rights instruments, the sheer indeterminacy of the scope of human rights obligations, but also tensions inherent to the human rights project, most notably between its individualist and deontological sensitivities on the one hand, and its collective and instrumental propensities on the other. This then leads on a path where it is democracy itself that is, this time on human rights grounds, propped up as the defining feature of the *domaine*, in ways that will be shown to be themselves still problematic.

3.1 *Do Human Rights Spell the End of the Domaine Réservé?*

As already examined in the first chapter, human rights are historically broadly associated with reconfiguring the *domaine réservé*, in ways that are generally understood as having shrunk it. This has been presented at times as a factual reconfiguration, and sometimes as a normative one, though it probably has elements of both. Human rights considerations are effectively reshaping what counts as part of the *domaine reservé* in a sociolegal sense; but they are also defining that scope from the purportedly superior axiological character of international human rights law. In other words, what counts is not only the ongoing, customary self-definition of the *domaine réservé* in terms of state practice (even though that too is happening), but the sheer immanent *autoritas* of human rights when it comes laying claim to domains heretofore largely considered as domestic. Notions like 'sovereignty as responsibility',[754] goes the

754 Roberta Cohen and Francis M Deng, 'Sovereignty as Responsibility' in Alex J Bellamy and Timothy Dunne (eds), *The Oxford Handbook of the Responsibility to Protect* (Oxford University Press 2016); Francis M Deng, 'From "Sovereignty as Responsibility" to the "Responsibility to Protect"' (2010) 2 Global Responsibility to Protect 353; Amitai Etzioni,

argument, fundamentally reshape the *domaine réservé* by making ruling over that domain dependent on compliance with prior international obligations.

Several dimensions of human rights concur, theoretically and doctrinally, to making them into potentially capacious vehicles for intervention and interference. First, the universalism of human rights means that intervening states can argue that international human rights standards are already the standards of the target state, thus belying any notion of the specificity of the *domaine réservé*. They are, moreover, shared standards, so that the otherwise interfering state is merely complaining about obligations that both are committed to. Second, the binding and even *jus cogens* nature of human rights means that intervening states are merely not violating international obligations when intervening, but actually complying with them. Not only are they not interfering, but they *must* in fact perform solicitousness in relation to the human rights or humanitarian record of others. Third, international human rights protections thoroughly cut across facile distinctions such as that between an internal and an external domain, so that nothing ever seems, given the wide scope of such protections and their overlap with most areas of domestic jurisdiction, like it is plausibly inherently national.

These ideas have been given striking credence in the European context, one in which the idea of the common concern for human rights is well entrenched and gives rise to sophisticated views of the European Convention on Human Rights as based on obligations 'essentially of an objective character'.[755] This has since at least the case brought by Scandinavian states and the Netherlands against colonels' regime in Greece justified the notion that states can sue others in the European system as part of an emerging *actio popularis* when other states violate the human rights of their own populations.[756] As the European Court of Human Rights (ECtHR) put it in a case on the Russian Registration Law to which we will return later:

'Sovereignty as Responsibility' (2006) 50 Orbis 71; Luke Glanville, 'The Antecedents of "Sovereignty as Responsibility"' (2011) 17 European Journal of International Relations 233.

755 *Austria v Italy* (1961) 4 YB 116, para 138. See also Frédéric Mégret, 'Nature of Obligations' in Daniel Moeckli and others (eds), *International Human Rights Law* (Oxford University Press 2014) 100.

756 Kristine Kjærsgaard, 'Confronting the Greek Military Junta: Scandinavian Joint Action under the European Commission on Human Rights, 1967–70' in Poul Villaume, Rasmus Mariager and Helle Porsdam (eds), *The 'Long 1970s': Human Rights, East-West Détente and Transnational Relations* (Routledge 2016); Mark E Villiger, 'Inter-State Applications (Article 33 of the Convention)' in Mark E Villiger, *Handbook on the European Convention on Human Rights* (Brill Nijhoff 2022).

> In essence, the regulation appears to be based on a notion that matters such as respect for human rights and the rule of law are 'internal affairs' of the State and that any external scrutiny of such matters is suspect and a potential threat to national interests. This notion is not compatible with the drafting history and underlying values of the Convention as an instrument of European public order and collective security: that the rights of all persons within the legal space of the Convention are a matter of concern to all member States of the Council of Europe.[757]

This idea of the widely shared interest in certain values has known of very specific applications in the international criminal justice contexts. It underscores the power of states to refer to the Court situations other than their own, as Argentina, Canada, Colombia, Chile Paraguay have done in relation to Venezuela, or many states against Israel, for example.

Still, the idea that all issues of human rights have essentially eviscerated the *domaine réservé* needs to be assessed critically and is worth better than formalist generalities. As seen in the previous chapter, this was never that obvious to Warsaw Pact states when ratifying the Helsinki Final Act. These states believed, erroneously it turns out, that notwithstanding human rights' universal character their implementation was essentially domestic so that no 'title—legal, moral or political—to claim compliance or to protest against non-compliance vis-à-vis the other participating States' would be created in favour of other participating states who would be 'the exclusive judge of [their] performance'.[758] At the time of the Helsinki Final Act, Arangio-Ruiz made a compelling case that the Soviet argument that international human rights law did not impose substantive obligations on states had already been overtaken by international law.[759] That Helsinki moment may have passed, but it problematizes any facile sense that the implementation of human rights must necessarily follow the same path as their proclamation. Simply because rights are hailed as being of common concern materially does not necessarily mean that they can justify any manner of foreign incursion. There seems to be a distinction worth maintaining, in particular, between the broadly symbolically intrusive character of human rights obligations themselves, and the necessary conversation about the sort of means that can be deployed by third states or supranational bodies to enforce them.

---

757 *Ecodefence and Others v Russia* App no 9988/13 and others (ECtHR 14 June 2022), para 139.

758 Gaetano Arangio-Ruiz, *Human Rights and Non-Intervention in the Helsinki Final Act* (Sijthoff & Noordhoff 1977) 209.

759 ibid 212.

The question remains, therefore, whether invoking human rights from outside a state can make legal those measures that would otherwise be an illegal form of interference. At one end of the spectrum, it is largely acknowledged that 'merely considering, debating, and making recommendations regarding a state's human rights record is not generally considered "intervention" in that state's internal affairs'.[760] At the other end of the spectrum, the most famous variant of that debate concerns humanitarian intervention, an area where some scholars have long sought to argue that the use of force, a particularly radical form of intervention, could be legal *in extremis* when engaged in to protect human rights.[761] That these conversations even arise is a reminder that, for states in particular, there is quite a gap between the recognition that certain areas are broadly subsumed under the notion of 'international concern' and the idea that intervention or interference are ipso facto inconceivable as soon as human rights are involved. Human rights lawyers are sometimes at fault for under-specifying the implications of the general recognition that human rights are of common concern, given that this can surely not be a licence for the interference by all in all others' affairs.

If nothing else, there is now a quite solid consensus that a human rights exception to the prohibition on the use of force has not materialized, been created, or been confirmed even to avoid international crimes, let alone in cases of more 'ordinary' human rights violations. This is so after more than a decade of R2P norm entrepreneurship failing to yield much more, when it comes to the narrow question of the use of force, than a confirmation of the status quo. The pushback, whether on pacifist, anti-imperial, prudential, or sovereignty-respecting grounds, has been quite consistent.[762] The dominant feeling has been that humanitarian intervention either resuscitates the 'standard of civilization', unduly erodes prohibitions on the use of force in the U.N. Charter, or is too discretionary a notion to provide guidance in international relations. At most, scholars have pointed to the ultimately undecidable character of the prohibition of humanitarian intervention, even as they have emphasized the rhetorical power of international law in occasionally legitimizing but also ruling it out[763] on the basis of discourses of morality and

760 Sean D Murphy, *Humanitarian Intervention: The United Nations in an Evolving World Order* (University of Pennsylvania Press 1996) 10.

761 Tesón (n 196).

762 Orford (n 27); Iain Atack, 'Ethical Objections to Humanitarian Intervention' (2002) 33 Security Dialogue 279; Mohammed Ayoob, 'Humanitarian Intervention and State Sovereignty' (2002) 6 The International Journal of Human Rights 81.

763 Ian Hurd, 'Is Humanitarian Intervention Legal? The Rule of Law in an Incoherent World' (2011) 25 Ethics & International Affairs 293; Martti Koskenniemi, '"The Lady Doth Protest

legitimacy.[764] The only saving grace for humanitarian intervention, then, is it having been decided by an international body—the U.N. Security Council—which already has the authority to decide upon the use of force on its own grounds anyhow.[765] In the end, the use of force component of the R2P debate amounted to very little,[766] although some of its other pillars do help restructure the understanding of what constitutes interference in international affairs.

There remains today a relatively marginal debate on the legality of armed intervention to rescue one's *own* nationals[767] (as opposed to humanitarian intervention which seeks to assist the nationals of another state), a distant legacy of imperial patterns of 'protection of nationals'. This is sometimes framed as not (so) easily suspected of being a nefarious intervention given states' evident jurisdictional interest in the fate of their own citizens, merely raising the question 'of the extent to which the right of one state to self-defence held sway over the right of another to independence'.[768] Nonetheless, it is doubtful that even cloaking the defense of one's nationals in human rights terms[769] will

---

Too Much" Kosovo, and the Turn to Ethics in International Law' (2002) 65 The Modern Law Review 159.

764 JE Linter, 'Humanitarian Intervention: Legitimising the Illegal?' (2005) 5 Defence Studies 271.

765 Jost Delbruck, 'A Fresh Look at Humanitarian Intervention under the Authority of the United Nations Commentary on International Law' (1991) 67 Indiana Law Journal 887.

766 Dele Jemirade, 'Humanitarian Intervention (HI) and the Responsibility to Protect (R2P): The United Nations and International Security' (2021) 30 African Security Review 48; Andrew Garwood-Gowers, 'China's "Responsible Protection" Concept: Reinterpreting the Responsibility to Protect (R2P) and Military Intervention for Humanitarian Purposes' (2016) 6 Asian Journal of International Law 89; Simon Chesterman, 'Humanitarian Intervention and R2P' in Thomas G Weiss and Rorden Wilkinson (eds), *International Organization and Global Governance* (3rd edn, Routledge 2023); Cristina Badescu, *Humanitarian Intervention and the Responsibility to Protect: Security and Human Rights* (Routledge 2010); Noele Crossley, 'Is R2P Still Controversial? Continuity and Change in the Debate on "Humanitarian Intervention"' (2018) 31 Cambridge Review of International Affairs 415.

767 Theodor Schweisfurth, 'Operations to Rescue Nationals in Third States Involving the Use of Force in Relation to the Protection of Human Rights' (1980) 23 German Yearbook of International Law 159; Tom Ruys, 'The "Protection of Nationals" Doctrine Revisited' (2008) 13 Journal of Conflict & Security Law 233; Raby (n 446); John R D'Angelo, 'Resort to Force by States to Protect Nationals: The U.S. Rescue Mission to Iran and Its Legality under International Law Note' (1980) 21 Virginia Journal of International Law 485; Abraham Abramovsky and Preston L Greene, 'Unilateral Intervention on Behalf of Hijacked American Nationals Held Abroad' (1979) 1979 Utah Law Review 231.

768 Vincent (n 69) 288.

769 Natalino Ronzitti, *Rescuing Nationals Abroad Through Military Coercion and Intervention on Grounds of Humanity* (Martinus Nijhoff Publishers 1985); Richard B Lillich, 'Forcible Self-Help by States to Protect Human Rights' (1967) 53 Iowa Law Review 325.

suffice to launder what remains otherwise very much a violation of the obligation not to use force and a form of blatant intervention.[770] Intervention to save one's nationals remains at best tolerated and often will be blatantly illegal, unless it otherwise fits within a self-defence paradigm or has been authorized by the Security Council.[771] In other words, not even the saving grace of minding the fate of one's nationals provides a plausible defense against the charge that in using force in violation of international law, one is doing anything else than unlawfully intervening in the affairs of another state.

At any rate the use of force is a peculiar taboo, one that was always unlikely to be overturned by mere invocations of human rights—not least of course because any use of force stands to negatively affect such rights. It is probably the case that the particularly restrictive approach when it comes to the use of force cannot easily be generalized to actions short of the use of force, such as non-forcible counter measures,[772] notably of an economic nature, where arguments taken from human rights may therefore, all other things being equal, have more traction. The broader question remains, then, as to the justificatory power of human rights in defense of a variety of incursions that do not make it to the level of the use of force in international law. This is especially the case in a decentralized international system marked by imperfect human rights compliance and where pressures will no doubt exist to effectuate some kind of decentralized enforcement through states' good citizenship.

The simple notion that human rights are of common interest and, in fact, *erga omnes* (or at least *erga omnes inter partes*), however, constantly needs to be recomplexified. It can operate on a very high level of abstraction which in practice hides considerable reluctance by most states to treat all matter of human rights as open to outside scrutiny. In fact, quite the contrary often seems to be the case: states seem uniquely piqued by criticism of their human rights record and particularly jealous to safeguard the implementation of human rights as part of their *domaine*. Consider, for example, that states often refrain from criticizing other states' human rights record, perhaps out of fear that other states will do the same; that they have agreed only reluctantly to do so eventually and only as part of highly institutionalized exercises such as the Human Rights Council's Universal Periodic Review, for example; and that human rights prying remains either very regional or quite asymmetric when

770 Schweisfurth (n 766).

771 Francis Grimal and Graham Melling, 'The Protection of Nationals Abroad: Lawfulness or Toleration? A Commentary' (2011) 16 Journal of Conflict & Security Law 541.

772 Elisabeth Zoller, *Peacetime Unilateral Remedies: An Analysis of Countermeasures* (Brill Nijhoff 2023).

unfolding in a more universal context. There remain considerable sensitivities about the legitimacy and validity of human rights criticism, not just because it may be wrong on the specifics or in bad faith but specifically because it is understood to involve a degree of interference.[773]

The fact that some states sometimes rise to the challenge of some *erga omnes* obligations, then, does not necessarily make such obligations the perfect heuristic to understand the international legal system's position when it comes to interference. There is a difference between the cosmology of international human rights law generally and the fact that certain matters of human rights have been specifically internationalized to the point that their collective character warrants meddling.[774] Even in the narrow context of diplomatic interference, it is hardly a foregone conclusion that merely invoking human rights or purporting to promote them will free one from the suspicion of interference. As Paul Behrens has underscored, it is not even clear that surveying another state's human rights performance properly falls within the range of functions anticipated by the Vienna Convention, although it could be subsumed under representation or observatory functions.[775] When it comes to unilateral coercive measures, there has been consistent resistance by the Third World that merely invoking human rights as a justification will make such measures legally unproblematic, despite a Western tendency to portray a range of measures purporting to enforce human rights as naturally legal.[776]

In short, human rights often help to 'launder' behavior that might otherwise appear to be an illegal form of interference by radically minimizing the scope of the *domaine réservé*. What human rights can do in this context is theoretically help shift the framing of interference away from a narrow emphasis on the protection of sovereignty towards one informed by the needs and aspirations of populations. In that, they do provide a potentially richer framing of what constitutes interference or not. Their incidence has generally been a reluctance to draw a firm line between the domestic and the international in democratic and open societies, thus further eroding any notion of the *domaine* as the sovereign's exclusive preserve.

---

773 Frédéric Mégret, 'Just Criticism? Human Rights, Inter-State Relations, and the Ethics of Finger Pointing' (2024) 12 The Canadian Journal of Human Rights.

774 Buergenthal (n 588).

775 Paul Behrens, 'Diplomatic Interference and Competing Interests in International Law' (2012) 82 British Yearbook of International Law 178.

776 Alexandra Hofer, 'The Developed/Developing Divide on Unilateral Coercive Measures: Legitimate Enforcement or Illegitimate Intervention?' (2017) 16 Chinese Journal of International Law 175.

But this push has also elicited significant resistance that is normatively principled and draws on the resources of the international legal order itself to push back against 'human rights meddling'. The idea of a 'human rights exception' to the rules of interference has long been contested, for example by the Soviet Union in its efforts to challenge Radio Free Europe or more recently by Iran against BBC Persian, essentially denying the notion that journalistic work reporting on these countries from outside should be particularly deferred to if it is perceived as meddling. In effect, proponents of human rights may be prone to underestimate the extent to which 'free' information can not only be contentious (especially when backed by states with evident geopolitical agendas) but, in the best of cases, is objectively destabilizing of receiving states' hold on power (which, for better or for worse, they consider to be within their *domaine*).

At the same time, human rights are deployed in more specific ways to buttress the case for relatively open societies, notably when it comes to forging connections between foreign states and local civil society forces. The issue there is not just the bromide that human rights are the concern of all but more specifically the idea that restrictions to certain flows violate human rights of at least some constituencies in the territorial state. A broad 'right to information' tied to freedom of opinion and expression has been invoked, for example, to suggest that populations cannot be deprived from access to continuing flows of outside media, in ways that evidently curtail states' attempts to prevent them from doing so.[777] Human rights luminaries have argued that 'NGOs have a right to receive foreign funding'.[778] Such inspiration also underscores programs such as the State Department's 'Internet Freedom' initiative which seek to facilitate the internet access of citizens living in authoritarian states.[779] Limitations to freedom of opinion and expression here are reimagined as relating not only to domestic sources of information but to foreign ones as well. The European Convention on Human Rights (hereafter, 'European Convention' or ECHR) notably anticipates that '[e]veryone has the right to freedom of expression. This right shall include freedom to hold opinions and to receive and impart

777 Michael Riegner, 'Access to Information as a Human Right and Constitutional Guarantee. A Comparative Perspective' (2017) 50 Verfassung und Recht in Übersee / Law and Politics in Africa, Asia and Latin America 332.

778 Kenneth Roth, 'NGOs Have a Right to Receive Foreign Funding' (*International Service for Human Rights*, 26 April 2014) <https://ishr.ch/latest-updates/ngos-have-a-right-to-receive-foreign-funding/> accessed 19 June 2023.

779 Fergus Hanson, 'Internet Freedom: The Role of the U.S. State Department' (Brookings 2012) <https://www.brookings.edu/articles/internet-freedom-the-role-of-the-u-s-state-department/> accessed 3 April 2024.

information and ideas without interference by public authority *and regardless of frontiers*'.[780] The notion that '[t]he right to freedom of expression applies 'regardless of frontiers' is also routinely invoked in the universal context.[781] It once justified a finding that a ban by Switzerland of a particular satellite dish that allowed access to Soviet TV was not 'necessary in a democratic society'.[782]

This right to enter in contact with and receive information from is, moreover, commonly tied to a particular common transnational information infrastructure. As the U.N. Human Rights Committee (HR Committee) put it, '[t]here is now a global network for exchanging ideas and opinions that does not necessarily rely on the traditional mass media intermediaries. States parties should take all necessary steps [...] to ensure access of individuals thereto'.[783] As a result, the Committee has for example expressed concern that in Tunisia 'during elections, the Electoral Code [...] prohibits anyone from using a private or foreign radio or television channel or one broadcasting from abroad with a view to encouraging listeners to vote or to abstain from voting for a candidate or list of candidates', urging the State party to abolish such restrictions.[784] Amidst growing talk of a 'human right to the internet'[785] and an 'international law of the internet',[786] it has been claimed, notably in the wake of the 2011 Arab

780 COE, Convention for the Protection of Human Rights and Fundamental Freedoms (European Convention on Human Rights, as amended) (4 November 1950) ETS 5 (ECHR) art 10, para 1. My emphasis.

781 U.N. Special Rapporteur on Freedom of Opinion and Expression, OSCE Representative on Freedom of the Media, OAS Special Rapporteur on Freedom of Expression and ACHPR Special Rapporteur on Freedom of Expression and Access to Information, 'Joint Declaration on Freedom of Expression and "Fake News", Disinformation and Propaganda' ('Joint Declaration on Disinformation') (2017), para H.

782 *Autronic Ag v Switzerland* (1990) Series A no 178, para 63.

783 U.N. Human Rights Committee (HR Committee), General Comment No 34, Article 19: Freedom of Opinion and Expression (12 September 2011) U.N. Doc CCPR/C/GC/34, para 15.

784 HR Committee, Concluding observations of the Human Rights Committee, Tunisia (23 April 2008) U.N. Doc CCPR/C/TUN/CO/5, para 19.

785 Brian Skepys, 'Is There a Human Right to the Internet' (2012) 5 Journal of Politics and Law 15; Ryan Shandler and Daphna Canetti, 'A Reality of Vulnerability and Dependence: Internet Access as a Human Right' (2019) 52 Israel Law Review 77; Merten Reglitz, 'The Socio-Economic Argument for the Human Right to Internet Access' (2023) 22 Politics, Philosophy & Economics 441; Abhinav Mehrotra, 'Access to Internet as a Human Right–Justification and Comparative Study' (2021) 27 Comparative Law Review 313; Kay Mathiesen, 'The Human Right to Internet Access: A Philosophical Defense' (2012) 18 The International Review of Information Ethics 9.

786 Molly Land, 'Toward an International Law of the Internet' (2013) 54 Harvard International Law Journal 393.

Spring, that populations have a right to not be cut off from such access, and that interventions to guarantee access cannot be labelled unlawful intervention.[787] Rather than interference with domestic affairs, then, it is 'interference with internet access' that is being portrayed as problematic. The argument is that 'a powerless group in an oppressive country should not be denied outside assistance in the group's attempted exercise of the political rights guaranteed by human rights law'.[788] This further erodes the notion of a *domaine* réservé from within as it were, through direct appeals to individuals' prerogative to not be denied certain forms of communication with the 'outside' of the state.

This sort of expansive deference to the right to impart and receive information even of a political nature has long militated for not considering behavior that would otherwise constitute interference to be illegal, 'laundered' as it is by its human rights goals. The Chinese (nationalist) member of the ILC for example, in proposing a crime of subversion as part of the Draft Code of Crimes against the Peace and Security of Mankind, had sought early on to distinguish between communist subversion and acceptable anti-communist statements on the basis of human rights. Hersch Lauterpacht went further, arguing that propaganda in favor of human rights, all the way to inciting revolution, could not be a crime:

> the international community was no longer a society for the mutual protection of established governments. A revolution might be a crime against the State, but it was no longer a crime against the international community. So long as international society did not effectively guarantee the rights of man against arbitrariness and oppression by governments, it could not oblige States to treat subversive activities, when they did not amount to hostile expeditions, as a crime. [...] [I]t would be most regrettable if the Commission adopted a provision which might lead to the restriction of the freedom of speech and political opinion. States should not allow their territory to be used as a base for armed raids, but propaganda in favour of a political theory was a very different matter.[789]

In such a context, John Linarelli argues, '[a]n overly broad intervention article can be viewed as based on outmoded principles of sovereignty' and 'may serve to immunize internal elites in a repressive regime from enforcement of

787 Steven R Swanson, 'Forcing Facebook on Foreign Dictators: A Violation of International Law' (2011) 79 Tennessee Law Review 851.

788 ibid 882.

789 Yearbook of the ILC (1954) vol I, 141, para 6.

emerging human rights law'.[790] In short, human rights, under one reading at least, can be construed not so much as justifying interference by third states as such as demanding a degree of openness of states to outside flows, for the benefit of their populations.

3.2 *Rehabilitating the 'Human Rights State'*

Even as human rights increasingly limit the imagined scope of the *domaine réservé* by laying claim to ever more areas of regulation and forging connections between civil society actors and the international public interest, however, human rights law's own dynamics potentially reinstate a degree of ambiguity. This is a familiar paradox of rights discourse of course, namely that it can be used, at least on its face, at cross-purpose,[791] in this case both to constrain but also to solidify the *domaine*. This is visible in the debate on unilateral sanctions which has increasingly been taken over by human rights considerations against sanctions, very much at odds with the tendency to invoke human rights to pry open the *domaine*. Whereas the traditional problem with unilateral sanctions was that they interfered with sovereignty, the creation of a Special Rapporteur on unilateral coercive measures has clearly shifted the emphasis on the negative and unjustifiable *human rights impact* of such sanctions.[792] Similarly, in the context of debates on spying, the traditional role devolved to considerations of sovereignty has arguably begun to be superseded, in a context where the meddlesomeness of espionage seems to be tolerated by sovereigns inter se, by considerations taken from the negative impact on the human rights of those being spied upon.[793] This shows a remarkable ability to internalize the language of human rights for the purposes of, in effect, buttressing sovereignty against interference.

A similar move has long been in evidence in the context of efforts to prohibit and regulate the use of mercenaries, where the initial emphasis on resisting foreign destabilization designs associated with the perturbation of sovereignty[794] has gradually since the 1990s given rise to an emphasis on their

790 Linarelli (n 24) 46.

791 See, for example, Frédéric Mégret, 'Human Rights Populism' (2022) 13 Humanity: An International Journal of Human Rights, Humanitarianism, and Development 240.

792 Human Rights Council (UNHRC) 'Human Rights and Unilateral Coercive Measures' (3 October 2014) U.N. Doc A/HRC/RES/27/21.

793 Forcese (n 532) 205.

794 FJ Hampson, 'Mercenaries: Diagnosis before Proscription' (1991) 22 Netherlands Yearbook of International Law 3.

negative human rights impact on populations.[795] In fact, Western targets of interference, are more generally prone, in what is quite a radical overturning of their preferred narrative, to defend non-interference more broadly on grounds of the protection of human rights at home. For example, the European Parliament has insisted that 'disinformation decreases the ability of citizens to take informed decisions and to freely participate in democratic processes' and thus creates a genuine rights challenge[796] because it 'disrupt[s] the free formation and expression of individuals' political will'.[797] Such a late rediscovery of the human rights significance of sovereignty is of course nothing new for the Global South where sovereignty has long been understood not only as its own shield but as ensuring the basic conditions for distinct cultures of rights.[798] But it does manage to fashion a new role for the human rights register in an age of interference, to the point that human rights considerations appear on both sides of the ledger of intervention.

As we will see, the problem is not principally that this argument cannot logically be made; in fact, it very much can be made in certain contexts and some version of it has been made for a long time by the Global South. This includes an evaluation of the sheer prima facie 'human rights respectability' of the state as a guarantor of human rights. Indeed, even international human rights law has obliquely and paradoxically long entrenched the role of the state by sanctifying some of its functions in guarding rights. The 'human rights state' must not only respect human rights, but also protect and guarantee them. Human rights therefore not only provide the impetus for an increasing inquisitiveness of states in the affairs of others; they also substantially contribute to refashioning a particular *domaine réservé*: ultimately, no actor, it seems, can quite replace the state when it comes to assuming responsibilities for rights.

Just as it is possible to justify interference on human rights grounds, then it is perfectly possible to retort that there can be no human rights without sovereignty, and therefore the ability to guard it robustly against outside interference. But it is at least worth noting that in making that point vociferously, the West is driven to concede (it should be said, as part of its own liberal tradition)

---

795 José L Gómez del Prado, 'Impact on Human Rights of a New Non-State Actor: Private Military and Security Companies' (2011) 18 The Brown Journal of World Affairs 151.

796 2023 Resolution on Foreign Interference in the E.U. (n 335), para T.

797 European Commission, 'Communication from the Commission to the European Parliament, the Council the European Economic and Social Committee and the Committee of the Regions, On the European Action Plan' COM(2020) 790 final, s 4.

798 A Dirk Moses, Marco Duranti and Roland Burke (eds), *Decolonization, Self-Determination, and the Rise of Global Human Rights Politics* (Cambridge University Press 2020).

the very point that decolonial states made persistently when opposing interference on the grounds of rights, namely that rights discourse also requires one to uphold a strong concept of the state's inherent sphere. Of course, the West's rights discourse may be more focused on individual rights whereas the Global South's discourse is more focused on the collective right of self-determination, but both exploit ambiguities long latent within overall rights discourse.

Indeed, on human rights' own account, sovereignty can be seen as both highly problematic for rights and crucial to them. On one (say, Lockean) view, the end of human rights understood as 'negative' liberty is protection from the excesses of the state. The need to protect at the very least the human right to be free from unwarranted violence is a powerful trope in justifying universal interference with the designs of oppressive states who have supposedly failed to protect it. This justifies a relatively reduced conception of the *domaine réservé*. However, on another (say, Rousseauan) view, the end or at least the basic precondition of human rights is collective self-determination and its corollary, sovereignty. 'Positive liberty' describes the ability to be one's master, and to choose one's destiny in company with others. It is typically understood as the ability, characteristic of collective self-determination, to choose one's government. As such and by contrast, it rather militates against interference, on collective liberty promoting grounds.[799] The positive liberty of a people, then, translates into a negative liberty understood as non-interference from fellow states.

As Uriel Abulof has pointed out, negative liberty focuses on what is ultimately legitimate (good and bad politics), whereas positive liberty focuses on who ultimately decides.[800] Paradigmatically putting popular will at the heart of the legitimacy of the state certainly magnifies the moral stature of Leviathans on the international stage and, all other things being equal, reinforces the prevention against interference in international affairs. Indeed, the tendency to neglect the normative foundations of sovereignty for the international order, including for the project of rights itself, has long been decried as simplistic and problematic. As RJ Vincent once put it, those calling for the end of sovereignty in the face of emerging global values:

799 Frédéric Mégret, 'Having It Both Ways: International Human Rights Law Cannot Both Be in Decline and Be (That) Problematic for International Law' (2018) 96 Texas Law Review Online 114.

800 Uriel Abulof, 'The Confused Compass: From Self-Determination to State-Determination' (2015) 14 Ethnopolitics 488, 489.

> tend to applaud the eclipse of sovereignty which they suppose to be taking place as an unqualified good, which exposes them to the danger of overlooking the function of the principle of sovereignty as an ordering device within and hence among states. It may be that the values to which the principle of nonintervention draws attention and which it legally protects are more tenacious and less uncivilized than progressive thought has allowed for.[801]

At any rate, the extent to which human rights also militate for non-intervention rather than intervention is typically eluded in the Western-dominated debate on intervention-for-rights, even as intervention can also clearly disrupt domestic order, sow chaos, and undermine the prospect of achieving even basic liberties.[802]

This explains why appealing to human rights cannot be the easy answer to either justifying or countering interference. Too much 'positive freedom' in this context can certainly reduce 'negative freedom' by holding a population hostage to some grand forward-looking collective design. But complete neglect of 'positive freedom' and the dignity of a collective life, as the imperfect but irreplaceable medium to forge one's collective destiny, can make the conquest of negative freedoms rather illusory. Both inviting outside influence and sealing it off completely, then, have their dangers for the domestic rights 'mix' that are irreducible to general international law but hardly conclusive. This of course goes to the heart of one of the most vexing tensions in the human rights project, namely its simultaneous guaranteeing of negative freedoms *and* its safeguarding of collective rights; its demands that civil and political rights be protected through *laissez faire*, just as economic and social rights be realized through welfare; or its emphasis on rights as trumps combined with heavy insistence on limitations based on the needs of society. Rights discourse can hardly lay claim to entirely and consistently police the frontiers of the open society as if some issues could, from a human rights perspective, be defined as inherently domestic or foreign. It may err on the side of openness because of its inherent cosmopolitanism, but it then will always risk eroding some of the very collective political bases on which rights rely; just as it can retreat to the fortress of self-determination but at the risk of denying its cosmopolitan promise.

---

801 Vincent (n 69) 310.

802 Ayoob (n 761) 93.

The discourse of non-interference, therefore, cannot be a discourse that simplistically pits 'sovereignty' against 'human rights' but one that will by necessity be rich with the occasional defense of sovereignty as essential to human rights as well as the insistence on human rights as necessary to legitimate sovereignty. An illustration is clearly visible, for example, in Chinese opposition to human rights interference on the grounds that human rights can only be achieved and entrenched domestically, leaving at best a very subsidiary role for the international community.[803] Although this can be pushed too far, it is also hardly a quirky understanding of the relationship between human rights and sovereignty. Positive international human rights law, in fact, consistently defers to the state as a necessary intermediary echelon for human rights promotion, establishing its centrality both as a holder of duties but also a repository of prerogatives.[804] As Poppe and Wolf have argued, 'resistance against foreign interference via democracy promotion also has a normative dimension, and claims to national sovereignty, self-determination, and non-interference are not only raised by self-serving autocrats'.[805] In short, defenders of pro-human rights or pro-democracy interference do not have a monopoly on human rights or democracy discourses.

And lest the emphasis on sovereignty as a determinant of human rights appear still very much grounded in a movement of bad faith resistance to human rights, it is worth noting that human rights include very specific injunctions to states to deploy their sovereignty so as to minimize certain forms of interference, thus powerfully connecting both registers. For example, the HR Committee in its General Comment 25 underlined that 'voters should be able to form opinions independently, free of violence or threat of violence, compulsion, inducement or manipulative interference of any kind'.[806] A never-adopted version of what would become Article 19 of the ICCPR anticipated that restrictions could be imposed on freedom of expression to prevent 'the systematic diffusion of deliberately false or distorted reports which undermine

---

803 Xue Hanqin, *Chinese Contemporary Perspectives on International Law: History, Culture and International Law* (Hague Academy of International Law 2012) 166.

804 Frédéric Mégret, 'The Apology of Utopia: Reflections on Some Koskenniemian Themes with Particular Emphasis on Massively Institutionalized Human Rights Law' (2013) 27 Temple International and Comparative Law Journal 455.

805 Annika Elena Poppe and Jonas Wolff, 'The Contested Spaces of Civil Society in a Plural World: Norm Contestation in the Debate about Restrictions on International Civil Society Support' (2017) 23 Contemporary Politics 469, 473.

806 HR Committee, General Comment No 25 (12 July 1996) U.N. Doc CCPR/C/21/Rev.1/Add.7, para 19.

friendly relations between peoples and States'.[807] More recently, the Joint Declaration on Freedom of Expression recharacterized disinformation and propaganda operations as 'designed and implemented so as to mislead a population, as well as to interfere with the public's right to know and the right of individuals to seek and receive, as well as to impart information and ideas of all kinds, regardless of frontiers'.[808]

This broader human rights inspired anti-interference register points to states' 'obligation to protect' from third parties that might violate rights, an obligation that could apply to foreign actors' interference. This is irrespective of whether the state interfering is itself violating its human rights obligations towards persons in the target state. Indeed, some of the most striking claims *against* electoral interference have been framed in the language of human rights itself. This was dramatically illustrated by a case brought by a coalition of British MPs and peers to challenge, on ECHR grounds, the U.K. government's refusal to investigate Russian interference in the 2016 Brexit referendum despite evidence to that effect.[809] Finally, some authors have long emphasized the existence of a 'human right to sovereignty' or 'human right to the state'.[810] Clearly this cautions against any facile cosmopolitan assertion that human rights provide a tool to systematically pry open sovereignty. It also endows sovereignty with a human rights respectability that can easily be used to resist wanton interference and mount a vigorous campaign against human rights cosmopolitanism.

A vision of human rights as a tool to interfere with sovereignty remains possible, then, but it does not exhaust the register of human rights. One can envision a role for human rights as simultaneously being deployed to resist interference of what is rightly considered domestic, with ricochet implications for the definition of interference. At the very least, it cautions against the overly simplistic view that human rights can be invoked entirely either way. To say that human rights are the concern of all and therefore provide occasional

807 Marc J Bossuyt, *Guide to the 'Travaux Préparatoires' of the International Covenant on Civil and Political Rights* (Martinus Nijhoff 1987) 387. Later, a ban was proposed on 'dissemination of slanderous rumours which undermined relations between states'. Wibke K Timmermann, *Incitement in International Law* (Routledge 2014) 73.

808 Joint Declaration on Disinformation (n 697).

809 Jamie Grierson, 'MPs Take Russian Election Interference Case to Human Rights Court' *The Guardian* (29 March 2022) <https://www.theguardian.com/law/2022/mar/29/european-court-urged-to-challenge-uk-failure-to-investigate-russia-interference> accessed 19 June 2023.

810 Eyal Benvenisti, 'Are There Any Inherently Public Functions for International Law?' (2021) 115 AJIL Unbound 302.

justification for interference, for example, is to trade in generalities: they may, but the whole question is to what extent, given that they cannot provide a blank cheque for types of interference that would conflict with a people's rights, including to self-determination and sovereignty. Acknowledging this is not particularly problematic from the point of view of human rights, but it may help rehabilitate, perhaps unwittingly, the idea that a relatively strong anti-interference stance can as much claim to be inspired by human rights as a strong pro-interference one.

In short, neither human rights nor sovereignty provide an incontrovertible case for interference or against it respectively, and both can be quite easily made to work 'at cross-purpose' as it were. If anything, they bring to the fore 'normative tensions that arise within a liberal universalism that is based on principles of both individual rights and collective self-determination'.[811] Although this certainly does not legitimize the 'new interference', it relativizes the claim that sovereignty should easily be sidelined when rights are at stake. In fact, the 'new interference' may put the West in a situation where it finds itself systematically granting the point that the Global South had been making all along in dealing with interference, namely that individual rights cannot be fully guaranteed in a political system that is entirely porous to outside meddling to the point of not offering a framework for democracy or, for that matter, sovereignty. The opposition, in that respect, is less between a Western and non-Western vision of the relationship between the two; it is intrinsic to the very relationship between sovereignty and human rights, on liberalism's own terms.

3.3 *Exceptionalizing Democracy?*

A popular view in the West to reclaim the upper ground, in this context, is that what is at stake in the *domaine réservé* is that part of sovereignty that is clearly worth protecting in the liberal tradition, namely democracy. This manages to move the conversation beyond both the traditional focus on sovereignty and the somewhat shaky terrain of human rights. Rather it locates the *domaine* in the sort of deliberative *entre soi* of equal citizens and to highlight something that is justifiably left to states. Where the pure defense of sovereignty as the basis of the *domaine* is henceforth vulnerable to the criticism that it serves to violate rights and where the pure defense of rights is vulnerable to the criticism that it serves to negate the politics of self-determination, the democracy argument operates on a sort of intermediary echelon.

811 Poppe and Wolff (n 804) 474.

This is not the same thing as claiming (dubiously, as we saw previously) that democracy is inherently national. Rather, it is an argument that democracy is one of the foundations of human rights and even legitimate sovereignty, and that therefore the entire debate about interference must be framed with an attention to it. This deference to democracy built into the international protection of human rights is also visible, more indirectly, in the holding up of democracy as the implicit standard by which all limitations to rights in the European Convention context ought to be evaluated,[812] as well as the inherent human rights desirability of regular and free elections.[813] It militates for an understanding of non-interference as a form of militant-democratic project dedicated, if nothing else, to stave off challenges to the peculiar character of that democracy.

Democracy, seems to be the argument, needs to simultaneously not be starved of outside influences, yet protected from pernicious interference. The United Nations General Assembly has, for example, claimed since the late 1980s that 'activities that attempt, directly or indirectly, to interference in the free development of national electoral processes [...] or that intend to sway the results of such processes, violate the spirit and letter of the principles of the [Friendly Relations Declaration]'.[814] More recently and notably after allegations of election tampering in the U.S., it has 'strongly condemn[ed] any manipulation of election processes, coercion and tampering with vote counts'.[815] The appeal to democracy could be seen as fusing concerns for self-determination, human rights and sovereignty in somewhat felicitous manner. It connects historical Third World concerns with the disruption of its electoral processes, with similar nascent concerns in the Global North more likely to be based on human rights. It provides an affirmation of the *domaine réservé* for the ages, one that is less fixated on sovereignty for sovereignty's sake.

Leaving aside that this may be a suspiciously late move from the West in this old debate, the idea that democracy is the real stake of non-interference is also one that departs, to be clear, from a tradition of international law devoted to protecting the sovereignty of *all* states, democratic or not. The reimagining

812 See ECHR, Preamble ('those fundamental freedoms which are the foundation of justice and peace in the world [...] are best maintained on the one hand by an effective political democracy and on the other by [...] observance of the Human Rights upon which they depend'). Also, Susan Marks, 'The European Convention on Human Rights and Its Democratic Society' (1996) 66 The British Year Book of International Law 209.

813 Protocol no 1 to the ECHR (20 March 1952) ETS 9, art 3.

814 UNGA Res 44/147 (15 December 1989).

815 UNGA Res 74/158 (18 December 2019) U.N. Doc A/RES/74/158.

of non-interference as 'non-interference (only) with democracy' rather than with a more conventional understanding of the *domaine réservé* seems almost designed to safeguard's the West meddling in the affairs of non-democratic states (understood as non-conforming), whilst minimizing interference in the affairs of Western states (assumed to be democratic). This is not to say that democracy does not deserve to be protected for the purposes of human rights, above and beyond sovereignty, but that clearly international law does not traditionally mandate the protection of sovereignty against interference only when it is a legitimate conduit for democracy; otherwise, the protection of sovereignty would amount to very little. Moreover, the emphasis on realizing democracy as the cornerstone of a theory of legitimate interference risks conflating democratic arrangements, self-determination, and human rights in ways that are ultimately impoverishing of the tradition of international law.[816]

There are several further ambiguities in making democracy the linchpin of a normative theory of non-interference, even in terms of democratic theory. To begin with, as mentioned previously, it is not clear that democracy 'belongs' to the *domaine réservé* entirely, at least as that notion was understood traditionally, namely as a series of prerogatives associated with sovereignty. Democracy is certainly organized by the state, but its sustenance implies a healthy distance from the powers of the state. Moreover, any notion of a rigid 'democratic entitlement' enforceable if need be by foreign powers is generally viewed with wariness under international law, at least to the extent that it might be understood to authorize otherwise unlawful interference and certainly the use of force.[817] This is a somewhat separate debate, but it relativizes the notion that the proper way to understand the problematic character of interference in the affairs of democratic states is, specifically, that it impinges on their democracy (or, by the same token, that interfering with the affairs of non-democratic states is not interference).

Indeed, is also worth noting that evolutions in democratic practice and theory on their own terms have made the idea that democracy is the singular province of the state where it operates at the expense of any foreign influence a slightly improbable and even unappealing one: whether it is debates about the right to vote of migrants, the importance of diasporic or dual nationality vote,

816 Vladyslav Lanovoy, 'Self-Determination in International Law: A Democratic Phenomenon or an Abuse of Right?' (2015) 4 Cambridge International Law Journal 388.

817 Oscar Schachter, 'The Legality of Pro-Democratic Invasion' (1984) 78 American Journal of International Law 645; Michael Byers and Simon Chesterman, '"You, the People": Pro-Democratic Intervention in International Law' in Brad R Roth and Gregory H Fox (eds), *Democratic Governance and International Law* (Cambridge University Press 2000).

transnational alliances of similarly minded political parties, or the increased imbrication of national democracy with supranational governance,[818] democracy has never seemed less in synch with a *domaine réservé* conception. It is almost a cliché of cosmopolitan accounts of democracy that it is destined to transcend its national cradle to be true to its very democratic ideals,[819] particularly in an environment where sovereignty itself is incessantly being transcended from above through global governance.[820] In such conditions, to insist that interference is primarily constituted by how it affects a particular conception of bounded national democracy at best sells both democracy and interference short, at worst contributes to sacralise a conception of democracy as jealously domestic precisely when its emancipation from that framework has never seemed more urgent, perhaps for the benefit of international law itself.[821]

As we will see later, the forceful renationalization of democracy could come dangerously close to enabling its authoritarian capture. Hence also the fundamental limits of 're-nationalizing' various spheres all be it on democratic grounds: social, political, or economic. States that have actively encouraged globalization and opened their borders may struggle to define any area as inherently domestic not just because it seems to contradict their earlier discourse but because there is no safe 'domestic' sphere to return to. This goes for democracy, perhaps more than any other sphere: although prohibitions on the foreign financing of political parties or the obligation to disclose that one is working for a foreign power may go some way to protect a particular national version of democracy, the definition of what part of the democratic process is fundamentally internal remains elusive in an era in which democracy has become partly supranational and extra-territorial.

To make matters more complicated, this remains an issue that is or should be fundamentally susceptible to democratic deliberation itself: in other words, we do not have a conception of what is the *domaine réservé* from a democratic

818 Klaus Eder and Hans-Jörg Trenz, 'Prerequisites of Transnational Democracy' in Beate Kohler-Koch and Berthold Rittberger (eds), *Debating the democratic legitimacy of the European Union* (Rowman & Littlefield 2007).

819 Jürgen Habermas, 'Democracy in Europe: Why the Development of the E.U. into a Transnational Democracy Is Necessary and How It Is Possible' (2015) 21 European Law Journal 546. For a non-domination, republican account along those lines, see James Bohman, 'Nondomination and Transnational Democracy' in Cécile Laborde and John W Maynor (eds), *Republicanism and Political Theory* (Blackwell 2008).

820 James Anderson, *Transnational Democracy: Political Spaces and Border Crossings* (Routledge 2002).

821 John S Dryzek, 'Transnational Democracy' (1999) 7 Journal of Political Philosophy 30.

point of view outside of each particular democracy's actualization of that notion. This is not only a general political or legal issue; what is a domestic and a foreign political interest has become hard to gauge in *normative* terms, from within conventional understandings of democracy itself. States and their populations, for example, stand to be impacted by each other's policies. They therefore have an inherent interest in the policies of other states being conducted in terms favorable to them and their *demos*: although this is certainly, again, no blank cheque for meddling, it somewhat relativizes the claim that states who interfere with other governments are fundamentally 'not minding their own business'. They may, on one reading at least, be very much minding their business against rigid Westphalian arrangements that would prevent them from doing so.

Consider the following hypothetical. A small island state threatened by disappearance as a result of rising oceans conducts a psychological operation in the U.S. to sway it away from massively subsidizing and consuming fossil energies. Leaving aside the question of the means used and focusing only on whether this encroaches with the U.S.'s reserved domain leads to perplexing interrogations. Under one view, how the U.S. organizes its energy consumption is fully within its sovereignty and the outside operation is a clear-cut case of interference (assuming, for the sake of argument, that it satisfies the other conditions of being interference), all the more so that U.S. policy was plausibly decided democratically; on another view, one can hardly claim that the U.S.'s massive over-consumption of fossil fuels, responsible as it is for a disproportionate share of global warming, ought to effectively belong to its *domaine réservé*. It is in effect producing considerable negative externalities and hugely so for certain states.

Again, the concern here is only with whether the notion of the *domaine réservé*, even as enhanced by appeals to democratic theory, provides, as such, a compelling rationale to justify prohibiting interference. The results are ambiguous, to say the least, especially in a context where issues such as climate change are forcefully shifting demands for democratic participation to the global level.[822] As soon as one's policies produce significant negatives

822 Daniel J Fiorino, *Can Democracy Handle Climate Change?* (John Wiley & Sons 2018); David Shearman and Joseph Wayne Smith, *The Climate Change Challenge and the Failure of Democracy* (Praeger Publishers 2007); Martin Albrow and Marlies Glasius, 'Democracy and the Possibility of a Global Public Sphere' in Martin Albrow and others (eds), *Global Civil Society 2007/8: Communicative Power and Democracy*, vol 8 (Sage Publications 2008); Ludvig Beckman, 'Climate Change Duties and the Human Right to Democracy' in Aaron Maltais and Catriona McKinnon (eds), *The Ethics of Climate Governance* (Rowman & Littlefield 2015).

externalities to others, it becomes difficult to argue that one's democratic pedigree provides a shield against interference. And of course, this slippage of the domestic into the global will be even more flagrant if the U.S. itself has long been making arguments along those lines.

Clearly election contestation and results in and of themselves would seem to represent a certain inviolable inner sanctum. In that respect, the crasser version of interference with voting is an intrusion on the *domaine*, although it may be a range of other things more specifically (e.g., a violation of domestic law, whether interference or not in the international legal sense) and although vote counting might be susceptible to all kinds of international contracts that belie any notion that it is inherently a sovereign prerogative in the strong sense. It is much less clear, however, that even hostile information operations are a violation of sovereignty, let alone a form of prohibited interference or intervention.[823] Aside from the issue of local constituencies being able to access information and opinions abroad, is it not legitimate for foreign constituencies that stand to be powerfully affected by the decisions of, particularly, hegemonic powers, to seek to influence *their* elections? In effect, it has already been argued for example that even foreign corporate financing of political parties and election campaigns should be allowed to better reflect the exigencies of an interdependent world wherein 'foreign corporations have a significant interest in the domestic policies of other countries and thus may have a legitimate right to express these interests in some manner'.[824] If sovereignty is already an illusion and has been lastingly undermined by appeals to common values, then what is to prevent this further, but perfectly natural, erosion of the last democratic redux, given the latter's evident porousness?[825] The attempt to sanctuarize the *domaine réservé* by an appeal to democracy thus ends up being very much a double-edged sword: on the one hand, giving normative substance to what sovereignty is supposed to stand for; on the other hand, replacing it by something that seems to invite outside influence even more.

Indeed, democratic theory itself does not necessarily offer a firm normative rebuttal to this treat, despite its idealized groundedness in a territorialized or

---

823 James Van de Velde, 'When Does Election Interference via Cyberspace Violate Sovereignty? Violations of Sovereignty, "Armed Attack," Acts of War, and Activities "Below the Threshold of Armed Conflict" via CyberspaceJames Van de Velde' in Jens David Ohlin and Duncan B Hollis (eds), *Defending Democracies: Combating Foreign Election Interference in a Digital Age* (Oxford University Press 2021) 165.

824 Jeffrey K Powell, 'Prohibitions on Campaign Contributions from Foreign Sources: Questioning Their Justification in a Global Interdependent Economy Comment' (1996) 17 University of Pennsylvania Journal of International Economic Law 957, 959–960.

825 ibid 5.3.

national demos, in a context where one cosmopolitan theorist after another has emphasized the extent to which we increasingly belong to 'communities of fate' on a global level and all persons should have a say in all politics that stand to impact them.[826] On the one hand, it is true that democratic theory is clearly indebted to the notion of a circumscribed polis, a body politic emanating from a particular people, albeit this is an always imperfectly realized ideal that has long come under attack most notably for its seemingly natural propensity to under-represent certain groups. On the other hand, the idea that there should be no government without representation suggests that affected extra-territorial constituencies should have a certain claim to the decision processes that are decisive for their lives, especially in a context where 'political decisions frequently ignite chains of causes that spill over the borders of nation states'.[827]

In effect, the exclusion of foreign states (and populations) from deliberations that crucially affect them can be recharacterized as itself a form of interference with their ability to govern[828] or even as granting an undue privilege to the local citizenry.[829] Hence for example a distinguished argument among cosmopolitan-leaning theorists of democracy is that 'all affected' by decisions should have a say in their adoption. Robert Dahl has suggested that we should take seriously the notion that Latin Americans should have the right to vote in U.S. elections because they stand to be uniquely affected by them.[830] Diasporas have also long made claims to extra-territorial representation in their country of origin, because of the way they are affected by its policies.[831] U.S. elections themselves have been described as 'megaevents' that increasingly draw

826 David Held, 'The Changing Contours of Political Community: Rethinking Democracy in the Context of Globalisation' [1999] Theoria: A Journal of Social and Political Theory 30; Will Kymlicka, *Politics in the Vernacular: Nationalism, Multiculturalism, and Citizenship* (New York University Press 2001) 320.

827 Ludvig Beckman, *The Frontiers of Democracy: The Right to Vote and Its Limits* (Palgrave Macmillan 2009) 41.

828 Duncan MacIntosh, 'Protecting Democracy by Commingling Polities: The Case for Accepting Foreign Influence and Interference in Democratic Processes' in Jens David Ohlin and Duncan B Hollis (eds), *Defending Democracies: Combating Foreign Election Interference in a Digital Age* (Oxford University Press 2021).

829 Powell (n 823) 990. (noting that '[a]llowing only domestic business entities to contribute [to political campaigns] provides them with an unfair advantage over their foreign competitors').

830 Robert Alan Dahl, *After the Revolution? Authority in a Good Society* (Yale University Press 1990) 51.

831 Mégret and Girard (n 652).

in global audiences[832] keen to participate in a debate that is also, in a sense, about them, and therefore ought not to proceed entirely without them. And it has been pointed out that 'if pluralist theory requires that an ideal democracy permit all interested groups to express their views, then any government purporting to be democratic must allow foreign corporations with significant domestic operations to convey their preferences'.[833]

There at times seem to be few limits to the sort of reconfiguration that notions of stakeholder democracy presage. Stefanie Walter has argued that referendums over whether states should pull out of certain international arrangements (e.g., Brexit) or even momentous national elections such as the 2016 U.S. elections that raise similar questions (e.g., withdrawal from the Paris agreement), create significant negative externalities abroad that should have democratic implications. In a context where 'democratically elected leaders, foreign policy makers are tasked to represent the interests of their citizens. [...] interventions in a foreign campaign with the intention to protect the country's own voters from harm may be legitimate'.[834] In Duncan MacIntosh's striking argument, what is necessary, then, far from sanctuarizing democracy further from all outside influences, is to create conditions wherein foreign nations can act as co-deliberators through the 'commingling [of] polities'.[835]

The dizzying possibility that becoming involved in the affairs of other states may actually be internationally or domestically mandated (to do anything less would be to fail one's own people) belies the notion that the question of interference can only be assessed democratically from the perspective of the target state. At the very least, the density of international inter-dependencies creates conditions of co-dependence between various national interests, suggesting that decisions about continued participation in politics may no longer be considered as purely domestic. Going further, for some cosmopolitan theorists, the solution lies not in re-delineating the sanctity of the *civis* (as the insistence on non-interference suggests), but very much in transcending the limitations of the nation state towards a true global or cosmopolitan democracy.[836] On this view, even a defense of non-interference energised by reference to democratic

832 Efe Sevin and Sarphan Uzunoğlu, 'Do Foreigners Count? Internationalization of Presidential Campaigns' (2017) 61 American Behavioral Scientist 315.

833 Powell (n 823) 989.

834 Stefanie Walter, 'National Votes with International Consequences: A Democratic Threat to Cooperation?' (2017) 3 <https://papers.ssrn.com/abstract=3057637> accessed 25 September 2018.

835 MacIntosh (n 827).

836 David Held, 'Democracy: From City-States to a Cosmopolitan Order?' (1992) 40 Political Studies 10.

arrangements provides no safe haven, as the latter should itself be increasingly understood as relational, global, and immersed in duties to others.[837] Various foreign public and private actors are not merely or even primarily imposing their politics when they are politically active in other states—as much as trying to gain access to the power centres that increasingly decide *their* fates, in line with an increasingly global 'not about U.S. without us'.

Of course, this is not to say that election meddling is a step towards the realization of cosmopolitan democracy, or that in trying to organize elections on its own terms, the U.S. is frustrating the legitimate foreign or global popular interest in their outcome. But one should at least consider that what is currently understood as interference under the Westphalian paradigm may manifest some of the very pathologies of an international system that continues, under the guise of sovereignty, to promote democracy as if it were a purely domestic affair. The idea that foreign funding of political parties or lobbies breaks the connection between a 'peoples' will' and their representative government, for example, is well ingrained[838] but in the end a bit of an abstraction. It could also be that it is local democratic forces that will lose out from lack of transnational engagement: who is to say that the realization of their democratic will does not entitle them to as deep and wide a menu of political options as they might have access to if diversified global participation in their political processes is allowed? Moreover, the increasingly nested and overlapping character of diverse claims to democratic processes, notably in regional contexts, certainly undermines some of the descriptive and normative foundations on which the critique of interference traditionally relies, since it blurs any sense that what is domestic and what is international is normatively unproblematic. This section has thus relativized the notion that either human rights or democracy, at least on their own terms, provide a full-proof or even particularly compelling underlying normative theory of the *domaine* réservé.

True, these cosmopolitan arguments are on one level mere normative visions, and one may think that they are unrelated to the legal question of what constitutes unlawful interference *in concreto* or at least legally. The difficulties of operationalizing a conception of electoral participation based on impact, for example, are hard to underestimate and make it easy to gently ridicule cosmopolitan plans as legally unworkable or to appeal to familiar notions of

837 Iris Marion Young, *Inclusion and Democracy* (Oxford University Press 2002) ch 7.

838 Daniel Scott Savrin, 'Curtailing Foreign Financial Participation in Domestic Elections: A Proposal to Reform the Federal Election Campaign Act' (1987) 28 Virginia Journal of International Law 783, 789.

the necessary privacy between the governed and the governing.[839] However, given the law's own deference to standards and practices beyond it and the uniquely normative nature of debates about sovereignty, rights and democracy, these interrogations undoubtedly suffuse the discursive field of interference. Transnational and cosmopolitan critiques of the state will instil a degree of legitimate doubt, radiating from democratic theory to the understanding of what legitimately constitutes the *domaine*, that lays waste to any notion that the construction of non-intervention is uncontentious. The point, moreover, is that interference as a notion has always been shot through and through with assumptions about the proper goal and process of political association, assumptions that are now being powerfully challenged and, in the process, further unsettle an already unstable legal conversation.

4 National Self-determination/Global Values

The limitations of defending and framing the *domaine réservé* on account of either the defense of sovereignty, human rights or democracy, then, lead to another, and in some ways more plausible option, which is to emphasize *self-determination* as the pivotal concept in framing the modern vision of non-interference. This reconnects with and does justice to a decolonial era leitmotiv,[840] now being rediscovered with gusto by some Western scholars.[841] Self-determination speaks to the fact that it is less the state itself in its sovereign dimension that is being targeted by the new interference than a complex set of society-to-state relations. Self-determination is also close to democracy whilst avoiding the pitfalls of tying a theory of non-intervention only to democratic arrangements. Defending non-intervention on the basis of self-determination, in fact, can provide a form of resistance to pro-democratic interventions, to the extent that the two concepts are not soluble: a pro-democracy intervention might still be in contradiction with a population's right to self-determination to the extent that it displaces the 'self' in the process of attempting to 'liberate' it.[842] Self-determination is often understood in the 21st Century as being

839 Teachout (n 323) 183–184.

840 See 1965 Declaration on the Inadmissibility of Intervention; 1970 Declaration on Friendly Relations.

841 Ohlin, *Election Interference: International Law and the Future of Democracy* (n 17).

842 Simone van den Driest, '"Pro-Democratic" Intervention and the Right to Political Self-Determination: The Case of Operation Iraqi Freedom' (2010) 57 Netherlands International Law Review 29.

denied to a minority by a majority *within* the state, but historically it has also evidently been denied from outside the state, notably as a result of occupation or colonization, but also of continued interference. Finally, self-determination, even more than democracy, has been highlighted as a cardinal human right and not simply as a general principle of international law.[843]

Far from being a new phenomenon in non-interference discourse, self-determination featured as a key pillar of its rejection as early as the 1949 General Assembly resolution on 'The Essentials of Peace' which condemned interference on the basis that, inter alia, it might 'subvert [...] the will of the people in any State'.[844] The Declaration on the Inadmissibility of Intervention also made the connection by highlighting that non-intervention was connected not only to State sovereignty but also to 'the right of self-determination and independence of peoples and nations, to be freely exercised without any foreign pressure'.[845] One can see the rudiments of such an approach echoed judicially in the ICJ's notion in *Nicaragua v United States* which, by analogy with the Corfu decision's old emphasis on 'territorial integrity',[846] insisted that states should respect the 'political integrity' of other states.[847] This evokes the idea, then, that behind the respect due to sovereignty and beyond the temptation to make democracy as the single marker of sovereignty-worth-respecting, it is really self-determination that stands for the true *domaine réservé*, potentially expanding the latter's scope to include complex societal processes of collective willing, and not just either the bare bones operation of the sovereign or a fully-fledged democratic system. Authors such as Jens Ohlin and Nicolas Tsagourias have most recently made the case, in the latest round of debates about electoral meddling, that interference is better understood as a violation of self-determination than of sovereignty.[848]

---

843 Allan Rosas, 'The Right of Self-Determination' in Asbjørn Eide, Catarina Krause and Allan Rosas (eds), *Economic, Social and Cultural Rights* (Brill Nijhoff 2001); Frank Przetacznik, 'The Basic Collective Human Right to Self-Determination of Peoples and Nations as a Prerequisite for Peace' (1990) 8 New York Law School Journal of Human Rights 49; Robert McCorquodale, 'Self-Determination: A Human Rights Approach' (1994) 43 International & Comparative Law Quarterly 857.

844 UNGA Res 290(IV) (1 December 1949) U.N. Doc A/RES/290(IV).

845 1965 Declaration on the Inadmissibility of Intervention, art 6.

846 *Corfu Channel Case* (n 488).

847 *Nicaragua v United States* (n 3) [202].

848 Ohlin, *Election Interference: International Law and the Future of Democracy* (n 17); Nicholas Tsagourias, 'Electoral Cyber-Interference, Self-Determination, and the Principle of Non-Intervention in Cyberspace' in Dennis Broeders and Bibi van den Berg (eds), *Governing Cyberspace: Behavior, Power and Diplomacy* (Rowman & Littlefield 2020). That argument has long been a recurring feature of the debate on intervention. See Damrosch (n 16) 37.

In doing so, they are arguably only reprising the cliché of Third World international law thinking that self-determination is central to the aspiration of peoples and in a sense prior to the spelling out of any non-intervention norm. For example, the foundation of the condemnation of intervention in the 1965 Declaration was that 'the use of force to deprive peoples of their national identity constitutes a violation of their inalienable rights'.[849] The incidence and centrality of the right to self-determination, moreover, goes beyond the peculiar legacies of decolonization to reconnect with the West's own heritage of anti-monarchism and anti-imperialism. The right of self-determination not only has a very strong pedigree in international human rights law; it has also long structured some of its core assumptions, including its methodological nationalism, the fundamentally subsidiary nature of global human rights protection arrangements or the deference to the margin of appreciation.[850] Connecting the elusive rule of non-intervention to the bedrock principle self-determination is a doctrinally powerful move since, as observed by Benedetto Conforti years before the current reappraisal of the concept, it anchors the former into the incontrovertible nature of the latter.[851] It also neatly suggests ways in which States' right to 'choose [their] political, economic, social and cultural systems' is indeed inalienable, as the 1970 Declaration proclaimed: because to alienate that freedom would be not only to undercut their own sovereignty, but also to undermine their peoples' self-determination.

4.1 *Self-determination: Impeding or Mandating Interference?*

The power of a self-determination analysis, then, is that it focuses on attempts to interfere with 'peoples' (or society), where the norm of non-intervention traditionally emphasized the state.[852] It thus leads to a potential decoupling of the typical targets of interference which can have quite opposite effects. On the one hand, it might reinforce the sanctity of sovereignty to the extent that it is or can be portrayed as aligned with self-determination in the first place. Focusing on self-determination as the linchpin of a rights-infused theory of non-interference at least guards against the notion that interference is wide open if one is dealing with a less-than-fully-self-determining state (whatever that is). However awkwardly, peoples self-determine even in authoritarian

849 1965 Declaration on the Inadmissibility of Intervention, art 3.

850 Frédéric Mégret, 'Ban on Religious Symbols in the Public Service: Quebec's Bill 21 in a Global Pluralist Perspective' (2022) 11 Global Constitutionalism 217.

851 Conforti (n 47) 471.

852 Jens David Ohlin, 'Did Russian Cyber Interference in the 2016 Election Violate International Law' (2017) 95 Texas Law Review 1579, 1591.

conditions through countless acts of will, a reality that reinforces the case that sovereignty is not merely an empty shell even when it is only a pale approximation of the ideal of popular self-determination. Governments can at the very least present themselves as better guardians of their peoples' self-determination than more or less disinterested third parties so that the argument from self-determination merely adds a gloss over the basic argument from sovereignty. For many Third World states, then, the emphasis on self-determination in the great anti-intervention instruments of the 60s and 70s was a way of safeguarding their newfound sovereignty as the embodiment of their will to decolonize.[853]

On the other hand, a theory of non-interference based on respect for self-determination can *also* justify countless encroachments on a state's sovereignty if the latter is 'found' not to be true to a people's aspiration to self-determination.[854] It could prevent a state from invoking non-interference when to do so would allegedly frustrate its population's will to self-determination; it could require outside parties to ascertain whether the state they are dealing with legitimately embodies the self-determination of its peoples; and it could of course provide ample ammunition to third states to intervene in the affairs of a state on the basis that it is not up to the task of self-determination. The more the 'political independence' of the state is understood as entailing not only freedom from external domination but also living up to an ideal of sovereign representation of a people, the more interference can, in fact, be recast as non-interference or at least as a form of emancipatory and therefore justifiable interference. The shield, in short, could and has regularly become a sword, as the 'political independence' of states is subtly recast as the 'independence' of its peoples.[855] This could extend not only to judging particular policies but to contesting the very authority of a foreign government.

A tell-tale incident reflective of the resulting tensions is the protracted tussle over the question of who is the legitimate leader of Venezuela. As seen, in earlier days the debate over (continued) recognition of governments had been dominated by attention to armed conflicts, the only type of incident susceptible of shaking the ordinarily massively ingrained assumption that the government is merely whatever faction effectively governs a territory. A prolonged

853 Roth, 'Democratization's Discontents' (n 559) 168–169. ('Given the prevalence of distrust and, especially, the history of colonialism and neo-colonialism, the presumption was that populations would perceive a greater confluence of interests with their own local tyrants than with foreigners pronouncing benevolent intentions').

854 Reisman (n 40).

855 Damrosch (n 16) s IV.

armed conflict, especially one in which a rebel movement challenged continued control over part of the territory, temporarily lifted—but barely—the veil of sovereignty and prescribed an attitude by third parties that can best be described as one of careful wait-and-see. It focused on hedging the international community's bets and avoiding the *faux pas* of treating with the wrong sovereign. At most, the normal indifference to the nature of the regime involved has of late been supplemented by attention to the degree to which the reining government, even if effectively challenged, may or may not embody its peoples' aspirations. What this emphatically did not extend to, however, was a sort of peace time, de novo assessment of who was the legitimate government merely on the basis of differing accounts of who won elections and had the best claim to embody self-determination.

Yet this is precisely what happened when a number of Latin American countries as well as the U.S. and the European Union decided to support Juan Guaidó against Nicolás Maduro as President of Venezuela by recognizing the former as the only legitimate head of the Venezuelan state. This was despite the failure of Guaidó's race to at least obtain accreditation for his representatives abroad and of course his lack of control of any of Venezuela's territory. The European Union High representative positioned himself very much as a sort of external guarantor of the Venezuelan Constitution which he claimed had been violated by Maduro's maintenance in power.[856] In doing so, third states were not entirely in *terra incognita* given the occasional practice in Haiti, Sierra Leone, Ivory Coast or the Gambia, of insisting that ousted leaders who were democratically elected remain the recognized government, although this is a different scenario than Venezuela's, notably because Guaidó was never the head of state in the first place and because of Security Council validation in those other cases. It might be argued that unilateral measures against the Maduro regime, then, are a form of collective counter-measure in the name of countering the violation of an *erga omnes* violation of the obligation to uphold self-determination. But as has been pointed out by Giuseppe Puma, 'while the violation of fundamental human rights surely amounts to an internationally wrongful act *erga omnes*, it seems highly questionable that the breach of democratic values also gives rise to such a wrongful situation'.[857]

---

856 'Declaration by the High Representative on Behalf of the E.U. on the Presidential and Regional Elections in Venezuela' (*Council of the EU*, 22 May 2018) <https://www.consilium.europa.eu/en/press/press-releases/2018/05/22/declaration-by-the-high-representative-on-behalf-of-the-eu-on-the-presidential-and-regional-elections-in-venezuela/> accessed 13 July 2024.

857 Puma (n 538) 15.

In other words, third states cannot *that* easily plead international law to engage in otherwise clearly hostile and intrusive conduct. The fact that Maduro's regime may be guilty of significant rights violations does not make him less, effectively, the leader of Venezuela in that case. Claiming that a government is not the government in this case, despite all appearances, because it does not represent the self-determination aspirations of a people involves a reduction of self-determination to the operation of democracy that could be problematic, even assuming that democracy had been corrupted in this case. A premature recognition of another contender is more than a fault of protocol; it is effectively a form of interference, even if not specifically coercive.[858] Finally, none of this excludes the possibility that third states could adopt a range of measures short of recognizing a *faux* leader (e.g., helping Venezuelan civil society). In doing so, they could effectively rebut charges that they were engaging in interference on the basis of the very same principles of self-determination, human rights and democratic entitlement. Whilst invoking self-determination to justify measures that are legal (for example, pointing out that financing an NGO from abroad is not illegal) will go a long way, then, doing the same will not suffice to launder behavior that is otherwise illegal (leaving aside, for the time being, the complex question of whether unilateral economic sanctions are illegal).

But note that, crucially, nor is this sort of interference-in-the-name-of-self-determination merely a manifestation of late Western imperialism. For example, the Third World itself was long energized around the notion that peoples seeking self-determination had a right to seek assistance and even that third states were obliged to give it to them.[859] Intervention in favor of decolonization was effectively recast as not intervention or as a legal form thereof. Resolution 2105 (XX) of 1965 even encouraged states to provide material and moral assistance to national liberation movements in colonial territories and Resolution 2160 (XX) and the Friendly Relations Declaration subsequently affirmed that peoples subject to colonial oppression were entitled to seek and receive moral and material support in their struggle.[860] The more general

858 Federica Paddeu and Alonso Gurmendi Dunkelberg, 'Recognition of Governments: Legitimacy and Control Six Months after Guaidó' (*Opinio Juris*, 18 July 2019) <https://opiniojuris.org/2019/07/18/recognition-of-governments-legitimacy-and-control-six-months-after-guaido/> accessed 11 July 2024.

859 Kader Asmal, 'The Legal Status of National Liberation Movements (with Particular Reference to South Africa)' (1983) 15 Zambia Law Journal 37.

860 See e.g., The Policies of Apartheid of the Government of the Republic of South Africa, UNGA Res 2307(XXII) (13 December 1967) U.N. Doc A/RES/2307(XXII) ('The General Assembly [...] [a]ppeals to all States and organizations to provide appropriate moral, political and material assistance to the people of South Africa in their legitimate struggle

move to making wars of national liberation into international armed conflicts, although operating as part of a humanitarian paradigm in Protocol I to the Geneva Conventions,[861] also clearly diminishes the scope of the *domaine réservé* and may still have some currency.[862] Although generally frowned upon in part as a form of interference, it has been mooted that foreign fighters could be seen as deserving on account of their contribution to host state self-determination.[863] Nonetheless, there remains persistent doubt, especially in the context of assistance to rebel groups, that appeals to self-determination of a people provide a way to override the nominal sovereignty of the state. This is not to mention that the more dramatic international statements in favor of self-determination, including foreign assistance thereto, were always confined to extra-maritime colonial domination and not to ordinary or secessionist political struggles within a state, legitimate as they may be.

What kind of support to rebel movements by third states this authorized has remained shrouded in ambiguity,[864] arguably all the more so now that the height of the first decolonial moment has passed. For example, whilst the 1974 definition of aggression anticipated that '[n]othing in this Definition [...] could in any way prejudice the right to self-determination, freedom and independence, as derived from the Charter, of peoples forcibly deprived of that right', it also insisted that '[n]othing in this Definition shall be construed as in any way enlarging or diminishing the scope of the Charter, including its provisions concerning cases in which the use of force is lawful'.[865] The idea that colonized or racially discriminated against peoples had an entitlement to outside assistance famously coexisted with both a larger wariness towards Western support for

---

for the rights recognized in the Charter'); Question of Southern Rhodesia, UNGA Res 2383 (XXIII) (7 November 1968) U.N. Doc A/RES/2383 (XXIII) ('The General Assembly [...] [u]rges all States, as a matter of urgency, to render all moral and material assistance to the national liberation movement of Zimbabwe, either directly or through the Organization of African Unity').

861 Jochen von Bernstorff, 'Defining Legal Subjectivities for a Postcolonial International Order: The International Legal Controversy over Wars of National Liberation' in Sebastian Thies, Susanne Goumegou and Georgina Cebey (eds), *The Routledge Handbook for Global South Studies on Subjectivities* (Routledge 2024).

862 Josalee S Deinla, 'International Law and Wars of National Liberation against Neo-Colonialism' (2014) 88 Philippine Law Journal 1.

863 Dara Conduit and Ben Rich, 'Foreign Fighters, Human Rights and Self-Determination in Syria and Iraq: Decoding the Humanitarian Impact of Foreign Fighters in Practice' (2016) 18 International Community Law Review 431.

864 Shaw (n 308).

865 UNGA Res 3314 (XXIX) 'Definition of Aggression' (14 December 1974) U.N. Doc A/RES/3314, art 6 and 7.

secessionist movements that would have disrupted the *uti possidetis* rule and an African willingness, from Katanga to Biafra, to repress separatism fiercely even when pursued on the grounds of self-determination. Nonetheless, this created a precedent that would oft be reprised by the superpowers during the Cold War to provide support to various 'freedom fighters'.

At any rate, the hiatus between self-determination and sovereignty creates genuine rupture in the discourse of international law, as well as significant potential instability. The emphasis on self-determination in the post-Cold War era has been taken up to highlight the specific validity of *pro-democratic* intervention. Already in the pivotal moment of the Helsinki Final Act, Arangio Ruiz had warned that contra a vision sometimes propounded by the Soviet bloc that self-determination entailed only freedom from external domination, it should also be understood as protecting *internal* self-determination from the yoke of tyranny:[866] not only decolonization, but liberation and perhaps even liberalization. The collapsing of the distinction between self-determination and democracy was, of course, not a foregone conclusion and it rests on shaky foundations intellectually. As was remarked in the previous section, this can have the effect of essentially nullify the principle of non-intervention for all but purportedly democratic states. There is much anecdotal evidence that support from outside of a 'people' that have risen against their state is still largely perceived as a blatant form of interference, notwithstanding the invocation of self-determination.[867]

Still, the point is that self-determination can clearly be invoked against sovereignty which is what makes it a double-edged sword for the purposes of propounding a coherent notion of non-interference. For example, the U.S. defends, not entirely improbably of course, a range of programs that Russia complains of as interference on the basis that, in fact, it 'does not view these programs as "manipulative" or threatening', but merely 'as enhancing existing desires by civil society to organize themselves and play a role in their own society'.[868] In that view, the outside power is merely helping a people self-determine themselves, all be it against their government. Particularly in revolutionary circumstances where the legitimacy of the government is weak, voices are bound to

866 Arangio-Ruiz (n 757) 225–227.

867 'Iran Protests: U.S. Accused of "grotesque" Interference' *BBC News* (4 January 2018) <https://www.bbc.com/news/world-middle-east-42563528> accessed 12 June 2024.

868 Cited in John Hudson, 'NO DEAL: How Secret Talks With Russia To Prevent Election Meddling Collapsed' *Buzzfeed.news* (12 August 2017) <https://www.buzzfeednews.com/article/johnhudson/no-deal-how-secret-talks-with-russia-to-prevent-election> accessed 3 April 2024.

be heard that will insist, for example, that the precocious recognition of popular resistance movements does not constitute interference since it merely gives voice to a fundamental aspiration to self-determination.[869] Much may depend, as was apparent in Libya, Syria[870] or Venezuela,[871] on nuances about whether what is being expressed is merely political support for certain constituencies (which is fully the prerogative of the states behind it even outside any consideration of the right of self-determination) or an actual legal act of recognition of what is deemed the legitimate government (which much more readily qualifies as interference).

The notion of intervention in favor of self-determination, just as intervention in favor of democracy, has a long and problematic history.[872] Although there has been no shortage of voices seeking to normalize coercion in the pursuit of collective goals,[873] one should intuitively guard against interpretations of non-interference that effectively transform it into a pretext for interference. Note that self-determination, even on its own terms, can be a tricky foothold for a theory of what should not be interfered with, precisely because of the way it potentially decouples the state and a people. What constitutes interference with sovereignty is fraught enough but interference with self-determination gives rise to a degree of perplexity given persistent controversies about the nature of self-determination under international law. The 'new interference', in particular, has prospered precisely as a result of being in a position to draw on local relays, whether local civil society groups, political operators, or communities who stand to gain from outside support and sometimes even seek it out, in the process confusing any sense that interference is effectively happening. Indeed, it has been claimed that 'interference pays off when it brings to power sympathizers in a target state eager to pursue a course favourable for the interfering state'.[874]

---

869 Jean Matringe, 'Les Révolutions et Le Principe de Non-Ingérence' (Institut de Relations Internationales et Stratégiques (IRIS) 2011) <https://www.iris-france.org/wp-content/uploads/2011/03/Les-r%C3%A9volutions-et-le-principe-de-non-ing%C3%A9rence.pdf> accessed 24 January 2024.

870 Stefan Talmon, 'Recognition of Opposition Groups as the Legitimate Representative of a People' (2013) 12 Chinese Journal of International Law 219; Olivier Corten, 'Déclarations Unilatérales d'indépendance et Reconnaissances Prématurées Du Kosovo à l'Ossétie Du Sud et à l'Abkhazie' (2008) 4 Revue générale de droit international public 721.

871 Ralph Janik, 'European Recognition Practice on Venezuela: The Devil in the Details' (*Opinio Juris*, 8 February 2019) <https://opiniojuris.org/2019/02/08/european-recognition-practice-on-venezuela-the-devil-in-the-details/> accessed 11 July 2024.

872 Schachter (n 816).

873 Reisman (n 40).

874 Istomin (n 315).

All arguments from self-determination, then, are very much a double-edged sword in terms of interference, both liable to oppose or justify it. As soon as one moves from the formal (sovereignty) to the substantive (self-determination), then one opens the possibility that interference might be justified precisely to further realize a repressed self-determination 'from outside' as it were. In effect, cases where self-determination is imagined denied are precisely the classic cases where the principle of non-interference has been argued to *not* apply, thus clearing the way for interference. Early decolonial arguments to that effect have since been reinforced by a logic of human rights that attempt to fuse both in not entirely wholesome ways. As Antonio Cassese once put it:

> the principle of non-interference [is] inapplicable where the right of a people to self-determination is at stake. States are no longer bound to remain silent, regardless of how a government behaves towards the people within its jurisdiction. They can denounce the government's repressive measures and publicly expose how it treats those subjected to its authority. In addition, [...] States can directly interfere in the authorities' relationship with the people entitled to external self-determination by aiding and assisting those people. In short, it is well settled that, under international law, the principle of non-interference must yield to the right of States to concern themselves with a peoples' legitimate quest for self-determination.[875]

In this view, self-determination provides a trump against interference only if self-determination is, in fact, guaranteed; if not, then outside states interfering can portray themselves as the artisans of a people's repressed aspiration to self-determination. They have the right and perhaps even the obligation to interfere. That sort of argument closely mimics the broader structure of international human rights law and the notion, sometimes entertained, that '[t]he oppressive government should not benefit from the non-intervention norm; rather, the country itself or its people deserve the norm's protection'.[876]

From that basis, one might consider that there is no interference if the acts in question are conducive to self-determination, but that there is if they are not.[877] Such reasoning is still highly prevalent in international legal thinking, where it has been suggested that '[i]t seems difficult to reconcile the imperative

875 Antonio Cassese, *Self-Determination of Peoples: A Legal Reappraisal* (Cambridge University Press 1995) 176.

876 Swanson (n 786) 882.

877 Damrosch (n 16).

of self-determination of peoples with a categorical prohibition on any form of intervention in the domestic affairs of states'.[878] One question is whether self-determination can be secured, or at least assisted, from outside, or whether interference does not by nature corrupt that which it claims to liberate. In that respect, Robespierre's promise that 'les Français n'useront de leurs forces et de leurs avantages que pour laisser à [tout] peuple la liberté de se donner la constitution qui lui paraîtra la plus convenable'[879] must be problematized in light of Bonaparte's two decades effort to shape conquered European nations in France's image;[880] or neo-conservative arguments about bringing democracy to Iraq in 2003, even in light of Saddam Hussein's undisputed dictatorial sway, should be assessed critically in light of their opportunism and the havoc wrecked on any meaningful prospect for self-determination in that country.[881]

Although views favorable to outside assistance may have been uncontroversial in the decolonial context (insofar as they justified solidarity with national liberation movements), transposing them outside this exceptional transition to a more multipolar moment may have the consequence of feeding the exact opposite politics. In effect, the turn to 'democracy promotion' in Western initiatives to the East and the South has often deftly presented the outsiders as the guarantors of self-determination rather than simply imposing democracy from outside. In some cases, this reasoning may be convincing: for example, few (today, at least) would argue that initiatives to undermine the Apartheid regime were interference in the self-determination of South Africans, given the egregious character of such a regime, the opposition to it by a majority of the population, and the commitment of the ANC to a policy of sanctions against the South African state.[882] But note that there is often a hefty dose of generality involved: whereas the argument that interference should not proceed because

878 Chimène I Keitner, 'Foreign Election Interference and International Law' in Jens David Ohlin and Duncan B Hollis (eds), *Defending Democracies: Combating Foreign Election Interference in a Digital Age* (Oxford University Press 2021) 186.

879 Maximilien Robespierre, *Oeuvres de Maximilien Robespierre avec une notice historique, des notes et des commentaires par Laponneraye* (Chez l'Éditeur 1840) 329.

880 Ouchakov (n 29) 7.

881 Alexander B Downes and Jonathan Monten, 'Forced to Be Free? Why Foreign-Imposed Regime Change Rarely Leads to Democratization' (2013) 37 International Security 90; Francis Fukuyama, *America at the Crossroads: Democracy, Power, and the Neoconservative Legacy* (Yale University Press 2006).

882 On the OAU and the non-applicability of the principle of non-interference to sanctions against 'clearly illegitimate apartheid regimes', see Elin Hellquist, 'Interpreting Sanctions in Africa and Southeast Asia' (2015) 29 International Relations 319, 323. See also UNGA Resolution 2307(XXII), calling for States to provide assistance 'to the people of South Africa in their legitimate struggle'.

it violates sovereignty provides a degree of relative clarity, what exactly does it mean to say that self-determination is denied? Is not self-determination always an imperfectly realized process? What threshold if any indicates that it has been denied beyond redemption? And what of the possibility that self-determination even denied to a degree (and it is arguably always denied to a degree) is at least still *self*-determination, the totality of outcomes engendered by the individual and collective decision of a people that is at least theirs?

4.2 *Interference by Invitation?*

The situation may be subtly different where an invitation to intervene is proffered locally and where the intervening power does not appear to be simply sitting in judgment from outside on the quality of self-determination in the host state. Governments can a priori invite foreign states to intervene on their territory and a fortiori to merely 'interfere' although in both cases the behavior in question ceases *ipso facto* to be either intervention or interference. This is especially if the intervener is an international organization such as the U.N., but arguably also if it is another state. What might otherwise qualify as intervention or interference functionally is redeemed by the invitation. The fact that the right of self-determination non-alienable does not mean that a state necessarily puts itself in a position where it has forfeited it merely by soliciting outside assistance. There is a history, for example, of quite far-reaching treaties by which states have put themselves under international tutelage. That is notably the case of a range of financial supervision arrangements concerning Egypt, Haiti or defeated Germany after the war: in application of the *volenti non fit injuria* maxim, states cannot object to supervision which they have themselves consented to via a 'traité permissif d'ingérence', although of course that consent may need to be relativized were it was granted in inherently coercive circumstances.[883]

An intervention by invitation is then very much at the host state's discretion, as shown in the *Uganda v Congo* case where the Court proceeded on the basis that 'a State may invite another State to assist it in using force in self-defence'.[884] In such cases, an invited power must of course not exceed the continued scope of such invitation and its intervention 'must not lead to the removal of the political control of the inviting government'[885] which in that case revolved around whether Uganda had continued to extend its welcome

883 Karl Strupp, *L'intervention En Matière Financière*, vol 8 (Brill Nijhoff 1925).

884 *Democratic Republic of the Congo v Uganda* (n 283) para 128.

885 Georg Nolte, 'Intervention by Invitation', *Max Planck Encyclopedia of Public International Law* (Oxford University Press 2011) para 20.

following a falling out with the DRC. It is not impossible, in fact, to think of forcible intervention by consent as relying, *stricto sensu*, on the vocabulary of international agreements.[886] The bottom line is that, as the Institut de Droit International put it in classic non-intervention jargon, '[m]ilitary assistance shall not constitute a coercive measure in order to obtain from a State the subordination of the exercise of its sovereign rights'.[887] Note, moreover, that interference does not lend itself particularly well to the register of invitation: something that is clandestine and subterranean cannot, by definition, have been invited.

Nonetheless, concerns about intervention have reached fever pitch even when it has been facilitated by governments in the target countries. There is, to begin with, a long history of governments being more or less coerced to issue 'invitations', especially retrospectively, to legitimize interventions, from the Anschluss to Hungary or Czechoslovakia's invitations to the Soviet Union or the invitation by the Chief of Santo Domingo's police to the U.S.[888] Even an invitation by a government may not alleviate concerns that it is problematic, especially if it used for repressive ends.[889] At any rate, one might argue that there has rarely been an intervention that has *not* under some conceivable reading been invited by local forces, with the attendant risks notably in a context of big power rivalry.[890] Invitations, it sometimes seems, can be conjured out of thin air. This is all the more so in a broad interference context in which some local relay welcoming interference can easily be found and provide some footing for claims that one is not intervening. There will always, in a sense, be a local politician, group or NGO to claim, rightly or wrongly, not so much that they invited an intervention (which is unlikely to be in their power to do) but that, from their perspective, said intervention is fully welcome and therefore not illegal.

The concern is, to begin with, about the very authority of those issuing the invitation, even in the name of a supposed government, to do so. In the midst of constitutional crises, it is sometimes not clear, for example, who within the

886 Eliav Lieblich, 'Intervention and Consent: Consensual Forcible Interventions in Internal Armed Conflicts as International Agreements' (2011) 29 Boston University International Law Journal 337.

887 Institut de Droit International, 'Present Problems of the Use of Force in International Law', *Session of Rhodes* (2011) art 6.3.

888 Louis B Sohn, 'Gradations of Intervention in Internal Conflicts' (1983) 13 Georgia Journal of International & Comparative Law 225, 225–227.

889 Irène Couzigou, 'Respect for State Sovereignty: Primacy of Intervention by Invitation over the Right to Self-Defence' (2019) 75 Heidelberg Journal of International Law 695.

890 Christakis and Bannelier, 'Volenti non fit injuria ?' (n 28).

apparatus of the state is doing the 'inviting' and whether they have the authority of the 'highest available State organ'. For example, the intervention of the OAS (an international organization, it is true, but leaving aside that nuance for now) in Ecuador in February 1997 was solicited by its President in the course of a campaign for his resignation, but opposed by members of Congress who saw it as an interference in the affairs of Ecuador (a similar scenario unfolded in Honduras some 12 years later).[891] More recently, severe concerns have been raised about former Ukrainian President Yanukovych's letter to the Russian Federation calling on it to intervene forcefully.[892] The fact that a government may be contested, have an imperfect hold on its territory or dubiously representative, however, do not normally suffice to impugn its quality of the government of that state under international law.[893]

Nor is it clear, in fact, that tolerance of interference by the executive itself, even assuming that its status is relatively undisputed, saves it from being problematic. Early doubts about whether Hungary had truly invited Soviet troops to intervene in 1956 or much later about whether Grenada had truly invited U.S. troops in 1983 are a reminder that such interventions are likely to radicalize questions about the legitimacy of governments and the degree to which they rightfully embody an aspiration to self-determination, let alone operate free of coercion by a foreign power. Even assuming that a government is rightly understood as the de jure and de facto leader, the conditions whereupon it came to power may add an extra layer of puzzlement about whether its apparent permission to interfere are entirely determinative of the interference question. Did interference by the U.S. in the affairs of Chile under Allende cease to be interference the minute Pinochet came to power through a coup and presumably laundered, retroactively, the effects of such interference? Or should an ill-acquired position of power be treated as inherently suspicious and as a continued manifestation of the interference that gave rise to it, insusceptible of being saved by an appeal to *de facto* and even *de jure* power going forward?

Invitations by governments to become involved, then, are bound to be evaluated against demands in the opposite direction (to not intervene or intervene on their behalf) by opposition groups and civil society. Interventions

891 Rubén M Perina, 'The Inter-American Democratic Charter: An Assessment and Ways to Strengthen It', *The Road to Hemispheric Cooperation: Beyond the Cartagema Summit of the Americas* (Brookings Institution 2012) <https://www.summit-americas.org/pubs/vi_summit_brookings.pdf> accessed 17 May 2024.

892 Thomas D Grant, 'The Yanukovych Letter: Intervention and Authority to Invite in International Law' (2015) 2 Indonesian Journal of International & Comparative Law 281.

893 de Wet (n 28).

by government invitation may certainly be viewed with a degree of skepticism if, for example, their finality is repressive, the government is little representative, or the suspicion is that the outside power is upending processes of self-determination by taking sides.[894] The international law of invitation, however, has struggled with these parameters. International lawyers have long disagreed, beyond the motivation or purpose of an invitation to intervene, on whether what matters is that a government be effective or that it be somehow legitimate, and in what proportions. As liberal arguments have risen in influence, both human rights and democracy have increasingly shaped expectations about governmental legitimacy and that states may exceptionally forfeit their right to invite outside intervention (notwithstanding their *de facto* and *de jure* control) if they are embroiled in the repression of groups engaged in legitimate rebellion.[895] Alternatively, governments may even compensate their lack of effective control by a surfeit of democratic or human rights legitimacy.

Notwithstanding, there is also a long tradition of wariness with intervention by governmental invitation especially in the context of the use of force, essentially denying foreign powers the ability to 'arbitrate' domestic conflicts.[896] In extremely contested settings, notably civil war, assistance to the nominal government, all be it at its technical invitation, may be seen as siding with it in violation of the obligation of non-intervention in civil wars. Indeed, the more decisive the intervention, the more it will appear to be resolutive of the very questions of contested authority that are at the root of whether intervention is legal in the first place—essentially functioning as a self-fulfilling prophecy. Especially in a context of 'frequent changes between incumbent governments and rebels' it may be difficult to 'maintain any meaningful distinction between them'.[897] The risk is that one will give too much salience to whoever happens to be relatively more in control of territory at any given time. At the same time, the international law on use of force by invitation is, if not in disarray, at least clearly in flux. States have not shied in to invoke the consent of host states when it suited them, for example in the context of Western strikes against Daesh in Iraq, not even hinting at a tradition of wariness with such interventions,[898]

894 Rein Mullerson, 'Intervention by Invitation' in Lori Fisler Damrosch and David J Scheffer (eds), *Law and Force in the New International Order* (Routledge 1992).

895 Redaelli (n 28).

896 Bennouna (n 28); Louise Doswald-Beck, 'The Legal Validity of Military Intervention by Invitation of the Government' (1985) 56 British Yearbook of International Law 189.

897 Friedmann, 'Intervention and the Developing Countries' (n 406) 210.

898 Akande and Vermeer (n 440).

and facing little 'negative opinio juris' in the process, although that may not be conclusive.[899]

Having said that, it is probably true that uses of force and armed conflict are a special case of intervention and quite remote from the concern with interference at the heart of this book. Reluctance to allow foreign meddling at the tipping point of a violent contestation over legitimate power raises particularly acute questions. Although emblematic and understandably a focus of attention, the focus on the use of force distorts the broader debate on intervention and interference by importing into it a specific prevention with the nature and impact of violence. Notably, the concern with intervention by invitation in civil wars is also the risk that outside forces may be 'betting on the wrong horse' to the extent that the entity claiming to invite no longer actually has that authority at all. Especially in the case of full-blown civil war where a rebel group controls part of the territory, then, this may militate towards prudentially denying requests for assistance from governments but also from said groups not out of the intrinsic nature of either (state or non-state), but on the basis of the indecisive character of the contest between them and the notion that an outside intervener should not 'tip the balance'.[900]

Outside such extreme scenarios, however, run-of-the-mill solicitations from governments (including for arms transfers for example) are likely to be seen as far less problematic in part because they are very difficult to distinguish from ordinary interaction and because it is hard to see on what grounds the state could not solicit assistance as part of its sovereignty. The more transparent, non-coercive and non-decisive the interference complained of is, the more unobjectionable it will be. It is also worth noting that much of the reasoning developed around the notion of intervention by invitation in domestic armed conflicts—where one can indeed imagine formal and decisive invitations—is quite inapposite when it comes to mere interference. Interference often happens if anything by osmosis, through the quiescence of local actors who see nothing untoward about it, may not claim any formal authority to channel foreign processes domestically, or see it as merely—and not unreasonably—a facet of international interdependence. In that respect, whereas an invitation to intervene in an armed conflict ought clearly to emanate from the government or some quasi-governmental authority, it is not even clear that when it comes to a range of behavior that is much less intrinsically harmful the government has a monopoly on such invitations. Not involving behaviour that is

899 Ferro (n 442).
900 Fox (n 28).

intrinsically illegal, proving that it is nonetheless illicit will be all the more difficult.[901] It is certainly far less problematic for non-state groups to ask for any degree of outside assistance when such assistance does not involve military support or the use of force. The solicitation of a mere interference as opposed to an intervention, let alone a forceful one, certainly frames that process in a very different light.

This could still entail that assistance in a civil war is not necessarily an intervention because it comes with an invitation; but it could also mean that peaceful interference at the solicitation of the government *is* capable of being an illicit interference as well. Indeed, even beyond the use of force realm, the tilting potential is still there, latently at least, and it is one that problematizes the idea of the sovereign's right and monopoly to invite outside influences. For example, a government that invited a foreign state to meddle in and disrupt its own elections is one whose otherwise uncontested governing authority would have to be weighed against the broad illegitimacy of undermining elections, be it one's own. By the same token, nor does this on its own make the case for civil society or opposition groups' ability to freely reach out to external actors for foreign support. For one thing, such actors will have to make do with the constraints of domestic law, at least so long as compatible with international human rights law and international law more generally, and its inherent tendency to defer first and foremost to governmental authority. States are free to impose reasonable limitations on the ability of their citizenry or groups in their midst to relate to external actors, notably those who would thereby seek to unduly sway domestic politics. For example, local actors could still use the leverage of their transnational relations to tilt processes of self-determination in problematic ways (imagine, for example, that a foreign power donates to a party's electoral campaign lavishly in ways that effectively decide an election).

Note that the problem is particularly fraught with the 'new interference' where, instead of a clear government-to-government invitation, one may witness situations where who issues the invitation to whom is elusive. Certain domestic constituencies—which could be part of the government but need not be—could signal discreetly to a range of shadowy actors, which could be part of a foreign government or not, that they would not oppose certain forms of domestic assistance, for example in elections. This could then have significant repercussions on what is imagined as an ideal self-determination process. It would essentially make it very difficult to assess the degree to which, as a result of such solicitations, self-determination is still national or not, or at least

901 Helal (n 408).

whether it has not been significantly channelled by outside forces. Merely benefiting from or not complaining of an interference is of course not acquiescing to it, but the point is that what counts as an invitation is yet another dimension of intervention that stands to be muddled by developments in the nature and quality of interference. This in a context where establishing exactly who is doing the inviting and in whose name has never been more important to ascertain the legitimacy of influence v the illegality of intervention.

This explains at any rate why rather than simple reliance on the consent of local actors, including the government, interference from outside has increasingly been further evaluated in terms of how compatible it is with certain international values, notably self-determination. Consent by the government may be a necessary but it is not a sufficient condition of lawful intervention. Such a trend has long been visible especially in the use of force realm where, for example, Karine Bannelier and Theodore Christakis have advanced the notion of a 'purpose based approach' acting as a further check on otherwise prima facie valid responses to government solicitation.[902] This is also reflected in the evolution of the IDI resolutions on the matter which, notably, henceforth anticipates that, outside situations of non-international armed conflict, '[m]ilitary assistance is prohibited when it is exercised in violation of the Charter of the United Nations, of the principles of non-intervention, of equal rights and self-determination of peoples and generally accepted standards of human rights *and in particular when its object is to support an established government against its own population*'.[903] It has been argued that states should at any rate not have the ability to invite an outside intervention when they are themselves compromised in R2P violations and in order to further such violations.[904]

This inevitably problematizes governments' authority in ways that also reshape how one might approach, mutatis mutandis, solicitations by non-governmental groups as well for purposes short of uses of force. The more it is the goal of and values animating interference that are emphasized, the less relevant the identity of the actor calling for it, all other things being equal, will matter. Although on some level assessing the degree to which an intervention is conducive to self-determination may seem like an unlikely abstraction to

902 Théodore Christakis and Karine Bannelier, 'Under the U.N. Security Council's Watchful Eyes: Military Intervention by Invitation in the Malian Conflict' (2013) 26 Leiden Journal of International Law 855.

903 Institut de Droit International, 'Present Problems of the Use of Force in International Law' (n 886) art 3.1.

904 Coman Kenny and Sean Butler, 'The Legality of Intervention by Invitation in Situations of R2P Violations' (2018) 51 New York University Journal of International Law and Politics 135.

assess the legitimacy of something as problematic as an outside intervention/interference, all assistance to a foreign government at its request will be prodded for the extent to which it objectively facilitates its maintenance in power and, as the case may be, its denial of self-determination of its peoples. The argument may be, by contrast, that support for an intervention by civil society, opposition groups or even rebels is more conducive to self-determination in some circumstances. Certainly, deference only to the government's openings reinforces a degree of sovereign rent-seeking that creates an obvious asymmetry with the position of non-state groups, especially those with significant popular backing.

This, however, underscores the complexity of debates about the finality of intervention and the stated purpose of invitation. Is it true that what matters not just who invites, but *what* they invite for? Where does that leave the normal authority of the government and the very purpose of statehood? One traditional response especially during the Cold War was, in a context of heightened sensitivity about merely pretextual invitations, that the motive of intervention was irrelevant. For example, the Friendly Declaration insisted unequivocally that 'no state shall organize, assist foment, finance, incite or tolerate subversive terrorist or armed activities directed towards the violence overthrow of the regime of another state, or interfere in civil strife in another state'.[905] Such a position, at a time when intervention was primarily seen as the doing of the superpowers, had the advantage of clarity, if not realism. It protected both states and populations from contrived interventions loosely 'on their behalf' by outsiders not necessarily in a very solid position to evaluate the degree to which self-determination was being achieved. But that discursive investment was also a product of its times: clearly the Third World was not deaf either to calls for assistance from anti-colonial or anti-Apartheid movements.

This has arguably given way to a much more flexible appreciation of different types and quality of motives. This is especially as a result of the possibility of multilateral validation, notably through the Security Council, of what counts as a legitimate invitation, for example to fight terrorism[906] but also possibly to reinstate democracy as in Haiti or Sierra Leone[907] (as well as, occasionally,

905 1970 Declaration on Friendly Relations. See also Institut de Droit International, 'The Principle of Non-Intervention in Civil Wars' (n 131).

906 Karine Bannelier-Christakis, 'Military Interventions against ISIL in Iraq, Syria and Libya, and the Legal Basis of Consent' (2016) 29 Leiden Journal of International Law 743.

907 Gregory H Fox, 'Invitations to Intervene after the Cold War: Towards a New Collective Model' in Dino Kritsiotis, Olivier Corten and Gregory H Fox (eds), *Armed Intervention and Consent* (Cambridge University Press 2023).

the identification of intervention by invitation and collective self-defence).[908] Of course, in such cases the invitation does not do all of the work of making an intervention legal and is in a sense transcended by the identification of a threat to international peace and security and the Security Council's Chapter vii powers. This can create confusion when invitation coexists as a possible justification for intervention with other possible rationales. But it equally stands to be a rough guide to what sort of invitations are not seen as prima facie invalid, and it has certainly contributed to enhancing the respectability of such invitations. In practice, moreover, invitations will not be the only reason for intervention and the argument for the latter will be reinforced through a range of arguments.

By the same token and from a deeper normative point of view, it is not clear that demands of assistance by *either* governments or opposition groups can ever be legitimate in terms of a canonical reading of self-determination, whatever their motives, to the extent that they disrupt what is imagined as the otherwise unmediated confrontation between national forces, inevitably tilting the balance one way or another on no account other than the moral chance of foreign help and its availability. As Oscar Schachter once put it, even when nominally in favor of self-determination, 'for a foreign State to support, with "force", one side or the other in an internal conflict is to deprive the people in some measure of their right to decide the issue by themselves'.[909] This is the logic that has long structured Mill's argument for non-intervention as, essentially, usurping the 'arduous struggle' of a people for liberation.[910] Deference to self-determination may then militate for a radical albeit consistent position of intervention neither in support of government nor non-government groups, regardless of their motivation. This is what has been described as the 'negative equality' principle, namely the position that the government is as disqualified as insurgent groups from inviting outside assistance.[911] It arguably militates for rigorous neutrality between both.[912]

908 Laura Visser, 'Intervention by Invitation and Collective Self-Defence: Two Sides of the Same Coin?' (2020) 7 Journal on the Use of Force and International Law 292.

909 Schachter (n 569) 160.

910 John Stuart Mill, 'A Few Words on Non-Intervention' (1859) 60 Fraser's Magazine for Town and Country 766, 775.

911 Independent International Fact-Finding Mission on the Conflict in Georgia, 'Report, Vol 2' (2009) 278 <https://www.mpil.de/files/pdf4/IIFFMCG_Volume_II1.pdf> accessed 13 July 2024.

912 Quoc Tan Trung Nguyen, 'Rethinking the Legality of Intervention by Invitation: Toward Neutrality' (2019) 24 Journal of Conflict and Security Law 201.

Still, from a traditional Westphalian standpoint, anxieties may be particularly high when the invitation is not by some organ of the state, however contested, but by opposition movements, not to mention amorphous civil society groups that may seek to undermine their government from within by promoting an alliance between internal and external forces. As the ICJ famously put it, 'it is difficult to see what would remain of the principle of non-intervention in international law if intervention, which is already allowable at the request of the government of a State, were also to be allowed at the request of the opposition'.[913] This non-equivalency thesis goes at the heart of international law and its relative sanctification of state sovereignty. It does not mean that states always have a presumptive claim to solicit assistance or that non-state groups can never do so, but it does distribute their ability to do so differentially, in line with their distinct statuses under international law.

It is sometimes interfering *states* themselves that have made much of the fact that they are responding to local actors, especially outside the limited context of the use of force, and their investment in a discourse of benign intervention is worth paying attention to. For example, the West has long sought to counteract claims that it is interfering in sovereign affairs by emphasizing that it is often civil society groups that are very much the ones calling for its support. In that respect, a clear line runs through the cosmopolitan vulgate of humanitarian intervention and a much more agentic theory of intervention at the request of the victims of oppression—a theory where victims are understood as fully constituted political agents. As the Spanish scholastic Suarez understood early on, war by a foreign power in defense of a foreign population is justified:

> on condition that the friend himself would be justified in waging the war, and consents thereto, either expressly or by implication. The reason for this limitation is that a wrong done to another does not give me the right to avenge him, unless he would be justified in avenging himself and actually proposes to do so. Assuming, however, that these conditions exist, my aid to him is an act of co-operation in a good and just deed; but if [the injured party] does not entertain such a wish, no one else may intervene, since he who committed the wrong has made himself subject not to every one indiscriminately, but only to the person who has been wronged.[914]

---

913 *Nicaragua v United States* (n 3) [246].

914 Francisco Suarez, *Selections from Three Works* (Thomas Pink ed, Liberty Fund 2014) 931.

Pufendorf adopted a similar standard, noting that 'we cannot lawfully undertake the defence of another's subjects, for any other reason than they themselves can rightfully advance, for taking up arms to protect themselves against the barbarous savagery of their superiors'.[915] This approach of seeing the right of intervention as fundamentally derivative of a right of a people to themselves resist their sovereign can be usefully contrasted to a tradition incarnated by the likes of Gentili, Grotius, Bodin or Hobbes who saw the power to intervene as relying only on the judgment of the intervener.[916]

International law has long hesitated between those positions, often outlining a sort of middle case. Although the ICJ did not ultimately find in *Nicaragua v United States* that a customary rule of international had materialized allowing assistance to rebels, it did at the time acknowledge that:

> there might be indications of a practice illustrative of belief in a kind of general right for States to intervene, directly or indirectly, with or without armed force, in support of an internal opposition in another State, whose cause appeared particularly worthy by reason of the political and moral values with which it was identified.[917]

In more recent times, this has occasionally given rise to robust proposals for allowing and deferring to invitations to intervene, if need be militarily, by rebel groups in lieu of their repressive state.[918] In the Syrian and Libyan contexts, one has witnessed the provision of non-lethal assistance by some Western states to groups that sought it, in ways that would have undoubtedly been treated as interventionist, notably on the basis of the ICJ's ruling in *Nicaragua v United States.*

Leaving aside the distinct possibility that such provision might expose contributing powers to accusations of complicity with crimes committed by said groups[919] or the separate debate on the violation of the prohibition of the use of force, there has been a very limited and cautious opening to the possibility that such assistance would not, in law, constitute an unlawful intervention.[920]

---

915 Samuel Pufendorf, *De Jure Naturae et Gentium Libri Octo, 1688 Ed (English Translation)*, vol 2 (Clarendon Press 1934) bk VIII, ch VI, s 14.

916 Tuck (n 90).

917 *Nicaragua v United States* (n 3) [206].

918 Michael Dressler Jr, 'I Have No Mouth, and I Must Scream: Interventions by Invitation in the Aftermath of Coup D'etats' (2022) 127 Penn State Law Review 237.

919 Georg Nolte and Helmut Philipp Aust, 'Equivocal Helpers—Complicit States, Mixed Messages and International Law' (2009) 58 International & Comparative Law Quarterly 1.

920 Redaelli (n 28).

However, some authors remain insistent that not even the human rights bona fides (such as it may be) of such assistance saves it from being basically in violation of international law; nor is it clear that invitation by local groups is even invoked as the decisive factor in justifying intervention. Expedients such as recognizing the Free Syrians as the legitimate representative of the Syrian people—which was at any rate engaged in very ambiguously, probably for good reason—[921] cannot ultimately overcome their lack of effective control and thus allow them to fulfill the legal criteria of governmentality.[922]

In effect, the tendency to ditch the historical rules of belligerency and their agnostic, regime neutral emphasis on the effectiveness of control for the benefit of an evaluation of the legitimacy of various actors' cause makes their agency relatively irrelevant—what matters, ultimately, is not so much that they called for intervention but that they had the legitimacy to do so, so that the decisive factor is ultimately the legitimacy of their cause. This has long led to an attendant impoverishment of a tradition of neutrality that at least sought to exclude direct military assistance to non-state groups as beyond the pale. If by contrast what matters is some loosely framed effort to promote self-determination, however, then third states are given a relatively free rein to decide who best incarnates that aspiration, even as against local opposition to intervention, by the government or non-governmental actors. The effort to prevent the internationalization of conflicts and the intrusion of third parties is then further weakened by the invocation of collective interests, in which invitation or consent, even by the government, ultimately plays a secondary role.[923] Although by no means an uncontested development, this is the blueprint not only for intervention in civil wars but more generally for all kinds of transnational assistance to civil society groups, namely that they concur to the goal of domestic self-determination as propounded by at least some groups (and there are almost always such groups).

Particularly when it comes to the use of force, however, the debate on 'intervention by invitation' sheds light on the dangers involved, especially

921 Michael N Schmitt, 'Legitimacy versus Legality Redux: Arming the Syrian Rebels' (2014) 7 Journal of National Security Law and Policy 139, 152–154.

922 Tom Ruys and Luca Ferro, 'The Enemy of My Enemy: Dutch Non-Lethal Assistance for "Moderate" Syrian Rebels and the Multilevel Violation of International Law' in Otto Spijkers, Wouter G Werner and Ramses A Wessel (eds), *Netherlands Yearbook of International Law 2019* (TMC Asser Press 2021).

923 Theodore Christakis and Karine Bannelier, 'French Military Intervention in Mali: It's Legal But … Why? Part II: Consent and UNSC Authorisation' (*EJIL: Talk!*, 25 January 2013) <https://www.ejiltalk.org/french-military-intervention-in-mali-its-legal-but-why-part-2-consent-and-unsc-authorisation/> accessed 10 July 2024.

the sometimes dubious status of those doing the inviting and the clear risk of abuse. Questions of the more or less representative character of *both* the government and opposition or civil society groups are thus bound to be central to any debate on locally invited interference.[924] It is not even clear, for example, that a government that requires outside assistance to prop itself up does not thereby forfeit or at least put in question its status as the de facto ruler. As William E Hall once put it, 'the fact that it has been necessary to call in foreign help is enough to show that the issue of the conflict would without it be uncertain, and consequently that there is doubt as to which side would ultimately establish itself as the legal representative of the state'.[925] A fortiori, non-state groups' status will be prodded closely given their lack of prima facie formal credentials. Of course, outside the solicitation of military help in a civil war there is less harm in the state seeking to maintain itself by enlisting foreign support at least so long as it does not do so to suppress the self-determination of its peoples, or of private groups doing more or less the same. Even there, however, questions are bound to arise about whether such outside solicitations are authorized and within the powers of the actors that make them.

Ironically, the Western emphasis on intervention by invitation echoes the long standing decolonial argument that peoples denied their right of self-determination 'are entitled to seek and to receive support in accordance with the purposes and principles of the Charter'.[926] This justification of intervention in response to calls for help from unjustly oppressed peoples was once a pillar of the non-aligned cause, as exemplified by the Declaration on Friendly Relations. Throughout the Cold War, there was no shortage of local groups aligned with one Superpower or the other and willing to call for assistance, more or less plausibly invoking international values, in ways that seemed to opportunistically justify intervention. Even in such a context, efforts were deployed to keep the genie in the box by consigning such forceful intervention to decolonial situations.[927] But concerns have not abated that 'intervention by invitation' is likely to be a continued 'tool of colonialism', in a context where willing local relays can always be found and provide a cover of legitimacy. Contra the notion that states can be oppressive to their people and therefore intervention is needed to reinstate internal self-determination, it is also the

924 John Lawrence Hargrove, 'Intervention by Invitation and the Politics of the New World Order' in Lori Fisler Damrosch and David J Scheffer (eds), *Law and Force in the New International Order* (Routledge 1992).

925 William Edward Hall, *A Treatise on International Law* (Clarendon Press 1884) 269.

926 1970 Declaration on Friendly Relations, 121.

927 Sohn (n 887) 229.

case that responding to a private invitation against the state can quickly lapse into a denial of external self-determination.[928]

Western states willing to instrumentalize the discourse of self-determination to justify their own form of interference should of course be mindful of how that discourse can, in turn, be adroitly deployed against them. For example, Azerbaijan has, through the creation of the 'Baku group' encouraged separatists from the French territories of Martinique, French Guiana, New Caledonia and French Polynesia to 'liberate' from France as part of an agenda of decolonization.[929] The point, of course, is that Azerbaijan is not entirely on shaky foundations when it makes such arguments, especially given the apparent willingness of some independentists to solicit its assistance. Such initiatives at least problematize what interference means by shedding some doubt on the representative character of the French government in some neo-colonial locales, even if the authority of a foreign state with its own agenda to engage in them is dubious. The willingness of any random local actor to call in outside interveners cannot be an official licence to interfere, especially where the use of force might be involved; the latter's representative character will be open to doubt and, at any rate, they are not the government and, arguably, a poor approximation of self-determination. Civil society thus does not necessarily hold the 'keys' to the *domaine réservé*.

Evacuating the problem of 'right authority' to call in the interveners or at least trying to address it through appeals to self-determination is not without its own pitfalls. The problem with 'self-determination paternalism' is the risk that it will set up outside observers as arbiters who 'know better' whether self-determination is being realized—outside, that is, of *actual* self-determination's processes. After all, during the Prague Spring, Warsaw Pact tanks intervened to 'protect' Czechoslovak sovereignty and self-determination against attempts to subvert it from within. As Kovalev put it in his famous Pravda article:

> Socialist forces in Czechoslovakia were in essence using talk about the right of self-determination to cover up demands for [...] Czechoslovakian withdrawal from the Socialist Commonwealth. But, implementation of such self-determination, that is, Czechoslovakia's separation from the

928 Farideh Shaygan, 'Intervention by Invitation as a Tool of New Colonialism' in James Crawford and others (eds), *The International Legal Order: Current Needs and Possible Responses* (Brill Nijhoff 2017).

929 Perina (n 890).

> Socialist Commonwealth, *would run counter to Czechoslovakia's fundamental interest.*[930]

The OAS's shift towards interventionist anti-Communism in the 1950s also created an environment ripe for abuse which reneged on the organization's non-interventionist tradition on account of a substantive, outcome-oriented view of self-determination. The problem was that, as Richard Falk put it, 'the assumption that Communism always derives from a foreign intervention involves a clear sacrifice of the principle of self-determination' given 'evidence [...] that Communism has, on occasion, been a genuine expression of self-determination'.[931]

Still, in a context where non-interference is simultaneously framed in terms of the need to safeguard self-determination and where human rights are increasingly presented as being of global concern, it seems inevitable that questions will be asked about who exactly is opposing interference and for what purpose. This will at least put states on the defensive when they deny outside assistance, especially of a non-lethal character. It will, in turn, be unclear whether the voice of those from within who are sympathetic to outside reaching-in can entirely be excluded. To be clear, interference almost always benefits some local constituencies and it has been adept, historically, at recruiting enablers, for example, the sort of 'political accomplices in the [E.U.] Member States who derive political and economic advantages from favouring foreign strategies' and thus are more than willing to assist them.[932] Famously, U.S. Presidential election candidate Donald Trump encouraged Russia to provide his campaign with intelligence on Hilary Clinton.[933] Indeed, the possibility of a local demand for outside interference even as there is a certain supply for it abroad stands to complicate the picture of what falls within self-determination. If the doors of the *domaine réservé* are constantly opened by local solicitations, then how much interference is truly going on? And where, exactly, is the locus of self-determination: in Western-aligned civil society, for example, de facto authorities or the de jure government?

---

930 Kovalov (n 151).

931 Falk, *Legal Order in a Violent World* (n 117) 177.

932 2022 Resolution on Foreign Interference in the E.U. (n 337), para F.

933 Michael S Schmidt, 'Trump Invited the Russians to Hack Clinton. Were They Listening?' *The New York Times* (13 July 2018) <https://www.nytimes.com/2018/07/13/us/politics/trump-russia-clinton-emails.html> accessed 11 December 2023.

Leaving aside the use of force question, civil society groups, even without democratic legitimacy, have the authority to seek to pry open some doors (those that should already, typically, be kept at least slightly ajar under international law), but nor can they open the door of sovereignty wide open if this contradicts the government's policy. The problem is of course that 'self-determination', however it is imagined, will rarely lead to homogeneous and easy-to-read outcomes that would allow to decipher an unproblematic invitation to meddle. At best, it will reveal contradictory impulses about whether outside solicitude is welcome solidarity or unwanted prying. There may be entirely self-serving demands for interference, for example, by local politicians who merely calculate that it can tip the scales of election processes in their favor. The fact that interference is apparently solicited or welcomed by such politicians (as seemed to be the case of candidate Donald Trump during the 2016 elections) hardly means that they stand for anything more than themselves, even if they are in government. By the same token, of course, there may be cases where local civil society gravitates towards foreign supporters because it is being repressed and starved of rights at home and can make a case that it is deserving of such assistance and perhaps even an *avant garde* of its peoples' self-determination.

This also potentially sets up a showdown between different recipients of international solidarity, in a context where all kinds of groups are being funded by outside states and, indeed, states themselves are often the recipients of significant outside largesse that could be seen as interfering with the free flow of self-determination. Is interference not interference when its beneficiary is a state actor? Why would it be necessarily wrong for private actors to solicit foreign help? Indeed, the inequity of governments receiving large amounts of foreign funding whilst prohibiting civil society from doing so is sometimes underlined to complain of its unfairness. As Kenneth Roth puts it:

> But why are foreign funds so nefarious when NGOs get them yet apparently uncontroversial when others do? The Ethiopian government is one of the largest aid recipients in Africa; does that make it subversive? The Russian government lives off its sale of oil and natural gas to foreign buyers; is that an act of treason? The Egyptian government receives billions of dollars in U.S. military assistance and is negotiating for billions more in loans from the IMF; is that an act of disloyalty? Of course not. So why is it wrong for NGOs to solicit financial support from foreign friends? Bolstered by foreign funds, governments routinely advance their political

> agendas. Militaries and businesses do the same. Why should NGOs be singled out for restriction?[934]

The obvious if facile answer, from an international law point of view, is that it is governments that represent their people, not civil society groups. Repeated appeals to self-determination 'from below' via civil society can, in fact, be seen as a crude way of undermining a state's sovereignty, a sort of Trojan horse for outside interests whose transparent goal is to displace the rightful—and legally unimpeachable—focus on the authorities. The rhetorical invocation of self-determination might bolster rather than weaken the case for interference.

This is a reminder that the contestation of the old interference was typically steeped in a Westphalian mindset that saw rights and self-determination, society and government, as presumptively aligned over a particular territory. This has gradually given way to a vision in which, although the state may in the best of cases be a vehicle conducive to self-determination, it can also be a significant obstacle to it, because it is dictatorial or otherwise seals its population off from welcome outside influences. Who will then say where self-determination lies, if we have decided that we can no longer equate self-determination and the state? Arguments from self-determination can thus end up reinforcing the state but also undermining it on the basis that it is failing in its vocation to embody self-determination, thus further confusing any notion of the appropriate perimeter of the *domaine*.

4.3 *Self-determination without Self-determination?*

It thus remains challenging to erect self-determination—as much as sovereignty or democracy—as the ultimate normative arbiter of whether a fundamentally domestic sphere is being interfered with, given persistent ambiguities about what self-determination even means. One ambiguity exposed by the new interference when it comes to self-determination concerns the nature of the process involved. For what *exactly* is being interfered with as part of the *domaine réservé*? The traditional vision of unlawful interference is quite Westphalian and envisages one state unlawfully interfering with another state by unduly weighing on the government or officials. The interference, if anything, is directed at a series of processes imagined as autonomous and self-constituted. In such conditions, the implicit image is one of a series of relatively autonomous public spheres, each with a life of its own whose delicate balance can presumably be disrupted by outside interferences.

---

934 Roth, 'NGOs Have a Right to Receive Foreign Funding' (n 777).

Particularly when it comes to self-determination and democracy, what is imagined, in the words of John Adams, is the danger that something 'partial or extraneous should infect the purity of our free, fair, virtuous and independent actions'.[935] Hence the goal of resisting interference is to stop the 'corruption' or at least the 'contamination' of one's own, exclusive and neatly delineated, public sphere—'to stop pollution of the "free market place of ideas" with nostrums promoted by undisclosed alien, totalitarian sources'.[936] As the Declaration on the Inadmissibility of Intervention put it, states should be able to exercise their self-determination 'without any foreign pressure'.[937] This is a fortiori the case with coercive intervention and uses of force that, in essence, 'rob' a polity of the outcome it would hypothetically have arrived at on its own terms. Quite aside from any concern one may have with the use of force per se, as Oscar Schachter put it, '[f]or a foreign state to support, with "force", one side or the other in an internal conflict, is to deprive the people in some measure of their right to decide the issue by themselves'.[938]

Even on the basis of classic Westphalian premises, however, this was always a fraught normative position because of the way it seemed to endow conflicts, both military and political, with a sort of immanent value for the purposes of self-determination. What reason does one have to think that an unimpeded contest of arms is in itself, duel-like, a meritorious ordeal to determine the political fate of a nation? Schachter suggested that governments had a presumptive right to receive military assistance but that if an 'organized insurgency occurs on a large scale' then third states should refrain from assisting either said insurgency of the government.[939] Why one would want to draw the line in exactly that way is unclear except perhaps on narrow prudential grounds. The danger is that one will fetishize a process merely because of its domestic credentials, which seems as problematic as assuming that internationally determined outcomes are always better, and which may ignore formidable domestic inequities. One may be opposed to intervention on self-determination grounds but still be wary of the idea of self-determination as a purely domestic process in an interconnected world. What can it possibly mean to exercise self-determination

935 John Adams, 'Inaugural Address of John Adams' <https://avalon.law.yale.edu/18th_century/adams.asp> accessed 30 January 2024.

936 Murray L Schwartz and James CN Paul, 'Foreign Communist Propaganda in the Mails: A Report on Some Problems of Federal Censorship' (1959) 107 University of Pennsylvania Law Review 621, 625.

937 1981 Declaration on the Inadmissibility of Intervention and Interference, para. 6.

938 Schachter (n 569) 160.

939 ibid 161.

without *any* foreign pressure, when the whole stake of self-determination is to wade through various forms of structural pressures? The point, at any rate, is that just as self-determination can be adduced to make a compelling case against intervention, it is also the very vocabulary that will sometimes be deployed convincingly to justify intervention.

The new interference certainly further calls into question the status of self-determination, not only in that it problematizes its factual premises, but also in that it challenges its normative assumptions. Increasingly, interference is not so much inter-governmental as it is government-to-society or even inter-social.[940] What is at stake is the attempt to broadly weaken the target society's ability to function on 'its own terms' (including, as the case may be, democratically), in ways that end up favouring certain interests, views, constituencies, or persons. But the idea that it is the public sphere that is being interfered with can be misleading in its simplicity, and at any rate does not immediately disclose why interfering with a sphere (as opposed to the state) should be illegal under international law, or whether the 'public sphere' is rightly seen as part of the *domaine réservé*. What is specifically national about public spheres, for example, against a background of circulation of political advisers, transnational alliances between political parties and the collectivization of campaigning and electoral platform models, as well as the complex transnational movement of money for the purposes of campaign financing? This is not to mention the scaling up of politics and the increasingly global character of many political debates.[941]

In conditions of globalization, in fact, public spheres, tend to become factually quite imbricated. What is foreign and what is domestic may be harder to discern, especially when each public sphere relies on a common informational infrastructure.[942] The days of purely national newspapers or media publishing for distinct national audiences, for example, are long gone, in conditions where virtually everything has become accessible from anywhere. Information flows liberally from one corner of cyberspace to another.[943] In a dilemma by

940 To use the expression recently put au goût du jour by Bertrand Badie. See Bertrand Badie, *Inter-socialités. Le monde n'est plus géopolitique* (CNRS editions 2020).

941 Nancy Fraser and others, *Transnationalizing the Public Sphere* (Kate Nash ed, Polity Press 2014).

942 Daniel C Hallin, 'Media, the Public Sphere, and the Globalization of Social Problems' in Erik Neveu and Muriel Surdez (eds), *Globalizing Issues: How Claims, Frames, and Problems Cross Borders* (Palgrave Macmillan 2020).

943 Stig Hjarvard (ed), *News in a Globalized Society* (Nordicom 2001); Oliver Boyd-Barrett and Terhi Rantanen, *The Globalization of News* (Sage Publications 1998).

now familiar in attempts to regulate cyberspace,[944] the deterritorialization of information production means that, whilst a power might be accused of seeking to interfere in the affairs of other states, it is also doing many other things at the same time. Russian TV may be seen as biased and touting the Kremlin line in Europe, but it is doing so from Russia (where obviously no one disputes its ability to be what it is on non-interference grounds) and for all kinds of non-European audiences. Attempts to limit its incidence will have ricochet effects in other polities, even as it becomes relatively harder to argue that it is specifically trying to interfere with one's political sphere, and even as limiting the perceived interference in one's system may only be achieved at the risk of engaging in interference in others'.

One might think that this confusion over the proper scope of public spheres could be easily remedied by a further appeal to self-determination. It is said that self-determination entails, at least, the ability to determine on one's own terms the circumference of one's public sphere even as that public sphere has no easily ascertainable boundaries of its own. Self-determination is indeed traditionally portrayed in this way: self-determining the self by deploying a protective mantle around it. 'Peoples', then, are imagined as better left to their own devices so as not to disturb their best efforts at deciding their fate.[945] Self-determination stands to potentially reenergize thinking about both sovereignty and interference, especially if it is understood not only in its external, decolonizing dimensions but also its internal, popular-will-producing dimensions. Certainly states have produced discourses of the *domaine réservé* including self-determination that are themselves a product of self-determination about the proper scope of the *domaine*.

But this leaves many questions unanswered. A first question concerns the degree to which the government can claim prima facie to embody self-determination. Under one reading at least, self-determination is vested in the state rather than the peoples as such, and any interference with sovereignty is necessarily an interference with its self-determination. A more popular view these days is that self-determination is vested in various peoples who pre-exist the state and whose fate is ultimately what international law is interested in. This introduces tremendous instability in the mix as, under that view, the question becomes one of adequacy between a government and its peoples. Although not necessarily leading down the path of a strict democratic entitlement, such an equation does serve to potentially delegitimize grossly

944 Horatia Muir Watt, 'Yahoo! Cyber-Collision of Cultures: Who Regulates?' (2002) 24 Michigan Journal of International Law 673.

945 See for example Mill's classic notion of an 'arduous struggle to become free'. Mill (n 909).

unrepresentative governments (even beyond the colonial context). It creates a persistent hiatus between international law's traditional bowing to the reality of effective power and its concern with good government. The only difference may be that governments can claim a sort of presumptive deference to their authority to solicit outside assistance where the onus is on non-state actors to prove that in soliciting such assistance they somehow have the authority to do so and are not thereby embroiling a foreign state in interference.

A second question concerns the nature of the 'self' that self-determination refers to, even if one can leave aside the above hiatus between government and peoples. Partly the complication is that self-determination is not the 'determination' of an already defined and stable 'self' but the very determination of what the self is in the first place. Who one acknowledges as the self, then, has considerable consequences for what one is imagined to be interfering with under a self-determination based theory of non-interference. As Dino Kritsiotis points out, drawing on the feminist analysis of Hilary Charlesworth and Christine Chinkin in the context of debates on forceful intervention by invitation, such an approach 'might work well to the extent that one can be confident of "a single relevant "self"" serving as the epistemic unit of any claim to self-determination'.[946] In a new interference environment, the fuzziness of the 'self' further lends itself to a very broad array of actors that can harness it to their benefit and claim a degree of representativeness of a 'people'. That is, assuming the precise contours of the latter are themselves uncontentious, something which one may very much doubt.

A third issue relates to the plausibility and desirability of the self, whatever it may be, insulating itself from its 'other' as an imagined condition of its preservation and prospering. This can be seen as neglecting the fact that states and, perhaps more importantly, societies constantly interact as a result of the global diffusion of technologies of communication, as well as the rise of global travel and even the establishment of durable diasporas significantly complicates that simple picture. A degree of interaction with the outside is not only normal and expected, but in fact desirable and to a large extent encouraged by the international system itself. Economic engagement with other states, for example, is not an impediment to one's development but at least in some respects an opportunity for such development. The more the set of challenges confronting public opinions everywhere is largely identical, global and connected, the more doubling down on some sort of inner sanctum of the self-determining

946 Dino Kritsiotis, 'Intervention and the Problematisation of Consent' in Dino Kritsiotis, Olivier Corten and Gregory H Fox (eds), *Armed Intervention and Consent* (Cambridge University Press 2023) 99.

self may seem to be part of the problem, certainly from the point of view of an international law of cooperation. This is why for example it has been argued that prohibitions on foreign campaign contributions may be an anachronic focus in a global and interdependent economy.[947]

Self-determination, then, does not occur in a social void but in complex interaction with its broader social environment. This subtly calls into question the problematic nationalist foundations of self-determination as a trump against interference understood as a sort of univocal 'right to be left alone'. Moving beyond a univocal concept of self-determination being realized or not—which is, at any rate, always a bit of a simplification—to the actual complex and contradictory processes by which it actually is, through contestation and struggle, exposes some of the concept's limits. Self-determination is more process than outcome, and more a certain quality of process than its postulated existence or its goal. Self-determination is reflexive in that it involves a degree of self-determination about self-determination. Furthermore, self-determination is not, put simply, a solipsistic exercise. On an individual psychological level, there is no pure 'ego' outside of its formation through family relations for example and, onwards, through engagement with society.

Collective self-determination, similarly, evolves not from some primitive fountain of identity, as in its dubious romantic variant, but as a result of the complex interaction with other, also self-determining 'selves'.[948] 'We' self-determine constantly in relation to and in interaction with others—we 'co-determine', as it were. Of course, not all of these outside influences have 'our' best interest at stake or particularly want 'us' to produce the best and most authentic versions of our self-determining selves. We largely tolerate these influences, nonetheless, because they constitute the dialectical core of self-determination and, in the process, provide U.S. with opportunities to determine for ourselves what our path ought to be. Subjectivity itself—the very subjectivity that, paradoxically, grounds the aspiration to self-determination—is the product of social relations and constructions.

This is especially relevant in a context where one does not know in advance the end-state of self-determination or even its best path: a context in which the point of self-determination is, in fact, to *self-determine*, not to head mindlessly towards an already determined outcome. If we knew where we were

947 Jeffrey K Powell, 'Prohibitions on Campaign Contributions from Foreign Sources: Questioning Their Justification in a Global Interdependent Economy' (1996) 17 University of Pennsylvania Journal of International Law 957.

948 Frédéric Mégret, 'The Right to Self-Determination: Earned, Not Inherent' in Fernando R Teson (ed), *The Theory of Self-Determination* (Cambridge University Press 2016).

going, so the thinking goes, we would not need to self-determine. As has been noted, for example, 'any reference to distortion necessarily presumes a set of electoral preferences that would exist absent foreign deception'[949]—but we do not know what the 'natural outcome of another state's internal political dynamic'[950] without interference would be. Unable to compare a freely self-determining path from one shaped by outside influence, we are left with only speculation and hypotheticals. The path of self-determination, especially of such complex bodies as nations, is radically indeterminate a priori: we cannot have already self-determined before we actually self-determine. Simply invoking self-determination as some mythologized inner core of a nation's being, then, no more addresses the challenge of interference than imagining what a political outcome would have been 'but for' coercion.

The sort of logical fallacy—or at least approximation—involved in supposing that there is such a thing as 'pure' self-determination before it is corrupted by 'foreign' influence can be exemplified very concretely by the attempts of some political systems to purge instances of supposed interference by rewinding their own processes. When the Qatargate came to the fore in the European Union (a slightly different, 'vertical' scenario of interference, but comparable for our purposes here), it emerged that a number of current and former European Parliament officials had received cash to influence the vote in favor of Qatar (and, possibly, other nations such as Mauritania and Morocco).[951] This created considerable uncertainty as to the deliberative and democratic legitimacy of Parliamentary deliberations in the recent past concerning these countries, for example the vote in support of a very favorable air transit agreement for Qatar Airways or of a fisheries agreement with Morocco. The European Parliament eventually voted to suspend all work involving Qatar, but it has been suggested that all legislative activity concerning Morocco should be scrutinized retrospectively to make sure that it was not the target of foreign interference.[952] Such an approach is welcome to a degree, but it also underscores the supreme difficulty of determining with precision when and how a deliberative process

949 Keitner (n 877) 191.

950 Damrosch (n 16) 50.

951 Eddy Wax, Elisa Braun and Gian Volpicelli, 'EU Failed to Tackle Corruption in Parliament, MEPs Say' *POLITICO* (13 December 2023) <https://www.politico.eu/article/qatargate-files-eu-corruption-scandal-mep-european-parliament/> accessed 22 December 2023.

952 Miguel Urbán Crespo, 'Moroccogate: Human Rights Are Not for Sale' (*The Left in the European Parliament*, 19 January 2023) <https://left.eu/moroccogate-human-rights-are-not-for-sale/> accessed 22 April 2024.

of self-determination veered off course or was compromised beyond recognition, let alone how one would go about rolling it back.

This is, then, what militates for a capacious and open conception of self-determination, rather than the monolithic idea of a process uniquely shepherded by the state. Even or especially within the most advanced democracies, we tolerate a range of forces (lobbies, private interests, cunning politicians, etc.) which could at any moment lead the polity 'astray' from what might be imagined/argued to be its ideally and most genuinely self-determined path, but who we refuse to disqualify a priori from participation in self-determination processes because to do so would assume that we already know what the proper outcome of self-determination should have been. We do so not just because we gullibly fetishize the unencumbered competition of ideas, but out of an acknowledgment that 'we' become 'ourselves' through a dialectical process of dealing with various contradictory influences, and that 'we' are the better for that process. *A contrario* imaginings of what 'might have been' simply do not provide U.S. with any kind of incontrovertible standard by which to measure the authenticity of 'what is' and may even contain the seeds of authoritarian reclamations of 'what ought to be'.

This immediately shapes interference, even of the new kind, in quite a different light. Even if the latter is ill-intentioned, we do not know this before we have been exposed to it and have had an opportunity to address it, and at any rate will disagree productively about its nefarious character. Now, it may be that the problem with interference is not its content but the fact that the actors engaging in trying to shape our self-determining thoughts are not authorized to be privy to that conversation in the first place (and of course the question of the covert nature of the interference, to which this book returns later, may be relevant). But that still raises the issue of why states should aspire to shield themselves from the political processes of others and should have the authority to exclude certain actors merely on the basis of their foreignness, on the basis of self-determination. States never fully knowing in advance what their unencumbered self-determination might lead to (such a notion may, in fact, be nonsensical), self-determine in conditions of inter-governmental and inter-societal interaction that are hard to second guess in advance. Indeed, if the state will not remain reasonably open for itself (because it is wary of the subversive potential of foreign messages), then it should theoretically be so for its peoples, and the latter should aspire to hold it to that ideal.

The point here is not to suggest that Russian attempts to meddle with U.S. politics are conducive to U.S. self-determination or vice versa. Rather, the argument here is that it is difficult, proceeding from liberal principles alone, to exclude these attempts merely on the basis of them emanating from a source that is outside the polity. This is partly on account of the fact that what is domestic and what is foreign may be particularly blurred, for example in the case of diaspora members that display complex dual allegiances. But it is also more fundamentally because the *domaine réservé* almost always already incorporates elements of foreignness, if only because a self-determining identity constantly constructs itself with and against others. If the heart of the *domaine réservé* is self-determination, then, it stands to be populated by a crowded set of contradictory forces that probably cannot be dismissed merely on the basis of their being foreign. The argument for the sanctuarization of self-determination, then, does not fare much better than the argument for the sanctuarization of democracy and, in fact, replicates some of its problematic assumptions. This suggests, in short, a normative need to keep a certain openness to outside interference on some of the very grounds—self-determination—that are sometimes suggested to limit it.

CHAPTER 4

The Nature of Interference: What Does It Take?

1 Introduction

Just as for the definition of the *domaine réservé*, there is an evident circularity in some of the standard definitions of what sort of behavior constitutes unlawful interference. Consider, for example, the ICJ's classic but question-begging statement that '[t]he principle of non-intervention involves the right of every sovereign State to conduct its affairs without outside interference'.[953] This hardly fares better than a concept of a *domaine réservé* entirely reliant for its definition on an evaluation of the 'development of international relations'. How exactly is that right to be free from foreign interference violated? Non-intervention is presented as dependent on a notion of interference that is itself undefined and which states have understood in widely different ways. Just as with defining the *domaine*, a range of analytical approaches exist that seek to define the essence of coercion or interpret it through some of its discrete manifestations

1.1 *The Policy Framing*

From a policy perspective, there is an inherent hazard in defining interference, namely the risk of making that definition under or over inclusive. Although the resulting framing is not reducible to law, it can certainly inform an understanding of how the law's content is produced and in some cases can be understood as going to the heart of what legal production entails.[954] As to the danger of being over inclusive, it remains important to understand that states do routinely seek to influence each other and that this is entirely acceptable as part of the ordinary operation of international relations. As noted in an Ottawa parliamentary discussion of the U.S. and Australian contexts:

> there is ambiguity in the use of the term foreign interference, and a tendency to lump many different kinds of activities that are broadly aligned with the objectives of the Chinese government as part of a PRC-sponsored interference effort. In fact, all governments engage in 'public diplomacy'

953 *Nicaragua v United States* (n 3) [202].
954 See, e.g., Tay (n 516).

 | DOI:10.1163/9789004532731_008

> abroad, for the very purpose of influencing the views of the host society and its leaders.[955]

The exercise of defining interference will not be served well, therefore, by more or less unwittingly ruling out a large part of legitimate international relations. A challenge for any valid definition of interference, then, is from the outset to distinguish it from mere influence, where we have every reason to think that the latter is a fundamental dimension of international interaction (and, what is more, far preferable to violent alternatives). This has long been a fundamental building block of the debate on interference and there is universal agreement in principle that mere influence is not problematic under international law, even if it be conceivably unfriendly. For example, at a meeting in Mexico in 1964 of the U.N. 'Special Committee on Principles of International Law Concerning Friendly Relations and Co-Operation between States', Western jurists emphasized that:

> [i]n considering the scope of the principle of non-intervention, it should be recognized that in an interdependent world it is inevitable and desirable that states be concerned with and try to influence the actions and policies of other states; and that the objective of international law is not to prevent such activity but rather to ensure that it be compatible with other principles of international law such as the sovereign equality of states and the self- determination of their peoples.[956]

Any contrary suggestion would incline international relations towards the autarchic end of the spectrum, a remedy worse than the ill, and one that may embarrass states that adopt too broad a concept of interference (one cannot hope to influence, under international conditions, if one is not open to being influenced). As was noted in the context of Canada's investigation of interference against it, the legitimacy of attempts at influencing is particularly well recognized in bilateral diplomatic environments:

> [i]t is both lawful and normal for states to have views on the policies of other states, to express those views publicly, and to attempt to convince

955 Senator Yuen Pau Woo, '"Chinese Interference" in Canada: What Do We Know and What Should We Do about It?' (Ottawa, 5 October 2018) <https://senatoryuenpauwoo.ca/en/media/press-releases/chinese-interference-in-canada-what-do-we-know-and-what-should-we-do-about-it/> accessed 10 July 2023.

956 McWhinney (n 33) 23.

> Canadian officials to adopt certain policies that align with those views. There is certainly nothing unusual about diplomats building relationships with elected officials and communicating their countries' views of issues to them. Canada conducts these types of activities throughout the world on issues that are important to Canada.[957]

This is why commentators have been adamant that 'criticism, public diplomacy, propaganda, retribution, mere maliciousness, and the like' should not be ordinarily equated with interference.[958] To the extent that action, such as mere criticism, falls below a certain *de minimis* threshold, it will be problematic as a matter of policy to describe it as interference. For example, Indian protests at Canadian Prime Minister Trudeau supporting farmers' demonstrations in India as a form of interference seem exaggerated: although potentially inimical to the Indian government, such a manifestation of solidarity with elements within Indian society falls well below a form of subversion. It can be seen as part-and-parcel of a robust international politics of speaking one's mind to interlocutors.[959] The reality is that states do have legitimate views about the performance of other states, particularly when it comes to shared standards of achievement, notably in human rights. Words are relatively inoffensive, and even harsh condemnation does not seem to reach the level of interference.[960]

The difficulty is nonetheless that legitimate influence and illegitimate interference will often be hard to disentangle, even as we would ideally not want a theory of what amounts to either to hang on specious casuistry. In practice, '[t]here is also a considerable "grey zone" in which activities that might appear largely benign (such as involvement between diplomats and diaspora community associations) can be leveraged by foreign adversaries'.[961] The same is true in the context of diplomatic interference where it has been said that 'the borderline between simple diplomatic pressure upon a foreign government and a forcible interference in its internal or external affairs is entirely fluid'.[962]

957 Johnston (n 352) 11.

958 *Tallinn Manual 2.0 on the International Law Applicable to Cyber Operations* (n 454) 318.

959 Vishwajeet Deshmukh, 'Political Comments as "Interference in Internal Affairs": The Farmers' Protest' (*BJIL*, 14 February 2021) <https://www.berkeleyjournalofinternationallaw.com/post/political-comments-as-interference-in-internal-affairs-the-farmers-protest> accessed 22 May 2024.

960 This is not exclusive, on a deeper level, of thinking about the ethics of criticizing other states' human rights performance for example. See Mégret, 'Just Criticism? Human Rights, Inter-State Relations, and the Ethics of Finger Pointing' (n 772).

961 Johnston (n 352) 11.

962 JHW Verzijl, *International Law in Historical Perspective* (Martinus Nijhoff Publishers 1968) 236–237.

Problematically, it is in this context that '[s]ophisticated malign actors [...] can attempt to achieve their objectives while still not doing anything unlawful'.[963] One therefore needs to be alert to the possibility that the rather large space conceded to mutual interaction between states is not abused for the purposes of interference.

Identifying that grey zone—albeit struggling to define its contours—has been an almost universal feature of the debate on interference in Canada, the U.S., France, or Australia.[964] It has often revealed the inadequacy of the vocabulary of international law to simultaneously encourage interaction yet seek to limit it. Consider, for example, the role of Confucius Institutes financed by China: even if those are indeed operating to encourage a positive view of China and its government, how is that wrong in international law or even particularly worrisome in itself? What makes mere influence tip into the realm of interference? In other words, 'although foreign interference is easy to define in principle, in practice it is not always straightforward to distinguish it from permissible diplomatic or political activity'.[965] Some have already suggested that one should think of foreign influence as operating on a continuum beyond the 'binary divide between "influence" and "interference"',[966] but it is not clear how this sort of continuum would operate as a matter of international law.

The converse danger of defining interference too broadly at the expense of international relations, of course, is that one will define it too narrowly, in ways that legitimize behavior that is indeed incompatible, under at least some normative theory, with some states' sovereignty. Extremely narrow definitions of what counts as intervention and the virtual exclusion of mere interference from the language of international law may be a way of safeguarding the specificity of the category, but also a way of minimizing the nefarious character of much problematic behavior. States have fought long and hard for adequately expansive conceptions of the rule of non-intervention which they feel protect their sovereignty at an adequate level. To deny the interference or intervention label to all but the more grotesque versions of it can amount to little more than encouraging an actual agenda of interference or intervention. The very

963 Johnston (n 352) 13.

964 Katherine Mansted, 'The Domestic Security Grey Zone: Navigating the Space Between Foreign Influence and Foreign Interference' [2021] Occasional Paper Series, National Security College <https://nsc.crawford.anu.edu.au/publication/18456/domestic-security-grey-zone-navigating-space-between-foreign-influence-and-foreign> accessed 21 November 2023.

965 Johnston (n 352) 11.

966 Mansted (n 963) 1.

notion of sovereign independence demands that a range of threats beyond that threshold be taken seriously and in their own terms. As often, international legal discourse seems imprisoned by the categories it has created, which take a life of their own and can become roadblocks in addressing a problem that is widely perceived to be there, but for which an adequate vocabulary does not (quite) exist.

1.2 *The Limits of Reasoning by Analogy*

One danger, in the process of finding the right mix, is that the debate about interference will be constantly conflated with other, close debates as part of the 'tendency on the part of lawyers, when confronted with difficult questions [...], to fall back on familiar concepts and criteria drawn from other contexts'.[967] For example, the discussion has long seemed to get its cues from the related debate on the use of force in international relations and the definition of aggression with which intervention is sometimes confused. Where the confusion with influence threatens to excessively broaden the scope of interference, the assimilation to the use of fore risks unduly narrowing it.

Indeed, it is sometimes important to retrace one's steps and elucidate why a debate took the direction that it did. For example, the focus on intervention as closely related to the use of force may be in part a function of the fact that the leading ICJ case on the matter, *Nicaragua v United States*, dealt precisely with a complex use of force in the shadow of which arose a number of issues of intervention. Even though the Court was cautious to note that it only dealt with 'those aspects of the principle which appear to be relevant to the resolution of the dispute',[968] the doctrinal tendency since has very much been to minimize the extent to which that particular judicial resolution was overdetermined by the set of facts that gave rise to it, in effect treating it as an exhaustive treatment of the issue when it is in fact by now quite unsuited to addressing some of the challenges of the moment.

Again, arguments about intervention being akin to the use of force do not always come from where one would expect. It was not the Third World that was the first to insist that 'economic aggression' was a reality that the international law order should tackle but the British delegation at the Paris Conference of 1916 which insisted that German post-war economic dumping should not be

967 Stephen C Neff, 'The Law of Economic Coercion: Lessons from the Past and Indications of the Future' (1981) 20 Columbia Journal of Transnational Law 411, 411.
968 *Nicaragua v United States* (n 3) [205].

allowed to proceed.[969] Much later, it was the Soviet Union that insisted that any definition of aggression should include whenever a State 'takes against another State measures of economic pressure violating its sovereignty and economic independence and threatening the bases of its economic life'.[970] Today, the conflation between unilateral economic sanctions and the use of force is more typically associated with the Global South[971] and one can wonder whether it does not involve a degree of overkill, given the largely non-violent character of such sanctions, whatever their otherwise problematic character.

It is also true, especially in the emblematic cyber context, that there has sometimes been a blurring of the line between mere intervention and uses of force, for example in the form of cyber-attacks. But as has already been pointed out generally, this is evidently a distinct debate, dealing with its own set of specific challenges. Whilst it shares some framing concepts with intervention, it can lead to very categorical findings where the debate on interference requires much more subtlety. The debate on interference, at any rate, is ill-served on various levels by an emphasis on physical compulsion which is increasingly the exception.[972] As Mohamed Helal has noted, even the understanding of coercion for the purposes of the ILC's Articles on State Responsibility as essentially vitiating the agency of the state being coerced is not particularly helpful to understand the nuances of coercion beyond its particular scope. A state may be coerced and not thereby become a mere 'instrument' of the coercing state.[973] In practice, coercion often occurs along a continuum and force or even the threat of force is rarely its defining feature or a useful analog to understand its complexity.[974]

There is a related risk that concerns about espionage, legitimate as they may be, will be confused with concerns with interference. This is evident for example in the designation of Huawei as a security risk, sometimes invoking the specter of interference but in ways that ultimately have much more to do with fears about spying and the collection of data via networks. Of course, in practice both can go hand in hand and espionage is clearly problematic on

---

969 James Brown Scott, 'Economic Conference of the Allied Powers' (1916) 10 American Journal of International Law 845, 849.

970 UNGA, *Report of the 1956 Special Committee on the Question of Defining Aggression* (United Nations 1957).

971 For a scholarly treatment that maintains that ambiguity, see Iryna Bogdanova, *Unilateral Sanctions in International Law and the Enforcement of Human Rights: The Impact of the Principle of Common Concern of Humankind* (Brill Nijhoff 2022) ch 2.

972 Helal (n 408) 75–76.

973 ibid 77.

974 ibid IV.

its own grounds, but something is lost by assimilating the two. Espionage has long been the object of a certain tolerance by states and does not capture the more actively intrusive component of interference, which need not rely on espionage at all. There is an evident distortion involved in assimilating the two which can end up being problematic for our understanding of both interference and espionage.

Also note that, if anything, the move towards theories of what is wrong about interference focused on self-determination rather than sovereignty can have the perhaps unintended effect of further complicating our understanding of what it takes to interfere. Self-determination is not a neatly delineated sphere the way the *domaine réservé* could at least be imagined to be; rather it is a collective, deliberative and, indeed, largely open *process*. From thereon, to 'interfere' with self-determination (unless one reduces it, again, to the sovereign *domaine réservé*, which seems to defeat the point) is a somewhat hazardous enterprise intellectually, given how much more difficult it is to delineate the outer contours of self-determination and to understand what coercion of that process might entail. Of course, those doubts do not extend to blatantly tinkering with voting machines, but who can say with any certainty where self-determination ends and where interference begins? Clearly the line between merely engaging another state's self-determination and usurping it is likely to be a blurry one.

Again, this need not paralyze us: it is perfectly possible for a principle of international law to have strikingly distinct understandings over time and still emerge as a structuring principle. We may not be able to predict how the principle will be used on the force of the principle alone, or to define a more legally valid or 'authentic' understanding of it, but we can conceptualize whatever falls into interference at any given time as the product of competing social forces engaged in highly dense and even volatile normative debates, notwithstanding their clear social consequences. In that respect, this chapter will be less concerned than others have been with keeping the 'politics' of what constitutes unlawful interference at bay,[975] and will instead explore these politics as the necessary antechamber of the law, on the understanding that what constitutes interference has never been riper for debate.

This still leaves ample space for specifically legal reasoning about the nature of the non-intervention rule. That reasoning will be per necessity grounded in a systemic understanding of the place that non-intervention occupies within a broader edifice of international law that has long sacralised sovereignty even

975 Jamnejad and Wood (n 29).

as it constantly demonizes it. Although it is difficult to simply infer the content of non-intervention from first principles and the rights of states[976] or from the observation of state practice and *opinio juris*, it may be that the rule also occupies a more intermediary status as a kind of logical connector between different claims. Even if its pedigree is more customary and jurisprudential than the result of any particular treaty, one can speculate that fundamental principles of statutory interpretation still have a role to play in our understanding of it. The suggestion, then, is as follows: for the rule of non-intervention—and there is little doubt that the starting point is that there is such a rule—to have any meaning it must have a meaning of its own that is not reducible to some already existing independent rules. To the extent that there are such close primary rules (the prohibition on the use of force, the prohibition on prematurely recognizing states or governments and, as we will see, the rule of non-interference), the ambit of the rule of non-intervention may lie in the near periphery of said rules but cannot be equated with them. In essence and if nothing else, non-intervention must have a meaning of its own.

1.3 *Interference in the Shadow of Intervention?*

As was mentioned in the introduction, this book deliberately chose 'interference' over 'intervention' to describe its object as one that, precisely, pushes the boundaries of what is going on beyond a well-recognized rule of international law. This will no doubt be an unorthodox and even contentious choice. Interference is the broader and woollier term for sure, but it also seems to capture more of what is going on, on an almost constant basis in the international system. It is not as if concerns about interference have not long been rife in the international system, but it is true that the notion of intervention has come to describe the more conspicuous and stylized violation of international law. Emphasis on a strict construction of the rule of non-intervention, nonetheless, is not free of a certain conservative politics, and it is worth asking whose interest is served by keeping the genie in the bottle. This section will remain a priori committed to the traditional task of elucidating what constitutes prohibited intervention and acknowledge that it continues to provide much of the intellectual framing for how one defines a particular genre of problematic inter-state conduct. But the suspicion of many[977] is that classic cases of such intervention are becoming few and far between and that, even as the evolving definition of non-interference borrows from the definition of

976 Aloupi (n 411); Tzanakopoulos (n 24).

977 Milanovic (n 463); Ido Kilovaty, 'The Elephant in the Room: Coercion' (2019) 113 AJIL Unbound 87.

non-intervention, the former needs to be understood distinctly from the latter. This is not merely a normative project, but a descriptive one, one committed to legal categories that actually describe the world as it is.

Much of the earlier 'decolonial' efforts to outlaw interference, in fact, named it as such and did not stop at 'illegal intervention'. This was part of a Third World driven agenda to prohibit intervention 'considéré non stricto sensu, mais lato sensu' as 'le simple fait d'essayer de porter atteinte aux droits souverains de [cet] Etat'.[978] The General Assembly, notably, insisted on the sovereign's right to 'develop its international relations [...] without outside intervention, interference, subversion, coercion or threat in any form whatsoever', a very broad definition if ever there was one.[979] Eric David went as far as to define intervention as 'le fait pour U.N. Etat de chercher à "subordonner" la souveraineté d'un autre Etat mais aussi dans le simple fait d'essayer de porter atteinte aux droits souverains de cet Etat', which meant that it included any measure 'destinée, soit, à empêcher U.N. Etat de faire ce qu'il est en droit de faire, soit, à obliger U.N. Etat à faire ce qu'il est en droit de ne pas faire'.[980] This very capacious and unorthodox, but arguably conceptually sound, definition of intervention essentially evacuates the notion of coercion, which as we will see is central to its conventional definition, as a necessary feature of the definition of intervention (although of course coercive interference remains a sort of particularly blatant case of intervention).

This tendency to not strongly distinguish between intervention and interference has been particularly evident in regional contexts, where formulations depart from a strict understanding of intervention as coercion to one that emphasizes the undesirability and indeed the illegality of interference more broadly construed. This has long been evident in the Inter-American context where the Charter of the OAS prohibits very broadly 'any other form of interference or attempted threat against the personality of the State or against its political, economic, and cultural elements'.[981] China itself, as part of its promotion of the Five Principles of Peaceful Coexistence since early treaties signed with the Soviet Union and India, uses the term non-interference rather than

978 David (n 536) 354.

979 UNGA Res 36/103 (9 December 1981) art 2(b).

980 David (n 536) 354.

981 See OAS Charter, art 19. See also Organization of African Unity, Constitutive Act of the African Union (adopted 1 July 2000, entered into force 26 May 2001) 2158 UNTS 3 (AU Constitutive Act), art 4 (g), proclaiming the '[n]on-interference by any Member State in the internal affairs of another'.

non-intervention, even though the two are presented as equivalent.[982] In more recent times, the Shanghai Cooperation Organization defines interference in its revised 2015 International Code of Conduct for Information Security as including the very broad 'use of information and communications technologies and information and communications networks to interfere in the internal affairs of other States or with the aim of undermining their political, economic and social stability'.[983] Also, albeit not always with a very explicit legal intent, the European Union itself has spoken of the problem of 'foreign interference' rather than of 'intervention'.[984]

It is of course not clear that these discourses are all uttered with international law in mind. But they do suggest that one may want to take seriously the notion that non-interference exists as a separate rule of international law from that of non-intervention. Recognizing this will have the non-negligible advantage that it will avoid tying ourselves in knots trying to redefine coercion as involving something quite different from what was traditionally understood.[985] It will also significantly update the international law of sovereignty to take into account the much more variegated phenomena that make defining intervention/interference a challenge.

Whether interference and intervention operate on a continuum, are the same or distinct norms, a factual predicate or a self-contained legal prohibition, note also that there is evidently a politics to that debate. The emphasis on intervention (with coercion as the litmus test) as the only strictly prohibited behavior in international law tends to put the bar quite high. It militates for a certain tolerance of behavior that may be hostile but should not be considered illegal.[986] Behavior may be problematic, but it is not ipso facto illegal and one should resist the temptation to make it so, except perhaps *de lege ferenda*. This has historically favored Western interests and may continue to do so, ensuring that a significant part of their projection does not fall under the intervention

982 Zhang Naigen, 'The Principle of Non-Interference and Its Application in Practices of Contemporary International Law' (2016) 9 Fudan Journal of the Humanities and Social Sciences 449, 450.

983 UNGA 'Annex to the letter dated 9 January 2015 from the Permanent Representatives of China, Kazakhstan, Kyrgyzstan, the Russian Federation, Tajikistan and Uzbekistan to the United Nations addressed to the Secretary-General' (13 January 2015) U.N. Doc A/69/723, principle 3.

984 Jones (n 495).

985 For such an effort, otherwise conceptually laudable as it may be, see Milanovic (n 463).

986 Luca Ferro, 'No Interference, No Problem: Voter Influence Operations and International Law' (2020) 53 Revue Belge de Droit International / Belgian Review of International Law 323.

label. It has been argued, for example, that some states' effort at 'forcing Facebook on foreign dictators' in the context of the Arab Spring is not a violation of international law given its non-coercive character.[987] This is because:

> Providing access to the Internet may amount to a political act, but it does not necessarily amount to coercion. Access to an information system that allows all points of view to be represented is too unfocused to be considered coercive. Even allowing access to specific social networking sites fails the coerciveness test. The outside country is merely providing a forum for the exchange of ideas, both supportive and critical of the government.[988]

The point is not to discuss the specifics of that argument here, merely to note that it is part of a lineage which, in emphasizing that coercion should be the litmus test of intervention, objectively favors relatively more interventionist and not always entirely benign agendas. To its credit, such a view also resists the temptation of dealing with behavior under international law that is not clearly illegal and that should best, if need be, be resisted by political means.[989]

By contrast, a broader conception of the illegality of interference speaks to traditional Global South concerns and, perhaps, emerging Western ones that more than intervention stricto sensu should be prohibited; that coercion should, in fact, not be *that* decisive in an age where various forms of manipulation or subversion are at least as toxic as coercion. This hints at a renewed appetite normatively to pry open intervention and reinstate an older, more expansive understanding of it that runs from the Bogota Charter to the General Assembly practice starting in the 1960s. In other words, whereas '[i]nterference pure and simple is not intervention',[990] it is at least interference and may be prohibited as such. This would certainly significantly expand, potentially, the range of unlawful international conduct, whether by including non-coercive interference within intervention or creating a distinct, self-standing category of prohibited interference.

As with earlier debates about whether the use of force included non-forceful intervention (which were largely resolved against), there is a certain logic to the notion that interference should be kept separate from intervention as, ultimately, quite different. Not collapsing the various categories of international law is key to making sure that that language remains capable of fine and

987 Swanson (n 786).

988 ibid 886.

989 Tzanakopoulos (n 24).

990 Jennings and Watts (n 397) 432.

important distinctions. But the continued uncertainty around these issues is sure to intensify long dormant debates in international law about the tension between sovereignty and international engagement. These debates are in a sense magnified, furthermore, by the redoubling of arguments that interference, even if it be prima facie interference, can be 'saved' by the fact that it is in the pursuit of international law, whether it be a form of self-defence, a corrective response in the form of counter-measures against an initially illegal intervention or, more ambitiously, 'interference' in the discharge of international prerogatives and obligations including human rights.

No doubt interference, especially in its subterranean and clandestine version, is an implausible tool to enforce international law because of its failure to signal what wrong is being corrected, but it is at least preferable to the use of force. In the best of cases, it might emerge as a manifestation of self-help in a decentralized system, not least because of the limitations and failures of international organizations. Some have long sought to reappraise the value of unilateral coercion to the international system based on its origin or goal.[991] For example for Michael Reisman '[t]hough all interventions are lamentable, the fact is that some may serve, in terms of aggregate consequences, to increase the probability of the free choice of peoples about their government and political structure'.[992] It has also been pointed out that the threshold for economic coercion to be legal and legitimate is 'not so much whether [a state] was obeying the law but whether it was *promoting* the law'.[993]

Nonetheless, any broad and automatic claim to intervention on behalf of the international community was supposed to have been sunk long ago by the ICJ in the Corfu Channel case: states cannot simply drape themselves in a sense of international *service public* to claim exception from the ordinary rules that apply to inter-state conduct. Such an argument hardly needs to be made when it comes to the use of force, but it should also be axiomatic when it comes to intervention and even interference. Note that more generally, it will ill-serve the definition of intervention to assess it on the basis of either its motivation or its success. As to the former, it is not liable to make an otherwise illegal intervention legal, outside cases of course where said motivation aligns with known exceptions to the rule of non-intervention (in which case it is the exception that is decisive, not the motivation); as to the latter, it cannot be that the condemnation of the unlawful character of an intervention relies on the

991 Reisman (n 40).
992 ibid 643–644.
993 Neff (n 966) 413.

moral chance of whether it reached its goal (operations of intervention have been successfully fought back and nonetheless assessed as illegal).[994]

At any rate, the 'new interference', because of its often shadowy and diffuse quality, but also because it challenges the underlying politics of international law, is set to further challenge the definition of what is alleged to be unlawful. Whereas the old interference was very much focused on a notion of intergovernmental coercion, the new interference involves something more akin to inter-societal disruption. Therein, the model is less the use of force or coercive imposition of will than a diffuse, shadowy elbowing into the political, democratic, and informational processes of another nation. This, against a background where, as explained in the previous section, the baseline, especially in conditions of relatively heightened globalization, is one in which interdependence and the porosity of borders have been normalized so that what is domestic and foreign, and what is welcome and unwelcome, is already quite blurry.

2 Coercion/Disruption

An obvious strategy to define unlawful meddling, then, is to highlight a special category of interference as particularly noxious. This can be done in a variety of ways that typically seek to set apart mere influence (legal) from interference, and certain forms of interference as more blatantly illegal than others. Consider the following statement before the committee on un-American activities by Adolf A. Berle, a member of Roosevelt's 'brain trust', as an example of that sort of effort along traditional Westphalian lines:

> Countries do have a right to endeavor to build a civilization not based on private property—if that is what their people want. As long as they observe international law, mind their own business, and do not seek to conquer or subvert other countries, the United States has not, I think, any real reason to object—though we may take a dim view of the success of these experiments. When however, they finance, first, subversive propaganda, then guerrilla movements, and finally build up and foment civil wars in other countries, aiming to take over power themselves, we do have a fight to object and, of course, doubly so when attempt is made

994 Helal (n 408) 79.

> to attack the United States abroad or to interfere in the internal affairs of the United States.[995]

This is of course just one statement of this kind uttered in a particular historical context, but it does point to the kind of behavior that has at various times been understood to be beyond the pale as including instances that range from propaganda to fomenting civil war. The 'laundry list' approach to defining prohibited interference seeks to emphasize discrete 'categories of action' as particularly problematic.[996] Note the tendency to portray these things as occurring along a continuum in ways that suggest a slippery slope, even though they are of a quite different nature. Note, also, the long shadow of armed intervention as the implicit reference of the definitional exercise. And note, finally, the typological nature of this sort of exercise where one might think that one would be better served by a broad analytical definition.

2.1 *The Definitional Challenge*

The typical danger identified in the introduction to this chapter, then, tends to be replicated at every junction, namely that one will set the bar too low (at the risk of hampering international relations), or too high (at the risk of, in fact, condoning interference). For many Socialist and Third World states, the dominant concern was historically the latter, worried as they were that much interaction that they, in fact, perceived as structurally coercive would be understood as par for the course in a post-colonial context, and that the definition of intervention would only capture behavior almost akin to a use of force. Nonetheless, sensitivity to the former danger is clearly discernible in the West, where it has long been feared that too punctilious an attitude to interference might in effect compromise the very ability to entertain international relations (including, presumably, relations comporting a hefty dose of domination). For example, the Declaration on the Inadmissibility of Intervention's prohibition of 'all other forms of interference or attempted threats against the personality of the State' has been described as 'over-inclusive' where '[i]n a world woven so tightly by interdependence, the interchange of political and economic influence among nations is unavoidable'.[997]

---

995 United States Congress House Committee on Un-American Activities, 'Statement of Honourable Adolf A Berle', *Hearings, Reports and Prints of the House Committee on Un-American Activities* (US Government Printing Office 1964) 1482.

996 Townley (n 62) 1177.

997 Christopher C Joyner, 'The Transnational Boycott as Economic Coercion in International Law: Policy, Place, and Practice' (1984) 17 Vanderbilt Journal of Transnational Law 205, 243.

Indeed, it may be that describing a range of mild and ordinary behaviour as interference cheapens the term unduly and could have a genuinely chilling effect on open, if robust, international interaction and foreign policy. Historically, many of the main Cold War resolutions are notable for their tendency to describe what constitutes unlawful interference in ever broader ways, as if constantly chasing new developments. The General Assembly clearly did not think that intervention needed to be coercive. For example, Resolution 31/91, deplored 'a wide range of direct and indirect techniques, including withholding assistance and the threat of withholding assistance, subtle and sophisticated forms of economic coercion, subversion and defamation with a view to destabilization' being deployed against states seeking to assert their economic sovereignty.[998] Among the manifestations of unlawful interference that frequently made the list featured fomenting subversive or terrorist activity or imposing one's will through economic means. By contrast, Western states at the time argued for a narrow understanding of intervention characterized only in the case of 'forcible measures'.[999] The twin dangers here can be understood as a trivialization of the meaning of intervention on the one hand, and such a concentration of its meaning on exceptional behavior that it almost never applies and ceases to have any real-world incidence on the other. As an example of the former, one proposal entertained during the drafting of the Declaration on Friendly Relations was to the effect that states should be prohibited from undertaking actions that would have 'harmful effects on other states'[1000]—obviously going much further than the regime of state responsibility under international law and probably much further than normatively cogent. States would essentially constantly walk on eggs lest merely throwing their weight around destabilize or in any way affect the trajectory of other states even as, in a billiard ball system, negative externalities are unavoidable.

There is of course something a bit rhetorical in such absurd scenarios, but they do capture a point, namely the possibility that if intervention is both defined broadly and 'interpreted literally, it might be wondered if much of customary diplomatic intercourse would remain lawful'.[1001] Schwebel was almost derisive in pointing out that '[t]o obviate "any" foreign pressure is to do a great deal, since the mere existence of powerful foreign States may give rise to a degree of pressure upon other States'.[1002] Indeed, the goal of defining

998 UNGA Res 31/91 (14 December 1976).

999 Jamnejad and Wood (n 29) 353.

1000 Houben (n 452) 728.

1001 Sthephen M Schwebel, *Aggression, Intervention and Self-Defence in Modern International Law*, vol 136 (Brill Nijhoff 1972) 454.

1002 ibid.

intervention cannot be to attempt 'to impose moral perfection, not to mention social stagnation, on humanity'.[1003] By the same token, if intervention is defined too narrowly as effectively equated with force that could belie its relevance as a category of international law altogether (an absurd result, if nothing else, from an interpretative *effet utile*) and leave unprotected the sort of presumptive interest it seeks to safeguard.[1004] This was very much the danger to which the Third World was alerted historically and that gave rise to the effort, embodied in Resolution 2625, to give its *lettres de noblesse* to intervention as a concept distinct from the use of force already prohibited in the U.N. Charter.

The underlying stake of that debate is nothing less, ideally typically, than the extent to which state/society constellations should interact freely with each other, on whose terms, and to what effect. What is most problematic is the wide range of behavior between mere influence-seeking and the use of force. One can always sketch the debate as occurring between stylized extremes, even as one suspects that the real problems arise in the middle. At one end of the spectrum, interference requires more than simply disruption, let alone mere influence. Seeking to influence is, after all, the very condition of international politics and diplomacy and thus not something that international lawyers would want to discourage. For the British delegate, at the General Assembly on the occasion of the negotiation of Resolution 2131 (XX):

> In considering the scope of 'intervention', it should be recognized that, in an interdependent world, it is inevitable and desirable that States will be concerned with and seek to influence the actions and policies of other States, and that the objective of international law is not to prevent such activity but rather to ensure that it is compatible with the sovereign equality of States and self-determination of their peoples.[1005]

As Marcelo Kohen put it, 'the mere adoption by states of certain political positions with regard to domestic situations, although often unfriendly, is not illegal'.[1006] A degree of influence may well be necessary precisely to foster cordial diplomatic relations. It cannot be, for example, that 'the mere mention

---

1003 Myres S McDougal and Florentino P Feliciano, *The International Law of War: Transnational Coercion and World Public Order* (Brill Nijhoff 1994) 197.

1004 Zemanek (n 407) 954.

1005 UNGA Special Committee on Principles of International Law Concerning Friendly Relations and Co-operation among States, 'United Kingdom: Proposal' (31 August 1964) U.N. Doc A/AC.119/L.8, 7.

1006 Kohen (n 29) 161.

of another country's internal affairs could be an unlawful intervention'.[1007] As Conforti has argued, moreover, 'when a State simply criticizes, or even condemns the conduct of another State, its political or economic system, or its foreign policy, it cannot be considered guilty of unlawful interference in the affairs of another State'.[1008]

Finally, to lower the standard of coercion so low as to make all kind of inequality or asymmetry in the international system a cause for concern would be to render the scope of coercion so vast as to make the concept meaningless. For instance, as Matthew Craven notes, one typical retort to the invocation of 'unequal treaties' is that 'every treaty, in some respects, is a manifestation of inequality' so that 'in absence of some substantive agreement as to what forms of inequality are tolerable or intolerable, ultimately undermine the conditions for certainty and stability in international relations'.[1009] Inequality should be criticized on its own terms, so the argument goes, but that is not the same thing as seeing a world constantly afflicted by intervention. Intervention is based on a critique of power but it is not so much a critique of power generally as an attempt to focus on one of its impermissible manifestations.

In short, too much intervention could kill intervention as a meaningful category. Accordingly, it has been pointed out that there are clear dangers, for example, to 'watering down' the requirement of coercion 'at the risk of hindering basic interstate relations' or even making them 'unlawful'.[1010] This was one of the main reasons, paradoxically, for criminalizing intervention and subversion as part of the Draft code of Crimes against the Peace and Security and Mankind.[1011] The trade-off involved in prohibiting intervention and a fortiori interference (otherwise clearly a limitation on states' freedom) must surely be a renewed commitment to allowing 'mere' influence. The 'sole expression of its opinion by a State as long as it is not followed by action of any kind' is presumptively lawful and even when it comes to economic measures for example, 'these would have to take the form of an economic blockade, the sudden interruption of a sizeable proportion of trade relations or the abandonment of a vast programme of technical assistance or development aid in order to be considered as an interference with a view to coercion'.[1012]

1007 Swanson (n 786) 887.
1008 Conforti (n 47) 472.
1009 Matthew Craven, 'What Happened to Unequal Treaties? The Continuities of Informal Empire' (2005) 74 Nordic Journal of International Law 335, 337–338.
1010 Moulin (n 461) 443.
1011 Linarelli (n 24) 27.
1012 Conforti (n 47) 472.

At the other end of the spectrum is the use of force, which is universally condemned not only on its own violence-producing terms, but also as a particularly blatant violation of the principle of non-intervention.[1013] The focus on force in discussions of intervention is a by-product of the centrality of Article 2(4) of the U.N. Charter, which is traditionally understood to exclude economic or political pressures, especially since a proposed Brazilian amendment that would have extended the prohibition beyond the use of force was rejected in 1945.[1014] Associating intervention with the use of force is an objective that has been pursued both by the Global South and the West at different points in time for their separate ends: the former by seeking to expand the understanding of the use of force to various forms of unilateral economic pressure; the latter by seeking to restrict intervention to something very close analytically to actual uses of force. As the ICJ has pointed out, it is certainly true that '[t]he element of coercion, which defines, and indeed forms the very essence of, prohibited intervention, is particularly obvious in the case of an intervention which uses force, either in the direct form of military action, or in the indirect form of support for subversive or terrorist armed activities within another State'.[1015]

The problem is, as already mentioned, that the use of force is problematic for its own reasons, and raises specific issues and condemnation that are not reducible to its interfering dimension.[1016] At any rate, the whole point of developing a distinct conception of intervention or interference in the post-Second World War era was to move beyond and expand on the prohibition of force alone (if the two terms are synonymous than their distinction collapses and only one is necessary). This, in a context where it was widely perceived that, given the prohibition of force, states might evolve towards alternative, even secretive, but just as corrosive forms of intervention. As the 1980s ILC rapporteur on the Code, Doudou Thiam of Senegal, put it: 'powerful States seek ways of challenging [the independence of small states]—not at the formal level, since colonialism has officially been buried, but by devious and insidious routes'.[1017] Indeed, it is not even that clear that force encompasses only physical force (in ordinary parlance, for example, one may 'force' someone to do

1013 Mégret, 'What Is the Specific Evil of Aggression?' (n 489).

1014 Derek W Bowett, *Self-Defence in International Law* (Manchester University Press 1958) 148, n 7.

1015 *Nicaragua v United States* (n 3) [205].

1016 Laura Visser, 'May the Force Be with You: The Legal Classification of Intervention by Invitation' (2019) 66 Netherlands International Law Review 21.

1017 ILC, 'Third Report on the Draft Code of Offenses Against the Peace and Security of Mankind, by Mr Doudou Thiam, Special Rapporteur' (1985) U.N. Doc A/CN.4/387, 12.

something without physical compulsion). Although every use of force is simultaneously an intervention, it does not follow that every intervention involves a use of force.

This, then, went to the heart of the Third World's insistence, notably, that economic intervention ought to be just as illegal as the use of force, as illustrated for example in the consistent advocacy of Jesús Yepes of Colombia (or Hsu Shuhsi from the Republic of China who sought the banning of subversion and sabotage) in the early discussions by the ILC of the prohibited intervention provision of a Draft Code of Crimes against the Peace and Security of Mankind.[1018] The Charter of Economic Rights and Duties of States, a central plank of the once-ambitioned New International Economic Order (NIEO), excludes 'outside interference, coercion or threat in any form whatsoever' and, as part of the recognition of the right to create producer cartels, an obligation 'to respect that right by refraining from applying economic and political measures that would limit it'.[1019] That conversation about the inherent acceptability of economic sanctions is related to the discussion about whether there is any baseline duty to engage economically with other states in the first place, as discussed in the final chapter of this book, but it also involves a more fundamental conversation about the characterization of economic pressure as a candidate for intervention.

On the one hand, economic sanctions, although they adopt the terminology of sanctioning, may look more like a variant of the power to influence and shape than a form of coercion stricto sensu. In many cases, they rely on merely 'withdrawing' something (a good, the benefit of an open trade regime, etc.) rather than actively disrupting another state's economy. They operate against fairly deeply held assumptions about the power of states to decide who they interact with. They may not be ill-intentioned (the aim may not be 'to punish the former recipient or to exert coercion regarding its domestic politics, but rather to cultivate more promising relationships elsewhere').[1020] And they rely on private actors as intermediaries in ways that may make them seem as involving mostly private relations inter se. Finally, an argument might be that economic sanctions are at least preferable to more blatantly coercive threats not to mention the use of force. On the other hand, economic sanctions, especially the unilateral sort, can radically impinge on the ability of target states

1018 Yearbook of the ILC (1950) vol I, 110, paras 33–33a (Jesús Yepes). Also, ibid, 130, para 5a (Hsu Shuhsi).

1019 UNGA Res 3281 (XXIX) 'Charter of Economic Rights and Duties' (12 December 1974) U.N. Doc A/RES/3281(XXIX), arts 1, 5.

1020 Damrosch (n 16) 47.

to exercise their sovereignty as they see fit, undermine their ability to foster their peoples' well-being and manifest some of the most striking inequalities of power in the international system. They also compromise the ability to self-determine.

Whether mere economic pressure can violate the obligation of non-intervention is an issue over which the Global South and the West have repeatedly sparred to the point of often arguing at counter-purpose. Whilst today the Global South is most associated with the position that economic pressure, notably in the form of unilateral sanctions, is almost scandalously a violation of the norm of non-interference, such a position was not always consistently held. When Arab nations adopted an oil embargo following the Yom Kippur war, they were adamant that economic coercion was not in itself a form of interference. The more sober Western observers felt in fact compelled to acknowledge that the non-intervention resolutions had never had the effect of making economic coercion illegal under international law because they were never followed by practice to that effect, as the boycott itself well showed.[1021] A case could even be made that, given the primitive character of the international legal system, the importance of self-help as a way of obtaining redress should not be underestimated and that the OPEP embargo might be justifiable as a widely contemplated form of retorsion.[1022]

By contrast, a chorus of Western authors, much at odds with what had until then and would subsequently become their dominant position, were prompt to denounce the embargo as in principle an illicit form of economic intervention. Jordan J Paust and Albert P Blaustein found unequivocally that the use of the 'Arab Oil Weapon' was a form of blackmail that placed 'intense pressure upon [other states'] freedom of choice' and, especially if viewed in light of its 'diplomatic and ideological instruments'[1023] Others pointed that it was probably in violation of the obligation to submit disputes to judicial settlement.[1024] Paul Dempsey argued, somewhat tenuously, that:

1021 Bilder (n 311) 41.

1022 Joyner (n 996) 231.

1023 Jordan J Paust and Albert P Blaustein, 'The Arab Oil Weapon—A Threat to International Peace' (1974) 68 American Journal of International Law 410, 412.

1024 Yehuda Z Blum, 'Economic Boycotts in International Law' (1977) 12 Texas International Law Journal 5. Admittedly, that argument has been made consistently, including to problematize the US's own practice of unilateral sanctions. See J Curtis Henderson, 'Legality of Economic Sanctions under International Law: The Case of Nicaragua Note' (1986) 43 Washington and Lee Law Review 167, 182–183.

> It does not appear desirable to constrain all forms of persuasive activity initiative by one State over another, for in an interdependent world it is necessary (or, indeed, vital as a sanctioning device in international law) that States be permitted to exercise some measure of influence over the policies and conduct of their neighbors in the world community. It does appear desirable, however, in an efficient system of world public order, that forms of coercive activity, which might be unnecessarily or unreasonably destructive to the essential values of an innocent target State, or which might significantly endanger international peace and security, be effectively regulated or even prohibited.[1025]

A few years after the OPEP oil embargo, the American Journal of International Law in turn published a protest by a South African international law academic after the American Society of International Law had decided to divest itself of investments in South Africa. The argument, again, did not hesitate to invoke none other than the Declaration on the Inadmissibility of Intervention in the Domestic Affairs of States and the Friendly Relations Declaration strongly gestured against economic coercion against states.[1026] Outside situations of self-defense, George N Barrie concluded, 'an economic boycott violates well-established principles of international law and is a direct and unjustifiable interference in the affairs of a nonconsenting target state'.[1027]

The essential reversibility and opportunistic character of such positioning is evident in that the long-term default position of Western international legal scholars has rather been that interference should not be defined too broadly and that, in fact, broad definitions do not comport with existing international law. Egon Schwebel, for example, was characteristically dismissive in his Hague lectures of some of the broad claims about interference that had emanated from the General Assembly on the occasion of the 1965 Declaration on the Inadmissibility of Intervention, noting that it 'may be doubted whether so sweeping an interdiction comports with the realities and current necessities of contemporary international life'. Ad absurdum, he seemed to hint that the Third World understanding of intervention involved conflating that term with having any negative impact: 'Does this mean, for example, that devaluation by one State of its currency is condemned, because that threatens an economic element of another State —and devaluation may certainly threaten the

1025 Dempsey (n 434) 261.

1026 George N Barrie, 'The Action Violates International Law and Policy' (1988) 82 American Journal of International Law 311, 312.

1027 ibid 313.

exports of other States?'[1028] The caricature is not necessarily a fair representation of even the Third World at the time, but it does hint at an abiding concern for international lawyers.

2.2 *Coercion and Its Limits*

The difficulty in elucidating the unlawful character of interference based on its nature alone (force, economic, political), then, has long shifted the debate towards the search for a sort of magic qualifier of unlawful intervention or interference that would make something indistinguishable from ordinary interaction into a cardinal contravention of international law. To be clear, intervention does not exist in the absolute so much as it is created by these conversations as part of an eminently political exercise that is nonetheless driven by the peculiar logic of the law's discursive economy. Particularly central to efforts to define interference has been the notion that it is illegal primarily when it is *coercive*, a much broader notion than merely the use of force. The classic, oft-quoted statement in Oppenheim is to the effect that:

> Although states often use the term 'intervention' loosely to cover such matters as criticism of another state's conduct, in international law it has a stricter meaning, according to which intervention is *forcible or dictatorial* interference by a state in the affairs of another state, calculated to impose certain conduct or consequences on that other state.[1029]

Even the General Assembly in its anti-interventionist heyday was quite clear about the significance of coercion for the purposes of thinking about unlawful interference: '[n]o State may use or encourage the use of economic, political or any other type of measures to *coerce* another State in order to obtain from it the *subordination* of the exercise of its sovereign rights and to secure from it advantages of any kind'.[1030] Similarly, the ICJ has emphasized that '[i]ntervention is wrongful when it uses methods of coercion'.[1031] Unlawful intervention as coercion, then, steers very closely to the international law on the use of force from which it draws its inspiration and whose relative clarity ('forcible') it seeks to borrow, but it also manages to extract itself from the more violent

1028 Schwebel, *Aggression, Intervention and Self-Defence in Modern International Law* (n 1000) 453–454.
1029 Jennings and Watts (n 397) 430.
1030 1970 Declaration on Friendly Relations, 123. My emphasis.
1031 *Nicaragua v United States* (n 3) [205].

and kinetic dimensions of the latter ('dictatorial'). It has garnered a very solid status as the linchpin of the rule of non-intervention.

The key idea behind 'dictatorial interference' is that a state is being threatened with some consequence that is in itself illegal if it does not comply with the sovereign will of another state. In one of the leading monographs on the question, Olivier Corten and Pierre Klein made much of the fact that coercion required some kind of ultimatum.[1032] What made the U.S. embargo against Nicaragua not a form of intervention, *a contrario*, was that it seemed to be an end in itself. The U.S. in its diplomatic note to Nicaragua announcing the embargo simply highlighted that the 'totalitarian political system' of the latter was 'incompatible with normal commercial relations between the two countries',[1033] but without any particular attendant demand. The requirement of coercion had also earlier made it possible for the West to deny interference was involved when Radio Free Europe broadcasted programs to the Eastern bloc: after all, the targeted sovereigns were not particularly *threatened* with any harmful consequence; the propaganda, hostile as it may have been, was just that.[1034] There is no doubt, then, that the requirement of 'coercion' raises the bar of what constitutes unlawful intervention quite high. For example, it has quite cogently been argued that if coercion is indeed the standard, then Russia's conferral of citizenship to the Georgian citizens of Abkhazia may be problematic in other ways, but is not specifically coercive since it hardly *constrained* Georgia's policies.[1035]

This calls into question why a sort of 'gun to the head' form of coercion should play such a conspicuous role, when coercion is far more likely, in the ordinary circumstances of international relations, to be experienced a structural, i.e.: the accrued effect of persistently unequal relations. Note also that this argument about the necessarily coercive character of intervention can

---

1032 Olivier Corten and Pierre Klein, *Droit d'ingérence ou obligation de réaction? Les possibilités d'action visant à assurer le respect des droits de la personne face au principe de non-intervention* (2nd edn, 1996) 42.

1033 'United States: Economic Sanctions Against Nicaragua' (1985) 24 International Legal Materials 809, 812.

1034 Natalie David McDonald, 'Radio Free Europe and the Right to Be Informed: National Sovereignty and Freedom of Information During the Cold War' [2017] Claremont Colleges Library Undergraduate Research Award <https://scholarship.claremont.edu/cgi/viewcontent.cgi?article=1003&context=cclura_2017> accessed 4 January 2024.

1035 Benedikt C Harzl, 'The Arrow of Passports in the Quiver of Russia: Eastern Ukraine, Abkhazia and South Ossetia in Perspective' in Benedikt C Harzl and Roman Petrov (eds), *Unrecognized Entities: Perspectives in International, European and Constitutional Law* (Brill Nijhoff 2021).

then also perfectly be used by Russia or China when accused today of directing hostile propaganda or upsetting elections: neither are *threatening* the U.S., for example, with any particular consequence if it does not yield as a result of those communications; rather, (i) the propaganda is *already* the consequence *hic et nunc*, and it is not itself the product of a prior threat (the issue is clearly not: 'if you do not do X, then we will inundate you with fake news'); (ii) there is no implicit or explicit promise of foregoing the behavior if the West changes its ways—indeed the propaganda exhibits a strong open-ended character with no evident prospect of termination or indeed always readily ascertainable goal; and (iii) either the 'propaganda' is transparent and may appear for what it is as not particularly demanding anything in exchange; or it is covert in ways that then also belie any notion that some clear demand is being made as a result. In short, the 'new interference' seems to lay waste to the idea that coercion is a useful or identifiable marker of illicit intervention.

If anything, then, the question is how the disruption of an election, let alone of broader political and informational processes, might be *coercive* in and of itself, in a context where the most dramatic scenario for foreign meddling is probably one where a polity ends up electing someone else than it would conceivably otherwise have elected without realizing it is doing so. The book has already discussed the sheer difficulty of evaluating what the outcome of self-determination would have been had its processes not been discreetly tinkered with. To be clear, no one is claiming that interference in such a case is a friendly act. Take interference operations in U.S. elections, for example. These have been described by one report, notably when it comes to Iran's actions, as furthering the 'longstanding objectives of exacerbating divisions in the U.S., creating confusion, and undermining the legitimacy of U.S. elections and institutions'.[1036] But this sort of across-the-board, discrete undermining is clearly not the same thing as delivering an ultimatum. As has been pointed out 'disinformation campaigns are not coercive, but merely persuasive. They do not factually compel the target to voluntarily abandon preferred choices, and only mislead the target to believe those choices are no longer preferable'.[1037] The question, then, is what is gained by describing such operations as, specifically, coercive and by requiring that this be the defining feature of intervention.

The issue has been particularly salient in the cyberspace context and the difficulty of putting one's finger on what exactly is wrong about interference

1036 National Intelligence Council, 'Foreign Threats to the 2020 U.S. Federal Elections (Declassified)' 5 <https://www.dni.gov/files/ODNI/documents/assessments/ICA-declass-16MAR21.pdf> accessed 11 January 2024.

1037 Tay (n 424) 54.

that uses it as a vehicle. There is a distinct feeling in the literature that cyber information operations are the problem of the day, but one struggles to describe them as specifically coercive. 'In practice', as one author points out, 'democracy, freedom of expression or the proper functioning of infrastructures (among others) are hindered without a need for "compelling" a state through the deployment of "coercive methods"'.[1038] Cyber interference may be toxic, vengeful, retaliatory, and destructive—but it is not necessarily or specifically *coercive*. Does that mean that it is not in violation of the rule of non-intervention? Where does that leave international law and its capacity to address what is widely perceived to be a crucial threat? The majority of international lawyers have sought to fold, more or less creatively, these new forms of interference under a coercive intervention framework. Obviously, coercion is itself a quite capacious term and it may be that all that is needed is to move it from its earlier connection to demands that the target state change its policies.

One possibility in this context is that at least some hostile attempts at cyber interference are, in fact, close enough to uses of force.[1039] This then puts the argument on the very solid legal terrain prohibiting such uses. The temptation to equate intervention and the use of force has long been obvious, notably in the wake of the *Nicaragua v United States* case. One needs to tread carefully here, however, as lowering the threshold of what constitutes a 'use of force' to fit mere non-armed interventions may in turn trivialize actual uses of force, and justify further uses of force in response (via self-defence or countermeasures). This is not to mention that the analogy is inherently problematic in cases where the 'force' in question is largely metaphoric. This was clearly a concern at the U.N. when the definition of aggression was being mooted as early as the 1950s and a majority of the Sixth Committee came to the conclusion that the right of self-defence was triggered only on condition of an actual use of force, not mere economic coercion. At any rate, most forms of interference are certainly not coercive in such a spectacular way. Subsumption within a use of force model is therefore unhelpful in terms of apprehending both actual uses of force and interference. The risk is that it will considerably extend the scope of unlawful intervention or even diminish the specific incidence of interference.

Even short of force, some authors remain quite sanguine about the fact that, notably, cyber interference operations do cross the line into coercive territory, and some no doubt will. Ultimately, the coercion conundrum may sometimes

1038 Moulin (n 461) 441.

1039 *Tallinn Manual 2.0 on the International Law Applicable to Cyber Operations* (n 454).

be unavoidable and have to be confronted directly both under positive law and jurisprudentially, even if to better deny that coercion should more generally be the linchpin of interference. Election disruption may be a particularly clear case in point. Lawyers such as Steven Wheatley, Steven J Barela, Gary Corn, or Sonia Boulos have made a strong case that cyber and influence operations targeting elections should be considered as inherently coercive because of the way they 'force' the target state to do something which it would not have otherwise done, notwithstanding the fact that they do so through the unusual and perhaps unprecedented means of 'infrastructural' or 'societal' interference.[1040] This seems to properly reflect the level of social alarm connected to disinformation campaigns, but may stretch the meaning of what it means to be 'forced' to do something in a context where one is, if anything, only 'made to do' something.

The case for interference is arguably particularly clear cut when it is the very infrastructure of elections that is being targeted, rather than the broader informational or political environment. For Barela, Russia's doings in the U.S. for example have 'targeted the legitimacy of the electoral process itself' which results in 'weakened authority' of the government and therefore amounts to coercion.[1041] More complicated is the question of what Stephen Wheatley describes as the 'coercive manipulation of the target's decision process', a genre so vague as to potentially include legal influence and that may incorporate what is illegal but ultimately non-coercive interference.[1042] The Tallinn Manual 2.0 describes coercion as 'an affirmative act designed to deprive another State of its freedom of choice, that is, to force that State to act in an involuntary manner or involuntarily refrain from acting in a particular way'.[1043] Despite the language of 'forcing', this does manage to reframe coercion as objectively neutering 'freedom of choice', in ways that hint at foreign interference as a form of

1040 Steven Wheatley, 'Foreign Interference in Elections under the Non-Intervention Principle: We Need to Talk about "Coercion"' (2020) 31 Duke Journal of Comparative & International Law 161; Gary P Corn, 'Covert Deception, Strategic Fraud, and the Rule of Prohibited Intervention' in Jack Goldsmith (ed), *The United States' Defend Forward Cyber Strategy: A Comprehensive Legal Assessment* (Oxford University Press 2022); Steven J Barela, 'Cross-Border Cyber Ops to Erode Legitimacy: An Act of Coercion' (*Just Security*, 12 January 2017) <https://www.justsecurity.org/36212/cross-border-cyber-ops-erode-legitimacy-act-coercion/> accessed 28 August 2023; Sonia Boulos, 'Does Foreign Cyber Intervention in Electoral Processes Violate International Law?' in J Martín Ramírez and Bartolomé Bauzá-Abril (eds), *Security in the Global Commons and Beyond* (Springer 2021).

1041 Barela (n 1039).

1042 Wheatley (n 1039).

1043 *Tallinn Manual 2.0 on the International Law Applicable to Cyber Operations* (n 454) 317.

perversion, usurpation, or corruption more than anything else. To better distinguish between run-of-the-mill interference and actual violations of the rule of non-intervention, then, it is also sometimes argued that the decisive factor is the 'nature of State interests affected [...] the scale of effects the operation produces in the target State, and the reach in terms of number of actors involuntarily affected'.[1044] Every time a more parsimonious definition of interference seems within reach, it seems it is saddled with a further array of variables.

This renovated version of coercion does, at least, go quite far beyond its traditional usage, in an attempt at making sense of the sort of problems that the international system is actually confronting. For Baade, information operations are coercive because they '[constrain] one's freedom to act by making certain options and conclusions no longer seem viable or making others seem mandatory';[1045] for Lahmann, 'manipulative cognitive warfare does indeed amount to "coercion"' because of its impact on self-determination;[1046] Marko Milanovic has warned of the dangers of conflating coercion-as-extortion and coercion-as-control and urged states to better distinguish between the two and making the case that the former is also prohibited intervention;[1047] Ido Kilovaty emphasizes the need to 'focus on the deprivation of free choice, on which the current coercion standard only lightly touches';[1048] Nicolas Tsagourias has emphasized taking 'control' over another state as what is noxious about coercion and one of the pathways to it;[1049] and Thibault Moulin suggests that we should think of coercion as deprivation of a sovereign's 'control', whatever its sources, to the point of rendering it powerless.[1050] The point of such scholarly strategies is that they seek to move coercion understood by analogy with the use of force to coercion as a form of deception, manipulation or denial of sovereign *libre arbitre*. Such a move may be particularly apposite in combination with understandings, as explored in the previous chapter, that the heart of what is protected by non-interference is self-determination.

There are clearly strengths and weaknesses to such an approach which fosters a direct line with older understandings of intervention (notably as subversion or what Ibrahim Shihata one described as 'the subordinating of sovereign

1044 Watts (n 391) 257.
1045 Björnstjern Baade, 'Fake News and International Law' (2018) 29 European Journal of International Law 1357, 1364.
1046 Lahmann (n 322) 220.
1047 Milanovic (n 463).
1048 Kilovaty, 'The Elephant in the Room' (n 976) 90.
1049 Tsagourias (n 847) 53.
1050 Moulin (n 461).

rights of other states'),[1051] even as it potentially changes its content significantly. Its essence is not that intervention is based on an inherently coercive act but that it has 'the potential for compelling the target State to engage in an action that it would otherwise not take'.[1052] It thus speaks to sovereign anxieties about control and loss of it and, specifically, the importance of *governing* (rather than being governed) as a fundamental criterion of statehood and self-determination. It also seemingly lowers the standard of what constitutes intervention, providing the sort of supple and adaptive formula that the times seem to demand, whilst still helpfully clinging to an analytical core. And it refocuses on sovereignty less as a shield or an envelope and more as a process that can be disrupted through exogenous dynamics.

But this 'but for' theory of intervention (the state in question would have arrived at this or that policy outcome had it not been for intervention) is also particularly slippery and elusive because of the way it potentially blurs the line between intervention, interference and influence. As the canard goes, states are constantly losing control over things they previously had control over. Moreover, if the point of all international interaction is to influence other states' behavior, what is to distinguish the will to influence from the desire for control? How can one know, as discussed when examining self-determination as the potential linchpin of the *domaine réservé*, what that behavior would have been were it not for the intervention? And why is it necessarily problematic that a state has switched behavior as a result of an external operation? For example, it is not clear what it means for a state to act 'voluntarily' or 'involuntarily' as a result of information operations, and surely an act could still be voluntary even if it has been heavily influenced by efforts to shape a decisional environment.

The definitional exercise seems to require constant characterization of what 'makes coercion coercive' that may even defeat the purpose of having a rule. On some level, a theory of intervention based entirely on the illegitimacy of imposition of one's will to another state (what in international instruments is often referred to as the 'subordination' of other states' will) risks morphing into simply a general theory of domination and subordination—something for which there is no doubt much use in general, but not necessarily to flesh out a particular, notoriously difficult rule of international law. In highlighting the 'elusiveness' of the idea of intervention, for example, Wolfgang Friedmann once noted that:

1051 Shihata (n 310) 617.

1052 *Tallinn Manual 2.0 on the International Law Applicable to Cyber Operations* (n 454) 319.

> In a wide sense, intervention is simply a function of the power relationships between states. Every alliance, every trade agreement, every act of governmental insurance—or refusal to issue insurance—for private investment, is an act of intervention. A declaration of neutrality is not less an act of intervention than a military alliance. Every act—of commission or abstention—is a form of intervention in the intricate a complex pattern of military, political and economic relations between the states.[1053]

If such is the case, then intervention provides neither a potent theory of power in international relations (it sees power only through one of its manifestations), nor a compelling explanation of interference (if interference is merely power, then why not have a much-needed conversation about power?). By the same token, a theory of intervention that focuses on discrete behavior taken out of its broader political context may appear as if it is toothless and confuses the tree for the forest.

By the time the scope of coercion has been expanded beyond recognition, moreover, one may wonder whether the term still fulfils the need for clarity and parsimony that one expects of legal concepts. To make matters more complicated, McDougal and Feliciano once emphasized that 'a certain degree of coercion is inevitable in States' day-to-day interactions for values'[1054] and that therefore not even coercion may be quite the problem that it is made up to be. Indeed, there has long been a particular genre of international legal argument that has erred on the side of caution in tackling a range of international behavior, seeing coercion as inevitable in an international system chronically marked by conflict, and even as variable of adjustment in the absence of centralized enforcement machinery. This school essentially militates for a realist embrace of the inevitability of coercion and, in some circumstances, its permissibility on Lotus type grounds and even its desirability as a systemic vehicle for expressing politics. For example, Richard Falk took an early stance in favor of tolerating hostile propaganda as a form of 'coercive competition' which does not '[endanger] the basic peace and security of the world'.[1055]

Quite often, then, coercion will need to be further qualified and contextualized (the 'wrong' as opposed to the 'right' kind of coercion) to such an extent as

1053 Friedmann, 'Intervention and the Developing Countries' (n 406) 207.

1054 Myres S McDougal and Florentino P Feliciano, *Law and Minimum World Public Order: The Legal Regulation and International Coercion* (Yale University Press 1961) 197.

1055 Richard A Falk, 'On Regulating International Propaganda: A Plea for Moderate Aims' (1966) 31 Law and Contemporary Problems 622, 622.

to create doubt about whether it can have the decisive character that it is traditionally endowed with. Some of the more sophisticated theories, for example, try to reach for an essence of interference beyond narrow understandings of coercion. The Tallinn Manual 2.0 focuses on the idea of *usurpation* of 'essentially sovereign functions'[1056] as conclusive of coercion, perhaps unwittingly rekindling earlier Third World debates about 'subversion',[1057] and reprising a classic concern.[1058] At other times, it is the 'destabilizing' character of interference that is underscored.[1059] Yet another approach is to emphasize the scale and intensity of interference to identify, independently of the particular form it takes, when it reaches the stage of being actually coercive.[1060] For others, it is the *goal* of interference that is relevant in turning it into a coercive operation,[1061] effectively shifting the analysis from an objective evaluation of behavior to a subjective assessment of its motivations.[1062]

Aside from trying to define the predicate act of intervention, states and international lawyers have indeed long emphasized a certain intent or motive as characterizing what is problematic with interference.[1063] For example, the Declaration on Friendly Relations bans coercion specifically when it is '*in order* to obtain from it the subordination of the exercise of its sovereign rights and to secure from it advantages of any kind'.[1064] When discussing the lawfulness of 'economic coercion' in the 1980s, an expert group highlighted that '[t]here was general consensus that the intent of the sender country was an important criterion'.[1065] Indeed, it is hard to see how development aid should be classified in the same category as seeking the overthrow of local governments for example,

1056 *Tallinn Manual 2.0 on the International Law Applicable to Cyber Operations* (n 454) 20.

1057 See e.g., OAU, 'Resolutions adopted by the Second Ordinary Session of the Assembly of Heads of State and Government Held in Accra, Ghana, from 21 to 26 October 1965' (October 1965) AHG/Res 27 (II).

1058 Tay (n 424) s II. B.

1059 'Treasury Sanctions Russia-Linked Election Interference Actors' (*US Department of the Treasury*, 10 September 2020) <https://home.treasury.gov/news/press-releases/sm1118> accessed 25 January 2024.

1060 Milanovic (n 463).

1061 Duncan Hollis, 'The Influence of War; the War for Influence' (2018) 32 Temple International & Comparative Law Journal 31.

1062 Joyner (n 996) 230.

1063 Derek W Bowett, 'International Law and Economic Coercion Symposium on the New International Economic Order: Part One: Economic Coercion: Past and Present' (1975) 16 Virginia Journal of International Law 245; Zemanek (n 407).

1064 1970 Declaration on Friendly Relations, 5.

1065 U.N. Secretary-General, 'Economic Measures as a Means of Political and Economic Coercion Against Developing Countries' (10 October 1989) U.N. Doc A/44/510, para 9.

although the devil is in the details and economic assistance can come with its own destabilizing thrust.[1066] According to the Tallinn Manual 2.0, although propaganda in itself may not be a violation of sovereignty and probably should not be considered interference per se, 'propaganda *designed* to incite civil unrest in another State would likely violate the prohibition of intervention'.[1067]

In other words, ultimate intent, to the extent that it is ascertainable, taints any analysis of intervention. This can turn out to be subtly exculpatory for interveners who will profess their good intentions. For example, the specifically 'dictatorial' character of intervention has been denied, whatever form or manifestation it may take, when it is supposedly engaged in for the benefit of the target state and in the name of international law. Adam Roberts, in particular, has decried the use of the label even as it applies to military and thus otherwise evidently coercive interventions:

> Today [...] the word 'dictatorial' seldom appears in definitions of intervention. It is hardly the appropriate adjective to describe some of the interventions since 1990, the purposes of which have included: assisting delivery of humanitarian aid, preventing ethnic cleansing and genocide, and introducing democratic changes. 'Dictatorial' also seems especially inappropriate given that interventions today are often defended by their protagonists as implementing the principles of the international community as a whole, and as helping to liberate the inhabitants of the territory concerned from dictatorial government.[1068]

The problem is that theories of the nefarious character of interference based on motive or intent, whilst they may helpfully exclude unintentional interference as usefully described as such, are particularly hard to prove. As Henkin put it, '[i]t seems hopeless to attempt to distinguish interventions which are benevolent from those which are malevolent, those which are crassly egoistic from those which are altruistic or serving only a subtle and enlightened self-interest'.[1069] This is in part because of the thorough multiplicity of overlapping motives in any given intervention and the difficulty of parsing those that are actually operative. Relying on motive also runs the risk of deferring excessively to the very justificatory and self-serving rhetoric of states intervening and of reinforcing a sense that intervention gets to be subjectively defined by those

---

1066 Friedmann, 'Intervention and the Developing Countries' (n 406) 218–219.

1067 *Tallinn Manual 2.0 on the International Law Applicable to Cyber Operations* (n 454) 29.

1068 Roberts (n 19) 158.

1069 Henkin and others (n 67) 157.

who engage in it rather than objectively on the basis of international community interests. And one will still need to relate motive to a theory of what is normatively wrong or right about said motive. Given that wanting to change another state's attitude cannot be wrong in itself, one option goes, the wrongfulness of interference must, in turn, surely be partly on account of the means used, which brings U.S. back to square one. A further possibility is to emphasize the perception of the target state, for example that it is being 'destabilized' against its will, but this move seems to suffer from the same default that relying excessively on the purveyor of interference's intent does. It could open the gates to what counts as unlawful interference extremely broadly.

In short, such attempts at displacing the traditional focus on conventional coercion get U.S. closer, but they remain either vague, incomplete, or seem fail to capture the novelty of what is at stake. They tend to subsume under existing legal definitions what are in essence quite novel and challenging scenarios. They stretch 'coercion' beyond the ordinary meaning of the word in order to accommodate a plurality of situations. They may miss the fundamental nature of the new interference altogether, one that is less based on coercion all along than, as many alert observers have noted, *seduction*. As Paul Charon and Jean-Baptiste Jeangène Vilmer emphasize, for example, at the heart of the Chinese Communist Party's *dispositif* of influence/interference are operations that seek to woo rather than force.[1070] These authors argue that seduction 'can lead to a complete subjugation' of its targets.[1071] Seduction is a powerful prism in that it reminds U.S. that intervention is a two-way process and that there may be a degree of voluntary submission to its effects. Similarly, Helal points out that coercion is 'often exercised through a strategy of carrots and sticks. Threats of harm and offers of benefit are intertwined in a single process of coercion'.[1072] And Xuan Tay makes the case that 'persuasive interference' ought to be considered on a par with 'coercive interference'.[1073]

But, again, what is wrong with seduction from an international legal standpoint, characteristic as it is of much soft power? If seduction is the pivotal concept, this still begs the question of how presumably nefarious seduction understood as interference can be distinguished from legitimate seduction understood as merely influence. To ask of states that they neither coerce nor

1070 Paul Charon and Jean-Baptiste Jeangène Vilmer, 'Chinese Influence Operations: A Machiavellian Moment' (IRSEM 2021) <https://www.irsem.fr/report.html> accessed 1 February 2024.

1071 ibid 147.

1072 Helal (n 408) 7.

1073 Tay (n 424) s III.

seduce may seem contradictory, counterproductive, and in the end corrosive of international relations. And to merely argue that seduction is problematic because it does not say its name, is interested, or instrumental, is to impose a burden of good faith on seduction that nothing in international norms can currently justify.

2.3 *Beyond Coercion?*

One temptation, then, may be to move away from intervention altogether because of its problematic reliance on coercion. There has long been a frustration with the unduly narrow character of coercion as a determinant of intervention (let alone mere interference) in a context in which 'some subtle techniques of political influence may be as effective as cruder forms of domination'.[1074] As early as 1990, Eric David did not hesitate to argue, presciently, that:

> De toute façon, l'approche de la Cour [in *Nicaragua v U.S.*] nous paraît trop restreinte car elle ne rend pas compte de toutes les facettes de l'intervention mises en évidence par la pratique et d'où il ressort que des comportements habituellement qualifiés d'intervention et caractérisés par une atteinte aux droits souverains de l'Etat victime ne s'accompagnent pas nécessairement de mesures de contrainte.[1075]

Of late, there has been a recurrence of interest in thinking of intervention beyond the narrow confines of coercion. Xuan Tay, for instance, has challenged the uncontested assumption, since Nicaragua v. U.S., of intervention necessarily being coercive, and criticized the reductionism that has ensued.[1076] In part, this focus on the multifaceted nature of interference is not only subtly revisionist but ideologically dissonant since the emphasis on coercion has most starkly been defended, historically, by Western international lawyers. By contrast, it was Latin American states who first insisted that a range of interference and not simply coercive intervention was problematic from the point of view of international law, soon to be followed by the Third World at large. Reconnecting with these earlier genealogies is a crucial critical move.

Coercion, for one thing, seems strangely inadequate—perhaps all along, but especially now—to help U.S. understand what is potentially nefarious

1074 Damrosch (n 16) 5.
1075 David (n 536) 353.
1076 Tay (n 424).

about interference and is, in fact, a bit of a misnomer.[1077] Because the prohibition of intervention has historically gotten its cue from the use of force, it has arguably tended to overestimate the normative incidence of coercion. Curing the international law of intervention of that defect would involve a recognition that, whilst significant, intervention by coercion is no longer the problem of the day. Instead, if one imagines the default and certainly defining state of international relations to be one of a tense 'peace' marked by ongoing strategic competition on the economic, political and social domains, then a multifacetted concept of interference not requiring coercion seems to much better capture the peril of the moment. It will at least incline international lawyers to better understand the particular perversity of interference as something that is not specifically coercive, were it not for the particular interpretative strictures of international law. If self-determination is thrown into the mix, it becomes even less clear how a population—as opposed to a government—can collectively be coerced into doing something that it does not want to do.

In fact, one constant in the literature post-2016 has been a growing if grudging realization that 'coercion' has become more of an obstacle than anything else in efforts to pin down what is problematic with interference.[1078] To wit, the focus on the importance of an 'ultimatum', for example, seems strangely conspiratorial: surely it should not make such a difference that the U.S. launches an embargo against Nicaragua loudly telegraphing it to change its policies or that it launches such an embargo merely *because* of or to combat such policies. In both cases, Nicaragua will have heard loud and clear that it had incurred U.S. displeasure and that a change of its policies might bring about a reversal of the unfortunate consequences that followed. And even if it did not, Nicaragua might still be on the receiving end of a regime change operation that attempted to change it from outside without its knowledge—hardly more defensible normatively. The notion of coercion seems even more inadequate when it comes to diffuse forms of entryism that the new interference is concerned with. The point may precisely be that some states do not need to (nor particularly want to) coerce as much as they want to merely disrupt, not particularly asking for anything in exchange. Throwing a spanner in the works of self-determination does not so much coerce as it disorients.

Of course, simply because a notion in international law has seemingly outlived the conditions of its analytical and social utility does not mean that it can be wantonly discarded. One cannot merely have the concept of intervention

1077 Ohlin, 'Did Russian Cyber Interference in the 2016 Election Violate International Law' (n 851).

1078 Kilovaty, 'The Elephant in the Room' (n 976).

that one needs to address the problem of the times. Part of the discipline that international law imposes is 'living with' the legacies that state practice has bequeathed us. One can see, anyhow, how it is strategically tempting to subsume the new interference within the existing international legal framework of 'coercive' intervention, given the stigma that comes from the term, its pedigree and its associations. A coercion-based conception of intervention commends itself a priori to international lawyers as at least benefiting from a near universal recognition and as being the object of a minimal consensus. It may be that coercion as a concept still provides the requisite elasticity to encompass the ever-evolving range of tactics that are commonly associated with the new interference. Insisting that coercion is required by the definition of intervention is not necessarily incompatible, as was seen, with an effort to at least see coercion in a broader light. And defining coercion broadly, if it can be done successfully, stands to magnify the standing of a prohibition of ordinary interference by making it analytically equivalent to behavior, intervention, that is clearly condemned.

The feeling that the emphasis on coercion provides clarity and solidity to the definition of intervention, however, may be more apparent than real, given genuine and long evident ambiguities about what actually constitutes coercion. The risk is that one will neglect the extent to which target states are less strictly 'forced' to do something than it is their ability to self-determine from within that is being corroded.[1079] To say that 'fake news' is a form of democratic coercion, for example, sounds awkward and reductive. Disinformation operations are problematic, no doubt, but not in the same way nor for the same reasons as the old interference. Efforts to expand the meaning of coercion to do away with such complexities may ultimately distort the meaning of intervention without providing U.S. with a clear road map to interference. More importantly, as Xuan Tay points out, the idea that intervention needs to be coercive arguably does not even reflect the *lex lata* that the ICJ's ruling in Nicaragua v. U.S. is imagined as having saddled international law with.[1080] In effect:

> The textual history makes clear that the principle's content has been in perpetual motion, transforming from a limited rule against armed intervention into a broader one against various subtler interpositions in the

1079 Ohlin, 'Did Russian Cyber Interference in the 2016 Election Violate International Law' (n 851).

1080 Tay (n 516).

twentieth century context of increasing economic interdependence, decolonization, and the Cold War.[1081]

One possibility, then, is that international law is and ought to be moving away altogether from a single minded focused on the rule of non-intervention, to enrich the palette of what constitutes a renewed, irreducible concept of interference. This entails going beyond merely an expansion of coercion to recognize that cases of manipulation, perversion, and usurpation of the sovereign will are better understood as manifestations of the violation of a distinct rule of non-interference. Although Milanovic argues that this is not about to happen given prevailing inertias in state *opinio juris*, his own subsuming of quite different forms of coercion under the common framework of intervention suggests that such a reconceptualization may already be under way.[1082] In the context of cyberspace, which has proved quite susceptible to a general blurring of contours, the evolution is for example towards characterizing not only 'damage' but 'impairment' as problematic to the extent that 'has the effect of depriving the State of control over the matter in question', even though not strictly as prohibited intervention.[1083]

It might first be argued that, intervention or not, the behavior at stake is, de minimis, a *violation of the sovereignty* of the target state. This means that one can usefully lower the threshold at which behavior can be ruled as problematic and dealt with under an international law framework without further muddling the prohibition on intervention. Such a move has already been in evidence in the context of low-level cyber interference below what is necessary to violate the rule of non-intervention, and the argument that it is at least a violation of sovereignty[1084] (or, for some of the lawyers who have defended that distinction, is not).[1085] This has led to a spirited discussion about whether sovereignty is merely a principle of international law incapable as such of prohibiting interference, or whether it is more specifically a primary rule of international law already prohibiting interference.[1086] The latter is more likely to be true—after all, surely sovereignty is routinely invoked to protest outside

1081 ibid 43.
1082 Milanovic (n 463).
1083 *Tallinn Manual 2.0 on the International Law Applicable to Cyber Operations* (n 454) 318.
1084 Schmitt, 'In Defense of Sovereignty in Cyberspace' (n 521).
1085 Gary P Corn and Robert Taylor, 'Sovereignty in the Age of Cyber' (2017) 111 American Journal of International Law 207.
1086 Kevin Jon Heller, 'In Defense of Pure Sovereignty in Cyberspace' (2021) 97 International Law Studies 1432.

behavior that may not be more specifically prohibited under international law under a separate rule. In effect, scholars seem to have had little difficulty in describing forms of low-level interference as, if nothing else, a violation of sovereignty.[1087]

Even if sovereignty is more principle than rule, it still exudes 'rules' at every turn and can, in fact, be understood as a bundle of claims which other states are expected to respect. Sovereignty can be violated in itself and it would be ironic if the foundational rule of international law (that sovereignty ought to be respected) could only be violated through a range of discrete rules codifying it as it were. Interference that does not reach the level of violating the rule of non-intervention could clearly be, then, classified as a violation of sovereignty if nothing else, even when it does not also violate some distinct primary rule of international law. On some level, it may be simpler to deal even with blatant forms of coercive interference as merely violations of sovereignty. This meshes well with an understanding, contra the traditional dominant position, that coercion is ultimately a possible but not necessary element of all intervention. It also connects to a long line that has seen sovereignty as the cardinal value and rule protected by the principle. This then means that the problem of interference is properly understood, as 'celui de l'atteinte aux droits souverains qui sert de dénominateur commun à toutes les formes d'actes catalogués d'intervention'.[1088]

Here, however, the inverse problem arises than with taking the use of force as one's model: this time, that one will sell short interference and the tradition it represents by subsuming it within a much larger category of run-of-the-mill violations of sovereignty. Not only does this seem to relatively trivialize interference's gravity, but it also diminishes a sense of its specific evil (seeking to *displace* the sovereign rather than simply violating its rights). It also opens the door to potentially considering vast swaths of international behavior as illegal interference, robs the notion of interference (and perhaps even intervention) of its specificity. There is utility, it seems, in maintaining a distinction between ordinary violations of sovereignty and the particular perversity of interference, just as there is value in not conflating interference with a broad intervention framework, or the latter with the use of force.

Indeed, there may yet have always been another strategy, which is to more clearly spell out that there have in fact always been or at least now exist two rules alongside each other, one prohibiting intervention (based on coercion)

1087 Van de Velde (n 822).
1088 David (n 536) 351.

and one prohibiting interference (based on meddling). Detaching interference from the coercion that is widely understood to be defining of unlawful intervention, then, might make the most of the need to analytically distinguish the two, as well as simultaneously distinguishing them from garden variety violations of sovereignty. The governing issue when it comes to interference specifically, it is argued, is not so much that any particular governmental authority is being coerced to do anything under threat than the fact that the operation of a state's sovereignty is being corrupted from without. This makes it somewhat irrelevant to argue that states are being coerced when they may in fact be embracing certain outcomes on the basis of a particular environment and information, albeit a corrupted one.[1089]

It does also risk making interference as a concept quite elusive, stuck as it is between a coercive intervention on the one hand, and a violation of sovereignty on the other. Towards the lower end of the spectrum, the risk is that interference will come dangerously close to mere influence. An illustration of the problem is what to do with cyber operations that generally weaken the target state but do not seem to have any clear outcome let alone request beyond a general, possibly low level, degradation of critical infrastructure.[1090] Or consider election interference 'not aimed exclusively at influencing specific election results but at undermining or destroying citizens' long-term confidence in the legitimacy of their democratic institutions as well as their democratic processes':[1091] clearly undesirable, but also clearly elusive in its scope and incidence. This leaves the new interference even more in need of a theory of what then distinguishes it from (lawful) influence. Certainly, there could be behavior that is not strictly coercive but in fact far worse than coercion: compare, for example, a one-time threat by a foreign power to a single official to retaliate against him if they do not produce a certain outcome (coercion, but relatively less problematic), to the systematic bombardment of a polity with subtly misleading propaganda on social networks (not clearly coercion, but clearly very problematic). It would be concerning if international law were to end up condemning the lesser behavior because, strictly speaking, it manifests coercion, but were mum about the sort that is intuitively graver because it is hard technically to pin down its specifically coercive character.

Note that one strategy has been to seek to avoid the fundamental definitional quandary altogether by instead itemizing a sort of laundry list of

---

1089 Hollis (n 1060).

1090 Experts clearly disagree on the issue. *Tallinn Manual 2.0 on the International Law Applicable to Cyber Operations* (n 454) 318.

1091 2023 Resolution on Foreign Interference in the E.U. (n 335), para BA.

behavior that is portrayed as problematic. As the ILC noted when intervention was contemplated as part of the Code of Offences against the Peace and Security of Mankind, 'intervention in the affairs of another State was necessarily translated objectively into certain specific acts, such as fomenting internal troubles or exerting political or economic pressure. It would be wise for the Commission not to inscribe "intervention" as such as an offence in the code, but to break down the concept and list instead, as offences, the specific acts which constituted intervention'.[1092] This is a familiar drafting technique: we may not be able to fully define interference, but we at least recognize it when we see its concrete manifestations. It is part of a recurring, post-ontological move away from definition to manifestations, also visible in the definition of the *domaine*. Certain kinds of activities are then presented as unlawful because of their *form*. For example, Kuan Tai argues in favor of 'identify[ing] specific manifestations of the principle that take the form of concrete rules' such as the prohibition on the use of force, in an effort to produce a sort of quilt-work entrenching the norm of non-interference.[1093]

Such an approach has the advantage that it ostensibly wades through the rich thicket of state practice, a practice always more complicated and ambiguous than the principles it draws on. The hope is that interference can be described not on the basis of some general idea but on processes of international law making, not unlike what the New Haven school once recommended. As often with such definitional attempts, however, it has not fared unambiguously well.[1094] Although it manages to shift the focus away from a somewhat illusory insistence on rules, it replaces them by standards that seem endlessly pliable and manipulable. Take, for example, the case of propaganda, a good illustration of a practice that is not well characterized as being specifically coercive. Various statements differ significantly on what is meant by propaganda and what its status is, in a context where many states resort to it. The line between propaganda and communication is not a clear one, and one state's propaganda may easily appear to be another state's truth. The preamble to the 1976 General Assembly resolution on Non-Interference referred to 'campaigns of vilification' and 'subversion and defamation',[1095] and the 1981 Declaration on

1092 Report of the International Law Commission on the work of its thirty-seventh session, 6 May–26 July 1985, Official Records of the General Assembly, Fortieth session, Supplement No. 10, para. 85.

1093 Tay (n 424).

1094 In a very different context but with a similar line of argument in mind, see Frédéric Mégret, 'The Humanitarian Problem with Drones' (2013) 2013 Utah Law Review 1283.

1095 UNGA Res 31/91 (14 December 1976).

the Inadmissibility of Intervention and Interference denounced 'defamatory campaign[s], vilification or hostile propaganda for the purpose of intervening or interfering in the internal affairs of other States'.[1096] By contrast, the Tallinn Manual 2.0 notes that '[t]he International Group of Experts agreed that [propaganda] transmission into other States is generally not a violation of sovereignty'[1097] (note, however, the use of the word 'generally') and therefore not prohibited interference.

The question of whether certain communications are or not propaganda came up in the Russia Today (RT) France case, a case in which the European Court of Justice (ECJ) had to determine whether the withdrawal of that Russian channel's broadcasting licence was legal. The question was not specifically whether interference was involved under international law, but it came close given the sort of limitations analysis foregrounded by human rights (the restriction of RT would have been legal if it had been a 'necessary' measure to combat what was effectively interference). The Court had to decide whether the applicant 'had engaged in continuous and concerted propaganda actions targeted at civil society in the European Union and neighbouring countries in order, inter alia, to justify and support the Russian Federation's aggression against Ukraine'[1098] and was therefore rightly deprived of its authorization to broadcast.

A whole dossier of proof including articles and interviews was introduced in court. This included evidence that RT had presented the deployment of the Russian armed forces 'as a preventive action to defend the self-proclaimed republics of Donetsk and Luhansk', reports of the words of the Russian Minister of Foreign Affairs 'accusing the "West" of "creating insurmountable confrontation between Russia and NATO"', or referring to Ukrainian ethnic cleansing as having prepared the ground for the invasion.[1099] After the attack of Ukraine in February 2022, it was claimed that the applicant had:

> continued to adopt the official position of the authorities of the Russian Federation that the offensive [...] was a 'special operation', a preventive, defensive and limited action, caused by Western countries and by the aggressive attitude of NATO and also by Ukrainian provocation, aimed at defending the self-proclaimed republics of Donetsk and Luhansk.[1100]

1096 1981 Declaration on the Inadmissibility of Intervention and Interference, s II(j).

1097 *Tallinn Manual 2.0 on the International Law Applicable to Cyber Operations* (n 454) 27.

1098 Case T-125/22 *RT France v Council of the European Union* [2022] ECLI:EU:T:2022:483, para 175.

1099 ibid, para 177.

1100 ibid, para 178.

The judgment then detailed a number of ways in which RT France's content was systematically aligned with the Kremlin's claims, including by hosting outside guests whose arguments were not critically engaged with by RT journalists. The ECJ found that 'the applicant engaged in a systematic action of broadcasting "selected" information, including manifestly false or misleading information, revealing a manifest imbalance in the presentation of the different opposing viewpoints, with the specific aim of justifying and supporting that aggression'.[1101] This led to the conclusion that:

> The Council was [...] entitled to consider that the various items of evidence referred to above constituted a sufficiently concrete, precise and consistent body of evidence capable of demonstrating [...] that the applicant had, inter alia, broadcast information justifying the military aggression against Ukraine, capable of constituting a significant and direct threat to the Union's public order and security.[1102]

If this is good enough for the European Council to withdraw RT France's license, then it would probably be good enough for the European Union to complain of an interference vis-à-vis Russia.

If anything, however, even in this case propaganda sounds more like a form of persuasion than coercion and as a form of interference its status is ambiguous. It remains difficult to know whether propaganda is interference, in part because this depends on the weight one allots to sovereignty, human rights or international community interests. There are, for example, certainly those who will profess that 'information appraising [an oppressed people] about their human rights [...] may, indeed, be dangerous' but not illegitimate.[1103] Many approaches of what is wrong about propaganda specifically ultimately tackle the problem either by adding more qualifiers (malicious, defamatory, incendiary, etc.) and/or circularly returning to the notion that propaganda is illegal if, in fact, it constitutes interference. But making a theory of illicit interference depend largely on the ends it pursues is a sure recipe for international dissensus, both on account of general disagreement about ends and specific disagreement about whether they are, in this particular case, those pursued.

Rather than looking at certain types of behavior or its finality, then, it might be a particular generic quality that it has that is crucial in evaluating interference. The covert character of the way in which the influence is sought may be

1101 ibid, para 211.
1102 ibid, para 188.
1103 Farer, 'Political and Economic Coercion in Contemporary International Law' (n 433) 407.

a clue and is often what is seen as problematic about influence operations. For example, it is alleged that Russia has given more than $300 million to political parties internationally since 2014 using a web of shell companies and institutions to conceal the funds' origin.[1104] Russia is also active in financing secessionist movements in Europe such as Catalunya, often using intermediaries that make it difficult to determine who the ultimate payer is. From a national security or democratic perspective as well as, possibly, domestic law, these are obviously concerning developments. Chapter 6 will return to explore this question more fully, as a potentially meaningful extrapolation of existing trends. The point here is that the covert character of influence is not currently entirely conclusive under international law. There is no clear expectation in international relations that foreign actors will always be forthcoming about what exactly it is they are doing and even legitimate expectations, as already observed, about the confidentiality of one's domestic and foreign policy.

This suggests that secrecy in itself is a weak basis on which to hang an entire theory of illegal interference. States routinely shroud their policies, most notably their foreign policy as it relates to other states they seek to influence, in secrecy, in ways that are not normally cause for concern. For example, diplomats may well routinely seek to influence foreign officials or civil society without, evidently, explicitly broadcasting their ultimate intention. That is largely accepted in the international realm. It may be that this tolerance exists only for genuine foreign affairs and diplomatic activities, which might of course conserve a high degree of secrecy but are still identifiable as such. Concerns may arise with broader sovereign operations outside the normal scope of inter-state relations, notably as contemplated by the Vienna Convention on Diplomatic and Consular Relations. Jens Ohlin, for example, has argued that 'deception' is the litmus test, citing the example of the 2016 Russian social media campaign which 'masqueraded as inside members of the polity'.[1105] Similar concerns may exist in relation to diaspora manipulation to obtain certain electoral outcomes, namely that it involves a form of 'masked' intervention through intermediary actors.

As soon as one moves beyond the strict realm of interference with the electoral infrastructure to shadowy information-bending operations, however,

1104 Edward Wong, 'Russia Secretly Gave $300 Million to Political Parties and Officials Worldwide, U.S. Says' *The New York Times* (13 September 2022) <https://www.nytimes.com/2022/09/13/us/politics/russia-election-interference.html> accessed 19 June 2023.

1105 Jens David Ohlin, 'Election Interference: A Unique Harm Requiring Unique Solutions' in Jens David Ohlin and Duncan B Hollis (eds), *Defending Democracies: Combating Foreign Election Interference in a Digital Age* (Oxford University Press 2021) 251.

merely prejudicial but nonetheless political interference is hard to pin down—in ways, at least, that do not end up making all 'unfriendly' forms of influence illegal. Sensing that any other outcome would let Russia off the hook too easily, it has been argued that it is the unprecedented 'breadth' and 'scale' of the meddling that makes the interference coercive.[1106] Highlighting a 'threshold of harm'[1107] (as opposed to the specifically coercive intentionality of interference) may go some way to alleviating concerns that making all attempts to covertly influence other polities constitutes interference in the affairs of sovereign states will cheapen the concept at the cost of its utility. There remains a crucial difference, however, between targeting the electoral infrastructure itself (for example by corrupting voting machines: clearly illegal under international law) and more generally acting, even perversely, on the informational environment within which elections occur (less clearly illegal given the inherent malleability of such an environment). It is unclear that the intensity with which the latter is carried out helps make it equivalent to the former.

Reformulations beyond the coercion canon, at any rate, also pose problems of their own. 'Distortion', for example, has emerged as a key conceptual marker of interference. The European Parliament has insisted that what is specifically at stake with disinformation is that it 'distorts the public debate around elections and other democratic processes and can make it difficult for citizens to make informed choices'.[1108] It is not clear, however, whether the distortion argument as a normative theory of why interference is wrong works as well as a positive law criterion to identify actual interference. It supposes, somewhat problematically, that we have a way of knowing what the outcome of elections for example would have been 'but for' certain forms of distorting interference: this sort of counterfactual seems methodologically fraught, as was seen when critiquing the invocation of self-determination to outline the *domaine réservé*. Even assuming one has the requisite knowledge, how can one more fundamentally know if the democratic process was distorted and to what extent, in a context where the debate is in a sense always being distorted (there is no 'pure' debate outside any distortion by the standard of which distortions could be assessed)? Hence the argument made by Michael Schmitt in particular that the Russian actions, notably the release of DNC e-mails, operated in a 'grey zone'.[1109]

1106 Barela (n 55).
1107 Milanovic (n 463).
1108 2022 Resolution on Foreign Interference in the E.U. (n 337), para AD.
1109 Schmitt, 'Grey Zones in the International Law of Cyberspace' (n 55).

The 'hostile' nature of certain operations is sometimes highlighted as a marker, at least among others, of interference. To be sure, most interference is presumably hostile to some extent, but not all hostile behavior is interference. A range of diplomatic measures might be described as hostile (concluding a defense treaty to protect oneself from a state, scaling down or interrupting diplomatic relations, etc.) without being constitutive of interference. Moreover, hostility is clearly to some extent in the eyes of the beholder. Interfering in elections in liberal states through cyber operations might be commonly deemed hostile; but authoritarian states will also complain that support to civil society within their boundaries is also hostile. Hostility seems too vague a concept, again, on which to hang a theory of what constitutes interference (or what constitutes the harm of interference): either it merely describes the quotidian competition between sovereigns seeking to maximize their national interest to the point of being trivial; or it brings an unnecessary element of motivational pathos in ways that distract from what is going on; or it neglects the extent to which interference has often presented itself as 'friendly' and might still be problematic on some separate account.

Finally, as a sign of a worrying trend, it has occasionally become acceptable in political parlance to speak of even 'influence' as potentially problematic, suggesting that every international interaction is now susceptible to being seen from an interference lens. For example, David Johnston's report on foreign interference in Canadian elections speaks of the fact that 'foreign governments are attempting to influence candidates and voters' and suggests that this is 'a growing threat to our democratic system and must be resisted as effectively as possible by government'.[1110] Essentially what seems to be happening here is a slippage away from the discourse of international law (which, as was seen, speaks of intervention or at least interference as being problematic, but not influence) to a constitutional law discourse that is much more all-encompassing, albeit perhaps only in relation to elections. The idea that mere influence is now potentially problematic manifests a clear semantic shift that may be justifiable from a democratic perspective, but that will not translate easily into the language of international law. Rooting out all outside influence would incline polities towards the autarchic end of the spectrum in ways that could be worse than the ill it is trying to address.

1110 Johnston (n 352) 1.

3 Public/Private

Intervention is traditionally presented, particularly in the West, as a very *public* form of meddling. Whatever it is interfering with in the target state, it at least emanates from states. In that respect, intervention suggests a basic relation of symmetry between public actors interfering with other public actors. In effect, all the main components of the state can be involved in intervention. The executive of course can, directly or indirectly through the civil service, be a leading cause of interference. A notable example of this is of course so-called 'diplomatic interference' where members of the foreign service act as a sort of spearhead for their governments' typically covert efforts at shaping outcomes in the host state.[1111] International legal sources are most on point when it comes to this paradigmatic form of intervention, the very intervention that international law has, traditionally, guarded against. But the public sources of interference can be diverse and operate remotely. They can involve legislatures who adopt laws with extra-territorial reach or design a foreign policy framework that is geared towards interference. Courts can themselves become mired in their own form of interference with the affairs of other states, if they go along with or produce their own expansive interpretations of extra-territorial jurisdiction, especially absent any international authorization to do so.[1112]

The same is true of interference more generally, which is typically imagined as largely public in origin, along the model characteristic of intervention. An interesting special case of the rule is spelt out by the Vienna Convention on Diplomatic Relations which anticipates that 'it is the duty of all persons enjoying such privileges and immunities [...] not to interfere in the internal affairs of that State'.[1113] This is essentially the transposition to the individual diplomat's level of the general prohibition on state interference, with the nuance that it also applies to cases where said diplomats are not acting on instructions and the question is that of their individual interference (made problematic, nonetheless, by their embodying their state). Evidently, embassies and consulates are particularly well placed to engage in interference given their presence in the territory of the host state, and their occasional connection to opposition

1111 Behrens, *Diplomatic Interference and the Law* (n 112).

1112 Austen L Parrish, 'Evading Legislative Jurisdiction Federal Courts, Practice & Procedure: Essay' (2011) 87 Notre Dame Law Review 1673; Nico Krisch, 'Jurisdiction Unbound: (Extra)Territorial Regulation as Global Governance' (2022) 33 European Journal of International Law 481.

1113 Vienna Convention on Diplomatic Relations (adopted 18 April 1961, entered into force 24 April 1964) 500 UNTS 95 (Vienna Convention) art 41.

or diaspora groups. As such, they provide an interesting if not unique window into a sort of interference at close quarters.

There is a long tradition of 'indelicate' consular or embassy officials providing support to insurgents or rebels in ways that either betray a disregard of their professional obligations or an even more worrisome disregard of their state's obligation not to interfere. Perhaps one of the earliest reported incidents of such interference involved Lord Sackville, then British Minister in Washington, being caught writing a letter to a U.S. citizen purporting to be of British origin, that he should vote for a party favorable to British interests[1114] (although there was some dispute as to whether his expulsion was an appropriate remedy given the arguably private nature of his indiscretion).[1115] Such a case arose in an earlier era where interference of this kind was less likely to be excused on account of its human rights high mindedness. By the same token, there is a long tradition of significant reluctance to pronounce even on grave matters of humanitarian or rights concerns lest this be seen as transgressing the taboo of non-interference and interfering with bilateral relations. In some recent cases, consulates have appeared to be on the front lines of foreign interference, in ways that have raised eyebrows with states keen on insulating themselves from finger pointing, notably of their human rights record.

Today, indelicacy in diplomatic practice is likely to take quite different forms that manifest different degrees of impropriety and straddle the liberal/illiberal divide. On the one hand is a recurring complaint, typically by authoritarian states, that diplomats, notably Western, are involved in advanced contact with dissidents and sometimes participate in political events, whether it is British diplomats being swept up in anti Ceauşescu protests in Romania in 1989 or German diplomats allegedly involved in anti-government protests in Iran 2010.[1116] At stake here may be the individual behavior of said diplomats rather than a more deliberate effort by their state to embrace a democratic opposition. But of course, the supposed interference may be very much at the initiative of states. European embassies, for example, have long invited well known Cuban dissidents on festive occasions as part of what became known as the

1114 John M Gover, 'Some Recent Incidents in International Law' (1888) 14 Law Magazine and Law Review 109, 110.

1115 Charles S Campbell, Jr, 'The Dismissal of Lord Sackville' (1958) 44 The Mississippi Valley Historical Review 635, 645.

1116 Hossein Jaseb and Reza Derakhshi, 'Iran Official: German Diplomats Involved in "Riots"' *Reuters* (27 January 2010) <https://www.reuters.com/article/idUSTRE60Q1XY/> accessed 20 February 2024.

'cocktail wars',[1117] much to the chagrin of the Havana government. Although inviting dissidents to cocktails hardly ought to count as intervention, it may be that particularly close involvement of embassy staff with known dissidents can border on something problematic from an international legal point of view.[1118] By contrast, initiatives by some diplomats (again, possibly out of their own volition or at the, plausibly deniable, request of their state) to pressure host state politicians, typically critical of their state, or threaten members of the diaspora, are good candidates for interference.[1119]

3.1 *The Invisibility of Private Interference*

At any rate, one of the consequences of this perceived publicness of intervention has been the relative lack of attention historically to how private actors, by contrast, might become involved in interference. Indeed, under dominant understandings of international law, non-state actors cannot technically interfere any more than they can, for example, commit aggression[1120] or even violate the Charter prohibition on the use of force.[1121] As has been observed, '[t]echnically speaking, many non-state actors cannot commit internationally wrongful acts which could give rise to their responsibility, for they are not bound by primary norms of international law to begin with'.[1122] That clearly applies to the norm of non-intervention and, as the case may be, non-interference, making the responsibility of non-state actors in their own name (even if shared) under international law a challenge.

1117 Juergen Kleiner, *Diplomatic Practice: Between Tradition and Innovation* (World Scientific 2009) 107.

1118 Michael Weissenstein, 'Cuba Accuses U.S. Diplomat of Supporting Illegal Actions' *AP News* (20 November 2019) <https://apnews.com/article/ad164694f7794d4091be5a1d582ca331> accessed 20 February 2024; Michael R Pompeo, 'Cuban Government Allegations of Political Interference Against U.S. Chargé d'Affaires' (*US Department of State*, 23 November 2019) <https://2017-2021.state.gov/cuban-government-allegations-of-political-interference-against-u-s-charge-daffaires/> accessed 20 February 2024.

1119 Cecco (n 366).

1120 For a criticism, see Steve Beytenbrod, 'Defining Aggression: An Opportunity to Curtail the Criminal Activities of Non-State Actors Note' (2010) 36 Brooklyn Journal of International Law 647; Sasha Dominik Bachmann and Yasser Abdelkader, 'Reconciling Quasi-States with the Crime of Aggression under the ICC Statute' (2018) 33 Emory International Law Review 91.

1121 Lanovoy (n 815).

1122 Jean d'Aspremont and others, 'Sharing Responsibility Between Non-State Actors and States in International Law: Introduction' (2015) 62 Netherlands International Law Review 49, 54.

To this day, for example, the clearest prohibition on foreign political party funding in many domestic laws is by foreign *states*.[1123] When the American Society of International Law was criticized for having divested from South Africa to oppose the Apartheid regime, its answer was that intervention 'evidently applies only to the actions of states' and that '[n]othing suggests that these strictures against economic coercion were meant to apply to the actions of individuals or corporations, much less learned societies. These entities of domestic law remain free, as a matter of international law, to deal or not to deal with foreign entities or even with states as their self-interest or conscience dictates'.[1124] Even as interference is increasingly channelled through social media (and in some ways produced by them), domestic requirements of foreign registration remain unhelpfully fixated on a 20th Century vision of interference as dependent on sovereign operatives.[1125] At best, corporations are to be reined in by their state and not used as vectors of public interference. The 1981 Declaration, for example, anticipates that the state must prevent the use of 'transnational and multinational corporations under its jurisdiction and control as instruments of political pressure or coercion against another State, in violation of the Charter of the United Nations'.[1126] As Jamnejad and Wood put it, however, even there '[i]t ought to be emphasized that economic intervention is, like all other forms of intervention, a matter of state-to-state behaviour' and a company would not thereby 'be liable directly for its actions; responsibility would lie with the state for a failure to control'.[1127]

But what if, notwithstanding this slightly stodgy disdain for private actors, it is said actors that are effectively interfering with sovereign affairs, perhaps even unbeknownst to their state? Despite the little space that international law devotes to them (or thanks to it), private groups, out of their own volition or in the service of states, have long assumed a prominent role as facilitators, relays, or, perhaps most crucially, autonomous purveyors of interference. Already in the 1960s, Wolfgang Friedmann noted that '[p]rivate interests may no longer

1123 Indeed, in some cases the prohibition applies only to donations from foreign states and public foreign organs, to the exclusion of any other actor. See Ley orgánica 3/1987, de 2 de julio, sobre financiación de los partidos políticos (Vigencia desde 04 de Julio de 1987. Revisión vigente desde 12 de Marzo de 2003) (Spain), art 6.

1124 Paul C Szasz, 'The Action Does Not Violate International Law' (1988) 82 American Journal of International Law 314, 315.

1125 Joshua R Fattal, 'FARA on Facebook: Modernizing the Foreign Agents Registration Act to Address Propagandists on Social Media' (2018) 21 New York University Journal of Legislation & Public Policy 903.

1126 1981 Declaration on the Inadmissibility of Intervention and Interference, s II(k).

1127 Jamnejad and Wood (n 29) 371–372.

be in a position to invoke the military intervention of their home state for the protection of their economic interests; but they can still vitally influence or modify political action'.[1128] A corporation such as Toshiba, for example, was very active in the late 1980s in the U.S. to get it to rescind sanctions following its sale of electronic equipment to the Soviets, often finding support from U.S. corporations who themselves stood to lose from them.[1129] In fact, both states and corporations may be only too aware that the latter's relative invisibility in international law makes channelling otherwise prohibited financial aid to armed groups for example possible since, unlike similar state-origin aid, it 'is not covered by the prohibition of intervention'.[1130] Consider in recent times the role of the Wagner group in the Central African Republic: although there is much evidence that the group has significant Kremlin support and may even be a proxy, it also to some extent operates as an interference entrepreneur, engaging in deeply parasitic activities in other countries that are somewhat autonomous from Russia.[1131]

In doing so, of course, it is arguably merely reprising a much older playbook which has long seen Western companies, from Union Minière du Haut Katanga to United Fruit, from International Telegraph and Telephone Company to Total, act as champions of their own states' interventions but also, occasionally, as 'states within the state'. These groups have sometimes displaced, challenged or eroded the sovereignty of host states,[1132] reprising elements of the interference repertoire exactly as it was conceived by states. They have even arguably innovated in their interference techniques, unconstrained as they are by some public rules. Big Western oil companies, for example, long had a symbiotic relationship with their patron states and maneuvered to orient the latter's foreign policies to delay and minimize the impact of nationalization waves.[1133] More recently, some corporations have elevated themselves to the

---

1128 Friedmann, *The Changing Structure of International Law* (n 21) 28.

1129 Robert a Rosenblatt, 'Intense Lobbying Cools U.S. Anger at Toshiba' *Los Angeles Times* (1 May 1988) <https://www.latimes.com/archives/la-xpm-1988-05-01-fi-3406-story.html> accessed 6 September 2024.

1130 Beate Rudolf, 'Governance Without Government? Non-State Actors and International Law', *Working Paper, American Political Science Association (APSA) Annual Meeting* (2009) 30 <https://papers.ssrn.com/abstract=1449182> accessed 13 June 2024.

1131 Charamba and Mégret (n 695).

1132 Raymond Vernon, *Sovereignty at Bay: The Multinational Spread of U.S. Enterprises* (Basic Books 1971).

1133 See e.g., Shakiba Fadaie, 'Greed and Influence: The Role of the Anglo-American Oil Company in Iran's 1953 Coup D'etat' (*Shakiba Fadaie—UBC Blogs*, 6 August 2020) <https://blogs.ubc.ca/shakiba/2020/08/06/greed-and-influence-the-role-of-the-anglo-american-oil-company-in-irans-1953-coup-detat-shakiba-fadaie/> accessed 27 April 2024.

status of 'worldwide interest groups' in a context where, as one U.S. Deputy Undersecretary of State for Economic Affairs once put it, '[i]t becomes difficult to know where business ends and foreign policy, political and economic begins'.[1134] Their role as 'surrogate sovereigns'[1135] in some countries leads to a suspicion that they are not only challenging the sovereignty of the host state, but subverting it. In recent decades, MNCs have also appeared to be instrumentalized by civil society groups to make further incursions into the politics of host states.[1136]

This has long fed into a sense that the exclusive focus on state-to-state interference, central as that phenomenon may arguably be, may simply miss the mark when it comes to the multifarious activities of multinationals and other groups in the Global South. Before the General Assembly, Salvador Allende famously lambasted corporations, arguing that '[w]e are faced by a direct confrontation between the large transnational corporations and the states. The corporations are interfering in the fundamental political, economic and military decisions of the states'.[1137] In fact, one might argue that Third World opposition to interference was originally at least as much focused on Western private actors as Western states, whether corporate or non-profit. For Latin America, the Middle East or Africa, there is in fact nothing new about corporate interference as the point of the spear of Western imperialism.[1138] By contrast, the wave of nationalizations begun during the decolonization era and culminating in the rise of OPEP was a resounding success in those states precisely because it diminished the influence that big oil companies had had until then.

Hence late Western concerns about Cambridge Analytica or Facebook having an inordinate impact on domestic politics need to be heavily contextualized: what appears as pathological and new has arguably been the day-to-day experience of the Global South for decades, if not centuries. The novelty is that many of the concerns that were historically those of the Third World have gradually become those of industrialised nations as well. It is by the time Global South corporations began to hold significant investments in the West that the

---

1134 Cited in Jonathan F Galloway, 'Multinational Enterprises as Worldwide Interest Groups' (1971) 2 Politics & Society 1, 4–5.

1135 John M Kline, 'MNCs and Surrogate Sovereignty' (2006) 13 The Brown Journal of World Affairs 123.

1136 Marina Ottaway, 'Reluctant Missionaries' [2001] Foreign Policy 44.

1137 Cited in Hugo K Radice, *International Firms and Modern Imperialism: Selected Readings* (Penguin Books 1975) 342.

1138 Sundhya Pahuja, 'Corporations, Universalism, and the Domestication of Race in International Law' in Duncan Bell (ed), *Empire, Race and Global Justice* (Cambridge University Press 2019).

U.S. began to treat foreign owned companies warily as some came to be seen as 'moles, agents of their home governments, to be used in some unspecified scenario of the future to compromise the interests of the United States'.[1139] Among earlier U.S. concerns with foreign agents and foreign election financing have featured Philippine sugar producers or Japanese electronics makers engaged in transnational lobbying efforts given the importance of the U.S. regulatory framework for global trade.[1140] These can exercise considerable leverage, not unlike of course that of domestic firms, for example by promising the implantation of factories in particular districts. There is an evident historical irony here. Just as states in the Global South have long complained of influence from international NGOs and multinationals in their sovereign affairs, the West is in turn wary of interference by shadowy groups, including some taking a corporate form, whose connection to the state is sometimes difficult to establish.

A late realization of the importance of such phenomena has led to an increasingly alarmist discourse notably on both sides of the Atlantic as the problem of interference is understood as a sort of 360 degree, coordinated assault. The European Parliament speaks, somewhat ominously, of information manipulation 'serv[ing] the economic interests of state *and non-state actors and their proxies*' and suggests the importance of a 'whole-of-society approach' that includes coordination 'with civil society and the private sector',[1141] but without providing much clarity as to who these actors are. Chinese telecom company Huawei has often been in the crosshairs of Western regulators as entertaining deep ties with the Chinese government, raising concerns that it could be an indirect source of interference.[1142] It is quite clear, however, that persistent doubts about the private or public character of who one is facing do little to clarify the international law of non-intervention. In fact, the diversification of actors that *actually* engage in interference (even if they cannot *formally* do so) problematizes not only their own contribution to interference but the phenomenon's very definition.

3.2 *Issues of Attribution*

The difficulty in knowing who one is facing brings inherent risks for international law and stability, including the possibility that countermeasures will be abusively adopted or directed at the wrong actor, thus endangering bilateral

1139 Raymond Vernon, 'Sovereignty at Bay: Twenty Years After' (1991) 20 Millennium: Journal of International Studies 191, 193.

1140 Rosenblatt (n 1128).

1141 2022 Resolution on Foreign Interference in the E.U. (n 337), paras H, O, P.

1142 Moore (n 714).

relations. It will not always be clear that some sort of meddling by private actors is or should count as interference under international law, given its lack of connection, as the case may be, to a state. One growing and fairly familiar issue for international law in this context is the extent to which the acts of various semi-public groups ought to be attributable to certain states. Russia relies on semi-private or semi-public offices of dubious status; China is said to increasingly rely on its diaspora; and the West has long relied on government funded NGOs with an international ambition.

This trend has gradually drawn attention to obligations of monitoring by states. As Resolution 36/103 put it, states are bound to 'prevent the use of transnational and multinational corporations under its jurisdiction and control as instruments of political pressure or coercion against another State, in violation of the Charter of the United Nations'.[1143] Moreover, it is sometimes suggested, as in the Tallinn Manual 2.0, that '[a] State shall not knowingly allow the cyber infrastructure located in its territory or under its exclusive governmental control to be used for acts that adversely and unlawfully affect other States'.[1144] But interfering states may have policies that more or less deliberately obscure attribution, perhaps taking advantage of those laws' ambiguity and inherent statism.[1145] Even civil society can be instrumentalized for the purposes of interference. As one Canadian report points out, '[w]hile there is nothing wrong with grassroots community organizations expressing political preferences, they can be hard to discern from so-called "astro-turf" organizations that purport to be grassroots but exist for ulterior or illegitimate purposes'.[1146] And 'disinformation-for-hire, whereby providers offer disinformation services to government and non-government actors, for example over the dark web, setting out lists of services and prices',[1147] has emerged as a reality.

The European Parliament, moreover, has complained that interference relies 'on widespread use of artificial intelligence (AI) and erod[es] attributability'.[1148] It is an open secret that OpenAI is being used by Russia, China, Iran as well as Israeli companies to generate social media posts to sway public

1143 UNGA Res 36/103 (9 December 1981), para (k).
1144 *Tallinn Manual 2.0 on the International Law Applicable to Cyber Operations* (n 454) 29.
1145 Oona A Hathaway and others, 'Ensuring Responsibility: Common Article 1 and State Responsibility for Non-State Actors' (2016) 95 Texas Law Review 539.
1146 Johnston (n 352) 14.
1147 2023 Resolution on Foreign Interference in the E.U. (n 335), para 9.
1148 2022 Resolution on Foreign Interference in the E.U. (n 337), para K.

opinion against the background of certain conflicts.[1149] Fake profiles on social networks make it difficult to identify the source of heavily decentralized covert campaigns to influence public opinion. In this context, the categories of attribution and non-attribution are constantly being solicited for the purposes of demonstrating interference or detaching oneself from the suspicion that one is engaged in it, yet not always in the relatively familiar legal terms of state responsibility. The problem is that it is entire ecosystems of disinformation that have emerged, including actors very much deliberately producing such disinformation but also a host of innocent relayers and amplifiers.

One policy report has sought to distinguish between interference that is 'state-directed', 'state-encouraged' or merely 'state-aligned'[1150] in ways that suggest that the 'either/or' of state responsibility may not do justice to the complexity of issues, especially when based on effective control. Western states are adamant, for example, that NGOs operating from within their confines are separate and independent actors that cannot and should not be reined it as a result of misconceived complaints by authoritarian foreign states[1151] but this is an ongoing source of unresolved tension. There has been concern about whether attribution is even possible and relevant at all given both the amorphous nature of civil society actors, their formal independence, and the elusiveness of the interference they engage in. If nothing else, the problem will be one of proof and evidence in a context where states may not even know they have been the target of cyber interference,[1152] much more than the conceptual niceties of attribution.

As is well known, to make matters worse, the debate has more generally been confused in the background by a tendency to mix the registers of state

1149 Cade Metz, 'OpenAI Says Russia and China Used Its A.I. in Covert Campaigns' *The New York Times* (30 May 2024) <https://www.nytimes.com/2024/05/30/technology/openai-influence-campaigns-report.html> accessed 15 June 2024; Frenkel (n 383).

1150 Laura Galante and Shaun Ee, 'Defining Russian Election Interference: An Analysis of Select 2014 to 2018 Cyber Enabled Incidents' (Atlantic Council: Scowcroft Center for Strategy and Security 2018) 6 <https://www.atlanticcouncil.org/wp-content/uploads/2018/09/Defining_Russian_Election_Interference_web.pdf> accessed 25 January 2024.

1151 This is largely premised on the notion that NGOs are neither state agents nor controlled by the state. Although see Joanna Macrae, 'NGOs: Has the "N" Gone Missing?' [2003] *The Magazine of the International Red Cross and Red Crescent Movement* <https://web.archive.org/web/20201020222616/http://www.redcross.int/EN/mag/magazine1996_3/18-19.html> accessed 25 January 2024.

1152 François Delerue, 'Attribution to State of Cyber Operations Conducted by Non-State Actors' in Elena Carpanelli and Nicole Lazzerini (eds), *Use and Misuse of New Technologies: Contemporary Challenges in International and European Law* (Springer International Publishing 2019).

responsibility, the international law on the use of force and the characterization of conflicts as non-international or international.[1153] That debate stands to be further complicated by the extra-territorial operation of many non-state actors,[1154] perhaps especially those, such as corporations, involved in interference *in situ* on the territory of host states. This is not the place to re-explore the international law of attribution as a component of state liability comprehensively, except insofar as the question of interference stands to be complicated by ambiguities therein and, in turn, the prism of interference stands to further muddy the waters of attribution. Certainly, novel questions raised by the new interference would, all other things being equal, seem to militate for a loosening of the rules of attribution if states are to be actively encouraged to rein in private actors engaging in interference that they have control over. The sort of more expansive models that have been mooted in the context of the use of force[1155] (and that stand to be inherently less problematic, one would think, in the context of peaceful interference), including a lower standard of proof,[1156] might supply useful developments for how to think about the issue outside the box.

This is especially given the fear that a failure of international law to provide an adequate framework will provide a sort of free-for-all in which neither public nor private actors stand to be regulated. Nonetheless, it is worth considering that broadly holding states accountable for private initiatives may be harsh and unwarranted when the link is remote. As Zephyr Teachout has asked, 'can you really punish a country for "harboring election law violators?"'[1157] The risk of misattribution remains a very real danger, in a context where 'the indication that an ICT activity was launched or otherwise originates from the territory or the ICT infrastructure of a State may be insufficient in itself to attribute the activity to that State'.[1158] The problem, moreover, is not simply the factual one

1153 Jörn Griebel and Milan Plücken, 'New Developments Regarding the Rules of Attribution? The International Court of Justice's Decision in Bosnia v Serbia' (2008) 21 Leiden Journal of International Law 601; Marko Milanović, 'State Responsibility for Acts of Non-State Actors: A Comment on Griebel and Plücken' (2009) 22 Leiden Journal of International Law 307.

1154 Makaela Fehlhaber, 'The Evolution of "control" in Attributing Conduct of a Non-State Actor to a State in Public International Law' (2022) 29 Australian International Law Journal 21.

1155 See, for example, Vladyslav Lanovoy, 'The Use of Force by Non-State Actors and the Limits of Attribution of Conduct' (2017) 28 European Journal of International Law 563.

1156 M Emrah Tanyildizi, 'State Responsibility in Cyberspace: The Problem of Attribution of Cyberattacks Conducted by Non-State Actors' (2017) 8 Law & Justice Review.

1157 Teachout (n 323) 182–183.

1158 UNGA Report on International Security Developments in IT (2015) A/70/174, para 28(f).

of determining who lies behind interference, but the in some ways trickier normative one of assessing to what extent interference that is not clearly or wholly sovereign even falls within the categories of international law.

Certainly, for example the international law of counter measures, as set out by the ILC, does not envisage that states can sanction other states for the acts or private actors without meeting quite onerous criteria. The suggestion that states have broad duties of 'due diligence' when it comes to not letting their territory be exploited for the purposes of interference in the affairs of other states is a contentious one.[1159] Drawn from the fight against terrorism,[1160] it is particularly problematic when it slides into the terrain of justifying the use of force against states that are deemed to have failed in their obligations.[1161] Of concern is the fact that such duties have in the past been identified with a path (e.g., exercising self-defence against states that fail to rein in violent non-state actors) that is rife with dangers and a slippery slope for the use of force.[1162]

International law is of course not without tools to assign responsibility to the state, even when the actors involved are not state agents, although questions of state responsibility for corporate misbehavior have tended to focus on human rights violations rather than interference.[1163] The ILC's Articles on State Responsibility, in particular, provide a useful, if somewhat onerous and narrow, blueprint for holding states accountable for the acts of non-state actors

---

1159 Russell Buchan, 'Cyberspace, Non-State Actors and the Obligation to Prevent Transboundary Harm' (2016) 21 Journal of Conflict & Security Law 429.

1160 Ingvild Bode, '"Manifestly Failing" and "Unwilling or Unable" as Intervention Formulas: A Critical Assessment' in Aiden Warren and Damian Grenfell (eds), *Rethinking Humanitarian Intervention in the 21st Century* (Edinburgh University Press 2017).

1161 Jose Luis Aragon Cardiel, Amanda Davis and Lauranne Macherel, 'Modern Self-Defense: The Use of Force against Non-Military Threats' (2018) 49 Columbia Human Rights Law Review 99.

1162 In this sense, France has expressed concerns over the justification of the use of force via the claim that a State might have violated its due diligence obligations ('Le non-respect de l'obligation de diligence requise par U.N. État tiers ne suffit pas à fonder le droit de recourir à la force à son encontre dans le cadre de cyberattaques perpétrées depuis son territoire [...] la France ne reconnaît pas l'approche extensive de la légitime défense exprimée par une majorité des experts du Manuel de Tallinn') French Ministry of Armed Forces (Ministère des Armées), 'Droit International Appliqué aux Opérations dans le Cyberspace' (2019) 10 <https://www.defense.gouv.fr/sites/default/files/ministere-armees/Droit%20international%20appliqu%C3%A9%20aux%20op%C3%A9rations%20dans%20le%20cyberespace.pdf> accessed 31 January 2024.

1163 Robert McCorquodale and Penelope Simons, 'Responsibility Beyond Borders: State Responsibility for Extraterritorial Violations by Corporations of International Human Rights Law' (2007) 70 The Modern Law Review 598.

on the basis of customary rules of attribution.[1164] If interference cannot be committed as such by private actors, in fact, the only way in which they might be implicated is as conduits for a sovereign's designs. This may or may not be a fruitful hypothesis factually. The problem is that scenarios of attribution to the state are only as useful as the interference is understood to not be largely the doing of private actors. To impute responsibility to states for interference carried out fundamentally by private actors simply because such actors cannot be found liable in their own name, risks misrepresenting reality.

A state may be liable for the acts of private actors where those act on the 'instructions of, or under the direction or control' of a state.[1165] Cases where orders came from the top will be the easiest, assuming that there is indeed unlawful interference, although when it comes to interference such a scenario is not always very plausible. The involvement of state agents at some level will also make it easier to establish responsibility. 'Effective control' of private actors or acquiescence to their acts may also evidence state involvement, although it is notoriously a high threshold and may be harder to demonstrate. In the case of Confucius Institutes, for example, organic links include supervision by the Office of Chinese Language Council International which includes Chinese government organizations and suggests close ties to senior Chinese Communist Party officials as well as management by consulate and embassy staff.

Nonetheless, if the jurisprudence of the ICJ in *Nicaragua v United States* is still good law, it will prevent easy findings that a state is liable on the basis of effective control, potentially leaving corporation-mediated interference in a grey zone. This is especially so given that 'a State may operate strategically to evade the relevant standards of attribution, for example by ensuring that non-State actors do not, actually, act under its "effective control"'.[1166] It has been suggested that, when it comes to cyber operations, three standards of attribution coexist in Article 8 of the ILC's Articles on state Responsibility, including 'instructions, direction and control'.[1167] These might be combined. One possibility is that the relatively strict criteria of attribution for state responsibility are too demanding for the purposes of merely developing broader policies of protection against interference. *Sui generis* standards may need to be

1164 ILC 'Draft Articles on Responsibility of States for Internationally Wrongful Acts—With Commentaries' (2001) Yearbook of the ILC, vol 2, Part 2.

1165 ibid, art 8.

1166 Sander (n 390) 28.

1167 Kubo Mačák, 'Decoding Article 8 of the International Law Commission's Articles on State Responsibility: Attribution of Cyber Operations by Non-State Actors' (2016) 21 Journal of Conflict & Security Law 405, 405.

developed by states domestically that involve risk assessment much more than hard rules of attribution.

This suggests that the international law of interference may require not only the application but the reimagining of international standards, for example to include forms of complicity with private interference, in the form for example of a 'knowing and causal contribution'.[1168] In the context of Huawei, for example, the question is for all intents and purposes not so much whether its actions are imputable to China as a state but a complex understanding of the dependency of Huawei vis-à-vis the Chinese government, the fact that it is bound by Chinese law and that it could not, if pushed, refuse to disclose confidential information to it. This is considered by some Western states to pose an undue risk in terms of interference, but not in terms of strict attribution to China.[1169] On some level, taking into account risk is a perfectly legitimate pursuit for states, so long as it does not violate the letter or the spirit of countervailing obligations in international law (e.g., trade). At any rate, one cannot simply redraft the secondary rules of state responsibility to address a glitch in the operation of primary rules of non-intervention.[1170]

Note that the debate stands to be enriched and complicated by reading it through the exigencies of human rights, whatever classical international law may have to say on the matter. One challenge will be to not unduly attribute responsibility to states merely because of political support for certain independent actors, in ways that might then be replicated across situations and foster an exaggerated sense of the proximity of states and NGOs for example. In that respect, arguments focused on Russian interference in Western elections may neglect how they may unwittingly furnish tools for Russia to then protest support for human rights organization as itself a form of interference. Human Rights Watch (HRW) is funded by the U.S., and one may even think that it steers a course that is objectively too close to U.S. interests, but that does not mean that HRW campaigns abroad can be traced back to the U.S. as a state. Similarly, support for foreign local NGOs should not be considered per se to constitute interference. For example, the fact that the U.S. threatened to withhold 1.3 billion dollars in military assistance to Egypt as a result of its crackdown against civil society[1171] cannot in and of itself be seen as an endorsement

1168 Lanovoy (n 1154) 585.

1169 Moore (n 714).

1170 For that criticism, see Ilias Plakokefalos, 'The Use of Force by Non-State Actors and the Limits of Attribution of Conduct: A Reply to Vladyslav Lanovoy' (2017) 28 European Journal of International Law 587.

1171 Michael R Gordon and Mark Landler, 'In Crackdown Response, U.S. Temporarily Freezes Some Military Aid to Egypt' *The New York Times* (19 October 2018)

of the particular actions or positions of such NGOs that would further justify Egypt in its crackdown.

One possibility in this context is to nonetheless double down on the notion that even if a state has no direct or deliberate role in the interference orchestrated by a private actor, it does have a residual responsibility merely as a result of that actor operating from its territory. One standard, endorsed by the 2015 GGE Report, is that 'States must not use proxies to commit internationally wrongful acts using ICTs, and should seek to ensure that their territory is not used by non-State actors to commit such acts'.[1172] 'Proxies', is not a term of art in international law and it would seem to be much less demanding than the ordinary standards of attribution. It is true that the idea that states have a general duty not to act in such a way as to cause harm to other states from their territory is well established under international law, albeit in relation to existing primary obligations rather than a self-standing duty.[1173] This is sometimes considered to give rise to duties of due diligence, notably in the human rights field but also in the area of international peace and security, such that states that are unable or unwilling to control private actors on their territory may incur responsibility.

Something in the order of acquiescence or 'knowingly harboring' by the state, then, may be needed, based on the idea that states should not allow their territory to be used for harmful and unlawful international activities, but one should also be wary of the history of the notion and its inevitable slippages. Wolfgang Friedmann once argued that, in cases of hostile propaganda, it neither could nor should 'make any difference whether the offending broadcasting station is directly government-controlled or operates only by permission of the government' in an age (the Cold War) where certain private means of propaganda were necessarily the extension of a country's psychological warfare effort.[1174] This sort of automatic association of private actors and states seems acutely problematic today, denying as it does the substantial autonomy that private actors have even if they act in ways that are broadly consonant with their states' policies and from its territory. It may be that Western media are broadly aligned ideologically with the states from which they operate, but

<https://www.nytimes.com/2013/10/10/world/middleeast/obama-military-aid-to-egypt.html> accessed 14 February 2019.

1172 UNGA Report on International Security Developments in IT (2015) A/70/174, para 28(e).

1173 Beatrice Walton, 'Duties Owed: Low-Intensity Cyber Attacks and Liability for Transboundary Torts in International Law' (2017) 126 The Yale Law Journal 1460, 1496.

1174 W Friedmann, 'Some Impacts of Social Organization on International Law' (1956) 50 The American Journal of International Law 475, 500.

this does not mean that they merely parrot the 'party line', let alone that they are mere instruments of those states.

In the context of foreign fighters, it has been argued that 'States of origin that knowingly tolerate the departure of their nationals or habitual residents from their territory in order to participate in a foreign a conflict zone without destination-State consent commit an international wrong, so long as they possess the capacity to prevent or impede those departures'.[1175] This at least points to an obligation to prevent departure of foreign fighters when such a departure could be interpreted as intervention, especially when it occurs with the knowledge and acquiescence of the state of origin. It is arguable that during the Spanish Civil War, states' collective attempt to mitigate the problem of foreign fighters, notably through the Non-Intervention Committee, reflected an *opinio juris* to the effect that there was such an obligation. The obligation also arguably extends to repatriation as a way of retrospectively curtailing the problem of foreign fighters. In that vein, the Dayton accords required the withdrawal of all foreign fighters from Bosnia after the war.[1176]

Whether a duty of due diligence extends to reining in the acts of private actors alleged to have interfered nonetheless remains an open question, especially if such actors cannot in and of themselves be engaged in the proscribed conduct because the primary rule does not apply to them (i.e., if one considers that private actors cannot, strictly speaking, interfere in the affairs of a sovereign state). There is also a very real risk of slippage in making states liable for episodes of interference to which they have a relatively tenuous link through excessive amalgamation. It may be that a leading human rights NGO and the state within which it is incorporated have broadly consonant views when it comes to the human rights situation in another state (as one Chinese publication put it, 'Is Human Rights Watch an impartial NGO or a U.S. post-Cold War zombie?'),[1177] but that does not mean that there is no light of day between the two, and congruence of views does not mean control. Similarly, although foreign fighters are certainly nationals of their home states, it seems improbable that host states would have onerous duties or the capacity to rein in such traveling abroad by their nationals if it is largely voluntary. In fact, in recognition of

---

1175 Benjamin R Farley, 'Regulating the Foreign Fighter Problem' (2023) 64 Virginia Journal of International Law 69, 101.

1176 The General Framework Agreement for Peace in Bosnia and Herzegovina, Annex 1-A Agreement on the Military Aspects of the Peace Settlement, art 3(2) (14 December 1995).

1177 'GT Investigates: Is Human Rights Watch an Impartial NGO or a U.S. Post-Cold War Zombie?' [2021] *Global Times* <https://www.globaltimes.cn/page/202103/1216969.shtml> accessed 27 April 2024.

such limitations, Article 6 of Hague Convention (V) long anticipated that '[t]he responsibility of a neutral Power is not engaged by the fact of persons crossing the frontier separately to offer their services to one of the belligerents'.[1178]

Interestingly, although the question in international law, for the purposes of establishing state responsibility, is one of attribution, the question of the link between public and private actors can arise from different legal angles. The RT France case before the ECJ is relevant as an exploration of the links between that TV channel and Russia as a state. The point of that exploration was not to determine whether the acts of RT France were imputable to Russia in the sense of international law, but the closely related issue of whether RT France was rightly considered by the Council as 'media outlet under the permanent direct or indirect control of the leadership of the Russian Federation'.[1179] In finding that the Council had rightly come to the conclusion that it was indeed a mere propaganda organ for the Russian government, the Court pointed out that its capital belonged entirely to the Russian law association TV Novosty 'which is, in essence, entirely funded by the budget of the Russian State'. Even more damningly, it was largely acknowledged by the RT group itself that it was a:

> Russian State news outlet, 'an international channel representing the country', whose mission is, in particular, to build up a large audience beginning with the countries where its channels are operational and to be used, at crucial moments, for example in time of war, as an 'information arm' against the Western world.[1180]

This meant that the RT Group was not that different 'in essence, [from] the Russian Defence Ministry',[1181] and declarations of President Putin himself suggested that there was no daylight between the channel and the Russian state. Again, and to be clear, the question was not one of attribution but the reasoning proposed by the ECJ in this case does provide an interesting sense of how proximity between states and notionally independent actors might be construed to detect interference.

It may be worth heeding in passing the risk that, in seeking to strongly attribute the acts of corporations to the failures of their states, international law

---

1178 Hague Convention (V) Respecting the Rights and Duties of Neutral Powers and Persons in Case of War on Land (adopted 18 October 1907, entered into force 26 January 1910) 2 AJIL Supp 117, art 6.

1179 *RT France case* (n 938), para 171.

1180 ibid, para 172.

1181 ibid.

would contribute to reshaping states' domestic rapport to their own private sector. This could count as a perverse sui generis constitutional and human rights effect of trying to deal with interference. Certainly, a strong model of state responsibility for the acts of private actors might lead states, all other things being equal, to pre-empt that risk by asserting further control over said actors.[1182] The risk is that one will broadly enable that which many states are only too willing to do, namely to control civil society. Friedmann's extremely broad notion of state responsibility seemed to reflect a vision of an almost organic link between the state and private actors which would have extended international responsibility far beyond what is typically anticipated by essentially incorporating private actors into the sovereign.

What may be justifiable under a capacious model of state responsibility could thus have negative domestic constitutional ramifications, essentially justifying greater control of bodies which we have reason to think should retain their independence. There is also a very real risk that states will effectively be required to do other states' bidding, controlling their NGOs, corporations and even individuals for no other reason than to not incur the displeasure of third states who believe they are being interfered with. To rein in one's private actors, in that context, is to implicitly concede they had a point. In effect, many host states have actively refused to accede to foreign demands to discipline private actors on their territory, sometimes for bad but sometimes also for good reasons. In an extreme scenario, complaints about interference and attendant demands to better control private actors could itself become a form of interference, extending neo-authoritarian agendas to other states.

But this is, in a sense, the relatively easier problem, a way of subsuming all private acts under a capacious conception of state control. What, by contrast, of actors involved in interfering from outside that are, at least for the sake of discussion, truly private and independent and not more or less directly an extension of the state? International law often seems to remain wedded to the idea that 'there must surely be a state responsible somewhere' in a global environment where non-state actors, whether they be NGOs or corporations, have long developed agendas of their own that they are perfectly capable of implementing without the instigation of any particular sovereign power. It may, of course, be that there is a sinister foreign power lurking behind an interference operation, perhaps using a shell company or a so-called GONGO; but it may also be that this company or NGO is not a shell and, in fact, very much capable

1182 The possibility that anti-subversion or anti-propaganda treaties would have implications for the domestic law of ratifying states has long anticipated. Friedmann, *The Changing Structure of International Law* (n 21) 273.

of its own political agency and volition. Focusing on a hypothetical and elusive sovereign origin of interference, as the international law of intervention/interference seems wont to do, may direct responses in an outdated and misleading direction.[1183]

3.3 *Beyond Attribution?*

The challenge, ultimately, is that it is not inconceivable, under a 'new interference' model, that private actors—international political entrepreneurs of sorts—would launch attempts to influence foreign policies more or less out of their own initiative. For example, the larger-than-life role played by multi-billionaire Elon Musk in granting Ukrainians key access to the Starlink internet network and then withdrawing it[1184] or of ingratiating himself to authoritarian rulers through Twitter support to obtain certain industrial concessions,[1185] suggest the temptation of exercising such a leverage when one has it, even independently ofU.S. foreign policy. Some private and independent groups may today have as much capacity for interference as certain governments. For those, traditional standards of attributability based on a principal-agent relationship, especially as stereotypical one as effective control, may be difficult to establish, conceptually beside the point and even jurisprudentially misleading. The suggestion that more attention should be paid, beyond theories of de facto organs of states or effective control, to the possibility that private actors are performing acts or governmental functions by way of delegation[1186] may fully miss the mark: clearly Elon Musk is not engaging in interference for the benefit of the U.S., but for his own private interest.

At any rate, the elephant in the room is the extent to which private actors have the ability to and the duty to refrain from interference in their own right. The insistence on state responsibility does not necessarily exclude a residual

1183 Dov H Levin, 'The FEC Is Allowing "Foreign Entities" to Donate to U.S. Referendum Campaigns: That's a Problem' *The Washington Post* (19 November 2021) <https://www.washingtonpost.com/politics/2021/11/19/fec-is-allowing-foreign-entities-donate-us-referendum-campaigns-thats-problem/> accessed 7 September 2023.

1184 Victoria Kim, 'Elon Musk Acknowledges Withholding Satellite Service to Thwart Ukrainian Attack' *The New York Times* (8 September 2023) <https://www.nytimes.com/2023/09/08/world/europe/elon-musk-starlink-ukraine.html> accessed 27 April 2024.

1185 Ryan Mac, Jack Nicas and Alex Travelli, 'Elon Musk's Diplomacy: Woo Right-Wing World Leaders. Then Benefit' *The New York Times* (12 May 2024) <https://www.nytimes.com/2024/05/12/technology/elon-musk-world-leaders.html> accessed 13 June 2024.

1186 Constantine Antonopoulos, 'State Responsibility for Acts of Non-State Actors' in Photini Pazartzis and Panos Merkouris (eds), *Permutations of Responsibility in International Law* (Brill Nijhoff 2019).

obligation, if need be mediated by domestic law, on private actors. As has been suggested, although 'the obligation of non-intervention binds only the official organs of a State', it is also the case that 'the mass media, as well as non-governmental international and national organizations, have less strict obligations'.[1187] There remains the possibility that even though interference by private actors is not strictly a violation of the rule of non-intervention, it is generally considered inimical to host sovereignty and the object of specific prohibitions and protective measures, if nothing else under domestic, particularly constitutional, law. Of course, a Faustian bargain has long been in the works here, that of endowing non-state actors with more international subjectivity and respectability than, all things considered, might be thought wise on the basis of international law. A move to affirm that non-state actors can intervene or interfere is also one that, in the process of attempting to regulate them, contributes to elevate them to a quasi-public quality, a move that some are wary of[1188] just as others dismiss it as inconsequential.[1189]

Formalistic niceties aside, states can certainly find it in themselves to deal with asymmetric threats to their sovereignty from within and, if need be, outside international law's specific framing. Although such a move does not particularly need to invoke international law (except to point out that such counter-measures are not prohibited), it may also draw on international law by analogy to build a case that non-state actors are sometimes functionally equivalent to states when it comes to their homegrown interference policies. The blueprint for this can be found, for example, in the international law on the use of force, where even though it is widely acknowledged that non-state actors cannot strictly commit aggression as such, this is not considered to prevent their armed attacks from being repelled in self-defence or something closely akin to it.[1190] And although the consequences of finding a use of force are momentous and potentially perilous for the international legal order (in that use of force in response may be thereby justified), this is at least less of a problem when it comes to mere intervention.

1187 Hannikainen (n 174) 34.

1188 Mary Ellen O'Connell, 'Enhancing the Status of Non-State Actors through a Global War on Terror?' (2005) 43 Columbia Journal of Transnational Law 435; John H Knox, 'Horizontal Human Rights Law' (2008) 102 American Journal of International Law 1.

1189 Dawn Steinhoff, 'Talking to the Enemy: State Legitimacy Concerns with Engaging Non-State Armed Groups Note' (2009) 45 Texas International Law Journal 297; Lee McConnell, 'Assessing the Feasibility of a Business and Human Rights Treaty' (2017) 66 International & Comparative Law Quarterly 143.

1190 Eliav Lieblich, 'Internal Jus Ad Bellum' (2015) 67 Hastings Law Journal 687.

Note also that a phenomenon could be problematic for international law even though it is not clearly illegal under it. For example, the phenomenon of foreign fighters probably does not constitute an intervention or interference stricto sensu given its largely decentralized, private and independent character. As has been pointed out, there is 'a qualitative difference between merely allowing nationals to travel to a conflict zone and a State affirmatively organizing, arming, training, or supplying them with intelligence to facilitate their participation in a foreign armed conflict'.[1191] Yet tolerating such departures might still be considered broadly incompatible with 'friendly relations' and 'good neighborliness'.[1192] States have occasionally—as they did eventually during the Spanish Civil War—sought to proscribe, individually or collectively, their nationals from joining certain conflicts on such grounds.[1193] The new interference may not be strictly illegal as such, but it is a well-documented problem that is bound to give rise to demands that a range of tools be used to tackle it.

One may at any rate consider that a further move to more fully consider non-state actors as capable in their own right of interference is overdue and has, in fact and somewhat ironically, seriously been contemplated before. The debate on the direct applicability of primary rules of international law to non-state groups is a very broad one that cannot be covered here in any detail except insofar as it is impacted by and impacts on overarching conceptions of interference. In order to capture that intuition, one may want to go back to the 1970s and early 80s to the Draft United Nations Code of Conduct on Transnational Corporations, whose 1983 version, a document still steeped in the NIEO ethos, specifically anticipated, albeit in heavily redacted way, that:

> Transnational corporations should/shall not interfere [illegally] in the internal [political] affairs of the countries in which they operate [by resorting to] [They should refrain from any] [subversive and other [illicit] activities [aimed at] undermining the political and social systems in these countries.[1194]

1191 Farley (n 1174) 98.

1192 Marnie Lloydd, 'Retrieving Neutrality Law to Consider Other Foreign Fighters Under International Law', *European Society of International Law Conference Paper Series* (2017) 27.

1193 Nir Arielli, Gabriela A Frei and Inge Van Hulle, 'The Foreign Enlistment Act, International Law, and British Politics, 1819–2014' (2016) 38 The International History Review 636, 637. (pointing out that such laws 'bolster [...] both the domestic and international legal order, especially in the fields of recognition, non-intervention, and neutrality').

1194 U.N. Commission on Transnational Corporations, 'Draft United Nations Code of Conduct on Transnational Corporations' (1983) U.N. Doc E/1983/17/Rev.1, Annex II, para 15.

There is scattered evidence that some states continue to consider that corporations can interfere with their sovereignty in their own right, irrespective of any connection or attribution to a state. For example, Russia has considered the hosting of protest announcements by YouTube during the 2019 election as 'interference in the sovereign affairs of state and also as hostile and hindering to the conduction of democratic elections'.[1195]

It is interesting to note that the more recent shift to the regulation of corporations as a matter of human rights, labor law, or environmental standards, part of a broader move from the critique of corporations as imperial agents to their constitution as human rights actors, has an ambiguous effect on evaluating the potential of corporations as such to interfere with domestic affairs.[1196] On some level, the reinvention of corporations as responsible public actors could be seen as having encouraged them to assume responsibilities in lieu of host states which, in earlier times, would have been readily identified as a form of interference.[1197] Therefore, the shift towards a 'corporate social responsibility' model has multiple effects: regulating corporations but also endowing them with quasi-public functions which suggest that they could, like states, interfere; and yet also endowing their preferences with the imprimatur of international law in ways that may make it seem less like interference.[1198]

On a related note and as a measure of how far the world has come since coming close to prohibiting corporate interference in sovereign affairs as such, there is now serious talk of the problematic character of *host state* interference in the affairs of corporations.[1199] Faced with such unmistakable evolutions on the international stage, the move towards a more *sui generis*, post-attribution model of non-state actor responsibility, especially when it comes to the use of force, is one that has been tentatively made.[1200] One logic might be that if non-state actors are sufficiently subjects of international law to have broad

1195 'Russian Media Agency Complains YouTube Facilitates Protests' *The Associated Press* <https://apnews.com/general-news-bd7d7e67886a46cb8df6b407fc0dcc99> accessed 25 January 2024.

1196 Sarah Joseph and Joanna Kyriakakis, 'From Soft Law to Hard Law in Business and Human Rights and the Challenge of Corporate Power' (2023) 36 Leiden Journal of International Law 335, 338.

1197 Kline (n 362).

1198 Graham Knight and Jackie Smith, 'The Global Compact and Its Critics: Activism, Power Relations, and Corporate Social Responsibility' in Janie Leatherman (ed), *Discipline and Punishment in Global Politics: Illusions of Control* (Palgrave Macmillan 2008).

1199 Natasha Lomas, 'Legislators from Ten Parliaments Put the Squeeze on Facebook' *TechCrunch* (7 November 2019) <https://techcrunch.com/2019/11/07/legislators-from-ten-parliaments-put-the-squeeze-on-facebook/> accessed 19 December 2023.

1200 Lanovoy (n 1154).

humanitarian and human rights obligations, then surely they must be sufficiently subjects of international law for the purposes of interfering and not interfering.

Finally, it is worth noting that, in addition to being potentially agents of interference, corporations have increasingly been enlisted as purported agents of *non-interference* as well, thus further remodelling the public/private divide when it comes to the issue. Corporations have sometimes done so as a result of legal obligation or political pressure. For example, major Silicon Valley companies such as Alphabet, Reddit, Telegram, Meta, TikTok, and Twitter have been urged to 'assume a heightened posture towards exploitation of [their platform] by Russia and Russian-linked entities engaged in information operations'.[1201] As Senator Mark R Warner put it, corporations should, among other things, '[d]evote additional resources towards the identification of inauthentic accounts, and the removal or labeling of inauthentic content, associated with Russian influence operations'.[1202] Particularly in the E.U., the pressure is on hosts and content providers to minimize the risk of serving as a conduit for interference, for example by promptly informing public authorities of alleged illegal activities.[1203]

The enlisting of corporations as suppletive for the purposes of policing interference has yielded ambiguous results. On the one hand, it can be seen as prolonging state authority in cyberspace; on the other hand, it can appear as little more than a renouncement of state authority, entrusting its defences to front line private actors. Indeed, even outside such political pressure, corporations have increasingly engaged, presumably for their own purposes, in policing of the sort of semi-private semi-public sphere their activities have spun. For example, Facebook routinely removes accounts connected to Russian or Iranian troll farms. This also leaves space for hybrid forms of regulation of non-interference.

1201 Mark R Warner, 'Letter from Senator Mark Warner (VA) to Sundar Pichai, CEO of Alphabet Inc' (25 February 2022) <https://www.warner.senate.gov/public/_cache/files/4/a/4a3293e2-b07c-49fe-b052-3b3733ee586b/598A05F2F5B91764B6652B9ED516AD3B.google-final.pdf> accessed 1 February 2024. For copies of the letter sent to Meta, Reddit, Telegram, TikTok and Twitter see 'Warner Urges CEOs of Major Tech Companies to Take Actions to Curb Russian Information Operations' <https://www.warner.senate.gov/public/index.cfm/2022/2/warner-urges-ceos-of-major-tech-companies-to-take-actions-to-curb-russian-information-operations> accessed 17 December 2023.

1202 Warner (n 1200).

1203 European Parliament and Council Directive 2000/31/EC on certain legal aspects of information society services, in particular electronic commerce in the Internal Market [2000] OJ L178/1 ('Directive on electronic commerce'), art 15.

The 2022 Strengthened Code of Practice on Disinformation[1204] was adopted by major online platforms based on the European Commission's Guidance.[1205] Tik Tok, faced with aU.S. ban, has been eager to shore up its credentials as a self-policing and responsible corporate actor[1206] that can continue to exist whilst offering reassurances that it will not be exploited by ill-intentioned foreign forces.[1207] Corporations are keen to self-regulate, possibly because they see a trade off as against the risk of being regulated.

Reporting requirements remain difficult to enforce, however,[1208] and the diversity of actors involved can lead to a plethora of regulatory approaches.[1209] Many commitments, such as those under the Code of Practice on Disinformation, are voluntary, despite attempts to monitor them, and many digital actors are not party to them (Apple, Amazon, Telegram, etc.). Efforts at further monitoring private actors such as those suggested as part of the European Commission's proposal for a European Media Freedom Act, including the idea of a 'structured dialogue between platforms and the media sector to monitor platforms' compliance with self-regulatory initiatives',[1210] need to tread carefully lest they end up justifying intrusions to media independence. At the same time, private actors have occasionally bemoaned the fact that they are not up to the task on their own and need the support of states in dealing with interference.[1211] There have also been calls to include leading online

1204 '2022 Strengthened Code of Practice on Disinformation' (*European Commission*, 16 June 2022) <https://digital-strategy.ec.europa.eu/en/library/2022-strengthened-code-practice-disinformation> accessed 1 February 2024.

1205 European Commission, 'Guidance on Strengthening the Code of Practice on Disinformation', COM (2021) 262 final.

1206 Hadero Haleluya, 'TikTok Removes Russian State Media Accounts for "covert Influence Operations" Ahead of U.S. Election' [2024] AP News <https://apnews.com/article/tiktok-russia-media-election-interference-abd51ba03af439cf272888556f424d38> accessed 24 September 2024.

1207 Sapna Maheshwari, 'TikTok Lays Out Past Efforts to Address U.S. Concerns' *The New York Times* (20 June 2024) <https://www.nytimes.com/2024/06/20/business/media/tiktok-ban-biden.html> accessed 24 September 2024.

1208 Shannon C McGregor, Bridget Barrett and Daniel Kreiss, 'Questionably Legal: Digital Politics and Foreign Propaganda' (2022) 19 Journal of Information Technology & Politics 1.

1209 Kara Swisher, 'Google Changed Its Political Ad Policy. Will Facebook Be Next?' *The New York Times* (22 November 2019) <https://www.nytimes.com/2019/11/22/opinion/google-political-ads.html> accessed 19 December 2023.

1210 2023 Resolution on Foreign Interference in the E.U. (n 335), para 36.

1211 Salvador Rodriguez, 'Mark Zuckerberg: We Can't Stop Russian Election Interference by Ourselves, U.S. Government Must Help' *CNBC* (26 June 2019) <https://www.cnbc.com/2019/06/26/facebook-ceo-zuckerberg-slams-weak-us-response-to-russian-interference.html> accessed 17 December 2023. ('As a private company we don't have the tools to

media companies in any international drafting exercise in a context where 'the development of workable rules for the problem of the post-truth information ecosystem online can hardly be successful without taking into account the positions of private media companies as natural stakeholders'.[1212]

The problem is that the framework within which such regulation should occur is often obscure. In some cases, corporate actors have pushed back strongly against the notion that it is their job at all to police political conversations and be an arbiter of free speech.[1213] But corporate actors do end up, in part whilst dealing with the problem of foreign interference, regulating free speech or at least having significant influence on its exercise. They thus immerse themselves in the regulation of the public sphere through private means, in the name of an international phenomenon. They also do so in often unaccountable ways that have little patience for the sort of intricate human rights analysis that is typically required of states. Moreover, they find themselves entrusted with fiduciary obligations for the sake of something other (a polity, a democracy) than the corporate space that falls most evidently within their competency. Finally, they do so extra-territorially and with only indirect responsiveness to the polities whose democratic operations they affect (hence the European Parliament 'regret[ting] the fact that the E.U. is dependent on non-EU companies to help preserve the integrity of European elections',[1214] but the concern also feeds into the fear of e-colonialism).

Indeed, the very suggestion that deeply flawed corporate actors[1215] with their own political agendas should assume such a role has been lambasted by outside commentators as a dereliction of democratic duties.[1216] The corporatization and out-sourcing of non-interference create a world in which, paradoxically, interference has never been harder to pin down. The enrolment or volunteering of corporate actors in resisting foreign interference (itself, of

make the Russian government stop. We can defend as best as we can, but our government is the one that has the tools to apply pressure to Russia, not us').

1212 Lahmann (n 322) 220.

1213 Cecilia Kang and Mike Isaac, 'Defiant Zuckerberg Says Facebook Won't Police Political Speech' *The New York Times* (17 October 2019) <https://www.nytimes.com/2019/10/17/business/zuckerberg-facebook-free-speech.html> accessed 19 December 2023.

1214 2023 Resolution on Foreign Interference in the E.U. (n 335), para 44.

1215 Adrienne LaFrance, 'The Largest Autocracy on Earth' [2021] *The Atlantic* <https://www.theatlantic.com/magazine/archive/2021/11/facebook-authoritarian-hostile-foreign-power/620168/> accessed 19 December 2023.

1216 Natasha Tusikov and Blayne Haggart, 'Stop Outsourcing the Regulation of Hate Speech to Social Media' *The Conversation* (28 March 2019) <https://phys.org/news/2019-03-outsourcing-speech-social-media.html> accessed 19 December 2023.

course, increasingly privatized) can quickly become part of how that interference is perpetuated and prolonged—a case, perhaps, of the proverbial fox guarding the henhouse. As a result of such movements, it is at least an open question whether major digital corporate actors are merely doing states' bidding in seeking to protect the public sphere, or creating a transnational private sphere of their own, where basic freedoms may or may not be guaranteed, but where there should be increasingly little doubt as to who reigns supreme and, quite possibly, sovereign.

4 Unilateral/Supranational

A final area of confusion concerns the possibly redeeming nature of the international motives or values inspiring a *prima facie* interference. The scenario is one of behavior that is beyond the de minimis range of mere influence but that is saved by what it at least ostensibly or objectively pursues.[1217] In other words, collective values reappear not, as previously seen, as objectively shrinking the scope of the *domaine réservé*, but as providing a justification for intervention or interference based on some overriding authority. Just as international law normally militates against intervention or interference it can, on account of the very same international values, licence forms of intervention or interference. An obvious example here is the Vienna Convention on the Diplomatic and Consular Relations: evidently it cannot be interference to do that which is explicitly anticipated by that treaty, so long as one operates indeed within its perimeters. Similar action by persons who are not accredited diplomats might well be interference but it is not as long as it emanates from embassy staff. It is on that basis, for example, that China has defended itself, not implausibly, against accusations of interference by its consulates.[1218]

But the debate on the potentially habilitative nature of international law when it comes to intervention is potentially much broader as well as, it should

1217 For examples of that discursive strategy see William S Maddox, 'The Comprehensive Anti-Apartheid Act: A Case Study in the Legality of Economic Sanctions Note' (1987) 44 Washington and Lee Law Review 1415; Winston P Nagan, 'Economic Sanctions, U.S. Foreign Policy, International Law and the Anti-Apartheid Act of 1986' (1988) 4 Florida International Law Journal 85.

1218 'Remarks of the Spokesperson of the Chinese Consulate General in Vancouver on Some Canadian Politicians and Media's Accusations of "Interference" by China in Canadian Elections_Consulate-General of the People's Republic of China in Vancouver' <http://vancouver.china-consulate.gov.cn/eng/news/202303/t20230317_11043375.htm> accessed 23 September 2024.

be said, hazardous. It has long precipitated a debate on 'counter-intervention intervention', for example in relation to U.S. support to El Salvador against Nicaraguan support for a rebellion there. This is on some level logical: just as the use of force is prohibited only insofar as it is used to fight back against an illegal use of force, one may argue, by analogy, intervention to push back against intervention by another state may be justified under international law. John Stuart Mill long ago added the caveat, in his well-known defense of non-intervention, that 'intervention to enforce non-intervention is always rightful, if not always moral'.[1219] During the Cold War, both the USSR and the U.S. invoked the risk of intervention to intervene. Whether in Afghanistan or Nicaragua, this was on the basis of the dubious theory that even if 'an initial intervention is unlawful [...] once an unlawful initial intervention happens on either side, another power had the right to come in and take countermeasures to repel the first intervention and "even things up"'.[1220] Indeed it has been said that 'virtually all the interventions that occur today are carried out in the name of non-intervention; they are justified as responses to prior interventions by the other side'.[1221]

This sort of intuition harks back to the Spanish civil war, in particular, where France's (and eventually the U.K.'s) commitment to non-intervention in the face of Fascist support of General Franco had had the disastrous effect of depriving the Republicans of assistance[1222] and has subsequently been interpreted as an inept form of appeasement. One of the lessons of that episode is that there is something profoundly destabilizing about a situation in which some states play by the rules and desist from an intervention they might otherwise be tempted to engage in whilst others seize the advantage to further destabilize a situation. In effect and in that case '"non-intervention" was clearly a species of intervention'.[1223] Before long the argument can be (as it was when the U.S. alleged that Nicaragua was itself interfering in the affairs of El Salvador)[1224] that states need to and even must intervene in some states precisely to prevent others from doing so, as part of a praxis of counter-intervention.[1225] Such practices, which have their root in the Roosevelt Corollary, were in fact rife during the

1219 Mill (n 909).
1220 Rogers and others (n 159) 568.
1221 Schachter (n 569) 160.
1222 Norman J Padelford, 'The International Non-Intervention Agreement and the Spanish Civil War' (1937) 31 American Journal of International Law 578.
1223 Friedmann, 'Intervention and the Developing Countries' (n 406) 207.
1224 *Nicaragua v United States* (n 3) [186].
1225 Falk, *Legal Order in a Violent World* (n 117) 163. ('The interventionary context once established invites other states to counterintervene, at least to an offsetting degree'). Falk

Cold War and were, it was sometimes argued, compatible with international law and even a manifestation of international legal *noblesse oblige*.[1226] There is, it has been argued, a 'right of counterintervention'.[1227]

It is conceivable that intervention can theoretically compensate for intervention. Evidently, once a path to self-determination has been lastingly compromised by some exogenous interference then it stands to reason that some countervailing push might contribute to restoring conditions where a nation can chart its own course anew. But it is equally clear that every counter-intervention can quickly degenerate into an intervention of its own, in a context where it will not always be clear when the effects of the initial intervention have been offset. The counter-intervention may then come with a debt of gratitude to the intervener and produce its own distortions. Moreover, dosing such matters can quickly degenerate into a free for all where virtually no intervention is ever illegal since it can always invoke some antecedent intervention. Especially when use of force is at stake, counter-intervention has the potential to eviscerate the prohibition of non-intervention. This was quite evident in the obtuse invocation of counter-intervention as a motif by Russia to justify the invasion of Ukraine in response to the negotiation of an accession agreement with the European Union. There is more than a hint in the logic of foreign powers seeking to concurrently cancel out each other's interventions, in fact, of the old idea of the balance of power[1228] and the way it effectively nullified the sovereignty of affected countries. In an effort to curtail the expansive register of countermeasures against intervention, the ICJ made it clear in Nicaragua v. U.S. that the norm of non-intervention itself did not have *erga omnes* status. This meant that the U.S. could not adopt measures, including measures themselves having an interventionist character, to counter Nicaragua's own interference in El Salvador.[1229]

Translating that language into the practice of contemporary interference can further muddy the waters as it will often not even be clear who is interfering in the first place and for what purpose. This increases the risk of a tit-for-tat that loosely borrows the language of counter-intervention but in ways that fundamentally further free up the possibilities of intervention, with potentially

---

characterizes 'a unilateral determination to follow a policy of nonintervention equivalent to default'. ibid 167.

1226 Lloyd N Cutler, 'The Right to Intervene' (1985) 64 Foreign Affairs 96, 106–107.

1227 John A Perkins, 'The Right of Counterintervention' (1987) 17 Georgia Journal of International & Comparative Law 171.

1228 ibid s II.

1229 *Nicaragua v United States* (n 3) para 127.

very destructive repercussions for the international legal order. This may explain why a distinct move has been to seek more objectifiable and multilateral validations to justify what might otherwise be described as intervention or interference. Counter-intervention can be sublimated through appeal to collective values, cloaked in the language of counter-measures to enforce international law for example, and further 'legalized' through appeal to such criteria as necessity and proportionality.[1230] This basic deferral to community interests then provides some pointers to determine when what might seem to a priori constitute intervention or interference can be salvaged as something else. Evidently, for example, 'intervention' in times of war as part of the exercise of legitimate self-defence is entirely absorbed by the latter to the point of ceasing to even raise issues usefully treated under an intervention framework.

The debate on counter-intervention is more likely today to be based on the language of countermeasures, as they have been codified by the ILC in Article 22 of the Articles on State Responsibility, which are a recognized modality of enforcement of international law. Not all measures adopted as countermeasures to intervention are likely to themselves be described as intervention, but some clearly are (for example, unilateral economic sanctions) and, at any rate, the question remains as to whether countermeasures adopted on any other ground qualify independently as intervention. The international law of counter-measures, contested and vague as it is, does provide an a priori potentially useful conduit to justify behavior that would otherwise be illegal. As early as the discussion of the Friendly Relations Declaration, the possibility that responses by states to violation of their rights would not constitute intervention (even if on their face they otherwise had all the hallmarks of one) was mooted.[1231] More recently, the Tallin manual 2.0 signals at the possibility of countermeasures against cybernetic attacks.[1232] This requires that one prove that such attacks are themselves an illicit act and that measures are deployed as a response to it. Unilateral sanctions are also sometimes justified as lawful countermeasures against violations of international law by the target state. This is especially so when the norms violated are norms *erga omnes* and that third states can claim that they have not only the right to adopt such measure but the obligation to do so—and therefore cannot possibly be engaging in intervention/interference in the process.

1230 Perkins (n 1226).

1231 Zemanek (n 407) 969.

1232 Jakub Spáčil, 'Countermeasures against Cyber Operations: Moving Forward?' (2023) 23 International and Comparative Law Review 86.

But the international law of countermeasures also comes with significant limitations as a conceptual framework. It requires either a finding that the interfering state's rights have been violated or, even more contentiously, that the norms in questions are *erga omnes* and that unilateral measures by third states are an appropriate way to respond to them. In the latter case, the non-forcible character of measures adopted as countermeasures will at least assuage concerns that the prohibition on the use of force is being violated. Notwithstanding, concerns that intervention is a form of meddling on merely pretextual grounds will, rightly or wrongly, be at their highest point. A review of practice in 2020 suggested that there was as yet no case of responses to such attacks being specifically justified as countermeasures.[1233] Framing an intervention, especially a forceful one or one involving military assistance to rebels, as a counter-measure has not proved a very compelling argument. For example, although the notion that non-lethal assistance to Syrian rebels was a counter-measure has been mooted, it is unclear what obligation to outside states was violated by the Syrian government that would allow the former to support a rebellion against the latter under this banner.[1234] There are also well known general concerns with the doctrine of counter-measures including the risk of violence that are only likely to be magnified as the notion is being banded around as a plausible way of dealing with an initial interference.[1235] In conformity with Article 50 of the Articles, at any rate, any counter-measure could not violate the prohibition on the use of force or affect human rights.

There has long been a suspicion, especially in the Third World, that countermeasures is not only an unwieldy tool and a potential recipe for chaos, but one highly likely to be instrumentalized to justify the unjustifiable intervention of powerful states.[1236] So pronounced is the wariness with intervention that Special Rapporteur James Crawford had suggested in his report to the ILC the insertion of a 'provision to the effect that countermeasures may not endanger the territorial integrity *or amount to intervention in the domestic jurisdiction of the target State*'.[1237] In other words, countermeasures ultimately may not even be capable, whatever their motivation or proportionality, of ever

1233 Juan Jorge Piernas Lopez, 'Self-Help Measures against Cyber Threats in International Law: Special Reference to the Possible Adoption of Collective Countermeasures Estudios' (2024) 16 Cuadernos de Derecho Transnacional 10.

1234 Schmitt, 'Legitimacy versus Legality Redux: Arming the Syrian Rebels' (n 920) 155–156.

1235 Van De Velde (n 500).

1236 Martin Dawidowicz, *Third-Party Countermeasures in International Law* (Cambridge University Press 2017) 293–294.

1237 Third report on State responsibility, by Mr. James Crawford, Special Rapporteur, A/CN.4/507, para. 354. Author's emphasis.

justifying what is otherwise an intervention. Crawford cited to that effect the provision in the Friendly Relations Declaration that '[n]o State [...] has the right to intervene, directly or indirectly, *for any reason whatever*, in the internal or external affairs of any other State'.[1238] In a similar vein and on the first reading of the Articles, Arangio-Ruiz had suggested, albeit unsuccessfully, that an injured State could not resort by way of countermeasures to 'extreme economic or political coercion designed to endanger the territorial integrity or political independence of the State which has committed the internationally wrongful act'.[1239]

Precisely, however, this begs the question of what is an intervention in the first place. Crawford was keen to emphasize that, notwithstanding the fact that countermeasures could not be a mere 'excuse' for intervention, a State's obligation to comply 'with its international obligations of cessation and reparation is not a matter of its domestic jurisdiction'.[1240] A better argument, then, is that higher motives do not so much justify what is otherwise illegal, as in the international law of countermeasures but, as the case may be, remove the initial sting of illegality altogether from the measures imposed. The licencing of interference under international law relates to behavior being broadly justified *as legal in the first place*, on the basis of its concurring to the defense and promotion of certain international norms rather than as a countermeasure. This moves the debate beyond the quite formalistic regime of state responsibility and countermeasures (required when seeking to justify what is presumptively illegal), to one in which international legal discourse is deployed to preemptively neutralize claims about interference. For example, when a state defends itself against claims of interference as a result of funding, say, a human rights NGO in a foreign country, it is unlikely to be claiming that such funding is a legal countermeasure following a breach of human rights by that country, and much more likely to simply claim that such funding is largely justified under international human rights law to begin with.

4.1 *Foundations for the Permissibility of Internationally Justified Interference*

A first litmus test of whether certain behavior amounts to interference or not, is whether it is unilateral or emanates from the international community, i.e.: that it proceeds with multilateral authority. This was long evident in early debates on a 'droit d'intervention', with one late 19th Century Belgium

---

1238 Id, author's emphasis.

1239 Arangio-Ruiz, Third Report (n 1226), paras. 101–102.

1240 Third Report (n 1226), para. 354.

internationalist noting that 'un Etat isolé ne peut pas s'arroger le droit d'intervention; ce droit ne peut être exercé qu'au nom de l'humanité représentée par tous les autres Etats, ou tout au moins par le plus grand nombre des Etats civilisés, qui doivent se réunir en congrès ou U.N. tribunal pour prendre une décision collective'.[1241] As Richard Bilder would point out much later:

> It seems clearly more legitimate and less threatening to international community interests for global international organizations, such as the United Nations, for broad-based regional organizations, such as the Organization of American States, to use economic coercion than for individual nations or specialized blocs of nations to do so.[1242]

For example, the reinvention of the OAS in the 1950s as a potentially intervening organizations was described by Richard Falk as essentially multilateralizing the Monroe Doctrine to '[reduce], as it were, the likelihood of abuse by removing the interventionary decision from the power and whim of a single state'.[1243] It was later pointed out in the context of sanctions or boycott against Apartheid South Africa that 'the general prohibition against individual economic coercion is lifted when the world community acts collectively under the leadership of a competent U.N. organ', in this case the General Assembly.[1244]

By contrast, unilateral sanctions have long been the object of suspicion (and in some quarters, reviled) as much more likely to constitute intervention, especially, but not only, against the background of certain obligations of continued engagement (as will be examined in chapter 6). To many observers, for example, despite the litany of semi-plausible justifications—including human rights—invoked by the U.S., the economic embargo imposed on Nicaragua smacked of an effort to insist 'on the subordination of Nicaragua's sovereign right to determine Nicaragua's own course of government'.[1245] This wariness with unilateral sanctions is especially pronounced when, adding insult to injury, such sanctions seek to forcefully enlist the cooperation of third states, through

1241 Rolin-Jaequemyns (n 91) 675.

1242 Bilder (n 311) 43.

1243 Falk, *Legal Order in a Violent World* (n 117) 177.

1244 Szasz (n 1123) 316.

1245 Henderson, 'Legality of Economic Sanctions under International Law' (n 1023) 193; Sherrie Lipsky, 'The Legitimacy of Economic Coercion: The Carter Foreign Aid Policy and Nicaragua' (1982) 5 Loyola of Los Angeles International and Comparative Law Review 101.

further sanctions if need be. So-called 'secondary' sanctions that cannot claim to be rooted in some clear multilateral mandate have incurred particular hostility as a sort of doubling down on the original interference.

The argument is, for example, that unilateral U.S. sanctions of E.U. based entities for their trade with Cuba or Iran may well be in violation of WTO obligations[1246] and, indeed, the U.S. eventually granted E.U. Member States a waiver in relation to Iran and suspended part of the Helms-Burton Act as long as the E.U. sought to promote democracy in Cuba.[1247] At the same time, the E.U. sought to protect itself from the continuing potential for interference of such invasive practices.[1248] Not even the national security exception in the WTO seems to countenance unilateral sanctions involving a secondary boycott against third party private individuals and corporations that do not themselves directly endanger national security.[1249] In effect, a secondary boycott, in addition to possibly constituting an interference with the state that is being boycotted, is almost certainly an interference in the affairs of third states unless it is horizontal effect is largely justified by some vertical mandate, e.g.: a Security Council resolution.[1250]

Of course, to the extent that multilateralism does provide the authority for sanctions, this is bound to raise questions anew about the supranational level's legitimacy in initiating intervention. It will bring back memories in which particular groups (the Holy Alliance, the Concert of Europe, colonial powers) have historically decided multilaterally but, unmistakably, for others. As Richard Falk put it, one cannot assume that simply because multilateralization has occurred, the resulting decisions are beyond contest: '[The] preference for authorization, on as broad a basis as possible, does not deny that a given interventionary policy, no matter how collectivized by the relevant community, may on occasion subject the target state to abusive and arbitrary claims'.[1251]

1246 World Trade Organization (WTO), 'United States—The Cuban Liberty and Democratic Solidarity Act: Request for the Establishment of a Panel by the European Communities' (8 October 1996) WT/DS38/2.

1247 'European Union-United States: Memorandum of Understanding Concerning the U.S. Helms-Burton Act and the U.S. Iran and Libya Sanctions Act' (1997) 36 International Legal Materials 529.

1248 Council Regulation (EC) 2271/96 of 22 November 1996 protecting against the effects of the extra-territorial application of legislation [1996] OJ L309/1.

1249 Schmidt (n 655) 73; Timothy Dunning, 'D'Amato in a China Shop: Problems of Extraterritoriality with the Iran and Libya Sanctions Act of 1996' (1998) 19 University of Pennsylvania Journal of International Law 169, 194–195.

1250 Joyner (n 996) 233–234.

1251 Falk, *Legal Order in a Violent World* (n 117) 341.

Moreover, there may be suspicions about the degree to which an authorization is indeed multilateral, in a context where for example even Security Council mandates have been found to raise questions of legitimacy by some states. The question of whether the motive is 'basely' unilateral or 'nobly' multilateral is as much as anything else a question of process, involving consideration of the extent to which multilateral (if only regional) authorization or prior dispute settlement determination were obtained or even reasonably sought and the degree of compatibility of the sanctioning states' motivation with the international rules whose enforcement is invoked.[1252]

Absent any explicit multilateral authorization, states have tended to overcompensate by claiming the authority of international law more broadly to enforce their rights or international law generally through self-help. This is relatively easier when they can be seen as invoking their own interest in the implementation of international law, notably under the banner of counter-measures. In such a scenario, unilateral sanctions are subject to the international law of counter-measures and notably that they be adopted, outside the relatively narrow case of obligations *erga omnes*, by the party that was affected by the breach, lest 'giving states an unfettered ability to defend the rights of others could risk seriously destabilizing the principle of non-intervention'.[1253] Moreover counter-measures are subjected to further requirements of, for example, proportionality.

Chapter 6 will return to the kind of assumptions that underscore the debate over whether such unilateral sanctions are not only illegal but specifically a form of intervention. Suffice it to say here that there is a long tradition, particularly in the Global South, of nonetheless viewing all unilateral sanctions, even when purportedly in defense of international law, with suspicion as merely a way to 'change the political behavior' of target countries that violates, among others, the principle of non-intervention.[1254] The suggestion seems to be that, even if a state's behavior is in violation of international law, it is not the business of other states to intervene in its affairs to correct this. For example, the U.S. embargo on Cuba has long been condemned on the basis of the non-intervention principle.[1255] It has been suggested that even a *prima facie*

1252 Paust and Blaustein (n 1022) 428.

1253 Eliza Fitzgerald, 'Helping States Help Themselves: Rethinking the Doctrine of Countermeasures.' (2016) 16 Macquarie Law Journal 67, 96.

1254 Asian-African Legal Consultative Organization (AALCO), 'Unilateral and Secondary Sanctions: An International Law Perspective (Executive Summary)' <https://www.aalco.int/52ndsession/EXECUTIVE%20SUMMARY.pdf> accessed 12 July 2024.

1255 Nigel D White, *The Cuban Embargo under International Law: El Bloqueo* (Routledge 2014).

legal countermeasure may be illegal if it is used 'for an illegitimate end, namely an intervention' and notably if 'its coercive force is strong enough to pose a serious threat to the self-determination of the target State with regard to its *domaine réservé*'.[1256]

It is true that states have nonetheless justified unilateral interference by invoking the fundamentally collective nature of the values they are seeking to enforce in the process as essentially trumping any wariness with intervention. Various forms of otherwise unilateral coercion may plausibly claim some degree of international authority either under the specific language of counter-measures (justifying otherwise illegal behavior as legal) or more broadly to deny that there is any illegality in their interference to begin with. In a very imperfect international system, the argument is sometimes made that unilateral enforcement of general international law, a form of juridical self-help or vigilantism, is the only means available, although evidently not to the point of allowing something (e.g., the use of force) that is otherwise illegal. Nonetheless, unilateral countermeasures in the general interest presumptively have a high hurdle to clear especially if they cannot count from the outset on some obvious multilateral institutional mandate and rely exclusively on the authority of international law. The bottom line, is that 'un Etat ne saurait juridiquement exiger d'un autre Etat U.N. comportement actif ou passif ne découlant pas du droit international'[1257]—but that they stand a better chance if violations of international law are involved. In other words, international law provides both the authority for and the limit to unilateral coercive measures.

4.2 *Justifying Interference: From Decolonization to Human Rights*

The idea that measures that might otherwise constitute interference can be redeemed by virtue of their enforcing some kind of international community interest is, beyond the slightly idiosyncratic particulars of the international law of counter-measures, an enduring one, and its provenance is more complex than typically assumed. It was entertained both by the Third World in the decolonization era as a way of justifying assistance to national liberation movements in the name of self-determination (in apparent interference with the sovereignty of the colonizing state) and, after the Cold War, by the West in sustaining a sense that aspiring to promote human rights norms substantially pre-empts the accusation of interference. This has both reinforced the notion

1256 Thomas Giegerich, 'Retorsion', *Max Planck Encyclopedias of International Law* (Oxford University Press 2011) para 24.

1257 Philippe Cahier, *Changements et continuité du droit international: cours général de droit international public*, vol 195 (Brill Nijhoff 1985) 38.

that interference can be legal if in pursuit of collective interests but also rendered it fragile on account of divergences of view about what that collective interest is, and whether it actually allows the form of intervention or interference in question. For example, where Arab states saw the vindication of international law as regards Palestine when it came to the OPEP embargo, others saw the aim of destroying Israel and even anti-Semitism.[1258]

One of the neglected origins of the notion that states can intervene in the affairs of other states on account of some higher community interest is not human rights stricto sensu (at least in their contemporary form), but the 1960s-1970s insistence that the use of coercive measures—the OPEP oil embargo comes to mind—was legitimate when assisting peoples in their decolonial struggles.[1259] On that count, it was claimed that there was certainly nothing inherently untoward about economic reprisals sustained by the highest ideal of promoting the U.N. Charter, a fortiori if actually authorized, even more or less unwittingly, by the U.N. itself. As Ibrahim Shihata put it, '[f]ar from being a "weapon for blackmailing the West" or a "threat to international peace", [the embargo] has been employed as an instrument for the respect and promotion of the rule of law in an area of international relations where such a rule has long been forsaken for the rule of superior military force'.[1260] In fact, 'precluding [weaker states] from the use of their economic power in the settlement of political disputes before a general ban is imposed on armaments and in the absence of an effective collective security system could not serve the interests of international justice'.[1261] In short, the Third World was adamant that coercive economic measures in the name of remedying occupation of Palestinian lands was not interference. Along the same lines, it argued that military support of groups fighting national liberation was legal under international law because of its decolonial agenda.

Whether in relation to the oil embargo or to the South African divestment campaign, or instances of transnational support of national liberation movements, this stance attracted considerable hostility from many Western international lawyers who found themselves very much on the defensive, trying to argue that references by the Third World of community interests, often strongly relying on human rights but in reality heavily focused on a particular understanding of self-determination, were misguided and at counter-purpose. These authors invoked with gusto the very Third World sponsored instruments which

1258 Bilder (n 311) 45.
1259 Shihata (n 310) 617.
1260 ibid 625.
1261 ibid 626.

a few years later the West had found itself consistently opposing. For example, Jordan J Paust and Albert P Blaustein found unequivocally that the use of the 'Arab Oil Weapon' was a threat to the U.N. Charter and bordering on the terroristic.[1262] One will appreciate here the degree of role reversal involved. The Third World was willing to ditch its iron-clad commitment to non-interference in order to justify its policies against Israel; and the West was willing to forsake its tolerance for interference, when it was the one vulnerable to it. To top up the irony, today exactly the opposite argument is being made by each 'side', with the West arguing that unilateral coercive measures in defense of internationally recognized human rights are not interference whilst the Global South insists that they are.

This is not, of course, conclusive of the specifically legal argument involved in each and every case: simply because one invokes self-determination, does not mean that it is in play, that one has any business promoting it from outside, or that it overrides otherwise strong considerations about the impermissibility of intervention/interference. Even at the height of the 1970s, whether and the degree to which states could provide military assistance to national liberation movements, for example, was never settled conclusively generally or in particular cases. More recently, claims that the provision of even non-lethal assistance to moderate Syrian rebels was conducive to Syrian self-determination have been scoffed at even by Western authors.[1263] By the same token, far less controversial forms of assistance that do not raise any prima facie issues of illegality will be solidified, if only rhetorically, by their ability to cast themselves as conducive to self-determination. The idea that assistance to dissident groups, NGOs or political parties is interference, for example, can be readily countered by the appeal to international norms on the relevance of broad and inclusive participation to processes of governance.

The structure of the argument has at any rate remained remarkably stable over time, even as its exact tonality and ideological provenance have changed. Note that the point here is not, as in the previous chapter, that forces have refashioned the *domaine* réservé (although that too happens) but that international norms validate behavior that might otherwise be problematic as encroaching on the *domaine* but is understood as justified and perhaps even mandated by international law (Chapter 5 will return to a specific version of

---

1262 Paust and Blaustein (n 1022) 412.

1263 Tom Ruys, 'Of Arms, Funding and "Non-Lethal Assistance": Issues Surrounding Third-State Intervention in the Syrian Civil War' (2014) 13 Chinese Journal of International Law 13, 34–36; Schmitt, 'Legitimacy versus Legality Redux: Arming the Syrian Rebels' (n 920) s II.e.

this, namely intervention by international organizations themselves). In other words, rather than denying that there is interference at all through shrinkage of the *domaine*, it very much accepts that there is interference but doubles down on its grand justification through international law. That discourse has gradually migrated from a focus on decolonization and the fight against racist regimes to a much broader and all-encompassing concern with cosmopolitan values, notably informed by human rights. That the connection between the two is not a straight line or a natural evolution is a reminder that whilst the structure of the argument remains the same, what ends it is being put to can fundamentally alter the nature of the regime over time.[1264]

This pattern of legitimizing international intervention in the *domaine* through international law is evident, for example, in the rise of international criminal law. The obligation of states to 'respect and ensure respect' of the Geneva Conventions or to 'undertake to prevent and punish' the commission of genocide under the Genocide Convention clearly justify what might otherwise be seen as invasions of the *domaine*. It does so either on the basis of treaty law and the assent that all states parties have given in advance to such 'interference' or even on the basis of customary international law. This is evident in some transnational criminal law discourses as well. Similarly, in the transnational criminal law field, the point of the anti-bribery Convention is that 'traditional principles of respect for state sovereignty have to be abandoned in order to address effectively the problems that arise when public officials fail in their basic function of representing their people with integrity',[1265] at the risk of resurrecting a form of 'imperial anti-corruption law'.[1266] Ultimately, the obligation to criminalize bribery speaks louder than a pro forma proclamation of non-intervention: in effect, states parties (and nothing forces them to become states parties) have *ipso facto* divested themselves of the possibility of arguing that pressuring them to commit to their obligations is a form of intervention and for third states 'fulfilling (their) responsibility appears to inevitable require infringements upon the sovereignty of another state'.[1267]

But it is more broadly the human rights field that has renovated the tenor of the intervention and interference debate, powerfully reshuffling the lines and occasionally confusing the stakes. The discourse of the *erga omnes* character of certain international obligations, in that respect, has further fueled the

---

1264 Riley Case and Mégret (n 252).

1265 Kevin E Davis, *Between Impunity and Imperialism: The Regulation of Transnational Bribery* (Oxford University Press 2019) 202.

1266 ibid 2.

1267 ibid 58.

notion that states can intervene even when their direct interests have not been violated.[1268] By purporting to collectivize the interest, promotion and even enforcement of certain norms, it has provided a powerful trope to discursively justify incursions which might otherwise appear to be dangerously treading the line. The point of human rights obligations in the dominant liberal cosmopolitan vernacular, moreover, is not only that they are inertly *erga omnes* as it were, but that their *erga omnes* character comes with a degree of compulsion: not only that they *can* be enforced by third parties, but that they *should* be enforced by all.[1269] In that respect, references to the *erga omnes* character of certain obligations go hand in hand with the notion that not all coercion is bad (coercion is not 'malum in se'); indeed, that coercion can be a necessary means to implementing imperative international law on behalf of the international community.[1270] A fortiori, non-coercive interference in the promotion of human rights of others has long found the favors of some authors who consider that the ICJ's position in Nicaragua that the U.S. could not simply act as a sort of human rights vigilante was too stringent.[1271] This is because international political activism to promote the rights of other peoples, notably of political participation, need not even be understood as a permissible countermeasure: it is, quite simply, a form of *ipso facto* legal influence, saved as it were by its purpose.[1272]

One of the implicit stakes of that debate has been distinguishing one's practices from that of others' or, in some cases, to show how close a state's practice has, in fact, erred from those it claims to be different from (*tu quoque*). There is both a tactical element involved and a deeper normative dimension, as participants in those debates are led to draw on implicit assumptions about what is right about what they do, and wrong about what others do. One of the most formidable issues that the 'new interference' raises in that respect is the extent to which certain forms of authoritarian interference can be distinguished from efforts to justify interference on human rights grounds—or whether the two are merely the two sides of the same hegemonic coin. President Putin of Russia seemed to relish being accused of interference in the 2016 U.S. elections,

---

1268 Sarah H Cleveland, 'Norm Internalization and U.S. Economic Sanctions' (2001) 26 Yale Journal of International Law 1, 53–56.

1269 Lillich, 'Intervention to Protect Human Rights' (n 447).

1270 Omri Sender, 'Coercion', *Max Planck Encyclopedias of International Law* (Oxford University Press 2022) para 18.

1271 Damrosch (n 16) 39.

1272 ibid 42.

pointing out both that the U.S. constantly did the same on grounds of democracy,[1273] and that the foreign agents law was merely taken from the U.S. itself.[1274] Contra this kind of 'whataboutism', the issue of the difference between 'liberal' and 'illiberal' interference has been debated with renewed vengeance, as Western states seek to portray their own meddling as being of a fundamentally different nature than the sort of incursions they are now subjected to.

Old practices are defended and distinguished from new ones through appeals to liberal values, in ways that at least make it possible to highlight certain lines of battle. To be clear, the notion that certain *interventions d'humanité* should not count as interventions at all draws on very old international legal themes that have long seen certain states arrogate themselves interventionist prerogatives. As early as the French revolution, the République issued a declaration in which it proclaimed that it would grant 'fraternité et secours à tous les peuples qui voudront recouvrer leur liberté'.[1275] Not only was this a possible exception to the sovereignty of states, but it was typically draped in the progressist discourse of the Enlightenment. The incidence of such proclamations was soon amplified by the fact that monarchical powers also made claims exactly in the opposite direction, notably as part of the Holy Alliance, namely to intervene to protect threatened thrones on the basis that the public law of Europe forbade change of regime by revolution. The question is what becomes of such proclamations on the long run in an international system that has discursively at least become much more wary of intervention.

Certainly, the impartial provision of strictly humanitarian assistance—as distinct from the much more contentious questions of humanitarian intervention—can typically not be considered to be a form of unlawful interference, as recognized by the ICJ in the Nicaragua case.[1276] According to the *Institut de Droit International*:

> [a]n offer by a State, a group of States, an international organization or an impartial humanitarian body such as the International Committee of the Red Cross, of food or medical supplies to another State in whose territory

1273 Team of the Official Website of the President of Russia, 'Interview to American TV Channel NBC' (*President of Russia*, 12 March 2018) <http://en.kremlin.ru/events/president/news/57027> accessed 22 April 2024.

1274 'Transcript of NBC News' Exclusive Interview with Russia's Vladimir Putin' (*NBC News*, 14 June 2021) <https://www.nbcnews.com/news/world/transcript-nbc-news-exclusive-interview-russia-s-vladimir-putin-n1270649> accessed 22 April 2024.

1275 Convention Nationale (France), 'Archives Parlementaires' (1792) vol 53, 474 <https://sul-philologic.stanford.edu/philologic/archparl/navigate/53/3/27/> accessed 1 February 2024.

1276 *Nicaragua v United States* (n 3) [243].

> the life or health of the population is seriously threatened cannot be considered an unlawful intervention in the internal affairs of that State.[1277]

Assistance in the name of democracy or human rights, however, raises more complex questions because of its intrinsically political character. A useful prism here is provided by election meddling. It is generally agreed that both the U.S. and Russia (and before it the Soviet Union) have targeted a multiplicity of elections in the last decades (one out of 9 since the 1960s according to one study).[1278] This makes any argument that meddling by either is of a fundamentally different nature than the meddling by the other *a priori* suspicious. Of course, 'the mere fact that the United States itself may have violated the norm in prior occasions does not necessarily entail that the United States cannot be victimized by similarly illegal conduct or that the activity is not illegal'.[1279] Notwithstanding, some commentators have certainly sought to have it both ways, to argue that prior U.S. interventions were not unlawful interference, whereas Russian meddling in U.S. elections *is*. This is what might be called, contra a Russian *tu quoque* argument, the non-equivalency thesis, namely the idea that there is something fundamentally different about the two sets of practices. This at least begs a theory of why this might be so, a theory that has not always been very forthcoming except through appeal to legal generalities and liberal pieties.

At best, this has typically been provided by extolling pro human rights or democracy campaigns as being of a fundamentally different nature. For Jens Ohlin, for example, 'it is important to distinguish between political interference in dictatorships and other illiberal systems versus interference in genuinely democratic elections'.[1280] Similarly, it has been pointed out that 'election interference should not be confused with nonpartisan foreign assistance in support of principles enshrined in the Universal Declaration of Human Rights nor with efforts to strengthen democratic institutions'.[1281] The distinguishing feature here appears to be that liberal meddling helps to realize self-determination and democracy, whilst illiberal meddling does not, along the lines emphasized

1277 Institut de Droit International, 'The Protection of Human Rights and the Principle of Non-Intervention in Internal Affairs of States' (n 184).

1278 Dov H Levin, 'When the Great Power Gets a Vote: The Effects of Great Power Electoral Interventions on Election Results' (2016) 60 International Studies Quarterly 189.

1279 Ohlin, 'Did Russian Cyber Interference in the 2016 Election Violate International Law' (n 851) 1597.

1280 ibid.

1281 Vasu Mohan and Alan Wall, 'Foreign Electoral Interference: Past, Present, and Future' (2019) 20 Georgetown Journal of International Affairs 110, 110.

in the previous chapter in this book. Political scientists have notably distinguished between partisan (supporting one side) and process (supporting the democratic and electoral process) interventions,[1282] or between globally motivated and self-interested interventions.[1283] It has been argued that although '[i]t is true that the expansion of democratic participation can lead in some instances to a change of government and even, where the government in question is not democratic, to a change of regime', that this, at least, is 'not the goal of democracy promotion'.[1284]

4.3 *Can International Law Justify Interference?*

Much seems to hinge on the above sort of distinctions and their sustainability. Human rights initiatives, even state-to-state can be non-confrontational and non-invasive (e.g., inter-state human rights dialogue), just as they can be quite aggressive (e.g., pro-democratic ouster). There is certainly evidence, that some pro-democracy intervention has been relatively benign as a result of NGOs' non-confrontational stance and transparency,[1285] to the point of being accused, in fact, of failing to challenge entrenched authoritarian patterns. However, there is also evidence that pro-democracy intervention is powerful and effective, notably when it has the strong backing of foreign governments and especially powerful states.[1286] Is there a case that human rights or democracy promotion create an exception to the otherwise strict rule of non-intervention on account of their supposedly uniquely emancipatory character? Should foreign campaign contributions that are otherwise seen with wariness, for example, be acclaimed when they have the goal of supporting dissidents against oppressive regimes?[1287]

1282 Daniel Corstange and Nikolay Marinov, 'Taking Sides in Other People's Elections: The Polarizing Effect of Foreign Intervention' (2012) 56 American Journal of Political Science 655.

1283 Jonathan J Godinez, 'The Vested Interest Theory: Novel Methodology Examining US-Foreign Electoral Intervention' (2018) 11 Journal of Strategic Security 2.

1284 Gershman and Allen (n 294) 49. My emphasis.

1285 Sarah Sunn Bush, *The Taming of Democracy Assistance: Why Democracy Promotion Does Not Confront Dictators* (Cambridge University Press 2015) 44. (Noting the significance of 'regime-compatible programs', argues that 'Democracy practitioners […] will prefer to support practices and institutions that target countries will tolerate, if not embrace. Doing so allows them to obtain access and, arguably, make some progress'). Julian Oram and Deborah Doane, 'NGOs Are Adapting to Closing Space When They Must Push Back' (*Open Global Rights*, 19 December 2017) <https://www.openglobalrights.org/ngos-are-adapting-to-closing-space-when-they-must-push-back/> accessed 28 September 2018.

1286 Levin, 'Partisan Electoral Interventions by the Great Powers: Introducing the PEIG Dataset' (n 380).

1287 Powell (n 823) s 5.2.

To explore these questions is to test the solidity of international commitment to a norm of democracy promotion and entrenchment, even entitlement, a commitment that has certainly waxed and waned over time, notably in the long period opening with the end of the Cold War to the present (the 'post-post Cold War'). Although perhaps not rejected, the initial hubris of democracy promotion in the 1990s is certainly ripe for reassessments, both on account of its limited success (not least in promoting governments whose democratic credentials have been challenged) and its increasingly uncertain normative status, 'an artifact of an exuberant era gone by'.[1288] Still, democracy stands on the fault lines of interference and non-interference, a tantalizing promise for many but one that also stands to be exploited to gain footholds in the political dynamics of other states. The same is true for human rights whose associations with interference vary considerably from one state to another. For some, that conversation was already long closed and has settled that human rights justify a range of at least low-level interference since every state is, in a sense, 'its brother's keeper'; for others, ratifying international human rights instruments was never meant to actually allow international institutions, let alone foreign states, to weigh in on domestic matters.

Democracy promotion or human rights are of course hardly neutral when they are deployed, as they of course tend to be, in authoritarian or dictatorial regimes. Especially when support goes to groups that are heavily involved in protests against governments, as in the case of the 'color revolutions', it can quickly be understood locally as encouraging sedition and even revolution. It is also more often than not part of geopolitical calculations in which democracy/human rights are encouraged in some states but not others, in ways that may appear blatantly instrumental and reinforce the perception that was is involved is, at heart, a form of unlawful or illegitimate interference. Democracy promotion in the service of regime change against what are perceived as geopolitical foes may be particularly suspicious.[1289] Even when well intentioned, it involves a symbolic appropriation of another state's political destiny which, under the guise of *noblesse oblige*, has been described as 'palpably wrong' and as manifesting a transparent condescension.[1290] Certainly the sheer gall of substituting one's judgement of another state's domestic affairs to its own, especially when characterized by national chauvinism and liberal provincialism, is likely to inflame tensions between states.

1288 Roth, 'Democratization's Discontents' (n 559).

1289 Christopher I Clement, 'Confronting Hugo Chávez: United States "Democracy Promotion" in Latin America' (2005) 32 Latin American Perspectives 60.

1290 Diallo (n 269) 676.

Nonetheless, democracy promotion in particular is still defended by many, typically Western, lawyers as fundamentally *not* interference. The saving grace of democracy promotion, goes the argument, is that it seeks to enhance democracy whereas interference seeks to sabotage it. Consider, in this context, the argument made by Thomas Carothers of the Carnegie Endowment which can be understood as a sort of 'best case' in favor of the benign character of democracy promotion as opposed to Russian electoral interference:

> U.S. pro-democracy diplomacy and assistance do indeed seek to shape the political direction of other countries. And they are carried out with a strong sense of self-interest, not out of unalloyed idealism. They are driven by the belief that democratic outcomes abroad will generally be favorable to U.S. security and economic interests by producing stable governments amenable to deeper partnerships thanks to shared political values. But unlike Russian electoral meddling, U.S. democracy promotion does not seek to exacerbate sociopolitical divisions, systematically spread lies, favor particular candidates, or undercut the technical integrity of elections. On the whole, it seeks to help citizens exercise their basic political and civil rights in electoral processes, enhance the technical integrity of such processes, and increase electoral transparency.[1291]

One could of course discuss this as a description of the historical record, certainly during the Cold War. The idea that U.S. democracy promotion does not favor particular candidates would require significant validation, although it may be more credible that the U.S. does not routinely 'undercut the technical integrity of elections'.[1292] It is difficult not to read U.S. proclamations of innocence against an entire history of forceful meddling not just in elections but in the very structure of foreign governments, including of course support for or direct organization of *coups*. It is also important to listen to what countries targeted in this way have had to say about how they consider it displaces, if nothing else, their self-determination, even when conducted under the guise of purportedly democratic ambitions.[1293] Although support for coups may not

1291 Thomas Carothers, 'Is the U.S. Hypocritical to Criticize Russian Election Meddling?' [2018] *Foreign Affairs* <https://www.foreignaffairs.com/articles/united-states/2018-03-12/us-hypocritical-criticize-russian-election-meddling> accessed 1 September 2023.

1292 ibid.

1293 Anirban Chatterjee, '"Sovereign Democracy": Russian Response to Western Democracy Promotion in the Post-Soviet Space' (2023) 27 Jadavpur Journal of International Relations 143.

be as blatant as it once was, the practices of the new interference still sometimes err closely enough that they will attract strong alarm.

Even if one glosses over that troubling historical record, democracy and human rights promotion certainly favor a certain type of *regime*, which is unlikely to be seen by target states as innocuous. It may be 'outcome-neutral' in particular circumstances, but 'even pure democracy assistance—that is, foreign aid oriented at promoting democracy—constitutes a non-neutral measure that deliberately tries to shape the domestic political development of another country'.[1294] If anything, target states may be more concerned about interference in favor of an entire political system—typically a certain form of liberal market democracy—than they are with particular electoral outcomes, especially given their upper hand on such outcomes. And at any rate, it may be that, beyond the *a priori* neutral character of democratic politics, it is often quite clear who stands to gain from democracy promoting efforts, so that the distinction between the latter and interference in favor of a particular candidate is rather thin, at least in the circumstances of the moment. In that respect, as already alluded to, the close association of democracy promotion and a range of 'velvet' or 'color' revolutions in, particularly, Russia's near abroad, have long been understood to be closely and ominously inter-related, surreptitiously pushing regime change in favor of 'pro-Western' elites.

Moreover, the 'innocence' of pro-democracy intervention needs to be contextualized in a broader distributive—and thus eminently political—framework. In relation to a particular country, it may be that one can argue that democracy promotion is politically neutral in that it is not predisposed to a particular candidate; seen in a larger context, however, the fact that democracy is being promoted in this state, whereas dictatorship or authoritarianism are tolerated in this other (and a coup supported in yet another), suggests that some of what passes for democracy promotion has long had a deeper geostrategic dimension. Democracy is promoted aggressively where democracy's outcome is seen as beneficial in terms of national interest and neglected where it might endanger particularly prized bilateral relations (consider for example U.S.-Saudi or U.S.-Egyptian relations). Democracy promotion is also part of a discursive economy that feeds on the dynamics of a 'liberalism of restraint' (notably with allies) and a 'liberalism of imposition' (with foes) when it suits the intervener.[1295]

1294 Jonas Wolff and Iris Wurm, 'Towards a Theory of External Democracy Promotion: A Proposal for Theoretical Classification' (2011) 42 Security Dialogue 77, n 7.

1295 Jonathan Monten, 'The Roots of the Bush Doctrine: Power, Nationalism, and Democracy Promotion in U.S. Strategy' (2005) 29 International Security 112.

Of course, the criticism of double-standards is somewhat banal and the fact that a state promotes democracy in its own interest may not be entirely conclusive (if it is indeed promoting democracy); it is not inconceivable, at any rate, that one's support for democracy in a foreign country would have the unintended consequence of reinforcing a side other than the one favored by the interfering state, and certainly some democracy promoters have done so at their own (relative) national interest risk. But lack of consistency in democracy and rights promotion does suggest that liberal interference is less one of a kind than is often claimed and, to the extent it can easily be instrumentalized for foreign policy ends, still needs to be understood as part of a recurring tradition of interference, albeit one at least marginally less nefarious than fostering coups as well as deliberately distorting functional democracies. It also sheds light on 'who gets to promote democracy' in a context where that agenda has in effect been associated with only a narrow subset of powerful democratic states,[1296] in ways that caution against any suggestion that democracy promotion is the natural vocation of all democracies (one can, for example, be an 'isolationist democracy' not tempted by promoting that model to others).

This casts doubt on whether the more or less liberal character of interventions can truly form the linchpin of a theory of legitimate or illegitimate, let alone legal or illegal, interference. The debate also raises a deeper question of principle in relation to self-determination: even assuming an unquestioningly 'liberal' motivation if such a thing is possible, is such an influence necessarily conducive to self-determination? This is obviously a complex issue, but it is certainly conceivable that a people would broadly self-determine in non-liberal ways,[1297] or even adopt a liberal path that is not that broadly favored by foreign 'democracy promoters'. One problem with the generality of claims about 'liberal interference' is the fact that it typically packages a large degree of preferences for certain types of liberalism.[1298] Even within the liberal tradition, the U.S. or the European Union could be favoring a fairly peculiar form of human rights respecting democracy that is quite distinct, even in some ways incompatible, with the distinct liberal aspirations of other societies. The idea that self-determination and a certain version of liberalism somehow necessarily coincide can, then, run contrary to the very idea of self-determination: it

1296 Jonas Wolff, 'Power in Democracy Promotion' (2015) 40 Alternatives: Global, Local, Political 219.

1297 Thomas Carothers, 'Empirical Perspectives on the Emerging Norm of Democracy in International Law' (1992) 86 Proceedings of the ASIL Annual Meeting 261, 265.

1298 Jacques Barzun, 'Is Democratic Theory for Export?' (1987) 1 Ethics & International Affairs 53.

assumes, again, that we already know where the deliberative exercise of self-determining is taking a people to so that, in a sense, we do not need self-determination and can go straight to what we imagine it to lead to.

This is to say nothing of the incongruity of the posture whereby an outside intervener claims to know better what a foreign people aspire to than they do through their own, actual dialectical becoming.[1299] Such is the concern with the tension between democracy and self-determination, in fact, that a long-standing motif among commentators has been whether democracy promotion even makes logical sense. The idea of democracy as government by the people being promoted from outside can appear as a flagrant contradiction, especially when imposed by force.[1300] Not only is democratic imposition normatively contradictory, moreover, but it is unlikely to be successful, displacing as it does more local efforts at establishing a democratic path[1301] (although this is likely to be dependent on what kind of democracy is being promoted).[1302] The irony, as we will see, is that even as the need to reinstate self-determination is invoked to foster regime change on other states,[1303] self-determination is simultaneously held up as the ultimate foundation of non-intervention particularly in the Western inner-sanctum.

One therefore at least needs to nuance the idea that human rights or democracy promotion is generally not hegemonic or imperial, in addition to the fact that it may well have been undertaken in particular times and partly places as bluntly hegemonic or imperial. If nothing else democracy promotion brings attention to the fundamental hiatus between democratic aspirations and self-determination: although international and human rights lawyers are prone to think that two are intimately linked and that democracy is the natural conduit of self-determination,[1304] the fusion between the two evidenced in talk of a 'democratic entitlement' does violence to their quite distinct provenance and

1299 Diallo (n 269).

1300 David Beetham, 'The Contradictions of Democratization by Force: The Case of Iraq' (2009) 16 Democratization 443.

1301 Bruce Bueno de Mesquita and George W Downs, 'Intervention and Democracy' (2006) 60 International Organization 627.

1302 Hans Agné, 'Is Successful Democracy Promotion Possible? The Conceptual Problem' (2014) 21 Democratization 49.

1303 Matthew Saul, 'The Normative Status of Self-Determination in International Law: A Formula for Uncertainty in the Scope and Content of the Right?' (2011) 11 Human Rights Law Review 609, 629–630.

1304 Hua Fan, 'The Missing Link between Self-Determination and Democracy: The Case of East Timor' (2008) 6 Northwestern Journal of International Human Rights 176.

irreducibility, even and perhaps a fortiori in international law. As Amy Eckert points out:

> Ironically, an assertive pro-democratic position, which seeks to promote the protection of human rights, may undermine one of the most cherished rights, the right of a people to determine their political future through self-determination. To promote democracy as the only legitimate result of self-determination deprives that right of any meaning, because a "free" determination in which there is only one choice cannot be considered free.[1305]

In fact, vying to promote another state's democracy is also and paradoxically to displace its self-determination, understood as its ability to chart its own path (including, although not necessarily, towards a specifically democratic end state). One might think, consequently, that a genuine commitment to the practice of self-determination, even from within the liberal canon, has long required that one defer to a people's 'arduous struggle to become free by their own efforts',[1306]—that, in other words, one repress one's external urge to empower internal outcomes. From that peculiar Millian liberal perspective, political emancipation, such as it may be, is of value to the extent that it is conquered by a people's own devices. There is a rich tradition of thought that is wary of democracy being 'promoted' in other states as deeply incompatible with international liberal principles.[1307] Pro-democratic intervention, by contrast, is portrayed as a manifestation of political smugness.

This is especially in light of how democracy-oriented arguments have occasionally been used to justify force or even argue for the overthrow of leaders who were deemed not to have been democratically elected. For example, as early as the late 19th Century, Lawrence cautioned that '[i]t is easy to see that the right of a state to work out its own destiny in its own way would no longer exist, if International Law gave to other states a general right of interference whenever they were horrified at cruelties committed in the course of a war or an internal struggle'.[1308] This cautions against forms of heavy-handed outside

1305 Amy E Eckert, 'Free Determination or the Determination to Be Free? Self-Determination and the Democratic Entitlement' (1999) 4 UCLA Journal of International Law and Foreign Affairs 55, 78.

1306 Mill (n 909) 775.

1307 Michael Walzer, 'Mill's "A Few Words on Non-Intervention": A Commentary' [2007] JS Mill's Political Thought: A Bicentennial Reassessment 347.

1308 Lawrence (n 127) 132.

interference that would limit a people's ability to figure out for themselves whether they want a liberal regime (and which type), and to fight for it on their own terms. Indeed, one sees echoes of this emphasis on people sorting out their own political difficulties in the positions of China and Russia at the Security Council on the question of Venezuela for example.[1309]

None of this should be construed to imply that democracy may not be highly suitable to maximize self-determination, but that there is some value in maintaining a distinction between the two and that international lawyers dabble in such generalities at their peril. This would then relativize the claim that there is something fundamentally distinct about Western democracy promotion in terms of interference, although it would certainly not salvage Russian or Chinese interference either. Rather, instead of an equivalency of virtue as it were (illiberal interference is just as legitimate as liberal interference), this leads U.S. to a potential equivalency in harm (liberal interference is potentially as problematic the illiberal kind). The main point is that arguments that liberal interference is fundamentally distinct are at risk of mistaking political preferences for international law. They also tend to problematically prioritize relatively thicker notions of domestic liberalism oriented towards a certain vision of the 'right' political organization above relatively thinner concepts of international liberalism that lean towards tolerance for pluralism among nations and deferral to peoples' self-help.

This in turn helps problematize debates about human rights more generally as of the course the other great motif of interference in this day and age. As we saw in the first section, it is almost an article of faith in some quarters that actions undertaken in the name of international human rights law do not encroach on the *domaine réservé* as a result of dynamic developments in international law. The *Institut de Droit International*, for example, has insisted that '[s]tates, acting individually or collectively, are entitled to take diplomatic, economic and other measures towards any other State which has violated' human rights and that, provided such measures are legal under international law and do not involve the use of armed force, such 'diplomatic, economic and other measures cannot be considered an unlawful intervention in the internal affairs of that State'.[1310] The claim that interference justified by human rights is not

1309 Cecilia M Bailliet, 'Contesting Narratives on the Situation in Venezuela as a "Threat to Peace and Security"- Plural Interpretations of the Law of Peace within the U.N. Security Council' (24 September 2021) <https://papers.ssrn.com/abstract=4152422> accessed 3 April 2024.

1310 Institut de Droit International, 'The Protection of Human Rights and the Principle of Non-Intervention in Internal Affairs of States' (n 184) art 2.

illegal under international law, then, has been central to the modern reinvention of interference. There is much practice to that effect in a context where states routinely criticize each others' human rights performance without *pro tanto* eliciting strong international law-based protests. One can certainly agree with the Institut's contention that '[d]iplomatic representations as well as purely verbal expressions of concern or disapproval regarding any violations of human rights are lawful in all circumstances'.[1311]

Nonetheless, this does not mean that one should neglect the risk that human rights discourse can be abused to legitimize problematic interference or even the possibility that human rights claims are naturally abuse-prone in the international system. Of particular note here as expressing a traditional Third World sensitivity on the issue is the 1981 Declaration on the Inadmissibility of Intervention and Interference's insistence on '[t]he duty of a State to refrain from the exploitation and distortion of human rights issues as a means of interference in the internal affairs of States, of exerting pressure on other States or creating distrust and disorder within and among States or groups of States'.[1312] As Menno Kamminga has emphasized, this high point of the non-interference agenda, 'would of course provide any offending state with the perfect excuse to ward off legitimate expressions of concern by other states' since '[e]ven if the concerns were presented politely and diplomatically, the offending state would always be in a position to argue that the underlying motives of the interceding state were dishonorable'.[1313] That may be, but it still does not mean that motives are always pure simply because they invoke human rights.

Moreover, even in a case where human rights are not being manipulated to conduct interference in disguise, it remains wholly unclear that acting purportedly in pursuance of internationally guaranteed human rights always makes legal what would otherwise be an illegal interference. As the ICJ put it firmly in the Nicaragua case, 'the protection of human rights, a strictly humanitarian objective, cannot be compatible with the mining of ports, the destruction of oil installations, or again with the training. arming and equipping of the contras' so that 'the argument derived from the preservation of human rights in Nicaragua cannot afford a legal justification for the conduct of the United States'.[1314] Indeed, and even assuming that Nicaragua was becoming, as alleged by the U.S., a 'totalitarian state', Nicaragua did not owe it, on traditional

1311 ibid, art 3.

1312 1981 Declaration on the Inadmissibility of Intervention and Interference, s II(l).

1313 Menno T Kamminga, *Inter-State Accountability for Violations of Human Rights* (University of Pennsylvania Press 1992) 81.

1314 *Nicaragua v United States* (n 3) [268].

international law grounds at least, to the U.S. to remain democratic or rights-respecting. The U.S. thus had no ground to intervene in its sovereign affairs and 'to hold otherwise would make nonsense of the fundamental principle of State sovereignty on which the whole of international law rests, and the freedom of choice of the political, social, economic and cultural system of a State'.[1315]

Even when it comes to otherwise allowable interference in the affairs of states in the name of human rights, it is important to stress that international law never granted a blank cheque to other states to meddle with the affairs of sovereign states merely because they can invoke human rights. The entire architecture of international human rights law, including in its most institutionalized and vertical versions, is premised on the need to enforce human rights but also to protect the sovereignty of states. This is manifested in jurisdictional requirements from which international human rights courts are not exempted (most notoriously, the exhaustion of local remedies) and substantive concessions (most notoriously, the margin of appreciation) that reinstate if not a primacy, at least the utmost relevance of the state as the guardian of human rights.[1316] Not only have international courts largely internalized these dimensions but if they do not they will promptly be reminded of their responsibilities by states, through jurisdictional reform if need be, to further lessen any risk of interference.[1317]

This leans in favor of a healthy deference to the particular ways in which states organize their political systems and away from providing a licence for states to interfere in the affairs of others on the basis of marginal differences of view as to the best system.[1318] For example, third states might all other things being equal elect to prioritize assistance to the kind of processes that enable broad human rights governance and decision-making (democracy, the rule of law, etc.) rather than favoring any particular substantive understanding of human rights.[1319] Third states that do not defer to such arrangements will rightly be understood as engaging in or legitimizing forms of *ultra vires*

1315 ibid [263].

1316 Dominic McGoldrick, 'A Defence of the Margin of Appreciation and an Argument for its Application by the Human Rights Committee' (2016) 65 International & Comparative Law Quarterly 21.

1317 Kimberley Brayson, 'Securing the Future of the European Court of Human Rights in the Face of U.K. Opposition: Political Compromise and Restricted Rights' (2017) 6 International Human Rights Law Review 53; Ed Bates, 'Principled Criticism and a Warning from the "UK" to the ECtHR?' in Marten Breuer (ed), *Principled Resistance to ECtHR Judgments: A New Paradigm?* (Springer 2019).

1318 Damrosch (n 16) 44–45.

1319 ibid 46–47.

interference. In other words, rather than licensing interference lato sensu, international human rights law is largely dedicated to outlining in detail, both jurisdictionally and substantively, the conditions under which something will not be treated as interference and those in which it will.

That this is obviously a fine line is equally apparent in the related field of international criminal law, which one might otherwise think of as most radically licencing interference internationally. For example, in the 'vertical' context, the complementarity regime of the International Criminal Court (ICC) was very much produced so as to avoid accusations of interference:[1320] so long as the ICC stays within the bounds of complementarity, then it cannot be accused of interfering by displacing the criminal competence of the relevant state. However, a sign of how sensitive the matter is, is that, as a result of and sometimes even notwithstanding complementarity, states are routinely tempted to frame the Court's assertions of jurisdiction as a form of interference[1321] (especially, of course, when they are not states parties and therefore never consented to the Court's jurisdiction), even as the Court treads particularly carefully (some would say, too carefully) lest it be so accused of exceeding its competencies.[1322] The transnational criminal law field is even more attuned to the needs of preserving sovereignty through non-intervention, largely deferring to states' constitutional traditions or specificities when it comes to criminalization.

If anything, these concerns are magnified on a horizontal basis where there have been attempts at soft-law regulation of the exercise of universal jurisdiction so that again, notwithstanding a horizon of fundamental legality and legitimacy, it not unduly displace the jurisdiction of the natural sovereign (typically

1320 Steven Freeland, 'It's a Good Idea … Isn't It? The Impact of Complementarity at the International Criminal Court on Domestic Law, Politics and Perceptions of Sovereignty' in Marlene Wind (ed), *International Courts and Domestic Politics* (Cambridge University Press 2018).

1321 Yuval Shany and Amichai Cohen, 'The Prosecutor's Circumvention of Article 18 Complementarity? A Flaw in the ICC's Palestine Investigation' (*Just Security*, 1 June 2024) <https://www.justsecurity.org/96296/icc-article-18-complementarity/> accessed 12 July 2024.

1322 See Marika Giles Samson, 'On "Tempered Complementarity": The International Criminal Court and the Colombian Peace Process' (2019) 8 Canadian Journal of Human Rights 151; Marco Bocchese, 'El Coco Does Not Frighten Anymore: ICC Scrutiny and State Cooperation in Colombia' (2021) 26 Journal of Conflict and Security Law 157; Caroline D Kelly, 'Contextual Complementarity: Assessing Unwillingness and "Genuine" Prosecutions in Colombia's Special Jurisdiction for Peace' (2017) 48 Georgetown Journal of International Law 807.

that of the *locus delicti*).[1323] The same is true of universal civil jurisdiction, the underlying stake of which has not been, to say the least, wanton assertion but finding ways, through comity and restraint, to exercise it in ways that reasonably defer to the countervailing interests of the states primarily impacted.[1324] Interference and non-interference are thus, even within a framework of commitment to universal values, constantly being delimited and re-delimited so as to preserve something of sovereignty. The fact that the matter is never entirely or once and for all settled sheds light on the reality that the proclamation of universal shared interests was never a way to do away with sovereignty, but rather to continuously manage its complex implications. As part of that ongoing exercise, defenders of non-interference get at least as good an opportunity as those bent on justifying encroachments on the *domaine* at making their case as part of continued contestations.[1325]

Finally, there remains the challenging question of whether the content of human rights can be known with any degree of certainty and legitimacy from abroad without the mediation of self-determination and, as the case may be, national democratic arrangements to substantiate what human rights mean in particular circumstances. Interventions in the name of human rights are also based on a problematic epistemic claim to 'know better' from outside that ultimately disparage the centrality of self-determination in the realization of rights[1326] as well as the variety of national trajectories towards a culture of rights, just as with democracy. In other words, a high-strung approach to human rights promotion in other states can paradoxically end up undermining some of the very determinants of a culture of rights, including self-determination and democracy. This is why in reality the determination of human rights always defers to democratic or self-determining processes, rather than simply relying on a universalist or top-down vulgate.

Having said that, there remains one thorny issue already alluded to more generally, namely the possibility that interference in the affairs of a state is welcome by some constituencies within that state, specifically on human

---

1323 Devika Hovell, 'The Authority of Universal Jurisdiction' (2018) 29 European Journal of International Law 427.

1324 Serena Forlati and Pietro Franzina (eds), *Universal Civil Jurisdiction : Which Way Forward?* (Brill Nijhoff 2021).

1325 Julia Kapelańska-Pręgowska, 'Extraterritorial Jurisdiction of National Courts and Human Rights Enforcement: Quo Vadis Justitia?' (2015) 17 International Community Law Review 413.

1326 Richard Peterson, 'Dilemmas of Intervention: Human Rights and Neo-Colonialism' in Gail M Presbey (ed), *Philosophical Perspectives on the 'War on Terrorism'* (Brill 2007); Orford (n 27).

rights grounds. The combination of a local invitation *and* a human rights justification may prove a particularly alluring mix for would-be interveners. A government may see certain policies as interference that civil society groups may then see as a welcome show of solidarity in the face of human rights violations, for example. Domestic constituencies welcoming interference may merely be the 'dupes' that Jefferson spoke of but the fact that they are screaming (as the case may be) for assistance in safeguarding their rights may add a degree of genuineness to their call and urgency to interference. This is a question that can never be entirely avoided, and which problematizes the role of the host government in pushing back against interference when the people doing the calling are also those suffering the rights violations.

PART 3

Strategic Dilemmas of Interference

It may be that it is difficult, if not impossible, *in fine*, to draw a bright line between lawful and unlawful interference, both on account of the vagueness of the *domaine réservé* and our limited understanding of what could consistently be held to amount to an interference with it. Trying to pin down interference sometimes feels like staring into an abyss of dense inter-state rivalry from which little clarity emerges. Resort to human rights brings much needed nuance to the debate but also further perplexity. On some level, this may precipitate a flight from the norm. For example, in the cyberspace context, it has been noted that 'States may respond to the normative uncertainty about international rules [...] by regarding such rules as optional'.[1327] As will be seen further in this third and last part, the debate about interference is also a debate about how relevant international rules should be to determining the scope of the phenomenon and what to do about it. Nothing guarantees that international law will have a monopoly or even a pride of place in terms of how states address the resulting challenges.

1 The Function and Constraint of Arguments about Interference

By the same token, no dramatic flight from international law seems to have occurred, and the level of investment in defining the relevant norms suggests otherwise. Indeed, one of the enduring mysteries of international law is the extent to which it continues to be largely invoked by states and diplomats as the default language to frame and construct interference and intervention, despite evident doctrinal misgivings about the consistency of these categories. In many ways, this may be because interference and intervention are, literally, problems created by international law, or at least that cannot be understood outside of the analytical categories of a system that already posits that there is such a thing as sovereigns and that one of their claims to existence is not to be interfered/intervened with.[1328] This means that, at least as far as the project of international law is concerned, it cannot shy from the problem of defining interference/intervention because it is already ontologically committed to their centrality. There is simply too much credibility at stake for the system.

1327 Ossoff (n 341) 321.

1328 Frédéric Mégret, 'Is International Law Addressing Problems of Its Own Making?' in David Lefkowitz and Andreas Follesdal (eds), *The Philosophy of International Law* (Cambridge University Press Forthcoming).

 | DOI:10.1163/9789004532731_009

As to states, even as part of an often halting and inconclusive process, continued engagement with the norm has shown the value that they ascribe not so much to 'getting out on top' (although that too is understood to be the goal), but to maintaining the ability to denounce intervention and interference when need be as the very condition of their being sovereigns. Interestingly, however, the circle of social actors that have a vested interest in how interference and intervention are defined has significantly broadened. To be sure, states maintain the upper hand on efforts at definition, through international adjudication that only they can access, diplomatic practice that only they can produce, and international legal scholarship that largely defers to them as the cardinal reference points. But, as Part 2 has shown, interference and intervention also affect populations, corporations, individuals who are caught up in claims made about what it entails and who have increasingly raised questions of their own about where they fit into such processes. These actors are also part of the legally pluralist constitution of the notion of intervention/interference, even in circumstances where the law itself is unsure about their position therein. The diversification of actors, however, also increases the risk of normative dissonance between various interested parties.

One possibility is simply that interference and intervention will 'regulate themselves' out of nothing more than the occasional reconciliation of interests as part of international regimes of coexistence. There is an element of prisoners' dilemma involved in all attempts to extricate oneself from the bind of interference. States would all stand to gain from non-interference, but only if they could be reassured that other states would not take advantage of their desisting from interfering to, surreptitiously, engage in interference of their own. It is true that, tentatively and notably through the mediating and socializing role of international law itself, conciliation of interests may occur on an ad hoc basis. It is also true that the international system breeds its own type of self-restraint: for example, one of the points of interference is that it must be merely interference; too much interference kills the benefits of interference by making interference transparent and creating backlashes in the target state. Perhaps unsurprisingly, it has been argued that the most extreme form of interference—regime change—often backfires as foreign imposed leaders are exposed as mere stooges.[1329]

1329 Alexander B Downes and Lindsey A O'Rourke, 'You Can't Always Get What You Want: Why Foreign-Imposed Regime Change Seldom Improves Interstate Relations' (2016) 41 International Security 43.

Nonetheless, international law is more than the sum of rational behavior that animates its agents and, at any rate, the rational choice of actors stands to be greatly maximized by appropriate international legal sign posting and issue framing. Moving beyond the circularity of doctrinal arguments about interference or the solitary character of the state as the fountain of all international law, this final part seeks to shift the lens decisively by focusing on the extent to which interference, first and foremost, creates a range of *strategic dilemmas* for actors in the international system.[1330] Dilemmas are understood as strategic here because of the way they always involve more than the question seemingly (and confusingly) at hand: an implicit negotiation of the totality of the meaning of international law and one's symbolic place within it. In other words, contra a merely tactical vision of international legal disputes, a strategic vision insists that actors are not only maximizing their chances to 'win' certain cases but also the way in which their investment in the law at any given time constitutes them as actors and constrains the sort of investments they can make in the future.[1331] Legal argumentation, in that respect, is if nothing else path-driven: certain arguments are made necessary, or at least advantageous, by one's prior commitments, sense of self in the world and the contingency of international life (including who one interacts with).

This goes to the heart of international law as a discursive economy, with its rewards and sanctions. In foregrounding adaptive strategies rather than compliance, this approach will be less concerned with determining whether interference is legal or not once and for all in the abstract than understanding the rhetorical resources, potential and traps of international legal argumentation.[1332] As such it highlights normative investments in certain understandings of norms over time, and how these structure a certain *rapport* to law. By emphasizing such dilemmas, the goal is to re-root arguments about interference and intervention in the creative practices that this category of understanding, such as it is, makes possible thanks to its indeterminacy. These practices are neither entirely interest-driven nor exclusively value-constrained; rather, they express the complex coordination of changing preferences among a great many players in conditions of uncertainty and, simultaneously, the role of discourses in both stabilizing and destabilizing expectations about behavior. Over time,

1330 For an approach in terms of strategy, see, for example, Randall H Cook, 'Dynamic Content: The Strategic Contingency of International Law Notes' (2004) 14 Duke Journal of Comparative & International Law 89.

1331 See e.g., Frédéric Mégret, 'Immunities of Foreign Officials for International Crimes: The Dilemmas of Strategic Litigation' (2023) 15 Journal of Human Rights Practice 66.

1332 Scobbie (n 72).

they constitute the norm of interference much more than they are constituted by it: non-interference is not so much a general norm of international law as a norm that is constantly renegotiated bilaterally and multilaterally at arm's length as part of actual relations between states.

In that respect, arguments about interference can be seen as fulfilling several functions. First, they can serve as a rallying cry, allowing coalitions of states to emerge around certain stylized positions on the discursive spectrum of interference, often incarnated, at any one moment, by particular 'champions'. In that perspective, the goal of rhetoric is not so much to convince the reticent party but, as it were, to 'preach to the choir' for the purposes of loose alliance building. Thus, Russia and China have recently emerged as plausible 'norm entrepreneurs' in articulating a certain approach to non-interference. China, for example, has long promoted a model of relations with states in the Global South that emphasizes non-interference, in supposed explicit contrast to the approach that has traditionally structured North-South relations.[1333]

Of course the trenchancy of such a proposal is blunted by the fact that everyone (including, these days, the West) is emphasizing the importance of non-interference, but the importance of even minute differences in allowing differentiation between groups of states is key (everyone agrees superficially on the contours of non-intervention until at least the meaning of the expression needs to be concretized in a particular case).[1334] States can thus be seen as competing over certain models of interference/non-interference that are deployed instrumentally and strategically even as they may not, in fact, reflect actual practices (e.g., simply because China or Russia promote non-interference does not mean that they do not interfere). Over time, states seek to promote hegemonic alliances over the meaning of international legal concepts, thereby solidifying their claim to normativity through appeal to epistemic and sovereign communities.

A second and related function is more clearly adversarial and oppositional. Arguments about interference also help 'draw the lines of battle', to delineate and radicalize latent oppositions by formulating them in the jargon of international law. The point of this rhetoric is to emphasize how much one *disagrees* with the other party. For example, 'non-interference' emerged as a rallying cry in the 1960s to portray how Third World states wanted to organize their relations with each other in opposition to the West. It drew on the West's own

---

1333 Hirono, Jiang and Lanteigne (n 516); Zheng (n 326); Daniel Large, 'China and the Contradictions of "Non-Interference" in Sudan' (2008) 35 Review of African Political Economy 93.

1334 For an exploration in the cyber context, see Ossoff (n 341).

tradition of sovereignty but claimed to extend it to the whole world, even as the West was accused of wanting to depart from its own international legal canon in its relations with its former colonies. More recently, it is the European Union that has upped the ante of what it considers to be at stake in the debate over interference, portraying it as having 'the goal of destabilising European democracy, and therefore constitut[ing] a serious threat to E.U. security and sovereignty'.[1335] Contra a vision of international law as having a naturally unifying and universalizing role, appeals to non-interference radicalize a sense of international law, as Monika Hakimi has suggested, as an agonistic site of struggles in which states propound incommensurable visions of its stakes.[1336]

Third, arguments about interference evidently also have a more communicational and dialectical function, allowing states to 'put out feelers' about certain views of contested norms, test reactions and more generally embark on the complex process of identifying the best, or at least the most opportune, interpretation of norms. This is the tentative, experiential dimension of international law making; one should not assume that states always depart from totalizing conceptions of their interest when it comes to the law; rather, that interest is constituted in the process of formulating the norms that are designed to protect it. For example, there is a sort of 'wait and see' element to the processes by which norms in cyberspace for example are haggled over, many states adopting a tentative approach that is attuned to subtle dissonances from friend and foe alike and that leaves space for further adaptation as the stakes gradually come into further focus.[1337] Nothing guarantees, moreover, that states will always be comfortable accusing others of interference, and 'pulling one's punches' may also be an option when the stakes in terms of foreign relations are high.[1338] This may correspond to the best scenario for international lawyers, one in which the discipline at least mediates complex

1335 2022 Resolution on Foreign Interference in the E.U. (n 337), para E.

1336 Monica Hakimi, 'The Work of International Law' (2017) 58 Harvard International Law Journal 1.

1337 Consider for example the emphasis in France's major political statement on the issue that some behavior 'may' amount to intervention, a formula that seemingly keeps the door quite open as to what 'does' constitute such intervention. 'International Law Applied to Operations in Cyberspace' (n 530) 7.

1338 For example, it has been contended that the Canadian government has not aggressively taken China to task for its pressure campaign on certain Chinese Canadian politicians out of fear of deteriorating key relations. See Sean Boynton, 'China Will Be Emboldened to Target More Canadians If Diplomat Not Expelled: Chong' *Global News* (7 May 2023) <https://globalnews.ca/news/9677918/michael-chong-china-interference-west-block/> accessed 7 September 2023.

political claims through the pacifying and deferring language of law. It emphasizes the element of uncertainty and genuine and tentative search for meaning within and via legal exchanges.

The international law of non-interference, then, exists in the crucible of these political and rhetorical strategies and the sort of fragile and dynamic compromises that they occasionally make possible. As a result, arguments about interference operate under several constraints. In particular, they always come at some cost and are hamstrung by an implicit economy of argumentation. The constraints that weigh on that argumentation are multiple. For example, there are the costs of 'getting it wrong' both factually and normatively and claiming that another state interfered when it has a strong case (factual or normative) that it did not, thus harming productive bilateral relations and causing potential embarrassment. Trudeau's initially inconclusive accusations against India, to the effect that it murdered a Sikh activist on Canadian territory, are an example of the awkwardness that may result from unclear and unproven accusations. This is magnified when states, struggling with the elusive character of interference, adopt measures that are vague in scope but are widely understood to be targeting a particular state. It has been said, for example, that Australia's sweeping new anti-interference laws, however justified they may otherwise have been, 'have strained relations with Beijing, Australia's biggest trading partner, which has furiously denied claims of interference'.[1339] There is also evident a cost of 'getting it right' and denouncing a form of interference that has indeed occurred and whose visibility cannot then be undone. The costs to U.S./Russian bilateral relations of the allegations of Russian meddling in U.S. elections, in that respect, have been considerable.[1340] To accuse another state of intervention or interference is to compromise one's ability to entertain relations with it outside of those accusations; and to be accused of intervention or interference will require that one defend oneself from such accusations, at the expense of other productive engagements.

Against those costs, must of course be assessed the opportunity cost of *not* protesting and knowingly allowing interference to go unchecked for some ulterior motive. States that allow interference to go unchallenged to minimize embarrassment to adversaries and maintain good relations may find

1339 John Power, 'Australia's Spy Law Revamp Irks China' *Nikkei Asian Review* (20 June 2018) <https://asia.nikkei.com/Politics/Australia-s-spy-law-revamp-irks-China> accessed 12 February 2024.

1340 Timothy Farnsworth, 'China and Russia Submit Cyber Proposal' (*Arms Control Association*, 2 November 2011) <https://www.armscontrol.org/act/2011_11/China_and_Russia_Submit_Cyber_Proposal> accessed 11 March 2019.

that, over time, their sovereignty is diminished and may even amount to little. Sovereignty is also largely a performative exercise: one has sovereignty to the extent one is willing to assert it. There is deep resentment against and anxiety about the risk of unchallenged interference and what it means about one's continued destiny as a sovereign. As Russian President Vladimir Putin put it:

> The lesson all of U.S. should learn is that economic and government weakness and susceptibility to external shocks inevitably threaten sovereignty. We all know very well that, let's be honest, if you are weak, there will always be someone who will be eager to advise you on where to move, which policy to pursue and which development path to choose. These seemingly friendly and unobtrusive recommendations may look good, but in point of fact they camouflage diktat and gross interference in the affairs of sovereign states. We are perfectly aware of this.[1341]

It is within that narrow space between accepting interference as the cost of international interaction or seeking to aggressively fend it off that a number of strategic dilemmas arise. Through them, states are called upon to assess how their position on any one given instance of interference might affect their positionality in relation to the overall issue of interference. The reality of role reversal—many states are now potentially both interfered with and interfering in the affairs of others—only magnifies the tensions, both constitutional and in terms of foreign legal policy, that states are subjected to.

2 The Curse of Mimetism, the Hope of Reciprocity

Perhaps the most challenging element in that context stems from the fundamentally mimetic nature of the interference debate.[1342] Mimetism, consisting in the liberal 'borrowing' of practices along the non-interference/interference spectrum by states from each other, is not only a significant international social practice. It is also specifically a way of conceiving of meaning production.[1343] It

1341 Vladimir Putin, 'Prime Minister Vladimir Putin Delivers a Report on the Government's Performance in 2010 in the State Duma' (*The Official Site of the Prime Minister of the Russian Federation*, 20 April 2011) <http://archive.premier.gov.ru/eng/events/news/14898/print/> accessed 2 January 2024.

1342 On mimetism as a philosophical current inspired by French philosopher René Girard, see Maria Stella Barberi, *La spirale mimétique: dix-huit leçons sur René Girard* (Desclée de Brouwer 2001).

1343 Necati Polat, *International Relations, Meaning and Mimesis* (Routledge 2012).

includes the diverse genres of self-parody, ironic distance, *déjà vu*, or the 'narcissism of small differences'. An example is the early Belgian post-War militancy for the notion that Chapter xi of the U.N. Charter should apply to all peoples under some kind of colonial yoke and not just those suffering from such a fate in extra-maritime terms (the so-called 'salt water' test): although defensible on its own grounds, it was quite clear that this strategy of uber-internationalizing colonial questions was nothing more than an attempt by Belgium—which otherwise very much resisted any notion that it should report to the U.N. about its own possessions—to embarrass Third World states by daring them to follow that lead, which raised the specter of secessionism.[1344] Some Western states also thought twice, as a result of these Belgium shenanigans, about pushing the decolonial agenda too hard, lest this come back to haunt them.

Parties to international legal debates over time (as in other areas of international law) are called upon to tactically make the opposite argument to the one they had made earlier, at the risk of tying themselves into rhetorical knots. In other words, mimetism also involves a degree of role reversal over time and adopting the position of others one previously criticized. The West in particular now finds itself making strong arguments in favor of non-interference even as it has long sought to play down concerns about such interference and even as it seeks to strategically maintain its ability to, at least residually, engage in the sort of interference it desires. States that have been historically on the receiving end of interference, in turn, have sought to combine their traditional defense of the principle of non-interference with an increasingly blatant boldness about their own ability to interfere. Each, then, tends to echo the other and to adopt uncharacteristic arguments through mimetism.

Each of these positions has its drawbacks and can end up being invoked against the state that pushes it, putting it potentially in an uncomfortable space where its contradictions are exposed and it cannot, as it were, have its cake and eat it. Notwithstanding, as this book has underscored, there has been no shortage of situations where states have 'flipped' their position diametrically over time, sometimes without even bothering to argue for it, perhaps

1344 Claude, Jr (n 312). This was an 'effort to turn the tables on the anticolonials, to demonstrate they did not approach the task of supervising colonial policy with clean hands, to discourage the exploitation of chapter 11 by insisting that its most avid champions were themselves vulnerable to its impact. Belgium was attempting to combat the intensification of the application of chapter 11 by demanding the extension of its range of applicability. What Belgium and its cohorts really wanted was not to get all non-self-governing peoples under the protective umbrella of chapter 11, but to get their colonies out from under that umbrella—or, at any rate, to reduce the interference with their domestic jurisdiction resulting from the continued coverage of their colonies'. ibid 127–128.

relying on collective amnesia. This includes, for example, the double flip of the West first arguing that unilateral economic sanctions (for example, against the Soviet Union) were not a form of intervention; then discovering that they were (after the OPEP embargo); and finally reverting to its position that they are ultimately not (in relation to Cuba, for example). This was replicated, incidentally, in the realm of secondary sanctions where the U.S. originally complained of the secondary boycott of Israel implemented by the Arab League in 1948 but has since long become the leading purveyor of secondary sanctions.

The mimetic nature of the debate means that one always seems to be condemning in the 'other' that very behavior which one has simultaneously (elsewhere, at some other time) espoused. For example, having for many years strongly argued that propaganda, including hostile propaganda, destined to the Soviet bloc was *not* interference in those countries' domestic affairs, it is, all other things being equal, more difficult for the U.S. to now argue that Russian propaganda is a form of illegal interference. Although one may think today of Russia as the leading purveyor of cyber-interference, it is also, ironically, Moscow that has long spearheaded—for its own reasons and goals, no doubt, but still in ways that are at odds with its own behavior—the effort to fight off outside cyber-interference.[1345] And it remains tricky for the U.S. to criticize a type of legislation such as foreign agent registration that was fundamentally modelled on its own.[1346] Similarly, whilst Confucius Institutes have elicited concerns in the West, such concerns have been met by the retort that they are not that different from the U.K.'s British Council, France's Alliance française, or Germany's Goethe-Institut. There is an element of tit-for-tat involved in the interference debate, then, as when China produces an annual report on human rights in the U.S.,[1347] or when authoritarian states organize 'zombie monitoring' of their own elections by coopted Westerners,[1348] a sort of kitsch

1345 David Ignatius, 'Working with Russia on Cybercrime Is like Hiring a Burglar to Protect the Family Jewels' *Washington Post* (4 September 2018) <https://www.washingtonpost.com/opinions/global-opinions/working-with-russia-on-cyber-regulation-is-like-paying-a-bully-for-protection/2018/09/04/b16787ea-bc8e-11e8-9a6a-565d92a3585d_story.html> accessed 11 March 2019.

1346 Samuel Rebo, 'FARA in Focus: What Can Russia's Foreign Agent Law Tell U.S. about America's?' (2021) 12 Journal of National Security Law and Policy 277.

1347 'The Report on Human Rights Violations in the United States in 2022' (The State Council Information Office of the People's Republic of China 2023) <http://ge.china-embassy.gov.cn/eng/xwdt/202303/t20230328_11050361.htm> accessed 18 February 2024.

1348 Casey Michel, 'The Rise of the Zombie Monitors: They Came, They Saw, They Got It Completely Wrong' [2015] *The Diplomat* <https://thediplomat.com/2015/04/the-rise-of-the-zombie-monitors/> accessed 18 February 2024.

parody of other side's stance that suggests they have already anticipated and internalized the critique.

This can, in turn, reveal a tendency among states, especially liberal ones, to exaggerate the extent to which their own practices are distinct from those of others, notably authoritarian ones. For example, the European Union vaunts its approach to foreign registration as demonstrating its 'capacity to tackle this scourge while safeguarding and reinforcing the core principles of [its] democracies, including respect for fundamental rights and open democratic debate', and contrasts it to Singapore's Foreign Interference Act of 2021 which is said to be based on 'vague and wide-ranging offences'.[1349] Similarly, Europe has sought to distance its banning of RT France, the Russian TV channel accused of pro-Kremlin propaganda in relation to Ukraine, from similar moves by Russia. Western cultural institutes reply that unlike the Confucius Institutes they are stand-alone organizations that are also independent from their governments and not problematically niched within foreign universities. Whatever the merits of those particular comparisons—and evidently some of these differences are worth acknowledging—they suggest the troubling incidence of *déjà vu* when treading between democratic and authoritarian versions of the same playbook. They are also a reminder that either liberal states may have borrowed practices from authoritarian ones, or that that they are at risk of 'leading by example' with illiberal practices of their own.[1350]

The effort to distinguish lawful and unlawful interference from a substantive point of view is often rendered difficult, moreover, by the tendency of each side to essentially invoke the same fundamental normative references to justify interference or non-interference, in true mimetic fashion. Most strikingly, almost every argument can be (and indeed is) recast as an argument for human rights, sovereignty, or the international public interest. This may be the result of wily strategies by states, but it may also bring attention to something more profound and controversial, namely the difficulty of truly disentangling 'good' influence and 'bad' interference, especially on the basis of its motivation or goal, when both on the surface borrow from the same register. As we saw, the language of human rights provides arguments both to fight interference and to promote it. This can, for example, lead to a genuine puzzlement about 'the extent to which both [the Brezhnev and Reagan doctrines] represent examples

1349 Jones (n 495) 10.

1350 What the European Parliament describes as the 'danger that E.U. regulatory frameworks to combat disinformation may be copied and might be selectively used by other (authoritarian) countries in order to curb media freedom and freedom of expression'. 2023 Resolution on Foreign Interference in the E.U. (n 335), para CD.

of mirror-imaging by the two sides, of mocking behavior of one inspired by the action of the other'.[1351] It can also lead states into rhetorical battles where they appear to be arguing against themselves. For example, if the OPEP embargo or sanctions against South Africa are that inimical to international liberal sensitivities, then surely unilateral sanctions by the West are just as problematic?

This does not mean that it will be meaningless to seek to distinguish one's own practices from one's mimetic competitor, but that this is indeed the crucial challenge. It will often expose the degree to which ultimately form provides a poor guide to what can be credibly portrayed as interference. This is nowhere clearer than in 'foreign agent' registration laws which have blossomed both in more liberal and more authoritarian legal cultures, making it very difficult to make the argument that some are perfectly appropriate whilst others are not. Indeed, the much-criticized Russian law takes its title from the equivalent U.S. legislation of 1928. Subsequently, the Russian parliament adopted a bill designating all international media outlets as 'foreign agents' after a similar move was adopted by the U.S. Congress in relation to RT, Russia's state-funded news channel, which was required to register with the U.S. Justice Department.

The circulation of ideas and of provocative *répartie* is constant. Of course, too much can be made of the superficial similarities between laws. Simply because both the U.S. and Russia require foreign registration does not mean that they have the same laws or that they implement them in the same way. Certainly, some foreign agent laws have been enforced with more cynical gusto in authoritarian states.[1352] Notably, Russia's foreign registration requirements have been very broadly targeted at NGOs whereas the U.S. Foreign Agents Registration Act (FARA) has been relatively little used, requires a principal agent relationship (akin to being 'controlled' by foreign interests), includes many exceptions, and is mostly aimed at actual lobby groups.[1353] There is a sense that NGO registration has been particularly Orwellian in some countries and arises as a mere pretext to stamp out or control all civil society, be it meaningfully connected to the exterior or not, whereas some states have certainly adopted a lighter touch when it comes to registration.

1351 Rogers and others (n 159) 562.

1352 Jeff Vize, 'FARA's Double Life Abroad' (*International Center for Not-for-Profit Law* (ICNL), 21 October 2023) <https://www.icnl.org/post/analysis/faras-double-life-abroad> accessed 2 April 2024.

1353 Samantha Laufer, 'A Difference in Approach: Comparing the U.S. Foreign Agents Registration Act with Other Laws Targeting Internationally Funded Civil Society' (2017) 19 International Journal of Not-for-Profit Law 5.

Still, the superficial similarities are arresting and require going the extra length to explain just how different one's approach actually is. Efforts to distinguish 'malicious or authoritarian' or 'manipulative' or 'undue' interference[1354] from 'good faith' influence may not fare well in a context where broad linguistic practices are shared and hardly provide on their own terms a way to cut the Gordian knot. What is 'pernicious' is often in the eyes of the beholder. For example, as was seen in Part 2, the same behaviour might be described as positive influence in favor of the human rights of an oppressed population or negative interference with that population's right to self-determination. Over time, states may find themselves perilously close to contradiction as they use essentially the same justifications both for and against interference. Indeed, there is no reason to think that mimetism will lead to more reciprocity: not every attempt to reproduce what one is being a victim of or to turn arguments on their heads will lead to mutually beneficial results—mimetism may be part of a destructive tit for tat rather than the prolegomenon to stable reciprocity.[1355] The tension between the 'offensive' and 'defensive' potential of arguments about interference has been nowhere more visible than in the debate over whether interference below the non-intervention rule is even a violation of sovereignty, the negative response seemingly designed to safeguard the U.S.'s ability to carry out such operations even at the price, potentially, of being itself exposed to them.[1356]

If nothing else, this cautions against making certain arguments too forcefully, lest they come back to haunt those who make them. To attack others' human rights record on the basis that it is not part of the *domaine réservé* is to be vulnerable to other states doing the same. As noted by Barrie Sander, 'some States may have little desire to advance an expansive notion of non-intervention for fear that doing so might empower certain States to characterise the political activities of global civil society groups as coercive interventions'.[1357] As a result, the challenge is not just to think through what constitutes interference at home, but how every effort to define such interference might one day be used against oneself to portray what one does in relation to another sovereign. For example, if aggressively interfering states get caught red-handed, they may subsequently have trouble mounting a case against interference in their own

1354 Terms used as qualifiers by the European Parliament to describe Russian and Chinese interference. 2022 Resolution on Foreign Interference in the E.U. (n 337), paras E, F, 4.

1355 Frank C Richardson and Nicolette D Manglos, 'Reciprocity and Rivalry: A Critical Introduction to Mimetic Scapegoat Theory' (2013) 62 Pastoral Psychology 423, 426.

1356 Schmitt and Vihul (n 521).

1357 Sander (n 390) 54.

affairs. Alternatively, if states with relatively liberal leanings react too strongly to what they see as challenges of interference, they may unwittingly fall into the trap of reinforcing the hand of authoritarian regimes who have long been making exactly the argument that strong action is in order to protect one's political integrity. Thus for example when faced with a complaint in 1949 that the Spanish diplomatic mission in the U.S. was engaging in pro-fascist propaganda, Assistant Secretary of State Gross was at pains to emphasize that it would be 'embarrassing' for the State Department to object to Spanish activities to create a favourable sentiment for their government given that the U.S. diplomatic legation in Spain did the same.[1358]

The question, nonetheless, goes beyond the, ultimately quite self-serving, fear of being hamstrung in the future by one's rhetorical investments in the past or of giving ideas to one's adversaries. It points to the more strategic dimension of international law and one's repeated investments in it. One simply cannot change one's stance on weighty international legal matters at every hint of how they might affect one's interests because this undermines one's own stance. A certain constancy is required in staying the course to avoid getting caught in one's own rhetoric. That involves a hard look at one's own argumentative practices and not only for how they affect others' calculi but one's own standing, and the very possibility of international law. The resulting 'standpoint humility' as it were, hints at the need to not be fooled by one's own legal arguments and to understand them as part of patterns that are always in a sense precariously self-serving. Tom Franck intuited as much when he offered a stinging rebuke to U.S. protestations at Soviet intervention by showing the extent to which the Brezhnev Doctrine had itself been transparently inspired by the Monroe Doctrine:

> To show the parallels to the Brezhnev Doctrine in our own country's rhetoric is neither a pleasant task nor one our policymakers are likely to appreciate. The purpose of doing so is not to give comfort to the Russian violators of Czech independence, but rather to suggest the implications for future policymaking which can be drawn from our experience of having our own verbal formulas used by the Russians to our disadvantage. Just as one responsibility of a lawyer is to warn his client not to make allegations of principle or to assert rights if the concepts he espouses could be applied to his disadvantage, one purpose of this review of our

---

1358 Marjorie M Whitman, *Digest of International Law*, vol 7 (US Government Printing Office 1970) 145. Cited in Behrens, 'Diplomatic Interference and Competing Interests in International Law' (n 774) n 23.

> verbal strategy is to demonstrate the need to think through the reciprocal implications of the concepts by which our nation purports to conduct its foreign policy. Lawyers are obligated to reiterate to policymakers the wisdom of listening to themselves as if they were the enemy speaking. To some extent the legal profession's penchant for 'thinking reciprocally' reflects the rule that one should act in accordance with the principles one expects of one's peers, and should eschew principles of conduct one seeks to proscribe in others. That which is a moral imperative for philosophy and theology is a functional imperative for law; without a pattern of reciprocal application, law cannot grow.[1359]

3 Defining the Conditions of International Engagement

To complicate matters, not being caught red-handed in some embarrassing contradiction is a necessary but not sufficient component of a sound foreign legal policy. Beyond the purely discursive challenge is evidently a fundamental normative one. The welcome recognition that one 'engineers' the international legal system over time through one's interventions still leaves largely open the question of where states want to place the cursor of non-intervention, assuming that they have some control over that process. In stylized form, the challenge can be described as how one might maintain a relatively open international system in a context where openness is preyed upon by powerful foreign interests, often increasingly operating in collusion with domestic ones. All states, whether authoritarian or liberal, have to weigh how much they value continued engagement with other states against their desire to maintain the self-referential character of their sovereignty. Certainly, a consideration of not only domestic but the long-term international interests of states will be relevant here, for example between the risk of a further 'Westphalianization' of the internet as opposed to a 'free flow of information',[1360] with major geopolitical implications. At the same time, such simplistic images need to themselves be problematized in light of power asymmetries: it is certainly easier to be in favor of the free flow of information when one controls it, for example.

The dilemma is, no doubt, a complex one. States that are committed to a certain openness may decide that there is not much that they can do to fight interference in conditions of globalization—at the risk of the significant exposure

1359 Franck and Weisband (n 4) 980.

1360 Schmitt and Vihul (n 521) 217.

of some of their institutions, although in a way that reinforces their ability to make a strong case for certain types of interference—or they may emphasize the protection of their sovereignty in ways that protect their institutions better, but then also impair their own liberal expansionist instincts. It may be that an openness to outside influence is the price one has to pay for wanting other states to exhibit similar openness, and states may ultimately decide that in an open world they need to acclimatize themselves to more systematic meddling. But this will inevitably create trade-offs between domestic politics and foreign policy, the interest one has in keeping one's political sphere reasonably insulated whilst retaining tools to influence that of others. The dilemma is in a sense easier for states that oppose interference and deny that they are involved in any interference of their own—they are at least normatively consistent and do not create any noticeable tension between domestic and foreign goals. States that, by contrast, are caught insisting on a very national definition of their domestic sphere but are associated with a cavalier attitude to the domestic sphere of others will expose themselves to stinging rebukes.

Amidst all the recrimination, intermediary 'non-interference pacts' may arise across divides, based on a sort of equilibrium of fear and risk in relation to potential interference. After all, 'isolationism is prompted by a desire to induce respect for the internal autonomy of the state that has "isolated" itself' and that may have done so 'in exchange for the expectation that it will improve the prospect of securing reciprocal noninterference'.[1361] Reciprocity in what one does but also in what one does not do continues to provide one of the most appealing socio-legal foundations for international law because of the way it seems to reconcile state interest and a more societal vision of the international legal order. In fact, this is not entirely speculative as just such a deal—an *actual* non-interference agreement—was reportedly briefly contemplated between the U.S. and Russia.[1362]

Although that possibility was scuttled early, it has its realist defenders who, taking full cognizance of the asymmetry between the two and the relative vulnerability of the U.S. to cyberattacks, consider that this sort of 'mutual

1361 Falk, *Legal Order in a Violent World* (n 117) 169.

1362 Hudson (n 867); Jack Goldsmith, 'On the Russian Proposal for Mutual Noninterference in Domestic Politics' (*Lawfare*, 12 November 2017) <https://www.lawfaremedia.org/article/russian-proposal-mutual-noninterference-domestic-politics> accessed 3 April 2024. The possibility of an Australian-Chinese treaty has also been academically mooted. Daniel Mack, 'An Era of Foreign Political Interference: Impulsive, Overcompensation of Australia, and a Comparison of Legislative Schemes with the United States' (2020) 34 Emory International Law Review 367, s III.B.

forbearance' would be the least bad ill.[1363] It can be seen as having had precedents in the form of the 1933 Roosevelt-Litvinov exchange of letters committing the USSR to 'respect scrupulously the indisputable right of the United States to order its own life within its own jurisdiction in its own way and to refrain from interfering in any manner in the internal affairs of the United States, its territories or possessions' and vice versa.[1364] Note also that states desisting from inter-state litigation, particularly when it comes to human rights, has been explained as their being 'disinclined to embark on a path that could ultimately turn against them, and expose themselves to similar proceedings', especially against the background of 'a general culture of non-intervention'.[1365]

'Pulling one's punches', at any rate, remains a classic strategic gambit, both in the hope of drawing in other states to compromise and maintaining a certain deniability about one's own malfeasance. States may not want to attract too much attention on the interference they are subjected to, lest they be confronted with evidence of their own meddling in the affairs of others. They may thus decide that they are better off, all other things equal, by deciding to mutually not interfere with at least some states. They may further engage in exercises of protecting each other's back, for example by supporting other states wary of what they see as interference at the hands of international human rights bodies.[1366] In some ways, this is merely the rediscovery of international law redux and its dependence on expectations of similar treatment, except on a more limited bilateral basis (which, over time, can nonetheless accrue into something bigger). Whatever the case may be, such agreements will undoubtedly exact *normative* costs, the price of forfeiting one's ability to interfere in exchange for not being interfered with. As one U.S. official put it, for example, for a non-interference agreement to be concluded with Russia '[w]e would have to give up democracy promotion in Russia, which we're not

1363 Kimberly Marten, 'Digital Détente' *The New Republic* (28 November 2017) <https://newrepublic.com/article/145911/digital-detente-cyber-peace-russia> accessed 3 April 2024; Jack Goldsmith, 'Contrarian Thoughts on Russia and the Presidential Election' (*Default*, 1 October 2017) <https://www.lawfaremedia.org/article/contrarian-thoughts-russia-and-presidential-election> accessed 3 April 2024.

1364 'Exchange of Communications Between the President of the United States and Maxim M. Litvinov People's Commissar for Foreign Affairs of the Union of Soviet Socialist Republics' (1934) 28 American Journal of International Law 2.

1365 Tom Ruys, 'Legal Standing and Public Interest Litigation: Are All Erga Omnes Breaches Equal?' (2021) 20 Chinese Journal of International Law 457, 492.

1366 Ted Piccone, 'China's Long Game on Human Rights at the United Nations' (Brookings Institution 2018) <https://www.brookings.edu/wp-content/uploads/2018/09/FP_20181009_china_human_rights.pdf> accessed 12 July 2024.

willing to do'.[1367] The iron discipline of reciprocity can only be sustained on the condition of desisting from behavior that one might have thought is in one's interest to engage in.

At the other end of the spectrum, of course, the agreement may logically also be one about mutual interference because interference is simply too valuable to relinquish. As was once pointed out, '[s]o long [...] as insurrections and civil wars find big Powers behind competing factions, so long as competing interventions are a principal phenomenon of "Cold War", an agreed attitude towards subversion which can be said to be or to be becoming law is unlikely'.[1368] If no explicit agreement either way, the default attitude may be that of a strategic retreat into a position of plausible deniability, one leaving enough room of maneuver to extract oneself from tight spots whilst never fully conceding to a good faith engagement with the norm of non-intervention. This would not necessarily doom the clarification of a norm of interference, but it would keep it in a deliberate and permanent state of indeterminacy and indecisiveness.

There is certainly a level of strategic silence going on in the worldwide debate on interference, reminiscent, for example, of the status of espionage under international law (not exactly legal, but not exactly illegal either).[1369] It has even been suggested that states that rely too much on domestic and international law to frame their spying activities will incur a 'legal disability' where a 'policy of creative ambivalence' at least keeps options open.[1370] Some states will invariably decide that it is simply better to stay mum so as not to risk solidifying claims to the existence of interference either way, thus ensuring that they can continue to make contradictory arguments over time,[1371] and benefit from interference's 'constructive ambiguity'.[1372] This is evident in relation to the *cause célèbre* of economic sanctions as well, where it has been said that 'there are no rules of international law which categorically pronounce

1367 Hudson (n 867).

1368 Henkin and others (n 67) 158.

1369 Radsan (n 541); Iñaki Navarrete and Russell Buchan, 'Out of the Legal Wilderness: Peacetime Espionage, International Law and the Existence of Customary Exceptions' (2018) 51 Cornell International Law Journal 897; Asaf Lubin, 'The Liberty to Spy' (2020) 61 Harvard International Law Journal 185; Raphael Bitton, 'The Legitimacy of Spying among Nations' (2014) 29 American University International Law Review 1009.

1370 Forcese (n 532) 210.

1371 Sander (n 390).

1372 Keitner (n 877) 180.

either on the prima-facie legality or prima-facie illegality of economic coercion',[1373] a result that one can surmise may well be intentional.

It has been argued by the British Attorney General for example that, when it comes to the parameters of acceptable cyber-activity, '[a]round the world there are many who would not bother trying—some because they have scant regard for international law more generally and some because they see little advantage in being explicit about rules of acceptable behaviour'.[1374] As Christina Nowak argues in the context of intervention in civil wars:

> state practice has, slightly and imperceptibly, refocused, re-directed or varied the separation of what was formerly considered to be either strictly legal behaviour or obviously non-legal acts. As a result, it is increasingly difficult to accurately draw the line between an unfriendly but legal interference and an unlawful intervention.[1375]

There is thus a degree of 'strategic muddling' involved, wherein states cover their tracks and seek to not corner themselves into positions they may come to regret. Some debates may as a result appear to be in a permanent state of inconclusive stalemate not only because they espouse rigid lines of polarization, but because all sides have an interest in their inconclusive character. Craig Forcese has suggested in this context that the 'very fact' that there is so much disagreement in the debate on the legality of espionage in international law suggests that the position that it is 'neither legal nor illegal [...] lies closest to the truth' and that 'the international community seems content with an artful ambiguity on the question'.[1376]

Indeed, one of the main strategic dilemmas of dealing with interference is whether and to what extent it should be designated as such at all. Interference might be seen as problematic but only in certain contexts, and not worth denouncing, at least in a way that would allow systematization of claims about it. It is not even obvious that interference should be specifically prohibited in law even though, as the European Parliament has pointed out, making it a criminal offence would at least 'target and stigmatise this malign behaviour'.[1377] The

1373 Omer Yousif Elagab, *The Legality of Non-Forcible Counter-Measures in International Law* (University of Oxford 1986) 212.

1374 Jeremy Wright, 'Cyber and International Law in the 21st Century' (Chatham House, 23 May 2018) <https://www.gov.uk/government/speeches/cyber-and-international-law-in-the-21st-century> accessed 11 March 2019.

1375 Nowak (n 22) 75.

1376 Forcese (n 532) 204–205.

1377 2022 Resolution on Foreign Interference in the E.U. (n 337), CB.

inability to fully and consistently designate what one adamantly condemns in general terms, then, is surely one of the puzzles at the heart of interference. Debates such as that over unilateral coercive measures reveal both deep contradictions between groups of states, continuous institutional tensions and, ultimately at best, an 'agreement to disagree' about whether such measures are legal, tolerable, or legitimate.[1378] It may be that international law can never do better than the political contradictions it presides over; it is merely those contradictions made law, although it is at least *those* contradictions.

The end result is that the status of something as common as unilateral sanctions for example may remain shrouded in ambiguity and contestation, revealing hidden depths of dissensus.[1379] There has been some emerging scholarly recognition of how the complexity of the debates on interference has led many states to keep their cards close, prefer ambiguous positions or defer the adoption of international norms to inconclusive and open-ended processes. For Chimène Keitner, the result of 'the tension produced by states' conflicting desires to preserve the greatest possible freedom of action for themselves and to develop rules that constrain the behavior of others' is in fact that this has 'impeded the ability to formulate explicit treaty-based solutions to the problem of foreign election interference'.[1380] This is a reminder that, in the international arena, states may not always, despite claims to the contrary, aspire to the clarity and consistency of rules. This sometimes-tepid engagement with international law nonetheless creates a significant hiatus between what is considered binding and what is deemed merely desirable,[1381] maintaining a margin of manoeuvre to allow for unforeseen circumstances that can become as determinative as rule following.

What remains clear, despite the inconclusiveness of the debate on a general level, is that it will be particularly difficult over time for states to 'have it both ways', namely, to enjoy the fruits of interference in the affairs of other states whilst strongly objecting to interference in their own. If international law stands for something it must surely be at a minimum the equivalency and symmetry of fundamental international obligations of all. This is of course compatible with disagreeing on the facts about whether a particular interference falls into the unlawful category, and it is hardly a full proof guarantee that stable and equanimous outcomes will emerge over time. But it may be

1378 Hofer (n 775).
1379 Bogdanova (n 970) ch 2.
1380 Keitner (n 877) 180.
1381 Samuli Haataja, 'Cyber Operations against Critical Infrastructure under Norms of Responsible State Behaviour and International Law' (2022) 30 International Journal of Law and Information Technology 423, 430–432.

international law's saving grace when it comes to interference, and it does point to the basic reality that it has become increasingly problematic under the transparent current conditions of contemporary international discourse to have an international law standard for oneself, and another for others. This does not exhaust the totality of dilemmas that confront states, many of which involve them taking a stance on how the ongoing definition of interference affects their relationship to international law and organization and their own constitutional and political becoming. This third part will explore these dilemmas, notably as they involve states and other actors, through the constitution of 'interference', in complex arbitrages between the domestic and the international realm (Chapter 5) that ultimately require all participants to think hard about how their knowledge claims create the international legal world within which they operate (Chapter 6).

CHAPTER 5

Engaging the Dilemmas of the Domestic and the International

1 Introduction

One of the crucial strategic dilemmas of dealing with interference, particularly of the new kind, is the extent to which states should draw on international law at all. Every investment in international law is a relative disinvestment in domestic defenses against intervention, and vice versa. The investment in international law is a plausible one, as this chapter will show, but it is not a foregone conclusion. It commits one to a particular style of argumentation and, ultimately, a particular vision of sovereignty and what to interfere with it means. States must figure for themselves whether their investment in international law has a value of its own (being 'good citizens' of international law) or whether it only has instrumental value in terms of being more or less capable of offsetting interference. They must also be cautious about how their investments in international law can come back to haunt them and require an arbitrage between merely tactical and strategic victories.

Specifically, states must be aware of how the position one takes on these debates both relies on and may impact broader views about the relationship between the 'national' and the 'international', or the 'domestic' and the 'foreign' as productive categories of international legal thought. A strong emphasis on non-intervention, on the one hand, portrays states as systematically on the defensive, at the mercy of powerful outside forces, and constantly in need of the sort of international legal protection associated with sovereignty; an emphasis on interaction and interdependence, on the other hand, emphasizes the primacy of robust exchanges, states as naturally capable of guarding against undue influences, and the relatively secondary character of international legal protections against interference. Indeed, both attitudes echo deeper implicit normative commitments: at one end of the spectrum, a strong republican attachment to near-autarchic self-determination and therefore the need to not corrupt domestic (including democratic) processes through foreign influence; and, on the other end, an endorsement of the imbricated nature of international life, one in which it is quite difficult and perhaps deemed undesirable to disentangle the domestic and the foreign.

 | DOI:10.1163/9789004532731_010

1.1 *Interference as Crisis*

In other words, the 'new interference' goes at the heart of questions that have been asked insistently since the end of the Cold War about the sustainability of globalization. A world order marked by open borders, for the purposes of world trade and investment at least, has come repeatedly under threat as some of its contradictions have been exposed. The 'new interference' can be seen as only the latest in a number of lingering crises that have cast doubt on whether even those powers historically most enthusiastic about globalization were ever more than nominally committed to it, at least if it did not operate to their advantage. These crises include 9/11 and the fear of apocalyptic foreign terrorism, the immigration 'crisis' notably following the war in Syria, a global pandemic and the rise of China as the world's leading economic power, all of which have prompted sustained reaffirmation of borders. The interference scare fits very much in this pattern of seeing shadowy foreign forces as stripping one of one's autonomy and therefore security and privilege. Ironically in this context, it is 'populists' that seem least concerned about interference, either because they cynically exploit it to their tactical electoral advantage, or because they (rightly?) calculate that in precipitating the contradictions of the liberal international legal order it will more quickly bring about its demise.

The point here is not to engage in an extensive geopolitical analysis for its own sake but to emphasize that current debates about interference are inseparable from this broader context and that international lawyers study the question as one of mere legal technique at some risk. In particular, it should be clear that the interference 'moment' manifests a profound crisis of faith in the Western legal model. That model was based, in its hinterland at least, on the notion that reasonably autonomous territorialized communities (states) could interact with each other over time without fundamentally losing their autonomy or indeed their very identity qua self-directing polities. It heralded the state as a promise of self-referential emancipation that would not constantly be vulnerable to the whims of others. The model profoundly irrigated every idea of modern political thought, from democracy to constitutionalism, nationalism to rights, and sovereignty to law. It is that model that was sold to the world with tremendous success. It was compatible with entertaining thoughts about transcending sovereignty from above, although only to better constitute it supranationally on a regional basis. Of course, that model was always a bit of an illusion for most of the world, but the states that primarily benefited from it could at least comfort themselves into believing that it approximated what had been imagined as early as the 18th Century. The one thing the model could not countenance—or indeed, fathom—, however, was the possibility that it would bring about a world in which decisional power could no longer reliably be located or even ascribed to the heart of sovereignty, a world in which, in fact, the heart of sovereignty appeared rotten to the core. Behind the crisis of sovereignty, moreover, also lies a crisis of the ideas of peoplehood and self-determination, which cautions against offering up either as the solution to the epoch's ills.

1.2 *Two Models*

Two models have arisen to re-perform a sense of political autonomy in the context of its radical erosion: authoritarianism and populism. These are of course only reincarnations of earlier versions of themselves, but now increasingly fixated on the notion of interference. Nor are they incompatible, although they remain analytically severable. The authoritarian model seeks to reenergize sovereignty whilst the populist model seeks to reenergize peoplehood, both as antidotes against the perceived dispossession of self occasioned by globalization. To be clear and as per one of this book's fundamental intuitions, what is novel in this moment is that some of the forces unleashed in the 1990s are in a sense finally coming home to roost, laying waste to any notion that one could lastingly direct them at others whilst insulating oneself from their destructive effects. Economic liberalization allowed for huge economic gains, yet it now threatens to eviscerate the political basis of historically leading economies' dominance and the formal sovereignty that undergirded them. The globalization of media flows helped secure significant strides in terms of liberalization but it now threatens the very possibility of liberalism. Similarly, political overtures to the rest of the world, long initiated in a very unidirectional way, now threaten to undermine the very independence of states that pioneered it.

What both the authoritarian and populist model assume is that interference is fundamentally *foreign*. In this, they may well fall into the trap that they have laid for themselves, failing to see interference as essentially home grown, long internally welcome, and the result of a dispossession that is at least as much a transfer of decisional power to the economic sphere than it is the result of a mingling with other sovereigns. Were that reality seen for what it is, the common nature of the problem of interference, the fact that it straddles facile divisions between 'liberal' and 'illiberal' societies and even the domestic and the foreign, might lead to a moment of reckoning. In the meantime, the symbolic stake of debates about interference is whether one can (ever) recreate conditions of political self-mastery, even as such conditions are largely mythologized. The law has a considerable role to play in this gambit, both as what is protected (one's 'own' law, sovereign and national) and as what does the protection, reasserting a protective perimeter around its production. In that respect, the legal arsenals being deployed against interference are truly performative: they manifest, if nothing else, the sense that the law is what is being threatened by interference and that the law must therefore have a role to play in guarding against it.

The study of interference, then, radicalizes questions about the relevance of different regime types under international law and the way they stand to be differentially impacted by it. The problematic character of interference does cut across genres of government but for quite different reasons and in different ways. For authoritarian regimes, interference is perceived as a potential threat to their stranglehold on power, a manifestation of potentially ill-placed international solicitude that purports to displace their grasp in the name of superior international values. But at least in combating such interference, those states are merely extending a repressive playbook that they already ordinarily deploy internally. The threat, real or imagined, of interference may even be a 'divine surprise',[1382] one allowing them to do that which they would have wanted to do anyhow. In that respect, agendas of non-interference may be largely pretextual, harnessing the perceived threat of interference for domestic advantage, an ideal excuse for illiberal agendas.

For purportedly 'liberal' or 'open' societies, interference raises the more convoluted dilemma of how one can limit access to internal public life from outside whilst not appearing to and effectively violating the very principles that liberalism claims to stand for. In other words, how can one reconcile the commitment to an 'open society', central to the modern constitution of liberalism as it is presented, and an attitude bent on circumscribing and protecting sovereign power? This, in a context where every pushback against foreign meddling may end up furnishing arguments to autocrats elsewhere to justify cutting their own societies off from 'corrupting' and 'foreign' influences; but also where we have no reason to think that protection against foreign meddling, even in supposedly liberal societies, never borrows from paternalistic, populist or xenophobic playbooks. Indeed, one possibility is that the non-interference agenda will expose liberalism's hypocrisy or at least double standards: non-interference at home, but sustained only historically by an agenda of interference abroad; and non-interference as a domestic agenda of ideological repression (e.g., McCarthyism) and racism (anti-semitism, anti-Catholicism, Sinophobia, anti-black racism, etc.).[1383]

1382 Raymond Garreau, 'Maurras, 1940 et la "divine surprise"' *Le Monde.fr* (4 December 1975) <https://www.lemonde.fr/archives/article/1975/12/04/maurras-1940-et-la-divine-surprise_2587710_1819218.html> accessed 16 June 2024.

1383 Lila Corwin Berman, 'How a Citizen Becomes an Alien: Three Cases of American Jews and Citizenship Lost, Regained, and Lost Again' (2022) 5 Modern American History 289; Steven Waldman, 'The Ugly History of Dual-Loyalty Charges' [2019] *The Atlantic*

Indeed, citizens at home may be wary of how a heavy-handed response to foreign 'interference' may end up compromising their own rights given the difficulty of disentangling the domestic and the foreign and the possibility that they will be unjustly associated with the 'foreign'; and states that are on the receiving end of human rights and democracy promotion efforts will be the first to point to the hypocrisy of the discovery of the newly found travails of the open society. One of the concerns here will inevitably be the temptation of reinventing the domestic sphere as more domestic than it ever was, at the risk of damaging its necessary porosity; another will be mistaking one's shadow for the external problem one is trying to address or vice versa; yet another will be that of over-reaction to a perceived threat of interference, possibly feeding into a paranoia about foreign actors, that could have profoundly destructive impacts on democracy. This suggests that, rather than thinking about how international law can protect an already fully constituted *domaine réservé*, the better question is how the international norm of non-intervention or non-interference is constantly co-constituting a particular vision of the *domaine*. At heart, the challenge is to prod the evolving limits of the domestic sphere as a function of ongoing juxtapositions of claims about what is properly considered domestic and international.

1.3 *International Law's Calling?*

This is in a sense international law's calling, precariously maintaining conditions of autonomy and cooperation, independence and integration, in an effort to not wholly compromise itself. However, arbitrating the complex demands of sovereignty quickly risks contradiction. Claims about non-interference relate to what Vaughan Lowe has described as 'two things that people tend to expect from the law: that it keeps other people off their backs and leaves them free to organize their lives as they choose, and that it climbs onto other peoples backs so as to oblige them to do things for the common good'.[1384] Therein lies a fundamental tension of international law that speaks both to the value of minding one's own business and of organizing collectively, including as it manifests itself in the debate about interference: to not interfere is also, to a degree, to be required to not-interfere by an 'interfering' outside entity in the name of international values. There is no non-interference, that is, outside a degree of interference manifested in international community diktats to collectively

<https://www.theatlantic.com/ideas/archive/2019/03/ilhan-omar-and-ugly-history-dual-loyal-trope/584185/> accessed 16 June 2024.

1384 Vaughan Lowe, *International Law: A Very Short Introduction* (Oxford University Press 2015) 56.

sustain the norm of non-interference. This also speaks, presumably, to the fundamental utility of international law, namely that it makes it possible to formulate, in discursively generalizable categories, a claim about non-intervention or non-interference that is immediately recognizable to other states as the same claim they themselves make.

Yet it is difficult to ignore the fact that the era is also reactivating concerns about whether international law can be up to the task. In some quarters, international law has long been suspected of being a Trojan horse for sovereignty-dispossessing globalizing agenda, one that constantly minimizes and even ridicules the dangers of interference. This is somewhat ironic given international law's conservatism and its commitment to an equilibrium-state, yet as will be seen in this chapter there are reasons, including foundational ones, to be skeptical that international law can be part of the undoing of what it has itself brought about. Indeed, it is difficult to discuss interference as a purely international matter without taking into account the way the response to it almost always already structures societies domestically and raises a host of, inter alia, constitutional questions. Strikingly, international lawyers often do exactly that, relying on an exclusively international corpus of authority on the proper meaning of non-intervention, even as a more fine-grained attention to how it is processed constitutionally is not only interesting on its own terms, but a compelling source of practice and *opinio juris*.

The reality is that the *domaine réservé* is constantly being constituted by its domestic affirmation and delineation, through executive, legislative, and judicial agency, in the constitutional, criminal or civil fields. International law in such an environment is not exactly an afterthought, but it is typically resorted to when all else has failed; when the *domaine*, that is, has been breached despite its domestic delineation. International lawyers neglect that initial, intimate life of the *domaine* at some cost: often, when the issue becomes an international legal one, it will be after a gradual bubbling up of domestic developments that are the key to understanding why interference is being complained of, by whom, when and for what reason. This book has hinted as much when referencing the practice of 'sanctuarizing' certain areas of governance for example, in what must surely count as a useful and productive signaling practice, warning potential outside interveners that they encroach on a domain of sovereign life at their peril. This chapter will continue down that road by exploring ways in which the deployment of the law is used to further perform and reinstate its conditions of existence: law to the law's rescue.

2 Domestic v International Law?

The renewed debate about interference creates dilemmas, to begin with, for conceptualizing the relationship of domestic and international law. It is by no means a foregone conclusion that international law should have the upper hand in dealing with interference. The emergence of the new interference has if nothing else put into sharp relief the issue of whether international law has much to say on the issue of the day, or whether it is not hopelessly lagging behind developments that seem to belie some of its core assumptions. There is ultimately no reason in principle why states should seek the appropriate response to their perceived woes in international law, especially when they may aspire to fundamentally asymmetrical privileges that are hard to countenance within international law's structure. States will typically seek, if they can get away with it, to maximize their ability to interfere with the sovereign affairs of others whilst minimizing the ability of other states to interfere with theirs. In effect, many states have turned towards constitutional law, for example, to protect the operation of *their* democracy rather than making this an argument about international law to protect the sovereignty of all.

We should not assume that international law necessarily has anything particularly relevant to say about interference although nor, evidently, should we dismiss that possibility out of hand. If international law is found to be insufficiently protective of states, then they may simply choose to reframe the issue unilaterally as one of purely domestic, say constitutional or national security law. After all, states may decide that they cannot wait for international law to provide decisive guidance about how to protect them from an interference that they find unwanted, regardless of whether it is ascertainably illegal internationally or not. Simultaneously, although international law may in and of itself insufficiently protect states from interference, it is at least unlikely that it denies states the freedom to deal with what they see as threats to their sovereignty in the ways they see fit, in the spirit of the Lotus precedent. This is not to mention the fact that, as this book has pointed out, state sovereignty and the *domaine réservé* are to a large extent creatures of states' own making, and that making owes much to the day-to-day manifestations of the forces of domestic law.

2.1 *Privileging the Domestic*

A state may thus adopt a broad arsenal of domestic protective measures to fend off interference that are neither required but nor, more importantly, prohibited by international law. In that respect, international law's role may be permissive rather than imperative, which means in practice deferring significantly to domestic law, allowing states to carefully modulate their exposure to intrusion: non-interference, in short, as what states make of it.[1385] Domestic law ensures that there is no regulatory vacuum, only a multiplicity of not always reconcilable national positions on what constitutes or does not constitute interference through the ongoing and autopoeitic constitution of the *domaine réservé*. As Keitner has noted, '[i]n the future, these rules might coalesce into a body of international law',[1386] but the possibility that they might not is also real and should be acknowledged soberly. The accumulation of domestic legal praxis international law does not make. This suggests a view of the utility of international law that is quite minimalistic, even when it comes to the issue of the moment.

Historically, states have indeed occasionally chosen to not invest too much in international law's power as a shield against interference, often simply availing themselves of the ability to reinforce their own sovereign defenses via domestic initiatives. For example, as early as the 1930s and 1950s, when first Nazi and then Soviet propaganda threatened, the U.S. adopted a raft of administrative measures designed to deal with such threats that only loosely invoked the authority of international law and partook much more evidently in a homegrown tradition of domestic protection.[1387] Part of the latest wave of U.S. reaction to interference has, in fact, been to seek to revive old Cold War statutes such as the Foreign Agents Registration Act.[1388] The U.S.,[1389] Canada,[1390] the U.K.,[1391] Australia,[1392] and France[1393] have all adopted new legislative arsenals including new or expanded secrecy, sabotage, and treason related-offences. The European Union has recommended that interference be specifically criminalized, in line with U.S., U.K., and Australian developments. Corporations, particularly social media platforms, are to be obliged to detect interference. It has been argued in this context that such an offence, although its effectiveness is 'difficult to measure':

1385 This argument has most notably been made by Keitner (n 877).

1386 ibid 180.

1387 Nicholas J Cull, *The Cold War and the United States Information Agency: American Propaganda and Public Diplomacy, 1945–1989* (Cambridge University Press 2008).

1388 22 USC ch 11, subch II, ss 611–621 (1938).

1389 HR 7120/Public Law No 115–386 (2018).

1390 *Elections Modernization Act*, SC 2018, c 31, s 282.4.

1391 Data Protection Act 2018, c 12; Investigatory Powers Act 2016, c 25.

1392 National Security Legislation Amendment (Espionage and Foreign Interference) Act 2018 (Cth).

1393 Loi nº 2015-912 du 24 Juillet 2015 relative au renseignement; Loi nº2018-493 du 20 juin 2018 relative à la protection des données personnelles.

> will make it more difficult and more costly for foreign states to engage in foreign interference. The offence may curb criminal behaviour and deter third parties within the E.U. from supporting foreign actors in that behaviour. It will demonstrate the EU's perception that foreign interference is a criminal activity that should not be tolerated, and the EU's commitment to tackling it. [...] Criminalisation of foreign interference may also have indirect effect: it may encourage social media companies to devote more resource to detecting and tackling foreign interference on their platforms.[1394]

To be clear, moreover, the deployment of such arsenals is not limited to democracies. In 2017, the Russian Federation Council created a Commission 'on protecting state sovereignty and preventing interference in Russia's domestic affairs'. The project was endorsed by 152 senators, and only one abstention.[1395]

Across the board, at any rate, there is a remarkable constancy to the sort of measures that have been put in place by states.[1396] One of the goals of these new measures is, as seen in Chapter 3, to 're-nationalize' various domestic spheres, particularly the political and, as the case may be, democratic, and better protect them against real or perceived foreign incursions. Emblematic measures include bans on foreign financing of political parties or obligations of registration as foreign agents. As one Canadian lawyer put it, the Elections Modernization Act is meant to 'keep[...] it Canadian' by prohibiting all foreign funding of political activity.[1397] This process of demarcation is not unlike similar processes that have arisen in relation to states' physical borders and increasingly quixotic efforts to erect obstacles to migration: they involve, metaphorically, a sort of retreat into oneself. It is important to note that such measures are prima facie largely unilateral, do not draw on any particular international authorization and seem to flow from states' separate non-interference

1394 Jones (n 495) 15.

1395 'Russian Senate Creates Special Commission to Explore Ways to Prevent Western Political Interference' [2017] Meduza <https://meduza.io/en/news/2017/06/14/russian-senate-creates-special-commission-to-explore-ways-to-prevent-western-political-interference> accessed 14 February 2019.

1396 Ringhand (n 107); Scott J Shackelford and others, 'Making Democracy Harder to Hack' (2016) 50 University of Michigan Journal of Law Reform 629.

1397 Elisabeth Neelin, 'Keeping It Canadian: Guarding Against Foreign Interference in the Modernization of the Canada Elections Act' (*Langlois avocats*, 8 August 2019) <https://langlois.ca/keeping-canadian-guarding-foreign-interference-modernization-canada-elections-act/> accessed 28 August 2023.

agendas, even if these agendas, facing the same challenges, may have a similar inspiration and come up with similar measures.

2.2 *The Relative Irrelevance of International Law*

Much of the domestic response by states to the 'new interference', then, has been elaborated within international law but in ways that are not necessarily over determined by it. For example, banning foreign financing of political parties is certainly not prohibited under international law, but nor is it mandated by it. Conveniently collated IDEA data shows that, overall, about two thirds of the world's countries prohibit foreign financing of political parties whereas less than a third do nothing of the sort: significant, but perhaps not to the point of 'generalized practice' as would sustain a finding of a customary norm, especially given the conspicuous absence of *opinio juris*. The Venice Commission has also come to the conclusion that even under European human rights law, 'there cannot be only one answer to the question to what extent the prohibition of a foreign political party financing a political party may be consider "necessary in a democratic society"', so that 'every individual case has to be considered separately'.[1398]

One would certainly struggle to find states claiming that they ban foreign financing because they are *obliged* to, but nor, it should be said, would one find foreign states symmetrically protesting such bans on international law grounds. Of course, domestic, ground-up practice emerging from both constitutional and penal habitus (itself often relying on the 'best practices' of other states) might at some point coalesce towards the establishment of customary rules (at least about the legality of such initiatives rather than their binding character). As has been noted, 'conceivably, [the criminalization of interference by the E.U.] might be relevant in discussions on the extent to which foreign interference is or should be prohibited in public international law'.[1399] But it seems that we are simply not at the point where such uncoordinad initiatives, often taking as their point of reference constitutional or regional rather than universal values, are an unmistakable harbinger of customary international law.

In short, there is neither homogeneous practice nor *opinio juris* that suggests, for example, that banning foreign financing is anything else than an option under international law, one of the many things that states may but do

1398 Venice Commission, '66th Plenary Session, Venice, 17–18 March 2006, Opinion on the Prohibition of Financial Contributions to Political Parties from Foreign Sources' (2006) CDL-AD (2006)014 paras 32–34.

1399 Jones (n 495) 15.

not have to do as part of their sovereignty. International law, in fact, has not necessarily been at the forefront of the dynamics of insulation from foreign interference, except in a sort of default way as sanctioning the reality and, to a degree, the legitimacy of state unilateralism. This is clear, for example, in that the Group of Governmental Experts Developments in the Field of Information and Telecommunications in the Context of International Security (GGE), even as it has restated the applicability of international law in that context, has adopted norms that are voluntary and non-binding. The international contribution to the practice of countering interference—as opposed to its stating very broadly the terms under which such interference will be frowned upon—has been underwhelming and is better understood, especially when it comes to the new interference, as having been outsourced to domestic praxis, possibly as part of wait-and-see strategies by states.

One may speculate that the amorphous nature of the 'new interference' relatively diminishes the value of international legal arguments to denounce it on a bilateral basis and, conversely, relatively increases the utility of boosting available domestic defenses that are more tailored to the protective needs of particular states. This is especially in a context where there is little reason to think that states that sponsor the new interference will have much openness to entertaining international legal arguments about its illegality, even assuming that target states wanted to elevate the argument to the level of an explicit international legal dispute. The U.S. regime against election interference includes the possibility of sanctions decided following an intelligence assessment of whether elections have been tampered with, for example, which includes the U.S. Attorney-General, the Secretary of Homeland Security, and the Secretary of the Treasury in ways that do not seem particularly reliant on international legal counsel.[1400]

Opting to not specifically invoke international law when adopting domestic interference countermeasures, then, remains an avenue. This is especially in a context where, for example, the prospering of sovereign or quasi-sovereign cyber activity emerged thanks to the perceived paucity of international rules, and where the absence of clear international legal definition is seen as a boon by some actors. In other words, the relative poverty of international law on interference (or at least of actionable, determinate, and enforceable international law) may serve the designs of many states, allowing them to take advantage of confusion over the concept when accused of interfering, yet not depriving themselves of the ability to individually upgrade their defenses

1400 Executive Order No 13848, 31 CFR §579 (2018) (United States).

against interference that they individually deem noxious. The switch to largely domestic solutions could also reflect a shift from something that is seen as specifically illegal (in the tradition of the non-intervention rule) to something that is inimical, bothersome, but not meaningfully or at least usefully illegal under international law, and which states still maintain the possibility of making illegal domestically, on a need-basis. This would consecrate a marginalization of international law—possibly because it has been finally exposed as allowing no state to maximize interference vis-à-vis others whilst minimizing interference towards oneself—and an attendant hypertrophy of largely ad hoc, unilateral 'inside out' rather than 'outside in' responses designed to at least increase the cost of interference.

2.3 *The Unavoidability of International Law?*

Nonetheless, it is difficult to imagine that international law would have no role and that the international community's response to hostile interference would merely amount to the sum of isolated individual state practice not particularly informed by a sense of international obligation. This would be striking departure from the last decades of international experience which, as we saw, were heavily focused on trying to promote a central norm of non-intervention in international law and warranted significant investments to that effect in international fora. International law, presumably, calls upon states to repeatedly wear a double hat when it comes to interference: both arguing when it is problematic to protect states' sovereignty, and defending against allegations that it is problematic. In both cases, domestic law may be at the wheel when it comes to either legitimizing or challenging interference, but it is always only one step away from the objectivization of domestic responses through diplomatic channels in the terms of international law.

It may well be, for example, that the basic legal infrastructure of sanctions is rooted in domestic law (e.g., in the U.S., a number of Executive Orders by which the President can decide to adopt sanctions against certain states). In this day and age, interference has seemingly become as much an issue of domestic constitutional, administrative and criminal law, as states boost the immune system of their sovereignty. This makes sense so far as it goes on the basis of states' wide latitude to regulate their domestic affairs. However, such an infrastructure is basically irrelevant from the perspective of international law where it justifies nothing. One cannot oppose it to other states in one's dealings with them short of some theory of their legitimacy under international law, be it through a doctrine of jurisdiction, some version of the Lotus principle or some specifically enabling norm of international law. The fact that State A criminalizes a certain form of interference, for example, may work well within the confines of State A but it does not make it interference for the purposes of international law and may even render it vulnerable to the criticism that it is exceeding its authority. To the extent that State A wants to invoke this interference as a litigious issue with State B, the mere *fait accompli* of its criminal law will only go so far. States can no more invoke their domestic law to make something illegal under international law than they can invoke their domestic law to justify international law violations. State A may be able to claim that agents of State B violated its domestic law but not necessarily that State B interfered with its domestic affairs. State B may, in return, argue that what State A defines as criminal interference is such a mismatch with international law's definition that it cannot possibly constitute intervention/interference.

Moreover, to the extent that states adopt not only protective but also punitive and retaliatory measures, for example, they will inevitably be called upon to justify them under international law, including human rights law. For example, both the U.S. and Greece have responded to perceived meddling in elections by expulsing, respectively, 35 and 2 Russian diplomats, resorting to a classic riposte under international law.[1401] Similarly, when Venezuela declared the E.U. Representative in Caracas *persona non grata* it did so on the basis that the European sanctions regime against Maduro's regime had 'no legal basis in the shared norms of International Law'.[1402] Although such expulsions may occur in a grey zone of international law, they were certainly justified by reference to at least an inchoate sense of violation of an international obligation. Even in domestic law's own term, the inability to objectify what one is condemning ultimately harms a non-interference agenda. As Barrie Sander notes, for example, 'characterising a cyber influence operation as a domestic crime fails to reflect the State-sponsored form that such campaigns often are alleged to take',[1403] and thus robs the victim state of the ability to denounce an international wrong for what it is.

1401 Patrick Wintour, 'Greece to Expel Russian Diplomats over Alleged Macedonia Interference' *The Guardian* (11 July 2018) <https://www.theguardian.com/world/2018/jul/11/greece-to-expel-russian-diplomats-over-alleged-macedonia-interference> accessed 15 February 2019; Lauren Gambino, Sabrina Siddiqui and Shaun Walker, 'Obama Expels 35 Russian Diplomats in Retaliation for U.S. Election Hacking' *The Guardian* (30 December 2016) <https://www.theguardian.com/us-news/2016/dec/29/barack-obama-sanctions-russia-election-hack> accessed 15 February 2019.

1402 Bolivarian Republic of Venezuela, 'Venezuela Rejects the Imposition of New Unilateral Coercive Measures from the EU' (22 February 2021) <https://web.archive.org/web/20210612224651/http://www.mppre.gob.ve/en/comunicado/venezuela-rejects-imposition-new-unilateral-coercive-measures-from-eu/> accessed 12 July 2024.

1403 Sander (n 390) 15.

The international law of retorsion and countermeasures is also sure to remain relevant in assessing states' responses to cyber threats qua interference, where overreaction and escalation as a result of poor visibility are a constant risk. In the European context, it has been emphasized that '[a]ny sanctions regime must be compatible with public international law'[1404] especially when targeting individuals or media organisations. When it comes to countermeasures, one will by definition have to make a case that those are in response to a prior violation of international law, lest one run afoul of, as the case may be, prior international legal commitments. This will then inevitably raise questions of attribution since one cannot, for example, punish a state for an interference operation that one cannot actually compellingly trace back to it. The same goes for claims that an interference is not illegal because it is, in fact, merely an exercise of self-defence (and a preferrable one, incidentally, to one involving the use of force)[1405] or that there is no interference since the state is merely being pressured to comply with an international law obligation and is therefore not threatened with any illegal outcome.

Perhaps more importantly, international law still provides the basic grammar to at least frame claims about whether interference has, in fact, occurred. This is true both for international and domestic consumption, since measures to fend off interference have implications on both levels. This is evident, for example, in the context of U.N. efforts to deal with cybersecurity where the fact that cyber 'technologies and means can potentially be used for purposes that are inconsistent with the objectives of maintaining international stability and security and may adversely affect the security of States' has been the *de rigueur* starting point of the entire exercise.[1406] Contra what might have been a tendency to see hostile cyber activity as wholly exceptional and beyond international law, many states have predictably asserted the continued applicability of existing international obligations, both when it comes to the use of force but also to hostile acts less than the use of force. Moreover, they have insisted that '[m]aking cyberspace stable and secure can be achieved only through international cooperation, and the foundation of this cooperation must be international law and the principles of the Charter of the United Nations'.[1407]

The broad attempt to regulate cyber activity under both general international law and human rights law has centred predictably in part at least on the 'international law prohibition on intervention in the internal affairs of other

1404 Jones (n 495) 16.
1405 Fenwick, 'Intervention: Individual and Collective' (n 71).
1406 UNGA Res 53/70 (1999), Preamble.
1407 UNGA Report on International Security Developments in IT (2015) A/70/174, 4.

states' identified as being 'of particular importance in modern times when technology has an increasing role to play in every facet of our lives, including political campaigns and the conduct of elections'.[1408] This approach is complemented by the effort to regulate cyberspace in real time through, for example, the recommendation of 'voluntary, non-binding norms for responsible State behaviour'.[1409] There may still be opportunities to further define both regional and universal positions on the matter in ways that could clarify, through international cooperation, proper responses. If it takes a more institutional form, such a dialogue may be more productive than the sort of tit-for-tat, *ex post* and *ad hoc* responses that currently characterize states' attitude. One senses that a sort of race against time is involved in terms of whether the regime of interference ends up being determined by domestic or international law, and power politics or law at all.

It should be said, however, that the debate on interference is characterized by such a degree of mistrust and misunderstanding that it is open to doubt whether international law can offer much in the way of resolution where, if anything, the issues have become ever more complicated and fluid. For example, whilst the effort to regulate cyberspace under the auspices of the GGE was initially fairly consensual, deep rifts have of late appeared between a camp led by Russia and comprising many G77 states, and a group of Western states led by the U.S., which bodes ill of the ability to find common ground.[1410] It has been argued that '[a]nxiety over foreign interference is a two-way street and largely resembles the traditional logic of the security dilemma' where '[b]oth Russia and the United States present only their own concerns as legitimate while ridiculing the claims of the other side as unsubstantiated speculations for domestic consumption'.[1411] Needless to say, this is unlikely to lead to stable, general and explicit international norms. In fact, it is more likely to lead to forms of competitive lawyering whereby states seek to outsmart their adversaries rather than agreeing to rules that they can collectively live by. In such an environment, no headway is likely to be made that is not based on an earnest recognition of the extent to which the other has been interfered with—but this still seems a taboo.

To make matters more complicated, not everything is what it seems, and states may tout positions internationally that are fundamentally at odds with their own behavior. For example, a grand proposal to regulate cybercrime

1408 Wright, 'Cyber and International Law in the 21st Century' (n 1373).
1409 UNGA Report on International Security Developments in IT (2015) A/70/174, para 9.
1410 Grigsby (n 298).
1411 Istomin (n 44).

by Russia may in fact amount to little more than a diversionary tactic, just as emphasis on cyber sovereignty does not mean that its promoters actually intend to respect it. As has also been pointed out, '[o]ne of the CCP's foreign policy mantras is that states should practice non-interference in the affairs of other states, yet there is evidence that Chinese state actors such as the Ministry of State Security or PLA [...] do not consistently abide by this principle in their own work abroad'.[1412] In effect, interference in the affairs of some states may be paid at the cost of renewed interference with those interfering, in ways that pave the way for a breakdown of remaining mores of deferring to the sovereignty of others if only to better protect one's own.

In short, a 'business as usual' model, applying international law by inertia as it were, is one that could easily be overtaken by events, whilst a top-down approach to regulation may be one that will expose deep competition among states and the weakness of the UN's authority to legislate on the issue. What the overall response to the new interference suggests so far is a prudential investment in domestic responses, albeit one that remains framed by regular if hortatory invocations of international law when dealing with other states. The pushback against the new interference has also reinforced largely regional or alliance-based approaches that seek to coordinate between jurisdictions and present a united front in some of the normative fights of the moment. For example, the European Parliament has emphasized the 'utmost importance' of 'cooperation with like-minded partners, in relevant international forums, on common definitions of foreign interference in order to establish international norms and standards'.[1413] If nothing else, this suggests that, unsurprisingly, the international realm remains one of contestation and opposition when it comes to broad norm entrepreneurship surrounding interference, but also of the partial solidification of political 'blocs' around its meaning.

3 Horizontal v Vertical Interference?

A second way in which one might think how the relationship between the domestic and the international impacts of the definition of interference is by bringing attention to the tension between 'horizontal' (state-to-state) and vertical (international-organization-to-state) 'interference', and the way the two relate to each other. The debate about the evolving limits of legal interference

1412 Moore (n 714) 159.

1413 2022 Resolution on Foreign Interference in the E.U. (n 337), para J.

between states, in that respect, may be enriched by scrutinizing the close and related debate on interference by international organizations and bodies. Famously, Article 2(7) of the U.N. Charter anticipates that '[n]othing contained in the present Charter shall authorize the United Nations to intervene in matters which are essentially within the domestic jurisdiction of any state'. This evokes much earlier exhortations by Castlereagh, for example, that the early 19th Century Congress system was never 'intended as an Union for the Government of the World, or for the Superintendence of the International Affairs of other states',[1414] contra Russian and Austro-Hungarian appetite for doing just that. It is also in line with Article 15(8) of the Covenant of the League of Nations which at the time was suggested by Woodrow Wilson to encourage U.S. participation in the League. The Articles of Agreement of the World Bank also includes a specific admonition that '[t]he Bank and its officers shall not interfere in the political affairs of any member'.[1415] The question, though, is whether this language of vertical non-interference has anything to contribute to the older and continuing debate on horizontal interference.

3.1 *International Organizations' Interference with Domestic Affairs*

The difference between Article 15(8) in the league Covenant and Article 2(3) is that in the U.N. Charter the clause was inserted as a fundamental principle of the United Nations following a proposal to that effect at Dumbarton Oaks by the four Sponsoring Governments. The clause thus has a more significant reach than the League's because it is not consigned to specific dispute settlement procedures and applies to the entire operation of the United Nations. The use of the word 'essentially' also broadened the potential reach of the *domaine réservé* compared to the League use of the word 'solely'. Nor was international law specifically mentioned as the arbiter of the domestic character of disputes. Article 2(7) thus reflected the basic commitment to the U.N. dealing with governments and not directly with domestic matters.[1416] Reprising failed efforts at the League to cordon off domestic matters from international scrutiny (e.g.,

1414 Adolphus William Ward and George Peabody Gooch (eds), 'Appendix A: Lord Castlereagh's Confidential State Paper of May 5th, 1820', *The Cambridge History of British Foreign Policy, 1783–1919* (Cambridge University Press 1923) 627.

1415 International Bank for Reconstruction and Development, 'Articles of Agreement' (as amended effective 27 June 2012), art IV, s 10.

1416 DR Gilmour, 'The Meaning of "Intervene" within Article 2 (7) of the United Nations Charter: An Historical Perspective' (1967) 16 International & Comparative Law Quarterly 330, 337.

the so-called Lodge reservation),[1417] it also contributed to de-institutionalizing and de-judicializing the evaluation of the question.[1418] This once prompted Cançado Trindade to claim that 'there is ample evidence to assume that there is no strictly juridical answer to the problem of domestic jurisdiction' and that '[t]he political organs of international organisations have in fact done considerably more than the judicial organs to the development and clarification of that concept'.[1419]

Notwithstanding it longevity and solemnity, it has been argued that 'no article of the Charter has caused more trouble than this one'.[1420] Brierly once described the notion of 'domestic jurisdiction' as a 'new catchword' and a 'new fetish' whose 'extreme sanctity' was 'capable of proving as great a hindrance to the orderly development of [international law] as the somewhat battered idols of sovereignty'.[1421] At least Article 15(8) offered the prospect of claims about domestic jurisdiction being evaluated systematically under international law by an international organization. By contrast, it has sometimes been claimed that John Foster Dulles, representing the four Sponsoring Powers, deliberately ensured that the Article 2(7) would be treated as a political and flexible one.[1422] This is reinforced by the impression that the General Assembly and the Security Council, even when objectively interpreting said article, typically never refer to it, nor have laid out in any systematic way the criteria by which they (presumably) arrive at a determination that they are not encroaching on matters essentially within the jurisdiction of a state (or states), nor have ever sought, contra the League, guidance on such matters from the ICJ.[1423]

For all the early literature on the question and the decades debating the limits of Article 2(7), the most pessimistic reading of it was probably not the

1417 Leland M Goodrich, 'The United Nations and Domestic Jurisdiction' (1949) 3 International Organization 14, 17.

1418 Leo Gross, 'The Charter of the United Nations and the Lodge Reservations' (1947) 41 American Journal of International Law 531.

1419 Antônio Augusto Cançado Trindade, 'The Domestic Jurisdiction of States in the Practice of the United Nations and Regional Organisations' (1976) 25 International & Comparative Law Quarterly 715, 761.

1420 Gilmour (n 1415) 331.

1421 JL Brierly, 'Matters of Domestic Jurisdiction' (1925) 6 British Year Book of International Law 8.

1422 Rajan (n 568) 250.

1423 In that respect, the League at least went further in that its 1924 Protocol anticipated that disputes about the domestic question should be passed on to a special Committee of Arbitrators operating on the basis of advice by the Permanent Court of International Justice. League of Nations, 'Protocol for the Pacific Settlement of International Disputes' (2 October 1924), art 5.

most adequate one from the outset.[1424] And at any rate, the question probably no longer has the currency it once had. Even as interference between states remains a sore point, meddling by international organizations has become much more ingrained, despite the occasional effort to reassert the primacy of state sovereignty in the face of global governance.[1425] Sites and modes of intervention that were once out of bounds (or even unheard of) for the United Nations have long given way to manifold interventionist practices, that are not even evenly still seen as such by states. Ironically, although the omission of any reference to international law in Article 2(7) and the cross-cutting nature of the clause was meant at Dumbarton Oaks to safeguard the ability of states to put forth their own conceptions of what they considered to be essentially domestic[1426] it has, instead, served to expand the UN's own political understanding of what is or is not part of its own *domaine*,[1427] leaving little doubt that Article 2(7)'s impact was significantly diminished almost from the start.[1428]

If anything, reference to a neat, ontological distinction between domestic and international spheres, has now been replaced by late appeals to soft subsidiarity,[1429] as part of what is even sometimes viewed as a constitutional[1430] or quasi-federal[1431]—but, at any rate, integrated—system.[1432] If anything, the reproach when it comes to U.N. practice was for a long time that it did not go far enough, stopping on the edge of what might be a more meaningful engagement with the blind spots, as notably analyzed by feminists, of 'domestic

1424 Lawrence Preuss, *Article 2, Paragraph 7 of the Charter of the United Nations and Matters of Domestic Jurisdiction*, vol 74 (Brill Nijhoff 1949).

1425 JS Watson, 'Autointerpretation, Competence, and the Continuing Validity of Article 2(7) of the U.N. Charter' (1977) 71 American Journal of International Law 60.

1426 Gross (n 1417).

1427 Verdross (n 575) 35.

1428 Goodrich (n 1416) 27.

1429 Nicholas Tsagourias, 'Security Council Legislation, Article 2 (7) of the U.N. Charter, and the Principle of Subsidiarity' (2011) 24 Leiden Journal of International Law 539; Machiko Kanetake, 'Subsidiarity in the Maintenance of International Peace and Security Subsidiarity in Global Governance' (2016) 79 Law and Contemporary Problems 165.

1430 Bardo Fassbender, 'The United Nations Charter as Constitution of the International Community' (1998) 36 Columbia Journal of Transnational Law 529.

1431 Antonio F Perez, 'On the Way to the Forum: The Reconstruction of Article 2(7) and Rise of Federalism under the United Nations Charter' (1996) 31 Texas International Law Journal 353.

1432 Blaine Sloan, 'The United Nations Charter as a Constitution' (1989) 1 Pace Yearbook of International Law 61.

jurisdiction'.[1433] This may, in fact, suggest a narrow path for state-to-state interference as well: one in which over time such interference becomes less and less noticeable because it has been thoroughly normalized in international relations—although of course whether U.N. intervention is a valid precedent for vertical intervention remains precisely the question.

On its face, Article 2(7) is mostly about protecting a core sphere of member states' sovereignty and acts as familiar rehearsal on the theme of (non)intervention encased in the theory of international organizational subjecthood: the U.N. can do no more than its *compétence d'attribution* allows it to do. Any *ultra vires* action in relation to states' *domaine réservé* can thus hypothetically be characterized as an intervention of sorts, even if not of the same kind as would arise between states. Expansions of what can even be discussed by the General Assembly—starting, famously, with the question of Apartheid, of Franco Spain or of the Algeria war –[1434] were once read as very much raising pressing questions about the proper reach of the U.N. and vertical borders of the *domaine réservé*. As such, they were occasionally fiercely resisted by target states. Even the Security Council must in theory tread carefully and is bound by the economy of Chapters vi and vii. As has been pointed out when it comes to spelling out of the pivotal notion of international peace and security:

> if the Council were free to determine the meaning of Article 39, its involvement in the affairs of the Member States could become limitless. Clearly, neither had the Member States intended the Council to constitute a sort of world government, nor would the Council be equipped to fulfil such a role.[1435]

In earlier times, the League Council was clearly instructed to refrain from engaging in disputes 'solely' within the domestic jurisdiction of states, which meant that it should desist from even issuing recommendations. As was claimed by Judge Winiarski in the Advisory Opinion on Certain Expenses, in a now quite dated passage, '[t]he intention of those who drafted the [U.N. Charter] was

1433 Kristen Walker, 'An Exploration of Article 2(7) of the United Nations Charter as an Embodiment of the Public/Private Distinction in International Law' (1993) 26 New York University Journal of International Law and Politics 173.

1434 John M Howell, 'The French and South African Walkouts and Domestic Jurisdiction' (1956) 18 The Journal of Politics 95.

1435 Bernd Martenczuk, 'The Security Council, the International Court and Judicial Review: What Lessons from Lockerbie?' (1999) 10 European Journal of International Law 517, 542.

clearly to abandon the possibility of useful action rather than to sacrifice the balance of carefully established fields of competence'.[1436]

At the same time, this basic concern with keeping the genie in the bottle by emphasizing the constraints imposed on international organs and due respect for states' sovereignty, must *in fine* be understood against the background of assumptions about the purposes and mandate of the United Nations, as they have been assumed to licence quite extensive multilateral interventionism. *Ratione materiae*, this includes if nothing else the ability to discuss a wide swath of topics that deal with partly domestic affairs.[1437] Debates under the League of Nations about Article 15(8) did much to accredit the notion that very few matters involving more than one state, moreover, could rightly be considered as exclusively domestic (even as the League might, ultimately, not be in a position to do much about such matters). For example, the dispute over the Aaland island had led Finland to claim that the matter was an essentially domestic one falling within its domestic jurisdiction, but the Council, following legal advice, disagreed on the basis that the island's Swedish population and its right of self-determination internationalized the matter.[1438] Often, the mere emergence of an international dispute between at least two states is evidence enough that a matter is no longer strictly domestic, no matter that it may have its source on the territory of only one state.

If nothing else, then, the question of whether a matter is essentially domestic is potentially one for international bodies to decide.[1439] The General Assembly, for its part, has been loath to exclude much from its agenda, especially given its position that 'it is impossible to determine whether a proposed resolution would constitute intervention in the domestic jurisdiction of a state until the question has been discussed and the proposed resolution analyzed'.[1440] The fact that, contra the League, it is not particularly tasked with determining whether matters are domestic *under international law* seems to have been interpreted as a licence to interpret the issue from a broad, *sui generis*, teleological and institutional perspective. Indeed, even before the League an effort by

1436 *Certain Expenses of the United Nations (Article 17, paragraph 2, of the Charter)(Dissenting Opinion of President Winiarski)* [1962] ICJ Rep 151, 230.

1437 JK Feimpong and S Azadon Tiewel, 'Can Apartheid Successfully Defy the International Legal System' (1977) 5 Black Law Journal 287.

1438 Philip Marshall Brown, 'The Aaland Islands Question' (1921) 15 American Journal of International Law 268.

1439 Hans Kelsen, *The Law of the United Nations: A Critical Analysis of Its Fundamental Problems* (The Lawbook Exchange, Ltd 2000) 771.

1440 Quincy Wright, 'Is Discussion Intervention?' (1956) 50 American Journal of International Law 102, 108.

the British in 1926 to draw the line between international and domestic activities was strongly rejected by the French notably on account of the sheer difficulty of doing so in the abstract.[1441] The 'domestic jurisdiction clause' of the Charter, which had been vigorously challenged from the outset, has even been described as having entered a state of *désuétude*, given consistently expansive General Assembly and Security Council practice[1442] as well as a degree of state acquiescence to it over time. It has come to be understood as subjected to the UN's own determination of its competence rather than unilateral assertion by states of what they consider to be essentially domestic matters.

In addition to the shrinking of the *domaine réservé* for U.N. purposes, what constitutes interference with it has also been diluted as a result of the expansion of assumed U.N. powers. Lauterpacht insisted early on that the qualifier 'dictatorial' to interference applied both horizontally and vertically (meaning that only such dictatorial interference was prohibited even in the Charter context). Others have since argued that all interference is impermissible[1443] but that must be viewed in light of the many explicit powers of the UN[1444] that disqualify it almost statutorily from being 'dictatorial', notably given their largely non-coercive character (not to mention that it is improbable that states parties would have conferred upon the U.N. dictatorial powers in the first place). In other words, Article 2(7) anticipated a much broader range of permissible interference when it came to the United Nations than is considered legal under international law between states. The mere discussion by the U.N. of certain matters, but also the adoption of resolution, forms of dispute settlement or recommendations hardly carry any coercive character, especially given that they entail no tangible repercussion for said states' jurisdiction.[1445] This is the case even of sanctions applied by international organizations in the implementation of their mandates. In such situations, one need not rely on sophisticated considerations about the implementation of international law: the power to sanction, such as it may be, is a power presumably conferred by states themselves upon the organization and which they can little then claim to be a form of interference.

1441 Rajan (n 568) 256.

1442 Kawser Ahmed, 'The Domestic Jurisdiction Clause in the United Nations Charter: A Historical View' (2006) 10 Singapore Year Book of International Law 175.

1443 Gilmour (n 1415).

1444 Kelsen (n 1438) 787.

1445 Na Jiang, *China and International Human Rights: Harsh Punishments in the Context of the International Covenant on Civil and Political Rights* (Springer 2014) ch 1.

In turn, the political organs of the U.N., first among which is the Council, have over time crafted a regime of what is properly considered to be domestic matters and what counts as a legitimate space for international intervention that leaves considerable space to their subjective characterization.[1446] Indeed even beyond the Security Council, one witnesses a similar shrinking of the domestic exception, notably as a result of pretorian constructs such as the idea of 'international concern' since the Spanish question was raised after the Second World War. This is despite that expression not appearing anywhere in the Charter, and objectively obviating the need to resort to the Security Council's emergency powers.[1447] The U.N. has at every turn resisted any attempt to, for example, refer the question to the ICJ for juridical determination, thereby emphasizing its intention to treat such questions as ones of 'high politics' not susceptible to a legal straitjacket.[1448]

Early on, the mere fact that grave human rights violations were alleged sufficed, in the case of the treatment of Indians in South Africa,[1449] to come to the conclusion that the General Assembly's competence was largely established on the basis of the Charter, notwithstanding said states' effort to protest U.N. action as an intrusion. Similarly, the General Assembly satisfied itself that it could discuss the question of Franco Spain or the Hungarian government based on the nature of their political regimes as well as the potential for friction it entailed for other states.[1450] Spain had, through its particular choice of regime, effectively internationalized its own situation. This was a fortiori the case of non-self-governing territories, especially Indonesia in relation to the Netherlands and Tunisia, Morocco and, eventually, Algeria in relation to France, as well as Rhodesia in relation to the U.K., all situations built upon a colonial matrix that barely concealed its internationality[1451] and against which the Third World powerfully deployed Chapter xi of the Charter to 'penetrat[e] the colonial domain'.[1452]

1446 Paul C Szasz, 'Role of the United Nations in Internal Conflicts Panel III: The Role of International and Regional Organizations Responses to Internal Conflicts' (1983) 13 Georgia Journal of International and Comparative Law 345.

1447 John M Howell, 'A Matter of International Concern' (1969) 63 American Journal of International Law 771, 775–777.

1448 Rupert Emerson, 'Reflections on the Indonesian Case' (1948) 1 World Politics 59.

1449 'The "Domestic Jurisdiction" Limitation in the United Nations Charter' (1947) 47 Columbia Law Review 268.

1450 John A Houston, 'The United Nations and Spain' (1952) 14 The Journal of Politics 683.

1451 Goodrich (n 1416).

1452 Claude, Jr (n 312) 123.

There was little opposition, also, to the ECOSOC making recommendation of a social and economic nature that fell evidently within its remit, notwithstanding their potential domestic implications. The universality of the concern for refugees is also well recognized.[1453] Much later, crowning a series of evolutions in international criminal law,[1454] the ICTY would find that the occurrence of crimes that 'do not affect the interests of one State alone but shock the conscience of mankind'[1455] was all the more reason to think that no one state could invoke the domestic affairs exception all the way to the creation of international criminal tribunals by the Council. And although evidently strictures remain on the sort of measures that U.N. organs can decide, the General Assembly or the Secretary General have shown that they could exploit the considerable leeway that exists in the U.N. Charter to forge new understandings of their competencies, as illustrated for example by increasingly expansive understandings of peace keeping and a certain unmooring from strict state consent.

This basic evolution is replicated before regional organizations. For example, it has been pointed out that 'a multilateral assessment [by the OAS] of a situation that threatens democracy in a member state' would '[n]ot really [...] be considered interference in its internal affairs [...] since all members committed themselves to promote and defend democracy and all agreed voluntarily to respect the Charter's provisions'.[1456] Measures adopted against Poland or Hungary by the European Commission within its competences for failures of compliance with the rule of law do not constitute intervention since 'by joining the E.U. [these states] undertook legal obligations that removed these policy areas [...] from their *domaine réservé*'.[1457] And as far as the Organization of African States is concerned, it has been argued that Article 3(2)'s commitment to 'non-interference in the internal affairs of States' should be read in light of other principles of its Charter and that the practice of the organization should be directed at preventing human rights violations.[1458]

Note also, however, that just as it has been this book's contention that intervention has changed towards a more diffuse practice of interference, so

1453 Vera Gowlland-Debbas, 'The Expanding International Concern' (1993) 5 Peace Review 287.

1454 Roger S Clark, 'Offenses of International Concern: Multilateral State Treaty Practice in the Forty Years Since Nuremberg' (1988) 57 Nordic Journal of International Law 49.

1455 *Prosecutor v Tadic* (Decision on the Defence Motion for Interlocutory Appeal on Jurisdiction) ICTY-94-1-A (2 October 1995), para 57.

1456 Perina (n 890) 81.

1457 Helal (n 408) 67.

1458 UO Umozurike, 'The Domestic Jurisdiction Clause in the OAU Charter' (1979) 78 African Affairs 197.

have the practices of international organizations. The idea that international organizations engage in their own 'new interference' is one that has real analytical bite. Beyond well-worn modalities of action by international organizations that can hardly count anymore as a form of intervention, there are new tools in international organizations' 'toolkit' which, even though they are not strictly coercive let alone dictatorial, can be seen as subtly displacing traditional modes of sovereignty and would certainly qualify as interference if they emanated from states. For example, the U.N., notably its Secretary General, are increasingly prone to talk *directly* to civil society actors rather than through the mediation of their state (e.g., in the context of human rights treaty reporting). Moreover, the production of certain international norms such as the Ruggie principles has increasingly relied on the participation of private actors which, elevated to the rank of partner of the United Nations, graduate to an aggrandized role that allows them to bypass their own sovereign to push their priorities as part of 'non-state (if not private) normativity'.[1459]

In short, as the U.N. has become relatively less inter-governmental and more an institution that fancies itself as one of global governance involved in transnational regulation,[1460] it has blurred the contours of the domestic and international spheres of competence and what it can do to regulate both. Indeed, the global nature of the threats faced in an interdependent world suggests that the normative salience of freedom-from-interference (as opposed to the freedom to achieve certain ends) as an ideal is greatly diminished.[1461] A far-cry from the heavily institutionalized and almost doctrinal older concerns with international organization intervention seen earlier in this section, these forms of day-to-day interference suggest an expanded realm of intrusion. The category will of course not always be seen as less problematic simply because it emanates from the U.N. or the World Bank, especially if these are seen as proxies, in fact, for powerful states.

1459 Franck Latty, 'Non-State Authority: FIFA', *Global Private International Law* (Edward Elgar Publishing 2019).

1460 Bruce Cronin, 'The Two Faces of the United Nations: The Tension between Intergovernmentalism and Transnationalism' (2002) 8 Global Governance: A Review of Multilateralism and International Organizations 53.

1461 Eyal Benvenisti, 'The Future of Sovereignty: The Nation State in the Global Governance Space' in Sabino Cassese (ed), *Research Handbook on Global Administrative Law* (Edward Elgar Publishing 2016) 485.

3.2 *The Distinctiveness of International Organizations' Interference*

To be clear, supranational interference has its own history of being resisted strongly even in fields as interference-prone as human rights. For example, states long pushed back against the ability of the then Commission on Human Rights to hear complaints about systematic rights violations (let alone individual ones).[1462] When the main human rights treaties were adopted there was considerable pressure to have individual petitioning systems isolated in separate treaties and require an opt-in. There are countless instances of the Human Rights Commission or Council recommendations on human rights, being strongly opposed on the grounds that they involve interference. Even more clearly mandated instances of interference by regional organizations have nonetheless been met with a degree of resistance.[1463] The Council of Europe has for example been accused by Russia of engaging in interference in the affairs of states through 'country monitoring'.[1464]

Partly this may just be a function of the greater visibility and authority of multilateral interference. After all, a treaty body or a country special rapporteur's reports are likely to be quite precise and intrusive in scope, as well as quite public and, presumably, backed by the state's own consent. They will leave little to chance, where a bilateral critique of a state's human rights record might be more easily dismissed as interventionist. The occasional U.N. human rights special rapporteur that is made *persona non grata* after attacking a country's human rights record[1465] may attract more publicity than a discreet response to a discreet state-to-state voicing of concern about rights, but it will

1462 ME Tardu, 'United Nations Response to Gross Violations of Human Rights: The 1503 Procedure Syposium International Human Rights' (1980) 20 Santa Clara Law Review 559, 562. (Noting how the procedure was organized so as to alleviate concerns about 'undue interference').

1463 Notably, even in the highly jurisdictional and regional context of the European Convention on Human Rights, part of the opposition to the Court by the likes of the U.K. and Russia has been framed, if not quite in interference terms, in ways that were very close. The turn to 'subsidiarity' in the ECtHR, notably after the Brighton declaration, can be understood as a response by an international organization to these increasingly vocal concerns. Philip Leach and Alice Donald, 'Hostility to the European Court and the Risks of Contagion' (*UK Human Rights Blog*, 21 November 2013) <https://ukhumanrightsblog.com/2013/11/21/hostility-to-the-european-court-and-the-risks-of-contagion-philip-leach-and-alice-donald/> accessed 12 February 2019.

1464 'Volodin Urges Council of Europe to Stop Country Monitoring' *The Baltic Times* (9 October 2019) <https://www.baltictimes.com/volodin_urges_council_of_europe_to_stop_country_monitoring/> accessed 9 July 2023.

1465 David Smith, 'UN Torture Investigator Refused Entry to Zimbabwe' *The Guardian* (29 October 2009) <https://www.theguardian.com/world/2009/oct/29/zimbabwe-blocks-un-torture-investigator> accessed 11 March 2019.

also be harder to challenge. The multilateral and institutionalized character of such international interference is both what makes it more vulnerable to strident responses and what makes it harder to discredit. It may be paradoxically harder to rally the troops and curtail the mandate of an international organization than it is to stop a 'fellow' sovereign state from criticizing one's human rights performance.

Notwithstanding or perhaps because of the greater visibility and occasional extra bothersome character of multilateral interference for states, international organizations have long benefited from considerable tolerance when it comes to interference within the exercise of their founding instruments. Whatever one thinks of the original legal argument about who should interpret Article 2(7) and how, the reality is that the United Nations has largely forged ahead in developing its own very encompassing jurisprudence of what matters fall within its competence,[1466] and that this right is no longer particularly denied to it. This deference to the intervening ambitions of international organizations can be seen as a late variant of an earlier classical international law argument to the effect that states could intervene collectively in certain cases when they did so as members of an international society striving to protect its higher interest, for example the balance of power.[1467] The U.N. Charter, for its part, fundamentally reconceptualizes the debate about legitimate authority to engage in interference, in ways evocative of much older Medieval debates about Papal authority to evaluate the legitimacy of regimes.[1468] This it does particularly on the basis of discursive investments in an overarching conception of human rights as trumping sovereignty,[1469] but also as a result of the special nature of international organizations.

The broad deference to the powers of international organizations can be understood as flowing quite simply from their mandates, their theory of implicit powers, and their *kompetenz kompetenz*.[1470] In other words, not only is there an initial sovereign licence and a favorable a priori, but that licence is

1466 David R Gilmour, 'Article 2(7) of the United Nations Charter and the Practice of the Permanent Members of the Security Council' (1967) 3 Australian Year Book of International Law 153.

1467 Vincent (n 69) 290–293.

1468 Jonathan Havercroft, 'Was Westphalia "All That"? Hobbes, Bellarmine, and the Norm of Non-Intervention' (2012) 1 Global Constitutionalism 120.

1469 Paul Taylor, 'The United Nations in the 1990s: Proactive Cosmopolitanism and the Issue of Sovereignty' (1999) 47 Political Studies 538.

1470 Alf Ross, 'The Proviso Concerning" Domestic Jurisdiction" in Article 2 (7) of the Charter of the United Nations' (1949) 2 Osterreichische Zeitschrift fur Offentliches Recht/Austrian Journal of Public Law 562.

prolonged by the naturally dynamic exercise of their competencies by international organizations. The expansive powers of the Security Council under Chapters vi and vii belie any notion that even broad and previously unanticipated prerogatives (such as the creation of ad hoc international criminal tribunals) cross the threshold into undue intervention.[1471] Article 2(7), in fact, specifically excludes Council enforcement action from even the possibility of claiming interference in domestic matters,[1472] an exception that has in practice facilitated the assumption of broad powers by the Council notably when it comes to peace keeping missions[1473] and the UN's increasing involvement in non-international armed conflict.[1474] The broad deference to the resulting decisions was evident in the Tadic case, for example, where the appeal chamber found that Chapter vii was 'precisely the provisions under which the International Tribunal has been established'.[1475] This Security Council exception can be seen as building on the reality that many otherwise domestic matters do have international peace and security implications, a sort of exception that confirms the rule.

Chapter vii, in fact, can particularly effectively short circuit the modest strictures of Article 2(7) given its propensity to engulf all else. The broadening interpretation of what constitutes a breach or even merely a threat to international peace and security has facilitated a determination over time that there are few conflicts too domestically obscure for the Council not to intervene in them, leaving aside extraneous veto considerations.[1476] This has, predictably, been periodically challenged as abusive. But nor is this expansion of what counts as a breach or threat to international peace and security necessarily a manifestation of Council arbitrariness: it is true that few domestic conflicts have not had, whether through cross-border overspill, a colonial context and decolonizing motive, racial discrimination,[1477] grave humanitarian

1471 Charles G Fenwick, 'When Is There a Threat to the Peace?—Rhodesia' (1967) 61 American Journal of International Law 753.

1472 U.N. Charter, art 2(7) ('but this principle shall not prejudice the application of enforcement measures under Chapter vii').

1473 Leo Gross, 'Domestic Jurisdiction, Enforcement Measures and the Congo' (1965) 1 Australian Year Book of International Law 137.

1474 Ruth Gordon, 'United Nations Intervention in Internal Conflicts: Iraq, Somalia, and Beyond' (1993) 15 Michigan Journal of International Law 519.

1475 *Tadic* case (n 1384), para 56.

1476 James Gow, Natasha Kuhrt and Maria Varaki, 'International Peace and Security' in Michael S Goodman, Rachel Kerr and Matthew Moran (eds), *An Introduction to War Studies* (Edward Elgar Publishing 2024).

1477 McDougal and Reisman (n 590).

consequences[1478] or human rights impact, some actual international or transnational element that the Council could then seize upon as part of an evolutive and certainly not indefensible interpretative exercise.

Coupled with considerable ability in practice to define their agendas, then, it is no wonder that international organizations have been at the forefront of redefining what is or is not inherently domestic, for their own purposes at least. Indeed, international bodies' ability to resist expansive self-definition of the *domaine réservé* by states through their own broad definition of their competence is sometimes seen as the very condition of their existence[1479] even though it leaves something to be desired in terms of the consistency of international law.[1480] As Quincy Wright once observed, to allow states to have the last word on what are internal matters would effectively grant them a veto on the discussion of any matter that they deemed to constitute intervention in matters fundamentally within their domestic jurisdiction.[1481] Such a move would simply defer too much to capricious self-interpretation and self-characterization by states, in flagrant antinomy to principles of international law (*nemo iudex in sua causa*) and the *raison d'être* of the United Nations. Not even France's efforts to put the international community before the *fait accompli* of its assimilationist policies as regards Algeria[1482] (or Portugal's vis-à-vis Goa)[1483] could transform what was intrinsically an international situation into a formalized domestic one. As Myres McDougal and Michael Reisman put it:

> if states were to be permitted to impede the organized community's efforts to rectify situations by claims that activities, however threatening, are immune from inclusive concern because they are within domestic jurisdiction, the principal purpose for which the whole constitutive structure is established and maintained could be easily defeated.[1484]

1478 Cedric E Evans, 'The Concept of "Threat to Peace" and Humanitarian Concerns: Probing the Limits of Chapter VII of the U.N. Charter' (1995) 5 Transnational Law & Contemporary Problems 213.

1479 John M Howell, 'Domestic Questions in International Law' (1954) 48 Proceedings of the American Society of International Law at its annual meeting (1921–1969) 90.

1480 Abi-Saab (n 313) 87.

1481 Wright, 'Is Discussion Intervention?' (n 1440) 104–105.

1482 Flory (n 168).

1483 Quincy Wright, 'The Goa Incident' (1962) 56 American Journal of International Law 617.

1484 McDougal and Reisman (n 590) 14.

A similar concern has long manifested itself in relation to, for example, the Connally reservation[1485] (and previously the ill-fated fourth Lodge Reservation), and the possibility it heralded of the U.S. simply opting out of the ICJ's jurisdiction on the basis of its own determination of what constitute domestic matters.[1486] The ICJ has consistently found, by contrast, that invocations of domestic jurisdiction or national security are to be entertained at the merits but do not constitute a bar to its jurisdiction.[1487]

The 'self-judging' character of the 'national security exception' in Article XXI of the GATT is also sometimes mentioned in this connection as tilting the balance too far towards a residual state discretion ('a virtually unlimited escape clause')[1488] in matters that would be better ascertained by international bodies.[1489] This once led to a lesser known tussle between Nicaragua and the U.S., with the latter under President Reagan invoking the exception to cancel all trade with the former. Although a majority of states at the time took position in favor of the self-judging character of the exception, there was also significant pushback against its invocation in the circumstances given the difference in power and the absurdity of claiming that U.S. 'national security' was threatened by Nicaragua.[1490] The bottom line is that attempts to narrow the jurisdiction of international bodies, to the extent they go clearly against these bodies' competencies, will fall foul of the international law prohibition on invoking one's domestic law as a justification for breaching one's international obligations. So long, by contrast, as an international organization, based on a reasonable interpretation of its founding statute, finds that a matter rightly

---

1485 Carsten Stahn, 'Connally Reservation', *Max Planck Encyclopedias of International Law* (Oxford University Press 2006).

1486 Louis Henkin, 'The Connally Reservation Revisited and, Hopefully, Contained' (1971) 65 American Journal of International Law 374.

1487 Sebastián Mantilla Blanco and Alexander Pehl, 'The Second Generation of National Security Exceptions: Departing from the GATT Tradition?' in Sebastián Mantilla Blanco and Alexander Pehl (eds), *National Security Exceptions in International Trade and Investment Agreements: Justiciability and Standards of Review* (Springer International Publishing 2020).

1488 David T Shapiro, 'Be Careful What You Wish For: U.S. Politics and the Future of the National Security Exception to the GATT Note' (1997) 31 George Washington Journal of International Law and Economics 97, 98.

1489 Sarah Boutros, 'Addressing the Elephant in the Room: Discussing the WTO's Controversial Question Regarding the Application of Article XXI of GATT 1994' (2019) 34 Temple International & Comparative Law Journal 1.

1490 William J Gardner, Jr, 'Divergent Strategies: A Legal History of the WTO's National Security Exception in the Context of a Globalized Economy, 1983–2019' (2020) 28 University of Miami International and Comparative Law Review 181.

falls within its purview as a matter of 'international concern', then such a determination has much to commend it and should be broadly deferred to.[1491]

This has, it is true, long created concerns that international organizations, on the basis of an expanded vision of 'international concern', will favor a purely 'political' (indeed, 'anti-juridical') understanding of their powers. The fear is that the notion of 'domestic jurisdiction' in the Charter has been eviscerated of any specific legal meaning, not least by the refusal to ever refer its interpretation to the International Court of Justice[1492] (in fairness, this is the reverse concern of states doing the same thing by insisting capriciously that matters are domestic). This is to say nothing of the fear that inflation of U.N. encroachments on domestic affairs will create some more fundamental disconnect between the underlying reality of international politics and the organization's activities,[1493] thus precipitating a broader crisis of governance. At the same time, there has also long been an understanding that 'if we accept the postulate that intervention from outside, by the use of force, will never be absent from the affairs of nations' it is certainly preferable, especially from the point of view of developing nations, that 'intervention from outside, if necessary, should be in the hands of the organized international community rather than at the discretion of individual states'.[1494]

To be clear, there is no denying that, despite nominal state consent to the activities of international organizations and their superior multilateral standing, states have also routinely been piqued by what they see as international organizations crossing the line into what they understand in the moment to be interference. It is precisely in the context of the operation of international organizations that it is periodically suggested that 'all U.N. member states would appear to have a strong self-interest in developing and clarifying the concept of the rights of states in international law-in particular those which can be asserted against and which must be respected by other actors, including the Security Council', something which is 'especially true for smaller and developing states'.[1495] Despite the optimistic functionalist narrative of international organizations assuming ever-greater functions, there has long been

1491 Wright, 'Is Discussion Intervention?' (n 1439). Similarly, for Kelsen, the Security Council must have the power to determine if a matter is essentially domestic or not since if it 'could not assume this power, any Member could block the intervention of the Organisation in any dispute by pleading domestic jurisdiction'. Kelsen (n 1438) 790.

1492 Paul Eeckman, 'The Domestic Jurisdiction Clause of the Charter: A Belgian View' (1955) 9 International Organization 477.

1493 Watson (n 1425).

1494 Friedmann, 'Intervention and the Developing Countries' (n 406) 212.

1495 Joyner and Roscini (n 473) 479.

a corresponding tendency to seek to re-sanctify the *domaine réservé* against encroachment by said organizations, notably by small states.[1496] For example, the Security Council's ever-expansive conception of international peace and security has not gone unnoticed and has elicited recriminations from states that saw themselves as being on the receiving end of interference. This was visible, for example, as part of the creation of ad hoc international criminal tribunals, notably the ICTY, which seemed to some to disproportionately boost the *pouvoirs d'attribution* of the Security Council, at the expense of the former-Yugoslavia.

The particular amalgamation of dynamic international organization powers and expansive international peace and security agendas increasingly shaped by human rights considerations has not always been welcome. For example, before the General Assembly in 2013, the President of Ghana complained of 'so-called "humanitarian" interference by the United Nations, which, in reality, imposed political systems and democracies on the basis of hidden interests, disregarding the sacred principles of national sovereignty and the dignity of peoples'.[1497] Belarus has complained that the Human Rights Council had singled it out in violation of the principle of non-interference.[1498] In 2021, Algeria lashed out at the World Bank following a report that it found too critical of its leadership, describing it as a form of blatant 'immixtion'.[1499] Similar complaints of interference have emanated from left parties in India who wrote to the Prime Minister alleging that an internationally sponsored project to privatise water services in Delhi would constitute 'blatant interference'.[1500] As to

1496 See e.g.: Francisco-José Quintana, 'Small Powers, International Organizations and the Role of Law: Jorge Castañeda's Views from Mexico' (2023) 34 European Journal of International Law 319.

1497 'Africa No Longer Prey to Division by Those Bent on Disrupting Its Progress, Declares President of Ghana, as General Assembly Continues Debate' (*UN Meetings Coverage and Press Releases*) <https://press.un.org/en/2013/ga11428.doc.htm> accessed 26 May 2024.

1498 'Human Rights Council: United Nations High Commissioner for Human Rights Urges Government of Belarus to End Ongoing Human Rights Violations' (*OHCHR*, 4 December 2020) <https://www.ohchr.org/en/press-releases/2020/12/human-rights-council-united-nations-high-commissioner-human-rights-urges> accessed 26 May 2024.

1499 'Rapport Erroné de La BM: Une Tentative de Déstabilisation de l'Algérie' (*Algérie Presse Service*, 28 December 2021) <https://www.aps.dz/economie/133424-rapport-errone-de-la-banque-mondiale-une-tentative-de-destabilisation-de-l-algerie> accessed 26 May 2024.

1500 'Letter Written to the PM by Left Parties on 23 September 2005' (*Communist Party of India*, 8 August 2009) <https://cpim.org/privatisation-water-delhi/> accessed 23 December 2024.

complaints about interference by the ICC, they are almost routine, even from states parties.[1501]

Tensions reached boiling point in 2019 when the Security Council sought to assume an outsize role in relation to Venezuela, shattering any sense of international consensus. The Nicaraguan Representative insisted that even for the Council to meet was an interference in the affairs of Venezuela. Buzzwords such as 'sovereignty', 'independence', 'constructive engagement', or 'dialogue' (as opposed to 'regime change', 'responsibility to protect' or 'sanctions') pepper the declarations of those whose interpretation of sovereignty erred on the side of classicism on that occasion. Not even the European Union, operating as it does on the basis of decades of integration and capacious mandates, has escaped accusations that it is effectively interfering in the affairs of its member States.[1502]

There is, in other words, a constant, low volume, grumbling about international interference by international organizations that systematically reactivates the language of sovereignty and its associated prerogatives to complain of encroachments. Some of these complaints can no doubt be chalked up to autocrats disgruntled with the ordinary and entirely legitimate operation of international organizations, a rear-guard battle against the reality that what these do is not, in fact, interference. Others do raise genuine questions about whether the governance of international organizations has gone too far beyond voluntarism. And of course, the contestation of the governance powers of international organizations and what is seen as potentially excessively interfering agendas (but also insufficiently interfering ones) has long ceased to be a monopoly of states and includes, henceforth, NGOs and civil society.

Still, whether because international organizations have overall interpreted their powers conservatively or because there are built-in checks on their powers (e.g., majoritarian requirements, the Security Council veto), one cannot claim that there has been much of a sustained revolt against at least the U.N.'s exercise of its powers. Forays into domestic affairs that were once seen as innovative have gradually become normalized as par for the course. International

1501 John Victor D Ordoñez, 'Philippines Won't Tolerate ICC Meddling in Drug War, Says DoJ' *BusinessWorld* (2 March 2023) <https://www.bworldonline.com/the-nation/2023/03/02/508195/philippines-wont-tolerate-icc-meddling-in-drug-war-says-doj/> accessed 26 May 2024; 'Sudan Insists on Trying Darfur War Crime Suspects by Its Own' *Sudan Tribune* (22 November 2005) <https://sudantribune.com/article13267/> accessed 26 May 2024; 'Myanmar Rejects Interference by the International Criminal Court' (*Réseau Voltaire*, 9 August 2018) <https://www.voltairenet.org/article202513.html> accessed 26 May 2024.

1502 'Poland Referred to European Court over Judges' Forced Retirement' (24 September 2018) <https://www.bbc.com/news/world-europe-45628757> accessed 26 May 2024.

organizations' exercise of their powers has become largely accepted over time both in the absolute and, certainly, relative to similar behavior by states. When all is said and done, the mechanics of Charter operation are such that it has at least become very difficult to push back against ever-growing encroachments on the *domaine* emanating from the U.N. If nothing else, it is, henceforth, 'possible to override the prescriptions of non-interference and domestic jurisdiction in the interests of international peace and security'.[1503] International organizations have routinized their interventions even in circumstances where they might be deemed, *prima facie*, to be interfering in domestic affairs.

This suggests that the particular mix of voluntarism and autonomy that characterizes the law of international organizations has been a potent mix to settle the boundaries of the domestic and international domains. The International Labor Organization (ILO)'s investigation of Myanmar's practice of forced labor is in that respect instructive. The Myanmar government had alleged that the work of the Commission tasked with investigating such a violation would constitute an interference in its internal affairs and refused its in-country visit. The Commission responded to such an allegation that:

> by virtue of its Constitution the ILO was established to improve conditions of labour and [...] it follows that the matters dealt with by the Organization no longer fall within the exclusive sphere of competence of States (*domaine réservé*). Therefore, the action taken by the Organization in this case, namely the institution of a Commission of Inquiry with full fact-finding and investigative powers, cannot be considered to be undue interference in internal affairs, since it falls precisely within the terms of reference that the ILO has received from its Members with a view to attaining the aims assigned to it. Moreover, the establishment of such a Commission of Inquiry by the ILO is explicitly provided for in the Constitution of the ILO and is only possible in cases in which the Convention in question has been ratified by the State against which the complaint is made. Indeed, once a State has by a free and sovereign decision, not only joined the ILO but also ratified an international labour Convention, neither the establishment of a Commission of Inquiry nor its functioning are subject to the agreement or cooperation of the State

1503 Gow, Kuhrt and Varaki (n 1476) 101.

> concerned. The objection based on undue interference in the internal affairs of Myanmar is thus devoid of any legal validity.[1504]

At most, states who still believe that an international organization has exceeded its competence in improperly considering a matter can engage in a degree of non-compliance and self-help (for example, by staging a walkout at the General Assembly or ejecting a peacekeeping operation). This can temporarily paralyze the UN's action towards them and brings attention to the limits of checks and balances within international organizations to ascertain the validity of their assertions of competence or react to constitutional overreach. It cements the residual value of state sovereignty, at least de facto, albeit at some potential cost to the states involved. Specialized agencies have also occasionally pushed back on efforts by the U.N. to have them fall in line when it came to sanctions against their members.[1505] But this cannot obfuscate the fact that the U.N. has largely run roughshod over invocations of the domestic jurisdiction, perhaps all the more so that it can quite easily summon rather large majorities against the lone or isolated dissenter. This is typically understood as speaking to the replacement of strict principles of international legal voluntarism by an increased deference to the majority-infused mores of international organizations and their supposed promotion of the common international public interest, essentially making the U.N. the standard of its own practice.[1506]

3.3 *The Limited Relevance of International Organizations' Interference for State Interference*

What can one make of this carving out of a specific authority to reshape the *domaine* and what constitutes interference by international organizations? Clearly there is some affinity between vertical and horizontal interference. Article 2(7) was loosely modelled on states' traditional concern for safeguarding their domestic sphere. It has accordingly long been suggested that the UN's own arrangements around questions of respect for sovereignty and non-interference might indirectly influence the sort of arrangements that

1504 ILO Commission of Inquiry, 'Forced Labour in Myanmar (Burma)' (International Labour Organization 1998) paras 520–521 <https://webapps.ilo.org/public/libdoc/ilo/P/09604/09604(1998-81-serie-B-special-suppl).pdf> accessed 13 July 2024.

1505 Samuel A Bleicher, 'UN v IBRD: A Dilemma of Functionalism' (1970) 24 International Organization 31.

1506 For a skeptical view, see *Certain Expenses of the United Nations (Article 17, paragraph 2, of the Charter)(Separate Opinion of Sir Percy Spender)* [1962] ICJ Rep 151, 189, 195.

govern inter-state relations, given the similarities in formulation for example between Article 2(7) of the U.N. Charter and Resolution 2625 (XXV).[1507] The recognition of an inherent limit to the power of even broadly mandated international organizations does come troublingly close to the identification of a core domain of competence as lying with states.

As Chimène Keitner points out, '[a]s a textual matter, Article 2(4) addresses itself to states and Article 2(7) addresses itself to the United Nations', but 'both can be seen as protecting a core sphere of state activity from certain forms of external pressure'.[1508] In effect, Article 2(7) does provide a richly textured and ongoing approximation of what constitute domestic affairs and what amounts to interference, at least for the purposes of the Charter and United Nations practice. It has provided a laboratory of sorts for acceptable interference whose unmistakable thrust is the shrinking of the *domaine réservé* and the narrowing of what might actually constitute intervention. In short, there is a degree of at least symbolic back-and-forth between vertical and horizontal intervention that points to the reality that both, if nothing else, at least deal with the fundamental question of the proper scope of sovereignty broadly understood.

It is also true that the question of inherent domestic jurisdiction has sometimes been assessed by international organizations, elucidating their own vertical powers to be sure, but in the context of actual inter-state disputes (between Sweden and Finland in the Aaland island case, the U.K. and France in the Tunis-Morocco Decrees case, Greece and Turkey in the expulsion of the Oecumenical Patriarch case, etc.) in ways that suggest that the horizontal and vertical axes are not that irreducible. Even before the General Assembly, the examination of the record of particular states is typically triggered by other states which may only be too happy to do via the United Nations that which they may not do alone. This was the concern of the Soviet delegation at Dumbarton Oaks[1509] and clearly issues such as Apartheid and the Algeria war did not make their way into the UNGA agenda spontaneously without some referral by particular states, evidently with agendas of their own. This is not a concern that one can evacuate lightly. For example, the U.S. did organize the financial and economic blockade of Allende's Chile via the World Bank and the Inter-American Development Bank (superficially on account of Chile's lack of credit-worthiness, which was itself largely manufactured by the

1507 For a discussion, see Corten and Klein (n 1032) 42.

1508 Keitner (n 878) 183. See also Kamminga (n 1313) 2.

1509 United Nations Conference on International Organization (UNCIO), 'Summary Report of 9th meeting of Executive Committee' in *Documents of the United Nations Conference on International Organization: San Francisco 1945*, vol 5 (United Nations 1945) 522 ff.

refusal to lend to it).[1510] The multilateral structure of international organizations and their independent personality can be overrated when organizations such as the World Bank are particularly vulnerable to pressures from major contributors.[1511]

There are also concerns that the Security Council can be 'captured' by certain interests to effect interference that would have been patently illegal if effectuated on the horizontal level. During a particularly acrimonious debate on the Security Council's role in relation to the Venezuela crisis, Russia insisted that the U.S. was merely trying to destabilize the country by ousting its legitimately elected leader and that the item was not even on the Council's agenda—effectively accusing the U.S. and its allies of seeking to do via the Security Council that which would never be countenanced in bilateral relations. As the Russian ambassador put it:

> They completely disregard the sovereignty of Venezuela, while imposing decisions on it that they prefer. They have refused its people the right to resolve their problems on their own. [...] How would [France] feel if the Russian Federation proposed discussing in the Security Council the issue of [...] the protests staged by the gilets jaunes [...]? We call for, first, respect to legitimate authority; secondly, non-interference in the domestic affairs of the country; and, thirdly, the non-imposition of outside solutions on Venezuela. Instead, we propose that we help its people find a peaceful resolution to their problems on their own.[1512]

This form of 'diagonal' interference (allegedly using international fora to launder what under one reading might be seen as a form of state-to-state interference) is problematic to the extent that, even though its form its 'vertical', its motivation may be 'horizontal', essentially acting as a multilateral subterfuge for bilateral destabilization.

Some states have as a result long sought to portray, a little self-servingly, developments in vertical intervention as potentially licencing forms of problematic horizontal interference down the road. For example, as the French ambassador put it when the Third World sought to put a discussion of the Algeria war on the General Assembly agenda:

1510 Brosche (n 432).

1511 Bartram S Brown, *The United States and The Politicizatition of the World Bank: Issues of International Law and Policy* (Routledge 1992).

1512 UNSCOR, 74th Sess (26 January 2019) U.N. Doc S/PV.8452, 19.

> If it were decided to discuss here the French problem of Algeria, nothing would ever restrict, in the future, the right, which we would all have, to interfere in the internal affairs of any one of us, since this assembly would, henceforth, have recognized that very right. The territorial unity of any state, the treaties whether old or recent, relating to boundaries, could at any moment be challenged. For many it would be the end of security and for the weakest the end of independence.[1513]

By and large, however, this fear has emphatically not materialized and was at the very least exaggerated. It is simply not true that the internationalization of matters under the auspices of multilateral internationalism has been a Trojan horse for generalizing state-to-state interference, or that states more generally have engulfed themselves in the breach created by the U.N. to justify horizontal interference. This is despite the undoubted reality of state agency before international organizations. Of course, almost every international organization intervention is traceable to the initiative of some states. Nonetheless, third states who vote for resolutions that objectively encroach on the domestic affairs of others are not thereby doing through an international organization that which they could not do bilaterally: not only do international organizations have a juridical personality of their own, but in most cases—outside, perhaps, permanent Security Council members—the role of any given state is simply too undecisive to make the resulting intervention traceable, let alone attributable to it.

In truth, the broader translatability of legal developments in the vertical realm to horizontal matters remains inherently limited and the leakage of one category (vertical interference) into the other (horizontal interference) is hardly a foregone conclusion. To state the obvious, the U.N. Charter strictly speaking says nothing specific about inter-state interference and is only devoted to defining the U.N.'s own powers. Simply because the U.N., for its own reasons and on the basis of its own constitutional values, can interfere in the affairs of member states does not mean that said states can, without more, do the same in relation to each other. The scope of prohibited horizontal interference could be significantly wider than that of the vertical kind.[1514] As already remarked, some notions characteristic of horizontal interference (that it be, for example, 'dictatorial') do not make much sense in the vertical context, certainly even less so than in the horizontal one. This suggests that all along the

1513 Cited in Wright, 'Is Discussion Intervention?' (n 1440) 103.

1514 Zemanek (n 407) 955.

two realms have remained inherently distinct.[1515] Indeed Article 2(7), although it is sometimes 'viewed as a codification of the more general principle of non-interference as between sovereign states',[1516] has been described as 'entirely different' from the customary principle of non-intervention.[1517]

And there are good reasons for this to be so, linked to the fundamentally different nature of the power exercised and the nature of interference arising in the horizontal and vertical realms. Simply because the Security Council fancies itself as capable of engaging in quasi-humanitarian intervention[1518] (in itself a contested power that it must exercise in conformity with the Charter),[1519] for example, is certainly not conclusive of the parallel but largely irreducible debate on whether *states* can *suo sponte* do the same: quite the contrary, in fact, and the heart of the controversy has consisted in teasing out the differences between the two and the need to keep them neatly separated as formalized in R2P.[1520] As Wolfgang Friedmann once put it, 'in so far as the states have conferred certain powers upon the United Nations as the guardian of international peace and security, they have given it certain rights not available to any one of them individually'.[1521] Similarly, it is one thing the for the World Bank, representing 'common interests' and a multilateral forum of discussion from deciding the terms of an economic intervention, and another for states to do the same.[1522]

There are reasons to think that international organizations have legitimacy to intervene in ways that are simply not (and perhaps can never nor ought to be) replicated on a state-to-state level. States may consider United Nations interference relatively acceptable but not similar behavior when it comes to fellow states. To begin with, unlike interference on the horizontal level which

---

1515 Rajan (n 568) 254. (Noting that 'None of these actions or measures could be considered as "dictatorial interference" within the domestic jurisdiction of members and they are therefore altogether different from the intervention of one state within the internal affairs of the other which customary international law prohibits').

1516 Celeste Poltak, 'Humanitarian Intervention: A Contemporary Interpretation of the Charter of the United Nations' (2002) 60 University of Toronto Faculty of Law Review 1, 22.

1517 Gowlland-Debbas (n 1452) 290.

1518 Carrie Walling, *All Necessary Measures: The United Nations and Humanitarian Intervention* (University of Pennsylvania Press 2013).

1519 Lawrence Emeka Modeme, 'The Security Council and the Legal Limits of Humanitarian Military Intervention', *The Asian Yearbook of Human Rights and Humanitarian Law* (Brill Nijhoff 2018).

1520 Chesterman (n 766); Dorota Gierycz, 'From Humanitarian Intervention (HI) to Responsibility to Protect (R2P)' (2010) 29 Criminal Justice Ethics 110; Jemirade (n 766).

1521 Friedmann, *The Changing Structure of International Law* (n 21) 269–270.

1522 Friedmann, 'Intervention and the Developing Countries' (n 406) 222.

is rarely if ever formally welcomed and simply has no *a priori* legal status, the legitimacy of multilateral intervention can if nothing else be traced to an initial consent of even the state complaining of interference. For example, when the Soviet Union invoked the domestic jurisdiction exception to the U.N.'s scrutiny of its human rights record, the Egyptian delegate said that it was 'unquestionable that the competence of the General Assembly had been thoroughly established' since the Soviet delegation 'had taken part in the discussion of the draft' of the Universal Declaration.[1523] The protestations of colonial states in the decolonization era were all the more easily and justifiably brushed aside that they had, in ratifying the U.N. Charter including its chapter xi, already agreed in principle that the regulation of colonies had henceforth been internationalized, thus setting the United Nations on an irreversible path.[1524] Similarly, when the legality of the creation of the ICTY was challenged in the Tadic case, the Yugoslavia Tribunal merely noted that Yugoslavia had ratified the U.N. Charter and that it its successor states were bound in advance by decisions of the Security Council. Interference was all the less averred, moreover, that Bosnia Herzegovina itself had chosen to welcome the tribunal.[1525]

Note that this broad original consent can be actualized at various junctions, reinforcing the sense that, whatever tensions may arise on an ad hoc basis between particular states and international organizations, is still mitigated by a basic agreement by the former to the action of the latter. For example, it will be difficult for a host state to complain that a U.N. peacekeeping operation is interfering with its domestic affairs that this operation will, per hypothesis, have been agreed to in principle. This is all the more so that a part of the U.N.'s peacekeeping practice has increasingly erred towards the side of 'peace support' missions, wherein the U.N. takes a role that hews very closely to the interests of the host state[1526] and in fact occasionally seeks to curb outside interference.[1527] Similarly, it will be difficult to complain about World Bank meddlesomeness when one has agreed to the terms of a loan, or about European Union intrusion when one has largely already accepted its

1523 UNGA Sixth Committee (3rd Session), 'Summary records of the 136th meeting' (6 December 1948) U.N. Doc A/C.6/SR.136, 747.

1524 Claude, Jr (n 312) 124.

1525 *Tadic* case (n 1384), para 56.

1526 Touko Piiparinen, 'Intervening to Strengthen Sovereignty: The Lessons of the U.N. Intervention Brigade for Global Peacekeeping' (2016) 30 International Relations 154.

1527 Richard Gowan, 'Diplomatic Fallout: UN's "Intervention Brigade" Raises Cost of Interference in DRC' (*World Politics Review*, 8 April 2013) <https://www.worldpoliticsreview.com/diplomatic-fallout-u-n-s-intervention-brigade-raises-cost-of-interference-in-drc/> accessed 26 May 2024.

framework for foreign aid. By contrast, Belgrade can rightly claim that under no framework did Serbia ever consent to a military intervention by NATO on its territory.[1528] In short, parties to the U.N. have agreed to the dispositions of its Charter (including in how they legitimize in advance, within the organization's area of competency, fairly significant encroachments on the *domaine réservé*), whereas they are certainly not similarly bound vis-à-vis fellow states.

A second facet of the relative acceptability of international organizations' 'interference' is that they are traditionally seen as standing in for a certain international community interest. They are, in that respect, more than the sum of the consents that gave rise to them. Moreover, as deliberative organs based on the equality of state members, they are deemed to be more naturally inured from the excesses and politicization of state-to-state interference. As William Fenrick put it ahead of the adoption of the U.N. Charter, the debate changes significantly when one substitutes 'the collective action of the community in place of the unilateral action of the individual state' because, in reality:

> The true criticism of intervention is not that it has been in every case without justification, but rather that even in those cases in which, as time has gone by, it would appear that the particular intervention was undertaken in the interest of law and justice, the action of the intervening power has of necessity been arbitrary. For action is always arbitrary where the intervening state is the judge of its own case. Even where the results are good the use of force by the individual state must inevitably weaken the general structure of order and justice in the community.[1529]

By contrast:

> In the interest of international jurisprudence it would seem desirable not to use the term 'intervention' when speaking of the collective action of the whole body of states under circumstances where the action of an individual state would constitute intervention. What would be arbitrary for the individual state would in the case of the whole body of states be no more than the exercise of the higher right of the community to maintain law and order and to see to the observance by the separate states of their obligations as members of the community.[1530]

1528 Angel Angelov, 'Regional Involvement in Peace Operations: An Analysis of the Debate within the U.N. Security Council' (2010) 10 Conflict, Security & Development 599.
1529 Fenwick, 'Intervention: Individual and Collective' (n 71) 658.
1530 ibid 663.

In other words, it is not merely that states have consented to the operation of international organizations as they have ratified a number of treaties, but that in doing so they have endowed said organizations with a particular international legal personality that, in the best of cases at least, they will understand to be for some collective international benefit. International organizations stand in for a certain inchoate conception of the international community's interest that makes it harder to second guess their intentions or to dismiss them at the outset as hostile.

A third dimension is that, institutionally, international organizations also provide in-built limitations to their mandate that make their interventions more bearable, and which have no equivalent in inter-state relations. Under this view, supranational, often multilateral, and even universal bodies present greater representative, procedural and deliberative guarantees. They operate, at least in the best of cases, under systems of international checks and balances, institutional limitations and greater constraints of independence and impartiality than governments in their foreign relations. They are thus less easily suspected of pursuing some partisan agenda given their identification with the supposedly shared values of international society. It is as if multilateralism itself inoculated the U.N. from the worst forms of suspicion about horizontal interference.

A rough analogy is provided by international legal arguments over jurisdiction and immunities. Whilst the exercise of jurisdiction by domestic courts over former or incumbent officials invariably raises issues of immunities, international criminal tribunals have been much more likely to circumvent such procedural restrictions to their jurisdiction, in part at least by virtue of their very 'internationality';[1531] in that scenario, such internationality literally

---

1531 Robert Cryer, 'Immunities and International Criminal Tribunals' in Alexander Orakhelashvili (ed), *Research Handbook on Jurisdiction and Immunities in International Law* (Edward Elgar Publishing 2015); Astrid Reisinger Coracini and Jennifer Trahan, 'The Case for Creating a Special Tribunal to Prosecute the Crime of Aggression Committed Against Ukraine (Part VI): On the Non-Applicability of Personal Immunities' (*Just Security*, 8 November 2022) <https://www.justsecurity.org/84017/the-case-for-creating-a-special-tribunal-to-prosecute-the-crime-of-aggression-committed-against-ukraine-part-vi-on-the-non-applicability-of-personal-immunities/> accessed 22 March 2024; William A Schabas, 'The Special Tribunal for Lebanon: Is a 'Tribunal of an International Character'Equivalent to an "International Criminal Court"?' (2008) 21 Leiden Journal of International Law 513. Conversely, the intrusive character of such overriding is underscored by authors who stress the fact that this doctrinal explanation too easily ignores international law's colonial origins and its tendency to ride roughshod, historically, over colonized states' sovereignty. See Linda Mushoriwa, 'The Immunity Question before the International Criminal Court: Revisiting African Sovereignty and the Colonial Origins of International Law' (2021) 29 African Journal of International and Comparative Law 341.

becomes an argument to the effect that interference is minimized even as immunities are overridden. The argument is for example that the transfer of officials to international criminal tribunals only involves a 'surrender' rather than an 'extradition' and that the potential for noxious interference is much less than in the case of domestic or even universal jurisdiction. International criminal tribunals are not sovereign and therefore, paradoxically, cannot be strictly interfering in the sovereignty of a state.[1532]

Some authors have as a result argued that Article 2(7) 'is not of any help since it regulates the relations between the U.N. and the member States and not those among the States themselves'.[1533] It is one thing, for example, for the United Nations to supervise human rights, but quite another for individual states to critique other states' record (they may do so of course, but subject to different practices, such as inter-state petitions or diplomatic protests that have a logic of their own). Changes in the acceptability of 'interference' on one axis do not necessarily or even typically translate into changes in the acceptability of 'interference' on the other. It is theoretically perfectly possible to acknowledge the substantive ascendancy of human rights in international law as manifested by the rise of supranational supervisory or adjudicatory bodies, for example, yet to not *pro tanto* conclude that the norm of non-interference has been substantially modified when it comes to states' relations inter se. This is essentially what led the ICJ to recognize that 'statements whereby States avow their recognition of the principles of international law set forth in the United Nations Charter cannot strictly be interpreted as applying to the principle of nonintervention by States in the internal and external affairs of other States'.[1534]

Whatever redefinition of the scope of non-interference occurs as a result of international organizations' practice, then, can and should be neatly contained within that *sui generis* set of practices. The U.N.'s own evolving interpretation of its mandate is thus better understood as part of a *lex specialis* allowing U.N. intervention against the background of a *lex generalis* that continues to prohibit state intervention and adopt a much stricter stance on state interference. As Kunig puts it, 'Art. 2 (7) U.N. Charter explicitly applies only to the organs of the U.N. It cannot be transferred to the relations between Member States, because the extent of protection against acts of U.N. organs

1532 Frédéric Mégret, 'In Search of the "Vertical": An Exploration of What Makes International Criminal Tribunals Different (and Why)' in Carsten Stahn, Larissa Van den Herik and John Dugard (eds), *Future Perspectives on International Criminal Justice* (TMC Asser Press 2010).

1533 Ronzitti (n 115) 4.

1534 *Nicaragua v United States* (n 3) [106].

and against States is not necessarily identical'.[1535] For example, whilst states may be willing to recognize that the Council can *in extremis* use force as part of the 'responsibility to protect', they are not willing to extend this prerogative to states acting of their own initiative.[1536] As discussed, there are many normative, prudential and practical reasons why what is accepted for the U.N., operating as it does on the basis of quite strict safeguards and limitations, is not available even to some 'coalition of the willing'. This is even if it be one claiming to uphold international principles, be they the Charter's own, outside of the Charter's processes.

To conclude, there is nothing surprising about the fact that States may as a result tolerate forms of interference that come from supranational actors that they would not accept from unauthorized and tainted horizontal interveners—this, at least, is the relatively rosy internationalist observation of the fact that meddling by international organizations is routinely accepted that would be vigorously opposed if it came from fellow states. In that respect, although the paths opened by supranational scrutiny of human rights practices are likely to be soon also traveled by states emboldened to criticize others' human rights record, they remain very limited paths that hardly legitimize types of 'new interference' that are neither supranational, nor mandate-driven, nor process-constrained. Moreover, horizontal interference, even of the private and transnational kind, that receives significant support from international organizations will have a relatively stronger claim to being legal but only for that reason. Some NGOs, notably, are at least strongly embedded in the U.N.'s legitimacy, whose discourse they replicate and amplify. They may be supported by international or regional organizations that make their mandate both semi-public and somewhat supranational. As such, they can be distinguished from both purely private meddling and interventions that have the relatively dubious backing of a lone state.

4 International Law v Human Rights?

Finally, dilemmas of interference create tensions between a sovereign-oriented concept of the protection of the *domaine réservé*, and domestic and international human rights protections. In many ways, the discourse about interference was traditionally a quintessentially horizontal one that emphasized

1535 Kunig (n 563) para 12.

1536 UNGA '2005 World Summit Outcome' (20 September 2005) U.N. Doc A/60/L.1, para 139.

a kind of zero-sum game between equal and competing sovereigns, caught in a tense game of interfering-whilst-not-being-interfered-with. That left little space for attention to how the debate over interference also stood to be influenced by supranational norms on a more vertical axis. The turn to self-determination by the decolonizing world had given an early, tantalizing taste of what values might be harmed beyond sovereignty but self-determination itself has an ambiguous status in human rights law.[1537] In recent years, the 'militarization' of interference discourse has at times also served to distract from its broader human rights implications as its stakes in terms of sovereignty are magnified.[1538]

This left in the shadows interference's transnational effect on various populations, even though understanding interference from the perspective of human rights adds significant conceptual thickness to the debate and raises a quite different constellation of issues. Indeed, the discussion on interference stands to be reshaped by a human rights agenda which emphasizes both the necessity and the costs of limiting interference on human rights grounds. Human rights law finds itself, somewhat awkwardly, buttressing the basic case both for interference and non-interference: simultaneously trying to rein in states' excesses in combatting it, whilst legitimizing what might otherwise count as interference in the name of basic freedoms. This, in turn, triggers strategic dilemmas about the extent to which one is willing to engage in rights repressive agendas in order to preserve self-determination or even a culture of rights, or to ground non-interference in the broader deployment of rights discourse. The point is that arguments for or against interference are increasingly mediated not just by the traditional attention to sovereignty but by a concern, in good faith or not, with human rights.

4.1 *Pushing Back against Excessive Non-interference Agendas*

An obvious risk is that interference will be seen as a result of liberal societies being too open precisely because of their culture of rights, so that the sacrifice

---

1537 Matthew Saul, 'The Normative Status of Self-Determination in International Law: A Formula for Uncertainty in the Scope and Content of the Right?' (2011) 11 Human Rights Law Review 609; Richard A Falk, 'The Right of Self-Determination Under International Law: The Coherence of Doctrine Versus the Incoherence of Experience' in Wolfgang Danspeckgruber and Arthur Watts (eds), *Self-Determination and Self-Administration* (Lynne Rienner Publishers 1997); Eva Maria Belser and Alexandra Fang-Bär, 'Self-Determination: Historic and Current Ambiguities of International Law' in Eva Maria Belser and others (eds), *States Falling Apart? Secessionist and Autonomy Movements in Europe* (Stämpfli Verlag 2015).

1538 Douek (n 46).

of some rights is presented as justified in fending off interference. In fact, the West often seems like its inclination towards liberal political mores generally, and internet freedom in particular, leaves it vulnerable to some of the abuses that arise in cyberspace. This can precipitate a crisis of confidence in the ability of open societies to self-regulate and prompt the adoption of radical measures to guard against foreign interference. By contrast, Russian or Chinese notions of 'internet sovereignty' may appear to better guard against the threat of interference, at the risk of course of making them susceptible to the critique that they neglect rights and sacrifice the openness of the internet. The European Parliament has noted that 'authoritarian regimes have become more effective at co-opting or circumventing norms and institutions that support basic liberties'.[1539] One almost senses a degree of authoritarian-envy from liberal democracies that cannot afford to resort to some of the expedients that states less concerned with liberties routinely resort to.

It is true that basic freedoms such as of opinion, expression or association may be very much at risk as a result of anti-interference laws that are overbroad or unduly repressive. This is clear in authoritarian states, including such typical instances as foreign agent laws or broad definitions of 'espionage'. Human rights do provide a potent critique against such excesses. In some ways, 'foreign interference', like 'terrorism' before and alongside it, is the perfect excuse for an agenda of erosion of liberties and social control. Repressive agendas of fighting against interference have been implemented in a range of states but particularly in countries that lie somewhere in the middle of the liberal-illiberal spectrum. There, non-interference provides a veneer of respectability and urgency for measures that might be hard to adopt outside the manufacturing of panics about foreign preying. Because it is based on an amorphous and elusive threat, moreover, it can be instrumentalized very flexibly.

Singapore's Foreign Interference (Countermeasures) Bill (FICA) is a good example of a law with wide ranging implications for liberties that has been criticized as violating human rights principles of legality, necessity and proportionality. Its conflation of interference and national security betray an ambition that lies straightforwardly in a repressive register.[1540] Among other things, the law makes it a criminal offence to undertake 'clandestine electronic communications on behalf of a foreign principal' including when that activity 'diminishes or is likely to diminish public confidence in [...] the Government

1539 2023 Resolution on Foreign Interference in the E.U. (n 335), para BA.

1540 'Singapore: Withdraw Foreign Interference (Countermeasures) Bill | Human Rights Watch' (13 October 2021) <https://www.hrw.org/news/2021/10/13/singapore-withdraw-foreign-interference-countermeasures-bill> accessed 29 July 2024.

or a public authority' or 'is likely to be directed towards a political end in Singapore'.[1541] The Bill has been criticized as effectively making it impossible for social actors to know when they are treading the line between licit and illicit activity. The net effect may well be a chilling impact on international collaboration, especially as it affects scholars, activists or journalists. It may also 'increase the risk of individuals self-censoring and deliberately deciding not to participate in or engage with cross-border networks to avoid potentially falling foul of the law'.[1542]

Georgia also illustrated itself by adopting a wide-ranging anti-interference law ("Law on Transparency of Foreign Influence") that imposes onerous obligations of reporting to any organization with as little as 20% of foreign funding. The law was widely interpreted by both civil society and political parties there and human rights actors abroad as a pretext to firmly police NGOs more generally, leading to significant resistance and demonstrations, as well as legal challenges including by the President of Georgia herself.[1543] Its adoption was certainly seen as paradoxical: defended by the ruling party as a way to protect Georgian sovereignty, it has been widely derided as a form of surrender to Russia.[1544] This underscores that just as anti-interference agendas can have largely home-grown sources, the resistance against such as agendas is itself rooted in largely domestic struggles that may even avoid too conspicuous an invocation of international law lest they be further portrayed as beholden to foreign interests.

But the danger cuts across any neat sense of an illiberal/liberal divide among states. The latter, as has long already been evident in anti-terrorism or anti-migration frameworks, are also prone to react disproportionately and in ways at odds with the principles they claim to defend.[1545] There is, in fact, more than a hint of 'militant democracy' when it comes to the sort of measures that liberal democracies feel they should be able to deploy to deal with what is invariably portrayed (perhaps as a result of a shallow historical memory)

1541 Foreign Interference (Countermeasures) Bill, ss 17–19.

1542 'Singapore: Withdraw Foreign Interference (Countermeasures) Bill | Human Rights Watch' (n 1540).

1543 Dito Matcharadze, 'NGOs in Georgia Refuse to Register as "foreign Agents" under New Law' (*euronews*, 10 September 2024) <https://www.euronews.com/2024/09/10/majority-of-ngos-in-georgia-refuse-to-register-as-foreign-agents-under-new-law> accessed 22 September 2024.

1544 Maxim Krupskiy, 'The Power of Stigma' [2024] *Foreign Affairs* <https://www.foreignaffairs.com/georgia/power-stigma> accessed 22 September 2024.

1545 Michael Head, 'Australia's Anti-Democratic "Foreign Interference" Bills' (2018) 43 Alternative Law Journal 160.

as an exceptional threat. As the European Parliament points out, somewhat ambiguously: 'action against foreign interference and information manipulation must itself respect the fundamental freedoms of expression and information [...] in order to avoid disproportionate actions'; yet one limit seems to be the need to deal with 'actors carrying out foreign interference and information manipulation [who] misuse those freedoms to their advantage'.[1546] The level of social and political alarm generated about foreign interference can quickly lead to witch hunts, perhaps all the more severe that they invoke the language of democracy and rights.

In practice responses to interference do overreach and have the potential to damage the very values they are supposed to protect—and of course in some cases may be very much designed to damage those values. For example, the effort to ban Tik Tok in the U.S. or to force it to change its ownership structure has been assailed not so much on the basis that Tik Tok is not a conduit for Chinese meddling, but out of concerns with the First Amendment.[1547] The argument is that banning a platform that may channel foreign propaganda but is also a site of communication by millions of Americans would drastically curtail their freedom of expression.[1548] In that respect, it is the expansive construction of 'national security' that is challenged as potentially encroaching on vast areas of liberty, but also TikTok's own apparent willingness to offer the U.S. government a 'kill switch' in case in contravenes national security.[1549] At the same time, the argument is made more complex by the fact that one of the reasons for banning Tik Tok is itself taken from human rights, notably the need to curtail hate speech including anti-Semitism,[1550] including in response to the

1546 2022 Resolution on Foreign Interference in the E.U. (n 337), para D.

1547 Jameel Jaffer, 'Opinion | There's a Problem With Banning TikTok. It's Called the First Amendment.' *The New York Times* (24 March 2023) <https://www.nytimes.com/2023/03/24/opinion/tiktok-ban-first-amendment.html> accessed 24 September 2024.

1548 Alexander Paykin, 'A Tik-Tok Ban? The First Amendment Implications Should Not Be Underestimated' (*New York State Bar Association*, 26 August 2024) <https://nysba.org/a-tik-tok-ban-the-first-amendment-implications-should-not-be-underestimated/> accessed 24 September 2024.

1549 Andrew Ross Sorkin and others, 'TikTok's Legal Bet on the First Amendment' *The New York Times* (8 May 2024) <https://www.nytimes.com/2024/05/08/business/dealbook/tiktok-lawsuit-first-amendment.html> accessed 24 September 2024.

1550 'Jewish Teens on TikTok Say They Have to Brace for Anti-Semitic Comments When They Post about Judaism' (*NBC News*, 25 September 2020) <https://www.nbcnews.com/news/us-news/jewish-teens-say-life-tiktok-comes-anti-semitism-n1241033> accessed 24 September 2024.

proposed ban in the U.S.[1551]

In turn, internationally guaranteed human rights are routinely invoked to push back against the excesses of the anti-interference agenda. This is so both in relation to the rights of would-be interferers but also, crucially, of populations locally who are being dispossessed of an access to outside sources of information by measures supposedly designed to curtail interference. U.N. human rights treaty bodies, for example, have responded strongly to initiatives aimed at limiting the activities of civil society on the basis of the foreign support it receives. In 2015, the HR Committee, upon reviewing Russia's performance under the ICCPR, called on it to repeal or revise the foreign agent law, remove the term 'foreign agent' and better define political activity.[1552] The Venice Commission[1553] and the European Commissioner on Human rights[1554] have also denounced Russia's authoritarian (over) reaction to claims of interference. These various sources can be seen as doubling down on the notion that foreign funding of human rights work, even broadly understood, cannot be seen in and of itself as a form of interference given the collective interest in human rights.

Curtailments of freedom of association on account of interference have gradually made their way before courts, notably the Court of Justice of the European Union and the ECtHR, specifically in relation to foreign funding of civil society. The former found that Hungary's 'Transparency Act' was in violation of E.U. law. It constituted a limitation on freedom of association with strong dissuasive dimensions, including through the designation as an 'organisation in receipt of support from abroad' which would 'generalise climate of mistrust' and 'stigmatise' the relevant organizations.[1555] Although it found the goal of increasing the transparency of the financing of associations to be

---

1551 'TikTok Ban Feared, Antisemitic Conspiracy Theories Follow' (20 March 2024) <https://www.adl.org/resources/blog/tiktok-ban-feared-antisemitic-conspiracy-theories-follow> accessed 24 September 2024.

1552 HR Committee, 'Concluding observations on the seventh periodic report of the Russian Federation' (28 April 2015) U.N. Doc CCPR/C/RUS/CO/7 (HR Committee Concluding observations on the Russian Federation).

1553 Venice Commission, '99th Plenary Session, Venice, 13–14 June 2014, Opinion on Federal Law n 121-FZ on Non-Commercial Organisations ("Law on Foreign Agents"), on Federal Laws n 18-FZ and n 147-FZ and on Federal Law n 190-FZ on Making Amendments to the Criminal Code ("Law on Treason") of the Russian Federation' (2014) CDL-AD (2014)025.

1554 Opinion of the Commissioner on Human Rights on the legislation of the Russian Federation on non-commercial organizations in light of Council of Europe standards, 15/07/2013.

1555 Case C-78/18 *Commission v Hungary* [2020] ECLI:EU:C:2020:476 (Transparency of Associations), paras 118–119.

legitimate in principle, this did not warrant broad legislation that assumed, indiscriminately, that any foreign financial support was likely to jeopardize the host state's political and economic interests.[1556] This was all the more so that the financial thresholds triggering the law's application were fixed and unrelated to what might be considered a sufficiently serious threat to a fundamental interest of society which those obligations are supposed to prevent.[1557]

It is, however, the Russian registration law that has attracted most attention from both the Venice Commission,[1558] the Commissioner for Human Rights of the Council of Europe,[1559] treaty bodies of the United Nations[1560] and, eventually, the ECtHR, leading to quite a significant, largely converging corpus. Perhaps the most resounding rejection of the validity under human rights law of the Russian law has come from Strasbourg, which came out strongly in defense of freedom of assembly and association as, essentially, entailing a right to not be sanctioned for receiving foreign funding. Under the Russian law, NGOs could be denied registration if their 'goals and objectives [...] create a threat to the sovereignty, political independence, territorial integrity, national unity, unique character, cultural heritage and national interests of the Russian Federation'.[1561] The law and decisions based on it were challenged before Russian courts with limited success, the law being found to be constitutional by Russian Courts.[1562]

1556 ibid, para 86.

1557 ibid, para 94.

1558 Venice Commission, '99th Plenary Session, Venice, 13–14 June 2014, Opinion on Federal Law n 121-FZ on Non-Commercial Organisations ("Law on Foreign Agents"), on Federal Laws n 18-FZ and n 147-FZ and on Federal Law n 190-FZ on Making Amendments to the Criminal Code ("Law on Treason") of the Russian Federation' (n 1553).

1559 Commissioner for Human Rights, 'Opinion of the Commissioner of Human Rights on the Legislation of the Russian Federation on Non-Commercial Organisations in Light of Council of Europe Standards' (Council of Europe 2013) <https://rm.coe.int/opinion-of-the-commissioner-for-human-rights-on-the-legislation-of-the/16806da5b2> accessed 14 July 2024.

1560 HR Committee Concluding observations on the Russian Federation; U.N. Committee on Economic, Social and Cultural Rights (CESCR), 'Concluding observations on the sixth periodic report of the Russian Federation' (16 October 2017) E/C.12/EUS/CO/6, paras 7–8; U.N. Committee against Torture (CAT), 'Concluding observations on the 6th periodic report of the Russian Federation' (28 August 2018) CAT/RUS/CO/6, para 28.

1561 Katherin Machalek, 'Factsheet: Russia's NGO Laws' (Freedom House 2013) 10 <https://freedomhouse.org/sites/default/files/2020-02/SR_Contending_with_Putins_Russia_PDF.pdf> accessed 6 February 2024.

1562 Mercedes Malcomson, '"So Whose Agents Are We?" Defining (International) Human Rights in the Shadow of the "Foreign Agents" Law in Russia' (2020) 7 Birkbeck Law Review 122, 143–145.

In the *Ecodefence and Others v Russia* case before the ECtHR, 61 applications by 73 applicants complained of having been classified as 'foreign agents' as a result of the Russian Foreign Agents Act.[1563] The Court found that the Russian law undoubtedly affected freedom of association through 'a combination of inspections, new registration requirements, sanctions and restrictions on sources of funding and the nature of the activities' that they could undertake. Indeed, they had to 'alter their conduct significantly to reduce the risk of facing further penalties under the Act' and some even dissolved themselves.[1564] Essentially, the law confronted them with the impossible choice of either forfeiting significant funding at the cost of a reduction in the scope of their operations, or continuing to receive such funding but having to do so, henceforth, as 'foreign agents' subjected to onerous reporting and accounting obligations. The Court noted that 'to the extent that leaders and members of an association resolve to dissolve their organisation in the hope of avoiding adverse effects of domestic legislation or actions by the domestic authorities, such decisions cannot be said to have been made freely'.[1565]

In other words, the considerable chilling effect of the law was blamed on Russia and no amount of intervening agency by the NGOs themselves could change that reality (i.e.: NGOs could not be blamed for scuttling themselves rather than being subjected to oppressive legislation). Of course, the Court acknowledged that freedom of association could be limited, but it found that the Russian law failed the test of a permissible limitation on several counts. First, although it was clearly a law, it was formulated in such a way that it would be difficult for those concerned to 'foresee, to a degree that is reasonable in the circumstances, that certain conduct would lead to specific legal consequences or sanctions'.[1566] The definition of political activities, in particular, was 'very flexible' giving rise to 'extensive and unforeseeable interpretation' and allowed Russian authorities to requalify organizations working in environmental, cultural or social fields as engaged in such activities, even though they were supposed to be excluded. Second and more significantly for our purposes, 'the absence of clear and foreseeable criteria has given the authorities unfettered discretion to assert that the applicant organisations were in receipt of "foreign funding", no matter how remote or tenuous their association with a purported "foreign source" was'.[1567]

1563 *Ecodefence and Others v Russia* (n 673).
1564 ibid, para 87.
1565 ibid, para 85.
1566 ibid, para 95.
1567 ibid, para 110.

This validated the experience of targeted Russian NGOs. There was simply no criterion to determine the degree of foreign funding that would make one a foreign agent, such that 'token' donations might expose an organization to that characterization. Russian authorities had found, for example, that even for directors of an organisation to sit on the board of another organisation which was itself qualified as a foreign agent was enough for their own organisation to be branded as such.[1568] Under such circumstances, there was no way that the applicants could 'reasonably foresee' that risk, notwithstanding 'how many degrees of separation there were between the recipient organisation and the purported "foreign source"'.[1569] Not even availing themselves of the possibility of declining foreign funds, despite it being anticipated by the law, seemed to satisfy Russian authorities and courts that they were not foreign agents.

On the issue of whether it was 'prescribed by law' at all, then, the ECtHR concluded that the Russian registration law fell short given its intrinsic deficiencies, in itself a remarkable conclusion given how relatively low that threshold ordinarily is. Nevertheless, the Court went further and found that the interference was, in addition, not 'necessary in a democratic society'. Several NGOs had testified to the fact that 'the protection of sovereignty and security could not be relied upon as a lawful ground for imposing restrictions on civil society organisations'.[1570] Whilst accepting that the law served the 'objective of increasing transparency with regard to the funding of civil society organisations may correspond to the legitimate aim of the prevention of disorder',[1571] the Court found that this did not make the law 'necessary'. This was especially the case given the role of civil society as a democratic 'watchdog', the importance of freedom of association, the need to interpret exceptions to it strictly, and to use limitations sparingly only on the basis of 'convincing and compelling reasons'.[1572]

As the Court put it, '[w]here risks to [the democratic] process have been identified, foreign involvement in some sensitive areas—such as elections or funding of political movements—may justify stricter regulation or restrictions by the State'.[1573] Note the emphasis on the democratic process: non-interference laws must, in the eyes of the ECtHR, be protecting something that is worth protecting and certainly in principle democracy qualities on the basis of the

1568 ibid.
1569 ibid.
1570 ibid, para 121.
1571 ibid, para 122.
1572 ibid, para 123.
1573 ibid, para 139.

Court's own previous case law. One can imagine cases where groups are being financed directly by foreign powers with a view to interfering with the political processes of other states. For example, in the earlier *Parti Nationaliste Basque* case, the Court had found that a French law banning financial contributions from foreign governments to political parties did not offend the Convention since ensuring the financial independence of said parties from foreign states was necessary to ensure that they served solely the interests of the electorate.[1574] The European Parliament has noted, however, that 'any requirements imposed to guard against foreign influence, such as transparency of (civil society organization) funding, should not stigmatise or be unduly onerous for foreign-funded organisations'.[1575]

In the case of the Russian law, the abstract validity of the aim pursued could not justify 'a presumption, made in principle and applied indiscriminately, that any financial support by a non-national entity and any civil society organisation receiving such financial support are intrinsically liable to jeopardise the State's political and economic interests and the ability of its institutions to operate free from interference'.[1576] Indeed, the law's main fault was that it 'introduced a concept of agency in which the control of the donor over the recipient of funds was effectively presumed rather than established on a case-by-case basis, even in a situation where the recipient of funds retained full managerial and operational independence in terms of defining its programmes, policies and priorities'.[1577] Strikingly, 'neither the Ministry of Justice nor the courts considered it necessary to show that the applicant organisations had been acting in the interests of foreign sources, and deemed the fact that they had received foreign funding and had been carrying out political activities to constitute sufficient evidence of their being "foreign agents"'.[1578] Hence a number of organizations which clearly operated independently had nonetheless been found to be foreign agents merely as a result of having used a foreign embassy's premises for a conference, for example.

Much of the Court's reasoning and before it of various international bodies (who also intervened in the case) revolved around the question of whether the label 'foreign agent' was *itself* necessary in a democratic society, even if its tenor had been more precisely defined. The Venice Commission had already underlined that '[t]he use of the term "foreign agent" is highly controversial. By

1574 *Parti nationaliste basque—Organisation régionale d'Iparralde v France* ECHR 2007-II 349.
1575 Jones (n 495) 9.
1576 *Ecodefence and Others v Russia* (n 673), para 166.
1577 ibid, para 134.
1578 ibid, para 135.

bringing back the rhetoric used during the communist period and its hint of treasonous behavior,[1579] this term stigmatises the NGOs to which it is applied, tarnishing their reputation and seriously hampering their activities'.[1580] Even outside the Russian context, the term suggests a principal-agent relationship where the latter works at the behest of the former, typically in exchange for remuneration, that has dark undertones and comes close to suggesting treasonous behavior. Indeed, the law is specifically designed to activate dormant fears about hidden foreign enemies and agitates the specter of heavy reprisals for that purpose.[1581] The Court thus found that the use of the term *in itself* 'was unjustified and prejudicial and also liable to have a strong deterrent and stigmatising effect on [organizations'] operations'. In effect, it unfairly 'coloured them as being under foreign control, in disregard of the fact that they saw themselves as members of national civil society working to uphold respect for human rights, the rule of law and human development for the benefit of Russian society and its democratic system'.[1582]

Nothing in the arguments by Russia itself, moreover, even accounting for the margin of appreciation, suggested 'relevant and sufficient' reasons to adopt a label as 'stigmatizing' as that of 'foreign agent', one which had in effect marginalized from public life and engagement with authorities a range of NGOs involved in significant work for democracy and human rights. The Court further found that a range of assorted measures imposed on Russian NGOs were problematic including: (i) 'increased frequency of reporting and inspections, the obligation on "foreign agent" organisations to undergo a mandatory audit and publish it on a dedicated website, or the barring of such organisations from being able to benefit from simplified book-keeping';[1583] (ii) restricting access to funding which meant putting NGOs in front of an 'enforced choice between accepting foreign funding and soliciting domestic State funding'

1579 Chip Pitts and Anastasia Ovsuannikova, 'Russia's New Treason Statute, Anti-NGO and Other Repressive Laws: Sovereign Democracy or Renewed Autocracy' (2015) 37 Houston Journal of International Law 83.

1580 Venice Commission, '99th Plenary Session, Venice, 13–14 June 2014, Opinion on Federal Law n 121-FZ on Non-Commercial Organisations ("Law on Foreign Agents"), on Federal Laws n 18-FZ and n 147-FZ and on Federal Law n 190-FZ on Making Amendments to the Criminal Code ("Law on Treason") of the Russian Federation' (2014) CDL-AD (2014)025, para 132. On the 'stigmatising effect' of the term 'foreign agents', see also *Ecodefence and Others v Russia* (n 673) paras 129–130.

1581 Polina Malkova, 'Images and Perceptions of Human Rights Defenders in Russia: An Examination of Public Opinion in the Age of the "Foreign Agent" Law' (2020) 19 Journal of Human Rights 201.

1582 *Ecodefence and Others v Russia* (n 673), para 136.

1583 ibid, para 159.

which constituted a 'false alternative' in a context where they 'should be free to solicit and receive funding from a variety of sources' and where this might even enhance their independence;[1584] and (iii) disproportionate sanctions, including fines, for what was in the end merely a regulatory offence. The unmistakable conclusion was that:

> the cumulative effect of these restrictions—whether by design or effect—is a legal regime that places a significant 'chilling effect' on the choice to seek or accept any foreign funding, however insignificant the amount, in a context where opportunities for domestic funding are somewhat limited, especially in respect of politically or socially sensitive topics or domestically unpopular causes.[1585]

4.2 *Human Rights: Buttressing the Case for Non-interference?*

This hardly means, by the same token, that rights discourse cannot end up grounding quite significant limitations in the same sort of context to interference. Early on in this book, the case was made that, in principle, the 'human rights state' can be seen as naturally bent towards reducing interference that is harmful to democracy. Indeed, rights analysis can and has also been deployed in defense of anti-interference measures as part of strategic calculi that seek to invert the usual thrust of the human rights charge. Although historically the norm of non-interference was designed to protect state sovereignty as such, one can rediscover a sense of the centrality of non-interference to human rights themselves, perhaps even as a sort of indirect foundation for sovereignty. After all, the conceptual edifice of sovereignty, even in an age of human rights, is mired in ideas about its protective function (sovereignty as responsibility, R2P, the responsibility to not only respect but protect human rights from third parties, etc.). To be sovereign is not only to protect oneself *qua* sovereign from interference, but to shield one's population from its unwanted manifestations, even as one runs the risk of overreacting and harming rights in the process. In that respect, the reformulation of non-interference as, at least indirectly, a human rights norm is already apace and taking shape in intriguing ways. The ECtHR itself when faced with Russia's NGO law did of course not exclude the possibility that the law's finality might itself be legal, if it was not then so indiscriminate and overreaching.

1584 ibid, para 169.

1585 ibid, para 186.

It is particularly the European Union which in recent years, in mounting a vigorous defense of the sanctity of its democratic processes, has emphasized, through its Parliament, that 'interference, information manipulation and disinformation are an abuse of the fundamental freedoms of expression and information as laid down in Article 11 of the Charter and threaten these freedoms, as well as undermining democratic processes in the E.U. and its Member States, such as the holding of free and fair elections'.[1586] For the European Union, in fact, 'the right to freedom of expression does not include freedom to use manipulative practices to spread information' and '[a] state which tolerates widespread manipulation may be denying its population the freedom to receive information which is also an important element of the right to freedom of expression'.[1587] Moreover, since 'democracy depends on people making informed decisions',[1588] interference goes to the heart of the operation of a well-functioning democracy.

In other words, far from being merely a break on governmental attempts to resist interference, human rights could be their crucial engine. Emphasizing human rights these days is often a prelude to robust anti-interference agendas implemented in the name of protecting the right to information or the operation of democracy. The Council of Europe, through its Committee of Ministers, has taken the stance that foreign financial contributions to political parties can and should, in principle, be prohibited.[1589] The Venice Commission has found that prohibiting foreign financing can be seen as a limitation to freedom of association but that it is nonetheless 'necessary in a democratic society' (Article 11 of the ECHR).[1590] None of these justifications invoke the right to self-determination but there is no doubt that it could in theory at least in other contexts. And compared to the U.S. where the First Amendment serves as an at least *a priori* obstacle, the more flexible concept of rights dominant in Europe allows for limitations analysis to justify limitations for pressing social concerns.

1586 2022 Resolution on Foreign Interference in the E.U. (n 337), para B.

1587 Jones (n 495) 33.

1588 2022 Resolution on Foreign Interference in the E.U. (n 337), para D.

1589 Council of Europe, Recommendation Rec(2003)4 of the Committee of Ministers to member states on common rules against corruption in the funding of political parties and electoral campaigns (8 April 2003), art 7.

1590 Venice Commission, '66th Plenary Session, Venice, 17–18 March 2006, Opinion on the Prohibition of Financial Contributions to Political Parties from Foreign Sources' (n 1398); Venice Commission, '46th Plenary Meeting, Venice, 9–10 March 2001, Guidelines and Report on the Financing of Political Parties' (2001) CDL-INF (2001) 8.

It is not always clear, however, especially in a context that otherwise values openness as a function of democracy, what kind of contextual factors might justify limitations to interference. The Venice Commission has noted as reasons that have historically led states to want to limit foreign funding of political parties 'the international policies of extremist parties of the political right and left [...] the polarisation of the Western World on the one side and the Eastern on the other [...] the existence or fear of separatist movements', as well as a more general and unspecified 'wish to keep any provided funds within the country'.[1591] This is quite a varied list and, although it might suffice from a pure democratic policy angle, would probably not pass the test of necessity in human rights law. Indeed, the Commission did not actually take a stance on whether such motivations are to be seen as conclusive and ends up with the relatively question-begging stance that 'every individual case has to be considered separately' and that the issue is whether a foreign donation 'undermines the fairness or integrity of political competition or leads to distortions of the electoral process or poses a threat to national territorial integrity'.[1592]

The broad framework when it comes to limitations of the rights of interfering actors and even their targets is a familiar one. As the European Union puts it, drawing on the case law of the ECtHR:

> Measures that restrict foreign actors' capacity to express themselves freely, or to associate with whomsoever they please, are likely to infringe their human rights to freedom of expression and association respectively. Any such measures must therefore be prescribed by law, with sufficient precision that anyone affected can regulate their conduct accordingly and foresee the consequences of their actions. In addition, any measures must pursue a legitimate aim such as the interests of national security or prevention of disorder and must be necessary in a democratic society and proportionate to the legitimate aim pursued.[1593]

Specifically, when it comes to any measure that might limit freedom of expression, for example by criminalizing interference, such measure will not run afoul of human rights protections if:

1591 Venice Commission, '66th Plenary Session, Venice, 17–18 March 2006, Opinion on the Prohibition of Financial Contributions to Political Parties from Foreign Sources' (n 1398) para 22.

1592 ibid 33.

1593 Jones (n 495) 9.

> it is clearly defined and limited by law, serves the aim of protecting European democracy and political purposes from foreign threats, and is proportionate to that aim, including by being limited to activity perpetrated by, or connected with, a foreign power and constraining only activity that includes an element of deception, coercion or threat.[1594]

Similarly, if sanctions are implemented against 'interferers' in the European Union context, the ECJ will want to satisfy itself that such sanctions are 'clearly laid down by law; foreseeable and temporary; pursue an objective of general interest; and are proportionate, in other words appropriate and necessary to the aims to be achieved'.[1595] Crucially, it has been clarified that these limitations apply 'regardless of frontiers so as to limit restrictions not only within a jurisdiction but also those which affect media outlets and other communications systems operating from outside of the jurisdiction of a State'.[1596] If states can and indeed sometimes should limit the reach of outside media, they cannot do so more strictly than they would with domestic sources. Moreover, the ECtHR always stresses the importance of interpreting exceptions to Article 11 (on freedom of association) strictly so that 'only convincing and compelling reasons can justify restrictions'.[1597] As is quite clear then, the international human rights law of non-interference not only exists, it is more often than not more precise and operational than the general international law of non-interference, albeit on largely distinct grounds. Without necessarily providing a wide opening for non-interference purposes, it still manages to mark out a narrow path for legitimate non-interference agendas.

An interesting counterpoint to the Ecodefense case, in that respect, is the RT France case before the ECJ: interesting in itself but also interesting because it represents a European response to what might be broadly perceived as the same challenge, namely that of indirect foreign interference, albeit this time not through civil society but the media. RT France is a television company established in France whose capital is held by a not-for-profit association in the Russian Federation and which is entirely funded by the budget of the Russian State. It had initially been allowed to broadcast in France. It is worth noting that when it comes to freedom of expression, a group of special rapporteurs have insisted that:

1594 ibid 12.
1595 ibid 16.
1596 Joint Declaration on Disinformation (n 697), para 1(c).
1597 *The United Macedonian Organisation Ilinden and others v Bulgaria* App no 59491/00 (ECtHR 19 January 2006) para 57–62.

> jamming of signals from a broadcaster based in another jurisdiction, or the withdrawal of rebroadcasting rights in relation to that broadcaster's programmes, is legitimate only where the content disseminated by that broadcaster has been held by a court of law or another independent, authoritative and impartial oversight body to be in serious and persistent breach of a legitimate restriction on content [...] and other means of addressing the problem, including by contacting the relevant authorities of the host State, have proven to be demonstrably ineffective.[1598]

How did the European reaction to RT France, then, measure up to such a quite demanding standard? Following Russia's invasion of Ukraine, the Council adopted a regulation that deplored that '[t]he Russian Federation has engaged in a systematic, international campaign of media manipulation and distortion of facts in order to enhance its strategy of destabilisation of its neighbouring countries and of the Union and its Member States', and had 'repeatedly and consistently targeted European political parties, especially during election periods, as well as targeting civil society, asylum seekers, Russian ethnic minorities, gender minorities, and the functioning of democratic institutions in the Union and its Member States'.[1599] Moreover, Russia had 'engaged in continuous and concerted propaganda actions targeted at civil society in the Union and neighbouring countries, gravely distorting and manipulating facts'.[1600] This 'constituted a threat to the EU's public order and security'.[1601] As a result, RT France's name was added to a list of entities whose licence to broadcast should be suspended.

Lawyers for RT France did not fail to invoke arguments taken from human rights including 'the rights of the defence, freedom of expression and information, freedom to conduct a business and the principle of non-discrimination on grounds of nationality'.[1602] The ECJ was nonetheless unimpressed and framed its judgment in the context of the goal of the measures in 'safeguarding the values of the European Union and its security and to preserving international peace and security in compliance with international law and, in particular, the principles of the United Nations Charter'.[1603] Although the target of sanctions had the right to be heard, the Council was not required to jeopardise

1598 Joint Declaration on Disinformation (n 697), para 1(h).
1599 *RT France v Council* (n 938), para 22(6).
1600 ibid, para 22(7).
1601 ibid, para 21.
1602 ibid, para 45.
1603 ibid, para 85.

the effectiveness of sanctions' 'surprise effect' by giving them advance notice in a situation of 'extreme urgency'. Certainly, the Council had not erred in finding that RT broadcasts were essentially a form of Russian propaganda.

More delicate was the notion, advanced by the TV station's lawyers, that the suspension of the broadcasting licence violated the right of the public to access 'a variety of opinions and comments that reflect, in particular, the diversity of public opinion in the country and also to ensure that journalists and other audiovisual media professionals are protected against obstacles to the communication of that information and those comments'.[1604] The ECJ did find that there was an interference with the applicant's freedom of expression. That interference, however, was provided by law (and its consequences were foreseeable), and it did not violate the 'essence of freedom of expression' given its temporary and reversible character as well as territory-bound limitations.[1605] More importantly, the ECJ endorsed the Council's argument that 'the Union's public order and security [was] under threat from the systematic international propaganda campaign put in place by the Russian Federation, channelled through media outlets under the permanent direct or indirect control of its leadership, in order to destabilise neighbouring countries, the Union and its Member States and to support military aggression against Ukraine'.[1606]

Specifically, the Court found that 'propaganda and disinformation campaigns are capable of undermining the foundations of democratic societies and are an integral part of the arsenal of modern warfare'.[1607] In addition, 'the restrictive measures at issue may be understood as being the response, with the peaceful means at the Union's disposal and with a view to achieving the objectives laid down in Article 3(5) TEU, of a subject of international law faced with aggression in breach of Article 2(4) of the United Nations Charter and, consequently, a violation of the *opinio juris* obligations imposed by international law'.[1608] In other words, the measures were not only legal, they were perhaps even compulsory given the overall narrative of Russian aggression. It is thus legitimate to ask whether the case would have been decided the same way had it not been for the evidence of an international crime.

The ECJ also found that the decision to impose restrictive measures on RT was 'taken on a sufficiently solid factual basis' and derived from 'sufficiently specific and concrete evidence' given the near total alignment between the

1604 ibid, para 117.
1605 ibid, paras 153–159.
1606 ibid, para 161.
1607 ibid, para 162.
1608 ibid, para 164.

views touted by RT France and the Kremlin.[1609] The suspension of the broadcast licence was also an appropriate limitation given 'the broad discretion which the Council enjoys'.[1610] The Court found that less onerous restrictive measures would have been impractical given that that the Council was acting 'in an extraordinary context and one of extreme urgency'.[1611] Finally, the suspension of the licence involved a proportional 'weighing up of the competing interests',[1612] given the 'importance of the objective of maintaining peace and international security',[1613] and of 'safeguarding of the Union's values, fundamental interests, security and integrity'.[1614] This was, furthermore, in a context where 'the exercise of freedom of expression carries with it duties and responsibilities': RT France's propaganda was hardly of the sort that called for the 'enhanced protection afforded to press freedom',[1615] and the ICCPR specifically called for the banning of 'propaganda for war'.[1616]

In short, whilst human rights are typically seen as breaks to the sort of limitations that can be adopted to deal with interference, they are also entirely susceptible to justifying such limitations when they appear to be necessary and proportional in the circumstances. This is not altogether surprising, and on most occasions, human rights law is indeed about striking a delicate equilibrium between competing values, all of which can to some degree be recast as implicating human rights. Here, both a priori openness to outside flows of information and a certain aspiration to protect one's population from its excesses stand to be recast strategically from the perspective of human rights. Ultimately, the comparison of the Ecodefense and RT France cases makes for a particularly interesting exercise, where the former's foreign registration was found to be in violation of human rights, but the latter's prohibition was not. Observers will vary on their assessment of such case law and some no doubt will see a double standard at work. Nonetheless, both cases show the need for a grounded and contextualized analysis of what is really going on in a given case, beyond the fact that all parties will reflexively invoke rights discourse.

1609 ibid, para 170.
1610 ibid, para 193.
1611 ibid, para 198.
1612 ibid, para 201.
1613 ibid, para 203.
1614 ibid, para 205.
1615 ibid, para 206.
1616 ibid, para 209.

4.3 *The Problem of Stigmatizing Certain Populations*

Another, quite distinct concern connected to how human rights and interference play out, both to authorize and limit non-interference agendas, is in relation to certain national and ethnic minorities. Diasporic communities specifically have often been caught between a rock and a hard place in the context of claims about interference. On the one hand, they have been the target of transnational influence operations or even repression and pressure by their state of origin to behave in certain ways that conform to its interests, including in terms of their participation in local political affairs. On the other hand, they are susceptible to being branded as 'fifth columns' in the host state, little more than vaguely treasonous vehicles for foreign interference. In between, diasporas have shown much agency of their own, some inclined to further the interests of a state of origin (e.g., the Indian diaspora), others to oppose it vociferously (e.g., the Cuban diaspora in the U.S.). Diasporas are evidently often politically fragmented and so the suspicions that bear on them are themselves naturally suspect. But there is no doubt that debates about interference have reactivated with a vengeance questions of multiculturalism, multiple citizenship and complex allegiances.

International human rights law is notoriously slow at detecting more communitarian forms of discrimination, and needs to be supplemented here by an anti-racist attention to how both interference and agendas of non-interference play out distributively across various communities. Caught in-between states, there is a very real risk that perceived interference via foreign populations will reactivate latent racist and xenophobic agendas. Careless and unwarranted denunciation of foreign interference will end up branding entire communities as alien or a 'fifth column' in ways that resuscitate, for example, some of the dark traditions of antisemitism. The branding of some members of the European Parliament as 'Soros puppets' by the Slovenian Prime Minister, for example, was quickly denounced as anti-semitic.[1617] The movement in various U.S. states to prohibit Chinese nationals from even investing or buying farmland or even from being recruited in academic contexts is part of conspiratorial agendas that are at a high risk of leading to blatant discrimination.[1618]

1617 Sarantis Michalopoulos and Sebastijan R Maček, 'Slovenian PM's "Soros Puppets" Tweet Causes EU-Wide Political Storm' *Euractiv* (15 October 2021) <https://www.euractiv.com/section/eu-council-presidency/news/slovenian-pms-soros-puppets-tweet-causes-eu-wide-political-storm/> accessed 10 December 2023.

1618 Phelim Kine, 'US States Are Cutting off Chinese Citizens and Companies from Land Ownership' [2024] *Politico* <https://www.politico.com/news/2024/04/03/state-laws-china-land-buying-00150030> accessed 22 September 2024.

The topic is made particularly delicate by the fact that members of diasporas may well in some cases, wittingly or unwitting, serve as vectors of influence. The question of whether certain Jewish lobby groups working in close association with the state of Israel need to register as foreign agents is a long-simmering debate. The Eisenhower administration repeatedly asked the American Zionist Council to register as a foreign agent of the state of Israel and, of late, the American Israel Public Affairs Committee has come under similar occasional pressure.[1619] Still, one must tread carefully in a context where domestic politics have become increasingly diasporic[1620] and where there is nothing untoward, a priori, about members of diasporas acting as go-betweens. Members of diasporas or dual nationals may well be objectively favoring and promoting the goals of a foreign power, but does not make them agents of such a power without more and is, at any rate, their prerogative. And there is a very real risk that, in clamping down on diaspora politics, one will also neuter their ability to serve inter-civilizational and inter-national understanding.

There is certainly a risk that the foreign associations of some will be used against them, especially when these associations displease their governments. Past cases speak to this danger, as when WEB Du Bois, one of the leading African American intellectuals of his time and a keen supporter of world peace, was prosecuted at the height of McCarthyism (unsuccessfully, as it happens, for lack of evidence) for spreading foreign propaganda.[1621] This was even though the organization he worked with, the Peace Information Center, was composed entirely of Americans. There have also long been complaints from Irish Americans, Palestinians, or Salvadorans that their being forced to register as foreign agents was linked to the demands of U.S. foreign policy rather than any consideration of their impact on democracy, and that other groups

1619 Allan Brownfeld, 'AIPAC Election Role Raises Question of Foreign Agent Registration' [2022] *Washington Report on Middle East Affairs* <https://www.wrmea.org/north-america/aipac-election-role-raises-question-of-foreign-agent-registration.html> accessed 31 March 2024.

1620 James A Thurber, Colton C Campbell and David A Dulio (eds), *Congress and Diaspora Politics: The Influence of Ethnic and Foreign Lobbying* (State University of New York Press 2018); Jonathan Rynhold, 'Divide and Rule: Discursive Authority, Identity Dissonance, Ethnic Lobbies, and U.S. Foreign Policy, or How President Obama Defeated AIPAC over the 2015 Iran Deal' (2021) 17 Foreign Policy Analysis orab005; Shubha Kamala Prasad and Filip Savatic, 'Diasporic Foreign Policy Interest Groups in the United States: Democracy, Conflict, and Political Entrepreneurship' (2023) 21 Perspectives on Politics 831; Cody Levine, 'Bringing the Battle "Home": Protracted Conflicts and the Battle between Ethnic Lobbies' (2023) 22 Ethnopolitics 507.

1621 *United States v Peace Information Center*, 97 F Supp 255 (DDC 1951).

were not compelled to register in similar ways.[1622] The extent to which one is portrayed as susceptible to being manipulated by another state is a barometer of the degree to which one is accepted as a full and equal citizen of the host country.

The danger to diasporas has come into even sharper focus in the context of concerns about foreign interference by China in Australia, Canada, and the U.S. starting in the 2010s, raising delicate questions about how target states should reconcile their commitment to both non-interference and egalitarian, multicultural, and inclusive societies. On the one hand, suspicion of interference by China in elections has activated fears among Chinese immigrants that the entire community will be branded as alien and untrustworthy, with heightened discrimination as the result. Leading members of the Chinese diaspora in Canada have voiced the concern that '[f]or too many, "foreign interference" is simply a codeword for "Chinese" with all the racist overtones that have been imposed on that term'.[1623] The media have been accused of 'sensationalizing' a few 'disturbing stories' of interference.[1624] Specifically and as often with broad-based discrimination, the accusation is that sweeping laws or practices brand entire communities as problematic:[1625] if Chinese nationals are responsible for industrial espionage, for example, then clearly they should be dealt with as such, but it is quite clear that adopting laws that seem to presume that all Chinese nationals are untrustworthy is deeply discriminatory.

Some of the most prominent cases of coopted local politicians in Australia in the service of China's interests have not been of Chinese origin, suggesting that pointing the finger at the diaspora is inherently problematic and potentially toxic.[1626] Moreover, some of the language used often borrows heavily from some of the worst discriminating register (to wit, one Australian

---

1622 Collin P Poirot and Azadeh Shahshahani, 'The DOJ is Using "Foreign Agents" Accusations to Repress Black Liberation Organizers' [2023] *The Nation* <https://www.thenation.com/article/politics/foreign-agents-registration-act-political-repression/> accessed 2 April 2024.

1623 Open Letter from Canada-China Focus, 'An Open Letter to the Right Honorable David Johnston, Independent Special Rapporteur, Government of Canada' (21 March 2023) <https://onlineacademiccommunity.uvic.ca/ccf/open-letter-to-the-right-honorable-david-johnston/#open-letter> accessed 9 July 2023.

1624 Senator Yuen Pau Woo (n 946).

1625 Amy Qin, 'Florida Law Chills Chinese Student Recruitment' *The New York Times* (15 December 2023) <https://www.nytimes.com/2023/12/15/us/florida-law-chills-chinese-student-recruitment.html> accessed 22 September 2024.

1626 Andrew Greene, 'Long after Dastyari, China's Rapid Rise Will Be This Century's Big Story' *ABC News* (12 December 2017) <https://www.abc.net.au/news/2017-12-13/long-after-dastyari-chinas-rapid-rise-will-be-the-big-story/9253928> accessed 7 September 2023.

journalist's description, prefaced by a 'this has nothing to do with racism', of those in Australian politics with connections to China as 'rats, flies, mosquitoes and sparrows' and concluding: 'Pests. Who needs them?').[1627] Not only is such motivation blatantly racist even when it is not as explicit, but it can have a broader chilling effect on certain classes of foreign nationals. It can also, incidentally, involve a self-inflicted wound in terms of economic and technological competitiveness, not to mention the commitment to diverse societies.[1628] This is particularly the case when anti-interference legislation, rather than seeking to address the problem functionally and in a country-neutral way, focuses on one nationality, as the U.S.'s 'China initiative' did, catching into its dragnet a number of researchers from that country on often dubious charges.[1629] It is arguable that anti-interference agenda have licenced forms of broad and explicit 'racial profiling' that would be inconceivable in a normal context[1630] and that have been challenged as such by those targeted.[1631]

Of course, and on the other hand, it may well be that some sectors within diasporas are indeed tempted or coerced to serve as vectors of influence for their state of origin.[1632] It is true that 'as with our other values that underlie openness and freedom, the role of diasporas and their community organizations in domestic politics can be exploited by foreign interference actors. [...] [E]ven genuine organizations may be susceptible to being manipulated, induced or threatened to cross the line from legitimate democratic politics

1627 Peter Hartcher, 'The Chinese Interests Power Struggle Is about Sovereignty' *The Sydney Morning Herald* (5 September 2016) <https://www.smh.com.au/opinion/the-chinese-interests-power-struggle-is-about-sovereignty-20160905-gr94hs.html> accessed 8 September 2023.

1628 Amy Qin, 'As U.S. Hunts for Chinese Spies, University Scientists Warn of Backlash' *The New York Times* (28 November 2021) <https://www.nytimes.com/2021/11/28/world/asia/china-university-spies.html> accessed 22 September 2024.

1629 Matt Apuzzo, 'Former Espionage Suspect Sues, Accusing F.B.I. of Falsifying Evidence' *The New York Times* (10 May 2017) <https://www.nytimes.com/2017/05/10/us/politics/fbi-xi-xiaoxing.html> accessed 22 September 2024.

1630 Jenny J Lee and Xiaojie Li, 'Racial Profiling among Scientists of Chinese Descent and Consequences for the U.S. Scientific Community' (2021) 100 Committee of.

1631 See, e.g.: 'Asian Americans Advancing Justice | AAJC Delivers Petition of Nearly 30,000 Signatures Urging President Biden to End the "China Initiative" | Asian Americans Advancing Justice—AAJC' (12 April 2021) <https://www.advancingjustice-aajc.org/petition-delivered-end-china-initiative> accessed 22 September 2024.

1632 Robert Fife, Steven Chase and Xiao Xu, 'Security Experts Question Political Influence of Toronto Developer with Ties to Beijing' *The Globe and Mail* (3 December 2018) <https://www.theglobeandmail.com/politics/article-security-experts-question-political-influence-of-toronto-developer/> accessed 7 September 2023; Greene (n 1626).

into foreign interference'.[1633] The role of some Chinese consuls in apparently trying to sway the result of elections in Canada by pressuring the local diaspora to vote for certain candidates or to coordinate with students to oppose the hosting of event perceived as inimical to Chinese interests operates in an unprecedented grey zone and create concerns for the operation of democracy. Such episodes will raise difficult questions about the extent to which anti-Chinese sentiment is at stake or whether it is its invocation that is used to distract from serious accusations of interference.[1634] They also draw attention to the degree to which states of origin can themselves have a problematic role and objectively put their diaspora in an awkward spot.

Yet, aside from the risk of painting an entire community with the opprobrium associated with a few, the deeper issue is that it also remains amply within the rights of members of diasporas, including dual citizens, to have political views in their host countries that happen to be aligned with those of the government of their country of origin. This is even as it may lead them to promote policies that may be judged to objectively favor the interests of the latter (just as non-diaspora members may do the same). Certainly, Chinese Americans, Chinese Canadians or Chinese Australians are allowed to believe that Taiwan should not become independent, that Tibet is part of China or that the treatment of populations in Xinjiang is not a genocide without being suspected of being a fifth column. The same is true of Americans, Canadians or Australians who are not of Chinese origin. And it should go hand in hand with the possibility that Americans, Canadians, or Australians of Chinese origin may also have strongly anti-Beijing views. One does not go without the other.

As has been pointed out by David Johnston, a Canadian official tasked with investigating the issue, '[t]here is nothing wrong with a diaspora community or a community organization publicizing, objecting to, voting against, or encouraging others to vote against a political candidate whose policies about or posture towards that community's country of origin are seen as unfriendly or hostile'.[1635] Laws that seem destined to catch diaspora members in their nets could have a broader chilling effect on political participation and even neuter diasporas' traditional role as political and economic go-betweens in inter-state relations. The Chinese diaspora in Canada has already voiced concern that the

1633 Johnston (n 352) 14.

1634 Frederik Kelter, 'Canada Faces Questions over Alleged Chinese Interference' (*Al Jazeera*) <https://www.aljazeera.com/news/2023/4/13/canada-faces-questions-over-alleged-chinese-interference> accessed 23 September 2024.

1635 Johnston (n 352) 14.

climate against perceived Beijing influence will make it more difficult in the future to obtain Chinese-origin representation in Canadian politics.[1636]

Chinese Americans have strongly protested laws that would ban Chinese nationals them from owning property in some U.S. states such as Florida, pointing out that 'equating individuals with the country of their birth is a dangerous practice', as well as the abundant dark historical legacies of such practices.[1637] The federal appeals court temporarily blocked enforcement of that law, SB264 (23R), after a first ruling finding no fault with the law. Attorneys for the Florida government had sought to argue that the law was not about race but merely about nationality. By contrast, lawyers for plaintiffs argued that the law violates the U.S. Constitution's equal protection and due process clause.[1638] Although precedents in the U.S. had once allowed restrictions to property ownership of certain categories of aliens, these cases were deemed to be dated and to no longer really pass constitutional muster.

Ultimately, the problem of interference 'through' diasporas is a very sensitive one that also reflects the inability of international law and state sovereignty to think of allegiance as anything but exclusive. Coming after decades of migration, wide normalization of dual nationality, and in some cases active encouragement of multiculturalism, it can create a hiatus between a growing openness to fluid identifications and a newfound uneasiness with its implications. It can also reactivate dark registers familiar from a history of anti-semitism and anti-communism, from the Dreyfus to the Julius and Ethel Rosenberg cases.[1639] 'Dual Loyalty' is still more often than not wielded as an accusation,[1640] even as evidence has emerged that dual nationals may in fact be more loyal to each of their states than mono-nationals.[1641] The national panic around Australia's dual-national members of Parliament (and the fear

1636 Lisa Xing, 'Chinese Canadians Worry Foreign Interference Probe Could Stigmatize Politicians, Candidates' *CBC News* <https://www.cbc.ca/news/canada/foreign-interference-china-politicans-han-dong-justin-trudeau-1.6793763> accessed 9 July 2023.

1637 'Asian American Community and Allies Rally against Florida's Anti-Chinese Land Law after Court Hearings' (*CAA*) <https://caasf.org/press-release/asian-american-community-and-allies-rally-against-floridas-anti-chinese-land-law-after-court-hearings/> accessed 22 September 2024.

1638 Shen v. Commissioner, Florida Department of Agriculture, 11th U.S. Circuit Court of Appeals, No. 23-12737.

1639 Philip Mendes, *Jews and the Left: The Rise and Fall of a Political Alliance* (Palgrave Macmillan 2014) ch 5.

1640 Ilan Zvi Baron, 'The Problem of Dual Loyalty' (2009) 42 Canadian Journal of Political Science / Revue canadienne de science politique 1025.

1641 Andrea Schlenker, 'Divided Loyalty? Identification and Political Participation of Dual Citizens in Switzerland' (2016) 8 European Political Science Review 517.

of interference that it expressed), even though it has clear textual justification in the Australian constitution, seems like it is based on a henceforth dated, misguided and excessive wariness with foreignness as an indicator of imperfect allegiance.[1642] Similarly, the xenophobic rhetoric much in evidence in the Ivory Coast when it came to Presidential candidate Alassane Ouattara for supposedly being from Burkina Faso attests to the profoundly toxic nature of these sorts of suspicions.[1643] And this is saying nothing of the controversy over former President Obama's birthplace and its evidently racist inspiration.

One domain where excessive wariness of diaspora participation in politics as a result of concerns about interference has manifested itself problematically is in relation to dual nationals. Although being a dual national is not generally seen as an obstacle to exercising basic political rights, notably to vote in elections, it has emerged as a more sensitive issue when it comes to standing for office. 'Single citizenship' was long preferred, notably by newly independent countries, as better safeguarding against the continued hold of foreign states.[1644] The issue is sometimes framed as one of loyalty in the abstract, but there is little doubt that it is tied to 'anxiety about foreign interference'[1645] and a more general challenge to the 'exclusivity of sovereignty'.[1646] In effect, some states do use their dual nationals to promote their national interest abroad, in ways that can then strain international relations and make for somewhat awkward questions in the host state.[1647] Nonetheless, courts have resisted framing the issue as one wherein dual nationality should generally incite wariness towards dual nationals on account of their perceived diminished loyalty, let alone as vectors of foreign interference, absent of course specific proof to that effect.[1648] The embracing of civic forms of citizenship, multiple nationality, and multiculturalism does militate for a more inclusive approach to the

1642 Benjamen Franklen Gussen, 'A Pseudo Calabresian Sunset Down Under: The Anachronism of Disqualifying Australian Members of Parliament for Holding a Foreign Citizenship' (2019) 32 New York International Law Review 25.

1643 François Gaulme, 'L'"ivoirité", recette de guerre civile' (2001) 394 Études 292.

1644 Peter J Spiro, *At Home in Two Countries: The Past and Future of Dual Citizenship* (New York University Press 2016) 17.

1645 Ashley Kelaita, 'Section 44(i) of the Constitution: Where to from Here?' (*Constitutional Critique—Constitutional Reform Unit* (CRU), 5 June 2018) <https://conreform.sydney.edu.au/2018/06/section-44i-of-the-constitution-where-to-from-here/> accessed 18 December 2023.

1646 Nathan Glazer, *Sovereignty Under Challenge: How Governments Respond* (Routledge 2002) 34.

1647 Szabolcs Pogonyi, 'Dual Citizenship and Sovereignty' (2011) 39 Nationalities Papers 685.

1648 *Tănase v Moldova* ECHR 2010-III 361.

human right to stand for office,[1649] not to mention the generally inoffensive character of multiple identification.

Notably, the European Court of Human Rights has taken a strong stance against dual nationals being excluded from the ability to stand for high office at all as a result of suspicions of interference. In the *Tănase v Moldova* case, it concluded that the ban of a candidate in the parliamentary elections because he was a dual Romanian national was a violation of his rights. The law on the basis of which such an exclusion was justified was not necessary to 'ensure loyalty to the State' and was not proportional given that many states in the Council of Europe allowed their candidates in parliamentarian elections to have multiple nationalities.[1650] Even though dual nationals might pursue policies favorable to certain national minorities associated with their second nationality, this was simply to be expected in a democracy. There was no proven correlation between dual nationality and disloyalty and the law was, in fact, a transparent attempt to exclude a certain minority from representation.

Highlighting the positive human rights contributions that transnational populations can make to their various sovereigns has, in fact, become a somewhat urgent topic of reflection. As the authors of one open letter denouncing the Canadian government's anti-interference initiative put it, '[t]hrough their family connections, economic activities, and educational journeys, many Canadians are linked to people and institutions around the world in multiple, complex ways. Drawing lines between what and who is Canadian, and what or who is foreign can be extremely divisive'.[1651] It is inevitable and not necessarily problematic that some sectors of diasporas will be mobilized in their country of immigration by foreign policy issues that involve their state of origin. As David Johnston, the Canadian Independent Special Rapporteur on Foreign Interference, put it, 'one of our nation's strengths is multiculturalism, which arises because Canada is home to significant diaspora communities from around the world. It is not surprising that these diaspora communities wish to maintain links with their countries of origin. These connections are part of what enriches a multicultural society—they are not foreign interference'.[1652]

One way of combating interference in that respect is not to denounce some diaspora members' acquaintances with foreign regimes, but to think of ways

1649 Kim Rubenstein, 'Loyalty and Membership: Globalization and Its Impact on Citizenship, Multiculturalism and the Australian Community' in Geoffrey Brahm Levey (ed), *Political Theory and Australian Multiculturalism* (Berghahn Books 2012).

1650 *Tănase v Moldova* (n 1557).

1651 Open Letter from Canada-China Focus (n 1623).

1652 Johnston (n 352) 11.

in which members of diasporas may, in specific and delimited cases, require human rights protection from that same state of origin. In effect, members of diasporas are as much if not more likely to be coercively instrumentalized by their state of origin for the purposes of interference than they are to voluntarily act as vectors of such interference. Again, even there one must be careful that it is a priori legitimate for a state of origin to seek to influence the political opinions of its diaspora to be favorable to its interests. A line will be crossed, however, where for instance the diasporic vote is coerced to obtain certain outcomes in the host state or where members of the diaspora are being threatened.[1653]

This turns the tables on the debate and makes it a much more complex question of human rights in the home state. For David Johnston, for example, '[d]iaspora communities are largely victims of foreign interference activities'.[1654] In that respect, the issue is less with diasporas per se than with the occasional attempt by states of origin to instrumentalize them for political advantage in the host state, against said diasporas' own interests. This also brings attention to the role of the host state in simultaneously safeguarding certain diasporas in its midst *and* the integrity of its political processes. Indeed, host states increasingly have a recognized obligation to protect members of diasporas from transnational repression giving rise to violations on their territory.[1655]

1653 Siena Anstis, Noura Al-Jizawi and Ronald J Deibert, 'Transnational Repression and the Different Faces of Sovereignty' (2022) 95 Temp. L. Rev. 641.

1654 Mansted (n 964) 14.

1655 Siena Anstis, 'Regulating Transnational Dissident Cyber Espionage' (2024) 73 International & Comparative Law Quarterly 259.

CHAPTER 6

Imagining a Baseline

1 Introduction

Most of the debates on interference, and certainly those on armed intervention, focus on what states should *not* do. This is consonant with international law's general approach in a liberal system, and its focus on prohibiting behavior as illegal rather that outlining legal behavior. The problem, as we saw, is that the baseline expectation in international law—not interfering in ways that are coercive—is almost too narrow, asking too little, as it turns out, of states in the era of 'new interference'. The focus on intervention fails to see what is problematic about interference, its banal potential for compromising peaceful international relations and its negative ramifications for human rights. It also arguably fails to see how states should not only 'not interfere' in the negative sense but, ideally, ensure positively that they or their proxies do not interfere and perhaps proactively engage in non-interference. This suggests a genuine ethos that is potentially a far cry from *laissez faire* models. But what if what was interesting about the prohibition of interference was what it seems to presuppose *a contrario*, namely certain implicit understandings about the ideal course of international relations?

One avenue, then, is to take the problem from the other end, by attempting to define at a minimum what would *not* constitute interference. This includes, presumably, considerable realist acceptance (not alien to international law itself, of course) that states ordinarily seek to maximize their national interest and that this includes, as much as possible and however unseemly, bending other states to their will. This is carried out through perfectly legitimate channels such as public diplomacy. It is important for international lawyers to not appear to be seeking to outlaw practices that are fully part of the ordinary usages of diplomacy, including as they manifest themselves in new ways (for example, ambassadors have increasingly developed relations directly with local populations, without this being generally considered to offend international law). As the European Union has been keen to emphasize, '[f]oreign influence is distinct from foreign interference. It includes all activity by foreign powers which has the aim or effect of influencing E.U. politics and democracy. Foreign influence is a normal and legitimate aspect of international relations and

 DOI:10.1163/9789004532731_011

diplomacy'.[1656] A range of practices that go beyond government-to-government relations, such as engaging foreign parliamentarians directly, may raise eyebrows,[1657] but will be hard to exclude as beyond the pale.

Especially against a background where preventing violence in international relations is the overarching goal, turning practices of mere influence into forms of intervention or interference could both devalue the prohibition of the use of force and objectively discourage peaceful measures. As Stephen C. McCaffrey (U.S.) put it during the ILC's debates on a Draft Code of Crimes against Mankind, measures such as:

> the withholding of benefits, restrictions on exports of strategic goods and on exports of or access to natural sources, conditions imposed by international lending institutions, and import quotas [...] had always been regarded as legitimate means of diplomacy and should, if anything, be encouraged as non-violent means of making a political point or expressing displeasure *vis-à-vis* another State. Care should be taken not to do anything that would deprive States of the opportunity of having recourse to those peaceful measures.[1658]

As the U.S. put it in 1993, to do so would be 'not only be divorced from the practical relationship among nations, but [...] also an open invitation to criminalize disputes that should be more appropriately resolved by the careful and prudent practice of diplomacy'.[1659]

A similar approach is visible in the related field of diplomatic interference (i.e., interference by diplomats in host countries). One strategy to push back against accusations that diplomats are interfering (which they are prohibited from doing)[1660] has been to point to a baseline defined by the Vienna Convention on Diplomatic Relations of permissible diplomatic conduct which cannot therefore, by definition, amount to interference. This includes a range of representation functions that go to the core of diplomatic activity and, in less anodyne fashion, the promotion of friendly relations between states

1656 Jones (n 495) 7.
1657 Robert Fife, Steven Chase and Xiao Xu, 'Beijing Foots Bill for Canadian Senators, MPs to Visit China' *The Globe and Mail* (1 December 2017) <https://www.theglobeandmail.com/news/politics/beijing-foots-bill-for-visits-to-china-by-canadian-senators-mps/article37162592/> accessed 7 September 2023.
1658 Yearbook of the ILC (1985) vol 1, 55.
1659 Yearbook of the ILC (1993) vol 2, part 1, 102, para 10.
1660 See Vienna Convention, art 41(1).

'certainly cover[ing] direct engagement with political parties and people in the host country, even where such activities constitute, in the eyes of the diplomatic hosts, partisan conduct or propaganda'.[1661] As Paul Behrens points out, the Vienna Convention is quite capacious and includes a range of diplomatic activities that are conceivably related to the diplomatic interests of the sending state,[1662] although this does not *ipso facto* mean that these activities can be conducted without due concern for the domestic nature of the matter at stake.

The Vienna Convention is of course a special case, as already mentioned, of an international treaty licencing what would otherwise almost certainly count as interference, involving as it does the exercising of sovereign functions on the territory of another state. The question is whether one can up the ante beyond such a narrow regime of what states not only can but ought to do in their relations to others. This final chapter, therefore, explores the debate on the 'new interference' as an opportunity to raise the question of what is ordinarily expected of states under international law as a baseline of interaction with others. Rather than thinking merely in terms of prohibitions, it looks at the sort of social imaginaries of positive behavior that complaints about interference seem to evoke, and how one might draw on them to transcend the persistent limitations of a liberal international legal system. This includes certain positive duties in international law that can contribute to the reimagining of minimal expectations about international relations. The chapter seeks to conceptualize, based on neglected facets of international or foreign relations law, three possible duties (to engage, of transparency and of consistency), outlining their usefulness but also their precariousness.

2 A Duty to Engage?

International law is traditionally seen as protecting sovereignty understood as a freedom, not as imposing positive obligations to engage with other states. The default understanding has long been that the corollary of sovereignty is that, even as one cannot intervene in the affairs of other states, nor can one be compelled to enter into productive relations with such states. This maps out conveniently onto the interference debate: the goal is to protect states from a harm, not to prescribe some minimum content of international relations. The debate is very much mired in a liberal view of international law that

1661 Behrens, 'The Duty of Non-Interference' (n 555) 275.

1662 Behrens, *Diplomatic Interference and the Law* (n 112).

emphasizes states' basic freedom except to the extent it stands to interfere with the sovereignty of others. Yet the debate on interference *could* be a powerful prism to think about whether there is a degree of implicit openness required of states under normal conditions of international relations.

2.1 *The Liberal Acceptability of Non-engagement*

There is little global economic activity that does not involve some degree of competition and rivalry, and it takes a considerable effort of imagination, within the liberal presuppositions of mainstream international law, to rethink international economic relations otherwise. In a liberal international legal system, default conditions are imagined to be those of a sort of anarchic free-for-all where nothing is owed to others except respect for their freedom, in exchange for respect for one's own. This obviously characterizes economic competition and even 'warfare' that is largely tolerated as 'a fact of international life at least since the peace of Westphalia'.[1663] The Hobbesian premises of such a vision are then naturally complemented by either a neo-mercantilist or a neo-Hayekian vision of international economic relations that tolerate no interference in the way in which states organize their economic policies. The only thing susceptible of changing this *status quo* would be the existence, Lotus-like, of a norm of international law that would specifically prohibit non or withdrawal of engagement. The liberal argument, however, is emphatically that no such norm exists and that efforts to, for example, equate hostile economic relations with aggression, a use of force or intervention are ill-considered and have no grounding in international law.[1664]

This then contributes to a frame of mind that systematically minimizes any obligation to maintain, let alone engage in, any prescribed level of productive relations, notably of an economic nature, with other states. Take, for example, one of the enduring and symptomatic debates in international law of the last decades, namely whether disengagement as a result of the operation of conditionality, is a form of interference with other states' sovereignty. The dominant view is that, even as 'inducements and offers exploit the weaknesses and needs of the recipient state to induce it to alter its behavior':

> In an unequal world [...] nothing in international law prevents powerful states from leveraging the needs of weaker states to incentivize them to cooperate in the furtherance of their interests. Moreover, nothing in

1663 Lillich, 'The Status of Economic Coercion under International Law' (n 13) 17.
1664 ibid 18.

> international law entitles weak states to assistance from their powerful partners. Therefore, on their own, inducements such as official government aid and political support are not coercive.[1665]

It does seem difficult to deny the right of states to provide advantages on their terms. This cautions against the temptation of lowering the threshold of interference to include all kinds of not-particularly-friendly but not-fundamentally-illegal economic behavior in a context where states are constantly jousting for advantage, and where 'it would be ludicrous to characterize a State's economic action as illegal simply because it sought some advantage from another State'.[1666] This is particularly the case in areas such as development aid where no clear prior obligation to give exists, or where even when such an obligation exists it is still highly sensitive to a range of considerations.

It may be that rather than denying an advantage *ab initio* (non-engagement), then, it is withdrawal of engagement from ongoing relations (disengagement) that is tellingly wrong, notably in the form of 'unilateral sanctions'. Note that this is a more specific claim than the general critique of sanctions to the extent that it disrupts existing patterns of relations.[1667] It is largely in this form that the debate has often been construed. Disengaging or threatening to do so is a frequently enough resorted to tactic. A quite startling example of this was the major disengagement of the U.S. from Chile after the election of Salvador Allende, leading to the effective asphyxiation of the Chilean economy.[1668] In 2002, the U.S. Ambassador to Bolivia, Manual Rocha, warned the Bolivian electorate against voting for socialist candidate Evo Morales who ran on a platform of partly legalizing the production of coca leaves. The Ambassador insisted that to vote for the Socialist candidate would 'jeopardize American assistance and investment', which was widely interpreted as a threat of interference and, indeed itself a form of interference.[1669] As was seen earlier, the whole economy of the Lomé agreements is oriented towards the possibility of a cessation of cooperation on human rights or democracy grounds. The European Union

1665 Helal (n 408) 86.

1666 Derek W Bowett, 'Economic Coercion and Reprisals by States' (1972) 13 Virginia Journal of International Law 1, 3.

1667 Richard N Haass, 'Sanctioning Madness Essay' (1997) 76 Foreign Affairs 74.

1668 Weifeng Zhou and Ludo Cuyvers, 'Linking International Trade and Labour Standards: The Effectiveness of Sanctions under the European Union's GSP' (2011) 45 Journal of World Trade 63.

1669 Duncan Campbell, 'Bolivia's Leftwing Upstart Alarms US' *The Guardian* (15 July 2002) <https://www.theguardian.com/world/2002/jul/15/usa.duncancampbell> accessed 7 March 2024.

interrupted its Generalised Scheme of Preferences with Myanmar in 1997 and Belarus in 2006.[1670]

On the surface, this is the exact opposite of interference in that it merely involves a sort of withdrawal from engagement, not an active disruption of another state's sovereignty; but the net effect on states on the receiving end may be very similar to an actual intervention. The ensuing debate about intervention through disengagement has long been a motif in international relations. In the *Nicaragua v United States* case, counsel for Nicaragua had argued that the 'cessation of economic aid [...]; the 90 per cent reduction in the sugar quota for United States imports from Nicaragua [...]; and the trade embargo [...]', whilst 'not unlawful in themselves [...] add up to a systematic violation of the principle of non-intervention'.[1671] Iran has long claimed that the refusal of the U.S. to positively engage with it is a form of interference and has more recently launched legal action before the ICJ to that effect in the wake of the reimposition of sanctions following the U.S. pullout from the 2015 nuclear agreement.[1672] The embargo against Cuba—effectively, a refusal to engage with its government—is regularly denounced in the General Assembly as a violation of the principle of non-interference.[1673]

The irony is that this sort of argument had been to some extent pre-empted by the Third World itself, in an earlier era when it was quite content with touting its own power to withdraw from engagement with other parts of the world. This was notably the case during the OPEP oil embargo, when Third World scholars made short shrift of the notion that in refusing to sell oil Arab states were unlawfully interfering in the affairs of Western states. As Ibrahim Shihata

---

1670 Laura Beke and Nicolas Hachez, 'The E.U. GSP: A Preference for Human Rights and Good Governance? The Case of Myanmar' in Jan Wouters and others (eds), *Global Governance Through Trade: E.U. Policies and Approaches* (Edward Elgar Publishing 2015).

1671 *Nicaragua v United States* (n 3) [244].

1672 Rick Gladstone, 'Iran Takes U.S. to Court Over Nuclear Deal and Reimposed Sanctions' *The New York Times* (17 July 2018) <https://www.nytimes.com/2018/07/17/world/middleeast/iran-sues-us-over-sanctions.html> accessed 7 March 2024.

1673 UNGA Res 39/210 (18 December 1984) U.N. Doc A/RES/39/210; UNGA Res 40/185 (17 December 1985) U.N. Doc A/RES /40/185; UNGA Res 41/165 (5 December 1986) U.N. Doc A/RES/41/165; UNGA Res 42/173 (11 December 1987) U.N. Doc A/RES/42/173; UNGA Res 44/215 (22 December 1989) U.N. Doc A/RES/44/215; UNGA Res 46/210 (20 December 1991) U.N. Doc A/RES/46/210; UNGA Res 48/168 (21 December 1993) U.N. Doc A/RES/48/168; UNGA Res 52/181 (18 December 1997) U.N. Doc A/RES/52/181; UNGA Res 54/200 (22 December 1999) U.N. Doc A/RES/54/200; UNGA Res 56/179 (21 December 2001) U.N. Doc A/RES/56/179; UNGA Res 56/198 (23 December 2003) U.N. Doc A/RES/58/198; UNGA Res 60/185 (22 December 2005) U.N. Doc A/RES/60/185; UNGA Res 62/183 (19 December 2007) U.N. Doc A/RES/62/183.

put it, not only were Arab states adopting such a measure 'merely to discourage third countries from violating their obligations of neutrality toward them and from continuing their encouragement of, or their acquiescence in, an illegal situation' but, besides this show of good international citizenship, they 'were not to be expected [...], to do favors indefinitely for states which had refused to cooperate with them in putting an end to the illegal occupation' by keeping them continuously 'fueled with Arab exhaustible oil'.[1674] This was especially given their sovereignty over their natural resources. Even some good faith Western observers recognized that:

> it is unrealistic to expect or to require a nation, at least in the absence of a specific agreement otherwise, to continue to do business with another nation which it regards as its enemy or as helping its enemies. It seems even more unrealistic to attempt to require a nation to confer what it considers as gifts or favors, such as economic aid or trade concessions, upon other nations which it considers unfriendly.[1675]

Be that as it may, to accuse a state of interfering merely because it is disengaging may be paradoxical, but does it even make sense? Can refusing to engage outside any pre-existing obligation *really* be considered a form of interference as is often claimed? Is there, in other words, a right 'to be engaged with' or at least to be engaged with continuously once a certain level of engagement has created expectations to that effect? One situation is of course that in which the default between certain states has *already* been defined by substantive bilateral or multilateral obligations, for example in the trade realm. This creates a very different default assumption about international relations between said states. It may be that a pre-existing amity treaty will make withdrawal from continued engagement problematic under international law under the terms of that treaty. Whether doing less than fully engaging as per pre-existing obligations is actually or usefully understood as a form of intervention (as opposed to merely an instance of a violation of international law under its own *lex specialis*) remains to be seen, even in that case. It may be that this is one situation where the notion of interference short of intervention provides a particularly helpful key, but one should be wary of allowing that notion of interference to taint any violation of international law to the point of meaninglessness (interference cannot become synonymous with merely violating international law).

1674 Shihata (n 310) 626.
1675 Bilder (n 311) 42.

Even in that special case, it is not clear, on the basis of liberal premises alone, that disengagement is a violation of international law, let alone a form of interference or, *a fortiori*, intervention. If nothing else, many bilateral relations are susceptible to requirements of reciprocity which imply that they can be interrupted when reciprocity fails. Such reciprocity is built into a number of arrangements and inscribes any ensuing fallout within the economy of the relevant treaty regime and, more broadly, bilateral relations. In that spirit, the European Parliament has for example called for the 'establishment of "mirror clauses" whereby the openness of the European information space to third countries would be proportionate to the access European media outlets have in these countries'.[1676] Countermeasures, especially when adopted by a directly interested party, also manifest both international law's commitment to reciprocity and, if need be, self-help.

Even in the GATT context, the argument is sometimes made that trade sanctions, in addition to being potentially justified on some of the prescribed grounds, are adopted entirely within the jurisdiction of the state that adopts them and not directly against nationals or on the territory of foreign states.[1677] For example, in refusing to buy products derived from seal hunting, it has been argued that '[a]ll [the European Union] is doing is collectively refusing to purchase goods that it collectively does not want. […] Consumers, including countries as collective consumers, are not expected or required to buy what they do not want'.[1678] Finally, note the slightly unseemly dimension of asking the state to which one is manifestly hostile and on which one is problematically dependent to reengage with oneself as Iran did when it invoked the existence of an old, pre-revolution, friendship treaty between itself and the U.S. to protest sanctions.[1679]

Outside perhaps very solemn treaty commitments of amity, then, the default assumption in liberal international law is that a relationship of engagement is not an acquired right, such that a state that has once engaged with another is then bound to do so for eternity and in the same terms. This was already anticipated in no uncertain terms by Vattel:

1676 2023 Resolution on Foreign Interference in the E.U. (n 335), para 37.

1677 Lorand Bartels, 'Article XX of GATT and the Problem of Extraterritorial Jurisdiction the Case of Trade Measures for the Protection of Human Rights' (2002) 36 Journal of World Trade 353, 333.

1678 Philip I Levy and Donald H Regan, 'EC–Seal Products: Seals and Sensibilities (TBT Aspects of the Panel and Appellate Body Reports)' (2015) 14 World Trade Review 337, 373.

1679 *Alleged Violations of the 1955 Treaty of Amity, Economic Relations, and Consular Rights (Islamic Republic of Iran v United States of America) Provisional Measures, Order of 3 October 2018* [2018] ICJ Rep 623.

> Since [...] a nation cannot have a natural right to sell her merchandises to another that is unwilling to purchase them,—since she has only an imperfect right to buy what she wants of others,—since it belongs only to these last to judge whether it be proper for them to sell or not—and, finally, since commerce consists in mutually buying and selling all sorts of commodities,—it is evident that it depends on the will of any nation to carry on commerce with another, or to let it alone. [...] For in permitting another nation to trade with her, she grants that other a right; and every one is at liberty to affix what conditions he pleases to a right which he grants of his own accord.[1680]

Beyond cases where a certain intensity of relations is already anticipated, then, there is certainly something a little counter-intuitive about the idea that shunning another actor is, actually, 'interfering with it' if there is no *a priori* general obligation to engage.[1681] As Tom Farer pointed out, there is a clear distinction between 'threats not to give some benefit, or to withdraw one previously given, to which the threatened state is not legally entitled' and 'threats with respect to what could be called entitlements'.[1682] Only the latter case can be problematic. This is especially the case when it comes to measures of retorsion (as opposed to countermeasures) that in themselves entail no illegality and might at most be described as 'unfriendly': if there was not an obligation to engage in diplomatic relations or provide voluntary aid programmes in the first place, then it can no more be an obligation of international law to not terminate those. Such retorsion is merely an exercise by a state 'of its freedom of action to the extent that it has not undertaken any obligations to give the target state economic aid, for example, or to trade with it'.[1683]

This is what led to the conclusion in the Nicaragua case that the cessation of economic aid, notwithstanding its undoubted considerable impact, could not amount to illegal coercion even though it might be described as inimical ('A State is not required to continue particular trade relations longer than it sees fit to do so').[1684] As Oppenheim put it, in a classic statement of the liberal position:

1680 de Vattel (n 84) 134–135.
1681 Cleveland (n 1268) 53.
1682 Farer, 'Political and Economic Coercion in Contemporary International Law' (n 433) 405.
1683 Tzanakopoulos (n 24) 626.
1684 *Nicaragua v United States* (n 3) [276].

> a state may, without thereby committing an act of intervention (although it might be in breach of some other international obligation, for example under treaties such as the General Agreement on Tariffs and Trade which promote freedom of trade), sever diplomatic relations with another state, discontinue exports to it or a programme of aid, or organise a boycott of its products. Such measures are often in response to actions or policies of which the state taking the measures disapproves or regards as unlawful, and may be presented by it as a form of 'sanctions'. Although such measures may, at least indirectly and in part, be intended not only as a mark of displeasure but also to persuade the other state to pursue, or discontinue, a particular course of conduct, such pressure falls short of being dictatorial and does not amount to intervention.[1685]

Under liberal conditions, the assumption is that no onerous *a priori* duty of solidarity or engagement typically exists. Internationally, the liberal *locus classicus* at least is one of indifferent co-existence in which sovereigns a priori owe nothing to each other. This leads to a strong sense that:

> it could be argued that it is natural for states to be in competition with each other and that a state that imposes extra-territorial sanctions does nothing more than use its market power to exercise influence over others, and that this form of economic competition or coercion is part of the reality of international relations and needs to be endured or countered by others, in case they are powerful enough.[1686]

Indeed, as the U.S. put it in a case before the Iran-US Claims tribunal, '[e]very state has the right to grant or deny foreign assistance, to permit or deny exports, to grant or deny loans or credits, and to grant or deny participation in national procurement or financial management, on such terms as it finds appropriate'.[1687] It may be true, on a certain level, that for the U.S. not to trade with Cuba has a considerable impact on the latter country's economic and political destiny; but it is hard to argue that the U.S. is *interfering* with its

1685 Jennings and Watts (n 397) 432–434.

1686 Schmidt (n 655) 56.

1687 Iran–United States Claims Tribunal, Claim A/30 (1996), 57. See also ibid, n 38, referencing *Iran v United States*, Award No 382-B1-FT, 62, 19 Iran-US CTR 273 292 (31 August 1988) ('[The] President's exercise of discretion under Section 38 of the Arms Export Control Act to deny exports of defense articles and services is a "sovereign right which is not subject to review by an international Tribunal"').

sovereign affairs.[1688] As Jens Ohlin put it, drawing on a study of U.S. cases: 'how can it be coercive to remove something that you are not required to do in the first place?'[1689] Even Salvador Allende conceded that '[t]he United States has the sovereign right to grant or not to grant foreign aid to any country'.[1690] Reinforcing this point is a sense that to not trade with another state is an omission rather than an action[1691] and therefore meshes uneasily with the notion that it is a form of *intervention*, which seems to involve an operative dimension (although in fairness to *not trade* with a partner may involve quite active steps in practice, especially if secondary measures are involved).

A further argument against the idea of non-engagement as interference is that it creates a situation of 'damned if you do, damned if you don't' for the state accused of interference. If a state withdraws its engagement, it is interfering; but if it maintains that engagement, it may also be interfering in the eyes of some (e.g., propping up a regime that would not survive otherwise, possibly in violation of the right to self-determination of its peoples). The idea of a minimum obligation of positive engagement seems counter-intuitive on the economic or diplomatic planes. Withdrawal of diplomatic and consular representation may cause some hardships to populations and not be conducive to bilateral foreign policy, but no one has ever argued that ongoing relations are a due given the normal and largely accepted practice of occasionally breaking relations (the only due relates to the protection of the diplomatic and consular premises and persons if and once they are there). It may be, as we will see, that scenarios where there was previously sustained and binding engagement, for example in the form of considerable development assistance, are a special case where a sudden switch to non-engagement might be seen as exacting an excessive toll on the target country in terms of its sovereignty. For the most part, however, as recognized by the Special Rapporteur on the negative impact of unilateral coercive measures herself, 'States are free to choose their partners in trade, economic or other types of international relations. Customary

1688 UNGA '"Archaic, Punitive" Embargo Must Be Consigned to History Books, Say Speakers, as General Assembly, for Twenty-First Year, Demands End to Cuba Blockade' (13 November 2012) Meetings Coverage GA/11311.

1689 Ohlin, 'Did Russian Cyber Interference in the 2016 Election Violate International Law' (n 852) 1591.

1690 Radice (n 1137) 238.

1691 Clive Parry, 'Defining Economic Coercion in International Law' (1977) 12 Texas International Law Journal 1, 1.

international law provides for the possibility of unfriendly acts that do not violate international law'.[1692]

Indeed, there is yet another paradox linked to the idea of a hypothetical duty to engage: that, under the guise of limiting the interference in the sovereignty of, say, Cuba, it legitimizes a sort of broad incursion in the sovereignty of, say, the U.S., because it suggests that the U.S. has a sort of baseline duty, beyond its own self-determining choices, to engage in productive relations with Cuba. But this seems to go against sovereignty and, in particular, what is surely central to the realization of self-determination, namely the ability and freedom to choose one's 'friends' and, quite possibly, 'enemies'. Hence states have predictably justified sanctions 'as an assertion of their own sovereign right to regulate the trade relations with other nations based on a theory of "economic freedom"'.[1693] As the U.S. put it in response to draft resolutions on 'Human rights and unilateral coercive measures', such resolutions challenge 'the sovereign right of States to conduct their economic relations freely and to protect legitimate national interests, including by taking actions in response to national security concerns'.[1694] Although states occasionally complain that they have been the victims of embargos from third states, few of them would renounce the possibility of imposing embargoes if and when they could.

Finally, and perversely, a requirement that one never desist from a certain level of engagement with other states lest one be branded as having interfered in their sovereign affairs might lead certain states to think twice about ever entering in relations with other states in the first place. Ratcheting of bilateral or multilateral relations suggests neither party could ever downgrade alone a shared relation. Relations would only ever be unidirectional, towards ever greater closeness, essentially holding both states hostage to a commitment they may once have had but possibly no longer both share. Rather than imagining a base line of compulsory and proactive friendly relations between states, any departure from which is understood as a form of interference, therefore, it may be more plausible and helpful to imagine a world in which states constantly seek to exert power by offering or not offering engagement, and where this sort of behavior is better understood as not constituting interference. In

1692 UNHRC, 'Negative impact of unilateral coercive measures: priorities and road map' (21 July 2020) U.N. Doc A/HRC/45/7, para 27.

1693 Mohsen Rowhani, 'Rights-Based Boundaries of Unilateral Sanctions' (2022) 32 Washington International Law Journal 127, 141.

1694 UNGA Third Committee (70th Session) 'Summary record of the 52nd meeting' (20 November 2015) U.N. Doc A/C..3/70/SR.52, para 32.

short, the case for withholding one's engagement with others at one's discretion is certainly, under liberal conditions, quite strong.

2.2 *Questioning the Laissez Faire Bases of International Law*

Simply because there is a degradation or abandonment of relations that has a significant impact on one partner to a relationship, then, does not mean that there is, in the liberal understanding, interference with it. A fortiori, seems to be the logical inference, there can be no obligation to offer up a certain level or quality of relations. If no baseline of minimally engaged relations exists, then, it becomes much easier to dismiss behavior that may be hostile as nonetheless not illegal. A conversation may still be had on the level of international ethics, but international law has, perhaps precociously, exhausted its utility. Benign neglect or even malign neglect of another state probably does not translate into a well-justified claim to interference.

As the ICJ itself recognized, 'a state is not bound to continue particular trade relations longer than it sees fit to do so, in the absence of a treaty commitment or other specific legal obligations'.[1695] In fact, for Philip Levy and Donald H Regan, 'to force countries to buy what they do not want would be a serious interference in their internal affairs', at least outside a pre-existing treaty obligation to do so.[1696] Pushed to its extreme, the logic of economic non-interference can appear to merely reconduct the *status quo*, deferring the possibility of radical change by insisting on the fact that states owe each other nothing. Indeed, per the then Secretary General of the United Nations, it is 'difficult to see how such inequities, which arise from differences in situations, can be evened out short of changing the entire structure of international society'.[1697]

Still, for all its logical appeal, one should acknowledge that the hands-off approach to international relations is indeed deeply indebted to a particular legacy of liberal internationalism that gladly imagines a situation of relative and benign indifference of sovereigns to each other that is not unproblematic. To begin with, the argument that states are at liberty to simply disengage on liberal-sovereign grounds is an odd mix with the fact that such disengagements are often, paradoxically, justified through the invocation of liberal-collective values, as in the case of third-party sanctions for human rights violations. In such a scenario, states simultaneously affirm their right to back out from relations and their commitment to supposedly shared values. This not conclusive of the defensibility of the debate, but it inscribes it within a foundational

1695 Rowhani (n 1693) 141.
1696 Levy and Regan (n 1678) 373.
1697 UNGA, 'Question of Defining Aggression' (3 October 1952) U.N. Doc A/2211, para 446.

paradox. Nonetheless, it may be that international law—classical, liberal international law that is—does have resources of its own to, as it were, counter its own proclivities towards the solipsism of states. This sub-section will briefly mention three.

First, international law or something close to it is not unfamiliar with the notion of certain minimal prescribed levels of engagement. For example, states have long been encouraged to contribute a certain level of development aid as a percentage of their GNI. This is outside any firm contributory institutional framework (e.g., NATO, the World Bank) and seems to hang on little else than a sense that this sort of aid is owed as a result of economic differentials and historical legacies that have imposed a sort of debt of the developed West to much of the rest of the world. It is true that attempts to truly juridify such aspirational targets have largely floundered. Grand proclamations such as the Global Goals are not legally binding obligations to provide a certain level of effort to tackle poverty.[1698] Moreover, such demands are fundamentally directed at donor states per se and do not prejudge the identity of the beneficiaries of any such aid: even though a state is committed to contributing 0.7% of its GDI to international development assistance, as per the Millennium Development Goals, it is under no obligation to apportion this aid to all states on an equal level nor does it incur an obligation to provide for any particular state as a result.[1699] In other words, it would be hard to argue for a particular developing state that failing to benefit from a developed state's largesse was a failure by the latter to comply with its obligations towards it. Still, one can at least not claim that there has never been an attempt under international law to stipulate a certain level of engagement.

Second, unilateral sanctions might be thought of as precisely the kind of measures which, to use the reasoning originally promoted by Eric David, are basically legal at least until they are engaged in in bad faith or constitute an abuse of right.[1700] What if, for example, a state that otherwise had every right to scale down or even interrupt economic relations with another state was known, for whatever reason, to have done so specifically to debilitate another state's ability to make sovereign choices? This is not as farfetched as it

1698 Duncan French, 'The Global Goals: Formalism Foregone, Contested Legality and "Re-Imaginings" of International Law', *Ethiopian Yearbook of International Law* (Springer International Publishing 2016).

1699 Lawrence O Gostin and Robert Archer, 'The Duty of States to Assist Other States in Need: Ethics, Human Rights, and International Law' (2007) 35 Journal of Law, Medicine & Ethics 526.

1700 David (n 536).

seems: unilateral sanctions are in effect often accused of being deliberate ploys to establish neo-imperial relations of domination and subjugation. Obviously, on one realist, imperial or even liberal reading, it is within the discretion of states who can 'afford it' to want to establish such patterns of domination, and there is not much that international law can do about it. But the framing of international law might at least reveal some unilateral sanctions for what they are, namely not merely a general reassessment of economic opportunities or even the waning of ties but, occasionally at least, the subjective manifestation of a genuine will to interfere. Whether that does not bring the prohibition of interference too close to the prohibition of the exercise of any power is an open question, but one might draw a line between merely pressuring a state on the one hand, and seeking to totally subjugate it. This is all the more so of course that interruptions of relations may come with implicit promises of resumption dangled at target states and thus come ever-closer to a brutal register of coercion.

Third, the demand for a certain level of substantive engagement is increasingly made as part of global agendas of reparatory, transformative and transitional justice. For example, the Caribbean Community (CARICOM)'s 10 Point Plan for Reparatory Justice embraces an ambitious vision specifying how European governments should make amends for owning and trading slaves as well as committing genocide upon indigenous communities.[1701] This includes, for instance, a proposal for an 'indigenous peoples development program' to rehabilitate such communities or measures to deal with the public health crisis that has resulted from long term consequences of the import of slaves into the Caribbean. Similarly, the effort to fight climate change includes as part of the COP an emphasis on differentiated responsibilities and, in particular, how industrialized nations can assist developing ones in fending off some of the worst consequences of ocean rising.[1702] The point here is merely that agendas continue to emerge that refuse to imagine the international system as a sort of clean slate from which powerful states emerge free of any responsibilities for how they have contributed historically to shape the world to their advantage.

1701 Caribbean Community (CARICOM), 'CARICOM Ten Point Plan for Reparatory Justice' <https://caricom.org/caricom-ten-point-plan-for-reparatory-justice/> accessed 11 July 2024.

1702 Pieter Pauw and others, *Different Perspectives on Differentiated Responsibilities: A State-of-the-Art Review of the Notion of Common but Differentiated Responsibilities in International Negotiations* (German Development Institute 2014) <https://www.econstor.eu/handle/10419/199419> accessed 11 July 2024.

Perhaps more profoundly, in emphasizing sovereignty as a form of 'freedom', international legal *laissez faire* eludes the ways in which sovereignty of some has been earned as a result of the repression of that of others. It distinctly fails to problematize the historical distribution of territory, resources, population, and wealth as a function of the very operation of the international system. It is blind to the extent to which some states, from the Americas to Asia or Africa, have long been drawn into the international system on the basis that they owed strong duties of engagement with it (as Alvarez put it, himself a defender of non-intervention, one of its exceptions, 'approved by the whole civilized world' was that 'a State may not, on the ground that it is absolutely independent, isolate itself entirely from the other States or refuse to enter into relations with them').[1703] It minimizes the extent to which the ability to disengage is also a function of international privilege (indeed, disengagement, notably on human rights grounds, is almost always the doing of Western states). It eludes the depth of dependencies imposed on particular nations notably as a result of legacies of imperialism and colonialism that make non-engagement a losing proposition, particularly for the less powerful partner. And it assumes a world in which sovereigns have already emerged as fully free and self-sustaining rather than one in which their very (non)existence as sovereign is the hidden stake of the system.

'Paradoxically', as Richard Falk has noted, '"nonintervention" is one form of intervention'.[1704] Trade and financial vulnerabilities may be exploited by states that are less dependent, as part of deeply asymmetrical relationships. For example, the extensive, coordinated, and deliberate asphyxiation of some regimes by isolating them from the world economy, taking advantage of the huge infrastructural advantages of the U.S. (notably in terms of international payment instruments), may be a particularly troublesome case, especially if one computes its human and humanitarian consequences. At the very least, then, one should acknowledge that in reproducing tropes about there not being any *a priori* duty to engage, one is endorsing a certain legacy of international law that may be dated and in tension with what is otherwise the incessant proclamation of the finality of international law as deeply cooperative. Although states may not be expected to provide economic benefits to others *de plein droit*, they are certainly routinely expected to behave in ways (in the international environmental or human rights fields, for example) that manifest forms of good citizenship and the avoidance of avoidable harm to others.

1703 Alvarez (n 474) 124.

1704 Falk, *Legal Order in a Violent World* (n 117) 341.

Crucially, this is a strong motif in Western rhetoric in matters of international security where states are strongly encouraged not to create negative externalities for others (notably by hosting hostile armed groups).

It is precisely against these structural legacies, long and rightly identified as part and parcel of a problematic international legal order, that the Third World rose to propose a New International Economic Order in the 1970s. Seen against that light and, notably, a baseline duty to make long-standing economic inequities right, non-engagement or, specifically, destabilizing dis-engagement may be more readily characterized as interference. This led Christopher Joyner to once argue, based on the redistributive goals of the NIEO, that 'an economically coercive boycott' could be seen 'as a national instrument for antidevelopmentalism wielded by the developed minority against the developing majority'.[1705] The failure of that particular agenda in international law, sometimes dismissed as merely a footnote in its history, arguably makes no less pressing the task of addressing the underlying factors that render the ability to choose one's level of engagement with the international system a very unevenly distributed prerogative. Of late, an earlier attention to the iniquitous colonial legacies of the international system has been supplemented by a renewed attention to its racial economy and notably the international policing of a 'color line'.[1706]

All of these developments point to a baseline of international social life that is less Westphalian defiance and relative sovereign solipsism or neutral coexistence than the ambition to dismantle the inequities inherent to the international system and that chronically belie its liberal assumptions. In that light, it is also worth emphasizing that the liberal default position of international law is hardly unassailable on its own terms. Its particular *laissez faire* vision of the international legal order betrays its origins and is hardly ever consistent: exhortations to 'each his own' have frequently co-existed (and certainly when it suits some states) with the extolling of the inter-dependent character of the world (never more so than during the OPEP crisis). The effort to decolonize international law by the Third World in an earlier era was also an effort to put to waste such liberal sanctities by looking realistically and contextually at relations between states and the particular distributive economies they informed. It had at least a discreet echo in the ICJ's musing that '[t]he cessation of economic aid, the giving of which is more of a unilateral and voluntary nature, could be regarded as such a violation *only in exceptional circumstances*'.[1707]

1705 Joyner (n 997) 247.

1706 E Tendayi Achiume, 'Racial Borders' (2022) 110 Georgetown Law Journal 445.

1707 *Nicaragua v United States* (n 3) [276].

Quite what these circumstances are, however, has rarely been defined. But what if the pervasive nature of international power and injustice were the starting point rather than the supposed freedom of sovereignty? What if we understood the 'liberty to engage' against the background of centuries of forced engagement or forced shunning designed to generalize the Westphalian model, and some of its productivist, capitalistic, and exploitative proclivities? What if we understood sovereignty as a fundamentally differentiated, relational, and positional concept, such that the sovereignty of some paradoxically required both non-interference and a sustained and beneficial level of engagement?

First, arguments suggesting that international law, as a system of bare coexistence, imposes no positive obligations, have long co-existed with arguments that international law, in fact, very much imposes obligations of positive engagement with others . Even though the more ambitious demands of the NIEO (notably the 1970 Declaration on *Friendly* Relations) did not achieve universal consensus or customary status, many positive obligations have been recycled since as part of international human rights instruments guaranteeing the right to development, for example.[1708] This could suggest that one cannot brusquely disengage at will without falling afoul of at least some general if admittedly vague international legal obligation to cooperate multilaterally towards the attainment of beneficial development outcomes.[1709] This is all the more so if general international law obligations are supplemented by human rights ones. Indeed, some authors argue that unilateral sanctions violate target countries' right to development and therefore constitute an intolerable interference with their sovereign aspirations—a violation of the 'international norm prohibiting interference with a nation's right to develop',[1710] a

1708 Sigrun Skogly, 'Global Human Rights Obligations', *The Routledge handbook on extraterritorial human rights obligations* (Routledge 2021); Olivier De Schutter, 'A Duty to Negotiate in Good Faith as Part of the Duty to Cooperate to Establish "An International Legal Order in Which Human Rights Can Be Fully Realized": The New Frontier of the Right to Development' in Nehal Bhuta and others (eds), *The Struggle for Human Rights: Essays in Honour of Philip Alston* (Oxford University Press 2021); Noha Shawki, 'Global Basic Rights, Positive Duties, Extraterritorial Obligations, and Mediating Institutions: Do the Sustainable Development Goals Deepen the Institutionalisation of a Global Responsibility to End Poverty?' (2018) 37 Social Alternatives 3; Tahmina Karimova, *Human Rights and Development in International Law* (Routledge 2016); Dimitris Xenos, *The Positive Obligations of the State under the European Convention of Human Rights* (Routledge 2012).

1709 Evan J Criddle and Evan Fox-Decent, 'Mandatory Multilateralism' (2019) 113 American Journal of International Law 272.

1710 Benjamin Manchak, 'Comprehensive Economic Sanctions, the Right to Development, and Constitutionally Impermissible Violations of International Law' (2010) 30 Boston College Third World Law Journal 417, 450.

hindrance on human rights,[1711] a violation of the right to self-determination[1712] or, more simply, an interference 'in their ability to implement their own policy choices'.[1713] More often than not, then, 'not doing' something can have just as dramatic an impact as 'doing something'.

Second and more damningly, the West has its own tradition of emphasizing a priori positive duties, not least duties of hospitality, most famously towards the 'discoverers' of the Americas.[1714] Newly discovered lands were enjoined to trade with the Spaniards and Portuguese or face the consequences. The entire, vast exploitation of the world's mining resources, as Mario Prost points out, has long been justified by the notion that the South should be productive and, if not, allow itself to be subjected to the sovereignty of others.[1715] Notions of 'minimum treatment' owed to foreign nationals long structured a sense of intense obligation of the 'semi-periphery' to the 'centre'.[1716] The irony of the West portraying the notion of positive duties to other states as beyond the pale when much of the edifice of imperialism relied on precisely such onerous obligations will not have been missed. There is something a bit rich about the insistence, after centuries of forceful integration into the international system, that surely Third World nations should chart their own course, when in reality:

1711 Isabella D Bunn, 'The Right to Development: Implications for International Economic Law Conferences: Symposium: Interfaces: From International Trade to Economic Law' (1999) 15 American University of International Law Review 1425, 1459–1462; Rowhani (n 1693) 142–153.

1712 Idriss Jazairy, 'Unilateral Economic Sanctions, International Law, and Human Rights' (2019) 33 Ethics & International Affairs 291.

1713 Rahmat Mohamad, 'Unilateral Sanctions in International Law: A Quest for Legality' in Ali Z Marossi and Marisa R Bassett (eds), *Economic Sanctions under International Law: Unilateralism, Multilateralism, Legitimacy, and Consequences* (TMC Asser Press 2015) n 34.

1714 Martti Koskenniemi, 'International Law and the Emergence of Mercantile Capitalism: Grotius to Smith' in Vincent Chetail and Pierre-Marie Dupuy (eds), *The Roots of International Law/Les fondements du droit international* (Brill Nijhoff 2014); Antony Anghie, 'Civilization and Commerce: The Concept of Governance in Historical Perspective' (2000) 45 Villanova Law Review 887; Benjamin Straumann and Benedict Kingsbury, 'The State of Nature and Commercial Sociability in Early Modern International Legal Thought' (2010) 31 Grotiana 22.

1715 Mario Prost, '"One Vast Gasoline Station for Human Exploitation": Sovereignty as Anthropocentric Extraction', *The Routledge Handbook of International Law and Anthropocentrism* (Routledge 2023).

1716 Frédéric Mégret and Nicole Maylor, 'The US–Mexico Mixed Claims Commissions' in Chiara Giorgetti, Patrick W Pearsall and Hélène Ruiz-Fabri (eds), *Research Handbook on International Claims Commissions* (Edward Elgar Publishing 2023).

> Developing countries do not merely want self-government free from outside interference; they expect aid, without strings attached, from wealthy nations as well as release from obligations incurred under rules of law they did not help create and which in any case they find excessive.[1717]

This was nowhere more evident than when the West briefly experienced a taste of its own medicine following the OPEP oil embargo, promptly leading some commentators infuriated by this new 'economic warfare' to argue that industrialized nations should 'bend every effort to write some new rules of international law providing for equal access to raw materials into the GATT [and] and that we develop some multilateral sanctions against countries that violate these rules'.[1718] On that occasion, it was promptly argued that, pace the proclamation of permanent control over natural resources, the distribution of such resources had to be used to serve international peace.[1719] *Plus ça change, moins ça change.*

Third, the liberal status quo is heavily loaded ideologically. In conditions of fundamental asymmetry of power where the smaller party is highly dependent on the bigger one, the interruption of economic relations can have (deliberately) devastating impacts.[1720] There may be a difference between the idea that one does not have obligations to provide a certain level of engagement in the first place, and an understanding that one has no-harm obligations especially in the face of structured relations (except for good cause). Paradoxically, then, the greater the degree of existing interdependence the more problematic the breaking of relations.[1721] Note that a similar argument has been made even in relation to treaty-making where it has been pointed out that '[m]any underdeveloped countries have a single big commercial partner who is capable of dictating its integration into chains of commerce, and who, by blocking the trade of goods with the weaker State or shunning its access to international mechanisms' can produce a situation where 'the weak negotiating country has no alternative but to bow down'.[1722] This has led to calls for a recognition of a 'principle of equality in treaty relations' leading either to differential treatment

1717 Houben (n 452) 735.

1718 Cited in Brosche (n 432) 4.

1719 Paust and Blaustein (n 1023) 420.

1720 This is debated in the economics literature, but the impact is generally found to be sizeable.

1721 AK Abashidze, 'The negative impact of unilateral coercive measures on human rights, development, cooperation, international relations' [2015] RUDN Journal of Law 64.

1722 Del Negro (n 487) 57–58.

or, failing that, the renegotiation of treaties that are too unequal.[1723] In other words, even treaty formation is not unreceptive to the notion that it could have differentiated and corrective dimensions that take into account the actual reality of international relations and not simply formal equality between sovereigns.[1724]

2.3 *Friendly Relations?*

What would it mean for our understanding of interference, by contrast, to think of the default position of international relations not as a kind of insular solipsism, but as characterized by a sense that international society is defined by meaningful, if often difficult, engagement between states? What if one took seriously the idea that the baseline was 'friendly relations', a term notoriously promoted by the Third World to reimagine international relations starting in the 1970s? 'Friendly relations' may seem like a quaint term in the international legal jargon but it has quite the pedigree, including the well-known General Assembly Resolution 2625 of October 24 1970 on 'Principles of International Law concerning Friendly Relations and Co-operation among States'.[1725] That resolution, which sought to strike a delicate balance between non-interference and cooperation, independence and interaction, framed relations between states in an ambiguous way as both respectful of yet transcending their sovereignty.

But the concept crystalizes something beyond that middle-era. Earlier, the U.S.'s Good Neighbor Policy under Roosevelt had already introduced the notion that a particular kind of respectful relations could be based on the renunciation of intervention in the affairs of other states. Since then, Resolution 2625, the principle of friendly relations has occasionally been invoked even in the European context to guard against unwarranted assertions of jurisdiction, notably in relation to the 'passportization'[1726] and protection of ethnic kin[1727] debates, where it seems to provide a flexible formula to describe behavior that is not always evidently illegal, but can certainly be framed as inimical—whatever that means—in international law.

1723 Alice De Jonge, 'From Unequal Treaties to Differential Treatment: Is There a Role for Equality in Treaty Relations?' (2014) 4 Asian Journal of International Law 125.

1724 P Cullet, 'Differential Treatment in International Law: Towards a New Paradigm of Inter-State Relations' (1999) 10 European Journal of International Law 549.

1725 1970 Declaration on Friendly Relations, 123.

1726 Peters (n 643).

1727 Venice Commission, '48th Plenary Session, Venice, 19–20 October 2001, Report on the Preferential Treatment of National Minorities by Their Kin-State' (n 644) 19.

'Friendly' relations suggest an expectation of a certain degree and quality of engagement with other states, framed by comity but also cooperation and respect. It tends to lean away from purely liberal understandings of international relations that emphasize states' sovereignty and their ability to withdraw from international engagement at will. This opens the door for the possibility that the denial of good faith engagement with other states might constitute a form of interference. This would be even more the case in conditions of dependency reinforced by a long habitual engagement or support of another state and where the interruption of relations can have considerable asymmetrical effects. A connection has, moreover, increasingly been drawn by the General Assembly between the notion of friendly relations and respect for human rights, with unilateral measures 'in particular those of a coercive nature with all their extraterritorial effects, which create obstacles to trade relations among States' being presented as 'impeding the full realization of the rights set forth in the Universal Declaration of Human Rights'.[1728]

'Friendly relations', it should be said, has at times been a bit of a misnomer, 'in the wholly unromantic sense', as Brad Roth put it, 'of a framework of accommodation among bearers of potentially rival interests and values'.[1729] In the Third World-infused jargon of the General Assembly, it referred, for the most part, to relations that generously deferred to the sovereignty and self-determination of states and little else. Friendly relations was, in fact, about desisting from interfering with other states much more than doing things together. It was framed as a demand to be left alone rather than being engaged with. In other words, that 'friendship' was very much one that, on some level, was imagined as operating at arms' length—a polite friendship closer to comity perhaps than to a warm embrace of the other (friendly but not *too* friendly ...).

At the same time, the project of 'friendly relations' as it was spearheaded by the Third World and sought to impose itself on the West was also one of a strongly shared common purpose, if only that of remedying the system's legacies of inequality through decolonial solidarity. It could not itself have emerged without the solidarity of nations of the South. Its insistence on non-interference was arguably a prelude to, for example, a broader obligation of cooperation as anticipated in the Friendly Relations Declaration ('States have the duty to co-operate with one another, irrespective of the differences in their political, economic and social systems, in the various spheres of international relations'), all the way to sharing the benefits of the High Seas and even the

1728 UNGA Res 53/141 (8 March 1999) U.N. Doc A/RES/53/141, para 1.
1729 Roth, 'Democratization's Discontents' (n 559).

Deep Sea Bed under the U.N. Convention on the Law of the Sea as the 'common heritage of mankind'. In short, international law has certainly in the past produced thicker understandings of what the baseline of international relations is, and is not doomed to a minimalist vision of the liberal international legal order.

Friendliness, or at least a higher degree of community-feeling in a *gemeinschaft*, potentially raises the bar of what are expected to be 'normal' relations between states. This has been highlighted in the context of regional unions. On that count, for example, the Venice Commission found that there is nothing untoward from a democratic point of view about allowing parties located in one European Union member state to contribute financially to political parties in other states. Such an approach is 'reasonable and appropriate' because 'the legal system of the European Union differs from international public law' in which states have 'limited their sovereign rights', in a context where the Treaty of Rome itself has long emphasized that '[p]olitical parties at European level are important as a factor for integration within the Union'.[1730] A further consideration, characteristic of a close union between member states, is that freedom of capital movement is, in fact, a fundamental Treaty freedom. The European Union is of course atypical in that respect, imagining itself to proceed from a horizon of ever closer integration but the Venice Commission's findings at least suggest that, against the background of already particularly 'friendly' relations, the threshold of what constitutes interference could be substantially lowered.

Outside that limited regional context, however, it is less clear that there is an ascertainable obligation to have continued 'friendly' relations with other states under customary international law—and at any rate states will disagree about what friendliness entails in any given circumstance. Even in relatively institutionalized multilateral environments, notably those characteristic of international economic life, unilateral sanctions, especially when national security issues are concerned, are largely tolerated. The WTO and before it the GATT treaties, for example, which otherwise aspire to maintain unhindered international commerce, have long allowed states to adopt measures restricting trade to protect their essential security interests, even though this may seem to clash with 'what could be called entitlements'.[1731]

It is improbable that this clear allowance would then be reframed as a form of interference. For Sarah Cleveland, for example, sanctions seeking to enforce human rights are a special case that can be countenanced, in at least some

1730 Venice Commission (n 1191), s IV.

1731 Farer, 'Political and Economic Coercion in Contemporary International Law' (n 433) 405.

scenarios, under the WTO framework.[1732] Of course, it may be that loosely adopted cyber-sanctions, for example, do not even meet the national security exception because they are disproportionate or mistargeted[1733] or that sanctions of third parties for trading with a primary target are too remote from any credible invocation of national interest to fall under such an exception. Nonetheless, free trade rules only operate as a sort of exception to the default position (no obligation to engage in free trade) and reversion to that default position for good cause remains a possibility. The point is thus reinforced *a contrario* that outside any specific bilateral or multilateral commitment, there exists no a priori duty under customary international law to have any given degree of proactive relationship to other states.

One occasionally evoked possibility, however, is that withdrawal of an advantage once given is, in fact, worse than never having given that advantage in the first place: that, although there may not be an ingrained right to a certain level of exchange, there is a right to not have 'the rug pulled from under one's feet' economically. As Rosalyn Higgins put it, even though, 'one starts from the proposition that any state is free to trade with whomsoever it wants, and indeed free to terminate any trade arrangements that it has', it is also true that 'when trade patterns continue for a period of years expectations about the future are built up, and it is thus an over-simplification to say that one could therefore cut such relationships off at will'.[1734] This once led Richard Bilder to hint at the possibility that 'economic pressures or refusals to deal are improper where they are effective primarily because the state employing such pressures has induced the target state into a situation of economic dependence and vulnerability'.[1735] For example, bona fide trade partners from the Global South trading with nations of the North will in the process be durably adapting their system of production: for a partner state to then capriciously and unilaterally interrupt preferential policies may put the previously beneficiary state in a position worse than it was in before. Others have emphasized the suddenness

---

1732 Sarah H Cleveland, 'Human Rights Sanctions and International Trade: A Theory of Compatibility' (2002) 5 Journal of International Economic Law 133. See also Misha Boutilier, 'From Seal Welfare to Human Rights, Can Unilateral Sanctions in Response to Mass Atrocity Crimes Be Justified under the Article XX(A) Public Morals Exception Clause' (2017) 75 University of Toronto Faculty of Law Review 101.

1733 Iryna Bogdanova and Maria Vasquez Callo-Muller, 'Unilateral Cyber Sanctions: Between Questioned Legality and Normative Value' (2021) 54 Vanderbilt Journal of Transnational Law 911.

1734 Higgins, *Themes and Theories* (n 540) 275.

1735 Bilder (n 311) 44.

with which previously expected relations are withdrawn and hinted at some sort of acquired right to ongoing conditions. As Clive Parry put it, for example:

> If we look to economic coercion, is it not [...] the abruptness of this thing which is somehow objectionable? It would be difficult to maintain that state A must buy state B's sugar crop [...] or that state A must sell B as much oil as it wants [...]. But it is not unnecessarily unreasonable to suggest that the abrupt termination of or interference with an established trade pattern may approach the impermissible and may be capable of adequate enough definition.[1736]

Georges Abi-Saab hinted as much, emphasizing the doctrine of 'abuse of right', and pointing out that it is 'reasonable to consider that once established, if these relations create such a situation of dependence that a brutal rupture would inflict appreciable harm to the other party or even threaten its survival, this rupture would constitute an act of intervention by its effects and by the intention to harm that motivates it'.[1737] That danger even militated for 'the possibility of developing an obligation of "due diligence" with respect to the effect on others of what a State does or does not do within its own jurisdiction, an obligation whose violation will be more blatant if the harmful effect is intended'.[1738] This notion of the abrupt termination of existing relations was hinted at by the ICJ in the Nicaragua case, although admittedly only in relation to an existing treaty of friendship and commerce. The question of whether there is a right to not see continuous and dense relations interrupted unilaterally outside such a context is much less evident and, to be clear, some authors go by the proposition that 'however brutal or stupid a particular measure may be, legally, any country is free to restrict or prohibit economic relations'.[1739]

Nonetheless, conditions of extreme dependency and asymmetry, for example on financial markets necessary to be able to minimally trade for goods, create quite unique vulnerabilities. They reward partners in relationships who have historically accrued considerable leverage and can effectively interfere in the affairs of other states at little cost to themselves. On a certain level, disengagement may just be another word for an attempt to literally asphyxiate another state's economy and nullify its sovereignty because of dependencies on international infrastructure controlled by powerful states (for example,

1736 Parry (n 1691) 4.
1737 Abi-Saab (n 557) 233–234.
1738 ibid 234.
1739 Friedmann, 'Intervention and the Developing Countries' (n 406) 221.

inter-bank payment systems such as SWIFT).[1740] This is exactly what Salvador Allende denounced in his famous speech before the General Assembly, emphasizing this as a classic imperial subterfuge, namely intervention that did not even need to say its name because it could afford to cause great pain merely by disengaging:

> [w]e are the victims of a new expression of imperialism—more subtle, more sneaky, and terribly effective—to block the exercise of our rights as a sovereign state. [...] There have been efforts to isolate U.S. from the world, strangle the economy and paralyze the sale of copper, our main export product, and keep U.S. from access to sources of international financing. We realize that when we denounce the financial-economic blockade with which we were attacked, it is hard for international public opinion and even for many of our compatriots to easily understand the situation because it is not open aggression, publicly proclaimed before the whole world. Quite the contrary, it is a sneaky and double-crossing attack, which is just as damaging to Chile. We find ourselves opposed by forces that operate in the shadows, without a flag, with powerful weapons that are placed in a wide range of influential positions. We are not the object of any trade ban. Nobody has said that he seeks a confrontation with our country. [...] We are the victims of almost invisible actions, usually concealed with remarks and statements that pay lip service to respect for the sovereignty and dignity of our country. But we have first-hand knowledge of the great difference that there is between those statements and the specific actions we must endure.[1741]

A fortiori, an international human rights analysis would tend to reinforce a sense that unilateral sanctions that create considerable harm, for example by depriving a state (and its population) of the ability to provide basic foodstuffs, would be a particularly noxious and illegal. This is the case if one sees non-intervention as justified primarily on human rights grounds, although note that if behavior cancelling existing relations falls under the *lex specialis* of

1740 Mariam Majd, 'The Cost of a SWIFT Kick: Estimating the Cost of Financial Sanctions on Iran' in Gerald A Epstein (ed), *The Political Economy of International Finance in an Age of Inequality* (Edward Elgar Publishing 2018); Marco Cipriani, Linda S Goldberg and Gabriele La Spada, 'Financial Sanctions, SWIFT, and the Architecture of the International Payment System' (2023) 37 Journal of Economic Perspectives 31.

1741 Cited in Radice (n 1137) 236.

human rights violations it is not clear what is gained by seeking to characterize it as, in addition, a form of interference.

In conclusion, it is possible to *imagine* a vision of international law, contra liberal solipsism, wherein the baseline is a certain level of productive engagement, especially if that is understood as, say, merely an openness to trade rather than active provision of assistance, and especially if the focus in on interrupting long-standing relations capriciously rather than refusing to open new. ones. The argument from non-intervention when it comes to unilateral sanctions can certainly lay claim to a long line of vocal denunciation which helps to problematize the sort of power relations within which such sanctions occur. Interference may nonetheless not be the most evident ground to assess such rupture given the availability of, for example, human rights contestations of unilateral sanctions. Note, however, one final twist, on the state complaining of unilateral sanctions' own grounds. It is also the case, that the demand for engagement by some states who feel left out of the international community and of potentially productive bilateral relations is paradoxical: it calls for engagement with the target state but on the target state's own terms in ways that seem hard to sustain; and it testifies to a continued demand for social relations even by states who are otherwise defiant and proudly independent.

Therein lies the ultimate snag for states in the Global South who would insist on the continuity of relations with the imperial powers that have oppressed them: that it potentially prolongs those very relations. This shows the difficulty and perhaps the ambiguity of having it both ways, i.e., of seeking to maintain the bare relations necessary to one's survival in the global economy whilst keeping the hegemonic interferers at bay. As Allende put it after loudly denouncing the U.S. pullout from the Chilean economy, perhaps wary of what he might be seen to invite, '[w]e are not asking for those loans to be reinstated'.[1742] Indeed, awkwardly, insisting that states have a duty to guarantee a certain level of relations to others comes dangerously close to the sort of demands that the West once made to semi-periphery states as a condition of their participation in the international community, notably in terms of guaranteeing access to their markets. This goes against some of the very claims for independence that the Third World has long made, for itself at least.

1742 ibid 238.

3 A Duty of Transparency?

3.1 *Demanding Truth*

One criterion for assessing the illegality of the 'new interference' might be that it is systematically committed to spreading falsehoods. This was already apparent in 1950s efforts to curtail foreign influence in the U.S., with one report stating of communists and fascists that '[b]oth are willing to lie about their political views when it is convenient. They feel no obligation to come before the public openly and say who they are and what they really want'.[1743] Certainly, one of the concerns with 'new interference' has been trolling and fake news generally, and their unmistakable impact on respect for the public sphere.[1744] Several laws or projected laws specifically target the production of fake information.[1745] The European Union has promoted a very broad notion of 'information manipulation', including:

> spreading disinformation and completely false news, distorting facts, narratives and representations of opinion, suppression of certain information or opinions, taking information out of context, manipulating people's feelings, promoting hate speech, promoting some opinions at the expense of others, and harassing people to silence and oppress them; whereas one aim of information manipulation is to create chaos in order to encourage a loss of citizens' trust in the old and new 'gatekeepers' of information.[1746]

In that respect, the E.U. reconnects with earlier themes propounded by the Third World via the General Assembly, notably the 'right and duty of States',

1743 President's Committee on Civil Rights and Charles Erwin Wilson, *To Secure These Rights: The Report of the President's Committee on Civil Rights* (United States Government Printing Office 1947) 47. Also, ibid 51 ('one of the things which totalitarians of both left and right have in common is a reluctance to come before the people honestly and say who they are, what they work for and who supports them').

1744 Alison MacKenzie and Ibrar Bhatt, 'Opposing the Power of Lies, Bullshit and Fake News: The Value of Truth' (2020) 2 Postdigital Science and Education 217.

1745 *Loi* n° 2018-1202 du 22 décembre 2018 relative à la lutte contre la manipulation de l'information (France); Gaspar Pisanu and Javier Pallero, 'Brazil: "Fake News" Proposals Add Uncertainty to Institutional Crisis' *Access Now* (27 April 2018) <https://www.accessnow.org/brazil-fake-news-proposals-add-uncertainty-to-institutional-crisis/> accessed 15 February 2019; Kentaro Iwamoto, 'Singapore Set to Tackle Fake News with New Law' *Nikkei Asian Review* (20 September 2018) <https://asia.nikkei.com/Politics/Singapore-set-to-tackle-fake-news-with-new-law> accessed 15 February 2019.

1746 2022 Resolution on Foreign Interference in the E.U. (n 337), para W.

stipulated in the 1981 Declaration on the Inadmissibility of Intervention and Interference, 'to combat, within their constitutional prerogatives, the dissemination of false or distorted news which can be interpreted as interference in the internal affairs of other States'.[1747] This move harks back to some of the themes of the even older Conference on Freedom of Information and its goal, in the wake of the Cold War, of combating 'the diffusion of false or distorted reports likely to injure friendly relations between States'.[1748] In other words, the constituencies that have over time sought to fight fake news are varied and even include states that otherwise claim very much to be proponents of global freedom of information.

There are nonetheless difficulties with the notion that what is problematic about interference is that it is not truthful, and that something is not interference if it is truthful. First, the problem of truthfulness in the public sphere is clearly much broader than interference from outside and includes a range of private actors with perfectly domestic credentials engaging in exactly the same sort of practices. The debate over fake news is one that is now raging globally about how to regulate the public sphere in an age of digital media and seeming free-for-all on social networks.[1749] It is hardly restricted to outside interference. In fact, one readily available argument is that governments themselves have routinely become purveyors of fake news,[1750] in ways that should caution against making policies of speech regulation depend on whether information is reliably 'true' or 'false'. The danger is that foreign information operations, problematic as they may be, will be painted as 'uniquely pernicious, justifying more exceptional responses than manipulative or misleading domestic campaigns'[1751] and that a problem that runs much deeper will be dealt with through expedients targeting actors abroad rather than the rot at the core.

Indeed, if much lobbying of a purely domestic nature is itself not particularly held to an obligation of truthfulness, then on what basis exactly should one be

1747 1981 Declaration on the Inadmissibility of Intervention and Interference, s III(d).

1748 Department of State, *International Organization and Conference Series III, 1* (United States Government Printing Office 1948) 192.

1749 Jordan Guiao, 'Distorting the Public Square: Political Campaigning on Social Media Requires Greater Regulation' (The Australia Institute; Centre for Responsible Technology 2019) <https://apo.org.au/sites/default/files/resource-files/2019-11/apo-nid268891.pdf> accessed 19 December 2023; Kimberly Rhum, 'Information Fiduciaries and Political Microtargeting: A Legal Framework for Regulating Political Advertising on Digital Platforms Notes' (2020) 115 Northwestern University Law Review 1829.

1750 Sara L Ochs, 'Fake News & International Criminal Law' (2021) 66 Saint Louis University Law Journal 99.

1751 Douek (n 46) 266.

so shocked at foreign powers' similar practices? Is not domestic fake news just as toxic as the foreign-produced sort? In some ways, 'information manipulation' is the name of the game. Why should the transnational sphere be different? What makes states confident that they can distinguish the truthful and the non-truthful in cross-border propaganda, when they hesitate (probably for good cause) to do so domestically? The risk is that foreign actors would be held to a higher standard than is contemplated for domestic ones, on shaky grounds democratically, especially in circumstances where it is not inconceivable that domestic actors will be much more ill-intentioned than foreign ones.[1752] What might be required, by contrast, is a theory of interference of all actors in the life of the polity (and, quite conceivably, of interference of all actors with all actors) but, plainly, such a theory does not exist, at least under international law and, for the purposes of this book, one may have serious misgivings about whether it would be workable.

Second is the much more fundamental question of how we distinguish truth and untruth in democratic societies, without turning that exercise into a heavy-handed, authoritarian diktat about what can legitimately be thought, especially in a context of overall wariness with hard distinctions between truth and non-truth. The media and journalists are often considered to have a crucial role as 'watchdogs' both for the purposes of democracy in general and human rights specifically. This means that they are typically not held to impossible obligations of uttering the 'truth'. Although they should verify factual claims in accordance with the ethics of journalism,[1753] they are rightly not held to a perfect obligation of truthfulness beyond acting in 'good faith' and with 'due diligence', and especially not when it comes to value judgments.[1754] The ECHR certainly 'does not prohibit discussion or dissemination of information received even if it is strongly suspected that this information might not be truthful' and '[t]o suggest otherwise would […] place an unreasonable restriction on the freedom of expression'.[1755]

At most, international human rights bodies have validated the criminalization of very specific forms of untruthful information in the form of Holocaust or genocide denial, for example under the ECHR's so-called 'abuse clause'.[1756]

1752 Douek (n 46).

1753 *Goodwin v The United Kingdom* ECHR 1996-II 16, para 39.

1754 *Lingens v Austria* (1986) Series A 103, para 46.

1755 *Salov v Ukraine* ECHR 2005-VIII 143, para 113.

1756 ECHR, art 17 ('Nothing in this Convention may be interpreted as implying for any State, group or person any right to engage in any activity or perform any act aimed at the destruction of any of the rights and freedoms set forth herein').

Although the Parliamentary Assembly of the Council of Europe for example has expressed concern about abuses of online media designed to misguide the public, it has fallen clearly short of suggesting that journalists should be disciplined for propagating fake news.[1757] Very occasionally, the ECtHR has found that incendiary and misleading information was rightfully banned. In *Balsytė-Lideikienė v Lithuania*, the applicant had published a calendar that included a map of Lithuania laying claim to lands in Poland, Belarus, and Russia as 'ethnic Lithuanian lands under temporary occupation'.[1758] The Strasbourg Court accepted that the language of extreme nationalism in evidence, particularly in the light of complaints by foreign states, justified the confiscation of the calendar, because the factual claims were outrageous.[1759] Consider, by contrast, the banning of RT France: is the notion that Russia is engaged in a self-defence operation to protect Russian speakers literally and demonstrably 'fake'? Or is it no doubt what many would consider a shocking, ill thought out and biased view that nonetheless deserves to be discussed so that it can be discredited? The tendency of authoritarian regimes to routinely condemn dissidents for spreading false information should at least be pause for thought.[1760] Indeed, the West has its own tradition of punishing citizens for unpopular or controversial views, particularly in times of war, for example the U.S. under the 1917 Espionage Act.

It is surely difficult to differentiate systematically between truth and disinformation, especially without the benefit of the trial of information being aired, discussed and critically assessed in the public sphere. This is a distinction, in fact, that democracies ordinarily try to shun domestically in a context where it is deemed that to open the doors of free speech broadly is superior to punishing the occasional abuse of free speech. Initiatives such as the 'Joint Declaration on Freedom of Expression and "Fake News", Disinformation and Propaganda' have already made it clear that 'the human right to impart information and ideas is not limited to 'correct' statements' and that '[g]eneral prohibitions on the dissemination of information based on vague and ambiguous ideas, including 'false news' or 'non-objective information', are incompatible with international standards for restrictions on freedom of expression.[1761] This

1757 COE Parliamentary Assembly, 'Online media and journalism: challenges and accountability', Resolution 2143 (2017).

1758 *Balsytė-Lideikienė v Lithuania* App no 72596/01 (ECtHR 4 November 2008), para 10.

1759 ibid, para 85–86.

1760 Elena Sherstoboeva, 'Russian Bans on "Fake News" about the War in Ukraine: Conditional Truth and Unconditional Loyalty' (2024) 86 International Communication Gazette 36.

1761 Joint Declaration on Disinformation (n 697).

merely confirms what a variety of U.N. human rights bodies have been saying for some time.[1762]

In addition, the abuse of the notion of 'fake news' by populists or conspiracy theorists to undermine confidence in democratic institutions is well documented.[1763] Constant invocations of fake news can as much fragilize the public debate as actual fake news, creating a level of skepticism about the reliability of anything that is said in the public sphere and breeding a form of popular cynicism. Note that, beyond purely domestic reasons to be wary of making 'truth' the linchpin of a political theory of intervention, the concern with opening broadly the gates of idea circulation has always chimed well with the inherent liberalism of international law and its commitment to value-pluralism.[1764] Much diplomatic but also inter-societal intercourse depends on ideas being voiced widely and freely, even if the cost of this is that obnoxious or provocative views will also be expressed. Note that there is also a constant hesitation between thinking that the problem is that news is 'false' and that it is 'fake'. The latter points to an even more perplexing genuineness test that is very difficult to apply except perhaps, as seen below, to impose a requirement of transparency about source.

Third, the banning of information as 'fake' risks having ripple effects. Already, the prohibition of Russian propaganda channel RT France has been criticized as, if nothing else, making it more improbable that digital forensic reporters using open-source intelligence (OSINT), such as Bellingcat and Oryx, will be able to rely on the channel to understand what is happening in Ukraine. More importantly, the rush to ban Russian propaganda outlets assumes that European public opinions cannot make up their own minds about the war in Ukraine and minimizes the perverse effects that banning a broadcast will have. As pointed out by one U.S. commentator, such 'exclusions limit the view of the world available to the U.S. public and policymakers, and, by a well-understood and predictable process, they lead to the demonizing and silencing of valuable internal critics whose insights could help to improve the effectiveness of foreign and domestic policy'.[1765] It also bears mentioning that punishing

1762 Andrei Richter, 'Fake News and Freedom of the Media' (2018) 8 Journal of International Media and Entertainment Law 1, 13–14.

1763 Irini Katsirea, '"Fake News": Reconsidering the Value of Untruthful Expression in the Face of Regulatory Uncertainty' (2018) 10 Journal of Media Law 159.

1764 Frédéric Mégret, 'International Law as a System of Legal Pluralism' in Paul Schiff Berman (ed), *The Oxford Handbook of Global Legal Pluralism* (Oxford University Press 2020).

1765 Mark MacCarthy, 'Why a Push to Exclude Russian State Media Would Be Problematic for Free Speech and Democracy' *Brookings* (14 April 2022) <https://www.brookings.edu/articles/why-a-push-to-exclude-russian-state-media-would-be-problematic-for-free-speech-and-democracy/> accessed 17 December 2023.

the dissemination of 'fake' information will inevitably encourage other states, including authoritarian ones, to seize on this to engage in their own projects of repression.

Moreover, the issue with some of the information that is seen as problematically leaked is often not so much that it is false, but that it is inconvenient. The problem with the data leaked by the Russians during the 2016 election was not that it was false but at best that it was confidential. In fact, the DNC e-mails were very much real and pointed to events that had actually occurred. It is their reality that was problematic and that created tensions within the Democratic party which could be exploited by Republican opponents. It may be hard, in fact, to argue that this disclosure even ran against the best democratic interest of the U.S. population. The hack-and-leak revealed evidence of misconduct and lack of neutrality by the DNC, particularly against candidate Bernie Sanders. One might think it was in the public's interest to know this information. Had U.S. journalists found the emails themselves, they undoubtedly would have published them (indeed, they did publish them even when provided by the Russians).[1766] Aside from the illegality of the way in which the emails were obtained (which may only implicate the legal interests of, say, the DNC under domestic law), is it that obvious that the release constituted harmful interference in U.S. elections, given that the emails were real and arguably shed light on a crucial dimension of the campaign?

The same is true of the politics of leaks in general[1767] (e.g., on the Iraq war, on U.K.-U.S. trade):[1768] no doubt unfriendly and even illegal because of the way the information was obtained, but not necessarily problematic from a broader democratic perspective. As for many previous leaks punished under the Espionage Act such as those of Daniel Ellsberg (the former defense analyst who leaked the Pentagon Papers to various U.S. newspapers in 1973) or those of Edward Snowden in 2013, the issue was not that the information was fake or indeed that it was in itself prejudicial to the operation of democracy,

1766 Sydney Ember, 'Editors Defend Coverage of Stolen Emails After News of Russian Hacks' *The New York Times* (22 December 2017) <https://www.nytimes.com/2016/12/15/business/media/russian-hacking-stolen-emails.html> accessed 12 March 2019.

1767 Stephen Marmura, 'WikiLeaks, Russsiagate, and the Crisis of Democracy' in Oliver Boyd-Barrett and Stephen Marmura (eds), *Russiagate Revisited: The Aftermath of a Hoax* (Springer International Publishing 2023).

1768 Guy Faulconbridge, 'UK Says Russia Tried to Meddle in Election by Leaking U.S. Trade Documents' *Reuters* (16 July 2020) <https://www.reuters.com/article/idUSKCN24H1VS/> accessed 1 April 2024.

but merely that it was secret. Failed efforts to prosecute under the Act such as those against two AIPAC members who were accused of having trafficked information between Israel and the U.S. show more broadly the difficulty of prosecuting individuals for the mere conveying of information between states.[1769] In short, the focus on 'fake' news when coming from abroad may blind democracies to the extent to which they have always considered it problematic to aggressively police the border between what is true or false, in the spirit of letting the public decide for itself.

3.2 *Perfidy and the Requirement of Transparency*

It might be that it is less the lack of truthfulness of statements that should be seen as problematic than that they are often made whilst hiding their author's true identity. This could be seen as the peacetime equivalent of the prohibition on 'perfidy', enjoining actors to not appear as other than who they really are. Cyber deception has emerged as an abiding concern across the war/peace divide.[1770] Hence the central importance that concerns with transparency have gained in the last decade. Lack of transparency can crucially damage the confidence in political parties or the media and contribute to the erosion of democracy domestically. It can also create significant tensions internationally as states struggle to determine whether they have even been interfered with, how and by whom.

This also relates to 'truth' but not so much the truth of the statements proffered as truth (and transparency) about *authorship*, notably when local intermediaries are involved. Such a concern has a long history, notably in the young American republic, with George Washington in his farewell address warning against the possibility that 'tools and dupes' might be enlisted to propagate the 'insidious wiles of foreign influence', unbeknownst to the U.S. government.[1771] As the Truman Committee once put it:

> If these people wish to influence the public in our national forum of opinion they should be free to do so, regardless of how distasteful their views are to us. But the public must be able to evaluate these views. [...] The principle of disclosure is, we believe, the appropriate way to deal

1769 Neil A Lewis and David Johnston, 'US to Drop Spy Case Against Pro-Israel Lobbyists' *The New York Times* (1 May 2009) <https://www.nytimes.com/2009/05/02/us/politics/02aipac.html> accessed 17 December 2023.

1770 Vito Smyth, *The Best Defense Is a Good Offense: Conducting Offensive Cyber Operations and the Law of Armed Conflict* (Air War College 2014).

1771 Spalding and Garrity (n 100) 53.

> with those who would subvert our democracy by revolution or by encouraging disunity and destroying the civil rights of some groups. We have considered and rejected proposals which have been made to U.S. for censoring or prohibiting material which defames religious or racial minority groups. Our purpose is not to constrict anyone's freedom to speak; it is rather to enable the people better to judge the true motives of those who try to sway them.[1772]

More recently, it is specifically the 'clandestine' or 'deceptive' nature of some influence that has been highlighted as problematic for international law and in contravention of national security.[1773] The European Parliament has expressed concern that some 'political elites in E.U. Member States, for example in Germany, have advanced the agenda of Gazprom and expressed constant support for gas supplies from Russia'.[1774] Indeed according to the Australian Security Intelligence Organisation Act, lack of transparency should be the linchpin of a theory of non-interference:

> All foreign states seek to influence deliberations of importance to them. When those activities are conducted in an open and transparent manner they are not of concern. However when it is conducted covertly by, or on behalf of, a foreign actor; when it is clandestine, deceptive corrupting or threatening in nature and when it is contrary to Australia's sovereignty and interests, we classify this as foreign interference.[1775]

This then commends a raft of approaches that would impose 'transparency' as a remedy. The problem is not so much dissemination of information from abroad, but information that *passes* as domestic or at least as other than it really is.

1772 President's Committee on Civil Rights and Wilson (n 1743) 52.

1773 See for example the Canadian Security Intelligence Service Act (CSIS Act) (RSC 1985, c C-23), s 2, which defines 'threats to the security of Canada' as including 'foreign influenced activities within or relating to Canada that are detrimental to the interests of Canada and are clandestine, deceptive, or involve a threat to any person'. Also, the Australian Security Intelligence Organisation Act, which defines foreign interference as activities that are 'clandestine or deceptive'. Australian Security Intelligence Organisation Act (1979), s 4(a).

1774 2023 Resolution on Foreign Interference in the E.U. (n 335), para 66.

1775 'Counter-Espionage and Foreign Interference' (*Australian Security Intelligence Organisation (ASIO)*) <https://www.asio.gov.au/about/what-we-do/counter-espionage> accessed 16 February 2024.

The relevance of transparency is particularly glaring if one sees the foundation of the norm of non-interference as being the right to self-determination: in that context, it would seem that ordinary participants in the political process (who do not have the means of the sovereign at their disposal to parse *bona* and *mala fide* participants) have a particularly strong interest in knowing who they are 'self-determining with' and not being swayed by misleading external interlopers. Even assuming broad openness to outside ideas, one still needs to be able to locate them *as* foreign ideas. A fortiori if the intervener *claims* to be promoting self-determination, nothing seems more likely to arise suspicions than surreptitiously doing so, even if on some instrumental reading the outcome might conceivably be favorable to self-determination (although at that level of speculation, conduct truly consonant with respect for local self-determination would probably defer to a people's ability to see foreign assistance for what it is).

The argument is arguably even stronger when what would otherwise constitute interference is engaged in in the name of human rights: is there room, under international human rights norms, for *covert* human rights action? Is there not a contradiction in terms between the stealthiness of means and the claimed transparency of objectives? One must be mindful here, even outside broad principles, of the extent to which such a covert character will tend to impugn the intentions of its author when discovered and perhaps more readily discredit human rights assistance as the foreign ploy that authoritarians so incessantly denounce. It is true that receiving foreign assistance may endanger the position of local actors and that may militate, if not for clandestine, at least relatively discrete or stealthy assistance. But providing covert assistance, especially in a context of heighted anxiety about interference, is not necessarily the right solution. States wary of interfering should be mindful that local actors do not have the last word on the issue and that international law imposes on them distinct obligations on a bilateral level. Even if covert means are resorted to, the provision of assistance should be as far as possible severed from bodies associated with foreign policy or tied to other, strategic dimensions (for example, 'human rights assistance' provided covertly by the CIA is relatively more likely to trigger concerns that it rests on an instrumentalization of rights and constitutes a form of interference).

Still, the debate is bound to be complicated when the providers of information are nationals (George Washington's 'tools and dupes') who may have their own domestic agendas even as they are willing to relay a foreign power's propaganda, or members of diasporas who may, as seen previously, legitimately entertain relations with other sovereigns. It is this sort of concern that has long led to 'foreign agent' registration laws that require persons working for foreign powers to identify as such and whose lawfulness or legitimacy cannot be excluded a priori. The U.S. Foreign Agents Registration Act (FARA), which goes back all the way to 1930s fears about Nazi influence, requires '"agents of foreign principals" [...], who are engaged in covered activities, on behalf of their foreign principal' to register with the Department of Justice and disclose the nature of their relationships, including financial compensation.[1776] The Act did serve to prosecute 23 criminal cases during the war,[1777] although it then fell into desuetude. As a sign of how times have changed and how pregnant concerns about interference have become, its importance has been greatly revaluated, notably during the Trump administration. The normative incidence of FARA is that it does not police the content of expression but merely its origin, thus averting the Orwellian danger of making participation in political speech depend on its 'truthfulness'.

This practice has spread around the world over the decades, with clear 'cascading' effects in which policies are diffused transnationally through copying and adaptation. There is no reason to assume that copycat foreign agent registration initiatives will not be problematic. Most notoriously, Russia imposes onerous requirements on NGOs funded from abroad. Hungary's 'Transparency Act' also requires associations and foundations to apply to be on a special register if the foreign funding part of their budget exceeds approximately EUR 22,100 annually,[1778] and Israel's so-called 'NGOs Transparency Law' mandates that organisations which receive more than 50% of their funding from a foreign State or inter-State organisation must register this with the Ministry of Justice.[1779] Hungary, Kyrgyzstan, Slovakia, Ukraine and Georgia have also adopted equivalent legislation of their own.[1780] Foreign transparency requirements have been extended to a range of political activities. The Transatlantic Commission on Election Integrity has proposed a Pledge for Election Integrity whereby politicians commit not to aid and abet 'those who seek to undermine

1776 'US Attorneys' Manual: Foreign Agents Registration Act Enforcement' (*United States Department of Justice*, 7 December 2018) <https://www.justice.gov/archives/usam/criminal-resource-manual-2062-foreign-agents-registration-act-enforcement> accessed 8 February 2024.

1777 ibid.

1778 Law No LXXVI of 2017 on the Transparency of Organisations Financed from Abroad (*A külföldről támogatott szervezetek átláthatóságáról szóló 2017 évi LXXVI törvény*) (Hungary).

1779 Transparency Requirements for Parties Supported by Foreign State Entities Bill 5766-2016 (11 July 2016).

1780 Andrey Rikhter, '"Foreign Agents" in Media Regulation: Russia and Beyond' (2021) 64 Otázky žurnalistiky 12.

democracy',[1781] which targets those who might be tempted to become relays of foreign powers. The European Union has created a Transparency Register[1782] and the European Parliament has tightened its rules requiring its members to declare outside income over €5,000, potential conflicts of interests, as well as any meetings notably with non-E.U. representatives related to parliamentary business.[1783]

In other words, contemporary Russian efforts to establish the origin of political participation are not isolated or at least as uniquely egregious as is sometimes suggested. The requirement of transparency is also one that has been touted more specifically in the information and media context[1784] where onerous registration obligations may nonetheless turn out to be problematic.[1785] Transparency, it is argued, can at least minimize the risk of astroturfing writ-large, by forcing propaganda agents to appear for who they are. Interestingly, private social media platforms such as TikTok have also used labels such as 'Russia state-controlled media' to describe RT postings (so-called 'pre-bunking').[1786] However, the shift towards policing 'inauthentic behavior' that 'mislead[s] people or Facebook […] [a]bout the identity, purpose or origin of the entity that they represent',[1787] still leaves many questions unanswered, somewhere between the requirement of truth and transparency.

Facebook, for example, insists that it does 'not allow entities to engage in, or claim to engage in foreign or government interference, which is Coordinated Inauthentic Behavior conducted on behalf of a foreign or government actor'.[1788] Yet Facebook will also not police specific content or even the origin

---

1781 'The Pledge for Election Integrity' (*Election Pledge*) <https://www.electionpledge.eu/> accessed 5 September 2023.

1782 Justin Greenwood and Joanna Dreger, 'The Transparency Register: A European Vanguard of Strong Lobby Regulation?' (2013) 2 Interest Groups & Advocacy 139; Kim Fyhr, 'The Reform of the E.U. Transparency Register' (2021) 17 Croatian Yearbook of European Law & Policy 177.

1783 European Parliament decision of 13 September 2023 on amendments to Parliament's Rules of Procedure with a view to strengthening integrity, independence and accountability (2023/2095(REG)).

1784 Fattal (n 1125).

1785 Nick Robinson, 'Foreign Agents in an Interconnected World: FARA and the Weaponization of Transparency' (2019) 69 Duke Law Journal 1075.

1786 David Klepper, 'TikTok Propaganda Labels Fall Flat in "huge Win" for Russia' *AP News* (30 March 2023) <https://apnews.com/article/tiktok-russia-propaganda-labels-ukraine-kremlin-china-88ecd866a2c34218ebbaccb45e435c12> accessed 12 July 2024.

1787 'Inauthentic Behaviour' (*Transparency Center—Meta*) <https://transparency.fb.com/en-gb/policies/community-standards/inauthentic-behavior/> accessed 19 December 2023.

1788 ibid.

of postings as much as behavior that it judges suspicious. Indeed, it is often not the content of postings that is per se objectionable but, at best, the fact that what is spread is part of campaigns orchestrated by foreign actors. Even that, however, may prove difficult to prove given the voluntary and decentralized nature of much online reposting. This is not to mention concerns about making Facebook, a private company with monopolistic tendencies, the arbiter of what is problematic online interference.

There is certainly still a strong residual argument that, *de minimis*, the origin of influence in a state's political system should be clarified and that this can be done whilst maintaining a commitment to an open society. Individuals or groups who work surreptitiously for a foreign power are *de facto* lying about a key element that would allow democratic institutions to process their contributions. Democratic participation, in that respect, has a performative element: what matters is not only what is said, but who says it. It is not that foreign powers cannot under any circumstances have a say in the public life of other states; their leaders, might, for example and under the right conditions, speak directly to a foreign population; they might certainly say things in ways that ought to be unobjectionable. Nonetheless, for all the talk about the increasingly transnational moorings of democratic life, a sense of who is a legitimate member of the *civis* and who is not is surely an important ingredient for the purposes of public debate. Knowing that an argument (which on its face may be perfectly innocuous) is made directly at the instigation or for the benefit of a foreign power will be key to assessing its value, regardless of any inherent truth. In some cases, failure to disclose that one is working for a foreign government is clearly linked to the clandestine and subversive nature of the activities (as in the case of the 'Cuban five' who were convicted under, among others, FARA).

Foreign registration requirements stand to shape a particular conception of democracy at home. They send a strong signal to the local public when it comes to media networks such as RT America (now registered as a Russian agent) or the Xinhua News Agency and China Global Television Network (registered Chinese agents)[1789] that these are a very specific type of news providers. Transparency requirements could lead to the outlawing of some anonymous donations or ads. For example, in Israel, a judge barred anonymous ads ahead of elections in a judgment that also mandated identifying fake accounts.[1790]

1789 Bill Allison and Chris Strohm, 'US Orders Chinese Media to Register as Foreign Agents, Source Says' *Bloomberg.com* (18 September 2018) <https://www.bloomberg.com/politics/articles/2018-09-18/chinese-media-said-ordered-by-u-s-to-register-as-foreign-agents> accessed 2 April 2024.

1790 Staff (n 401).

As Jens Ohlin has argued, a requirement of transparency speaks specifically to the nature of the harm of interference as corrupting self-determination, rather than requiring a response based on the notion that a state has been 'coerced'.[1791]

3.3 *The Limits of Transparency*

Nonetheless, there have long been concerns about how transparency requirements can be implemented and what they mean more generally for democracy. To begin with, significant loopholes remain that make it relatively easy in various jurisdictions to pretend to be other than one is, notably when it comes to political financing. For example, FARA had a loophole until 1974 that allowed foreign contributions as long as not made through an agent operating in the U.S. enabling the Greek dictatorship to donate to Nixon's campaign. In India, foreign donors, including foreign companies, could, until the law was struck down by the Supreme Court of India,[1792] donate to Indian political parties by purchasing anonymous electoral bonds,[1793] effectively making it impossible to know the source of such foreign, often digital donations. In the U.K., even though funding from foreign states to political parties was banned by the Political Parties, Elections and Referendums Act of 2000, that law is said to allow for various loopholes such as funding from U.K.-registered companies that draw significant profits from abroad or the use of 'unincorporated associations'.[1794] In Australia, there have been concerns that, whilst Confucius Institutes' funding source are reported to the Department of Foreign Affairs and Trade under the Foreign Arrangements Scheme, they are not made public, despite a recommendation to that effect by the Inquiry into national security risks affecting the Australian higher education and research sector.[1795]

Of course, soliciting foreign donations may be criminalized (as in FARA since the 1960s, which targets U.S. companies) but there is no doubt that there

1791 Ohlin, 'Election Interference: A Unique Harm Requiring Unique Solutions' (n 1105).

1792 *Association for Democratic Reforms v Union of India* [2024] 2 SCR 420.

1793 The Indian electoral bonds scheme has recently been the object of a case in front of the Supreme Court of India, which determined its unconstitutionality. See 'Electoral Bonds' (*Supreme Court Observer*) <https://web.archive.org/web/20231127180413/https://www.scobserver.in/cases/association-for-democratic-reforms-electoral-bonds-case-background/> accessed 2 February 2024.

1794 John Johnston, 'Britain's Political Parties Are Quietly Raking in Millions. No One Will Say Where It's Coming from' *POLITICO* (8 June 2023) <https://www.politico.eu/article/how-to-pump-cash-into-british-politics-without-anybody-knowing-about-it/> accessed 28 August 2023.

1795 Parliamentary Joint Committee on Intelligence and Security (n 737) xvi.

is a demand as well as a supply side to such funding which points to its sustained character and the occasional deep imbrication of foreign and domestic interests. As a result, compulsory disclosure has occasionally been criticized as no panacea. To begin with, the point of influence-seeking in many foreign elections is that it often does not seek to hide itself and operates relatively publicly and legally, funnelling millions of dollars in plain view to lobbyists who plead their clients' case to the relevant political authorities.[1796] The fact that one registers as a foreign agent may thus change little to one's ability to donate to political campaigns.[1797] The line between lobbying, financially contributing, and even bribing as a way of buying influence may also be a fine one.[1798] That lobbyists, in fact, engage in influencing on behalf of foreign clients 'outside normal diplomatic channels' is so unobjectionable, that the argument barely needs to be made in international and domestic law that it is legal, even as such activities raise genuine political concerns.[1799]

Most importantly, foreign registration legislation has been criticized for its often fundamentally illiberal character, despite its stated intention of protecting the public sphere. The clearest example of foreign registration being taken too far is Russia, where being registered as foreign comes with onerous accounting obligations and allows the government to 'identify[...], label [...] and segregat[e] different types of NGOs [...] and degrad[e] and stigmatis[e] them via inspections, fines, juridical procedures and reputational damage' as 'deviant organisations'.[1800] This, in turn, rewards 'docile NGOs that adhere to disciplinary measures by, for example, providing them with government grants and enabling them to opt out from the 'foreign agents' register once they stop receiving foreign funding'.[1801] It leads to a broader strategy of

1796 Anu Narayanswamy, 'International Influence: Agents of Foreign Clients Report Thousands of Lobbying Contacts, Millions in Fees' (*Sunlight Foundation*, 21 September 2016) <https://sunlightfoundation.com/2010/12/02/top-players-2009/> accessed 2 February 2024.

1797 Anna Massoglia, 'Foreign Lobbyists Gave Millions to Influence 2020 Elections amid Foreign Influence Concerns' (*OpenSecrets News*, 19 August 2021) <https://www.opensecrets.org/news/2021/08/foreign-lobbyists-gave-millions-to-influence-2020-foreign-influence-concerns/> accessed 6 September 2024.

1798 Ben Freeman, *The Foreign Policy Auction: Foreign Lobbying in America* (CreateSpace 2012).

1799 Joe Oliver, 'Canada's Elections Are Already Being Infiltrated by Foreign Interests and, Shockingly, It's All Legal' *Financial Post* (16 May 2017) <https://financialpost.com/opinion/joe-oliver-canadas-elections-are-already-being-infiltrated-by-foreign-interests-and-shockingly-its-all-legal> accessed 25 September 2018.

1800 Galina Goncharenko and Iqbal Khadaroo, 'Disciplining Human Rights Organisations through an Accounting Regulation: A Case of the "Foreign Agents" Law in Russia' (2020) 72 Critical Perspectives on Accounting 102129.

1801 ibid.

co-optation of NGOs by the Russian government, where the latter's funding is substituted to that of the departed foreign donors (such as the U.S. Agency of International Development), with dramatic consequences for said organisations' independence.[1802]

Despite being in all likelihood in violation of international human rights requirements,[1803] and although it arguably creates conditions for a somewhat fruitful confrontation between civil society and state[1804] (and despite the possibility of some civil society ecosystem surviving against all odds),[1805] the law has persisted as a sword of Damocles over the head of civil society groups. The sheer vagueness of what constitutes 'political activity' has meant that NGOs can never be sure when or why they will be in the crosshairs of the authorities and thus are more likely to censor in relation to what ought to be innocuous activities. It *de facto* creates difficult binds for civil society groups who must decide whether to forfeit foreign funding or risk serious existential difficulties and are thus kept constantly on edge. In the process, it weakens solidarities between NGOs and their ability to offer a united front against the Russian state.[1806]

However, foreign agent registration requirements, which are widely denigrated when arising out of authoritarian cultures, clearly also have a potential for manipulation and instrumentalization in democracies. Just as one may need to acknowledge that laws such as the Russian one have some non-sinister motivations given the legitimacy of protecting sovereignty, one should not too readily assume that similar laws in the West are themselves free from the risk of authoritarian political manipulation.[1807] They will thus continue to be vulnerable to constitutional and international human rights challenges, in ways that caution against investing too much in them, and in favor of narrowing their application to only the most blatant cases of interference. There

---

1802 Suvi Salmenniemi, 'Civic Organizations and the State in Putin's Russia: Co-Operation, Co-Optation, Confrontation', *Civil Societies and Social Movements* (Routledge 2007); Alexander Nikitin and Jane Buchanan, 'The Kremlin's Civic Forum: Cooperation or Co-Optation for Civil Society in Russia?' (2002) 10 Demokratizatsiya 147.

1803 Alison Kamhi, 'The Russian NGO Law: Potential Conflicts with International, National, and Foreign Legislation' (2006) 9 International Journal of Not-for-Profit Law 34.

1804 Malcomson (n 1562) 146–150.Malcomson (n 1471) 146–150.

1805 Evelyn Moser and Anna Skripchenko, 'Russian NGOs and Their Struggle for Legitimacy in the Face of the "Foreign Agents" Law: Surviving in Small Ecologies' (2018) 70 Europe-Asia Studies 591.

1806 Françoise Daucé, 'The Duality of Coercion in Russia: Cracking Down on "Foreign Agents"' (2015) 23 Demokratizatsiya: The Journal of Post-Soviet Democratization 57.

1807 Robinson (n 1785); Rebo (n 1346).

has long been a concern, for example, that FARA can lead to what has been described as a 'weaponization of transparency' that makes it liable to being used against blameless nonprofits, especially if used to target disinformation.[1808] For example, the investigation by the House Committee on Natural Resources of tax-exempt organizations for manipulation by foreign entities on the basis that the latter sought to influence U.S. environmental policy (notably the Natural Resources Defense Council (NRDC) which was accused of unduly praising China at the expense of the U.S.).[1809] Arguing that 'China engages in an extensive perception-management campaign both domestically and internationally', it suspected the NRDC of 'aiding China's perception management efforts with respect to pollution control and its international standing on environmental issues in ways that may be detrimental to the United States', to the point of influence or coercion by foreign interests.[1810] The effort has been decried as little more than a 'witch hunt' and as hardly compatible with the independence of non-profits.[1811]

Furthermore, investigations by the DOJ of African Americans with leftist views in the wake of the Black Lives Matter movement have the potential to resuscitate the ghost of the earlier persecution of Du Bois.[1812] The general chilling effect and inherently problematic workability of U.S. foreign registration legislation, as a result, has been underlined by many civil society groups. In effect, foreign registration obligations require one to develop any one of: (i) a very neat distinction between what is foreign and domestic which may hardly be apposite in the case of transnational organizations making registration as a foreign actor 'unsuitable for our contemporary world—a world in which global interconnectivity is increasing and the roles of state and non-state actors are blurring';[1813] (ii) theories of the 'motivation' of such groups including whether they lean 'too much' towards a foreign power, even though such leaning may

1808 Robinson (n 1785).

1809 Jack Crowe, 'GOP Lawmakers Accuse Environmental Group of Aiding in Chinese Propaganda Efforts' (*National Review*, 7 June 2018) <https://www.nationalreview.com/news/gop-lawmakers-accuse-environmental-group-of-aiding-in-chinese-propaganda-efforts/> accessed 2 April 2024.

1810 Ibid.

1811 Brian Wanko, 'The Foreign Agents Registration Act's NGO Impact' (*InterAction*, 20 March 2019)<https://www.interaction.org/blog/the-foreign-agents-registration-acts-ngo-impact/> accessed 2 April 2024; 'EU Foreign Interference Law: Is Civil Society at Risk?' (*Netherlands Helsinki Committee*, 4 May 2023) <https://www.nhc.nl/eu-foreign-interference-law-is-civil-society-at-risk/> accessed 2 April 2024.

1812 Poirot and Shahshahani (n 1622).

1813 Wanko (n 1811).

simply be a function of their beliefs;[1814] and (iii) theories of principal-agent relations where the organization is, knowingly or even unknowingly, working at the behest of a foreign state (the U.S. FARA requires groups to register if they act 'at the [...] request [...] of a foreign principal or of a person any of whose activities are directly or indirectly, supervised, directed, controlled, financed, or subsidized in whole or in major part by a foreign principal').[1815]

This suggests that transparency is not the miracle cure that it is presented as being if the notion of a 'foreign agent' is itself so prone to abuse. It can lead to a culture of second guessing and suspicion that could be deeply debilitating of democratic arrangements, in the name of an arcane conception of sovereignty and democratic life as tightly bounded. A confluence of views between local and foreign actors is neither surprising nor suspicious and could be easily explained by innocent reasons that do not involve anything manipulative.[1816] For example, the fact that Earth Justice, a U.S. nonprofit environmental law firm, has advocated against relocating a U.S. base on Okinawa because of environmental concerns does not make that organization an agent of the Japanese government, simply because the latter also happens to oppose the relocation.[1817] Alignment is not always correlation, and correlation is not always causation.

Moreover, foreign registration laws may have a chilling effect on free speech by officially labeling some information as 'foreign' and denigrating it as such. In the Keene decision of the U.S. Supreme Court on Canadian NFB documentaries the plaintiff argued that, although the material was not censored, its labelling as 'foreign propaganda' was derogatory and would therefore impede him from exercising his right to share information.[1818] The Court nonetheless found that a mere label did not go too far in the direction of disclosure and fell short of infringing on the First Amendment.[1819] It may be that certain foreign influence is not welcome and that forcing it to reveal itself may have a salutary

1814 Timothy Cama, 'Top GOP Lawmaker Not Persuaded by Green Groups' Promises That They Aren't Foreign Agents' *The Hill* (28 June 2018) <https://thehill.com/policy/energy-environment/394717-top-gop-lawmaker-not-persuaded-by-green-groups-promises-that-they/> accessed 2 April 2024.

1815 22 USC § 611.

1816 Poirot and Shahshahani (n 1622).

1817 Emily Honstein, 'US Current Trend: Environmental Nonprofits Facing Lawfare Tactics' (*ICNL*, 15 October 2019) <https://www.icnl.org/post/analysis/environmental-nonprofits-facing-lawfare-tactics> accessed 2 April 2024.

1818 *Meese v Keene*, 481 U.S. 465 (1987).

1819 Ava Marion Plakins, 'Heat Not Light: The Foreign Agents Registration Act after Meese v. Keene Comment' (1987) 11 Fordham International Law Journal 184.

effect for democracy, but it may also have prejudicial consequences, for example a deterrent effect on domestic actors (who may consider that participating anonymously in the democratic debate is productive) and a paranoia about foreign authoritarian practices (as states see the hand of foreign states everywhere, and require foreign actors to register themselves).

And again, there is no reason to think that these risks will not manifest themselves as much in democracies, especially in a highly polarized and populist environment. In that respect, the possibility of moving to forms of restricted speech for foreign actors[1820] may have problematic repercussions for freedom of speech more generally. The emphasis on revealing one's identity may also impose a duty to identify themselves only on foreign agents, an obligation that typically does not apply to national actors, in ways that could be challenged as discriminatory. There may well be 'truth-saying' foreign agents, even as there is no shortage of perfectly 'national' participants in the democratic process who nonetheless make it their business to lie to the public. Strong associations between manipulation and foreignness may ultimately have debilitative effects on a culture of cosmopolitan openness. The problem of 'fake information', in the end, may well be a problem that international law can and ought to address,[1821] not least because of its implications for international peace and security,[1822] but that does not mean that non-interference is the appropriate prism to do so.

4 A Duty of Consistency?

Finally, one can conceptualize the normative underpinnings of strategizing about interference and non-interference as requiring a more fundamental attention to consistency. The consistency discussed here is not the vaunted but elusive consistency of rules between themselves[1823] or even of behavior and rules, but the consistency over time of various performative and symbolic investments in the rules. It refers to a sort of way of 'being in the law' that

1820 Matt A Vega, 'The First Amendment Lost in Translation: Preventing Foreign Influence in U.S. Elections after Citizens United v FEC' (2010) 44 Loyola of Los Angeles Law Review 951.

1821 Jingjin Huang, 'Information Warfare in the Digital Age: Legal Responses to the Spread of False Information under Public International Law' (2024) 28 Journal of Education, Humanities and Social Sciences 176.

1822 Hadi Salehi and Neda Kardouni, 'Fake News and Disinformation in the Perspective of International Peace and Security' (2023) 15 Journal of Legal Studies 321.

1823 Jaap Hage, 'Rule Consistency' (2000) 19 Law and Philosophy 369.

is non-contradictory and points to an ethos of good faith as a foundation of respect for international law. This dimension of consistency has been hinted at in the book so far, but in this sub-section the goal is to analyze its implications more systematically for our understanding of what passes and what ought to pass, at any given time, for unwanted, illegitimate, and ultimately illegal interference. The focus on consistency stresses the extent to which strategy is not only about achieving particular outcomes but also about structuring one's *rapport* to the law in ways that maximize its utility. It also connects agent-level concerns about optimal behavior with systemic concerns about the sustainability of the law, highlighting the very precarious relation between the two as a function of 'foreign legal policy'.[1824]

Consistency here can be understood as both horizontal and vertical. Horizontal consistency is the idea that one should not interfere with other states more than one is willing to be interfered with, or at least that one should be sensitive to the ways in which one interferes with the sovereign affairs of others will and ought to have consequences in terms of how much one can legitimately protest interference in one's affairs. This is the consistency, iterative and recursive, that shapes social expectations about how far one can reach to influence the affairs of equals. Vertical consistency refers to the idea that in promoting an international norm of non-interference in one's domestic affairs, one should be wary of how those efforts may interact with fundamental constitutional principles of one's own political organization: for example, when does promoting too much non-interference enter in tension with a domestic commitment to the open circulation of information? Ultimately this subsection will outline the extent to which the focus on consistency makes it possible to think about how claims of interference and non-interference constitute the sort of states that states want to be and how it is this, ultimately, that stands to structure the international law of non-intervention.

4.1 *Horizontal Consistency*

Horizontal consistency brings attention not only to the moral foundations of international law (one cannot expect of others what one is unwilling to concede to them), but also to its logical foundations. An interfering state is constantly undermining its very ability to protest interference in its own affairs by weakening the norm that it then seeks to invoke (as Thomas Franck and Edward Weisband pointed out long ago, '[i]t is not reasonable for the United States

---

1824 Mégret, 'Foreign Legal Policy as the Background to Foreign Relations Law? Revisiting Guy de Lacharrière's La Politique Juridique Extérieure' (n 78).

to expect Russia to refrain from acting on principles that we have espoused, or to abide by principles that we have declared inapplicable to our own conduct').[1825] Of course, one should not underestimate the relative shamelessness of states when it comes to complaining of the very behavior that they themselves have engaged in. For example, it was the USSR that put on the General Assembly's agenda 'The inadmissibility of intervention in the domestic affairs of States and the protection of their independence and sovereignty' after it had itself invaded both Hungary and Czechoslovakia. States have not exactly been frozen in their tracks because the hypocrisy of their international law stances have been exposed. It remains that, on a more fundamental normative level, one cannot have it both ways, not only because it is wrong but because it creates the conditions of a performative contradiction: the norm of non-interference is only so strong, especially for oneself, as one is willing to uphold it in one's foreign policy.

The 'boomerang' effect of rhetorical investments in the norm is almost guaranteed over time. In lowering the standard of what constitutes coercion, for instance, one has to be ready that others will also expect to be able to lower their own threshold: if propagating fake news in U.S. elections is coercive interference, then why should subsidizing liberal human rights NGOs in Russia not also be coercive? If the European Council can ban RT France, then why cannot Russia cut access to the BBC and Deutsche Welle on the basis that they spread 'false information' and 'anti-Russian' views?[1826] If states are serious about allowing corporate financing of elections abroad (for example, on account of the need to promote democracy in authoritarian states), then should they not, logically, be ready to allow it at home?[1827] It will be hard for states to complain of interference if they are previously on the record arguing that a certain type of behavior, when engaged by them, is not interference. It may be that such tit-for-tat is based on a false or misleading analogy and the point here does not relate to the ultimate merits of these contentions; but one must concede

1825 Franck and Weisband (n 4) 1014.

1826 'Russian Anger after E.U. Court Upholds Ban on RT' *France 24* (27 July 2022) <https://www.france24.com/en/live-news/20220727-russian-anger-after-eu-court-upholds-ban-on-rt> accessed 17 December 2023.

1827 For a rejection of the notion that the type of regime should make any difference to whether foreign political financing is allowed, see Powell (n 824) 988–990. (Noting that 'If governments are concerned that this would result in business exercising an undue amount of influence on the political process, then these countries should prohibit all corporate donations, regardless of their sources, and move towards a system of publicly financed election campaigns.').

that the politics of that analogy are precisely what is at stake rather than some improbable positivist interpretation of the law.

Similarly, as was long claimed by the Third World, it might be thought that the argument that states have no *a priori* obligation to engage with others is a high point of liberal classicism, one that is deeply inimical to the construction of an international legal order based on interdependence and solidarity. But note that the argument based on a duty to engage can also work both ways, including to the detriment of the Global South. It must be remembered that one of the foundational acts of decolonization was the proclamation of sovereignty over natural resources, thereby depriving the West of much of the access to such resources in its previous colonies that it had until then taken for granted. That singular act of emancipation was also an emphatic affirmation that the Third World certainly did not owe its resources to the North and that describing this denial as a form of interference with the West would have been almost laughable. Vulnerability to this sort of counter-argument, then, is certainly not all there is to international law but it can act as a powerful constraint on state behavior as Thomas Franck and Edward Weisband had intuited in their influential 'Verbal Strategies Among the Superpowers'.[1828] It may counsel against making too strident an argument for uninterrupted relations, for example, lest that claim be turned against oneself.

There are short term and long-term costs to being caught red-handed in the midst of contradiction, rhetorical or performative. For example, the Soviet Union exposed itself to significant legal discredit when it argued that Czechoslovak affairs were being interfered with by U.N. scrutiny, right after it had denied that Spain's or the Netherlands (in relation to Indonesia) were. Similarly, the tendency of colonial powers to support each other on mutually incompatible grounds should have created pause for thought: Belgium, for example, in flagrant contradistinction to its own thesis that colonial possessions could not be abstracted from international scrutiny merely by conferral of metropolitan status, opportunistically supported Portugal when it voted against General Assembly Resolution 1542 which made exactly the opposite claim. In other words, the political solidarity of colonial states was, unsurprisingly, stronger than their adherence to particular lines of legal thought about what constituted colonies or not. As Inis Claude put it, the point was that 'the colonial powers opted for a higher consistency [note: than that of legal arguments]—a consistent effort to find some shelter behind the wall of

1828 Franck and Weisband (n 414).

domestic jurisdiction from the winds of anticolonialism which had been funneled through the United Nations'.[1829]

States will ordinarily weather the charge of hypocrisy, which at times seems too woven into the fabric of international relations to make much of a dent. Nonetheless, they will also occasionally reach a point of no-return when, having staked their entire policy on a certain doctrinal claim, they then endorse the opposite position at considerable risk. Only historical amnesia will then sometimes save them from ridicule—but the exposure of deep contradictions between positions over time is a considerable risk to the ability to conduct one's foreign legal policy. This suggests a key dimension of strategizing about interference claims over time, in that every allegation of rule conformity or violation, especially in a decentralized system like international law, stands to over-determine the norm's content. It also suggests that in jostling for sustainable positions within the law, states need to arbitrate both between their interests, across time, and in relation to diversified constituencies, in conditions of imperfect information where they may never fully know in advance what position will effectively best promote their national interest on the long run. This is no apology for legal manipulation, but rather a reflection of how international law is what states make of it, and a recognition that what they make of it is structured by sometimes contradictory impulses.

Of course, consistency is always possible, but it comes at a cost that must also be reckoned with. States that claim that their desisting from relations through unilateral sanctions is *not* interference, for example, must be willing to forfeit such claims when they are themselves the target of disengagement. For example, when Canada was faced with a Saudi government-mandated massive pullout of its students from Canadian universities following declarations by the then Canada Foreign Minister that were deemed obnoxious by the Saudis, Canada did not try to make the argument that Saudi Arabia had some sort of obligation to maintain those students in place or that Saudi Arabia was somehow interfering in Canadian affairs (although it was certainly being inimical).[1830] This would have gone against the creed that no set level of engagement is ever owed to another state, outside of course an international legal obligation to do so. But forfeiting that claim clearly made Canada vulnerable to

1829 Claude, Jr (n 312) 132.

1830 Steven Chase, 'Saudi Arabia Withdrawing Students from Canadian Schools, Suspending Flights' *The Globe and Mail* (6 August 2018) <https://www.theglobeandmail.com/canada/article-saudi-arabia-to-withdraw-all-saudi-students-studying-at-canadian/> accessed 28 February 2024.

the pull-out, with little legal edge against a very prejudicial move. Consistency was paid at the cost of effectivity.

It remains that the adoption of certain arguments compromises one's ability to credibly make counter arguments at a later point; one is always, in short, at risk of being trapped by one's past rhetorical investments. States, perhaps riveted by a certain vision of the sort of interference they might be subject to, can in some cases end up producing such clear indictments of interference that they may compromise their ability to engage in similar behavior.[1831] Consider, for example, how France's claims that the Algerian war fell within its domestic affairs can be put in resonance with France's subsequently aggressive stance towards human rights violations committed by other states as part of a hypothetical 'droit d'ingérence'; or how the Third World's sacralization of the principle of self-determination to oppose interference has in some ways laid the groundwork for increasingly invasive claims from the outside based, precisely, on realizing that self-determination by supporting rebels or NGOs; or how the West's opposition to expansive conceptions of non-interference in the 70s and 80s is now paid at the cost of conceptual contortions when it comes to fighting back electoral interference by Russia or China; or how OPEP's insistence that it could turn off the oil tap on without engaging in interference might resonate decades later when the Global South would in turn complain of unilateral measures to punish it for violating human rights; or how traditional Global South complaints about unilateral economic sanctions seem to have fallen off the way side when Gulf states imposed sanctions against Qatar.

Over time, states find themselves surprisingly often on both sides of arguments for which they have previously registered strong opinions and from which it may be difficult to extricate themselves without losing face. In that respect, temporally inconsistent and asymmetrical propositions, where one state expects a strong ability to interfere with the sovereign affairs of others but denies that possibility to other states, are fundamentally vulnerable and are not salvaged by the supposedly more liberal or human rights-oriented nature of one's ambitions. For example, there is a certain irony in how Western states who have long opposed the notion that mere 'pressure' can constitute coercive interference in the economic realm are now so keen to argue that any 'disruption' to democracy or even compromission of the national character of the economy does qualify as such: over time, it is difficult to both ramp-up

1831 See Lahmann (n 322) 209. (Noting that 'Strikingly, if perhaps not at all surprisingly, the clearest qualification of foreign influence as generally being in conflict with international law has come from some of the countries that are most frequently accused of engaging in adversarial information operations themselves').

and dilute the conditions for what qualifies as interference. Indeed, questions of interference raise particularly acute dilemmas for societies that have long professed imperial ambitions but no longer have a monopoly on interference and seek to jealously protect a newly rediscovered *domaine réservé*, just as they raise questions for emerging powers that must shed part of their traditional investment in non-interference to free up their foreign policy's assertiveness.

Consistency, at least on a rhetorical level, is of course not simply a *vue de l'esprit*. It involves demands of non-contradiction made to any given locutor over time. It also involves a fundamental demand for equal treatment that resonates strongly with core concepts of international law such as sovereignty: if sovereignty is worth anything normatively, it is because, whatever its content and evolving interpretation at any given point in history, it is at least notionally the same sovereignty for all. This then leads to a rich vein of proclamations of at least nominal consistency in one's policy towards interference. Consider the classic case of the French revolution. The French Constitution of 1791 proclaimed that '[l]a Nation française renonce à entreprendre aucune guerre dans la vue de faire des conquêtes, et n'emploiera jamais ses forces contre la liberté d'aucun peuple'.[1832] The logic was, perfectly consistent in theory, that if '[Le peuple français] ne s'immisce point dans le gouvernement des autres Nations' then 'il ne souffre pas que les autres nations s'immiscent dans ses affaires'.[1833] The décret de la Convention of 13 April 1793 went even further, almost suggesting that its non-interference was only a *quid pro quo* for non-interference in its own affairs, noting that the Republic:

> ne s'immiscera en aucune manière dans le gouvernement des autres puissances; mais elle déclare en même temps qu'elle s'ensevelira plutôt sous ses propres ruines, que de souffrir qu'aucune puissance s'immisce dans le régime intérieur de la République, ou influence la création de la constitution qu'elle veut se donne.[1834]

Or consider, today, China's norm entrepreneurship around a strong reciprocal non-interference commitment (China will not interfere nor be interfered with).[1835] Superficial as it may be, it at least manages to offer strong and

1832 Constitution de 1791, ch 5, title 6.

1833 Acte constitutionnel du 24 juin 1793, art 119 (France).

1834 Cited in Jean-Baptiste Duvergier (ed), *Collection Complète Des Lois, Décrets, Ordonnances, Règlemens et Avis Du Conseil d'état (de 1788 à 1830 Inclusivement, Par Ordre Chronologique)*, vol 5 (A Guyot et Scribe 1834) 248.

1835 Zheng (n 326).

intuitive legibility for foreign partners. Strict non-interference may prosper in typically regional archipelagoes of like-minded states; and, paradoxically, it is not incompatible with the investment in international organizations that are themselves committed to non-interference.[1836]

Of course, there is often a gap between the rhetoric of non-interference and the reality of practices: 'champions' of non-interference in multilateral fora (the Soviet Union comes to mind) have evidently sometimes been strongly invested in remarkably heavy-handed patterns of actual interference.[1837] China's own actual practice has seemed to evolve away from its stated commitment to rigid non-interference.[1838] At the same time, states who engage in such inconsistencies (between different positions over time) and double standards (between the standards they apply to themselves and expect of others or between different others) expose themselves to having handed their enemies the tools to castigate them with. This will create tensions—minimal possibly, but genuine—over time to either adapt behavior or change one's normative stance to reduce that dissonance to the extent it is understood as a vulnerability. To suggest that international law emerges as a kind of self-regulated system that over time will strive to reduce dissonance is surely an exaggeration; but nor should one deny the vulnerability of state policy to being exposed as, perhaps systematically, fraudulent. Such constraints on the sort of horizon of consistency that states (must) strive for, then, point to a basic grammar of living by the law in international relations that cannot be easily ignored.

4.2 *Vertical Consistency*

Vertical consistency, by contrast, poses the question of the compatibility of foreign and domestic policy when it comes to non-interference. It raises particularly acute dilemmas for societies that are committed domestically to conditions of openness but nonetheless seek to protect their domestic affairs from interference. Hidden dangers are numerous as every move to shut down interference risks harming some of the very interests that interference is supposed to protect. The sort of hesitation this can lead to is illustrated in the European

---

1836 Ramcharan R, 'ASEAN and Non-Interference: A Principle Maintained' (2000) Contemporary Southeast Asia 60.

1837 Moore (n 714).

1838 Harry Verhoeven, 'Is Beijing's Non-Interference Policy History? How Africa Is Changing China' (2014) 37 The Washington Quarterly 55; Daniel Large, 'China & the Contradictions of "Non-Interference" in Sudan' (2008) 35 Review of African Political Economy; Alexandra Victorovna Khudaykulova, 'China as an Emerging Actor in Conflict Management: From Non-Interference in Internal Affairs to "Constructive" Engagement' (2019) 19 Vestnik RUDN. International Relations 420; Hirono, Jiang and Lanteigne (n 516).

Parliament's finding that 'it is key to ensure that democratic processes are not captured by private and external interests' but also that 'the ability of interest and group representatives to influence decision-making in Parliament by way of arguments is a vital part of European democracy'.[1839] Such dilemmas raise mixed questions of international and constitutional law. Reactions to the threat of the new interference range from under to over reaction, at the cost of significant disruption to self-determination, democracy, and human rights. One question, invariably, will be the extent to which governments can have it both ways on that axis as well, maintaining both conditions of non-interference and openness.

In addition to this vertical axis, note that there are further linkages between certain foreign policy aspirations and domestic principles when it comes to interference. Resisting interference is not simply a matter of general international law but also affects ways in which rights are protected at home (itself also increasingly an international law question).There is evidence that some states will shy from heavily protecting their own democratic sphere, lest this be held against them as part of allegations they are interfering in the affairs of other states.[1840] In at least consistently promoting openness, they may be able to mount a more powerful argument that they are not interfering in the affairs of others. As one U.S. official put, in rejecting the possibility of any bilateral deal with Russia over non-interference, '[t]he U.S. doesn't want to get into the world where we are censoring the U.S. press for things we view as investigative journalism but the Russians see as interference'.[1841] In other words, the goal of achieving reciprocal commitments is not such that it should lead one party to sacrifice something domestic that is evidently dear to it.

One should acknowledge, of course, that there is no necessary humility about getting the policy mix right in the process of resisting interference. The European Union in particular is adamant that precisely what distinguishes its own brand of non-interference is that 'the E.U. and its Member States are demonstrating their capacity to tackle this scourge while safeguarding and reinforcing the core principles of their democracies, including respect for fundamental rights and open democratic debate'.[1842] Nonetheless, it is clear that the new interference tests the compatibility, within liberal polities, between a

1839 2023 Resolution on Foreign Interference in the E.U. (n 335), para BR.

1840 Venice Commission (n 1191), para 23 (pointing out that some states 'seem to have deliberately avoided enacting legislation on prohibition in order to politically facilitate their own support of political movements in the Third World').

1841 Cited in Hudson (n 868).

1842 Jones (n 495) 10.

traditional commitment to sovereignty on the one hand, and to an open society and respect for liberties on the other. In that respect, polities that lean authoritarian at least have the advantage that their stated policy of non-interference is at one with their desire to maintain an uncontested hold on power at home by limiting contacts with the outside world; there is much less of a tension there.

In liberal leaning systems, or so the argument goes, so long as human rights provide the fundamental justification both for and to limit non-interference initiatives, then they will be broadly consonant with international law. Still, as has been seen, some non-interference laws in the West have long been decried as illiberal or undemocratic, or as undermining freedom of speech and political dissent, essentially overshooting in their eagerness to combat real or imagined interference.[1843] In that respect, interference may lay a trap for societies that pride themselves in their liberal principles, the trap that excessive remedies will lead to self-inflicted wounds. States, notably democracies, may engage in 'impulsive overcompensation' following episodes of perceived interference that lead them to needlessly cordon themselves off from their exterior and sometimes turn on themselves with a vengeance, possibly even exposing minorities to retaliation and stigma.[1844]

An extreme perversity would be if liberal societies, often tempted by their own authoritarian tendencies and more fragile than they appear, were to identify their openness and general valuation of freedoms as their key weakness in the international interference game. It may be that this is, in fact, precisely the goal of authoritarian interference: to activate a sort of self-destructive reflex in target societies that mistake their own defences for the problem as part of an indiscriminating auto-immune response. This is not to mention contagion effects given that efforts to curtail interference have broader structural ramifications for the international legal order. The response of liberal states, notably, may be eagerly awaited by more authoritarian-leaning ones to justify some of their own enterprises.

The key question, then, is how states steer the twin dangers of remaining steadfastly committed to their domestic principles at the risk of exposing themselves to further interference internationally or, conversely, compromise on their own principles to better insulate themselves from interference at significant domestic political cost. Some measures, such as the basic securitization of one's electoral infrastructure, do not seem to raise any particular concerns. The more one moves away from protecting 'elections' to protecting

1843 Head (n 1545).
1844 Mack (n 1362).

'democracy', however, the more situations may arise where that protection becomes heavy handed or otherwise inopportune. One of the ironies of the response to the 'new interference', for example, is that it occurs against a normative background in which Western promoters of human rights have long emphasized the centrality of freedom of expression and, indeed, what is sometimes imagined as its corollary, namely a right to receive information. Specifically, the U.S. has long stood for a particularly broad understanding of freedom of expression, including, incidentally, as it applies to non-natural legal persons (e.g., corporations). This has often been defended by invoking broad conceptions of the 'marketplace of ideas'.[1845] It has also been promoted internationally and formed the backbone of justifications for transnational liberal propaganda. One may therefore expect some tension between that commitment and moves to simultaneously establish a kind of 'political protectionism' from outside influences.

The costs at home of pursuing a vigorous non-interference policy, in fact, are potentially not negligible. The risk is that an overreaction may severely curtail domestic liberties and the very democratic institutions that non-interference measures seek to protect. In targeting *democracy* rather than the state, the 'new interference' also plays on a fundamental liberal vulnerability: whereas the sovereign, traditionally the primary beneficiary of the norm of non-intervention, is in its role when restricting outside flows, democracy, by contrast, requires a broad opening of channels of information and communication. This is not meant of course as an open invitation for foreign actors to interfere, but it does involve exposing oneself willingly and fairly constantly to outside influences (authoritarian states do not have that problem as much since they control the channels of access to information, but obviously at significant costs to their population). The reality *is* that it is some societies' very open character that makes them vulnerable to interference,[1846] and that it may be difficult to see how they can deal with that interference without mortally wounding that definingly open character.

In fact, one compelling view of the toxic character of the 'new interference' is that it may force an 'own goal', the self and gratuitously inflicted wound of states adopting exceptional measures to protect democracy that ironically end

1845 For example David Johnston emphasizes that '[r]obust protection for freedom of thought, belief, opinion, and expression means that discerning what is true and what is dis- or misinformation is predominantly left to what is sometimes referred to as the marketplace of ideas', Johnston (n 352) 13.

1846 ibid 12–13. ('[T]he openness of our democracy and media also provides an ideal forum for foreign actors that wish to disrupt our democratic process').

up undermining that very democracy.[1847] Foreign interference at times seems like it is destined to make liberal democracies trip and expose their ambiguities and their fragilities, perhaps of course because lurking beneath them has always been an authoritarian temptation. Ironically, following the ban of RT France, it is a Kremlin spokesperson who insisted that 'Europeans are trampling on their own ideals'.[1848] By contrast, the general thrust of human rights protections when it comes to the media and access to information is to typically leave the door wide open. The wariness with how curtailing 'foreign propaganda' might end up hampering cherished freedoms at home is an old one and exposes real disagreements between conceptions of liberal democracy that emphasize its internal resilience, and those that focus on its external vulnerabilities. As such, it may reactivate old debates about the extent to which democracies should be ready and willing to 'militantly' defend themselves against enemies of democracy,[1849] even at the cost of some compromises with principles.

The continued and even dogged embrace of both a culture of rights and openness has nonetheless long structured some liberal states' approach to interference. Truman's civil rights committee noted that it was 'as eager to guarantee [the civil rights of Communists and Fascists] as those of the people they attack',[1850] and defended freedom of expression as:

> an expression of confidence in the ability of freemen to learn the truth through the unhampered interplay of competing ideas. Where the right is generally exercised, the public benefits from the selective process of winnowing truth from falsehood, desirable ideas from evil ones. If the people are to govern themselves their only hope of doing so wisely lies in the collective wisdom derived from the fullest possible information, and in the fair presentation of differing opinions.[1851]

Writing in 1950 Arthur E Sutherland noted that '[e]xposure by eager and shrewd journalists, inquests by congressional committee, trials [...]—these

1847 Sarah Sorial, Shireen Morris and Peter Greste, 'Foreign Interference and the Incremental Chilling of Free Speech' (2024) 52 Federal Law Review 103.

1848 'Russian Anger after E.U. Court Upholds Ban on RT' (n 1826).

1849 Karl Loewenstein, 'Militant Democracy and Fundamental Rights, I' (1937) 31 American Political Science Review 417; Patrick Macklem, 'Militant Democracy, Legal Pluralism, and the Paradox of Self-Determination' (2006) 4 International Journal of Constitutional Law 488.

1850 President's Committee on Civil Rights and Wilson (n 1743) 51.

1851 ibid 47.

and like measures may more adequately show to the people of the country what is genuine and what is spurious in sponsorship'.[1852] More recently, the European Parliament has stressed that, for all the worrisome trend towards information manipulation and its framing as a security issue, 'high-quality, sustainably and transparently financed, and independent news media and professional journalism [...] are [...]the best antidote to disinformation'.[1853]

Contra this more liberal tendency, however, there have also long been calls emphasizing the special nature of the threat interference poses for democracy to justify making exceptions to the wide availability of information and opinions. In the 1950s, the President's Committee on Civil Rights, even as it sought to guard against an anti-Communist 'state of near hysteria [that] now threatens to inhibit the freedom of genuine democrats', did highlight the relevance of the 'clear and present danger' doctrine as a possible ground to curtail expression.[1854] The rhetoric is one characteristic of militant democracy: 'To expect people to reject totalitarians, when we do not provide mechanisms to guarantee that essential information is available, is foolhardy'.[1855] In the event, the outcome was McCarthyism which stemmed from the perceived need to stamp out Soviet interference, one of the worst descents into illiberality of the Post-War U.S.

In the response to the latest round of foreign interference in the West, there have been concerns that legislative measures to curtail it may have a widespread negative incidence on rights. After recognizing that '[f]oreign interference in democratic and electoral processes is a serious issue that threatens some of the most precious civil liberties: the right to vote and to representational democracy', for example, a consortium of Australian civil rights NGOs insisted in a submission to the Parliamentary Joint Committee on Intelligence and Security that:

> legislative response must be proportional to the nature of the threat, and it is not clear from the Bill [...] what increased threats of foreign interference have been raised in relation to Australian elections and democratic processes that might explain the introduction of much broader offences which, in many instances, carry increased and very serious penalties.[1856]

1852 Arthur E Jr Sutherland, 'Freedom and Internal Security' (1951) 64 Harvard Law Review 383, 385.

1853 2022 Resolution on Foreign Interference in the E.U. (n 337), para R.

1854 President's Committee on Civil Rights and Wilson (n 1743) 49.

1855 ibid 51.

1856 NSW Council for Civil Liberties and others, 'Submission to PJCIS Inquiry into the National Security Legislation Amendment (Espionage and Foreign Interference) Bill 2017' (2018)

Of particular concern were a set of new secrecy offences described as 'unwarrantedly and dangerously expansive, excessively punitive and lack[ing] necessary clarity', with potential chilling effects for the press, whistleblowers and democracy.[1857] In that respect, it must surely be a cause of concern that such encroachments on liberties in reacting to interference seem to loosely mimic some of the strong Russian or Chinese response to civil society interference that Western states have so vigorously deplored.

4.3 *Beyond Consistency: On Seeing Oneself in the Mirror*

Moreover, calls for restricting foreign interference may ultimately be a case of not liking what one sees in the mirror, to the extent that what is perceived as problematic about such interference are, in fact, questionable developments within democratic processes themselves. The destabilization of Western democracies, for one thing, only occurs because Western democracies are eminently destabilizable in the first place as a result of persistent tensions and inequalities. The debate on interference focuses the attention on shadowy manipulations imagined as coming from outside; but this occurs at a time when it is also domestic and equally shadowy manipulations that have reached new heights. For example, although Russian interference may be an ingredient in the corrosion of the political debate in Western democracies, that debate is already deeply corroded on its own terms and as a result of largely domestic factors to which foreign actors merely opportunistically graft themselves.[1858]

Interference may be very much a self-inflicted wound to the extent that it results from broader patterns of deregulation that have made corporate preying on democratic processes, *both from outside* but also *from within* only possible but likely. For example, in the U.S., the legacy of Dobbs in allowing PACs to invest almost unlimited amounts in elections, the superficiality of the Lobbyist Disclosure Act of 1995, and the outdated character of FARA not only create loopholes within which foreign actors can engulf themselves, but have come to characterize the political system's proclivities more broadly as one open to the highest bidder. In some cases, the worst that can be said about foreign actors

4 <https://www.nswccl.org.au/submission_to_pjcis_inquiry_into_the_national_security_legislation_amendment_espionage_and_foreign_interference_bill_2017_february_2018> accessed 8 February 2024.

1857 ibid 6.

1858 W Lance Bennett and Steven Livingston, 'A Brief History of the Disinformation Age: Information Wars and the Decline of Institutional Authority' in Susana Salgado and Stylianos Papathanassopoulos (eds), *Streamlining Political Communication Concepts: Updates, Changes, Normalcies* (Springer International Publishing 2023).

is that they 'exploit' already gaping frailties in the domestic public discourse, rather than creating such frailties.[1859] To blame 'fake news' or the spread of conspiracy theories entirely on ill-intentioned foreign powers, then, is to risk fundamentally mistaking the nature of the problem. In the West, that misdiagnosis can lead to an underestimation of, for example, the centrality of far-right networks to the production of conspiratorial, inflammatory and racist content that has relatively little need for outside support. As noted, the concern is that:

> popular understandings of disinformation problems, along with the related solutions, tend to focus on the symptoms and not on the causes of contemporary communication disorders. Locating the trouble in social media, confused citizens, or with foreign governments fails to explain the deeper origins of the problem [namely] decades of capture and erosion of governing institutions by wealthy interests and aligned political elites who could never sell their actual agendas to the publics without increasing levels of propaganda and disinformation.[1860]

This raises the question of whether the problem was ever truly about *foreign* interference, or whether it is about interference *tout court* and, once one reaches that realization, whether interference is even apposite as a term altogether given the relative implausibility of the notion of interference 'from within'. 'Fake news' is fake news, whether it is produced in Moscow or somewhere in the U.S., by a foreign state or by a local individual troll.[1861] In the end, the question may well be whether there is anything specific to interference as a foreign phenomenon that is not already endemic to and problematic in democratic life. This makes quixotic efforts at guarding against foreign interference—notably the attempt by U.S. states to prevent Chinese nationals from buying land there—appear for what they are, namely 'a solution in search of a problem' when the real issue is that 'rapid increase over the last 15 years in agricultural land ownership by wealthy individuals, pension funds, and multinational corporations'.[1862]

1859 Aman Bajwa, 'Information Disorder, the Triumvirate, and COVID-19: How Media Outlets, Foreign State Intrusion, and the Far-Right Diaspora Drive the COVID-19 Anti-Vaccination Movement' (2021) 4 The Journal of Intelligence, Conflict, and Warfare 16.

1860 Bennett and Livingston (n 1858) 48.

1861 Hal Berghel, 'Oh, What a Tangled Web: Russian Hacking, Fake News, and the 2016 U.S. Presidential Election' (2017) 50 Computer 87.

1862 Blaise Malley, 'Do Laws Preventing Chinese from Buying U.S. Land Even Make Sense?' (*Responsible Statecraft*, 20 June 2023) <https://responsiblestatecraft.org/2023/06/20/whats-driving-surge-in-efforts-to-restrict-chinese-land-ownership/> accessed 23 September 2024.

The reality is that attempts to rig democratic systems—from without but, most likely, from within—have long characterized their evolution, as those in power try to manipulate rules to their benefit (through gerrymandering, corruption, partisan nominations or voter suppression). As Richard Falk put it already in 1966, 'it will appear that the most coercive forms of propaganda are not connected with the manipulation of foreign audiences but with the manipulation of domestic public opinion'.[1863] To oppose an imagined 'pure' domestic democracy to 'impure' foreign interference may, in addition to its undertone of xenophobia, fundamentally misunderstand what has made democracy vulnerable in the first place. As has been pointed out, it may simply be that '[w]hat foreign interests have learned is if they want to try to obtain influence in Washington, they ought to do it the same way that corporations do it'.[1864] In that respect, the effort to protect the integrity of the domestic political debate from outside interference may distract from a necessary conversation about the undermining of that debate from within.

Corporate pressures on public life may certainly come from abroad, but they have also long come from inside. Problems of inappropriate meddling might just as well be recharacterized as inappropriate lobbying generally. This could, but need not necessarily be, foreign.[1865] Fake news may be spouted by foreign vehicles, but it is also very much alive and relayed on social media in ways that are largely domestic or at least not distinctively foreign. What remains unclear, then, is what is specific about foreign political hacking and whether it is not being held to higher standards than the domestic political processes ever were or could be. Of course, it may still be that foreign actors should be held to different standards, but there is a constant risk of over-evaluating the specificity of foreign and public interference as opposed to very domestic and private disruption. Justifying that differential treatment may therefore require more work than is typically assumed, at least from the point of view of democracy rather than sovereignty. And, on the more liberal end of the spectrum,

---

1863 Falk, 'On Regulating International Propaganda' (n 1055) 624.

1864 Dan Froomkin, 'How Foreign Money Can Find Its Way Into Political Campaigns' *HuffPost* (18 July 2011) <https://www.huffingtonpost.com/2011/07/18/foreign-money-campaign-finance-lobbying_n_897189.html> accessed 28 September 2018.

1865 See, for example, on the margins of the pay-for-access scandal involving prominent members of the Chinese Canadian community: Robert Fife and Steven Chase, 'Lobbying Watchdog Probes Liberal "Pay-for-Access" Fundraisers' *The Globe and Mail* (27 October 2016) <https://www.theglobeandmail.com/news/politics/lobbying-watchdog-investigates-liberal-fundraisers/article32544638/> accessed 7 September 2023.

some authors hint at the possibility that foreign actors should be allowed to do whatever domestic actors are legally allowed to do: no more, certainly, but no less either. It is only when they cross the threshold of unauthorized activity (but such activity is unauthorized just as much for a range of domestic actors) that they can be found to have interfered.[1866]

One contribution of the 'new interference' debate, then, may be precisely relativizing the notion of *interference* (as, traditionally, specifically focused on inter-state coercion), and broadening the debate to a range of measures that are deemed inimical to sovereignty, self-determination, or democracy not so much by reason of their foreignness but of their *corrupting* nature. This could contribute to further eroding the internal/external, domestic/international, and even private/public divides that were so central to the conversation about intervention, for the benefit of an analysis that sees interference as arising 'all the time and everywhere' and having as its central stake the capture by external actors (foreign states but also, for example, corporate agents) of the public agenda. In effect, for example, voter suppression in the U.S. is as much if not more a consequence of laws making it harder for certain populations to vote than it is of misleading foreign propaganda by Russia;[1867] the obsessive and to some extent justified denunciation of the latter should not obfuscate the fact that the right to vote is also being threatened in very domestic ways. A recalibration may thus be overdue, one adopting a more comprehensive and earnest view of what threats truly weigh on democracy. This may already be evident in some of the European Union's initiatives, which have stressed that 'online manipulative practices' should be dealt with 'regardless of their origin'—i.e., including when they are fully domestic. The approach is one where it is merely the 'availability' of such practices that makes them tempting for outside powers.

But if that is the case, then it is highly unlikely that international law alone would have the response to that particular threat, as opposed to domestic and international law operating on a continuum to safeguard political processes from rampant privatization, information manipulation and, indeed, unwelcome foreign meddling as well. The problem of foreign interference, it turns out, is in reality much deeper than foreign interference. True, the latter may lead to a reinforcement of racist, antisemitic, anti-feminist, or anti-gender discourses, but those discourses almost always pre-exist and outlast their revival as a result of foreign meddling. A richer reflection on interference would

1866 Van de Velde (n 823).
1867 Ferro (n 986) 353.

therefore foreground the extent to which it is often culpably and objectively 'invited' from within as a result of fundamental political and democratic deficiencies on which it merely sheds a new light.[1868] It would also shed light on the painful ordinariness of private, transnational and internal interference.

1868 Richard L Hasen, 'How to Keep the Rising Tide of Fake News from Drowning Our Democracy' *The New York Times* (7 March 2022) <https://www.nytimes.com/2022/03/07/opinion/cheap-speech-fake-news-democracy.html> accessed 18 February 2024; Hans Kundnani, 'Foreign Interference Starts at Home' (*Foreign Policy*, 22 February 2024) <https://foreignpolicy.com/2020/02/24/russia-china-foreign-interference-starts-at-home-trump-sanders/> accessed 20 February 2024.

Conclusion: Routinized Interference: The Unravelling of Sovereignty?

This book has sought to put the debates on illegal interference within a broader historical and theoretical perspective in order to highlight what exactly is new about the current phase of seemingly conspicuous and ubiquitous meddling in the affairs of sovereign states. It has erred on the side of historical caution, highlighting deep continuities with previous instantiations of the debate, whilst also noting some elements of rupture. Its central intuition was that much can be gained by discussing the relevant issues in an integrated and interdisciplinary fashion in order to elucidate the contours of interference, but also to radicalize some underlying questions about international law and relations. The norm of non-intervention's precise dimensions have never been so intensely debated even as they remain, perhaps inevitably, elusive. Overall, however, it is hard to avoid a sense that such discussions are channelling tremendously urgent and elemental debates about the very nature not only of international relations and sovereignty but also democracy, self-determination and human rights. Both agendas of interference and non-interference as, essentially, two sides of the same coin, raise questions not only about themselves but about the entire edifice of international law in the process.

Far from *désuétude*, the norm of non-intervention is being rejuvenated by a new round of conversations that highlight its continued and, in truth, existential relevance for the international legal order. Indeed, towards the early 2020s, one senses a renewed appetite for reinstating the central value of the norm of non-intervention, as if to compensate earlier excesses that had perhaps too precociously dismissed its relevance. To be sure, the debate is as much a regional as it is a universal one, and much be gained by paying attention to how, for example, non-intervention is not what it was in Africa or Latin America, but still very much defining in Southeast Asia.[1869] The latest swing of the pendulum involves a sometimes bold reassertion of the resilience of the idea of non-intervention and its greater orientation towards the pluralist end of international society.[1870] This may be a development befitting a more

1869 Brooke Coe, 'Sovereignty Regimes and the Norm of Noninterference in the Global South: Regional and Temporal Variation' (2015) 21 Global Governance 275; Hitoshi Nasu, 'Revisiting the Principle of Non-Intervention: A Structural Principle of International Law or a Political Obstacle to Regional Security in Asia?' (2013) 3 Asian Journal of International Law 25.

1870 Roth, 'Democratization's Discontents' (n 559); Yue Wu (n 18).

 | DOI:10.1163/9789004532731_012

polyarchic world, one in which the decline of superpower dominance makes thinking in terms of old-fashioned unilateral intervention ever less plausible and appealing. It potentially reinstates a degree of regime neutrality or at least agnosticism and reverts to more elemental 'Montevideo' identifiers of effective rule as the markers of legitimate statehood, as opposed to compliance with a demanding compact of international values.

At the same time, the situation is less one of 'non-intervention winning over intervention than one of intensification of the claims being made in the name of both, perhaps as a global and legal manifestation of the oft deplored polarization of public debate. To be sure, claims on behalf of broad intervention, although they may have passed their point of highest popularity, recur and are reinvented in the process.[1871] In a world in which the norm of non-intervention is reflexively invoked at every turn, the most that may be said in the end is that at various junctions any given state may think it is not intervening in the affairs of other states, or that other states are intervening in its affairs. But at least, no state claims that they are intervening in the affairs of other states or fails to claim that others are when it suits it. This subjects claims to interference to the constant pressure of legal argumentation, in itself a salutary exercise that may be an improvement on grandstanding, "values" talk or the perceived needs of the system. But the rule of non-intervention, precarious such as it always was, has in the process been the object of significant normalization and even dilution. The decades long effort to ensure that intervention as a stylized claim in international law is restricted to purely coercive imposition has gradually been replaced by expansive claims against mere interference. This is the terrain that states henceforth confront and although it is very much *that*—the terrain within which their arguments must perforce unfold—it is as yet unclear whose designs are reinforced by a relatively expansive vision of non-interference.

Indeed, and most spectacularly, both the reassertion of the norm of non-intervention and claims to transcend it also sits oddly with a sense that its factual and normative predicates have never been more vacuous. The reflexive shield is now at risk, if not of protecting an empty shell, at least of being raised against a threat more diffuse and elusive than ever. There is a growing misfit between the norm of non-intervention as it has been bequeathed by the international law of an earlier era, and the reality of pervasive, low-level interference that escapes detection and falls through the cracks. If sovereignty is not what it seems and if its appeal is being normalized (a range of actors can be quasi-sovereign), then the concept's ability to distinguish meaningfully

1871 Emma van den Boogaard, 'Environmental Intervention: An Activist Idea or a Legal Tool? An Analysis of the Possibilities of Environmental Protection in Light of the Principle of Non-Intervention' [2024] Netherlands International Law Review.

between a domestic and a foreign sphere both descriptively and normatively will be significantly curtailed. This is bound to paradoxically not only further facilitate intervention, but also make it more difficult to point to what is actually wrong with it. It could lead to world configurations where interference is merely synonymous with power, to the point of normative absurdity. This is why the book has argued that we should take seriously the idea that a distinct norm of non-interference now shadows the norm of non-intervention. Although such a norm comes with its own challenges, it arguably enriches our ability to describe problematic behavior for what it is.

A mere nostalgic appeal to the Friendly Relations Declaration, to be sure, will not do justice to the exigencies of the moment. The defiant, flag-raising version of the defense of sovereignty[1872] is hardly the most adequate in a context where intervention is less and less about a head-on clash between sovereigns, does not always involve the traditional civilizational smugness, and is the doing of a great many actors (corporate, supranational, individual). The fact that it is also not confined to neo imperial relations—or at least contributes to invent new ones—also suggests that a conventional 'Third World Approach to International Law' (TWAIL) approach risks missing some of the role-reversal involved and the genuine power that parts of the Global South wield, henceforth, in the heart of the hegemon and associated powers. As imperialism becomes more diffuse, many states that would have historically had mostly to complain about interference in their domestic affairs become at least part time interferers in the affairs of others as well. Moreover, they increasingly and willingly partake in discourses of global cooperation, governance and burden sharing—all be it sometimes as part of a form of voluntary subservience—that alleviate some of the pressure that traditionally bore on the invocation of non-intervention.

Indeed, it also bears mentioning that the occasional effacement of sovereignty is a complex function of the increased needs of international collaboration, foreign policy calculations that not insisting on one's sovereignty via interference is the right card to play at any given moment, and the more or less voluntary surrendering of sovereignty by coopted local elites. In some cases, what would in other times have been described as interference can even be recast, as part of a 'discursive shift from political autonomy and non-intervention to state capacity', to the point that 'international compacts to build governance capacity make sovereignty real, meaningful and effective,

1872 See for example Yue Wu (n 18).

precisely, by abandoning atavistic, retrograde aspirations to political autonomy'.[1873] In effect, the entire discourse of international 'state building' can be understood, quite paradoxically,[1874] as a form of institutionalized intervention in order to prop up sovereignty and therefore, at least potentially, to make states more resilient in the face of interference.[1875] Intervention and interference, in other words, are not always where one expects them to be.

This then drives a neo-liberal 'post-interventionist' discourse that is a far cry from international law's traditional posture. That discourse essentially erases any distinction between intervention and sovereignty by emphasizing the agency of local actors in soliciting programs of outside assistance:[1876] intervention becomes the condition prior to sovereignty rather than its negation, all in the name of 'state building'. In that view, the problem is not that one is being interfered with but that one is allowed to fall by the wayside of a global economy of attention. Despite all the clamor about interference, clearly some states are only too happy to monetize their openness to outside forces for their own ends and to compete on a sort of international market for intervention. That this may lead down a path of impoverished sovereignty is, at least, their sovereign choice and, besides, it is not inevitable. And to be clear, the global agenda of top-down state building is not the only one and coexists with a neo-authoritarian one which, in Africa notably, sees China[1877] or Russia[1878] offer

1873 Finkenbusch (n 369) 316.

1874 Shahida Aman and Shagufta Aman, 'Theory and Practice of Interventionist State Building: Paradoxes and Limitations' (2014) 21 Journal of Political Studies 27.

1875 David Chandler, 'Post-Conflict Statebuilding: Governance Without Government' in Michael Pugh, Neil Cooper and Mandy Turner (eds), *Whose Peace? Critical Perspectives on the Political Economy of Peacebuilding* (Palgrave Macmillan U.K. 2008) <https://doi.org/10.1057/9780230228740_20> accessed 10 July 2024.

1876 Chandler (n 395).

1877 Dan Banik and Benedicte Bull, 'Chinese Engagement in Africa and Latin America: Does It Matter for State Capacity?' (2018) 3 Third World Thematics: A TWQ Journal 532; Christof Hartmann, 'China's Contribution to African Governance: Some Conceptual Thoughts' in Christof Hartmann and Nele Noesselt (eds), *China's New Role in African Politics: From Non-Intervention towards Stabilization?* (Routledge 2019); Kevin Woods, 'Ceasefire Capitalism: Military–Private Partnerships, Resource Concessions and Military–State Building in the Burma–China Borderlands' in Nancy Lee Peluso and Christian Lund (eds), *New Frontiers of Land Control* (Routledge 2013).

1878 Viktor Marsai, 'Fragile States and the Issue of Foreign Interventions in the Sahel' (*European Institute of the Mediterranean (IEMed)*, 9 February 2018) <https://www.iemed.org/publication/fragile-states-and-the-issue-of-foreign-interventions-in-the-sahel/> accessed 12 July 2024; Pierre Englebert, 'State Capture and State Building as Stress Factors in African Conflicts' in Pamela Aall and Chester A Crocker (eds), *The fabric of peace in Africa: Looking beyond the state*, vol 17 (Centre for International Governance Innovation 2017); Catriona

their substantial economic or military support to prop up states—at a cost. That these sorts of offers have long had takers is a reminder that sovereignty was always less a given (notwithstanding international law's tendency to idealize it) and more a constant struggle at the interface between the domestic and the foreign. In short, interference happens not only because states interfere but because other states—as part of unequal international relations, no doubt, but also shrewd politics and evolving ideational frameworks—allow them to interfere.

At the same time, as a deliberate ploy to reinstate a strong sense of the value of sovereignty,[1879] the recurrent appeal to non-intervention may yet will the conditions of its realization into existence. It could still emerge as a real project to reassess the value of self-determination for the ages. That renewed interest for the norm of non-intervention can, at any rate, serve as frontispiece to this conclusion, one that raises questions about imperial nostalgia, legal pluralism, and the degree to which one is invested in rules as the be-all and end-all of international law. It involves the difficult work, as often for international lawyers, of seeking to reconcile conflicting values in ways that are not too formally unseemly. For example, it highlights both the promise and the pitfalls of seeking to balance a theory of non-intervention and non-interference on the basis of self-determination. As was seen, self-determination fundamentally reenergizes a sense of what is at stake when we speak of interference and what values it potentially conflicts with beyond a somewhat sterile and repetitious emphasis on sovereignty; at the same time a mere 'fishbowl' vision of self-determination, one in which the fish lives in an entirely self-contained environment whilst not even being aware of the world beyond it, was always both an implausible and unappealing as a metaphor for what non-interference as a value seeks to protect.

It is worth noting that non-intervention and non-interference refer, ultimately, to quite different political and symbolic registers whose tensions sometimes explode in the open. On the one hand, they purport to reassert a strong stranglehold of the state over domestic affairs, imagining 'its' interventions at least as legitimate. In that respect, the agenda is clearly, even if nostalgically and misleadingly, a statist one. On the other hand, the fetishization of the free operation of the domestic public sphere borrows from a neo-liberal register that condemns intervention or interference on the basis of the need to respect

Craven-Matthews and Pierre Englebert, 'A Potemkin State in the Sahel? The Empirical and the Fictional in Malian State Reconstruction' (2018) 11 African Security 1.

1879 On disenchantment with sovereignty, see Martti Koskenniemi, 'What Use for Sovereignty Today?' (2011) 1 Asian Journal of International Law 61.

the natural equilibria to which society is normally expected to lead. Barely hidden behind that model is a sense of not disrupting the optimal outcomes to which states will or would arrive by their own means if left undisturbed. This begs the question of what is so wrong about intervention and why one would have reason to systematically defer to the policy outcomes imagined to be produced, more or less unhindered, by states or populations, especially when those are either corrupted or otherwise problematic. Although self-determination is sometimes presented as the magic answer to that interrogation, it begs the question of why it is those particularly entities (i.e., states) that are its primary and perhaps exclusive locus, why the 'self' is being constructed in the way it is, and why self-determination cannot be a much more collective and relational exercise.

To make matters worse and as examined in the book, States are only beginning to grapple with something that is as yet nameless but already highly problematic: a form of interference that is neither specifically coercive and nor necessarily violent, but nonetheless widely perceived as potentially harmful. It is as if that interference deliberately eluded the fragile defenses of the international legal system and its elaborate—if, it should be conceded, indecisive—debates on what constitutes intervention. In doing so, they stand to shape both interference and practices deployed to resist it; blur the line between the principle of non-intervention and ongoing if scattered claims about the prohibition of interference; and all the while complicate their own ability to take a stance on the issue. In the process, they will and have already contributed to the ongoing reshaping of sovereignty, independence, equality, the *domaine réservé*, understandings of the use of force and self-determination. If it is true, as Anaxagoras once put it, that 'everything is in everything',[1880] then that is surely true of a principle as amorphous and over-extended as non-interference. All the more reason to try to understand what it *signifies*, beyond the strictly positivist exercise of seeking to pin down its meaning.

To be sure, as the book has cautioned, the debate on the new interference must be taken with a pinch of salt: part genuine phenomenon, part merely discourse, it also reflects anxieties about sovereignty, self-determination, and democracy as much as real threats to all of the above. Quite aside from the reality of interference (whatever that may be), there is certainly a 'discourse on interference' that can lead to self-inflicted wounds, confuse domestic problems and their external abuse, and risks constantly framing the category of

1880 Anna Marmodoro, *Everything in Everything: Anaxagoras's Metaphysics* (Oxford University Press 2017).

the foreign as problematic, inauthentic, and unwelcome. It is not hard to see how this could feed into structural patterns of xenophobia and racism that long predate the current debate on interference (this sort of age-old division of the world into the 'civilized' and the 'uncivilized' once justified intervention; it now buttresses the case for non-interference). This is despite the fact that there is reason to be somewhat temperate about the actual risk of interference,[1881] especially in a context where the consequences of an overreaction need to be themselves understood as not negligible. The fear of interference is at least as causal of the dynamics of states' politics as interference itself, and the two may only have a loosely correlated relationship just as, for example, domestically perceptions of crime and crime statistics can become disjointed in public opinion.

In that respect, the book has been devoted less to assessing the exact contours of the classic rule of non-intervention or the emerging rule of non-interference than it has been to elucidating what kind of world is constantly being produced by the assumption that such rules *exist*. For example, one might argue that the *domaine réservé* does not exist—there is no such thing. Or, a little less provocatively: the *domaine* does not pre-exist claims about non-interference; rather, claims about interference (or its absence), reverse engineer, as part of an ongoing process of social construction, what the *domaine* is and perhaps can and even ought to be. In the process, the *domaine* is being problematized rather than sanctified, perhaps along the line of Georges Abi Saab's distinction between a hardcore (a purely internal phenomenon that long gave rise to the 'impression that [international law] was indifferent to all that took place within the State, an expanse [...] beyond its reach'), 'a penumbra or transition zone' ('operating in a kind of limbo or space between States or on the external margins of the opaque billiard balls that are the States'), and a state's '"external affair", the proper ambit of international law'.[1882]

This is hardly a reason to give up on attempting to capture what makes interference relevant as a category of problematic behavior in international relations and law. As Lou Henkin once noted even as 'the lawyer struggling to find some meaningful role for international law in today's society might be tempted to reject "intervention" as an unmanageable and unhelpful concept', it remains that 'nations, all nations, think there is something in it, and the lawyer

1881 Johnston (n 352) 2. (Pointing out that 'when the intelligence is reviewed and considered in the context of all relevant intelligence, the specific instances raised are less concerning than some media reporting has suggested, and in some cases tell a different story from what has been reported to date').

1882 Abi-Saab (n 557) 229.

ought at least to attempt to contribute clarity to the problem at which the concept of intervention was directed, and to explore whether some areas at least may be subject to some meaningful order by law'.[1883] It may be of that the rule-like nature of non-intervention is over-stated; that in lieu of an actual rule, it is more a principle (so closely tied is it to sovereignty), but this does not mean that one should tire of delineating its contours or at least producing meaning through it. Quite the contrary, in fact, anchoring non-interference to a principle or treating it like a principle is a reminder of what it expresses and how it stands to be rejuvenated by constant appeals to that mooring in something resembling the 'living tree' of sovereignty.

But one should also be aware that one's interventions—particularly the interventions of the international law professional class—are not innocent of the thing they purport to pin down, and the agendas they promote in the process. International lawyers may have a relatively marginal role in the development of international law—notwithstanding the profession's occasionally inflated sense of self—but they do specialize in orienting conversations by furnishing its jargon and mannerisms. In that respect, the interference/intervention dyad raises a classic regulatory dilemma as well as a form of political responsibility. Should international lawyers: (i) take full stock of the evolution of international social conditions and, seeing that intervention is already fundamentally changing nature, redeploy their energies towards tackling the distinct problem of interference, thus fundamentally framing their role as one of accompanying social phenomena? Or (ii) reassert a strong norm of non-intervention *only*, based on the most prudent reading of the international legal canon, in the process boosting a sense of that norm's distinctiveness and perhaps maintaining its rarity, at the risk of international law's relative irrelevance to one of the defining phenomena of the era.

There will invariably be anxieties involved: that, on the one hand, one may precipitate the coming of precisely that which one is trying to regulate by stooping down to the phenomena one claims to control; and, on the other hand, that one may miss the train entirely by clinging to an outdated vision of the international system more interested in projecting a mythical core than dealing with the conditions of the real. In terms of the political economy of rules, there will also be questions well worth asking: is it better to have rarefied rules that can exceptionally and relatively clearly be breached, but at the risk of being overtaken by facts on the ground? Or is it better to embrace standards or principles that seek to address intimate and discrete dimensions of

1883 Henkin and others (n 67) 156.

international relations, but at the risk of a dilution of the force of rules? And, in turn, one needs to have an eye not just on one's immediate regulatory object but on how the rules construct the world that they imagine: one of relative fear of other states, at the risk of capturing behavior that is either innocent or, under some theory, positively helpful; or one of relative embrace of other states, at the risk of turning a blind eye to what remain distinct and problematic patterns of abuse of power. And one needs to have those conversations both with a view to particular cases and the general orientation of the system, it being clear that one of the saving graces of international law is that one must learn to live with the arguments that one propounds in any given context.

In this scenario, neither the worst nor the best are always the most likely. A concern with relatively under-the-radar interference should not be allowed to degenerate into a sort of conspiracy-theory writ-large approach to international relations where the "hand of Moscow", the "hand of Washington" or "the hand of Beijing" is seen behind every move. By the same token, a kind of imperialism illiteracy or naiveté also leads some observers to never see hegemonic interference for what it is, assuming that what is tagged as interference is merely normal robust interaction. Worse, it has led some to see the imperialism in others whilst not acknowledging it in themselves. International law's usefulness in those conversations is that it provides a framework that asks a series of pointed questions and provides parameters to understand whether interference is occurring and what is its nature. This is no magic bullet and the questions may not know of facile answers. But it should make one wary of the tendency to depart from the premise one is trying to prove, or the kind of confirmation bias that seems so widespread in international politics.

For example, whether foreign states are interfering with the affairs of Venezuela may ultimately depend on who actually won the elections, how quickly foreign powers came to the conclusion either way and on what basis, and even existing legacies of interference. One may have an interest in a certain outcome and still believe that this outcome is validated by the record; but one could also have an interest in a certain outcome and allow that interest to shape the facts to one's advantage. In the wake of the 2024 elections, one Chinese observer asked rhetorically 'Do American politicians know the will of the Venezuelan people better than the people themselves? Obviously not'. But this presumes that the Venezuelan people know what they want or that their vote was not stolen, ultimately a difficult question of evidence.[1884] There is no

1884 Lun Su, 'US Has Less Space to Intervene in Venezuela' *Global Times* (30 July 2024) <https://www.globaltimes.cn/page/202407/1317003.shtml>.

reason to automatically defer to whatever outcome is promulgated by a politically dominant group simply because it is in power, even as there is no reason to take the opposition one happens to support's word for it. By the same token, it could of course be that one is naturally tempted to think that those one supports did win the election because it is in one's interest. Even if one cannot know for sure who won the election, it may be that what decides positions either way can be treated with an adequate degree of circumspection.

Nor, however, will this ever merely be a question of fact to be evaluated forensically and clinically independently of the presuppositions that determine what a relevant "fact" is.[1885] When it comes to the rule of non-intervention, widespread agreement about its existence doctrinally must be reconciled with depths of ambivalence about its foundation, status, and scope. The norm's status, somewhere at the pinnacle of the international legal canon, cannot obviate its inherent ambiguity. Various constituencies will differ about how quickly a foreign power should recognize the outcome of an election, on what basis and for what purpose. They will do so on the basis of competing theories of who can make that judgment call, what it means for a state to be sovereign or for a population to self-determine, and with varying attention to how international rules shape all of these dimensions. The rule, in the best of cases, never obviates the need for or the temptation to revisit some of the underlying conversations.

The norm may yet falter through strategic misunderstanding, lack of clear sightedness and short-termism. Non-intervention is both embraced and ill-loved, the object of passionate defenses and incipient wariness. Every violation, every inopportune invocation of the norm contributes to its erosion, although it should also be said that there is no reason to think that the norm is not, to use Henkin's aphorism, respected most of the time by most states[1886] and does not feed, in other ways, on every invocation. It is worth remembering that norms, even cherished norms, *do* 'degenerate' incrementally[1887] through neglect, exceptions, or even excessively strident invocation. If that is true of the rule on the prohibition of the use of force, then it may be true *a fortiori* of a norm whose status is far less assured. To make matters more complicated, the norm of non-interference that this book has argued co-exists precariously

---

1885 Frédéric Mégret, 'Do Facts Exist, Can They Be "Found," and Does It Matter?' in Sarah Knuckey and Philip Alston (eds), *The Transformation of Human Rights Fact Finding* (2016) <https://philpapers.org/rec/MGRDFE> accessed 5 September 2024.

1886 Henkin, *How Nations Behave* (n 417) 47.

1887 Diana Panke and Ulrich Petersohn, 'Why International Norms Disappear Sometimes' (2012) 18 European Journal of International Relations 719.

in the shadow of non-intervention stands to further problematize all of the assumptions on which the theory of non-intervention precariously rested. If it is no longer clear what non-intervention protects, it will be harder to know when it has been violated; and if interference happens everywhere, all the time, it may be wondered whether the quest to neutralize it will not be illusory or trivial.

There may also be specifically international legal reasons why intervention and, *a fortiori*, interference is so hard to capture. In trying to designate, stigmatize and regulate both, international law is called upon not only to regulate state behavior (as is assumed in the standard account) but, to a degree, to 'regulate itself'. In other words, the definition of intervention/interference touches upon the very core of international law, namely the fundamental nature of sovereignty. It requires, therefore, a form of real time surgery by international law on international law, an intervention that in any circumstance would stretch the capability of any legal system and maximizes the risks of unexpected outcomes. But in constantly defining what is supposed to be at its base, or at least a more or less fixed component, international law is at risk of entering a vortex of circularity in which it defines itself in relation to itself. Failure to point to any external dimension beyond international law makes its discursive economy deeply self-referential, at the risk of staring down an abyss of perplexity.

Notwithstanding, it remains difficult to imagine an international legal system in which a norm against both intervention and interference would *not* have some analytical purchase and rhetorical traction or where, *a contrario*, assumptions of free-wheeling intervention or interference prevailed. At least, it remains difficult to imagine how such a system might still be described as *specifically international* in the Westphalian sense, as opposed to imperial or cosmopolitan (or both), involving a sort of constant *droit de regard* by powerful nations or hegemons over the destinies of weaker ones. The norms of non-intervention and non-interference must continue to play an outsize role *if* sovereignty is to conserve its value as the nominal linchpin of an international legal system based on states. Sovereignty is evidently a flexible and evolving concept, but 'what sovereign equality shall doubtless protect is the existence of the State as a self-determined human community, because it would otherwise cease to be *imperator regni sui*'.[1888] It is of course possible to argue that this ship sailed long ago, and that international law was only ever a fig leaf to hide the brutal reality of asymmetric patterns of interference. Be that as it may, the norm will only ever exist to the extent that states are willing to protest its

1888 Zemanek (n 407) 956.

violation, even as they may occasionally have no choice but to swallow their pride as the price of conducting international business.

Detlev Vagts, in outlining the contours of a conception of a hypothetical hegemonic international law insisted that it would 'require [...] setting aside the norm of nonintervention into the internal affairs of states', as hegemons today (the U.S.) or yesterday (Germany) have decreed occasionally.[1889] Clearly a number of regional powers are tempted by reinvigorating their own version of spheres of influence, which are often just a polite way of reinstating a prerogative of intervention in their neighbours. But international lawyers would be the first to concede that international law was always a *normative project* rather than a descriptive map, so that evidence of states having sought to game the system to their advantage or to push their vision of international order against the grain is not necessarily evidence of the law's decay. International law is constantly seeking to shape powerful proclivities that are enmeshed deeply within the system, and one cannot entirely fault it for its imperfect reach in doing so. At any rate, as Vagts argues, '[a] true hegemon would have reverted to the practice of overt intervention and would have demonstrated its unapologetic and implacable will by not canceling air cover for the Bay of Pigs invasion'.[1890] That the U.S. did not really suggests that hegemony, even regional, remains imperfect, and that the norm of non-intervention, as a formal injunction, a manifestation of some deeper logic of the system, or a prudential strategy, is not entirely dead letter yet.

At the other end of the spectrum, the whole notion of non-intervention could of course still be overtaken by a renewed globalization of the world or a surfeit of multilateral enthusiasm. Although this seems less likely now than it did in the 1990s, the accumulated effect of supranational and imperative norms has gone some way towards making this a self-fulfilling reality. The Security Council, for example, has had a leading role in reshaping, via expansive notions of international peace and security, a sense of what the legitimate realm of international intervention is, so much so that '[w]hat was once seen as interference by the Security Council in domestic matters [is] now viewed as the coming together of states for a common cause'.[1891] Internationally ordained human rights, moreover, have historically provided a Trojan horse of sorts to

1889 Detlev F Vagts, 'Hegemonic International Law' (2001) 95 American Journal of International Law 843, 845–846.

1890 ibid 846.

1891 UNSC, 'What Was Once Seen as Security Council Interference in Domestic Affairs Now Viewed as States "Coming Together for Common Cause", 1540 Review Hears Upon Closing' (2 October 2009) Meetings Coverage SC/9758.

undercut vigorous assertions of sovereignty against interference, typically on the basis of states' own treaty commitments. They have made it relatively easier for international organizations to claim that they are merely executing their mandates since a degree of prying is not only allowed under human rights but rendered *de rigueur*.

This has arguably, in turn, opened the way for much enhanced—and relatively acceptable—state scrutiny of other states' affairs. In a much more integrated world, one can speculate that interference would be much less likely to be perceived as such because its logical predicates would be missing. As Lori Damrosch once suggested at the dawn of globalization, '[s]ince influencing and target states are likely to have areas of overlapping interest—economic, social, cultural, ethnic or linguistic, as well as political—it may be preferable to accept transnational political activities that reflect common concerns on both sides of the boundary than to insist upon artificial political barriers'.[1892] In other words, the very continued condition of open societies may require a strategic lowering of the guard so that one not risk sawing the branch on which one is (historically) sitting in an effort to stamp off any sense of interference. It may be that efforts at sorting appropriate influence from disruptive interference simply come at too much of a transactional cost.

The need to take interference with a hefty dose of fortitude is even more pronounced in supranationally integrated groupings whose *raison d'être* has always seemed to be their openness and even denial of a strong sense of the *domaine réservé*—although, even there, some border delimitation may occur. Characteristically, for example, the European Regulation on funding of political parties at the European level envisages that such parties can be financed out of the European Union budget (even if they have domestic roots, they are active in the European political space). It does also, however, prohibit 'the direct or indirect funding of other political parties, and in particular national parties or candidates' which 'shall continue to be governed by national rules'.[1893] This sort of ambivalence about where to place the cursor between legitimate community interest and unwarranted interference is particularly visible in the context of regional integration premised on an effort to dilute meaningful borders between the domestic and the supranational in the first place. It highlights the continuing tension between an international law of coexistence and an international law of cooperation[1894] or even integration as it manifests itself

1892 Damrosch (n 16) 48–49.

1893 European Parliament and Council Regulation (EU, Euratom) 1141/2014 of 22 October 2014 on the statute and funding of European political parties and European political foundations [2014] OJ L317/1, art 22(1).

1894 Friedmann, *The Changing Structure of International Law* (n 21).

through attention to cardinal principles such as non-intervention and the policing of non-interference.

At the same time, the notion that interference is either the doing of big powers intent on maximizing their way at any cost or the transcending of sovereign interest through supranational organization may both already be thoroughly outdated: increasingly, interference assumes a largely private nature that is even more corrosive of sovereignty in that it is ideal-typically its negation and not merely a competition over its dominance. International law not only fails to see or stigmatize corporations as agents of interference, it loses much energy focusing on improbable issues of attribution, when all the while the problem of private interference is staring at it in the face. One danger, however, is that in the process of regulating private interference, one will endow corporate actors with more power than it may be wise to concede to them. In that respect, for private actors to either complain of interference or constitute themselves as its regulators is, implicitly, to make a claim to be sovereignty: I am sovereign, because I can be interfered with or address the problem of interference.

Of course, to the extent that the fate of a notion such as interference is closely tied to the notion sovereignty, then it is vulnerable to the well-known vagaries of that notion's own constant redefinition. We have no more reason, at the closing of this book, to think that sovereignty itself is more of a fixed concept than interference. Sovereignty, to be sure, has never been quite what it seems, and its socio-legal reality has always been more complex than lawyers' simplified rendering of it. It may be high time for the discipline of international law to acknowledge that this was always the case, although no doubt in the process some sacred cows will need to be sacrificed. A better understanding of interference may assist in this process, with the norm pointing as it does to the depths of complexity that characterize the 'intimate life' of sovereignty.

Although better pinpointing the exact point at which interference becomes problematic will probably not suffice to reinstate particular conceptions of sovereignty, nor should one be oblivious of the extent to which today's sovereignty is being built, block by block, as a result of protest and acquiescence to its implicit or explicit denial. Certainly, the angst with which the 'new interference' has been met testifies to the fact that some social actors very much consider a certain conception of sovereignty worth defending. But this may be a case of too little too late: sovereignty could still drift elsewhere than the state or be so thoroughly normalized (a form of power among forms of power) as to make the effort to highlight 'intervention' or 'interference' for particular status a self-defeating effort.

1 Reclaiming and Transcending the Ironies of Interference

What has often been missing from international lawyers' efforts to reassert a strong notion of sovereignty to face the challenge of interference, often mediated by the same well-worn formulas that have not served the discipline very well (or at least not served anyone who was not already at its ideological center of gravity), is any sense of irony—one of the running threads of this book. Irony—not to be mistaken with cynicism or nihilism—is an opening to the extent to which the secret of the law's discipline lies in something else than what law typically purports it to be, or the way in which 'the law's crooked timber occasionally produces the opposite of its intended effect'.[1895] Beyond the slightly tired conservative *cliché* of the perverse effect, perhaps the ultimate irony, the irony of the *connaisseurs* as it were, is that the law, in fact, produces *exactly* the effect that was intended—just not the one that it constantly proclaims. In that respect, it is worth underlining that the international law of non-interference is always simultaneously an international law *of interference*; or, at least, an international law that requalifies what might otherwise be considered interference as merely 'influence', 'human rights promotion', or 'private behavior', a law, in short, that constitutes what it merely claims to capture.

Contra modernist international law's 'serious' desire to reduce reality to its formal terms (interference/non-interference, *domaine réservé/erga omnes* obligations, domestic/international, sovereignty/non-sovereignty, etc.), and contra even the critique's dead seriousness about the actual nefarious effects of interference (or non-interference), the ironist adopts the stance of 'practical humanity', one prompt to denounce law's indistinguishability from politics, to ridicule false idols, and to deconstruct claims of authority.[1896] Although the ironist does not too readily assume that international law necessarily has the answers to the questions it raises, nor does it give up too easily on the effort to hammer out meaning from the law, cognizant that the refusal to engage in international law's word games is also often the first refuge of the scoundrel. In this conclusion, I want to suggest that the debate over interference confronts the discipline of international law with at least three, deep-seated ironies.

First, it was pointed out that in invoking the register of non-interference, states find themselves hamstrung by some of their past investment and

1895 Neil M Gorsuch, 'Law's Irony Thirteenth Annual Barbara K. Olson Memorial Lecture' (2014) 37 Harvard Journal of Law & Public Policy 743, 743.

1896 John Stuart Mill, 'A Few Words on Non-Intervention' (1859) 60 Fraser's Magazine for Town and Country, 1830–1869 766, 176.

disinvestments in the notion. This casts a long shadow over their attempts to reinvent themselves through appeals to norms of interference and non-interference alike. One of the enduring motifs of the book has been the extent to which one cannot have it both ways: to interfere and expect not to be interfered with. In that respect, it is not least of the ironies of the current debate about interference that it brings states who have historically been on the giving end of interference much pause for thought, as they discover their own vulnerabilities to a newfound willingness to interfere from non-Western big powers (Russia and China most notoriously), but also a range of other state and non-state smaller players. After insistently imposing the conditions of the open society, it will be very difficult for the West to cower under a reinvented notion of sovereignty-as-shield.

This significantly limits the incidence of arguments purporting to indignantly reaffirm a sense of the *domaine réserve* that was never clearly there, and which Western states are now ill positioned to claim. The kind of feverish erection of barriers to cyber and diasporic interference evident in the Western dominated debate on these questions often displays what one might describe as a certain lack of dignity in light of past histories of meddling in the affairs of other states. Some have even suggested that, when it comes to relations with China, a form of 'digital orientalism' is involved, one that 'others' these powers as particularly and uniquely nefarious when it comes to interference.[1897] Evidently, states that have historically been on the receiving end of interference do not necessarily fare much better: their willingness to use some of the very tools that they have long decried puts them in a rhetorically weak space, one in which the double-standards of their discourse is constantly revealed. How seriously can one really take indignant proclamations of the importance of non-interference by states willing to run the whole gamut of interference technologies when it suits them?

A second Irony of the debate is how it focuses attention on the integrity of the political process within states, precisely as that process has never been so relatively weak and under threat not just from external actors, but also as a result of domestic forces of corruption, the diversification of the potential sites of politics,[1898] and the globalization of democratic processes. The risk is

---

1897 Introducing the concept of 'Digital Orientalism' see Maximilian Mayer, 'China's Authoritarian Internet and Digital Orientalism' in Denise Feldner (ed), *Redesigning Organizations: Concepts for the Connected Society* (Springer International Publishing 2020). See also Josef Gregory Mahoney, 'China's Rise as an Advanced Technological Society and the Rise of Digital Orientalism' (2023) 28 Journal of Chinese Political Science 1.

1898 Andreas Georg Scherer and Guido Palazzo, 'The New Political Role of Business in a Globalized World: A Review of a New Perspective on CSR and Its Implications for the Firm, Governance, and Democracy' (2011) 48 Journal of Management Studies 899.

that one will romanticize and lionize a purist conception of democracy or self-determination that exists only in the minds of its defenders, and that one will confuse some idealized republican conception of the *civis* and the reality of complex collective will-formation. In conditions of globalization, many of the features that previously characterized interference have been so thoroughly reshuffled as to make both the defense against interference and the protection of normal interaction between states appear as problematic propositions. That may well be precisely the point from the point of view of those would put up walls against influence: the perceived need to re-establish boundaries in order to make sense of the operating software that international law has bequeathed us, and its reliance on sovereignty, self-determination, and rights. The norm of non-interference, in that respect, is the norm that the system needs to hold together, the norm that its existence posits.

Of course, this also risks getting things exactly inverted: we establish rules not only deductively to make sense of the demands of a system of norms, but inductively to make sense of the world that surrounds us. The question is whether it is only the 'new interference' that is the problem, or the very international legal vocabulary with which we seek to tackle it. In international law treatments of the issue, one senses at times as much of an interest in maintaining the relevance and salience of international law than in addressing the 'problem' squarely on its own terms. The risk is, for one, that one will overemphasize elements such as coercion that have a pedigree largely based on the idiosyncratic politics of the history of international law. It is also that one will pay too much attention to the element of foreignness in the corrosion of the public sphere, at the expense of its domestic determinants. In some ways, as was seen, foreign interference is only so successful as it can draw on existing polarities and even invitation as well as inherent frailties. This relativizes the notion that foreign interference is the prime mover as opposed to fractures already deeply embedded and increasingly apparent domestically. It can also lead to a politics of designation of foreign interference that overemphasizes its relevance at the expense of the heart of the problem, one that involves both corruption of public debate but also considerable normative doubts about its proper location.

Finally, note that the degree to which interference is adequately conceptualized as interference against the state at all may be open to doubt. Indeed, the notion that interference is even specifically tied to the *domaine réservé* of the *sovereign* is limited and may need to be significantly updated in an age of international organizations and integration. This is not altogether surprising: the more sovereignty drifts upwards to supranational spheres, the more one can expect those spheres to be the target of interference and to, in turn, claim that they have a right not to be interfered with. In that respect, the European Union's 'Qatargate'[1899] or revelations that the International Criminal Court was being spied from within[1900] suggest that international bodies are just if not more likely to be interfered with, both on account of the leverage they provide and their inherent vulnerability.

More surprisingly perhaps, there is now evidence that sub-state entities may equally be direct targets of foreign interference in and of themselves, as shown by revelations concerning New York mayor Eric Adams[1901] or efforts at tipping municipal elections in Vancouver.[1902] Indeed, a number of sub-state entities have developed their own anti-interference agendas independently of their state. This is the case of a number of U.S. states including Arizona, Oklahoma, Utah and Georgia, which have adopted or sought to adopt legislation based on the federal FARA but that potentially goes even further. This comes on the heels of laws or proposed laws by dozens of Republican dominated states restricting certain nationals from "countries of concern" (notably, Russia and China) from buying land and real estate.[1903]

If nothing else, such laws, in claiming a prerogative to fight interference, implicitly challenge the Federal government's traditional stranglehold on national security matters. More generally, in claiming a kind of *domaine réservé* of their own at least vis-à-vis foreign powers, they are part of a testy performance of quasi-sovereignty—constituting them into sovereigns in the process of claiming not to be interfered with. This may speak to a gradual uncoupling of interference from traditional notions of statehood, even as the latter is becoming relatively less crucial and is being transcended from above. To be clear, there can be interference without anything as solemn (or seemingly so) as the *domaine réservé*: one's competences can be interfered with

---

1899 Jeanne Ollivier, 'Brussels Dispatches: Foreign Interference in the Spotlight' (*EUobserver*, 12 April 2024) <https://euobserver.com/eu-elections/ar0b091c2f> accessed 22 April 2024.

1900 Shaun Walker, 'US Indicts Alleged Russian Spy Who Tried to Infiltrate ICC in The Hague' *The Guardian* (26 March 2023) <https://www.theguardian.com/world/2023/mar/26/us-indicts-alleged-russian-spy-sergey-cherkasov-who-tried-to-infiltrate-icc-in-the-hague> accessed 11 July 2024.

1901 Casey Michel and Vishakha Darbha, 'Opinion | Eric Adams and the Creeping Threat of Foreign Interference' *The New York Times* (1 October 2024) <https://www.nytimes.com/2024/10/01/opinion/eric-adams-foreign-interference-democracy.html> accessed 3 October 2024.

1902 Dan Bilefsky, 'Did China Help Vancouver's Mayor Win Election?' *The New York Times* (7 May 2023) <https://www.nytimes.com/2023/05/07/world/canada/ken-sim-vancouver-china.html> accessed 3 October 2024.

1903 Kine (n 1618).

even if they are not territorially exclusive. Along similar lines, it is not inconceivable that corporations would invoke the language of non-interference as a way of establishing their own quasi-sovereign credentials. The problem is that if everyone can be interfered with then the relative distinctiveness of the rule of non-intervention, such as it was once imagined to exist by international lawyers, will be a bit of a pipe dream.

Interference, under one expansive view, need not even be particularly related to the sovereign configuration at all. It could be reconceptualized as meddling with any form of power whose deliberative processes are understood as having a *prima facie* claim to being self-contained and self-referential. Interference of that kind, to be sure, already arises across the board: states are accused of interfering with human rights; regional organizations of interfering with their member states; federations of interfering with their composite entities; central governments with autonomous regions, executives with judiciaries, etc. Outside the specific jargon of international law, interference could be merely the term one uses to describe an attitude of wrongfully overstepping boundaries. But if the defining mark of interference is not that it affects any rigid idea of *domaine réservé* at all (because subjects outside the state have no or little *domaine* as such), then does this not change our prevailing conception of interference (not to mention intervention) beyond recognition?

Rather than interference being the specific mode of meddling associated with sovereignty, it becomes a broader metaphor for meddling with any constituted power and its authority both domestically and supranationally. Interference, then, would reflect less the highly unusual claims of a horizontal system of equals and, instead, merely manifest a banal form of encroachment on competencies, the likes of which are very familiar already on many levels of governance. Thus detached from the specific claims of statehood, it is open to conjecture whether the existing apparatus of international law when it comes to interference would still mean much and at any rate, a theory of interference-of-all-by-all would need an entirely different conceptual apparatus to sustain it. The paradox, then, is that the success of the notion of interference would be its demise.

A third irony is the extent to which some of the strategies deployed to fight back against interference risk undermining some of the very things that non-interference is designed to protect. For example, the urgent and insistent desire to reduce interference may well, if taken to its logical extreme, end up fueling interference via the argument from 'counter-intervention intervention'. The more other states interfere with one's domestic affairs, the more one may feel legitimized in interfering with theirs. Moreover, the more states interfere in the domestic affairs of other states, the more third states may feel or claim they are duty bound to interfere in the affairs of the interferers as a sort of compensatory move. The 'right of counter-intervention' could easily, in a new interference environment in which a wide range of actors can be suspected of interfering, furnish a plethora of pretexts for further 'corrective' interference. It could end up being reminiscent of the old 'right of intervention'—an exception that swallows the rule.

On a vertical plane, the same danger of 'too much non-interference killing non-interference' is apparent. The more liberal and open societies are inclined to adopt exceptional measures to deal with interference, including onerous registration obligations, banning of 'fake' news or a broad renationalization of democracy, the more they may appear inimical to the values of liberalism and openness that lie at their foundation. Indeed, the more they rupture what was always a delicate balance between the bonded, territorialized, and methodologically nationalist nature of the state on the one hand, and the open and free aspirations of democracy on the other, the more the universal cosmopolitanism to which some states claim to aspire to (including for others) will be exposed as a dangerous hypocrisy. Responses to foreign interference may entail their own risks in terms of marshalling resources that should remain, ideally, independent. For example, an all-of-society rather than merely a governmental response commends itself to the extent that protection from interference cannot be the monopoly of the executive or intelligence services; but in its embrace of civil society or academic research as 'partners' in resisting interference, for example, it may lead to a totalizing instrumentalization and excessive control of universities.

These strategies could end up (and may even turn out to have had the goal of) corrupting the very independence of the spheres they seek to protect. There is, niched deep into the effort to fight back against interference, a discreet totalitarian temptation, one perhaps most evident in countries like Russia but certainly not alien to liberal democracies. The more or less forceful cooptation of industry, the media, political parties, universities, or civil society into autarchic strategies of bracing against interference carries the seeds of liberalism's further corruption. In that respect, strategies of non-interference are a 'great leveller', bringing otherwise quite diverse regimes closer to each other in their joint effort to reassert their domestic bondedness. This aligns with similar patterns in terms of international trade for example: that, to guard against dumping, states are called upon to adopt their own protectionist measures, at the risk ultimately of collapsing the entire system of free trade in a self-destructive tit-for-tat. Even though this may be more against nature for some than others and there will inevitably be disputes about 'who started interfering first', it is quite clear that interference is activating powerful reflexes to make self-determination and sovereignty 'great again'.

A further irony is that breathless attempts to protect one's polity from outside interference may simultaneously represent a vote of non-confidence in the very ability of such a polity to sift the chaff from the grain and figure out for itself what is convincing and what is not, what is problematically foreign and what is helpful circulation of information and ideas, or what is 'authentic' or 'fake'.[1904] In being allowed to make up their minds on their own, populations would merely be doing what they are often expected to do and which one may have reasons to think they can do best. To engage in the deployment of a massive legal and police infrastructure to protect the polity from outside influences, by contrast, is more evocative of the authoritarian than the democratic toolbox and at any rate a manifestation of a problematic democratic paternalism. Recognizing the halting, iterative and open-ended character of self-determination, at any rate, seems far preferrable to assuming one knows where it is leading and reverse-engineering polities to deliver certain outcomes.

This, then, is the junction where international relations stand and, if nothing else, it risks further shaking the faith in the international legal order. For one thing, a recurring motif in this book has been that the norm of non-intervention in public international law imagined a fairly fixed world of concrete sovereigns violating the sovereignty of other concrete sovereigns. It certainly struggled with the horizontal and inter-subjective dimensions of that project on its own grounds, but at least it proceeded from readily ascertainable terms of the debate, illusory and partial as they may have been even at the time. Instead, all we seem to have, henceforth, are evanescent actors interfering with elusive spheres of competence through ubiquitous devices. It is as if, where the norm of non-interference previously pushed against the walls, it is now witnessing the collapse of its floor and the shattering of its ceiling. This is undoubtedly precipitating a crisis of adaptation, even if the entire history of international law can be summed up as itself a chronic crisis of adaptation.

If the riddle of globalization was that the local and the global converge, then the curse of defining interference in such conditions is that interference is everywhere and, therefore, nowhere. In short, if everyone is interfering with everyone, then the (highly relative) clarity that international law historically sought to bring to the question remains at best as a nostalgic framework to interrogate the deeply changing circumstances of the current international legal order. Rather than sovereignty providing the bulwark against which

---

1904 Mack (n 1362) 391–392.

notions of interference can be evaluated, it is the ongoing physiognomy of interference that provides tantalizing questions about the evolving notion of sovereignty.[1905] Already always slippery as a foundation for international law, sovereignty threatens to become ever more elusive until, either as its vanishing point or its neurotic obsession, it provides only a caricature of itself. Sovereignty, however, will not be reenchanted merely through the hortatory power of words, or legal exorcisms, or perhaps not even through sacrifice.

One pivotal idea in this book has been the extent to which the traditional 'horizontal' framing of interference is increasingly replaced by a 'vertical' one that emphasizes the extent to which sovereignty is not only constrained by its peers but kept under constant pressure by the force of domestic interests on the one hand, and supranational discipline on the other. First among the latter has probably been the attention paid to international human rights law and the extent to which interference can be framed as both necessary to and problematic for a culture of rights. The emphasis on human rights can rejuvenate and radicalize some of the underlying conversations about international law, at least clarifying the reasons for some of the persistent difficulties encountered in pinning down interference.

Perhaps unsurprisingly, however, human rights law does not provide the magic wand that will allow U.S. to transcend the aporia of interference's definition. In many ways, debates about global human rights always replicate debates about the state, its status, and its place. They tell U.S. both why interference is problematic and why it may be a form of salvation; why non-interference is worth defending and why it may be excessive; how to interfere and how not to interfere. In short, international human rights law attempts to tell U.S. too many things at once until it is hard to distinguish from the liberal international legal project within which it is embedded.[1906] It is also chronically suspected of being sovereignty's gravedigger, an accusation that may be unfair but that makes it an unlikely contender for shoring up the state's authority.

2 Non-interference: Rule, Praxis or Ethos?

What seems particularly necessary in this context is an effort at candidness in analyzing both past and new interference, and how they relate to each other. Whilst there is something obviously disingenuous about the Russian

1905 Mégret, 'Are There "Inherently Sovereign Functions" in International Law?' (n 571).

1906 Mégret, 'The Apology of Utopia: Reflections on Some Koskenniemian Themes with Particular Emphasis on Massively Institutionalized Human Rights Law' (n 804).

protestations of innocence at accusations of interference, there is also something self-righteous about the West's reluctance to confront its own legacy of interference and how it has long structured the asymmetrical paths of international law. Lucidity about the fact that, for example, 'since the United States in recent years has itself used a variety of techniques of economic pressure, embargo, and boycott, it would be difficult for it now to claim that such economic pressures are illegal'[1907] is not only morally appealing but legally sound. When it came to the OPEP oil boycott, as Richard Bilder recognized, Arab countries were only doing in relation to the West and Israel what the U.S. itself had long advocated in relation to Communist countries.[1908] Similarly, Andreas Lowenfeld noted that '[h]aving implemented all these programs [note: of unilateral economic sanctions] the United States surely would be contradicting itself if it were to adopt the position that it is somehow immoral to impose controls on economic activity on the basis of political motives'.[1909]

Yet a further and deeper historical reckoning with legacies of interference and how they continue to compromise today's debate remains long overdue and hardly ever discussed. An aggiornamento of interference is almost inconceivable without it: to this day, memories of spectacular interference and their persistent denial, from the overthrow of Mossadegh[1910] or Nagy,[1911] to that of Lumumba,[1912] Dubcek,[1913] Allende[1914] or Sankara[1915] continue to haunt the

---

1907 Bilder (n 311) 41.

1908 ibid.

1909 Andreas F Lowenfeld, 'Sauce for the Gander: The Arab Boycott and United States Political Trade Controls' (1977) 12 Texas International Law Journal 25, 30.

1910 Arash Norouzi, 'White House Asked If Apology For 1953 Iran Coup Planned' (*The Mossadegh Project*, 22 May 2015) <http://www.mohammadmossadegh.com/news/us-apology-for-1953-coup/> accessed 5 September 2023.

1911 Erika Laszlo, 'Hungary Wants Soviet Apology' *UPI* (23 July 1990) <https://www.upi.com/Archives/1990/07/23/Hungary-wants-Soviet-apology/6498648705600/> accessed 15 April 2024.

1912 Agence France-Presse, 'Europe: Belgium: Apology For Lumumba Killing' *The New York Times* (6 February 2002) <https://www.nytimes.com/2002/02/06/world/world-briefing-europe-belgium-apology-for-lumumba-killing.html> accessed 5 September 2023.

1913 Bruce Konsiver, 'Moscow to Say Sorry to Prague in Public' *The Irish Times* (22 August 1998) <https://www.irishtimes.com/news/moscow-to-say-sorry-to-prague-in-public-1.185513> accessed 15 April 2024.

1914 Dan Griffin, 'Envoy Is Disavowed After Apology for U.S. Role in Chile' *Washington Post* (9 March 1977) <https://www.washingtonpost.com/archive/politics/1977/03/09/envoy-is-disavowed-after-apology-for-us-role-in-chile/c5a0e252-1f0f-4818-967c-3c7181be6caf/> accessed 5 September 2023.

1915 United World International, 'How Thomas Sankara, "Africa's Che Guevara", Was Killed to Fulfill French Neocolonialist Ambitions' *United World International* (28 October

memory of nations.[1916] These too are legacies of international law, and they are always at risk of painfully exposing its double standards. Attempting to purge them will help at least problematize the gravest forms of interference and how they continue to structure the long memory of peoples who have too often been painfully on the receiving end of hegemony. The legacies from which such interference springs are legacies of superpower politics, no doubt. But in more ways than one, they also tell stories about the relatively pliability of international law to such politics.

Talking in the early 1970s, Thomas Franck already intuited the need for a reckoning with both:

> United States and Soviet practice have culminated in the most sophisticated expression of this rule of superpower supremacy—the Brezhnev Doctrine. Although our role in this development is not generally acknowledged in Washington, virtually every concept of the Brezhnev Doctrine can be traced to an earlier assertion of identical rights by the United States vis-à-vis Latin America. If one finds distasteful the rule under which the Dubcek regime was removed by Soviet aggressive might, the search for a new standard of relations between superpowers and their neighbors must begin with a clear understanding that we, as much as the Russians, were instrumental in conceptualizing the Brezhnev norm.[1917]

That sort of lucidity ('listening to ourselves as if we were the enemy speaking', as Franck put it) has not frequently been in evidence since, even less so arguably in the long—but not eternal—unipolar moment. The fact that the flows of interference have been partly reversed could be an opportunity to double down on old recriminations and to engage in persistent misunderstandings; but it could also provide, quite uniquely, circumstances in which a great variety of states have now felt the sting of interference and may be more inclined over time to negotiate concerted and rational platforms about it.

Ultimately, what is involved may be a veritable competition over the preferred modalities of international relations, a competition of 'models' of

---

2021) <https://unitedworldint.com/how-thomas-sankara-africas-che-guevara-was-killed-to-fulfill-french-neocolonialist-ambitions/> accessed 6 September 2023.

1916 David Smith, 'AOC Urges U.S. to Apologize for Meddling in Latin America: "We'Re Here to Reset Relationships"' *The Guardian* (2 September 2023) <https://www.theguardian.com/us-news/2023/sep/02/aoc-us-apology-latin-america-coup-chile> accessed 5 September 2023.

1917 Franck and Weisband (n 4) 980.

interference or non-interference. Whilst in some liberal circles it has long been fashionable to deplore the West's failure to interfere more in cases of problematic human rights predicaments, others make a virtue of the fact that, as far as they are concerned, interference will not be an issue. For example, China often presents itself and is praised by others, as a state that, unlike Western countries, will not interfere in the affairs of states it does business with.[1918] Both approaches have their strengths and will have their backers and critics, but none is necessarily ever quite what it seems: Chinese or Russian rhetorical professions of non-interference are only that, and amply belied by their own neo-imperialist meddling in Africa for example; just as Western professions of intervention have in practice coexisted with systematic patterns of restraint vis-à-vis at least some states and strategic isolationism.

Nonetheless, states can be seen as performing certain attitudes towards interference or non-interference that have a broad signaling function and are part of a worldwide competition over the preferred modalities of international relations. Global leadership stands to be increasingly evaluated in terms of what broad patterns of more or less mutually agreed and, possibly, asymmetrical, interference it can be expected to rely upon. The promotion of certain models of non-interference is a competition sustained by ambition and politics, but also by a degree of *credibility*. It will be harder for a superpower associated with a long history of unwanted interventions to recast itself as a paragon of non-interference. There is a deep, experiential quality to the degree to which one can portray oneself as more or less non-interfering, seared in the memories of nations. Some legacies of intervention will only overcome by a compensatory performance of sustained non-intervention.

What this reality underscores is that it takes two to interfere and, whilst opposing interference that is directed one's way is one way to deal with the problem, work to reduce the 'supply side' of interference is also needed. This can take international routes such as sanctions, all the more so of course that interference, as this book has tried to show, contravenes general and *sui generis* principles of international law. But it could also include a degree of self-control and self-restraint in every state where interference is susceptible to originate. Executive, legislatures, and courts all have a responsibility to minimize undue interference in the affairs of other states through control of foreign policy but also of a range of public and private actors operating transnationally. This is true of course of states' obligations to minimize private interference

1918 Pang (n 326); Large (n 1333); Chris Alden, Daniel Large and Ricardo Soares de Oliveira (eds), *China Returns to Africa: A Rising Power and a Continent Embrace* (Columbia University Press 2008). See also Forum on China-Africa Cooperation [FOCAC] (n 247).

originating in their territory (for example, prohibiting nationals from serving abroad as 'foreign fighters'), but it is also true of the organs of the state itself. There is thus a place for extra-territorial disciplining of oneself, as it were, or of ones' nationals, on the understanding that interference is problematic and might bring disrepute.

In that respect, the most intrusive, finger pointing reaction to human rights violations by another state is hardly a foregone or necessarily desirable outcome, and states will 'often prefer less confrontational avenues, e.g., by pursuing quiet forms of diplomacy or restricting financial assistance with the State concerned, or will prefer to leave the matter to be tackled through other available procedures'.[1919] This broader form of comity goes to the heart of the interfering predicament as something that must be checked at the source and that cannot only be litigated by the weakest states in a desperate effort to be treated as equal sovereigns. It can take root in obligations that states may impose on *themselves* not to engage in certain forms of interference. Hence U.S. courts, for example, in interpreting the extra-territorial scope of laws, have engaged in a balancing test weighing 'the relative interests of the United States against those of other states affected by a particular exercise of U.S. jurisdiction'.[1920] It has been argued that said courts should even more explicitly take into account the principle of non-interference.[1921] And courts, which have their own domestic reasons for not encroaching on the domain of other states, could provide a blueprint for how legislatures and, particularly, executives could further develop domestic and perhaps even unilateral doctrines of non-interference.

In effect, states have sometimes backpedaled policies of interference that were outed as such, notably in relation to supposed allies. For example, the U.S. eventually prohibited the use of funds by the National Endowment for Democracy to dissident groups, after finding that said funds had been used to tip an election in Panama.[1922] The origins of the international bribery regime lie in U.S. anti-bribery laws that were adopted following the Lockheed scandal which exposed how a U.S. company had effectively interfered in the affairs of a range of U.S. allies to secure contracts.[1923] It effectively proscribes

1919 Ruys, 'Legal Standing and Public Interest Litigation: Are All Erga Omnes Breaches Equal?' (n 1365) 492–493.

1920 Gerber (n 519) 185.

1921 Gerber (n 519).

1922 Lori Fisler Damrosch, 'Covert Operations' (1989) 83 American Journal of International Law 795, 802.

1923 A Timothy Martin, 'The Development of International Bribery Law' (1999) 14 Natural Resources & Environment 95.

U.S. corporations from getting involved in corruption of foreign officials understood as a form of foreign interference.[1924] There is a nascent interest in how the extra-territorial application of human rights law might nip interference in the bud, as it were, by preventing states from engaging in operations that would violate their own obligations. Developing that law remains subject to the broader debate on the conditions under which foreign states might be held to have extra-territorial human rights obligations, but it is a promising avenue.[1925]

Non-intervention, then, perhaps is more ethos than rule, a form of self-restraint rather than just a form of protest. But if it be an ethos, then it should be an active ethos of not doing—one should deliberately 'non-intervene' or 'non-interfere'—that one must put one's mind to. Just as under human rights for example, one should not merely 'not commit torture' but organize one's entire state apparatus to minimize the risk of torture, the same goes for interference. The burden of non-interference, at any rate, is not only the destination state whose threshold of tolerance to interference has been crossed and is required to manifest its displeasure, but the would-be interfering state that must desist from doing what it might. This points to a broader 'culture of non-interference' as, potentially, one of the more decisive determinants of respect for other states' sovereignty, one that has only ever been imperfectly realized. Intervention is problematic, incidentally, not just for the society that directly receives it but also for the society that spreads itself thin, trivializes some of its own liberal accomplishments and even acts at odds with some of its underlying foundations in the process of intervening 'on behalf' of others.

Although such a model of self-restraint has evident limits, it has received some juridical recognition.[1926] Cedric Ryngaert has pled for exercises of jurisdiction that are consonant with the regulatory interests of the international community and in which not only courts but regulators 'are willing to rise above nationalist reflexes and [exercise] jurisdictional restraint if another State's sovereignty is encroached upon'.[1927] It of course remains relatively easier to engage in such self-restraint in a judicial context and in relation to suspicions of jurisdiction-creep (as was underlined, courts rely on a number of doctrines to not encroach on the sovereignty of other states, many of which are tied to

1924 Powell (n 824) s 4.

1925 Kilovaty, 'Cybersecurity Abroad' (n 499).

1926 F Hoffmann-La Roche Ltd v Empagran SA 542 U.S. 155 (2004). This was a significant improvement from the traditional U.S. Position. See Akehurst (n 635) 208.

1927 Cedric Ryngaert, *Jurisdiction in international law* (2nd edn, Oxford University Press 2015) 6.

the need to respect separation of powers equilibria) than in an executive context and in relation to the broader field of the 'new interference'. But the idea is a powerful one, and it has the merit of making purveyors of interference part of the solution in at least some measure. For example, the 1981 Declaration on the Inadmissibility of Intervention and Interference in the Internal Affairs of States already anticipated the 'right and duty of States to combat, within their constitutional prerogatives, the dissemination of false or distorted news which can be interpreted as interference in the internal affairs of other States'. The goal of stopping interference at the source is a reminder that the 'supply side' of interference also needs to be problematized as expressing a form of sovereign and national aggrandizement at the expense of others, although clearly that possibility was always written into the very genetics of international law.

At the same time, one should occasionally be wary of states protesting too much that they do not want to interfere, when it suits them. If self-restraint can be a healthy manifestation of keeping to oneself jurisdictionally, it can also translate into the odd abdication or at least shirking of one's responsibilities, notably for the harm produced by one's national subjects. There is an entire discursive economy of interference and non-interference which begs to be explicated in terms of what it relates to, when and how, along with an attention to its distributive impact.[1928] It could simply be too easy to 'wash one's hands clean' of responsibilities one has to one's exterior. Especially if the measure of appropriate exercises of jurisdiction is something approximating the international legal interest, then there are circumstances in which home states should think seriously about exercising jurisdiction over matters to which they have some connection, lest they be suspected of strategically instrumentalizing non-interference to maintain conditions of impunity.

Hence it has sometimes been deplored that somewhat staged misgivings about interference in host nations are evoked by states to better decline to exercise jurisdiction over some of their corporations and the latter's extraterritorial wrongdoing. The problem, even from a TWAIL perspective, is far more complicated,[1929] and whilst one may welcome the scruple about not interfering, one can also see it as occasionally opportunistic and self-serving. A similar debate arises in relation to states' obligations for their troops acting abroad and the argument by such states that they would not want, through

1928 See e.g., Uta Kohl, 'Corporate Human Rights Accountability: The Objections of Western Governments to the Alien Tort Statute' (2014) 63 International & Comparative Law Quarterly 665.

1929 Sara L Seck, 'Transnational Business and Environmental Harm: A TWAIL Analysis of Home State Obligations' (2011) 3 Trade, Law and Development 164.

such a medium, to impose 'their' standards to other nations: again, the concern may be welcome in the abstract, but not if it is instrumentalized to deny transnational responsibility when it suits. Similarly, the notion that Western states do not want to exercise jurisdiction over 'foreign fighters' in Iraq or Syria as a result of a prevention over these states' sovereignty evokes significant skepticism in light of obligations to prosecute war crimes or human rights violations when facing host state inertia.[1930] It may be that exercise of jurisdiction by 'home' states will in fact concur towards reinforcing the sovereignty of 'host' states which for a range of reasons may not be in a position to exercise their jurisdiction.[1931]

If states' record is scrutinized in this way when it comes to their potential for interference, as this book has shown, then it also stands to be examined in terms of their record in fighting off interference. Indeed, this is a relatively new and henceforth perhaps decisive front for the global conversation on intervention. Whilst traditionally states were more concerned about agendas of interference than agendas of non-interference, the latter very much condition the range of responses that can be deployed to respond to the phenomenon. States eye each other in their responses, copy some of their policies and look for evolving signals about how far one can go in justifying domestic responses to interference. It should be underscored that non-interference agendas can have very pretextual and opportunistic dimensions, essentially allowing states to do that which they would have wanted to do for other reasons anyhow, e.g., disciplining civil society. This suggests that states are never alone even in their domestic responses to interference and that these responses will be scrutinized and emulated. They may thus want to think about how they might lead by example or at least not create too much dissonance between their domestic and foreign constitutions. Failure to live up to their stated ambitions, for example, will give opportunities to 'authoritarian' states to lecture 'liberal' ones for not living up to their claimed principles.[1932]

1930 David McKeever, 'Repatriating Foreign Terrorist Fighters and Their Family Members: What International Law Requires, and What National Courts Will Do' (2023) 28 Journal of Conflict and Security Law 67.

1931 Lucas Roorda and Cedric Ryngaert, 'Public International Law Constraints on the Exercise of Adjudicatory Jurisdiction in Civil Matters' in Serena Forlati and Pietro Franzina (eds), *Universal Civil Jurisdiction: Which Way Forward?* (Brill Nijhoff 2020).

1932 Lily Kuo, 'Beijing Complains as U.S. "Orders Chinese Media to Register as Foreign Agents"' *The Guardian* (20 September 2018) <https://www.theguardian.com/world/2018/sep/20/beijing-complains-as-us-orders-chinese-media-to-register-as-foreign-agents> accessed 2 April 2024.

3 The Meaning of Interference for, rather than in International Law

Leaving aside a hypothetical self-restraint by interfering states, the response to interference, conceived as a response that mostly originates in target states, has often taken a perhaps surprisingly haphazard, ad hoc, and even anemic aspect. As was seen, there is no reason to think that international law is necessarily the decisive response in dealing with interference. It may be, for example, that ultimately states are more likely to desist from intervening in the affairs of others simply because 'even under the best possible conditions, interference in the politics of a major power [...] is a questionable gamble', one that exposes its originators to backlash and resentment and ultimately offers 'limited payoffs'.[1933]

Even in relation to small states and in asymmetric contexts, interference has hardly been an unmitigated success, as shown by the challenges the U.S. experienced in changing regimes in the Caribbean or Eastern Europe for example.[1934] Reliance on proxies of dubious allegiance can mean that interference is simultaneously invited and resisted. Revelations that Israel sought to engage in a covert operation to shift the narrative on the Gaza war after the 7th October have exposed the occasional amateurishness of some psychological operations and the embarrassment they can create for their originators.[1935] This suggests that, through rational choice alone, states may ultimately come to the conclusion that interference does not serve them particularly well and desist from such practices on such grounds, rather than because it is mandated under international law.

Furthermore, there is no reason why a state's response should be one under international rather than regional or domestic law. The beating heart of anti-interference efforts has typically been domestic, evidencing often knee-jerk unilateral responses to perceived threats by panicked political elites keen on boosting the body politics immune response. There have been a plethora of domestic commissions and investigations concerning interference, for example, all raising the alarm and suggesting the need for new regulation: the U.S. Mueller investigation which delivered the 'Report on the Investigation Into Russian Interference in the 2016 Presidential Election';[1936] Canada's

1933 Istomin (n 315).
1934 Lindsey A O'Rourke, *Covert Regime Change: America's Secret Cold War* (Cornell University Press 2018).
1935 Sheera Frenkel, 'Israel Secretly Targets U.S. Lawmakers With Influence Campaign on Gaza War' *The New York Times* (5 June 2024) <https://www.nytimes.com/2024/06/05/technology/israel-campaign-gaza-social-media.html> accessed 6 September 2024.
1936 Mueller (n 330).

'Public Inquiry into Foreign Interference in Federal Electoral Processes and Democratic Institutions';[1937] annual reports of the French 'Parliamentary Delegation for Intelligence'; the European Parliament's Committee on Foreign Interference,[1938] etc. Advancing more or less in unison, Western states have rushed to adopt domestic constitutional, criminal, and human rights agendas tailored to their needs, often borrowing loosely from each others' policy registers, but in ways that bypass any explicit or more than *pro forma* reference to international law. Their efforts to develop common positions on the universal level have been hampered by persistent polarities, second-guessing, and uncertainty about where holding any given position on the matter might land them in the future.

In the process, they have occasionally found themselves in strange company, essentially emulating or reprising policy responses which, in other circumstances, they might have found less than commendable. Fighting interference, moreover, may require a degree of cooperation in a context where such cooperation has never been harder because of the zero-sum game quality of interference. This, in a strategic playing field where states are wary of each others' intentions and what they might be asked to sign onto. The 2017 breakdown of the U.N. Group of Governmental Expert's process on state cyber-operations was an early indication that for many states universal agreement might come at too high a cost—either dilution of norms to the point of their irrelevance or hyping up of stances that are ultimately seen as incompatible with domestic values or even departing from acceptable international interaction. This leaves regional actors (the E.U., the Shanghai Cooperation Council) as perhaps the best way to achieve a modicum of consensus, although at the risk of a very self-defeating limitation on the scale of application. However, not even domestic law has been consistently resorted to. For example, in the U.S., FARA prosecutions remain very much the exception, as if authorities hesitated to use the tools at their disposal.[1939]

1937 Marie-Josée Hogue, 'Initial Report' (Public Inquiry into Foreign Interference in Federal Electoral Processes and Democratic Institutions (Canada) 2024) <https://foreigninterferencecommission.ca/fileadmin/user_upload/Foreign_Interference_Commission_-_Initial_Report__May_2024__-_Digital.pdf> accessed 28 May 2024.

1938 Sandra Kalniete, 'Report on Foreign Interference in All Democratic Processes in the European Union, Including Disinformation' (Special Committee on foreign interference in all democratic processes in the European Union, including disinformation (INGE 2) 2023) <https://www.europarl.europa.eu/doceo/document/A-9-2023-0187_EN.html#_section1> accessed 28 May 2024.

1939 Wright, 'Reexamining Criminal Prosecutions under the Foreign Nationals Ban' (n 344).

This could be due to technical or evidentiary hurdles, but it could point to a deeper *malaise* about resort to very powerful medicine against interference and its side effects. It is worth stressing that there is no reason why the resistance to interference should necessarily and always even be framed in *legal* terms at all. Indeed, political actors are periodically tempted to depart from the legal script (flexible as it may be), for example by repeatedly referring to interference as 'illegitimate' rather than specifically 'illegal'.[1940] Much of the response already and appropriately belongs to the policy realm.[1941] The European Union in particular has mooted a so-called 'whole of society' response that includes cyber hygiene, the creation of 'focal points and strategic responses to foreign interference', the need to 'follow the money',[1942] etc. Canadian sources also speak of strengthening 'the capacity to detect, deter and counter foreign interference in our elections'[1943] and an 'electoral ecosystem approach to disinformation and cyber threats',[1944] without necessarily making international law a central plank of that effort. Many issues related to interference involve matters of ethics and good behavior that need not solicit something as dramatic and weighty as bilateral accusations of interference under international law.[1945] There is and will continue to be a considerable defense and national security component to dealing with interference[1946] that is not saturated, to say the least, by references to legal arguments.

The shortcomings of international law and law in general are only too obvious, including the hangover and perpetual haggling over definitions, the somewhat illusory emphasis on accountability, and the general ineffectuality of international legal arrangements. A jaundiced or jaded view about the possibility of making sense of the norm, however, is no more warranted than a

1940 Jones (n 495) 11.

1941 Adam Henschke, Matthew Sussex and Courteney O'Connor, 'Countering Foreign Interference: Election Integrity Lessons for Liberal Democracies' (2020) 5 Journal of Cyber Policy 180.

1942 Jones (n 495) 11.

1943 Johnston (n 352) 1.

1944 Yasmin Dawood, 'Combatting Foreign Election Interference: Canada's Electoral Ecosystem Approach to Disinformation and Cyber Threats' (2021) 20 Election Law Journal: Rules, Politics, and Policy 10.

1945 Ashifa Kassam, 'Trudeau to Be Questioned by Ethics Watchdog over Reports of Cash for Access' *The Guardian* (15 December 2016) <https://www.theguardian.com/world/2016/dec/15/justin-trudeau-to-be-questioned-political-fundraisers-ethics> accessed 7 September 2023; Fife, Chase and Xu (n 1657).

1946 Julian E Barnes, 'US Cyber Command Expands Operations to Hunt Hackers from Russia, Iran and China' *The New York Times* (2 November 2020) <https://www.nytimes.com/2020/11/02/us/politics/cyber-command-hackers-russia.html> accessed 18 December 2023.

naïve formalistic one. The norm lives through, if nothing else, efforts to prop it up and to contest it. Although some may deplore the rule of non-intervention as an 'unhelpful generality', the constructive incidence of generalities should not be lightly dismissed. In a sense, international law writ-large is an unhelpful generality that nonetheless finds meaning in the crucible of history and the needs of the moment. Generalities are needed as points of communicational reference, and they undoubtedly produce important effects. Indeed, despite that character:

> the nonintervention principle lives on in contemporary international law as a rule which states have bound themselves to observe in various international instruments, as a slogan lodged in the minds and frequenting the sayings of statesmen, and as a doctrine which has received the imprimatur of the United Nations.[1947]

Generalities are also starting points that betray, if nothing else, the common sense of a discipline.

The typical move in that context is to double down on the exercise of further specifying what interference is. This book has cautioned against that temptation and what it can realistically achieve. It has suggested that intellectual oxygen is to be found less by drilling down than by opening new vistas; less by interpreting canonical texts than by contextualizing the significance of interference for the times; and less by arguing over definitions than imagining the sort of underlying concepts that the law needs to thrive. One adjacent temptation here is the further deformalization of international rules towards a more general embrace of various 'standards' of conduct that are voluntary and implicate comity. This is the move suggested for example by Stephen Townley, namely to think of non-intervention less as a strict rule than as a standard by which to evaluate state conduct in ways that might 'help square the circle between those who see the principle of non-intervention as rigid and clear, and those who dismiss it as Delphic'.[1948] The idea is, essentially, that the rule of non-intervention always promised more than it could deliver and that its ambiguities and inconsistencies recommend a flexible and case based approach. Other scholars had previously spoken of thinking of violations of the norm of intervention in terms of degrees of 'seriousness'.[1949]

1947 Vincent (n 69) 313.

1948 Townley (n 62).

1949 Falk, *Legal Order in a Violent World* (n 117) 204.

Such a path may yet help deal with interference's pesky antinomies, although it is hard to see how these antinomies would not resurface somehow, whether one called non-interference a rule, a standard, a principle, a goal or a value. It would also mark a shift away from a straightforward sense of transgression towards a certain conception of idealized behavior and degrees of departure from it. This move away from principles or rules to standards is well on its way and could still lead to a semi-juridified notion of 'friendly' relations. For example, a group of human rights Special Rapporteurs has called for 'State actors [to] not make, sponsor, encourage or further disseminate statements which they know or reasonably should know to be false (disinformation) or which demonstrate a reckless disregard for verifiable information (propaganda)'.[1950] This sort of exhortation will go some way, but questions will inevitably be asked about its authority (what is special rapporteurs' special claim to expertise on the issue?) and its impact, as well as its status (is there not a risk of further weakening an already debilitated rule?).

On one level, the overall posture of the West may appear as one of strategic retreat from international law at a time when it is no longer clear what can be gained and what might be lost as a result of too blind an investment in it. Notably, the reaction to persistent election meddling by Russia, China, and others has *not* been strident assertions that international law was violated as much as a remarkably mute withdrawal to familiar domestic legal tools.[1951] Perhaps one of the prices of maintaining relatively open societies is that, over time, one will simply need to get used to being subjected to the constant grind of day-to-day, low-level interference—death by a thousand cuts rather than a single blatant operation. This would suggest that many societies are in it for the long haul and that interference is not about to disappear, a scourge one has to learn to live with, like pandemics or inflation, rather than an intolerable attack on the system. The alternative, one of incessant clamping down on not just 'interference' but also on what is (imagined as) 'foreign' arguably carries far greater risks. As has been seen, it reactivates not just democratic and sovereign, but also nationalist and racist tendencies that are at one, politically, with the broader populist-authoritarian project of affirming one's autonomy at all costs. In that respect, for all its emancipatory pedigree, one of this book's findings is that self-determination is at least an ambiguous tool when it comes to idealizing non-interference.

1950 Joint Declaration on Disinformation (n 697), para 2(c).

1951 Lahmann (n 322) 210–211.

On another level, the challenge of interference can be seen as mostly a challenge to sovereignty rather than international law per se, and perhaps as an opportunity for the latter. Paradoxically, the argument for respecting sovereignty for sovereignty's sake, despite the many caveats that such a statement is bound to elicit, may better approximate intuitions about non-intervention and non-interference than countless attempts to circumvent sovereignty by highlighting its ultimate purpose. These arguably open highways for interference and, what is more, breach the fundamental principle of equality of states by making the question of whether they are worthy of non-intervention uniquely dependent on the sort of regime they have embraced. Sovereignty is sovereignty, goes the argument, whatever flavour it comes in. At the same time, the argument from sovereignty needs to be grounded in a particular understanding of sovereignty in human rights, peoples' agency, and the demands of international law that have long led to chicken-and-egg problems. There is no incontrovertible meaning of sovereignty to which one can return to define intervention and interference. One must thus contend both with the unavoidability of sovereignty as the referent, and the evidence of its slippery and changing meaning.

Maybe, then, international law can switch from prohibiting intervention to regulating interference, promising less the black-and-white allure of rule by rules than a complex algorithm to channel interference and protect the leftovers of sovereignty. Indeed, one should not forget that it is just as much sovereignty that has long been a challenge to international law, both conceptually and practically. This is not so much in the traditional sense that states jealously guard their independence behind invocations of voluntarism, but in the sense that sovereignty is fluid and fluctuating, never quite what it seems, and not always as evidently and assuredly self-constituted in the first place as assumed. We should not too readily assume, for example, that states will always champion their own sovereignty in the face of interference, especially when the state is already, to a degree, a fiction. Nor is it clear that sovereignty can survive through the sheer force of international law, absent a compelling and ongoing political theory of why we would want to respect it.

In practice, some actors within the state may stand to gain from allowing at least some forms of benign interference in their favor. As was remarked, it is not the least of ironies that it is some of the most outspoken populist voices for sovereignty that have shown themselves to be only too happy to accept handouts and leaks from foreign sources. Some countries, in fact, may 'lack [the] political will [...] to take concrete steps to protect the integrity of their own countries' information environments'.[1952] This may be true *a fortiori* of regional

1952 Keitner (n 878) 180.

bodies such as the European Union, whose own reaction to interference via corruption has sometimes appeared tepid.[1953] Others will already have been deeply undermined from within by actors keen to 'invite' the interference of foreign powers for their benefit but also for the purposes of state building and elite cooptation. In that respect, sovereignty is constituted by the will to be sovereign, as it expresses itself—or not—including through the solicitation or liberal tolerance of some interference fluxes. Sovereignty, then, is better understood at any given time as relative: one might theoretically be able to reassert its former grandeur, but on a day-to-day basis one is more likely to simply live with its remains.

To be clear and having said that, a sort of wide open-door to all outside influences can be tantamount to an abandonment of any sovereignty, an abdication in front of elusive forces that the state gives up on controlling at the risk, ultimately, of undermining its very claim to be sovereign. This will inevitably raise questions about the state's legitimacy and even authority, in the process of highlighting its vulnerabilities. In that respect, democratic states and open societies may feel that they are particularly vulnerable, keen as they are on simultaneously defending their sovereignty but remaining porous to outside influences. There is a strong sense in the reaction to the new interference in Canada, for example, that 'democracy, the rule of law, federalism and respect for minorities' are 'foundational principles' but that 'they are also the very features that leave our institutions open to manipulation by foreign actors and states that work to undermine the integrity of our system for their own purposes'.[1954] In particular, 'the openness of our democracy and media also provides an ideal forum for foreign actors that wish to disrupt our democratic process'.[1955] As to the rule of law, it also creates its own set of vulnerabilities as '[s]ophisticated malign actors understand how to operate in the grey zone of legality, in which they can attempt to achieve their objectives while still not doing anything unlawful'.[1956]

The interpretative challenges this raises make it very difficult to imagine a response to interference that is not mediated at least in part by *legal* claims about what it is that interference encroaches on and why it is problematic,

---

1953 Eddy Wax and Sarah Wheaton, 'The EU's Reply to Qatargate: Nips, Tucks and Paperwork' *POLITICO* (31 July 2023) <https://www.politico.eu/article/qatargate-qatar-corruption-scandal-eu-european-parliament-eva-kaili-marc-tarabella-roberta-metsola/> accessed 22 December 2023.

1954 Johnston (n 352) 13.

1955 ibid.

1956 ibid.

even under a flexible and reactive model of rule-by-standards. For example, some remedies to interference specifically deploy on the international plane and therefore necessarily involve debates about international law. This is the case, for example, of sanctions regimes such as already exist in the U.S. which allow the U.S. Attorney-General and the Secretary of Homeland Security to assess evidence and order asset freezes, travel bans and restrictions on large business entities (more than a hundred such sanctions have been pronounced already).[1957] A proposed European sanctions regime including trade measures to punish individuals engaged in particularly egregious and repeated forms of interference raises similar issues.[1958] As we saw, if only on account of unilateral sanctions' potential to themselves qualify as a form of illegal interference, much thinking will have to go into how such initiatives can be compatible with international law including human rights.[1959] It nonetheless seems natural—if a little paradoxical—that approaches to dealing with interference in sovereign affairs will actually have to up the ante in terms of multilateral consultation and the development of specifically international modalities of response.

So, what of the future of interference? In an age of populist backlash, one might expect a range of different outcomes. On the one hand, a reassertion of the centrality of non-interference as part of a renewed insistence on internal sovereignty as a vehicle for self-determination and democracy, but also a sort of kneejerk insistence on the 'purity' of domestic political life with potentially nauseating undertones; on the other hand, a callousness about interference abroad in a context of reassertion of external sovereignty and the right of states to promote their views and pursue their national interest aggressively in an interdependent world. Both these moves, of course, will tend to be visible simultaneously in the argumentative arsenal of any one party, although in relation to different facets of (their) sovereignty, in different bilateral relations and in different contexts. They will create at least moderate—as befits international law—stress among their authors as the ability to simultaneously hold positions in relation to interference abroad and counter-interference at home will be strained.

The odds are that these two movements may roughly cancel each other out as normative claims over time and make it even more difficult to assert the rule's contours, leaving only a series of significant but consistently contradictory set of endlessly repeated practices. But they will also expose discursively and perhaps unwittingly the very contradictions on which an international

1957 Executive Order No 13848, 31 CFR §579 (2018) (United States).
1958 2022 Resolution on Foreign Interference in the E.U. (n 337), paras CH-CJ.
1959 Jones (n 495) 16.

system devoted to both closure and openness, pluralism and centralism, nationalism and cosmopolitanism has always relied. Pinning down these contradictions may ultimately be one of the most useful contributions that international lawyers can make, in at least making it relatively difficult for states to reject interference when simultaneously engaging in it and vice versa, but leaving no one in any doubt in the process that these contradictions are embedded in international law itself. In between those contradictions, at any rate, lies a vast transnational space of diffuse and decentralized interference that will not simply go away, and that will require international law to significantly adapt, if it is not to whittle away.

Index

If you have any questions regarding this title, please contact:

Koninklijke Brill BV
Plantijnstraat 2
2321 JC Leiden
Email: info@brill.com

Batch number: 08075597